Lecture Notes in Computer Science 16492

Founding Editors

Gerhard Goos
Juris Hartmanis

Editorial Board Members

Elisa Bertino, *Purdue University, West Lafayette, IN, USA*
Wen Gao, *Peking University, Beijing, China*
Bernhard Steffen, *TU Dortmund University, Dortmund, Germany*
Moti Yung, *Columbia University, New York, NY, USA*

Magali Bardet · Ruben Niederhagen
Editors

Post-Quantum Cryptography

17th International Workshop, PQCrypto 2026
Saint-Malo, France, April 14–16, 2026
Proceedings, Part II

 Springer

Editors
Magali Bardet
Université de Rouen Normandie
Mont-Saint-Aignan, France

Ruben Niederhagen
Academia Sinica and University of Southern
Denmark
Taipei, Taiwan

ISSN 0302-9743   ISSN 1611-3349 (electronic)
Lecture Notes in Computer Science
ISBN 978-3-032-22697-6   ISBN 978-3-032-22698-3 (eBook)
https://doi.org/10.1007/978-3-032-22698-3

This Springer imprint is published by the registered company Springer Nature Switzerland AG
The registered company address is: Gewerbestrasse 11, 6330 Cham, Switzerland

If disposing of this product, please recycle the paper.

Preface

PQCrypto 2026, the 17th International Conference on Post-Quantum Cryptography, was held from April 14–16, 2026, at the Palais du Grand Large in Saint-Malo, France. The PQCrypto conference series serves as a platform for sharing research on cryptography designed to withstand the capabilities of large-scale quantum computers. Over the years, PQCrypto has expanded its focus to encompass not only academic and theoretical work but also applied research, emphasizing practical implementation and deployment of post-quantum cryptographic schemes.

For PQCrypto 2026, a single-blind review process was employed, meaning submissions were not anonymized. Sixty-six papers by 180 authors from 28 countries fulfilled the technical criteria and were accepted for peer review. Each submission was rigorously evaluated by at least three members of the program committee (five for contributions co-authored by any committee members). The committee, comprising 62 members and supported by 33 subreviewers, conducted a total of 243 reviews. Following an intensive online discussion phase, 27 high-quality papers were selected for inclusion in the conference program and these proceedings.

The accepted papers showcase a diverse range of topics within the field of post-quantum cryptography, including:

- code-based cryptography,
- multivariate cryptography,
- lattice-based cryptography,
- isogeny-based cryptography,
- cryptanalysis,
- quantum security,
- side-channel attacks, and
- security notions.

The success of PQCrypto 2026 would not have been possible without the contributions of many individuals and organizations. We extend our deepest gratitude to the authors, whose submissions reflected exceptional quality, and to the program committee and external reviewers for their dedicated effort in evaluating and discussing the papers. Their commitment was essential to assembling a strong technical program.

A special acknowledgment goes to our General Chairs, Pierre-Alain Fouque, Pierre Loidreau, and Yixin Shen, who played a key role in organizing this event. Additionally, we would like to thank the IRISA administrative team (Antoine, Aurélie, Éléonora, Lucien, and Benoît) for their help with the local organization of the event and the people from the Palais du Grand Large at Saint-Malo. Finally, we express our appreciation to Springer for publishing these proceedings.

April 2026

Magali Bardet
Ruben Niederhagen

Organization

General Chairs

Pierre-Alain Fouque   Université de Rennes, IRISA, Inria, France
Pierre Loidreau   DGA MI, Université de Rennes, CNRS, IRMAR, France
Yixin Shen   Inria, Université de Rennes, IRISA, France

Program Committee Chairs

Magali Bardet   Université de Rouen Normandie, France
Ruben Niederhagen   Academia Sinica, Taiwan and University of Southern Denmark, Denmark

Program Committee

Gorjan Alagic   University of Maryland, USA
Sarah Arpin   Virginia Polytechnic Institute and State University, USA
Lejla Batina   Radboud University, Netherlands
Daniel J. Bernstein   University of Illinois at Chicago, USA
Loïc Bidoux   Technology Innovation Institute, United Arab Emirates
Olivier Blazy   École Polytechnique, France
Daniel Cabarcas   Universidad Nacional de Colombia, Medellín, Columbia
Fabio Campos   Darmstadt University of Applied Sciences, Germany
Sanjit Chatterjee   Indian Institute of Science, India
Céline Chevalier   Université Panthéon-Assas Paris 2 and ENS Ulm, France
Łukasz Chmielewski   Masaryk University, Czechia
Alain Couvreur   Inria and École Polytechnique, France
Thomas Debris-Alazard   Inria and École Polytechnique, France
Thomas Decru   KU Leuven, Belgium
Martin Ekerå   Swedish NCSA, Swedish Armed Forces, Sweden

Andre Esser   Technology Innovation Institute, United Arab
                                   Emirates
Thibauld Feneuil   CryptoExperts, France
Scott Fluhrer   Cisco Systems, USA
Philippe Gaborit   University of Limoges, France
Tommaso Gagliardoni   Horizen Labs, Switzerland
Qian Guo   Lund University, Sweden
Julius Hermelink   Max Planck Institute for Security and Privacy,
                                   Germany
David Jao   University of Waterloo, Canada
John Kelsey   National Institute of Standards and Technology,
                                   USA
Juliane Krämer   University of Regensburg, Germany
Momonari Kudo   Fukuoka Institute of Technology, Japan
Sabrina Kunzweiler   Inria Bordeaux, France
Russell W. F. Lai   Aalto University, Finland
Pierre Loidreau   DGA MI, Université de Rennes, CNRS, IRMAR,
                                   France
Luciano Maino   University of Birmingham, UK
Chloe Martindale   University of Bristol, UK
Dustin Moody   National Institute of Standards and Technology,
                                   USA
Phong Nguyen   Inria and ENS, France
Ayoub Otmani   University of Rouen Normandy, France
Kostas Papagiannopoulos   Radboud University, Netherlands
Ray Perlner   National Institute of Standards and Technology,
                                   USA
Edoardo Persichetti   Florida Atlantic University, USA and Sapienza
                                   University, Italy
Peter Pessl   Infineon Technologies, Germany
Angela Robinson   National Institute of Standards and Technology,
                                   USA
Mélissa Rossi   CryptoExperts, France
Adeline Roux-Langlois   CNRS, France
Markku-Juhani O. Saarinen   Tampere University, Finland
Amin Sakzad   Monash University, Australia
Simona Samardjiska   Radboud University, Netherlands
Palash Sarkar   Indian Statistical Institute, India
Nicolas Sendrier   Inria, France
Yixin Shen   Inria, Université de Rennes, IRISA, France
Benjamin Smith   Inria and École Polytechnique, France
Daniel Smith-Tone   University of Louisville and NIST, USA
Rainer Steinwandt   University of Alabama in Huntsville, USA

Tsuyoshi Takagi   University of Tokyo, Japan
Atsushi Takayasu   University of Tokyo, Japan
Jean-Pierre Tillich   Inria, France
Monika Trimoska   Eindhoven University of Technology, Netherlands
Javier Verbel   Technology Innovation Institute, United Arab
                                    Emirates
Antonia Wachter-Zeh   Technical University of Munich, Germany
Alexandre Wallet   PQShield, Germany
Violetta Weger   Technical University of Munich, Germany
Thom Wiggers   PQShield, Netherlands
Yang Yu   Tsinghua University, China

Additional Reviewers

Nicolas Aragon
Valentina Astore
Thomas Aulbach
Henry Bambury
Sebastian Bitzer
Pierre Briaud
Jan Brinkmann
André Chailloux
Jean-Christophe Deneuville
Antoine Douteau
Jonathan Komada Eriksen
Hiroki Furuc
Joel Gärtner
Yasufumi Hashimoto
Johan Håstad
Kaisei Kajita
Elena Kirshanova
Peigen Li
Youcef Mokrani
Tomoki Moriya
Denis Nabokov
Romaric Neveu
Shinya Okumura
Hiroshi Onuki
Tapas Pandit
Amaury Pouly
Emeline Repel
Leonardo Spreafico
Ricardo Villanueva
Ivy K. Y. Woo
Yan, Bo Ti
Masaya Yasuda
Floyd Zweydinger

Contents

Cryptanalysis and Fault Attacks

Isogeny- and Group-Action-Based Cryptography

Endomorphisms via Splittings

Sabrina Kunzweiler[1,2(✉)] and Min-Yi Shen[1,2]

[1] Centre Inria de l'université de Bordeaux, Université de Bordeaux,
Bordeaux, France
[2] Université de Bordeaux, Bordeaux, France
`sabrina.kunzweiler@math.u-bordeaux.fr`

Abstract. One of the fundamental hardness assumptions underlying isogeny-based cryptography is the problem of finding a non-trivial endomorphism of a given supersingular elliptic curve. We show that this problem is related to the problem of finding a *good* splitting of a principally polarized superspecial abelian surface. We provide formal security reductions, as well as a proof-of-concept implementation of an algorithm to compute endomorphisms of elliptic curves by solving the splitting problem.

Keywords: Isogeny-based cryptography · abelian varieties · security assumptions · implementation

1   Introduction

Computing the endomorphism ring of a supersingular elliptic curve is one of the fundamental problems underlying the security of isogeny-based cryptography. The best known algorithms to solve this problem rely on finding enough non-trivial endomorphisms. Indeed, one can show that the so-called `OneEnd` problem which asks to find one non-trivial endomorphism is equivalent to the problem of computing the entire endomorphism ring [30].

Algorithmic solutions to `OneEnd` mostly rely on finding cycles in suitably chosen isogeny graphs. Given a supersingular elliptic curve $E/\mathbb{F}_p^2$, all of these algorithms have exponential runtime: In 1996, Kohel [21] first gave an algorithm with running time $O(p^{1+\epsilon})$, $\epsilon > 0$, for computing a non-trivial endomorphism of E. In 2016, Delfs and Galbraith [13] analyzed the structure of the isogeny graphs over $\mathbb{F}_p$ and gave a path finding algorithm in this graph which runs in $\tilde{O}(p^{1/4})$. This algorithm is then used as a subroutine in order to find an endomorphism for some elliptic curve over $\mathbb{F}_p^2$. First one computes two distinct isogeny paths to the $\mathbb{F}_p$-subgraph, and then one applies Delfs-Galbraith to obtain a path between the two $\mathbb{F}_p$-curves. The overall complexity is dominated by the first step, and it is given by $\tilde{O}(p^{1/2})$ under the generalized Riemann hypothesis (GRH). Further improvements of the algorithm (with the same asymptotic complexity) were provided by Corte-Real Santos, Castello and Shi in [9]. In 2020, Eisenträger,

M. Bardet and R. Niederhagen (Eds.): PQCrypto 2026, LNCS 16492, pp. 3–38, 2026.
https://doi.org/10.1007/978-3-032-22698-3_1

4   S. Kunzweiler and M.-Y. Shen

Hallgren, Leonardi, Morrison and Park [15] introduced a new cycle-finding algorithm that requires less memory, but still runs in time $\tilde{O}(p^{1/2})$. Recently, Fuselier, Iezzi, Kozek, Morrison and Namoijam [18] provided a new algorithm to compute an inseparable endomorphism of a E. This algorithm is faster in practice than Delfs-Galbraith method and the cycle-finding algorithm because it only needs one path from the given curve over $\mathbb{F}_p^2$ to another curve over $\mathbb{F}_p$.

Another seemingly unrelated hardness assumption appears in isogeny-based protocols that work in the isogeny graphs of abelian surfaces. Given a (superspecial) irreducible principally polarized abelian surface A, it is presumably hard to find a splitting, i.e. an isogeny to a product of elliptic curves $\phi : A \to E_1 \times E_2$. We refer to this problem as the $\texttt{Splitting}$ problem.

$\texttt{Splitting}$ first appeared in the cryptanalysis of the 2-dimensional version of the Charles-Goren-Lauter (CGL) hash function [7,37]. An important security assumption underlying this hash function is the hardness of finding an isogeny between superspecial principally polarized (p.p.) abelian surfaces, $\Phi : A \to A'$. In [10], Costello and Smith observed that this problem can be reduced to a problem in dimension one, by finding splittings $\phi : A \to E_1 \times E_2$ and $\phi' : A' \to E_1' \times E_2'$. The best known attack to solve $\texttt{Splitting}$ relies on a random walk in the superspecial isogeny graph, and has heuristic time complexity $\tilde{O}(p)$ when working over the finite field $\mathbb{F}_{p^2}$. Improvements on the concrete running time for this attack are provided by Corte-Real Santos, Costello and Frengley in [8].

Our Contribution.

In this work, we propose a new algorithm to find a non-trivial endormorphism of an elliptic curve. Our algorithm uses the connection between isogeny diamonds of elliptic curves with 2-dimensional product isogenies that was established by Kani [20]. To make this more precise, consider an elliptic curve E, a separable endomorphism $\phi \in \mathrm{End}(E)$, and choose a (potentially trivial) decomposition $\phi = \psi_2 \circ \phi_1$. These isogenies fit into a commutative diagram:

$$
\begin{array}{ccc}
E & \xrightarrow{\phi_1} & E_1 \\
\downarrow{\scriptstyle\phi_2} & & \downarrow{\scriptstyle\psi_2} \\
E_2 & \xrightarrow{\psi_1} & E
\end{array}
$$

Here $\deg(\phi_i) = \deg(\psi_i)$ for $i = 1, 2$. Such a configuration induces a product isogeny $\Phi : E \times E \to E_1 \times E_2$ defined as

$$
\Phi : \begin{pmatrix} P \\ Q \end{pmatrix} \mapsto \begin{pmatrix} \phi_1 & \hat{\psi}_2 \\ -\phi_2 & \hat{\psi}_1 \end{pmatrix} \cdot \begin{pmatrix} P \\ Q \end{pmatrix}.
$$

Instead of searching for cycles in the isogeny graph involving the elliptic curve E, we will search for product isogenies in the isogeny graph of dimension 2. A rough outline of our appraoch is provided in Algorithm 1 (FindEndomorphism). The idea is simple, first we compute a gluing $E \times E \to \mathrm{Jac}(C)$, and then search for a *good* splitting $\mathrm{Jac}(C) \to E_1 \times E_2$ for some elliptic curves E_1, E_2 (see Problem 4.5).

Algorithm 1. FindEndomorphism *(sketch of the general idea)*

Input: E a supersingular elliptic curve over a finite field $\mathbb{F}_{p^2}$.
Output: $\phi \in End(E)$.
  1: Compute an (N_1, N_1)-gluing $f_1 : E \times E \to \mathrm{Jac}(C)$ for some genus-2 curve C, and some $N_1 \in \mathbb{N}$
  2: Find a *good* (N_2, N_2)-splitting $f_2 : \mathrm{Jac}(C) \to E_1 \times E_2$ for some $N_2 \in \mathbb{N}$, i.e. it is required that

$$f_2 \circ f_1 : E \times E \to E_1 \times E_2$$

  is an $(N_1 N_2, N_1 N_2)$-isogeny.
  3: Use Kani's lemma to translate the product isogeny $f_2 \circ f_1$ to an endomorphism $\phi : E \to E$.

In order to be a solution to the **OneEnd** problem, it is required that the output of FindEndomorphism is a *non-trivial* endomorphism. While this might not be the case in general, we provide an explicit version of the algorithm using chains of $(2, 2)$-isogenies, where this subtlety is resolved naturally (Algorithm 6).

The dominating step in Algorithm 1 is Step 2 which requires to solve the **Splitting** problem. With the currently best known methods to solve this problem, our algorithm is not competitive with state-of-the-art methods to solve **OneEnd**. Instead, the main purpose of our paper is to provide new insight into the endomorphism problem. In particular, it proves a reduction of **OneEnd** to **Splitting**. The problem **OneEnd** is well-studied and also appears in classical algorithmic number theory, whereas the **Splitting** problem is less studied. Moreover **Splitting** is a very different problem in nature. It can be phrased as a more geometric problem which means that there are completely different tools that could be helpful to solve the problem. An example is given by the use of refined Humbert invariants (see for example [8, 23]).

We make the reduction of **OneEnd** to a variant of **GoodSplitting** explicit. While the focus of our paper is on the **OneEnd** problem, we also provide an analogous algorithm which can be used to prove a reduction from the isogeny-finding problem **Isogeny** to **Splitting**. Furthermore, we provide a proof-of-concept implementation in SageMath. This implementation can be used to find an efficient representation of a non-scalar endomorphism of a supersingular elliptic curve defined over $\mathbb{F}_{p^2}$ (provided that $p \cong 3 \pmod 4$). The code is publicly available in our GitHub repository

https://github.com/easonmath/endomorphisms-via-splittings

Using this implementation, we conducted experiments over different finite fields. We compare two different versions of the algorithm to find a *good* splitting in our setting: the faster method is based on a long random walk. The second method is slower but has asymptotically the same runtime. It searches splittings of bounded degree. The latter yields an efficient representation of the corresponding endomorphism. Interestingly, the degrees of the recovered endomorphisms seem to be smaller than the degrees obtained from other methods in the literature. Moreover there is no reason for the degrees to be smooth and our method even allows to find endomorphisms of prime degree.

Conclusion and Future Work

One of the main takeaways of this work should be that it is important to understand the splitting problem (in dimension 2) in order to understand the hardness of the endomorphism ring problem (in dimension 1). This claim is supported by a concrete algorithm (including an implementation) to compute endomorphisms via splittings, as well as proven security reductions. We refer to Fig. 4 for an overview.

While the resulting algorithm to compute endomorphisms is asymptotically slower than state-of-the-art algorithms, we believe that the general method could lead to new competitive algorithms. For instance, the following idea was pitched to us by Damien Robert: In Step 1 of Algorithm 1, one could replace $E \times E$ by $E \times E^\sigma$, where E^σ is the Frobenius twist of E. This p.p. abelian surface is defined over $\mathbb{F}_p$, hence one can search for a splitting in a much smaller isogeny graph. A concrete analysis of the running time and an implementation of this modification are a work in progress.

An open problem for future research is the study of the relation of $\mathtt{Splitting}$ with other hardness assumptions in dimension 2. We briefly elaborate on the relation with the endomorphism ring problem in dimension 2 (Remark 4.13). A more complete analysis and formal reductions are left for future work.

Related Work

The first time Kani's lemma appeared in isogeny-based cryptography was in the attacks on the key exchange protocol SIDH in 2022 [5,25,32]. Since then, many constructions appeared that make use of the bridge between isogenies of dimension one and isogenies in higher dimensions, most prominently the signature scheme SQISignHD [11], and its 2-dimensional variants [3,14,29].

Regarding the connection between one-dimensional problems and two-dimensional problems, there is a recent preprint by Kırımlı and Martindale [23]. Under GRH, they show that finding an isogeny between two given supersingular elliptic curves E_1 and E_2 over $\mathbb{F}_{p^2}$ is equivalent to computing the coefficients of a *refined Humbert invariant* $q_{(E_1 \times E_2, \theta_{E_1} \times \theta_{E_2})}$ of the p.p. abelian surface $(E_1 \times E_2, \theta_{E_1} \times \theta_{E_2})$. The former, referred to as $\mathtt{Isogeny}$ in this paper, is a well-known hard problem in dimension one. The latter asks one to compute an isomorphism invariant, introduced by Kani [19], on the polarized Néron-Severi group of a given p.p. abelian surface.

Outline

In Sect. 2, we recall results from the literature related to isogenies of p.p. abelian surfaces. In Sect. 3, we provide an explicit description of Algorithm 1 that builds the basis of our implementation. In Sect. 4, we prove reductions between isogeny problems in dimension 1 and the splitting problem in dimension 2. In Sect. 5, we discuss data collected in our experiments for finding endomorphisms. Furthermore, the appendix contains more details on our implementation.

2   Preliminaries

In this section, we introduce terminology and recall some results from the literature related to isogenies of (superspecial) principally polarized abelian surface. In particular, we recall Kani's lemma, and a method to compute 2-isogenies using theta coordinates which forms the basis of our implementation. A reader only interested in the formal reductions in Sect. 4 may skip the part about theta coordinates (and Sect. 3).

2.1   Isogenies of Principally Polarized Abelian Surfaces

Let A be a principally polarized abelian surface. An isogeny $f : A \to B$ is defined by its kernel $K = \ker(f)$ up to isomorphism. The latter is a maximal N-isotropic subgroup of A for some $N \in \mathbb{N}$. We say that f is an (N, N)-*isogeny* if the kernel K has rank 2, equivalently $\ker(f) \cong \mathbb{Z}/N\mathbb{Z} \times \mathbb{Z}/N\mathbb{Z}$. Similarly, an isogeny of elliptic curves $f : E \to E'$ is called an N-*isogeny* if the kernel is a cyclic group of order N.

Consider an (N_1, N_1)-isogeny $f_1 : A \to B$ and an (N_2, N_2)-isogeny $f_2 : B \to C$. We say that f_2 is a *good extension* of f_1 if $f_2 \circ f_1$ is an $(N_1 N_2, N_1 N_2)$-isogeny. Note that if $\gcd(N_2, N_1) = 1$, then any f_2 is necessarily a good extension of f_1 (in the above setting). This is not true if $\gcd(N_1, N_2) > 1$, see for example [4, Section 2.2].

2.2   Kani's Lemma

In [20], Kani studied genus-2 curves that admit an elliptic subcover. Among other results, the paper contains an equivalence relation between certain product isogenies in dimension 2 and isogeny-diamond configurations.

Definition 2.1. *Let $d_1, d_2 \in \mathbb{N}$ be two positive integers. A (d_1, d_2)-isogeny diamond is given by the decomposition of a $d_1 \cdot d_2$-isogeny $\phi : E \to E'$ as*

$$\phi = \psi_2 \circ \phi_1 = \psi_1 \circ \phi_2,$$

with

$$\deg(\phi_1) = \deg(\psi_1) = d_1, \quad \deg(\phi_2) = \deg(\psi_2) = d_2.$$

We represent (d_1, d_2)-isogeny diamonds by a commutative diagram:

$$
\begin{array}{ccc}
E & \xrightarrow{\ \phi_1\ } & E_1 \\
\downarrow{\phi_2} & & \downarrow{\psi_2} \\
E_2 & \xrightarrow{\ \psi_1\ } & E'
\end{array}
$$

Further, we say that the above configuration is an isogeny diamond configuration *of order $N = d_1 + d_2$ from E to E'.*

We remark that in [20], there is an additional condition that $\ker(\phi_1) \cap \ker(\phi_2) = \{0\}$. This leads to a correspondence with more specific product isogenies [20, Corollary 2.4]. Instead, here we use the more general setting.

Lemma 2.2. *Given two elliptic curves E, E', there is a 1-to-1 correspondence between equivalence classes of isogeny diamond configurations of order N from E to E', and maximal N-isotropic subgroups $G \subset (E \times E')[N]$ defining a non-diagonal product isogeny with domain $E \times E'$.*

Explicitly, given a (d_1, d_2)-isogeny diamond with notation as in Definition 2.1, the induced product isogeny is given by

$$F : E \times E' \longrightarrow E_1 \times E_2 \quad with \; F = \begin{pmatrix} \phi_1 & \tilde{\psi}_2 \\ -\phi_2 & \tilde{\psi}_1 \end{pmatrix}.$$

Proof. This follows from Theorem 2.3 in [20].

2.3   Level-2 Theta Coordinates

For the instantiation of our algorithm, we use $(2,2)$-isogenies. Such computations can be performed efficiently using level-2 theta coordinates. Here, we informally introduce the theory of level-2 theta coordinates, and briefly summarize the necessary algorithms from the literature.

Theta functions provide a convenient way to work with principally polarized (p.p.) abelian varieties in any dimension. In this manuscript, we denote by θ^A a *level*-2 theta structure attached to the abelian variety A of dimension g. This defines an embedding of the Kummer variety, $A/\langle \pm 1 \rangle$, into the projective space $\mathbb{P}^{2^g - 1}$. This means that a point of an elliptic curve E is represented by two projective coordinates, $\theta^E(P) = (x_0 : x_1)$, and a point on an abelian surface A is represented by four projective coordinates $\theta^A(P) = (x_0 : x_1 : x_2 : x_3)$.[1] We refer to these as (level-2) theta coordinates.

Theta Null Point. We say that the theta coordinates of the zero element, $\theta^A(0_A)$, is the (level-2) *theta null point* of A. We denote $\theta^A(0_A) = (a_0 : a_1)$ for elliptic curves, and $\theta^A(0_A) = (a_0 : a_1 : a_2 : a_3)$ for p.p. abelian surfaces. Remarkably, the theta null point $\theta^A(0_A)$ determines the underlying p.p. abelian variety A up to isomorphism if A is irreducible [17,39] or $g \leq 3$ [26]. This is the case in all of our applications.

Product Structure. For a reducible abelian variety $A = A_1 \times A_2$, the theta structures on A_1 and A_2 induce a theta structure on A via the Segre embedding. A theta structure obtained in this way is called *product theta structure*. More explicitly, consider two elliptic curves equipped with a level-2 theta structure

---

[1] Of course, this representation is only well defined up to sign.

(E, θ^E) and $(E', \theta^{E'})$, and their product $A = E \times E'$. We write $\theta^A = \theta^E \times \theta^{E'}$ for the product theta structure. For a point $(P, P') \in A$, we have

$$\theta^A((P, P')) = (x_0 x_0' : x_0 x_1' : x_1 x_0' : x_1 x_1'),$$

where $\theta^E(P) = (x_0 : x_1)$, $\theta^{E'}(P') = (x_0' : x_1')$.

Symplectic Transformations. Different level-2 theta structures for the same abelian variety are related by symplectic transformations. Roughly, such transformations consist of scaling the coordinates by a 4th root of unity, applying a Hadamard transformation, or permuting the coordinates. For details on such transformations, we refer to [31, Appendix B] for a general description, and [22, Appendix A.1] for a description specific to theta structures of level 2. In our applications, this will become important when computing non-generic isogenies. In these cases, we need to either compute a non-product structure (gluings) or recover the product structure (splittings).

2.4   Radical Isogeny Formulas

Here, we summarize the radical isogeny formulas from [22], see also [31]. In any dimension g, a radical 2-isogeny $f : A \to B$ can be computed as the composition of three simple operations: coordinate-wise squaring, a Hadamard transform and taking coordinate-wise square-roots. The in- and output are theta null points $a = \theta^A(0_A)$ and $b = \theta^B(0_B)$, respectively. This is sketched in Fig. 1.

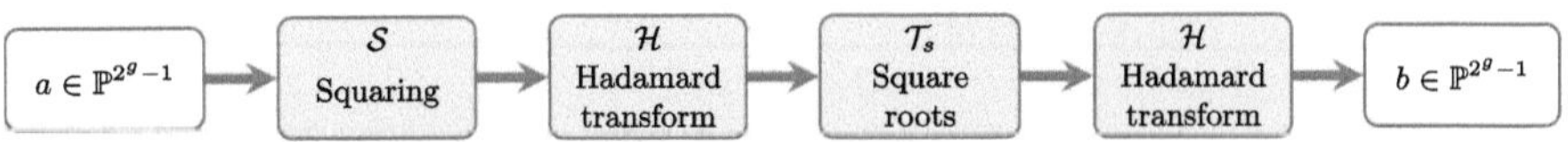

Fig. 1. Radical 2-isogeny $f : A \to B$ with $a = \theta^A(0_A)$ and $b = \theta^B(0_B)$ as described in [22, p.2].

In full generality, the definition of the square-root function, $\mathcal{T}_s$, is not straightforward, since certain square-roots have to be chosen compatibly. In this article, we only work with radical isogenies in dimension $g = 2$, where these subtleties do not arise yet. Thus, the description for these isogenies is particularly simple. It is outlined in Algorithm 2.

Note that the case distinction in Line 3 of Algorithm 2 is necessary to include non-generic isogenies. More precisely, the coordinates $x_0, \ldots, x_3$ computed in Line 2 are all non-zero if the input A is irreducible, and at most one coordinate may vanish if A is reducible.

Remark 2.3. The kernel of the isogeny $f : A \to B$ computed in Algorithm 2 is given by

$$\ker(f) = \langle (a_0 : -a_1 : a_2 : -a_3), (a_0 : a_1 : -a_2 : -a_3) \rangle.$$

This means that the isomorphism class of the codomain B does not depend on the choice of signs s_1, s_2, s_3. However, the choice of signs does determine the level-2 theta structure induced on B. In particular, it determines the kernel of the next $(2, 2)$-isogeny computation if a chain of $(2, 2)$-isogenies is computed, see [22, Section 2.5].

Algorithm 2. Radical2Isogeny (see [22, Algorithm 2] and [22, Appendix B])

Input: A level-2 theta null point $\theta^A(0_A) = (a_0 : a_1 : a_2 : a_3)$ of an abelian surface A
   and choice bits $s_i \in \{-1, 1\}^3$

Output: A level-2 theta null point $\theta^B(0_B) = (b_0 : b_1 : b_2 : b_3)$

1: $a_0', a_1', a_2', a_3' \leftarrow a_0^2, a_1^2, a_2^3, a_3^2$ $\triangleright$ Squaring

2: $x_0, x_1, x_2, x_3 \leftarrow a_0' + a_1' + a_2' + a_3',\ a_0' - a_1' + a_2' - a_3',\ a_0' + a_1' - a_2' - a_3',\ a_0' - a_1' - a_2' + a_3'$

                                                             $\triangleright$ Hadamard

3: **if** $x_0 \neq 0$ **then**

4:      $y_0, y_1, y_2, y_3 \leftarrow x_0, s_1 \cdot \sqrt{x_0 x_1}, s_2 \cdot \sqrt{x_0 x_2}, s_3 \cdot \sqrt{x_0 x_3}$ $\triangleright$ Square-roots

5: **else**

6:      $y_0, y_1, y_2, y_3 \leftarrow 0, x_1, s_2 \cdot \sqrt{x_1 x_2}, s_3 \cdot \sqrt{x_1 x_3}$

7: **end if**

8: $b_0, b_1, b_2, b_3 \leftarrow y_0 + y_1 + y_2 + y_3,\ y_0 - y_1 + y_2 - y_3,\ y_0 + y_1 - y_2 - y_3,\ y_0 - y_1 - y_2 + y_3$

                                                             $\triangleright$ Hadamard

9: **return** $(b_0 : b_1 : b_2 : b_3)$

Remark 2.4. Let (A, θ^A) be a reducible p.p. abelian surface $A = E \times E'$ equipped with the product theta structure $\theta^A = \theta^E \times \theta^{E'}$, and consider the isogeny $f : A \to B$ computed as described in Algorithm 2.

From Remark 2.3, we know the kernel of this isogeny. Writing $\theta^E(0) = (e_0 : e_1)$ and $\theta^{E'}(0) = (e_0' : e_1')$, we obtain

$$\ker(f) = \langle (e_0 e_0' : -e_0 e_1' : e_1 e_0' : -e_1 e_1'),\ (e_0 e_0' : e_0 e_1' : -e_1 e_0' : -e_1 e_1') \rangle$$
$$= \langle ((e_0 : e_1), (e_0' : -e_1')),\ ((e_0 : -e_1), (e_0' : e_1')) \rangle.$$

This shows that f is a diagonal isogeny and the codomain is again a product of elliptic curves:

$$f : E \times E' \to E / \langle (e_0 : -e_1) \rangle \times E' / \langle (e_0' : e_1') \rangle.$$

Note that the induced theta structure on the codomain is not necessarily a *product* theta structure, hence iteratively applying the radical isogeny formula still leads to irreducible p.p. abelian surfaces. In our applications, it will be preferable to compute a radical gluing immediately. This can be achieved by applying a symplectic automorphism in order to change the underlying theta structure. We make this explicit in Algorithm 3 (Gluing).

2.5   Evaluation of Isogenies

For evaluating a 2-isogeny which was computed by a radical formula, we apply the algorithms developed in [12], see also [31]. Given a radical 2-isogeny $f : A \to B$ computed as in Fig. 1 (see also Algorithm 2), then (in the generic case) the evaluation of this isogeny at a point can be expressed in a similar way. Only the coordinate-wise square-roots are replaced by coordinate-wise scaling by the dual theta null point of the codomain, $\tilde{b}$. We recall that $\tilde{b}$ is obtained from the null point $b = \theta^B(0_B)$ by applying a Hadamard transformation. The evaluation of the 2-isogeny f is sketched in Fig. 2.

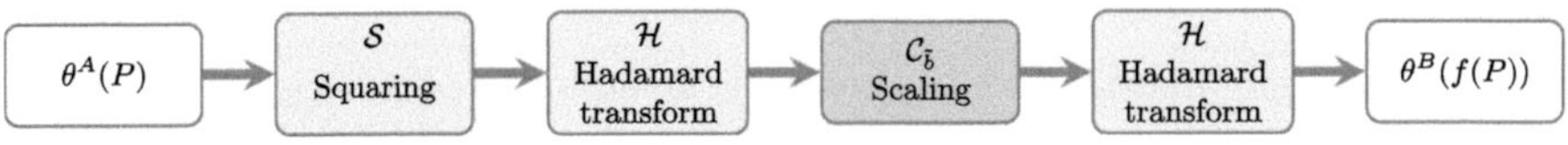

Fig. 2. Evaluation of a (generic) 2-isogeny $f : A \to B$ at a point $P \in A$, following [31, §5].

Remark 2.5. The description in Fig. 2 applies to all 2-isogenies $f : A \to B$ where A is irreducible. On the other hand, when A is the product of elliptic curves, then one of the coordinates of the dual theta null point, $\tilde{b}$, might vanish. In this case, the scaling step $\mathcal{C}_{\tilde{b}}$ is not well-defined, and the evaluation of isogenies requires more care. One possibility is to work with additional information on a 4-torsion point that lies above the kernel of the isogeny f. This idea, which we use in our implementation (Algorithm 14), is explained in [12, pp. 17-18].

In our applications, it is also required to evaluate the dual isogeny of some isogeny $f : A \to B$ (computed as in Fig. 1). Similarly to the evaluation of f, it can be decomposed into 4 basic operations. This is depicted in Fig. 3. The description follows immediately from the duplication formulas [31].

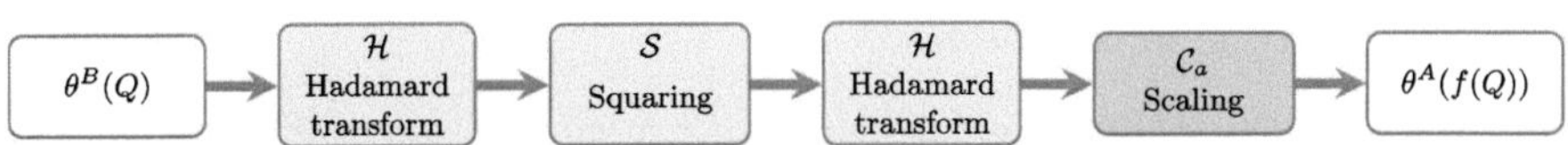

Fig. 3. Evaluation of the dual isogeny $\hat{f} : B \to A$ at a point $Q \in B$, where $f : A \to B$ is as in Fig. 2.

We remark that this description is only valid when none of the coordinates of the theta null point $a = \theta^A(0)$ vanishes. Here, the case that needs to be treated separately is when B is reducible (i.e. $\hat{f}$ is a gluing isogeny).

3   A Concrete Algorithm: Endomorphisms via Splittings

Our general idea to find an endomorphism of an elliptic curve is sketched in Algorithm 1 in the introduction. First, we compute an (N_1, N_1)-gluing $E \times E \to \mathrm{Jac}(C)$ for some $N_1 \in \mathbb{N}$. And then we find a (good) (N_2, N_2)-splitting $\mathrm{Jac}(C) \to E_1 \times E_2$. Composition yields an $(N_1 N_2, N_1 N_2)$-isogeny $E \times E \to E_1 \times E_2$ which is necessarily induced by an isogeny diamond:

$$
\begin{array}{ccc}
E & \xrightarrow{\phi_1} & E_1 \\
\Big\downarrow{\phi_2} & & \Big\downarrow{\psi_2} \\
E_2 & \xrightarrow{\psi_1} & E
\end{array}
$$

From this isogeny diamond we can read off the endomorphism $\psi_2 \circ \phi_1 \in \mathrm{End}(E)$.

3.1   Instantiation of Algorithm 1

There are several choices that can be made in the implementation of Algorithm 1. In the following, we describe a solution based on the computation of $(2,2)$-isogenies in level-2 theta coordinates. The computed isogeny chain will be of the form

$$
E \times E \xrightarrow{\sigma} (E \times E)_\sigma \xrightarrow{f_1} A_1 \to \ldots \to A_{n-1} \xrightarrow{f_n} (E_1 \times E_2)_{\tau^{-1}} \xrightarrow{\tau} E_1 \times E_2, \quad (1)
$$

where σ and τ are automorphisms that change the underlying theta structure, $f_1, \ldots, f_n$ are $(2,2)$-isogenies, and $A_1 \ldots A_{n-1}$ are irreducible p.p. abelian surfaces.

Remark 3.1. We say the isogeny chain (Eq. 1) is of length n, since σ and τ are isomorphisms. We also fix the notation of σ and τ in this paper; note that σ is a fixed automorphism discussed below while τ depends on the surface $(E_1 \times E_2)_{\tau^{-1}}$.

Gluing. The first steps, applying the autmorphism σ and computing the isogeny f_1, are summarized in Algorithm 3.

Lemma 3.2. *On input theta null points of two elliptic curves $\theta^E(0) = (e_0 : e_1)$ and $\theta^{E'}(0) = (e_0' : e_1')$, Algorithm 3 (Gluing) outputs:*

- NL_0, *theta null point of $E \times E'$ equipped with the product theta structure,*
- NL_0', *theta null point equivalent to NL_0 obtained via a symplectic transformation,*
- NL_1, *theta null point of a p.p. abelian surface B that is 2-isogenous to $E \times E'$.*

Moreover, the kernel of the $(2,2)$-isogeny $f : E \times E' \to B$ is given by

$$
\ker(f) = \langle ((e_1 : e_0), (-e_0' : e_1')), ((-e_0 : e_1), (e_1' : e_0')) \rangle.
$$

The codomain B is irreducible if one of the following conditions holds:

Algorithm 3. Gluing

Input: Theta null points of two elliptic curves $\theta^E(0) = (e_0 : e_1)$ and $\theta^{E'}(0) = (e'_0 : e'_1)$, with $j(E) \neq 0, 1728$ or $j(E') \neq 0, 1728$.

Output: Theta null point of an irreducible p.p. abelian surface $\theta(B) = (b_0 : b_1 : b_2 : b_3)$ that is 2-isogenous to $E \times E'$.

1: $\mathsf{NL}'_0 = (a'_0 : a'_1 : a'_2 : a'_3) \leftarrow (e_0 e'_0 : e_0 e'_1 : e_1 e'_0 : e_1 e'_1)$ ▷ Segre embedding

2: $\mathsf{NL}_0 = (a_0 : a_1 : a_2 : a_3) \leftarrow (a'_0 + a'_1 + a'_2 - a'_3 : -i(a'_0 - a'_1 + a'_2 + a'_3) : a'_0 - a'_1 - a'_2 - a'_3 : -i(a'_0 + a'_1 - a'_2 + a'_3))$ ▷ symplectic automorphism

3: $\mathsf{NL}_1 = (b_0 : b_1 : b_2 : b_3) \leftarrow \mathsf{Radical2Isogeny}(a_0 : a_1 : a_2 : a_3)$

4: **return** $\mathsf{NL}'_0, \mathsf{NL}_0, \mathsf{NL}_1$

---

1. $E \not\cong E'$.
2. $j(E) = j(E') \notin \{0, 1728\}$, and $(e_0 : e_1) = (e'_0 : e'_1)$.

Proof. First, we note that the computation in Line 2 corresponds to applying a symplectic automorphism σ with matrix representation

$$M(\sigma) = \begin{pmatrix} 1 & 1 & 1 & -1 \\ -i & i & -i & -i \\ 1 & -1 & -1 & -1 \\ -i & -i & i & -i \end{pmatrix}.$$

One can verify that

$$\sigma(\iota((e_1 : e_0), (-e'_0 : e'_1))) = (-a_0 : -a_1 : a_2 : a_3),$$
$$\sigma(\iota((-e_0 : e_1), (e'_1 : e'_0))) = (-a_0 : a_1 : a_2 : -a_3),$$

where ι denotes the Segre embedding. These elements generate the kernel of the radical isogeny applied in Line 3 (see Remark 2.3).

It remains to show that the codomain of the isogeny f is irreducible. As we have just shown, the kernel of f is non-diagonal. If $E \not\cong E'$, this readily implies that f is a gluing. On the other hand, when $E \cong E'$, there exists an isogeny diamond of degree-1 isogenies which induces a product isogeny $\tilde{f}$. As long as $j(E) = j(E') \notin \{0, 1728\}$, this product isogeny is unique with kernel

$$\ker(\tilde{f}) = \langle((-e_0 : e_1), (-e_0 : e_1)), ((e_1 : e_0), (e_1 : e_0))\rangle,$$

assuming $(e'_0 : e'_1) = (e_0 : e_1)$ (see also [12, Appendix A.3]). In particular $\ker(\tilde{f}) \neq \ker(f)$.

For simplicity, the case $j(E) = j(E') \in \{0, 1728\}$ is excluded in Lemma 3.2, since it does not appear in our applications (we already know non-trivial endomorphisms of these elliptic curves). The reader is referred to the description of $(2, 2)$-isogenies with domain $E \times E$ in Weierstrass coordinates provided in [16, Tables 9 and 10].

Finding a Good Splitting. The next step is the bottleneck of our method. Given a superspecial irreducible p.p. abelian surface, we want to find a splitting. Asymptotically, the best known method to do this is by taking random walks in the superspecial isogeny graph [8, 10]. A basic method is outlined in Algorithm 4 (FindSplitting). This algorithm is expected to return an isogeny after $\tilde{O}(p)$ steps. The reasoning behind this is that the proportion of reducible p.p. abelian surfaces in the superspecial isogeny graph over $\mathbb{F}_{p^2}$ is $O(1/p)$.

Algorithm 4. FindSplitting

Input: The theta null point $\mathsf{NL}_1 = \theta^{A_1}(0)$ of an irreducible superspecial p.p. abelian surface encoding an incoming $(2, 2)$-isogeny $f_1 : A_0 \to A_1$

Output: A $(2^{n-1}, 2^{n-1})$-isogeny $g : A_1 \to E_1 \times E_2$ for some $n \in \mathbb{N}$ and elliptic curves E_1, E_2, so that $g \circ f_1$ is a $(2^n, 2^n)$-isogeny. The isogeny chain is described by a chain of theta null points $\mathsf{NL}_1, \ldots, \mathsf{NL}_n$.

1: $i \leftarrow 1$
2: **while** True **do**
3:      $S_i \xleftarrow{\$} \{-1, 1\}^3$
4:      $\mathsf{NL}_{i+1} \leftarrow \mathsf{Radical2Isogeny}(\mathsf{NL}_i, S_i)$
5:      **if** IsReducible(NL_{i+1}) **then**
6:          **return** $\mathsf{NL}_1, \ldots, \mathsf{NL}_{i+1}$
7:      **end if**
8:      $i \leftarrow i + 1$
9: **end while**

A drawback of Algorithm 4 is that the output is long and hence the evaluation of the corresponding endomorphism inefficient. In order to obtain a splitting that can be evaluated efficiently, we propose Algorithm 5 (FindSmallSplitting) which takes walks of bounded length N until a splitting is found. More precisely, it searches a splitting in a subtree of the superspecial isogeny graph with root $\mathsf{NL}_1 = \theta^{A_1}(0)$. The algorithm fails if none of the $O(8^N)$ inspected p.p. abelian surfaces in the neighborhood of the starting vertex is reducible.

Algorithm 5. FindSmallSplitting

Input: The theta null point $\mathsf{NL}_1 = \theta^{A_1}(0)$ of an irreducible superspecial p.p. abelian surface encoding an incoming $(2,2)$-isogeny $f_1 : A_0 \to A_1$, and a bound $N \in \mathbb{N}$.

Output: A $(2^{n-1}, 2^{n-1})$-isogeny $g : A_1 \to E_1 \times E_2$ for some $1 \le n \le N$ and elliptic curves E_1, E_2, so that $g \circ f_1$ is a $(2^n, 2^n)$-isogeny. The isogeny chain is described by a chain of theta null points $\mathsf{NL}_1, \ldots, \mathsf{NL}_n$. If no such isogeny exists[2] the algorithm returns $\perp$.

```
 1:  S = S_0, ..., S_7 ← {-1,1}^3                        ▷ list of sign choices
 2:  i ← 1                                               ▷ current depth
 3:  j_1 ← 0                                             ▷ sign choice at step i
 4:  while i > 0 do
 5:      if j_i = 8 or i = N - 1 then
 6:          j_{i-1} ← j_{i-1} + 1
 7:          i ← i - 1
 8:      else
 9:          NL_{i+1} ← Radical2Isogeny(NL_i, S_{j_i})
10:          if IsReducible(NL_{i+1}) then
11:              return NL_1, ..., NL_{i+1}
12:          end if
13:          j_{i+1} ← 0
14:          i ← i + 1
15:      end if
16:  end while
17:  return ⊥
```

Lemma 3.3. *If Algorithms 4 or 5 terminate successfully, then the output is correct.*

Proof. The only non-trivial part is to make sure that g is a $(2^{n-1}, 2^{n-1})$-isogeny, and the composition $g \circ f_1$ a $(2^n, 2^n)$-isogeny. This is an immediate consequence of [22, Section 3.4], where it is shown that the composition of the radical $(2,2)$-isogeny formulas underlying Algorithm 2 (Radical2Isogeny) yields a $(2^k, 2^k)$-isogeny. Note that the gluing $E \times E \to A$ is computed using the same formulas (after applying the isomorphism σ). $\square$

Explicit Endomorphism Finding Algorithm. Our explicit version of the endomorphism finding algorithm is just a combination of the explicit gluing algorithm (Algorithm 3) and one of the splitting algorithms (Algorithms 4 and 5). For future reference, we state this explicitly in Algorithm 6. The output of this algorithm provides a list of theta null points NL. This output provides a representation of the endomorphism which is an *efficient representation* if the length of the chain is polynomial in $\log p$ (see also Definition 4.1).

---

[2] Note that we do not test all possible $(2^n, 2^n)$-isogenies, see Remark 2.3.

Algorithm 6. FindEndomorphismExplicit

Input: E a supersingular elliptic curve over a finite field $\mathbb{F}_{p^2}$ with level-2 theta null point $(e_0 : e_1)$ and $j(E) \neq 0, 1728$

Output: A list of theta null points of abelian surfaces that represent a *non-trivial* endomorphism of E via Algorithm 14.

1: $\mathsf{NL}_0', \mathsf{NL}_0, \mathsf{NL}_1 \leftarrow \mathsf{Gluing}((e_0 : e_1), (e_0 : e_1))$ $\triangleright$ Algorithm 3

2: $\mathsf{NL}_1, \ldots, \mathsf{NL}_n \leftarrow \mathsf{FindSplitting}(\mathsf{NL}_1)$ or $\mathsf{FindSmallSplitting}(\mathsf{NL}_1)$

                         $\triangleright$ Algorithm 4 or Algorithm 5

3: **return** $\mathsf{NL}_0', \mathsf{NL}_0, \ldots, \mathsf{NL}_n$

Extracting the Endomorphism from a Product Isogeny. Assume we are given a chain of theta null points outputted by Algorithm 6. This chain induces a product isogeny $F \colon E \times E \to E_1 \times E_2$ with matrix representation

$$F = \begin{pmatrix} \phi_1 & \hat{\psi}_2 \\ -\phi_2 & \hat{\psi}_1 \end{pmatrix}.$$

By [33, Lemma 3], the adjoint isogeny $\tilde{F}$ has the matrix form $\begin{pmatrix} \hat{\phi}_1 & -\hat{\phi}_2 \\ \psi_2 & \psi_1 \end{pmatrix}$. With the knowledge of F and $\tilde{F}$, we are able to 'extract' the endomorphism $\psi_2 \circ \phi_1$. By 'extract' an endomorphism, we mean being able to evaluate the map on a given point. Briefly, we first compute $\phi_1(P)$ from the first component of $F \cdot \begin{pmatrix} P \\ 0_E \end{pmatrix}$ and then obtain the desired $\psi_2 \circ \phi_1(P)$ from

$$\tilde{F} \cdot \begin{pmatrix} \phi_1(P) \\ 0_{E_2} \end{pmatrix} = \begin{pmatrix} [\deg \phi_1](P) \\ -\psi_2 \circ \phi_1(P) \end{pmatrix}. \tag{2}$$

Recall that F was computed as a chain of $(2,2)$-isogenies (and two additional isomorphisms), more precisely $F = \tau \circ f_n \circ \cdots \circ f_1 \circ \sigma$ as in Eq. 1. The evaluation of the individual $(2,2)$-isogenies is efficiently computed as $\mathcal{H} \circ \mathcal{C}_{\tilde{b}} \circ \mathcal{H} \circ \mathcal{S}$, where b is the theta null point of the corresponding codomain (see Fig. 2). Only in the first step, i.e. for the gluing isogeny f_1, this approach does not work (Remark 2.5). We explain the necessary modifications in detail in Appendix A.1. In particular, we describe the algorithm ChainEvaluation (Algorithm 13). The latter takes as input a chain of theta null points NL describing F as in (Eq. 1), and a point $(P, Q) \in E \times E$, and outputs the image $F((P,Q)) \in E_1 \times E_2$.

Similarly, the adjoint isogeny $\tilde{F} : E_1 \times E_2 \to E \times E$ is given by

$$\tilde{F} = \sigma^{-1} \circ \hat{f}_1 \circ \cdots \circ \hat{f}_n \circ \tau^{-1}.$$

The evaluation of the individual steps is efficiently computed as $\mathcal{C}_a \circ \mathcal{H} \circ \mathcal{S} \circ \mathcal{H}$ as in Fig. 3. Similar to before, only the first isogeny, here $\hat{f}_n$, requires special treatment since it represents a gluing isogeny. The details for this step are provided in Appendix A.2.

3.2 Constructing *Non-scalar Endomorphisms*

Assume we found an endomorphism $\psi_2 \circ \phi_1 \in \mathrm{End}(E)$ using Algorithm 6. In order for this to be a solution to the `OneEnd` problem, we require that the endomorphism is non-scalar. In this subsection, we prove that scalar endomorphisms are naturally avoided in our setup.

Lemma 3.4. *Let E be an elliptic curve and $F : E \times E \to E_1 \times E_2$ a $(2^n, 2^n)$-product isogeny. If $\psi_2 \circ \phi_1$ is scalar, then all $\phi_1, \phi_2, \psi_1, \psi_2$ are cyclic isogenies of degree 2^{n-1}.*

Proof. We denote $\psi_2 \circ \phi_1 = [N]$, and use the decompositions

$$\phi_1 = [a] \circ \phi_1', \quad \psi_2 = [b] \circ \psi_2',$$

where $[a], [b]$ denote scalar multiplications (by positive integers a, b) and ϕ_1', ψ_2' are cyclic isogenies. Note that

$$[N] = \psi_2 \circ \phi_1 = [ab] \circ \psi_2' \circ \phi_1'$$

which implies that $\hat{\psi}_2' = \pm\phi_1'$. In particular $\deg(\psi_2') = \deg(\phi_1')$. This provides us with a condition on the degrees:

$$2^n = \deg(\phi_1) + \deg(\psi_2) = \deg(\phi_1') \cdot (a^2 + b^2).$$

It follows that $\deg(\phi_1') = 2^{k_1}$ for some $k_1 < n$, and $a^2 + b^2 = 2^{n-k_1}$. The only solution to the latter is $a = b = 2^{k_1'}$ with $k_1' = (n - k_1 - 1)/2$.[2] Similarly, we write

$$\phi_2 = [c] \circ \phi_2', \quad \psi_1 = [d] \circ \psi_1',$$

where $[c], [d]$ denote scalar multiplications and ϕ_2', ψ_1' are cyclic isogenies, and obtain the condition $\deg(\phi_2') = 2^{k_2}$ for some $k_2 < n$ and $c = d = 2^{k_2'}$ with $k_2' = (n - k_2 - 1)/2$.

In conclusion, the product isogeny is of the form

$$F = \begin{pmatrix} [2^{k_1'}]\phi_1' & \pm[2^{k_1'}]\phi_1' \\ [2^{k_2'}]\phi_2' & \pm[2^{k_2'}]\phi_2' \end{pmatrix}.$$

By assumption, F is a $(2^n, 2^n)$-isogeny. In particular, $\ker(F)[2] \subset (E \times E)[2]$ is maximal 2-isotropic. Now if $k_1' > 0$ or $k_2' > 0$, then the rank of $\ker(F)[2]$ is greater than 2. This proves that $k_1' = k_2' = 0$, hence $k_1 = k_2 = n - 1$.

Lemma 3.5. *Let $f : E \times E \to A$ be a $(2, 2)$-isogeny with kernel*

$$\ker(f) = \{(P, P) \mid P \in E[2]\},$$

then $A \cong E \times E$.

---

[2] One way to see this is writing $a = 2^\alpha(1 + 2a')$, $b = 2^\beta(1 + 2b')$ for some a', b', and w.l.o.g. $\beta \geq \alpha$. Then $a^2 + b^2 = 2^{2\alpha}(1 + 4(a' + a'^2) + 2^{2(\beta-\alpha)}(1 + 4(b' + b'^2)))$. So $a^2 + b^2$ can only be a power of two if $a' = b' = 0$ and $\alpha = \beta$.

Proof. Consider the Kani diagram

$$
\begin{array}{ccc}
E & \xrightarrow{\;\cong\;} & E \\
{\scriptstyle\cong}\downarrow & & \downarrow{\scriptstyle\cong} \\
E & \xrightarrow{\;\cong\;} & E
\end{array}\;.
$$

This induces the $(2,2)$-isogeny

$$
F : E \times E \to E \times E \quad \text{with } F = \begin{pmatrix} 1 & 1 \\ -1 & 1 \end{pmatrix}.
$$

Note that

$$
F(P,P) = (P+P, -P+P) = ([2]P, 0) \quad \text{for all } P \in E.
$$

Consequently,

$$
\ker(F) = \{(P,P) \mid P \in E[2]\},
$$

and the isogenies F and f coincide (up to isomorphism).

Using the preceding lemmas, we can now show that Algorithm 6 finds a non-scalar endomorphism.

Proposition 3.6. *Let $\psi_2 \circ \phi_1 \in \mathrm{End}(E)$ be an endomorphism outputted by Algorithm 6. Then $\psi_2 \circ \phi_1$ is non-scalar.*

Proof. Let $F : E \times E \to E_1 \times E_2$ be a $(2^n, 2^n)$-product isogeny constructed in Algorithm 6, and let $F = f_n \circ \cdots \circ f_1$, i.e.

$$
E \times E \xrightarrow{f_1} A_1 \xrightarrow{f_2} \ldots \xrightarrow{f_{n-1}} A_{n-1} \xrightarrow{f_n} E_1 \times E_2
$$

be the decomposition into $(2,2)$-isogenies. Assume that $\psi_2 \circ \phi_1$ is a scalar endomorphism. Note that in our algorithm, the isogeny f_1 is a gluing, i.e. A_1 is irreducible. On the other hand, it follows from Lemma 3.4 that $F = \begin{pmatrix} \phi_1 & \pm\phi_1 \\ -\phi_2 & \pm\phi_2 \end{pmatrix}$ for some 2^{n-1}-isogenies ϕ_1, ϕ_2. For a 2-torsion point $P \in E[2]$, it holds that

$$
F((P,P)) = \begin{pmatrix} \phi_1(P) \pm \phi_1(P) \\ -\phi_2(P) \pm \phi_2(P) \end{pmatrix} = \begin{pmatrix} \phi_1(P \pm P) \\ \phi_2(-P \pm P) \end{pmatrix} = \begin{pmatrix} \phi_1(0) \\ \phi_2(0) \end{pmatrix} = 0
$$

Now Lemma 3.5 implies that the codomain of f_1 is $A_1 = E \times E$. This contradicts the fact that f_1 is a gluing, hence the endomorphism $\psi_2 \circ \phi_1$ is non-scalar.

3.3 Analyzing the Degree of the Endomorphism

The degree of the endomorphism that we find using Algorithm 6, depends on the degree of the $(2^n, 2^n)$-product isogeny. More precisely, we find an endomorphism $\psi_2 \circ \phi_1$ of degree $d = \deg(\psi_2) \cdot \deg(\phi_1)$, where $\deg(\psi_2) + \deg(\phi_1) = 2^n$. This provides us with the bounds

$$
2^n < d < 2^{2n}.
$$

Order of Magnitude. We know that the proportion of products of supersingular curves in the superspecial isogeny graph [10, Section 6] is

$$\frac{\#S_2(p)^E}{\#S_2(p)} \approx \frac{10}{p},$$

We expect to find a splitting after inspecting $O(p)$ vertices in the graph. Using Algorithm 4 to find a (long) splitting, we expect to succeed for a $(2^n, 2^n)$-isogeny with $n \approx p$. The degree of the resulting endomorphism is exponential in p.

On the other hand, using Algorithm 5 to find a (short) $(2^n, 2^n)$-splitting bounded by $n \leq N$, we visit $O(8^N)$ vertices in the neighborhood of the starting vertex. Under the (strong) assumption that these vertices behave sufficiently random, we would expect that a value of $N = \log_2(p)/3$ suffices to find a product. In this case, the degree of the endomorphism that we find is bounded by

$$\deg(\psi_2) \cdot \deg(\phi_1) < p^{2/3}.$$

Interestingly, this upper bound is similar to the lower bound on the degree of the smallest endomorphism of a general supersingular elliptic curve. More precisely, [24, Proposition B.5] states that every supersingular elliptic curve over $\mathbb{F}_{p^2}$ has an endomorphism of reduced norm at most $1/2p^{2/3} + 1/4$, and that the exponent $2/3$ is optimal. However, we point out that not any arbitrary endomorphism can be detected by our algorithm. In contrast, we require that an endomorphism $\alpha \in \mathrm{End}(E)$ has a decomposition $\alpha = \alpha_2 \circ \alpha_1$ with isogenies $\alpha_1 : E \to E'$ and $\alpha_2 : E' \to E$ so that $\deg(\alpha_1) + \deg(\alpha_2) = 2^n$.

The underlying assumption for the (optimistic) upper bound described above is that vertices in the neighborhood of a product behave like random vertices. This assumption is clearly too strong. In our experiments, the bound $N = \log_2(p)/2$ works well. In this case, the degree of the resulting endomorphism is upper bounded by p. For further experimental data concerning the degree of the endomorphism, we refer to Sect. 5.

Smoothness. We also note that the degree of the isogeny (resp. endomorphism) outputted by Algorithm 7 (resp. Algorithm 6) is of the form $\deg \phi_1 \cdot (2^n - \deg \phi_1)$ and there is no reason for it to be smooth. This is in contrast to other endomorphism or isogeny finding algorithms, where the result is usually described as the composition of low-degree isogenies, and very smooth.

Below, we describe two scenarios where this is a particularly useful output:

1. Given two supersingular elliptic curves E and E', Algorithm 7 finds an isogeny (namely $\psi_2 \circ \phi_1$) of degree $\deg \phi_1 \cdot (2^n - \deg \phi_1)$ between the two curves. In particular, when $\deg \phi_1$ is a prime, the extracted isogeny might be interesting: In the new cryptosystem *PRISM* [2], the degrees of the isogenies are of the form $q \cdot (2^a - q)$ where q is a prime of a bits. To implement a forgery attack (see [28]), one needs to generate an isogeny of this particular form.

2. Given a supersingular elliptic curve E, Algorithm 6 (or Algorithm 7) outputs two isogenies with domain E (namely ϕ_1 and ϕ_2) of degree $\deg \phi_1$ and $2^n - \deg \phi_1$, respectively. When $\deg \phi_1$ or $2^n - \deg \phi_1$ are prime, our algorithm gives a method to construct an isogeny of large prime degree.

Computing the Degree of the Endomorphism Explicitly. Assume we have recovered the endomorphism $\psi_2 \circ \phi_1$ by Algorithm 6, the degree of $\psi_2 \circ \phi_1$ can be computed explicitly by computing pairings.

Consider an isogeny $\phi \colon E \to E'$ between elliptic curves, for $P_N, Q_N \in E[N]$, recall the following relation ([36, III Proposition 8.1])

$$e_N(P_N, Q_N)^{\deg \phi} = e'_N(\phi(P_N), \phi(Q_N)) \tag{3}$$

where e_N (resp. e'_N) is the N-Weil pairing on E (resp. E'). In our case, given P_N, Q_N and their images under an isogeny, we can recover $\deg \phi \mod N$ from Equation (3). We provide pseudo-code for our implementation of this method in Appendix A.3. This method requires that the endomorphism was computed using Algorithm 5 as a subroutine, i.e. the output is an endomorphism of small degree.

3.4   Finding Isogenies via Splittings

A small change in our algorithm FindEndomorphism allows us to find isogenies between two given elliptic curves E and E'. This is outlined in Algorithm 7. Essentially, the only difference is that we now start on the product surface $E \times E'$, and need to find a non-diagonal product isogeny $F : E \times E' \to E_1 \times E_2$ from which we can extract an isogeny $E \to E'$.

Algorithm 7. FindIsogeny

Input: $E \not\cong E'$ two supersingular elliptic curves over a finite field $\mathbb{F}_{p^2}$
Output: an isogeny $\phi \colon E \to E'$
 1: Compute a $(2,2)$-gluing $f_1 \colon E \times E' \to \mathrm{Jac}(C)$ for some genus-2 curve $C \triangleright$ Algorithm 3
 2: Find a good $(2^{n-1}, 2^{n-1})$-splitting $\mathrm{Jac}(C) \to E_1 \times E_2$ for some $n > 1$. It is required that the composition is a $(2^n, 2^n)$-isogeny $F \colon E \times E' \to E_1 \times E_2 \triangleright$ Algorithm 4 or Algorithm 5
 3: Use Kani's lemma to extract the isogeny $\psi_2 \circ \phi_1 \colon E \to E'$ from the product isogeny
$$F = \begin{pmatrix} \phi_1 & \hat{\psi}_2 \\ -\phi_2 & \hat{\psi}_1 \end{pmatrix}$$

The analysis of the output of Algorithm 7 is considerably easier than that of 6 (see Subsect. 3.2). There do not exist "trivial" isogenies between elliptic curves. We only need to ensure that the output is not the zero map.

Proposition 3.7. *Let $\psi_2 \circ \phi_1 : E \to E'$ be a map outputted by Algorithm 6. Then $\psi_2 \circ \phi_1$ is non-zero, in particular, it is an isogeny.*

Proof. First note that Line 3 holds because the isogeny is induced by the isogeny diamond:

$$
\begin{array}{ccc}
E & \xrightarrow{\phi_1} & E_1 \\
\downarrow{\scriptstyle\phi_2} & & \downarrow{\scriptstyle\psi_2} \\
E_2 & \xrightarrow{\psi_1} & E'
\end{array}
$$

The only subtlety is to exclude the possibility that $\psi_2 \circ \phi_1$ is trivial, i.e. the zero map. This can only happen if one of ϕ_1 or ψ_2 vanish, in other words, if the product isogeny F is a diagonal isogeny. However, this is not possible since F is a $(2^n, 2^n)$-isogeny (i.e. has kernel of rank 2), and the first step of the isogeny chain is a gluing, whereas for a diagonal $(2^n, 2^n)$-isogeny, each $(2,2)$-isogeny is diagonal as well.

4 Reductions Between Different Hardness Assumptions

There are numerous articles studying the connection between different hardness assumptions underlying isogeny-based cryptography. For recent results on the relation between the problems, we refer to [15,27,30].

In this section, we apply the main ideas underlying Algorithms 1 and 7 to include the Splitting problem in the landscape of equivalent hardness assumptions. Our results are sketched in Fig. 4.

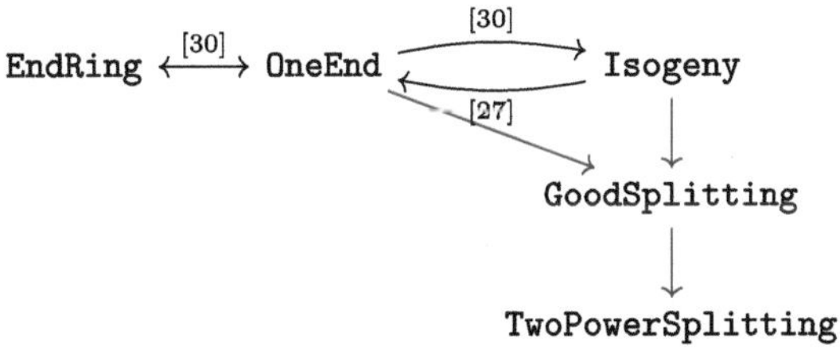

Fig. 4. Relation among different hardness assumptions in isogeny-based cryptography. The first row corresponds to a part of [27, Fig. 1]; the blue arrows are new.

4.1 Definitions of the Hardness Assumptions

Before we study the reductions between different problems, we provide more formal definitions.

First, we point out that whenever we ask to "find" an isogeny (including endomorphisms or splittings), we ask for an *efficient representation* in the following sense (cf. [1, Definition 3.1]):

Definition 4.1. *(Efficient representation) Let* $\varphi\colon A \to B$ *be an isogeny between two abelian varieties defined over a finite field* $\mathbb{F}_q$. *An* efficient representation *of* φ *with respect to a given algorithm is some data* $D_\varphi \in \{0,1\}^*$ *such that, on input* D_φ *and* $P \in A(\mathbb{F}_q)$, *the algorithm returns the evaluation* $\varphi(P)$ *in polynomial time in* $\log q$ *and the length of* D_φ.

In particular, we formally state the `OneEnd` and `Isogeny` problems as follows.

Problem 4.2. (`OneEnd`) Given a supersingular elliptic curve E, find an efficient representation of a non-trivial endomorphism of E.

Problem 4.3. (`Isogeny`) Given two supersingular elliptic curves E and E', find an an efficient representation of an isogeny $\phi\colon E \to E'$.

In its most general form, `Splitting` asks to find an efficient representation of an arbitrary splitting $A \to E_1 \times E_2$ on inputting a p.p. abelian surface A. We consider the following two more restrictive variants of this problem:

Problem 4.4. (`TwoPowerSplitting`) Given a principally polarized abelian surface A together with a maximal isotropic subgroup $K \subset A[2]$, find an efficient representation of a *good* $(2^{n-1}, 2^{n-1})$-splitting $F : A \to E_1 \times E_2$ for some $n > 1$. Here *good* means that $K \cap \ker(F) = \emptyset$.

We note that the meaning of *good splitting* here coincides with the terminology from Sect. 3. In the latter setting, the group $K \subset A[2]$ would be the kernel of the dual of the gluing isogeny.

Problem 4.5. (`GoodSplitting`) Given a principally polarized abelian surface A and a maximal m-isotropic group $K \subset A[m]$ for some integer $m \in \mathbb{N}$, find efficient representations of a good (N, N)-splitting $F : A \to E_1 \times E_2$ for some N.

Note that any (N, N)-splitting $F : A \to E_1 \times E_2$ with $\gcd(N, m) = 1$ is a solution to `GoodSplitting`. However, our definition also includes the case $\gcd(N, m) > 1$.

4.2   Reductions to `TwoPowerSplitting`

The idea for the reduction from `OneEnd` to `TwoPowerSplitting` lies at the heart of our paper. Algorithm 8 which uses only one call to the `RadicalSplitting` oracle, provides a polynomial time reduction.

Proposition 4.6. `OneEnd` *reduces to* `TwoPowerSplitting`.

Proof. The reduction is sketched in Algorithm 8. This is a slightly more abstract version of Algorithm 6. The correctness of this reduction, namely that ϕ is non-scalar, was proved in Proposition 3.6. We note that the extraction of the endomorphism $\psi_2 \circ \phi_1$ from the product isogeny requires that we can evaluate F and its adjoint $\tilde{F}$ efficiently. By assumption, we know that this is true for F. Since

---

Algorithm 8. Reduction from `OneEnd` to `TwoPowerSplitting`

Input: A supersingular elliptic curve E defined over $\mathbb{F}_{p^2}$
Output: A non-trivial endomorphism $\phi \in \mathrm{End}(E)$
  1: Compute a $(2,2)$-gluing $f_0 : E \times E \to A$, and let $K \subset A[2]$ be the maximal isotropic subgroup defining the dual isogeny $\hat{f}_0 : A \to E \times E$.
  2: Run the `TwoPowerSplitting` oracle on input (A, K) to obtain a good $(2^{n-1}, 2^{n-1})$-splitting $f_1 : A \to E_1 \times E_2$
  3: Return the non-trivial endomorphism $\psi_2 \circ \phi_1$ embedded in the product isogeny
$$F = f_1 \circ f_0 = \begin{pmatrix} \phi_1 & \tilde{\psi}_2 \\ -\phi_2 & \tilde{\psi}_1 \end{pmatrix}.$$

F is a composition of 2-isogeny, one may easily compute the adjoint of each 2-isogeny, and thereby obtains an efficient representation of $\tilde{F}$ as well. Apart from this, the proof does not use any specific properties of the implementation, and immediately translates to the setting here.

The reduction from `Isogeny` to `TwoPowerSplitting` is described in Algorithm 9. It is an abstract version of Algorithm 7, and as the previous reduction, it only requires one call to the `TwoPowerSplitting` oracle.

Algorithm 9. Reduction from `Isogeny` to `TwoPowerSplitting`

Input: Two supersingular elliptic curves E and E'
Output: An isogeny $\phi \colon E \to E'$
  1: Compute a $(2,2)$-gluing $f_0 : E \times E' \to A$, and let $K \subset A[2]$ be the maximal isotropic subgroup defining the dual isogeny $\hat{f}_0 : A \to E \times E'$.
  2: Run the `TwoPowerSplitting` oracle on input (A, K) to obtain a splitting $f_1 : A \to E_1 \times E_2$
  3: Return the isogeny $\psi_2 \circ \phi_1$ embedded in the product isogeny
  4: $F = f_1 \circ f_0 = \begin{pmatrix} \phi_1 & \tilde{\psi}_2 \\ -\phi_2 & \tilde{\psi}_1 \end{pmatrix}.$

Proposition 4.7. *Isogeny reduces to TwoPowerSplitting.*

Proof. The reduction is sketched in Algorithm 9. This is a slightly more abstract version of Algorithm 7. As in the proof of Proposition 4.6, one can show that the evaluation of the adjoint isogeny $\tilde{F}$ is efficient.

The only remaining subtlety when proving the correctness of the reduction is to make sure that $\psi_2 \circ \phi_1 \neq 0$. This follows from the fact that the product isogeny factors through a gluing, hence it cannot be diagonal.

4.3 Generalization of the Reductions

One might feel that the problem (`TwoPowerSplitting`) that we discussed is quite specific. In fact, most parts of the reductions also work in more general settings. In particular, the only restriction for extracting an elliptic curve isogeny from a product isogeny using Algorithm 14 (ExtractEndomorphism) is that the product isogeny and its adjoint can be evaluated efficiently which motivated the definition of the problem GoodSplitting (Problem 4.5). The more delicate part is making sure that the result is non-trivial.

Proposition 4.8. *Isogeny reduces to GoodSplitting.*

Proof. The reduction is almost the same as the reduction from Isogeny to TwoPowerSplitting sketched in Algorithm 9. The only difference occurs in Line 2, where we now call the oracle for GoodSplitting on input (A, K) which returns an (N, N)-splitting $f_1 : A \to E_1 \times E_2$ so that $F = f_1 \circ f_0$ is a $(2N, 2N)$-product isogeny $F : E \times E' \to E_1 \times E_2$. By assumption, we can evaluate both F and $\tilde{F}$ efficiently, hence we can extract an efficient representation of $\psi_2 \circ \phi_1$.

Moreover, as in the proof of Proposition 4.7, we find that $\psi_2 \circ \phi_1$ is non-zero since it factors through a gluing and the kernel of F has rank 2.

We remark that the fact that the GoodSplitting-oracle returns a *good* splitting is essential in the proof of the reduction. This not only avoids that the returned splitting is the dual of the gluing computed in the first step, but it also ensures that other trivial cycles in the isogeny graph are avoided.

This condition becomes even more important in the next reduction, where it helps us to exclude certain special cases that would result in scalar endomorphisms. We first prove a technical lemma about diagonal isogenies appearing in the factorization of product isogenies.

Lemma 4.9. *Let $F : E \times E' \to E_1 \times E_2$ be an (N, N)-isogeny for some integer N which is induced be an isogeny diamond confiuation*

$$\phi = \psi_2 \circ \phi_1 = \psi_1 \circ \phi_2,$$

with notation as in Definition 2.1.

Then $\ker(\phi_1) \cap \ker(\phi_2)$ is a cyclic group of order m for some $m \mid N$. If $m \neq 1$, then F factors through a diagonal (m, m)-isogeny $F_1 : E \times E' \to \tilde{E} \times \tilde{E}'$ for some elliptic curves $\tilde{E}, \tilde{E}'$ i.e.

$$E \times E' \xrightarrow{\ F_1\ } \tilde{E} \times \tilde{E}' \xrightarrow{\ \star\ } E_1 \times E_2.$$
$$\underset{F}{\underbrace{\hspace{4cm}}}$$

If, moreover, ϕ factors through $[m]$, i.e. $\phi = [m]\phi'$ for some isogeny $\phi' : E \to E'$, then F also factors through a diagonal (m, m)-isogeny $F_2' : \tilde{E}_1 \times \tilde{E}_2 \to E_1 \times E_2$, i.e.

$$E \times E' \xrightarrow{\ \star\ } \tilde{E}_1 \times \tilde{E}_2 \xrightarrow{\ F_2'\ } E_1 \times E_2.$$
$$\underset{F}{\underbrace{\hspace{4cm}}}$$

Proof. First, we note that $\ker(F)$ would be a rank-3 group if $\ker(\phi_1) \cap \ker(\phi_2)$ had rank 2. This is a contradiction to F being an (N, N)-isogeny. Hence,

$$\ker(\phi_1) \cap \ker(\phi_2) = \langle P \rangle, \quad \text{for some } P \in E[m],\ \mathrm{ord}(P) = m.$$

Necessarily $m \mid N$, and since F is an (N, N)-isogeny, $\ker(F)[m]$ is a maximal isotropic subgroup of $(E \times E')[m]$. Moreover $\langle (P, 0) \rangle \subset \ker(F)[m]$ by the definition of P. From the isotropy condition it then follows that $\ker(F)[m] = \langle (P, 0), (0, P') \rangle$ for some $P' \in E'[m]$. This is a diagonal kernel which means that F factors through a diagonal isogeny $F_1 : E \times E' \to \tilde{E} \times \tilde{E}'$.

For the second part, assume that $\phi = [m]\phi'$ for some $\phi' : E \to E'$, and consider the adjoint isogeny $\hat{F} = \begin{pmatrix} \hat{\phi}_1 & -\hat{\phi}_2 \\ \psi_2 & \psi_1 \end{pmatrix}$. Using the first part of the lemma, it suffices to show that $\ker(\hat{\phi}_1) \cap \ker(\psi_2)$ contains a point of order m. Denote $E[m] = \langle P, Q \rangle$ with P as above. Then we claim that $\phi_1(Q) \in \ker(\hat{\phi}_1) \cap \ker(\psi_2)$. First, note that $\hat{\phi}_1 \circ \phi_1(Q) = 0$, since $m \mid \deg(\phi_1)$; and $\psi_2 \circ \phi_1(Q) = 0$ since $\phi = \psi_2 \circ \phi_1$ factors through $[m]$ by our assumption. Second, note that $\mathrm{ord}(\phi_1(Q)) = m$. Otherwise, there would exist an integer $m' \mid m$ greater than 1 with $\phi_1 = [m'] \circ \phi_1'$. But then $\ker(F)[m']$ would have rank 3 which is a contradiction to our assumptions.

Proposition 4.10. `OneEnd` *reduces to* `GoodSplitting`.

Proof. The reduction algorithm is almost the same as in the reduction from `OneEnd` to `TwoPowerSplitting` sketched in Algorithm 8. The only difference occurs in Line 2, where we now call the oracle for `GoodSplitting` on input (A, K) which returns an (N, N)-splitting $f_1 : A \to E_1 \times E_2$ so that $F = f_1 \circ f_0$ is a $(2N, 2N)$-product isogeny $F : E \times E \to E_1 \times E_2$. By assumption, we can evaluate both F and $\tilde{F}$ efficiently, hence we can extract an efficient representation of $\psi_2 \circ \phi_1$. Let us now show that the endomorphism is non-trivial. We proceed by contradiction, i.e. assume that $\psi_2 \circ \phi_1 = [M]$ for some scalar $M \in \mathbb{Z}$.

First, if $\ker(\phi_1) \cap \ker(\phi_2) = \langle P \rangle$ with $\mathrm{ord}(P) = m \neq 0$, then we apply Lemma 4.9. That is we decompose $F = F_2 \circ F_1$, where F_2 is a diagonal isogeny $F_2 : \tilde{E}_1 \times \tilde{E}_2 \to E_1 \times E_2$, and $F_1 : E \times E \to \tilde{E}_1 \times \tilde{E}_2$ is a product isogeny induced by an isogeny diamond of order N/m. It suffices to show that this isogeny diamond induces a non-scalar product isogeny. Having this in mind, we may and do assume that

$$\ker(\phi_1) \cap \ker(\phi_2) = \{0\}.$$

Now, similar to the proof of Proposition 3.6, we write

$$\phi_1 = [a] \circ \phi_1', \quad \psi_2 = [b] \circ \hat{\phi}_1'$$

and

$$\phi_2 = [b] \circ \phi_2', \quad \psi_1 = [a] \circ \hat{\phi}_2'$$

for some cyclic isogenies ϕ_1' and ϕ_2' (here we use the fact that $\ker(\phi_1) \cap \ker(\phi_2) = \{0\}$). We further remark that

$$2N = \deg(\phi_1) + \deg(\phi_2) = d \cdot (a^2 + b^2),$$

where $d = \deg(\phi_1') = \deg(\phi_2')$.

Consequently, the product isogeny is of the form

$$F = \begin{pmatrix} [a]\phi_1' & [b]\phi_1' \\ -[b]\phi_2' & [a]\phi_2' \end{pmatrix}.$$

We distinguish two cases.

If $a \equiv b \pmod 2$, then both a and b are odd (and coprime), since $\ker(\phi_1) \cap \ker(\phi_2) = \{0\}$. In this case

$$F : \begin{pmatrix} P \\ P \end{pmatrix} \mapsto \begin{pmatrix} \phi_1'([2]P) \\ \phi_2'([2]P) \end{pmatrix} = \begin{pmatrix} 0 \\ 0 \end{pmatrix} \quad \text{for all } P \in E[2].$$

This means $\ker(F)[2] = \{(P, P) \mid P \in E[2]\}$ which is a contradiction by Lemma 3.5.

If $a \not\equiv b \pmod 2$, assume without loss of generality that a is even and b is odd. Then

$$F : \begin{pmatrix} P \\ Q \end{pmatrix} \mapsto \begin{pmatrix} \phi_1'(Q) \\ \phi_2'(P) \end{pmatrix} = \begin{pmatrix} 0 \\ 0 \end{pmatrix} \quad \text{for } (P, Q) \in \ker(\phi_2') \times \ker(\phi_1') \subset (E \times E)[2].$$

This means that $\ker(F)[2]$ is the kernel of a diagonal $(2,2)$-isogeny in contradiction with our construction.

Remark 4.11. Note that in the reduction `Isogeny` to `GoodSplitting`, we did not make use of the fact that the first step is a $(2,2)$-gluing. Indeed, one could use an arbitrary (n,n)-gluing provided that the splitting is *good* with respect to this gluing.

This is different from the reduction `OneEnd` to `GoodSplitting`. Here, the fact that the first step is a $(2,2)$-gluing is essential in the proof. And indeed, it cannot be generalized to arbitrary gluings in an obvious way. We show this in Example 4.12.

Example 4.12. Let E be an arbitrary elliptic curve and denote $E[3] = \langle P, Q \rangle$. We consider the isogeny diamond

$$
\begin{array}{ccc}
E & \xrightarrow{\;\phi_1\;} & E_1 \\
{\scriptstyle [2]\phi_2}\downarrow & & \downarrow{\scriptstyle [2]\hat{\phi}_1} \\
E_2 & \xrightarrow{\;\hat{\phi}_2\;} & E
\end{array}
$$

where $\ker(\phi_1) = \langle P \rangle$ and $\ker(\phi_2) = \langle Q \rangle$.

This isogeny diamond induces a $(15, 15)$-product isogeny $F = f_1 \circ f_0$. Without loss of generality assume that f_0 is a $(3,3)$-isogeny. Then f_0 is necessarily a gluing unless there exists a 2-isogeny $E \to E$.

This is an example for a nontrivial (N, N)-product isogeny with domain $E \times E$ which induces a scalar endomorphism, here $([2]\hat{\phi}_1) \circ \phi_1 = [6]$.

Remark 4.13. We have shown that computing endomorphisms in dimension 1 essentially reduces to finding splittings in dimension 2. It is natural to wonder about the relation with finding a non-trivial endomorphism in dimension 2. To make this question more precise, we recall that the endomorphism ring of a super-special product of elliptic curves, $E_1 \times E_2$, is of the form $\begin{pmatrix} \mathrm{End}(E_1) & \mathrm{Hom}(E_2,E_1) \\ \mathrm{Hom}(E_1,E_2) & \mathrm{End}(E_2) \end{pmatrix}$.

Using a `GoodSplitting` oracle, we can find a non-trivial isogeny for each entry by the methods outlined in this article. Moreover, given an irreducible superspecial A, using the `GoodSplitting` oracle again, allows us to find $\varphi \colon A \to E \times E'$ for some E and E'. Let $\psi \in \mathrm{End}(E \times E')$ be an endomorphism found as described above, then the composition $\tilde{\varphi} \circ \psi \circ \varphi \in \mathrm{End}(A)$ is an endomorphism. This suggests a possible reduction from `OneEndDim2` to `GoodSplitting`, where `OneEndDim2` asks to find a non-trivial endomorphism of a principally polarized abelian surface. However, we note that the map $\tilde{\varphi} \circ \psi \circ \varphi$ is not necessarily an (N, N)-isogeny for some $N \in \mathbb{N}$, and it might not even be an isogeny of principally polarized abelian surfaces. More advanced techniques are necessary, to find an endomorphism of $\mathrm{End}(A)$ which is compatible with the polarization.

Another reduction related to this setting was suggested by one of the reviewers of this article: If we had an oracle to compute $\mathrm{End}(A)$ on input A, then we could use KLPT^2 [6] in order to construct a splitting $A \to E \times E'$.

Further analysis of the relation of `Splitting` with the `OneEnd` and `EndRing` problem in dimension 2 are left for future work.

5 Experimental Results

We implemented our algorithms in SageMath 10.5 [38], and conducted different experiments. The main goal of the experiments is to get a better understanding on the distribution of endomorphisms embedded in 2-dimensional product isogenies.

For these experiments we use the following primes

$$p = 4099, 8219, 16411, 32771, 65539, 131111, 262147, 524347, 1048703.$$

These are the smallest primes of bit length $12, \ldots, 20$ respectively, for which the supersingular elliptic curves over $\mathbb{F}_{p^2}$ have full rational 4-torsion. This guarantees that all level-2 theta null points computed in our experiments are $\mathbb{F}_{p^2}$-rational (see [22, Example 30]). The experimental data is summarized in Figs. 5 and 6.

In Fig. 5 we compare our methods `FindEndomorphism` and `FindSmallEndomorphism`. Both algorithms have asymptotic running time $\tilde{O}(p)$, and as expected `FindEndomorphism` which computes an endomorphism of arbitrary degree is faster than `FindSmallEndomorphism` which computes an endomorphism of degree bounded by $N = \log_2(p)$. As a reference for state-of-the-art algorithms in dimension one, we use the `CycleFinding` approach from [15]. Having asymptotic complexity $O(\sqrt{p})$, the performance is clearly better than that of our new methods.

In Fig. 6, we compare the degree of the endomorphism computed with different methods. We exclude the algorithm `FindEndomorphism` as it typically

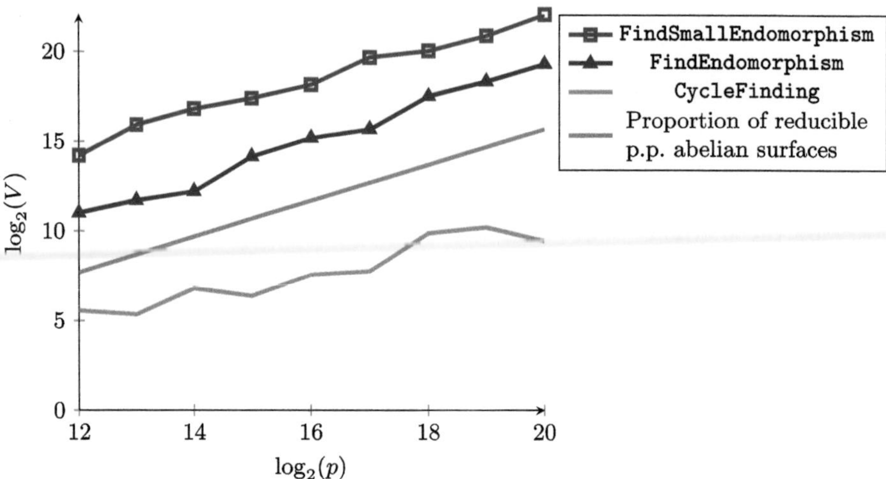

Fig. 5. Vertices visited in the isogeny graph (V) until an endomorphism is found. Comparison between the methods `FindEndomorphism`, `FindSmallEndomorphism` and `CycleFinding`.

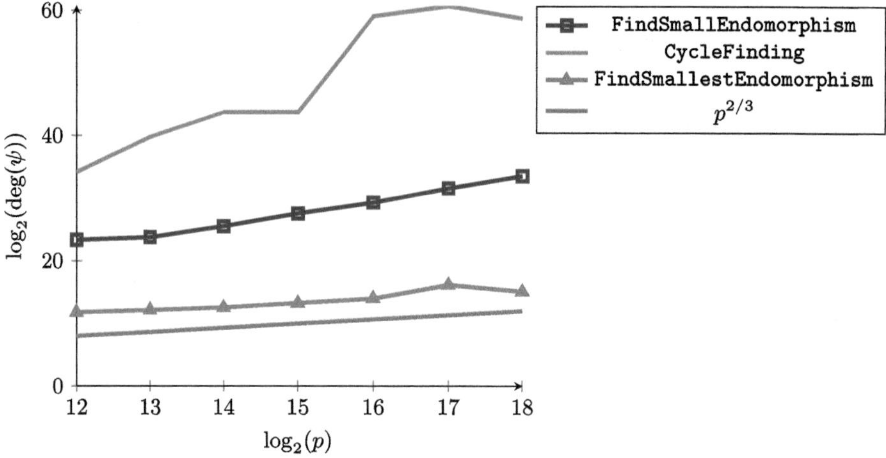

Fig. 6. Comparison of the degrees of the endomorphism, between `FindSmallEndomorphism`, `CycleFinding` and the smallest possible degree of an endomorphism embedded in a $(2^n, 2^n)$-isogeny.

produces an endomorphism of degree $\approx 2^p$, and it is not clear how to determine the exact degree from the 2-dimensional representation in this case (cf. Subsection 5.2). Instead, we compare the degree of the endomorphism found with `FindSmallEndomorphism` with the smallest endomorphism embedded in a $(2^n, 2^n)$-isogeny. For comparison, we further added the degree of the endomorphism found with the 1-dimensional cycle finding method from [15]. Here, we observe that the degree of the smallest endomorphism embedded in a $(2^n, 2^n)$-product isogeny is close to the upper bound on the degree of the smallest endomorphism of an elliptic curve (cf. Subsection 3.3). In our experiments, the degree of the endomorphism found with our methods is typically larger, but it is still significantly smaller than the degree of the endomorphisms found with the cycle finding method.

More details including explicit running times and implementation details are provided in the remainder of this section. Experiments were run on a computer with an Intel i7-1365U processor running Ubuntu version 22.04 with SageMath version 10.5 installed. All code is made available in our GitHub repository [34]:

https://github.com/easonmath/endomorphisms-via-splittings

5.1   The Cycle-Finding Algorithm

For reference, we included a comparison to one of the state-of-the-art algorithms to compute endomorphisms of elliptic curves: the cycle-finding algorithm from [15]. We briefly summarize this method here. It computes an endomorphism on input a supersingular j-invariant j_0.

1. Starting from j_0, take a random walk on the isogeny graph.
2. Repeating Step, stop when j_k is adjacent to j_k^p.
3. Appending $\{j_0, \cdots, j_k\}$ with $\{j_k^p, \cdots, j_0^p\}$.
4. Repeating the steps above (if necessary) to obtain another $\{j_0, \cdots, j_k', j_k'^p, \cdots, j_0^p\}$.
5. Return $\{j_0, j_1, \cdots, j_k, j_k^p, \cdots, j_0^p, j_1'^p, \cdots, j_k'^p, j_k', \cdots, j_0\}$.

If a pair of j-invariants (j, j') is a root of the modular polynomial, then so is (j^p, j'^p), which means the third step is automatic.

Remark 5.1. First, we remark that the algorithms from [15] work for ℓ-isogeny graphs where ℓ needs not be 2. In the comparison with our method, we only consider a version based on 2-isogenies. Further, we note that their finding-algorithm

Table 1. Numbers of visited vertices

Prime	$\log_2(p)$	FindEndomorphism	FindSmallEndomorphism	CycleFinding
4099	12	2055	18692	47
8219	13	3330	61475	40
16411	14	4712	115281	111
32771	15	18145	172265	83
65539	16	36772	291312	186
131111	17	52065	826845	214
262147	18	186309	1073583	940
524347	19	332190	1923937	1186

actually finds $j_k \in \mathbb{F}_p$, i.e., $j_k = j_k^p$. Thus, the degree of the endomorphism is always a power of 2.

In Fig. 5, we compare the number of vertices visited in the isogeny graph until an endomorphism is found. This Figure is based on the values from Table 1. For each prime p, we compute the average over 10 randomly chosen elliptic curves as input.

Counting the number of inspected vertices is an implementation independent way to analyze the complexity of the algorithm. One should have in mind that in the cycle finding method each step is the computation of an isogeny in dimension 1, while in our method for each vertex, we need to compute an isogeny in dimension 2. The cost differs by a constant factor. More precisely, if one uses radical 2-isogenies than the cost of an isogeny in dimension 2 is roughly three times as high as for a one-dimensional isogeny.

Another detail to have in mind is that in the method `FindSmall Endomorphism` certain square-root computations in the evaluation of the radical isogeny formulas can be reused. This reduces the average cost of an isogeny computation at each step.

In our implementation, we observe the following running times: For a prime of bitlength $\log_2(p) \approx 12$, the algorithm `FindEndomorphism` needs about 0.27 seconds, while it takes about 88.01 seconds if $\log_2(p) = 20$. The algorithm `FindSmallEndomorphism` requires about 1.17 seconds if $\log_2(p) \approx 12$, and 628.52 seconds if $\log_2(p) \approx 20$.

5.2   Comparing the Degree and Smallest Possible Degree

In Fig. 6, we provide some details on the degree of the endomorphism found with our methods. We recall that any supersingular elliptic curve over $\mathbb{F}_{p^2}$, has a non-scalar endomorphism of degree at most $p^{2/3}$. As we discussed in Subsect. 3.3, our method cannot detect endomorphisms of arbitrary degree. In Fig. 6, we illustrate the average degree of an endomorphism found with `FindSmallEndomorphism` for

Table 2. Comparison: degree d_α of the endomorphism found with FindEndomorphism and the smallest possible degree $d_{\alpha,min}$ of an endomorphism embedded in a $(2^n, 2^n)$-product isogeny

Prime	$\log_2(p)$	d_α	$d_{\alpha,min}$
4099	12	10576473	3599
8219	13	14129172	4628
16411	14	47044451	5956
32771	15	195023255	9794
65539	16	666093523	16481
131111	17	3189167810	73185
262147	18	12866882456	34944

primes of different sizes. We compare this to the degree of the smallest endomorphism embedded in a $(2^n, 2^n)$-isogeny (assuming that we fixed the first gluing in the isogeny chain), and with the generic lower bound. The Figure is based on the values from Table 2.

In order to find the degree of an endomorphism, we use the Weil pairing (cf. Subsection 3.3). And to find the smallest good $(2^k, 2^k)$-splitting of a given p.p. abelian surface, we repeatedly use FindSmallSplitting with decreasing bound N.

Acknowledgments. Sabrina Kunzweiler received funding from the French National Research Agency (ANR) under the ANR CIAO with reference ANR-19-CE48-0008, and the France 2030 program under grant ANR-22-PETQ-0008 (PQ-TLS).

Disclaimer. Part of this article is published in the second author's Master's thesis [35].

A   Implementation Details

In our implementation of the endomorphism finding algorithms, we had to adapt several algorithms from the literature. The high-level idea of our computations are described in Sect. 3. Here, we provide more details on the concrete modifications. We recall that our implementation is available at

$$\text{https://github.com/easonmath/endomorphisms-via-splittings}$$

A.1   Evaluating Isogeny Chains

In our implementation, isogenies are computed using radical formulas and level-2 theta coordinates. In particular, the resulting isogenies are represented by the level-2 coordinates of the domain, and codomain of the isogeny (see Fig. 1). In most cases, this information is enough to evaluate the corresponding isogeny efficiently on any input (see Fig. 2). However, when the domain is reducible, several subtleties appear (see Remark 2.5). In this section, we describe these subtle points in more detail, and explain the solution followed in our implementation. In particular, we describe the following algorithms

- SpecialEvaluation (Algorithm 10): This describes the evaluation of an isogeny when one of the theta null values vanishes.
- Find4Torsion (Algorithm 11): The computation of 4-torsion points lying above a specified 2-torsion point.
- GluingEvaluation (Algorithm 12): This method is based on the previous two algorithms, and describes the evaluation of the gluing isogeny at an arbitrary point.
- ChainEvaluation (Algorithm 13): This is the resulting algorithm to evaluate a $(2^n, 2^n)$-isogeny represented as a chain of theta null values.
- EvaluateEndomorphism (Algorithm 14): Given a chain of theta null values representing a product isogeny $F : E \times E \to E_1 \times E_2$, the algorithm explains the evaluation of the endomorphism represented by this chain.

Regarding the first gluing, we apply the idea in [12], which is stated in Algorithm 10: To evaluate a gluing $f\colon E \times E' \to A_1$, where $\tilde{\theta}^{A_1}(0)$ has a zero, we require a 4-torsion point T_1' lying above T_1, where $\ker(f) = \langle (a_0 : -a_1 : a_2 : -a_3), (a_0 : a_1 : -a_2 : -a_3) \rangle := \langle T_1, T_2 \rangle$; that is $2T_1' = T_1 \in \ker(f)$. The key reason is the *translation formula*, given a 2-torsion point S which corresponds to $(j, \chi) \in (\mathbb{Z}/2\mathbb{Z})^g \times \widehat{(\mathbb{Z}/2\mathbb{Z})^g}$ and any point P, we have

$$(\theta_i(P + S))_i = (\chi(i)\theta_{i+j}(P))_i. \tag{4}$$

So, writing

$$\tilde{\theta}^{A_1}(f(P)) = \left(\tilde{\theta}^{A_1}_{00}(f(P)) : \tilde{\theta}^{A_1}_{10}(f(P)) : \tilde{\theta}^{A_1}_{01}(f(P)) : \tilde{\theta}^{A_1}_{11}(f(P)) \right),$$

we have

$$\mathcal{H} \circ \mathcal{S}(\theta^A(P + T_1')) = \tilde{\theta}^{A_1}(0) \star \tilde{\theta}^{A_1}\left(f(P) + f(T_1') \right)$$
$$= \tilde{\theta}^{A_1}(0) \star \left(\tilde{\theta}^{A_1}_{10}(f(P)) : \tilde{\theta}^{A_1}_{00}(f(P)) : \tilde{\theta}^{A_1}_{11}(f(P)) : \tilde{\theta}^{A_1}_{01}(f(P)) \right),$$

where $(x_i)_i \star (y_i)_i = (x_i y_i)_i$. The second equality comes from the translation formula because $f(T_1') \in A_1[2]$ corresponds to $((0,0), \chi_{(1,0)})$. In other words, T_1' helps us to swap the desired components and therefore one could recover the missing coordinate from the zero coordinate in $\mathcal{H} \circ \mathcal{S}(\theta^{E \times E'}(P))$. Hence, it remains to find $\theta^{E \times E'}(T_1')$ and $\theta^{E \times E'}(P + T_1')$.

Algorithm 10. SpecialEvaluation as $\alpha = 0$ ([12, Algorithm 9])

Input: $\theta^{E \times E'}(P)$, $\theta^{E \times E'}(P + T_1')$ and $\tilde{\theta}^{A_1}(0) = (\alpha, \beta, \gamma, \delta)$ where $\alpha = 0$
Output: $\theta^B(f(P))$

1: $X_P, Y_P, 0, W_P \leftarrow \mathcal{H} \circ \mathcal{S}(\theta^{E \times E'}(P))$
2: $X_{PT}, Y_{PT}, 0, W_{PT} \leftarrow \mathcal{H} \circ \mathcal{S}(\theta^{E \times E'}(P + T_1'))$
3: $Y, Z, W \leftarrow Y_P/\beta, Z_P/\gamma, W_P/\delta$
4: **if** $Z \neq 0$ **then**
5:     $Z \leftarrow Z/\delta$
6:     $\lambda^{-1} \leftarrow Z/W_{PT}$
7: **else**
8:     $Z' \leftarrow Z/\gamma$
9:     $\lambda \leftarrow W/Z'$
10: **end if**
11: $X' \leftarrow Y_{PT}/\beta$
12: $X \leftarrow X \cdot \lambda^{-1}$
13: $X, Y, Z, W \leftarrow \mathcal{H}(X, Y, Z, W)$
14: **return** (X, Y, Z, W)

Finding the Four-torsion Point. To find a compatible 4-torsion point T_1' on a reducible p.p. abelian surface D (not necessarily in the product structure), we first note that we know the form of $\theta^D(T_1')$ from the relation $T_1' + T_1 = -T_1'$:

$$\theta^D(-T_1') = \theta^D(T_1') = (s_0 : s_1 : s_2 : s_3)$$

$$= (s_0 : -s_1 : s_2 : -s_3)$$

where the second equality comes from the translation formula (Eq. (4)). So the torsion point is of the form $(x : 0 : 1 : 0) \in \mathbb{P}^3$ for some x in the base field. It remains to solve for x from the fact $\tilde{f} \circ f(\theta^D(T_1')) = \theta^D(T_1)$. We provide the pseudo-code in Algorithm 11.

Algorithm 11. Find4Torsion

Input: A theta null point $(a_0 : a_1 : a_2 : a_3)$ of a reducible p.p. abelian surface (not necessarily in the product structure)

Output: The theta coordinates of a 4-torsion point lying above $(a_0 : -a_1 : a_2 : -a_3)$

1: Compute the automorphism μ such that $(E \times E')_\mu$ is in the product structure and $a \leftarrow \theta^{(E \times E')_\mu}$

2: Doubling $\mu \cdot (x, 0, 1, 0)$ by applying the radical-2 isogeny and its adjoint. Denote the result by (X, Y, Z, W) where the coordinates is represented by the unknown x

3: Solve for x from $\mu^{-1}(X : Y : Z : W) = (a_0 : -a_1 : a_2 : -a_3)$ in the projective space

4: **return** $(x : 0 : 1 : 0)$

Evaluation of the Gluing. Computing $\theta^{E \times E'}(P + T_1')$ from $\theta^{E \times E'}(P)$ and $\theta^{E \times E'}(T_1')$ is not possible because one needs to know $\theta^{E \times E'}(P - T_1')$ to do the differential addition. A method is to compute the addition in Weierstrass coordinates before turning into the theta model. By combining this idea with the two algorithms above, we provide the pseudo-code of the gluing-evaluation in Algorithm 12.

Algorithm 12. GluingEvaluation

Input: $\theta^{(E \times E')_\sigma}(0)$, $\theta^{A_1}(0)$ and $(P, Q) \in E \times E'$

Output: $\theta^{A_1}(f \circ \iota(P))$ where f is a $(2,2)$-gluing and $\iota \in \{[\pm 1] \times [\pm 1]\}$

1: $\theta^\sigma(T_1') \leftarrow$ Find4Torsion on $(E \times E')_\sigma$

2: $\theta(T_1') \leftarrow \sigma^{-1}\theta^\sigma(T_1')$

3: Recover (T_{11}', T_{12}') in Weierstrass coordinates from $\theta(T_1')$

4: Compute $(P + T_{11}', Q + T_{12}')$ and transform it to the theta model

5: $\theta^\sigma(P), \theta^\sigma(P + T_1') \leftarrow \sigma\theta(P), \sigma\theta(P + T_1')$

6: $(X, Y, Z, W) \leftarrow$ SpecialEvaluation$(\theta^\sigma(P), \theta^\sigma(P + T_1'), \tilde{\theta}^{A_1}(0))$

7: **return** (X, Y, Z, W)

Notice that in Step 3, one actually recovers four valid points $(\pm T_{11}', \pm T_{12}') \in E \times E'$ from a single $\theta(T_1')$. The four ι's in the output actually correspond to the different choices in Step 3.

Lemma A.1. *The four choices in Step 4 of Algorithm 12*

$$(P + T_{11}', Q + T_{12}'), (P - T_{11}', Q - T_{12}'), (P + T_{11}', Q - T_{12}'), (P - T_{11}', Q + T_{12}')$$

correspond to right-composition of the gluing isogeny with the four isomorphism $[\pm 1] \times [\pm 1]$.

Proof. Using the notation from Algorithm 12. Recall that we are working on a Kummer variety $E/\pm 1$ (resp. $E'/\pm 1$), so P and $-P$ (resp. Q and $-Q$) give the same theta coordinates. Therefore, for example,

$$\theta(P - T'_{11}, Q + T'_{12}) = \theta(-P + T_{11'}, Q + T'_{12}).$$

In other words, if we say the first choice leads to $f((P,Q))$ then the last choice actually gives $f((-P,Q))$.

Although we know the relation between the choices, there is no reason to say that the first choice yields $\theta(f((P,Q)))$, so Algorithm 12 actually compute $f \circ \iota$ for an $\iota \in \{[\pm 1] \times [\pm 1]\}$.

The overall evaluating-algorithm is stated in Algorithm 13 and Evaluation used there is simply the formula $\mathcal{H} \circ \mathcal{C}_{\tilde{b}} \circ \mathcal{H} \circ \mathcal{S}$. A subtle thing is that the effect of ι produced by GluingEvaluation can be ignored because the theta coordinates originally represent a point up to a sign.

Algorithm 13. ChainEvaluation

Input: A chain $\mathsf{NL} = (\mathsf{NL}'_0, \mathsf{NL}_0, \mathsf{NL}_1, \ldots, \mathsf{NL}_n)$ containing the theta null points of an isogeny chain as in (Eq. 1), and $\theta^{E \times E'}((P,Q))$
Output: $F(P,Q)$ in Weierstrass model where F is induced by NL
  1: $\theta(F((P,Q))) \leftarrow$ GluingEvaluation($\mathsf{NL}[1], \mathsf{NL}[2], (P,Q)$)
  2: **for** $i \in \{0, \cdots, \#\mathsf{NL} - 3\}$ **do**
  3:     $\theta(F((P,Q))) \leftarrow$ Evaluation($\mathsf{NL}[i+3], \theta(F((P,Q)))$)
  4: **end for**
  5: $\theta(F_\tau((P,Q))) \leftarrow \tau\theta(F((P,Q)))$
  6: Recover the pair $F_\tau(P,Q) \in E_1 \times E_2$ from its theta coordinates
  7: **return** $F_\tau((P,Q))$

A.2   The Adjoint Isogeny

Assume that we are given an efficient representation of an isogeny as the composition of small-degree isogenies. Then we can also find an efficient representation of the adjoint isogeny. The reason is that the latter can be decomposed as a composition of small-degree isogenies as well. Furthermore the computation of the adjoints can be done step-by-step. Here we describe these computations in more detail for the isogeny chain considered in Subsect. A.1.

To extract the endomorphism, we also need to evaluate the adjoint isogeny induced by the same chain. Due to the symmetry of our chain (1), the algorithms AdjointSpecialEvaluation, AdjointFind4Torsion, AdjointGluingEvaluation and AdjointChainEvaluation are quite similar to the corresponding algorithms. For simplicity, we only note three important points here.

1. To evaluate a point via the adjoint of $f \colon A \to B$, one applies the formula $\mathcal{C}_a \circ \mathcal{H} \circ \mathcal{S} \circ \mathcal{H}$ instead.

2. The auxiliary 4-torsion point S_1' in AdjointSpecialEvaluation lies above S_1 where $\ker(\tilde{f}) = \langle (a_1 : a_0 : a_3 : a_2), (a_2 : a_3 : a_0 : a_1) \rangle := \langle S_1, S_2 \rangle$. Again, one can show that $S_1' = (y : y : 1 : 1)$ for some y in the base field, and use the same strategy to find y.
3. AdjointGluingEvaluation only computes the dual-gluing up to some $\iota' \in \{[\pm 1] \times [\pm 1]\}$, and again, it does not affect the output of AdjointChainEvaluation.

Using the described subroutines, the evaluation of the endomorphism is described in Algorithm 14.

Algorithm 14. EvaluateEndomorphism

Input: A chain $\mathsf{NL} = (\mathsf{NL}_0', \mathsf{NL}_0, \mathsf{NL}_1, \ldots, \mathsf{NL}_n)$ containing the theta null points of an isogeny chain as in (Eq. 1), and $P \in E$
Output: The image of P under the endomorphism (namely $\psi_2 \circ \phi_1$) induced by the chain.
  1: $(\phi_1(P), *) \leftarrow \mathsf{ChainEvaluation}(\mathsf{NL}, (P, 0_E))$
  2: $(*, -\psi_2 \circ \phi_1(P)) \leftarrow \mathsf{AdjointChainEvaluation}(\mathsf{NL}, (\phi_1(P), 0_{E_2}))$
  3: **return** $\psi_2 \circ \phi_1(P)$

A.3 Computing the Degree of the Endomorphism

Once, we found an endomorphism, we would also like to know its degree. As we mentioned in Sect. 3.3, we can recover the degree by evaluating the Weil pairing on pairs of points on the domain and codomain. More precisely, we use the relation given in Eq. 3. We used this idea in our implementation of the experiments in Subsect. 5.2. Here, we make this explicit by describing our implementation.

Algorithm 15 summarizes the idea for the ϕ_1-entry, and we note that one can easily adapt the algorithm to compute the values for the other entries.

Algorithm 15. WeilConstraint

Input: A null list inducing the $(2^s, 2^s)$-isogeny $F = \begin{pmatrix} \phi_1 & \hat{\psi}_2 \\ -\phi_2 & \hat{\psi}_1 \end{pmatrix}$ and a positive integer
    $N \mid p + 1$
Output: r_1 where $r_1 \equiv \deg \phi_1 \mod N$
  1: Generate $P_N, Q_N \in E[N]$ where $N \mid p + 1$
  2: Compute $F(P_N, 0)^\top = (\phi_1(P_N), \phi_2(P_N))^\top$
  3: Compute $F(Q_N, 0)^\top = (\phi_1(Q_N), \phi_2(Q_N))^\top$
  4: Using Equation 3 on P_N, Q_N and their images under ϕ_1, we obtain $r_1 \equiv \deg \phi_1 \mod N$
  5: **return** r_1

Furthermore, since we work with theta coordinates, we can only compute the pairing up to a sign (or see Remark A.3 for another approach); more precisely,

$$e_N(\pm \phi(P_N), \pm \phi(Q_N)) = e_N(P_N, \pm Q_N)^{\deg \phi} = e_N(P_N, Q_N)^{\pm \deg \phi}$$

as we can only recover $\pm\phi(P_N)$ and $\pm\phi(Q_N)$ from their theta coordinates. This is the reason for the signs in Line 4 of Algorithm 16.

In Algorithm 16, we apply the idea discussed above in our case to find $\deg\phi_1\deg\psi_2$ up to a multiple of $p+1$: For a supersingular elliptic curve $E/\mathbb{F}_p$, we have $E(\mathbb{F}_{p^2}) \cong \mathbb{Z}/(p+1)\mathbb{Z} \times \mathbb{Z}/(p+1)\mathbb{Z}$ and

$$(\phi + m[p+1])P = \phi(P) + m[p+1]P = \phi(P)$$

for any $m \in \mathbb{Z}$ and $P \in E(\mathbb{F}_{p^2})$.

Algorithm 16. FindDegree

Input: A null list NL inducing the $(2^s, 2^s)$-isogeny $F = \begin{pmatrix} \phi_1 & \hat{\psi}_2 \\ -\phi_2 & \hat{\psi}_1 \end{pmatrix} : E \times E \to E_1 \times E_2$

Output: $\deg\psi_2\deg\phi_1$
1: Generate $P \in E[p+1]$ and fix $N \mid p+1$
2: Compute $[\deg\phi_1](P)$ from Eq. (2), and compute $[\deg\phi_2](P)$ similarly
3: $r_1 \leftarrow$ `WeilConstraint(NL)`
4: Solve $xP = [\deg\phi_1](P)$ for one x where $x \equiv \pm r_1 \mod N$. If $[2^s - x](P) = [\deg\phi_2](P)$ ruturn $x(2^s - x)$; otherwise, find another x

---

Remark A.2. In general, given an endomorphism η, one way to compute $\deg\eta$ is by considering field extensions. Over a sufficiently large extension, one gains access to N-torsion points for larger N. With this additional information, one can find the explicit $\deg\eta$ from Equation (3).

Remark A.3. To address the sign issue, one may additionally compute $\theta(\phi(P_N + Q_N))$ and recover $\pm\phi(P_N + Q_N)$ from it. By determining the signs of $\phi(P_N), \phi(Q_N)$ and $\phi(P_N + Q_N)$ such that $\phi(P_N) + \phi(Q_N) - \phi(P_N + Q_N) = 0$, one can identify a correct combination.

References

1. Anni, S., Bisson, G., Iezzi, A., Garcia, E.L., Wesolowski, B.: On the computation of endomorphism rings of abelian surfaces over finite fields (2025). arXiv: https://arxiv.org/pdf/2503.08925v1
2. Basso, A., et al.: PRISM: simple and compact identification and signatures from large prime degree isogenies. In: Jager, T., Pan, J., (eds.), Public-Key Cryptography – PKC 2025, pp. 300–332. Springer Nature Switzerland, Cham (2025)
3. Basso, A., et al.: SQIsign2D-West - the fast, the small, and the safer. In Advances in Cryptology - ASIACRYPT 2024 - 30th International Conference on the Theory and Application of Cryptology and Information Security(2024), Proceedings, Part III, vol. 15486 of Lecture Notes in Computer Science, pp. 339–370. Springer, Kolkata, December 9-13 (2024)
4. Castryck, W., Decru, T.: Multiradical isogenies. In: 18th International Conference Arithmetic, Geometry, Cryptography, and Coding Theory, vol. 779, pp. 57–89. American Mathematical Society (2022)

5. Castryck, W., Decru, T.: An efficient key recovery attack on SIDH. In: Annual International Conference on the Theory and Applications of Cryptographic Techniques, pp. 423–447. Springer (2023)
6. Castryck, W., Decru, T., Kutas, P., Laval, A., Petit, C., Ti, Y.B.: KLPT^2: algebraic pathfinding in dimension two and applications. In: Annual International Cryptology Conference, pp. 167–200. Springer (2025)
7. Castryck, W., Decru, T., Smith, B.: Hash functions from superspecial genus-2 curves using Richelot isogenies. J. Math. Cryptol. **14**(1), 268–292 (2020)
8. Corte-Real Santos, M., Costello, C., Frengley, S.: Efficient algorithms for the detection of (N, N)-splittings and endomorphisms. Cryptology ePrint Archive, Paper 2025/147 (2025)
9. Corte-Real Santos, M., Costello, C., Shi, J.: Accelerating the delfs–galbraith algorithm with fast subfield root detection. In: Dodis, Y., Shrimpton, T., (eds.), Advances in Cryptology – CRYPTO 2022, pp. 285–314. Springer Nature Switzerland, Cham (2022)
10. Costello, C., Smith, B.: The supersingular isogeny problem in genus 2 and beyond. In: Ding, J., Tillich, J.B., (eds.), Post-Quantum Cryptography, pp. 151–168. Springer International Publishing, Cham (2020) , Cham (2020)
11. Dartois, P., Leroux, A., Robert, D., Wesolowski, B.: SQISignHD: new dimensions in cryptography. In: Annual International Conference on the Theory and Applications of Cryptographic Techniques, pp. 3–32. Springer (2024)
12. Dartois, P., Maino, L., Pope, G., Robert, D.: An algorithmic approach to (2, 2)-isogenies in the theta model and applications to isogeny-based cryptography. In: International Conference on the Theory and Application of Cryptology and Information Security, pp. 304–338. Springer (2024)
13. Delfs, C., Galbraith, S.D.: Computing isogenies between supersingular elliptic curves over $\mathbb{F}_p$. Des. Codes Cryptography **78**(2), 425–440 (2016)
14. Duparc, M., Fouotsa, T.B.: SQIPrime: a dimension 2 variant of SQISignHD with non-smooth challenge isogenies. In: Advances in Cryptology - ASIACRYPT 2024 - 30th International Conference on the Theory and Application of Cryptology and Information Security, Proceedings, Part III, vol. 15486 of Lecture Notes in Computer Science, pp. 396–429. Springer, Kolkata, December 9-13 (2024) (2024)
15. Eisenträger, K., Hallgren, S., Leonardi, C., Morrison, T., Park, J.: Computing endomorphism rings of supersingular elliptic curves and connections to path-finding in isogeny graphs. In: Open Book Series 4 (2020)
16. Florit, E., Smith, B.: An atlas of the richelot isogeny graph. RIMS Kôkyûroku Bessatsu **90**, 195–219 (2022)
17. Freitag, E.: Siegelsche Modulfunktionen, vol. 254 of Grundlehren der mathematischen Wissenschaften. Springer-Verlag (2013)
18. Fuselier, J., Iezzi, A., Kozek, M., Morrison, T., Namoijam, C.: Computing supersingular endomorphism rings using inseparable endomorphisms. J. Algebra **668**, 145–189 (2025)
19. Kani, E.: Elliptic curves on abelian surfaces. Manuscripta Math. **84**, 199–223 (1994)
20. Kani, E.: The number of curves of genus two with elliptic differentials. J. für die reine und angewandte Mathematik **485**, 93–122 (1997)
21. Kohel, D.: Endomorphism rings of elliptic curves over finite fields. PhD thesis, University of California at Berkeley (1996)
22. Kunzweiler, S., et al.: Radical 2-isogenies and cryptographic hash functions in dimensions 1, 2 and 3. In: IACR International Conference on Public-Key Cryptography, pp. 265–299. Springer (2025)

23. Kırımlı, E., Martindale, C.: The computational refined humbert invariant problem is equivalent to the computational isogeny problem. Cryptology ePrint Archive, Paper 2025/1295 (2025)
24. Love, J., Boneh, D.: Supersingular curves with small non-integer endomorphisms. ANTS, pp. 7–22 (2020)
25. Maino, L., Martindale, C., Panny, L., Pope, G., Wesolowski, B.: A direct key recovery attack on SIDH. In: Annual International Conference on the Theory and Applications of Cryptographic Techniques, pp. 448–471. Springer (2023)
26. Salvati Manni, R.: On the projective varieties associated with some subrings of the ring of Thetanullwerte. Nagoya Mathemat. J. **133**, 71–83 (1994)
27. Herlédan Le Merdy, A., Wesolowski, B.: Unconditional foundations for supersingular isogeny-based cryptography. Cryptology ePrint Archive, Paper 2025/271 (2025)
28. Nakagawa, K., Onuki, H.: Attacks on PRISM-id via torsion over small extension fields. Cryptology ePrint Archive, Paper 2025/1602 (2025)
29. Nakagawa, K., et al.: SQIsign2D-East: a new signature scheme using 2-dimensional isogenies. In: Advances in Cryptology - ASIACRYPT 2024 - 30th International Conference on the Theory and Application of Cryptology and Information Security (2024), Proceedings, Part III, vol. 15486 of Lecture Notes in Computer Science, pp. 272–303. Springer, Kolkata, December 9-13 (2024)
30. Page, A., Wesolowski, B.: The supersingular endomorphism ring and one endomorphism problems are equivalent. In: Joye, M., Leander, G., (eds.), Advances in Cryptology – EUROCRYPT 2024, pp. 388–417. Springer Nature Switzerland, Cham (2024)
31. Robert, D.: A note on optimising 2^n-isogenies in higher dimension (2023)
32. Robert, D.: Breaking SIDH in polynomial time. In: Annual International Conference on the Theory and Applications of Cryptographic Techniques, pp. 472–503. Springer (2023)
33. Robert, D.: Breaking SIDH in polynomial time. In: Hazay, C., Stam, M., (eds.), Advances in Cryptology – EUROCRYPT 2023, pp. 472–503. Springer Nature Switzerland, Cham (2023)
34. Shen, M.S.: Github repository: endomorphisms via splittings (2025)
35. Shen, M.Y.: A two-dimensinoal method for representing an endomorphism of an elliptic curve. Master's thesis, National Tsing Hua University (2025)
36. Joseph, H.: Silverman. The Arithmetic of Elliptic Curves. Graduate texts in mathematics. Springer, New York (2009)
37. Takashima, K.: Efficient algorithms for isogeny sequences and their cryptographic applications. In: Mathematical Modelling for Next-Generation Cryptography: CREST Crypto-Math Project, pp. 97–114. Springer (2017)
38. The Sage Developers. SageMath, the Sage Mathematics Software System (Version 10.5) (2025). https://www.sagemath.org
39. van Geemen, B., van der Geer, G.: Kummer varieties and the moduli spaces of abelian varieties. Am. J. Math. **108**(3), 615–641 (1986)

On the Use of Atkin and Weber Modular Polynomials in Isogeny Proofs of Knowledge

Thomas den Hollander[iD], Marzio Mula[iD], Daniel Slamanig[iD],
and Sebastian A. Spindler[(✉)][iD]

Research Institute CODE, Universität der Bundeswehr München, München, Germany
{thomasdh,marzio.mula,daniel.slamanig,s.spindler}@unibw.de

Abstract. Zero-knowledge proofs of knowledge of isogenies constitute a key building block in the design of isogeny-based signature schemes and have numerous other practical applications. A recent line of work investigated such proofs based on generic proof systems, e.g., zk-SNARKs, along with a suitable arithmetization and in particular rank-1 constraint systems (R1CS). Cong, Lai and Levin (ACNS'23) considered proving the knowledge of an isogeny of degree 2^k between supersingular elliptic curves via modular polynomial relations. Recently, den Hollander et al. (CRYPTO'25) have shown that the use of canonical modular polynomials instead of the classical ones allows to improve on the number of constraints for the same types of isogenies, and further allows to extend this approach to isogenies of higher (though limited) degrees. Another recent work by Levin and Pedersen (ASIACRYPT'25) showed that switching from modular polynomials to radical isogeny formulas also leads to significant improvements (at least for the case of the prime $\ell = 2$).

A natural question that remained open is whether sticking with the modular polynomial-based approach, but switching to other candidates of modular polynomials, and in particular Atkin and Weber polynomials, is possible and gives improvements and flexibility. In this paper we show that the use of the Atkin modular polynomials enables the use of degrees not covered by existing works and improves the number of constraints for $\ell > 2$ by up to 27%, while the Weber polynomials allow up to 39% sparser constraint systems than the current state of the art. As in our prior work on canonical modular polynomials, the adaption of well-known results to the Atkin and Weber modular polynomials also requires some technical work, especially when going to positive characteristic. To this end we expand and optimize our previous resultant-based methodology, resulting in much simpler proofs for our multiplicity theorems.

1 Introduction

The use of zero-knowledge proofs of knowledge of a secret isogeny has various applications, ranging from the design of digital signatures [4,8,25,30], over the generation of supersingular elliptic curves of unknown endomorphism ring [5],

M. Bardet and R. Niederhagen (Eds.): PQCrypto 2026, LNCS 16492, pp. 39–73, 2026.
https://doi.org/10.1007/978-3-032-22698-3_2

to various applications in the design of cryptographic protocols and real world deployments (cf. [33] for a discussion). Most of these works construct dedicated zero-knowledge proofs via sigma protocols, typically having a small challenge space and thus require a significant number or parallel repetitions (cf. [7] for a rather recent survey). An alternative approach is to not design a sigma protocol for a certain hard relation, but to rely on alternative possibly more generic proof systems along with suitable representations of isogenies.

In [18] the authors for the first time deviated from the aforementioned strategy and proposed the use of succinct non-interactive arguments (SNARGs) for isogeny proofs. In particular, they suggested to use a sumcheck protocol based on modular polynomial relations in the 2-isogeny graph. However, due to their focus on verifiable delay function (VDF), they did not require knowledge soundness nor the zero-knowledge property and a practical assessment was left open. Cong, Lai and Levin [21] then deepened the study of proving modular polynomial relations. Instead of using any tailored (or ad-hoc) proof system, the authors express modular polynomial relations, and in particular the knowledge of an isogeny of degree 2^k between supersingular elliptic curves, as a rank-1 constraint system (R1CS). This allows them to rely on existing zero-knowledge succinct non-interactive arguments of knowledge (zk-SNARKs) that support R1CS arithmetization such as Aurora [6], Ligero [2] or Limbo [26]. The authors managed to construct a proof system for a NIST-level I instance that runs in just above a second, which for use-cases such as the generation of supersingular elliptic curves of unknown endomorphism ring [5] significantly improved over the state of the art. These developments in turn motivated further efforts to optimize R1CS constraints, with two concurrent lines of work pursuing different reduction strategies.

In [33], the authors propose replacing standard modular polynomials with canonical modular polynomials, achieving a further decrease in the number of constraints for the same classes of isogenies. They additionally construct constraint systems for higher-degree isogenies with $\ell \in \{3, 5, 7, 13\}$. An alternative direction is taken in [41], which replaces the modular polynomial representation altogether by the recently introduced radical isogeny formulas [15–17] for $\ell = 2$. These formulas have a particularly simple form and require no auxiliary conditions to prevent backtracking, yielding once again a more efficient proof system.

For completeness, we also note the approach of [45], which arithmetizes isogeny walks via Vélu's formulas and employs the Nova folding scheme [37] to recursively aggregate proofs. However, their construction rests on discrete-logarithm assumptions. Adapting it to the post-quantum setting, e.g., relying on [10], would require additional lattice-based assumptions for isogeny proofs of knowledge, where such a mix of assumptions seems undesirable.

Given that the use of (canonical) modular polynomials seems to provide the most general setting that does not impose any particular restrictions, a natural question is whether other classes of modular polynomials allow to further improve the arithmetization via R1CS in terms of the constraint system and to extend the list of supported primes ℓ.

1.1 Technical Overview and Our Contributions

We focus on ℓ^n-isogenies between supersingular elliptic curves over $\mathbb{F}_{p^2}$, represented as sequences of ℓ-isogenies between j-invariants $j_0 \to j_1 \to \cdots \to j_n$.

The reason why R1CS can be effectively used to prove knowledge of ℓ^n-isogenies is that they can be expressed as 'chains' of solutions of suitable equations: For example, Cong, Lai and Levin [21] use the classical modular polynomial, leveraging the well-known fact that two elliptic curves are ℓ-isogenous (over a fixed algebraic closure) if and only if their j-invariants are roots of the classical modular polynomial Φ_ℓ. In this way, one can view an ℓ^n-isogeny as a chain of solutions $\{(j_i, j_{i+1})\}_{i=0}^{n-1}$ of the equation $\Phi_\ell(J_0, J_1) = 0$.

A natural question is whether other equations can be used to concretely improve the resulting R1CS, especially when working with a slightly larger prime ℓ – a question that is affirmatively answered in [33], by showing that the use of canonical modular polynomials leads to a 48% improvement over [21].

In this work, we follow a similar footprint as [21,33]: We select and study suitable modular equations to encode ℓ^n-isogenies, optimize them for R1CS, and evaluate the performance of the resulting zk-SNARK. Our goal is to extend the picture of [21,33] by considering two more families of modular polynomials.

Atkin and Weber Modular Polynomials. We study Atkin modular polynomials, denoted as $\Phi_\ell^A(Y, J_0)$, and Weber modular polynomials, denoted as $\Phi_\ell^W(F_0, F_1)$. For both families we provide new proofs for some of their basic features, building on our previous results on canonical modular polynomials in [33] and combining resultant theory with tools from the theory of modular functions. In particular, with the Atkin Multiplicity Theorem we illustrate how, for $\ell \leq 31$ or $\ell \in \{41, 47, 59, 71\}$, the ℓ^n-isogeny relation can be expressed as a chain of solutions $\{(t_i^+, j_i, j_{i+1})\}_{i=0}^{n-1}$ of the system

$$\Phi_\ell^A(Y, J_0) = 0 = \frac{\Phi_\ell^A(Y, J_1) - \Phi_\ell^A(Y, J_0)}{J_1 - J_0},$$

while the Weber Multiplicity Theorem proves that, for $\ell \geq 5$, an ℓ^n-isogeny can be expressed as a chain of solutions $\{(\mathfrak{f}_i, \mathfrak{f}_{i+1})\}_{i=0}^{n-1}$ of the equation

$$\Phi_\ell^W(F_0, F_1) = 0,$$

with the further constraint that $(\mathfrak{f}_1, j_1)$ and $(\mathfrak{f}_n, j_n)$ are solutions of the equation $(F^{24} - 16)^3 - F^{24} \cdot J = 0$. We also confirm that in both cases the chains of solutions always lie in $\mathbb{F}_{p^2}$ for the supersingular case. Throughout the paper, we highlight how the modular equations we encounter, as well as the restrictions we impose to the choice of ℓ, relate to the properties of certain complex modular function fields.

Automated R1CS Optimization. We generalize some of the optimizations described in our previous work [33] and present an algorithm that can perform these and more in a systematic way (cf. Sect. 5.3). We provide a framework in Rust which is used to describe, optimize and measure the number of constraints, variables and non-zero entries in the R1CS constraint matrices[1]. We expect this framework to be useful for describing and comparing constraint systems consistently, especially in the context of isogeny walks.

Finally, to verify the computational claims on which some of our proofs rely, we provide SageMath scripts in an accompanying GitHub repository[2].

2 Preliminaries

2.1 Resultants

Let R be an integral domain and let $g, h \in R[X]$ be non-zero polynomials. The *resultant* of g and h is an important algebraic tool to detect common divisors between these two polynomials. We state its necessary properties here and give the theoretical background in the full version of this article [34, Appendix A], where we expand upon the results of [33, Section 2.2].

Proposition 1 ([33, **Proposition 1**]). *Let $g, h \in R[X]$ be non-zero polynomials, and let $\varphi \colon R \to S$ be a ring homomorphism, extended to a ring homomorphism $\varphi \colon R[X] \to S[X]$ via coefficient-wise application. If φ preserves the degrees of g and h, then we have*

$$\varphi(\mathrm{res}(g, h)) = \mathrm{res}(\varphi(g), \varphi(h)).$$

Moreover, we have $\mathrm{res}(g, h) = 0$ if and only if g and h share a common divisor of positive degree.

Theorem 1. *Let K be a field, let $g \in K[X]$ and $h \in K[u, X]$ be non-zero polynomials, and let $u_0 \in K$ such that $\deg_X h(u_0, X) = \deg_X h$. Further write*

$$m = \#\{\!\{ \textit{Roots } x \in \overline{K} \textit{ of } g \textit{ such that } h(u_0, x) = 0 \}\!\}$$

where the double bracket notation indicates a multiset, i.e. we count each root of g with its multiplicity. Then

$$\left. \frac{\partial^k}{\partial u^k} \right|_{u=u_0} \mathrm{res}_X(g, h) = 0 \quad \textit{for } k \in \{0, \dots, m - 1\}.$$

2.2 Elliptic Curves

We assume some familiarity with isogenies of elliptic curves and refer to [51] for the main definitions. Throughout, we work over perfect fields K of characteristic $\mathrm{char}(K) \neq \ell$ and consider isogenies of ℓ-power degree defined over the algebraic closure $\overline{K}$, which are hence always separable. We identify elliptic curves up to isomorphism over $\overline{K}$ – labelling them by their j-invariant – and we regard two isogenies as equivalent if they differ by post-composition with an isomorphism.

---

[1] https://github.com/QuSAC/isogeny-walk-constraint-counter.

[2] https://github.com/QuSAC/IsogenyPoKviaVariousModPolys.

This lets us view an ℓ^n-isogeny as a chain of ℓ-isogenies between j-invariants, i.e., an *isogeny walk*. When we refer to the *number of non-equivalent ℓ-isogenies* $j_0 \to j_1$, we are talking about the number of equivalence classes of ℓ-isogenies from a fixed curve E_0 over $\overline{K}$ of j-invariant j_0 that map to some elliptic curve E_1 over $\overline{K}$ of j-invariant j_1; note that this number does not depend on the choice of representatives.

2.3   Modular Curves

We briefly recall the definitions of $X_0(N)$ and $X_0^+(N)$ following [27, Chapters 1–2], [24, §11.B], [29, §3], and [22, §4].

For any $N \in \mathbb{N}$, we denote by $\Gamma(N)$ the *principal congruence subgroup of level N*, i.e. the subgroup of the *modular group* $\mathrm{SL}_2(\mathbb{Z})$ given by

$$\Gamma(N) := \left\{ \begin{pmatrix} a & b \\ c & d \end{pmatrix} \in \mathrm{SL}_2(\mathbb{Z}) \colon \begin{pmatrix} a & b \\ c & d \end{pmatrix} = \begin{pmatrix} 1 & 0 \\ 0 & 1 \end{pmatrix} \bmod N \right\}.$$

A *congruence subgroup* of $\mathrm{SL}_2(\mathbb{Z})$ is a subgroup $\Gamma \subseteq \mathrm{SL}_2(\mathbb{Z})$ such that there is an $N \in \mathbb{N}$ with $\Gamma(N) \subseteq \Gamma$, and the minimal such N is called the *level* of Γ. According to the following result, this minimality can be understood equivalently in terms of size or in terms of divisibility; its proof can be found in the full version of this article [34, Proposition 5].

Proposition 2. *For $M, N \in \mathbb{N}$ we have $\Gamma(M) \cdot \Gamma(N) = \Gamma(\gcd(M, N))$.*

An important example of a level N congruence subgroup is the group

$$\Gamma_0(N) = \left\{ \begin{pmatrix} a & b \\ c & d \end{pmatrix} \in \mathrm{SL}_2(\mathbb{Z}) \colon \begin{pmatrix} a & b \\ c & d \end{pmatrix} = \begin{pmatrix} * & * \\ 0 & * \end{pmatrix} \bmod N \right\}.$$

The group $\mathrm{SL}_2(\mathbb{Z})$ acts (from the left) on the complex upper half plane $\mathfrak{H}$ via Möbius transformations, which are defined as

$$\begin{pmatrix} a & b \\ c & d \end{pmatrix} (\tau) = \frac{a\tau + b}{c\tau + d} \quad \text{for } \tau \in \mathfrak{H}.$$

We denote by $Y(1)$ the quotient space $\mathrm{SL}_2(\mathbb{Z}) \backslash \mathfrak{H}$, i.e. the set of orbits of $\mathfrak{H}$ under $\mathrm{SL}_2(\mathbb{Z})$. Importantly, the j-invariant $j(\tau) \colon \mathfrak{H} \to \mathbb{C}$ is invariant under the action of $\mathrm{SL}_2(\mathbb{Z})$ and thus induces a function $Y(1) \to \mathbb{C}$. With this, one can prove that $Y(1)$ is in bijection with the *moduli space* of complex elliptic curves up to isomorphism. The compactification of $Y(1)$ is

$$X(1) = Y(1) \cup \mathrm{SL}_2(\mathbb{Z}) \backslash (\mathbb{Q} \cup \{\infty\}).$$

Similarly, we denote by $Y_0(N)$ the quotient space $\Gamma_0(N) \backslash \mathfrak{H}$, i.e. the set of orbits of $\mathfrak{H}$ under $\Gamma_0(N)$. One can prove that $Y_0(N)$ is in bijection with the moduli space of N-isogenies, that is the set of equivalence classes of pairs (E, C), where E is a complex elliptic curve, C is a cyclic subgroup of E of order N, and two pairs (E, C) and (E', C') are equivalent if and only if there is an isomorphism $\varphi \colon E \to E'$ such that $\varphi(C) = C'$. The compactification of $Y_0(N)$ is

$$X_0(N) = Y_0(N) \cup \Gamma_0(N)\backslash(\mathbb{Q} \cup \{\infty\}).$$

Quotients of $\mathfrak{H}$ by subgroups of $\mathrm{SL}_2(\mathbb{Z})$ containing $\Gamma(N)$ for some N, and their compactifications, are called *modular curves*. In particular, $X(1)$ and $X_0(N)$ are modular curves.

To see how $X_0^+(N)$ is constructed, we consider the *Fricke involution* ω_N – a special case of an *Atkin–Lehner involution* – given as the Möbius transformation by the matrix

$$w_N = \begin{pmatrix} 0 & -1 \\ N & 0 \end{pmatrix}.$$

Importantly, due to the following result this is an involution on $X_0(N)$:

Lemma 1 ([47, **Proposition 2.2**]). *We have $w_N \Gamma_0(N) w_N^{-1} = \Gamma_0(N)$.*

In terms of isogenies, the Fricke involution corresponds to dualization since $j \circ \omega_N(\tau) = j(N\tau)$. Now $X_0^+(N)$ is obtained by quotienting $X_0(N)$ by the Fricke involution ω_N. Equivalently,

$$X_0^+(N) = (\Gamma_0(N) \cup w_N \Gamma_0(N))\backslash(\mathfrak{H} \cup \mathbb{Q} \cup \{\infty\}),$$

where the above quotient makes sense since, more generally, matrices with positive determinant act on $\mathfrak{H} \cup \mathbb{Q}\{\infty\}$ via Möbius transformations. We stress, however, that this is not a modular curve since $w_n \notin \mathrm{SL}_2(\mathbb{Z})$.

A *modular function* for a congruence subgroup $\Gamma \subseteq \mathrm{SL}_2(\mathbb{Z})$ is a function $t \colon \mathfrak{H} \cup \{\infty\} \to \mathbb{C}$ which is invariant under Γ, meromorphic on $\mathfrak{H}$, and meromorphic at the cusps – i.e., for each $\gamma \in \mathrm{SL}_2(\mathbb{Z})$ the Fourier expansion of $t(\gamma\tau)$ has the form $\sum_{n=-m}^{\infty} a(n)e^{2\pi i n\tau}$. Equivalently, a modular function is a rational function on the modular curve $X(\Gamma)$. As for $X_0^+(N)$, we define modular functions as modular functions on $X_0(N)$ that are invariant under the Atkin–Lehner involution ω_N. Note that these correspond to rational functions on $X_0^+(N)$ via precomposition with the quotient map $X_0(N) \to X_0^+(N)$. Hence, for all the curves X we consider, we can canonically identify the field $\mathbb{C}(X)$ of modular functions on X with the function field of X as an algebraic curve – this connection will be crucial for our approach, as it allows us to understand these curves equivalently through their modular functions due to the correspondence between algebraic curves and function fields (cf. [27, Theorems 7.2.5–6]). We can give explicit generators for the function fields we will consider:

Theorem 2. *Let $N \in \mathbb{N}$. Then*

$$\mathbb{C}(X_0(N)) = \mathbb{C}(j(\tau), j(N\tau)) \ \text{ and } \ \mathbb{C}(X_0^+(N)) = \mathbb{C}(j(\tau) + j(N\tau), j(\tau) \cdot j(N\tau)).$$

In particular, for $N = 1$ we have $\mathbb{C}(X(1)) = \mathbb{C}(j(\tau))$.

Proof. The first equation is proven in [46, Theorem 6.1]. Further ω_N swaps $j(\tau)$ and $j(N\tau)$ as $j(\tau)$ is invariant under $\left(\begin{smallmatrix} 0 & -1 \\ 1 & 0 \end{smallmatrix}\right)$, so $j(\tau) + j(N\tau)$ and $j(\tau) \cdot j(N\tau)$ are invariant under ω_N and clearly generate a degree 2 subfield of $\mathbb{C}(X_0(N))$ for $N > 1$; as the quotient map $X_0(N) \to X_0^+(N)$ has degree 2 since ω_N is a non-trivial involution (unless $N = 1$), we obtain the second claim. $\qquad\square$

Finally, we recall that the *classical modular polynomial* $\Phi_N(J)$ is defined as the minimal polynomial of $j(N\tau) \in \mathbb{C}(X_0(N))$ over $\mathbb{C}(X(1)) = \mathbb{C}(j(\tau))$. Explicitly, given representatives $a_0, \ldots, a_k$ of the cosets $\mathrm{SL}_2(\mathbb{Z})/\Gamma_0(N)$, it can be factored as

$$\Phi_N(J) = \prod_{i=0}^{k} (J - j(Na_i(\tau))). \tag{1}$$

As $\Phi_N(J)$ turns out to have coefficients in $\mathbb{Z}[j(\tau)]$, we can equivalently consider it as a bivariate polynomial $\Phi_N(J_0, J_1) \in \mathbb{Z}[J_0, J_1]$.

Finally, for $N = \ell$ prime we see that $j(\ell a_i(\tau))$, $i = 0, \ldots, \ell$, give the j-invariants that are ℓ-isogenous to $j(\tau)$, i.e. for a curve E_τ of j-invariant $j(\tau)$ they give the j-invariants of the quotients of E_τ by order ℓ subgroups. This leads to the following result over $\mathbb{C}$, which was extended to positive characteristic by Igusa [36]:

Classical Multiplicity Theorem. *Let ℓ be a prime and let K be a perfect field with* $\mathrm{char}(K) \neq \ell$. *Then, for any $j_0, j_1 \in K$, the number of non-equivalent ℓ-isogenies $j_0 \to j_1$ coincides with the multiplicity of j_1 as a root of $\Phi_\ell(j_0, J_1)$.*

3 Atkin Modular Polynomials

In this section we focus on the so-called *supersingular primes*, which are the primes $\ell \in \mathbb{N}$ such that $X_0^+(\ell)$ has genus 0. The list of supersingular primes, denoted by $\mathcal{L}$, contains in particular those for which $X_0(\ell)$ has genus 0 or 1 – this follows from the Riemann-Hurwitz formula (see e.g. [49, Proposition 1]). The complete list, which also includes some primes for which $X_0(\ell)$ has larger genus, was determined by Lehner and Newman [39, Theorems 8 and 9]:

$$\mathcal{L} = \{2, 3, 5, 7, 11, 13, 17, 19, 23, 29, 31, 41, 47, 59, 71\}.$$

The reason why the genus 0 case is particularly relevant for our application boils down to the existence of a *Hauptmodul* for $X_0^+(\ell)$. We will now recall what this means exactly: Let X be a modular curve, or the quotient of a modular curve by some Atkin–Lehner involution. When X has genus 0, its function field $\mathbb{C}(X)$ is generated by a (unique up to translation) modular function with a unique simple pole of residue 1 at ∞. Such a function is called a *Hauptmodul*, and it can be shifted to obtain a (unique) *normalized Hauptmodul*, i.e., a Hauptmodul whose q-expansion has constant term 0. A classic example is $X(1)$, for which a Hauptmodul is the j-invariant modular function $j(\tau)$. Another relevant example is $X_0(\ell)$, which has genus 0 if and only if $\ell \in \{2, 3, 5, 7, 13\}$; in this case, a Hauptmodul is

$$t_\ell(\tau) := \left(\frac{\eta(\tau)}{\eta(\ell\tau)} \right)^{2s} \tag{2}$$

where $s = 12/(\ell - 1)$ and $\eta(\tau) = e^{\frac{\pi i \tau}{12}} \cdot \prod_{n=1}^{\infty}(1 - e^{2n\pi i \tau})$ is the Dedekind eta function. In particular, for each such ℓ, the j-invariant $j(\tau)$ can be expressed as a rational function of $t_\ell(\tau)$. If we view $X_0(\ell)$ as a moduli space, this means that $t_\ell(\tau)$ parametrizes ℓ-isogenies and, consequently, one can project $X_0(\ell)$ onto $X(1)$ by mapping each value of $t_\ell(\tau)$ to the j-invariant of the domain of the corresponding isogeny. Notably, the Fricke involution identifies an isogeny with its dual: Therefore we do not expect an analogue projection to map a Hauptmodul $t_\ell^+(\tau)$ for $X_0^+(\ell)$ to the j-invariant. Indeed, due to $j(\ell\tau) \neq j(\tau)$, $j(\tau)$ does not descend to a function on $X_0^+(\ell)$. Nevertheless, as we will see, $t_\ell^+(\tau)$ identifies a *pair* of j-invariants – which are the domains/codomains of the dual pair of isogenies represented by $t_\ell^+(\tau)$.

Finding the Normalized Hauptmodul for $X_0^+(\ell)$. We will now describe how to obtain explicit generators $t_\ell^+(\tau)$ of $\mathbb{C}(X_0^+(\ell))$ for $\ell \in \mathcal{L}$. When $X_0(\ell)$ has genus 0, a Hauptmodul for $X_0^+(\ell)$ is easily obtained from a Hauptmodul of $X_0(\ell)$.

Proposition 3. *Suppose that $X_0(\ell)$ has genus 0 and let $t_\ell(\tau)$ be as in Equation (2). Then*

$$t_\ell^+(\tau) = t_\ell(\tau) + 2\,s + \ell^s/t_\ell(\tau)$$

is the normalized Hauptmodul for $X_0^+(\ell)$.

Proof. By Theorem 2 $\mathbb{C}(X_0(\ell))$ is a degree-2 field extension of $\mathbb{C}(X_0^+(\ell))$ since $j(\tau)$ is not invariant under ω_ℓ. Moreover, as an immediate consequence of the properties of η [48, Lemma 5.5], we have

$$t_\ell\tau\left(-\frac{1}{\ell\tau}\right) = \frac{\ell^s}{t_\ell(\tau)}, \tag{3}$$

which shows that $t_\ell^+ \circ \omega_\ell(\tau) = t_\ell^+(\tau)$ and therefore $\mathbb{C}(t_\ell^+(\tau)) \subseteq \mathbb{C}(X_0^+(\ell))$. Since

$$t_\ell(\tau)^2 - t_\ell(\tau)(t_\ell^+(\tau) - 2s) + \ell^s = 0,$$

we have that $\mathbb{C}(X_0(\ell))$ is a degree 2 extension of $\mathbb{C}(t_\ell^+(\tau))$, which implies that $t_\ell^+(\tau)$ generates $\mathbb{C}(X_0^+(\ell))$.

To conclude, we need to show that $t_\ell^+(\tau)$ is normalized and has a unique pole of order 1 at ∞, but this follows immediately from the q-expansion

$$t_\ell^+(\tau) = q^{-1} + \sum_{n \geq 1} a_n q^n$$

of $t_\ell^+(\tau)$, which can be verified via direct computation using low precision (see also the SageMath script `qExpansions.sage`). $\qquad\square$

A harder task is giving explicit formulas for the supersingular primes such that $X_0(\ell)$ has genus > 0, i.e. for $\ell \in \mathcal{L} \setminus \{2, 3, 5, 7, 13\}$. A first approach, conjectured in [22] and proved in [11, Theorem 1.1], is to use suitable *Thompson series*, whose q-expansions are determined by the so-called *head characters* of the *Monster group* (the largest sporadic simple group). Another approach is to use a technique developed by Atkin called *blanchiment*, consisting in combining powers of functions of the form

$$\frac{\sum_{m,n} q^{am^2+bmn+cn^2}}{\eta(\tau)\eta(\ell\tau)}$$

for suitable integers a, b, c to obtain generators of $X_0^+(\ell)$ with small order at ∞ (see [40, §3.3.2] and [47, §2.3.1]). A third approach, explored in [19, Table 1], uses combinations of generalized Dedekind eta functions.

For our purposes, it will be sufficient to refer to the former construction. The corresponding q-expansions have been pre-computed up to the first hundreds of coefficients by G. C. Greubel on https://oeis.org/ as the McKay–Thompson series of the class ℓA for the Monster group.

The Atkin Modular Polynomial. Fixing $\ell \in \mathcal{L}$, we can now consider the minimal polynomial $\Phi_\ell^A(Y)$ of the normalized Hauptmodul $t_\ell^+(\tau) \in \mathbb{C}(X_0^+(\ell))$ over the field $\mathbb{C}(j(\tau)) = \mathbb{C}(X(1))$, which is called the ℓth *Atkin modular polynomial* as (a variation of) it was originally considered by Atkin [3, §2.2] for the optimization of Schoof's point counting algorithm [50]. Following the presentation of Lercier [40, §3.3.2] and Morain [47, §2.3], we can give its construction more explicitly: The finitely many cosets of $\mathrm{SL}_2(\mathbb{Z})/\Gamma_0(\ell)$ are represented by the matrices

$$a_n = \begin{pmatrix} 0 & -1 \\ 1 & n \end{pmatrix}, \ 0 \le n < \ell, \ \text{and} \ a_\ell = \begin{pmatrix} 1 & 0 \\ 0 & 1 \end{pmatrix},$$

and, as $t_\ell^+(\tau)$ generates $\mathbb{C}(X_0(\ell))$ over $\mathbb{C}(X(1)) = \mathbb{C}(j(\tau))$ by Theorem 2, the Atkin modular polynomial is given by

$$\Phi_\ell^A(Y) = \prod_{n=0}^{\ell} \left(Y - t_\ell^+(a_n(\tau))\right) = \left(Y - t_\ell^+(\tau)\right) \prod_{n=0}^{\ell-1} \left(Y - t_\ell^+\tau\left(\frac{-1}{\tau+n}\right)\right).$$

Note that, due to the fact that $t_\ell^+(\tau)$ is a modular function for $\Gamma_0(\ell)$, one can choose any representatives $a_0, \ldots, a_\ell$ of this collection of cosets to factor $\Phi_\ell^A(Y)$.

Moving from the modular interpretation to a more explicit approach, we first describe, for the supersingular primes $\ell \in \mathcal{L}$, the form of the Atkin modular polynomial in more detail. Via direct inspection we can see that $\Phi_\ell^A(Y)$ has coefficients in $\mathbb{Z}[j(\tau)]$, and can thus be considered as a bivariate polynomial $\Phi_\ell^A(Y, j) \in \mathbb{Z}[Y, j]$, which we list in the script `AtkinModularPolys.sage`. These polynomials were computed by Kohel[3]; however, the exact polynomials $\Xi_\ell(Y, j)$ given by Kohel, which are also integrated into SageMath as a database, are not

---

[3] https://www.i2m.univ-amu.fr/perso/david.kohel/dbs/atkin_polynomials.html.

exactly the minimal polynomials of the respective normalized Hauptmoduln. In fact, they are related to the above minimal polynomials via

$$\Xi_\ell(Y, j) = \begin{cases} \Phi_\ell^A(Y, j), & \ell \leq 19 \\ \Phi_\ell^A(Y - 1, j), & \ell \geq 23 \end{cases}.$$

For uniformity we stick to our original definition $\Phi_\ell^A(Y, j)$, but we note that all our results, being invariant with respect to integer shifts of the variable Y, also apply to the polynomials in Kohel's database.

Proposition 4. *Let $\ell \in \mathcal{L}$. Then the ℓth Atkin modular polynomial $\Phi_\ell^A(Y, j)$ is of the form*

$$\Phi_\ell^A(Y, j) = j^2 - j \cdot \left(Y^\ell + \sum_{i=0}^{\ell-1} a_i Y^i \right) + Y^{\ell+1} + \sum_{i=0}^{\ell} b_i Y^i$$

with integer coefficients $a_i, b_i \in \mathbb{Z}$.

We note that we can also see $\deg_j \Phi_\ell^A(Y, j) = 2$ from the fact that the field extension $\mathbb{C}(X_0^+(\ell)) \subseteq \mathbb{C}(X_0(\ell))$ is a degree 2 extension. With this we can understand the modular picture better:

Corollary 1. *Let $\ell \in \mathcal{L}$. Then*

$$\Phi_\ell^A(t_\ell^+(\tau), j) = (j - j(\tau)) \cdot (j - j(\ell\tau)).$$

Proof. By Proposition 4 we know that $\Phi_\ell^A(t_\ell^+(\tau), j)$ is monic of degree 2 in j, and by definition it has $j(\tau)$ as a root. Moreover, applying (the action of) ω_ℓ to the expression $\Phi_\ell^A(t_\ell^+(\tau), j(\tau)) = 0$ yields $\Phi_\ell^A(t_\ell^+(\tau), j(\ell\tau)) = 0$ due to the ω_ℓ-invariance of $t_\ell^+(\tau)$. Thus $\Phi_\ell^A(t_\ell^+(\tau), j)$ has the two distinct roots $j(\tau)$ and $j(\ell\tau)$, as claimed. $\qquad\square$

To capture the above factorization arithmetically, we will also need the difference quotient polynomial

$$\delta_\ell(Y, J_0, J_1) := \frac{\Phi_\ell^A(Y, J_1) - \Phi_\ell^A(Y, J_0)}{J_1 - J_0} = J_0 + J_1 - \left(Y^\ell + \sum_{i=0}^{\ell-1} a_i Y^i \right).$$

Corollary 2. *Let K be a field and $j_0, j_1, j_2 \in K$ with $j_1 \neq j_2$. Then, for each $\ell \in \mathcal{L}$,*

$$\gcd(\Phi_\ell^A(Y, j_0), \delta_\ell(Y, j_0, j_1), \delta_\ell(Y, j_0, j_2)) = 1.$$

Proof. For any $t^+ \in \overline{K}$ the polynomial $\Phi_\ell^A(t^+, j) \in \overline{K}[j]$ can have at most two (not necessarily distinct) roots by Proposition 4; hence, if t^+ is a root of $\Phi_\ell^A(Y, j_0)$, then either j_0 is a double root of $\Phi_\ell^A(t^+, j)$ or there is a unique $j_1 \in \overline{K}$ with $j_1 \neq j_0$ such that $\Phi_\ell^A(t^+, j_1) = 0$. Stated equivalently, there is a unique $j_1 \in \overline{K}$ such that t^+ is a common root of $\Phi_\ell^A(Y, j_0)$ and $\delta_\ell(Y, j_0, j_1)$. $\qquad\square$

3.1 The Atkin Multiplicity Theorem

Motivated by Corollary 1, we relate the Atkin modular polynomial to the classical modular polynomial via resultant theory.

Proposition 5. *For any $\ell \in \mathcal{L}$ we have*

$$\mathrm{res}_Y\big(\Phi_\ell^A(Y, J_0), \delta_\ell(Y, J_0, J_1)\big) = \Phi_\ell(J_0, J_1)$$

where the resultant is computed over the coefficient ring $R = \mathbb{Z}[J_0, J_1]$ of bivariate polynomials.

Proof. This can be verified via direct computation (cf. the SageMath script `AtkinModularPolys.sage`). However, as this computation is somewhat expensive, we also give a modular proof in the full version of this article [34, Proposition 12]. $\square$

Remark 1. Using the invariance $\mathrm{res}_Y(f, g) = \mathrm{res}_Y(f, g - f)$ of the resultant together with the multiplicativity of the resultant (see [34, Proposition 2]), one can show that the equation of Proposition 5 is equivalent to

$$\mathrm{res}_Y\big(\Phi_\ell^A(Y, J_0), \Phi_\ell^A(Y, J_1)\big) = (J_1 - J_0)^{\ell+1} \cdot \Phi_\ell(J_0, J_1);$$

see also [32, p. 8] for this latter equation, up to a sign error for $\ell = 2$. This highlights why we need to consider the difference quotient as our second equation: If we want to detect loops, i.e. evaluate J_0 and J_1 at the same j-invariant j_0, then we need to check whether $\Phi_\ell^A(t^+, j)$ has a double root at j_0 for some t^+. However, this will not be possible just using the polynomial $\Phi_\ell^A(Y, j_0)$ twice, but we instead also need to consider its j-derivative; to elegantly capture this case and the case of two distinct j-invariants in the same equation, we thus opt for the difference quotient.

In view of our general result on derivatives of resultants, we can use the above equation to prove a crucial relation between the Atkin modular polynomial and ℓ-isogenies. We note that a partial version of this result also appears in [32, Proposition 2.9] purely in the language of modular curves.

Atkin Multiplicity Theorem. *Let $\ell \in \mathcal{L}$, let K be a field of characteristic $\mathrm{char}(K) \notin [\ell] = \{1, \ldots, \ell\}$ and let $j_0, j_1 \in K$. Then the number of (non-equivalent) ℓ-isogenies $j_0 \to j_1$ is equal to the cardinality of the multiset*

$$\left\{\!\!\left\{ \text{Roots } t^+ \in \overline{K} \text{ of } \Phi_\ell^A(Y, j_0) \text{ such that } \delta_\ell(t^+, j_0, j_1) = 0 \right\}\!\!\right\}.$$

In particular, j_0 and j_1 are ℓ-isogenous if and only if there exists $t^+ \in \overline{K}$ such that

$$\Phi_\ell^A(t^+, j_0) = 0 = \delta_\ell(t^+, j_0, j_1). \tag{AM}$$

Proof. To simplify notation we may assume that K is algebraically closed. For any $j_0, j_1 \in K$ we now write $\chi_\ell(j_0, j_1)$ for the number of roots of $\Phi_\ell^A(Y, j_0)$ (counted with multiplicity) that are roots of $\delta_\ell(Y, j_0, j_1)$, and we write $\nu_\ell(j_0, j_1)$ for the number of non-equivalent ℓ-isogenies from j_0 to j_1. Hence our goal is to show that $\chi_\ell(j_0, j_1) = \nu_\ell(j_0, j_1)$; however, it suffices to prove the inequality

$$\chi_\ell(j_0, j_1) \leq \nu_\ell(j_0, j_1) \tag{4}$$

for all $j_0, j_1 \in K$ since summing both quantities over all possible j_1 for a fixed $j_0 \in K$ then yields

$$\ell + 1 = \deg_Y(\Phi_\ell^A(Y, j_0)) = \sum_{j_1 \in K} \chi_\ell(j_0, j_1) \leq \sum_{j_1 \in K} \nu_\ell(j_0, j_1) = \ell + 1$$

in view of the Classical Multiplicity Theorem and Corollary 2, so all inequalities will have to be equalities.

To prove the inequality (4) we can use our previous results: Indeed, as $\delta_\ell(Y, J_0, J_1)$ has leading Y-coefficient -1, Propositions 1 and 5 yield the identity

$$\mathrm{res}_Y(\Phi_\ell^A(Y, j_0), \delta_\ell(Y, j_0, J_1)) = \Phi_\ell(j_0, J_1)$$

in the polynomial ring $K[J_1]$, and applying Theorem 1 to the K-linear evaluation $J_1 \mapsto j_1$ shows that for any $k \in \{0, \ldots, \chi_\ell(j_0, j_1) - 1\}$ the kth J_1-derivative of this resultant vanishes at $J_1 = j_1$. Due to our assumption $\mathrm{char}(K) \notin [\ell]$, this means that $\Phi_\ell(j_0, J_1)$ has a root of multiplicity at least $\chi_\ell(j_0, j_1)$ at $J_1 = j_1$, and inequality (4) follows. $\qquad\square$

3.2 Atkin Root Computation

Similarly to [33, §3], the Atkin Multiplicity Theorem leads us to the question of how to compute the additional invariants $t_1^+, \ldots, t_k^+ \in \overline{\mathbb{F}_p}$ for a path

$$j_0 \xrightarrow{t_1^+} j_1 \xrightarrow{t_2^+} \cdots \xrightarrow{t_{k-1}^+} j_{k-1} \xrightarrow{t_k^+} j_k$$

of j-invariants; to this end we derive a low-degree equation for t_i^+ over $\mathbb{F}_p(j_{i-1}, j_i)$.

Corollary 3. *Let $\ell \in \mathcal{L}$, let $j_0, j_1 \in \overline{\mathbb{F}_p}$ for a prime $p > \ell$, and consider the gcd-polynomial*

$$\Lambda_\ell(j_0, j_1) := \gcd(\Phi_\ell^A(Y, j_0), \delta_\ell(Y, j_0, j_1)) \in \mathbb{F}_p(j_0, j_1)[Y].$$

Writing $\nu_\ell(j, j')$ for the number of non-equivalent ℓ-isogenies $j \to j'$, we then have

$$\deg \Lambda_\ell(j_0, j_1) \leq \min\{\nu_\ell(j_0, j_1), \nu_\ell(j_1, j_0)\}.$$

Moreover:

(a) $\deg \Lambda_\ell(j_0, j_1) \geq 1$ *if and only if j_0 and j_1 are ℓ-isogenous.*
(b) *If j_0 is ordinary or $p > 4\ell^3$, then $\deg \Lambda_\ell(j_0, j_1) \leq 2$.*

Proof. From the Atkin Multiplicity Theorem we directly see that $\deg \Lambda_\ell(j_0, j_1)$ is bounded above by $\nu_\ell(j_0, j_1)$ since $\Lambda_\ell(j_0, j_1)$ is a divisor of $\Phi_\ell^A(Y, j_0)$ such that each of its roots is also a root of $\delta_\ell(Y, j_0, j_1)$. Moreover, Λ_ℓ is symmetric in (j_0, j_1). Indeed, for $j_0 \neq j_1$ we have

$$
\begin{aligned}
\Lambda_\ell(j_0, j_1) &= \gcd(\Phi_\ell^A(Y, j_0), (j_1 - j_0)\delta_\ell(Y, j_0, j_1)) \\
&= \gcd(\Phi_\ell^A(Y, j_0), \Phi_\ell^A(Y, j_1) - \Phi_\ell^A(Y, j_0)) = \gcd(\Phi_\ell^A(Y, j_0), \Phi_\ell^A(Y, j_1)),
\end{aligned}
$$

which clearly is symmetric in (j_0, j_1). Together with the prior analysis we therefore obtain the general upper bound on the degree of $\Lambda_\ell(j_0, j_1)$. Furthermore, claim (a) follows immediately from the Atkin Multiplicity Theorem. Finally, suppose that j_0 is ordinary or that $p > 4\ell^3$. Then there are at most two non-equivalent ℓ-isogenies $j_0 \to j_1$ or at most two non-equivalent ℓ-isogenies $j_1 \to j_0$: In the supersingular case with $p > 4\ell^3$ this follows from [12, Corollary 16] for $j_0 \neq 0$ and from [42, Theorem 2(2)] for $j_0 = 0$, and in the ordinary case this follows from the structure of ordinary isogeny volcanoes (cf. [12, Corollary 27]), using throughout the asymmetry [12, Proposition 4] of isogeny graphs. Therefore our general degree bound yields claim (b). $\qquad\square$

Contrary to [33, Corollary 2], the inequality in Corollary 3 is generally not an equality, as the following example shows:

Example 1. For $\ell = 3$, $p = 13$ and $j_0 = 5$ we have $\Phi_\ell^A(Y, j_0) = (Y - 5)^2 \cdot (Y - 9)^2$ and $\delta_\ell(Y, j_0, j_0) = -(Y - 5) \cdot (Y - 9) \cdot (Y - 12)$. Therefore there are four non-equivalent ℓ-isogenies $j_0 \to j_0$, double the degree of $\Lambda_\ell(j_0, j_0) = (Y - 5) \cdot (Y - 9)$.

The issue in the above example is that, in contrast to the canonical modular polynomial Φ_ℓ^c, the Atkin modular polynomial Φ_ℓ^A can have roots of higher multiplicity even away from the special j-invariants 0 and 1728. On the modular side, these additional multi-roots come from the ramification of the quotient map $X_0(\ell) \to X_0^+(\ell)$ at degree ℓ endomorphisms that are not equivalent to their dual. This also motivates the following result, which we include for completeness; we give its proof, which can be performed with some involved resultant computations, only in the full version of this article [34, Lemma 14] as we do not need this result in the sequel.

Lemma 2. *Let $\ell \in \mathcal{L}$ and let K be a field of characteristic $\mathrm{char}(K) \neq \ell$. Furthermore let $j_0 \in K$ such that $j_0 \notin \{0, 1728\}$ and suppose that $t^+ \in K$ is a double root of $\Phi_\ell^A(Y, j_0)$. Then the following holds:*

(a) t^+ *is not a root of $\Phi_\ell^A(Y, j_1)$ for any $j_1 \in K$ with $j_1 \neq j_0$.*
(b) t^+ *is not a triple root of $\Phi_\ell^A(Y, j_0)$, i.e. its multiplicity as a root is exactly 2.*

Additionally, the polynomials $\Phi_\ell^A(Y, 0)$ and $\Phi_\ell^A(Y, 1728)$ have a factorization analogous to [33, Lemma 3]:

Lemma 3. *Let $\ell \in \mathcal{L}$. Then there are integers $t_0^+, t_{1728}^+ \in \mathbb{Z}$ as well as monic non-constant irreducible polynomials h_0 and h_{1728} in $\mathbb{Z}[Y]$ such that*

$$\Phi_\ell^A(Y,0) = (Y - t_0^+)^{e_0} \cdot h_0^3 \quad and \quad \Phi_\ell^A(Y,1728) = (Y - t_{1728}^+)^{e_{1728}} \cdot h_{1728}^2,$$

where

$$e_0 = \begin{cases} 1, & \ell = 3 \\ 2, & \ell \equiv 1 \bmod 3 \\ 0, & \ell \equiv 2 \bmod 3 \end{cases} \quad and \quad e_{1728} = \begin{cases} 1, & \ell = 2 \\ 2, & \ell \equiv 1 \bmod 4 \\ 0, & \ell \equiv 3 \bmod 4 \end{cases}.$$

Moreover, the following holds for a field K and $j^* \in \{0, 1728\} \subseteq K$:

(a) $\Phi_\ell^A(t_{j^*}^+, j) = (j - j^*)^2$.

(b) If $\mathrm{char}(K) \notin \{2, 3, \ell\}$, then $t_{j^*}^+ \in K$ is not a root of h_{j^*}.

(c) If $\mathrm{char}(K) \notin [4\ell]$, then h_{j^*} does not have a double root in $\overline{K}$.

Proof. In the SageMath script `AtkinModularPolys.sage` we confirm the above factorization of $\Phi_\ell^A(Y,0)$ and $\Phi_\ell^A(Y,1728)$, as well as the additional claims (a) and (b) by evaluation, where we check for claim (b) that $h_{j^*}(t_{j^*}^+)$ only has prime factors in $\{2, 3, \ell\}$. Finally, for claim (c) one confirms computationally that the discriminant $\mathrm{res}(h_{j^*}, \frac{\partial}{\partial Y} h_{j^*})$ of h_{j^*} only has prime divisors in $[4\ell]$; then, as applying $\mathbb{Z} \to K$ coefficient-wise preserves the degrees of h_{j^*} and its derivative, we conclude the claim with Proposition 1. $\qquad\square$

Remark 2. Lemma 3(c) can be seen as the analogue of Lemma 2(a) for the special j-invariants: Indeed, for $\mathrm{char}(K) \notin [4\ell]$ the loops at $j^* \in \{0, 1728\} \subseteq K$ are exactly given by the root $t_{j^*}^+$ according to the Atkin Multiplicity Theorem and [12, Lemma 29]. Therefore any root of h_{j^*} will encode an ℓ-isogeny to a different j-invariant, and the exponents 3 resp. 2 correctly account for the asymmetry in isogeny graphs (cf. [12, Proposition 4]); if the target j-invariant does not lie in $\{0, 1728\}$, one can thus immediately obtain the claim from Lemma 2(a).

Remark 3. To get a gcd-polynomial for which the degree coincides with the minimal number of ℓ-isogenies between the two j-invariants, one can instead consider

$$\begin{cases} \gcd(\Phi_\ell^A(Y, j_0), \Phi_\ell^A(Y, j_1)), & \text{if } j_0 \neq j_1 \\ \gcd(\Phi_\ell^A(Y, j_0), \delta_\ell(Y, j_0, j_0)^2), & \text{if } j_0 = j_1. \end{cases}$$

to account for the reduction of root multiplicities caused by the derivative.

3.3   The (Supersingular) Splitting Behavior of $\Phi_\ell^A(Y, j_0)$

To apply the Atkin modular polynomials for a R1CS-based proof of knowledge, we also need to understand the splitting behavior of $\Phi_\ell^A(Y, j_0) \in \mathbb{F}_{p^2}[Y]$ for a supersingular j-invariant $j_0 \in \mathbb{F}_{p^2}$. For the small primes $\ell \in \{2, 3, 5, 7, 13\}$ for which $X_0(\ell)$ has genus 0 and for which we understand the splitting behavior of the canonical modular polynomial[4] due to [33, Theorem 2], we can transfer Proposition 3 to the case of positive characteristic.

---

[4] We recall the theory of canonical modular polynomials in the full version of this article [34, Appendix B].

Proposition 6. *Let $\ell \in \{2, 3, 5, 7, 13\}$, let K be an algebraically closed field with $\operatorname{char}(K) \neq \ell$, write $s = 12/(\ell - 1)$ as before and define on $K^\times$ the rational map*

$$\epsilon_\ell \colon K^\times \to K, \ f \mapsto f + 2s + \ell^s/f.$$

Then ϵ_ℓ is invariant with respect to the involution $\iota_\ell \colon K^\times \to K^\times$, $f \mapsto \ell^s/f$ and induces a bijection

$$\bar{\epsilon}_\ell \colon K^\times/\iota_\ell \xrightarrow{\sim} K.$$

Furthermore this rational map ϵ_ℓ satisfies

$$\Phi_\ell^A(\epsilon_\ell(T), j) = (j - \mathcal{J}_\ell(T)) \cdot (j - \mathcal{J}_\ell(\ell^s/T)) \tag{5}$$

where $\mathcal{J}_\ell(T) = \Phi_\ell^c(T, 0)/T$ represents the j-invariant in terms of T. Thus, for $\bar{\epsilon}_\ell(\{f, \ell^s/f\}) = \epsilon_\ell(f)$, the roots of $\Phi_\ell^A(\epsilon_\ell(f), j)$ are precisely $\{\mathcal{J}_\ell(f), \mathcal{J}_\ell(\ell^s/f)\}$.

Proof. It is immediate that ϵ_ℓ is invariant under the involution ι_ℓ. Furthermore, for any $a \in K$ we have $\epsilon_\ell(f) = a$ if and only if f satisfies the polynomial equation $T^2 + (2s - a)T + \ell^s = 0$, and from the constant term we deduce that this polynomial factors as $(T - f)(T - \ell^s/f)$ for some $f \in K^\times$ since K is algebraically closed. Altogether, ϵ_ℓ indeed induces the claimed bijection. Finally, to verify Eq. (5), we consider the ring homomorphism

$$\varphi \colon \mathbb{Q}(T)[j] \to \mathbb{C}(t_\ell(\tau))[j], \ T \mapsto t_\ell(\tau),$$

which is an embedding since $t_\ell(\tau)$ is transcendental. In view of Proposition 3 and Corollary 1 we now obtain

$$
\begin{aligned}
\varphi(\Phi_\ell^A(\epsilon_\ell(T), j)) &= \Phi_\ell^A(\epsilon_\ell(\varphi(T)), j) = \Phi_\ell^A(\epsilon_\ell(t_\ell(\tau)), j) \\
&= \Phi_\ell^A(t_\ell^+(\tau), j) = (j - j(\tau)) \cdot (j - j(\ell\tau)) \\
&= (j - \mathcal{J}_\ell(t_\ell(\tau))) \cdot (j - \mathcal{J}_\ell(\ell^s/t_\ell(\tau))) \\
&= \varphi\left((j - \mathcal{J}_\ell(T)) \cdot (j - \mathcal{J}_\ell(\ell^s/T))\right),
\end{aligned}
$$

and the injectivity of φ yields the remaining claims. $\qquad\square$

With the help of the rational maps ϵ_ℓ and the theory of canonical modular polynomials we can directly derive the following splitting theorem for the Atkin modular polynomials at supersingular j-invariants for $\ell \in \{2, 3, 5, 7, 13\}$:

Corollary 4. *Let $\ell \in \{2, 3, 5, 7, 13\}$, let $p \neq \ell$ be a prime and let $j_0 \in \mathbb{F}_{p^2}$ be a supersingular j-invariant. Then $\Phi_\ell^A(Y, j_0)$ splits over $\mathbb{F}_{p^2}$.*

Proof. Let $t^+ \in \overline{\mathbb{F}_p}$ be a root of $\Phi_\ell^A(Y, j_0)$. By Proposition 6 we then find an element $f \in \overline{\mathbb{F}_p}^\times$ such that $\epsilon_\ell(f) = t^+$ as well as $j_0 \in \{\mathcal{J}_\ell(f), \mathcal{J}_\ell(\ell^s/f)\}$. Switching f for ℓ^s/f if necessary, we may assume $j_0 = \mathcal{J}_\ell(f)$, i.e. $\Phi_\ell^c(f, j_0) = 0$. But then [33, Theorem 2] yields $f \in \mathbb{F}_{p^2}$, and we obtain $t^+ = \epsilon_\ell(f) \in \mathbb{F}_{p^2}$. $\qquad\square$

To analyze the splitting behavior of the Atkin modular polynomials for all $\ell \in \mathcal{L}$, one would hope to directly adapt the techniques of [33, Section 3.3] to arrive at an analogous *Atkin Reconstruction Theorem*. However, this approach runs into multiple computational issues since the Hauptmodul does not determine the j-invariant uniquely anymore.

For this reason we will turn to a graph-theoretic approach to prove the splitting theorem for supersingular j-invariants. First we handle the special j-invariants 0 and 1728 separately:

Proposition 7. *Let $\ell \in \mathcal{L}$, let $p \neq \ell$ be a prime and let $j^* \in \{0, 1728\} \subseteq \mathbb{F}_{p^2}$ be supersingular. Then $\Phi_\ell^A(Y, j^*)$ splits over $\mathbb{F}_{p^2}$.*

Proof. In the script `AtkinModularPolys.sage` we confirm that the claim holds for $p \leq 4\ell^2$, so we may assume $p > 4\ell^2$. Moreover, in view of Corollary 4 we may assume $\ell > 3$. Now let $t^+ \in \overline{\mathbb{F}_p}$ be a root of $\Phi_\ell^A(Y, j^*)$, and let $j_1 \in \overline{\mathbb{F}_p}$ be the unique j-invariant satisfying $\delta_\ell(t^+, j^*, j_1) = 0$ (cf. Corollary 2). Then j_1 is ℓ-isogenous to j^* by the Atkin Multiplicity Theorem, so $j_1 \in \mathbb{F}_{p^2}$ is a supersingular j-invariant. Noting that for $j^* = 0$ (resp. $j^* = 1728$) we necessarily have $p \equiv 2 \bmod 3$ (resp. $p \equiv 3 \bmod 4$), we can now use the explicit knowledge of the neighborhood of j^* in the supersingular ℓ-isogeny graph as discussed in [42]:

- For $j_1 \notin \{0, 1728\}$ there is exactly one ℓ-isogeny $j_1 \to j^*$ (up to equivalence) by [42, Theorem 2].
- If $\{j^*, j_1\} = \{0, 1728\}$, then there are exactly two non-equivalent ℓ-isogenies $1728 \to 0$ by [42, Theorem 2].
- If $j^* = j_1$, then there are at most two non-equivalent ℓ-isogenies $j^* \to j_1$ by [42, Theorem 1].

By Corollary 3 the gcd-polynomial $\Lambda_\ell(j^*, j_1) \in \mathbb{F}_p(j^*, j_1)[Y]$ thus is either a linear polynomial over $\mathbb{F}_{p^2}$ or a polynomial of degree at most two over $\mathbb{F}_p$, so $\Lambda_\ell(j^*, j_1)(t^+) = 0$ gives $t^+ \in \mathbb{F}_{p^2}$. $\qquad\square$

For sufficiently large prime characteristics we can now easily obtain the desired splitting behavior via analysis of the supersingular ℓ-isogeny graph:

Theorem 3. *Let $\ell \in \mathcal{L}$, let $p > 4\ell^4$ be a prime and let $j_0 \in \mathbb{F}_{p^2}$ be a supersingular j-invariant. Then $\Phi_\ell^A(Y, j_0)$ splits over $\mathbb{F}_{p^2}$.*

Proof. Due to Proposition 1 we may assume $j_0 \notin \{0, 1728\}$. Hence [12, Corollaries 16 & 18] show that there is at most one double edge, and otherwise only simple edges, at the vertex j_0 in the supersingular ℓ-isogeny graph. Thus Corollary 3 shows that $\Phi_\ell^A(Y, j_0)$ splits completely over $\mathbb{F}_{p^2}$ except possibly for a single irreducible factor of degree 2. However, via direct inspection one sees that the discriminant of $\Phi_\ell^A(Y, j_0)$ is a square in $\mathbb{F}_{p^2}$ (for $\ell = 2$ due to the fact that $j_0 - 1728 \in \mathbb{F}_{p^2}$ is a square, see [33, Corollary 3]), so it cannot have this single irreducible factor of degree 2 by [31, Theorem 1.8], and we obtain our claim. $\quad\square$

Remark 4. Due to the fact that $X_0(\ell)$ parametrizes ℓ-isogenies, which can always be defined over $\mathbb{F}_{p^2}$ for supersingular curves after an appropriate choice of models for the elliptic curves (cf. [1, Theorem 6]), it is certain that the above splitting claim also holds for all smaller characteristics $\ell \neq p < 4\ell^4$ (see also [20, Theorem 5.36]); checking this claim manually, however, is computationally infeasible. Alternatively, one could prove it by computing a model for $X_0(\ell)$, explicitly realizing the quotient map $X_0(\ell) \to X_0^+(\ell)$ as a rational map and explicitly associating to a kernel polynomial of an ℓ-isogeny the correct point on $X_0(\ell)$. As we will only be interested in sufficiently large characteristics for our application due to attacks on path-finding in the supersingular ℓ-isogeny graph, we omit these computations here. Moreover, as previously mentioned, there are also multiple hurdles when trying to adapt the reconstruction approach pursued in [33, Section 3.3]; this adaption would be very similar to the alternative approach sketched above.

4 Weber Modular Polynomials

In [52, §125–144] Weber defined a modular function of level 48 – denoted by $\mathfrak{f}$ – for a suitable modular group Γ_W of index 72 in $\mathrm{SL}_2(\mathbb{Z})$. His main goal was to study the Hilbert class field, i.e., the maximal unramified abelian extension of imaginary quadratic number fields (see [9] and [24, §12.B]). He noted that, for any CM (i.e., imaginary quadratic) point τ, the element $\mathfrak{f}(\tau)$ generated a small-degree extension of the Hilbert class field of $\mathbb{Q}(\tau)$. Moreover, the minimal polynomial of $\mathfrak{f}(\tau)$ was more compact than that of $j(\tau)$. This feature was further explored in several other works [14,35,43,53], which assess how 'optimal' the logarithmic height of $\mathfrak{f}(\tau)$ is at CM points.

The intuition that modular equations are in general more compact for $\mathfrak{f}(\tau)$ than they are for $j(\tau)$ led Bröker, Lauter, and Sutherland [14] to construct, for every $\ell \geq 5$, the *Weber modular polynomial* $\Phi_\ell^W(F_0, F_1)$. As we will see in this section, Φ_ℓ^W captures the ℓ-isogeny relation in the same way as the classical modular polynomials. More precisely, we will prove that a chain of ℓ-isogenies over a finite field can be viewed as a chain of consecutive roots of $\Phi_\ell^W(F_0, F_1)$. This is already illustrated in [23], leveraging the observation that $\mathfrak{f}$ parametrizes elliptic curves with a level 48 structure. In this way, isogenies between $\mathfrak{f}$-invariants can be interpreted as isogenies between the corresponding j-invariants that respect this level structure.

A further reason to consider Φ_ℓ^W in our work is that it enjoys a (heuristically) 72 times smaller logarithmic height and a sparser structure than Φ_ℓ. More precisely, the coefficient of $F_0^a F_1^b$ in $\Phi_\ell^W(F_0, F_1)$ can be nonzero only when $\ell a + b \equiv \ell + 1 \bmod 24$ [14, §7.3].

The Weber Modular Curve. We start by introducing the Weber modular function(s):

Definition 1. *The* Weber modular function $\mathfrak{f}(\tau)$ *is defined by*

$$\mathfrak{f}(\tau) := \frac{\eta(\tau)^2}{\eta\left(\frac{\tau}{2}\right)\eta(2\tau)}.$$

For reference we also define the other Weber modular functions[5]

$$\mathfrak{f}_+(\tau) := \frac{\eta\left(\frac{\tau}{2}\right)}{\eta(\tau)} \quad and \quad \mathfrak{f}_-(\tau) := \frac{\sqrt{2}\eta(2\tau)}{\eta(\tau)}.$$

These functions satisfy the following cover equations over $\mathbb{C}(X(1)) = \mathbb{C}(j(\tau))$:

Lemma 4 ([24, **Theorem 12.17 and Corollary 12.19**]). *We have*

$$(\mathfrak{f}(\tau)^{24} - 16)^3 - \mathfrak{f}(\tau)^{24}j(\tau) = 0 = (\mathfrak{f}_\pm(\tau)^{24} + 16)^3 - \mathfrak{f}_\pm(\tau)^{24}j(\tau).$$

Furthermore we have

$$\mathfrak{f}(\tau + 2) = e^{-2\pi i/24}\mathfrak{f}(\tau), \quad \mathfrak{f}\left(-\tfrac{1}{\tau}\right) = \mathfrak{f}(\tau) \quad and \quad \mathfrak{f}_\pm\left(\tfrac{-1}{\tau}\right) = \mathfrak{f}_\mp(\tau).$$

Throughout this section we will highlight multiple reasons for why we start from the function $\mathfrak{f}(\tau)$ instead of the functions $\mathfrak{f}_\pm(\tau)$; for now, let us describe its corresponding modular curve in more detail:

Proposition 8. *The invariance subgroup*

$$\Gamma_W = \{M \in \mathrm{SL}_2(\mathbb{Z}) : \mathfrak{f}(M\tau) = \mathfrak{f}(\tau)\}$$

of the Weber modular function $\mathfrak{f}(\tau)$ is a level 48 congruence subgroup generated by $\Gamma(48)$ and the five matrices

$$\begin{pmatrix} 10 & 103 \\ 13 & 134 \end{pmatrix}, \begin{pmatrix} 13 & 72 \\ 24 & 133 \end{pmatrix}, \begin{pmatrix} -77 & -90 \\ 6 & 7 \end{pmatrix}, \begin{pmatrix} -25 & 14 \\ -34 & 19 \end{pmatrix}, \begin{pmatrix} 0 & -1 \\ 1 & 0 \end{pmatrix}.$$

We refer to $X(\Gamma_W)$ as the Weber modular curve.

Proof. The fact that Γ_W contains $\Gamma(48)$ follows from Lemma 4, though it can also be verified through computation by checking that a (finite) family of generators of $\Gamma(48)$, which can be computed using SageMath, keeps $\mathfrak{f}(\tau)$ invariant. Furthermore one computationally checks that the five matrices given above keep $\mathfrak{f}(\tau)$ invariant as well, e.g. by comparing q-expansions. Therefore Γ_W at least contains the group Γ' we claim it to be equal to, and Γ' has index 72 in $\mathrm{SL}_2(\mathbb{Z})$ since the five matrices above generate an index 72 subgroup of $\mathrm{SL}_2(\mathbb{Z}/48)$.

Finally, the equation

$$\Psi^W(F, j) := (F^{24} - 16)^3 - F^{24} \cdot j \in \mathbb{Z}[F, j]$$

is irreducible over $\mathbb{C}(j)$: If we could factor $\Psi^W(F, j) = g \cdot h$ with $g, h \in \mathbb{C}[j][F]$, then we would necessarily have $\deg_j(g) + \deg_j(h) = 1$, i.e. $\Psi^W(F, j) = (a \cdot j + b) \cdot h$ where $a, b, h \in \mathbb{C}[F]$. However, as $(F^{24} - 16)^3$ and F^{24} are coprime in $\mathbb{C}[F]$, this forces h to be a unit. Therefore $\Psi^W(F, j)$ is irreducible as a polynomial over $\mathbb{C}[j]$,

---

[5] Historically these functions are denoted $\mathfrak{f}_1(\tau)$ and $\mathfrak{f}_2(\tau)$, respectively, but we switch the notation to avoid confusion with the later notation for roots of the Weber modular polynomial.

and with Gauss's lemma we conclude that it is also irreducible over $\mathbb{C}(j)$. As $j(\tau)$ is transcendental over $\mathbb{C}$, Lemma 4 thus shows that $\Psi^W(F, j(\tau))$ is the minimal polynomial of $\mathfrak{f}(\tau)$ over $\mathbb{C}(j(\tau))$, i.e. $\mathbb{C}(j(\tau)) \subseteq \mathbb{C}(\mathfrak{f}(\tau))$ is a field extension of degree $72 = [\mathrm{SL}_2(\mathbb{Z}) : \Gamma_W]$ due to [20, Proposition 1.33]. In conclusion, $\Gamma' \subseteq \Gamma_W$ both are index 72 subgroups of $\mathrm{SL}_2(\mathbb{Z})$, and the claim $\Gamma_W = \Gamma'$ follows. $\qquad\square$

Remark 5. [44, Modular curve 48.72.0.d.1] gives $\mathrm{GL}_2(\mathbb{Z}/48)$ generators of a curve isomorphic to the Weber modular curve $X(\Gamma_W)$. By computing enough words of determinant 1 in these generators and constructively lifting across the reduction $\mathrm{SL}_2(\mathbb{Z}) \to \mathrm{SL}_2(\mathbb{Z}/48)$, one then obtains a congruence subgroup of level 48 and index 72 in $\mathrm{SL}_2(\mathbb{Z})$. This, however, is not the group Γ_W; in fact, it is the invariance subgroup of $\mathfrak{f}_-(\tau)$, but from this one can derive the subgroup Γ_W via the matrix $S = \left(\begin{smallmatrix} 1 & 0 \\ -1 & 1 \end{smallmatrix}\right)$. Indeed, $S^{-1} \cdot \Gamma_W \cdot S$ is the invariance subgroup of $\mathfrak{f}_-(\tau)$ by [40, Proposition 7] since $\mathfrak{f}(S\tau)/\mathfrak{f}_-(\tau)$ is a constant function due to the transformation properties given in [24, Corollary 12.19]. This also shows that (the invariance subgroup of) $\mathfrak{f}_-(\tau)$ has level 48 and not 24 as claimed in [20, Proposition 3.57][6], which can also be verified by checking that $\mathfrak{f}_-(\tau)$ is *not* invariant with respect to the matrix $\left(\begin{smallmatrix} 25 & 24 \\ -24 & -23 \end{smallmatrix}\right) \in \Gamma(24)$.

The Weber Modular Polynomial. The following result is the crucial reason why we can use the Weber function $\mathfrak{f}(\tau)$ 'like' the j-invariant $j(\tau)$ to construct a modular polynomial for ℓ-isogenies.

Corollary 5. *Let $N \in \mathbb{N}$ with $\gcd(N, 48) = 1$. Then the Weber subgroup Γ_W satisfies*

$$\Gamma_W \cdot \Gamma_0(N) = \mathrm{SL}_2(\mathbb{Z}),$$

and the inclusion $\Gamma_W \subseteq \mathrm{SL}_2(\mathbb{Z})$ thus induces a bijection

$$\Gamma_W/(\Gamma_W \cap \Gamma_0(N)) \simeq \mathrm{SL}_2(\mathbb{Z})/\Gamma_0(N).$$

Proof. Due to $\Gamma(48) \subseteq \Gamma_W$ and $\Gamma(N) \subseteq \Gamma_0(N)$ we have

$$\mathrm{SL}_2(\mathbb{Z}) \supseteq \Gamma_W \cdot \Gamma_0(N) \supseteq \Gamma(48) \cdot \Gamma(N) = \mathrm{SL}_2(\mathbb{Z})$$

by Proposition 2 since $\gcd(48, N) = 1$. $\qquad\square$

Geometrically, the above result states that the modular curve $X(\Gamma_W \cap \Gamma_0(N))$ is the pullback of the two covers $\mathcal{W}: X(\Gamma_W) \to X(1)$ and $X_0(N) \to X(1)$, the latter being given by taking the domain j-invariant of the isogeny. Equivalently, the function field of the curve $X(\Gamma_W \cap \Gamma_0(N))$ is generated by $\mathfrak{f}(\tau)$ and $j(N\tau)$, noting that $j(\tau)$ is also contained in $\mathbb{C}(\mathfrak{f}(\tau))$.

The following description of the function field grounds the Weber modular polynomial as the analogue of the classical modular polynomial:

---

[6] The issue is that $\mathfrak{f}_+(\tau) = \mathfrak{f}_-(S\tau)$ is not invariant under shifts of the argument by multiples of 24.

Theorem 4. *Let $N \in \mathbb{N}$ with $\gcd(N, 48) = 1$. Then we have*

$$\mathbb{C}(X(\Gamma_W \cap \Gamma_0(N))) = \mathbb{C}(\mathfrak{f}(\tau), \mathfrak{f}(N\tau)).$$

Proof. This follows analogously to Theorem 2 (see again [46, Theorem 6.1]); note that this uses the fact that $\mathfrak{f}(N\tau) = \omega_N^* \mathfrak{f}(\tau)$ since $\left(\begin{smallmatrix} 0 & -1 \\ 1 & 0 \end{smallmatrix}\right) \in \Gamma_W$. $\qquad\square$

We now define, for $N \in \mathbb{N}$ coprime to 48, the N-th *Weber modular polynomial* $\Phi_N^W(F) \in \mathbb{C}(\mathfrak{f}(\tau))[F]$ to be the minimal polynomial of $\mathfrak{f}(N\tau)$ over $\mathbb{C}(\mathfrak{f}(\tau))$. We collect its properties, noting that the proofs are analogous to the classical case:

Theorem 5. *Let $N \in \mathbb{N}$ with $\gcd(N, 48) = 1$. Then the Weber modular polynomial $\Phi_N^W(F)$ has coefficients in $\mathbb{Z}[\mathfrak{f}(\tau)]$ and satisfies*

$$\Phi_N^W(F) = \prod_{i=0}^{k} (F - \mathfrak{f}(Na_i(\tau)))$$

for any matrices $a_0, \ldots, a_k \in \Gamma_W$ representing the cosets $\Gamma_W/(\Gamma_W \cap \Gamma_0(N))$. Moreover, viewed as a bivariate polynomial $\Phi_N^W(F_0, F_1) \in \mathbb{Z}[F_0, F_1]$, it satisfies the following:

(a) $\deg_{F_1} \Phi_N^W(F_0, F_1) = \deg_{J_1} \Phi_N(J_0, J_1)$.
(b) *If $N > 1$, then $\Phi_N^W(F_0, F_1) = \Phi_N^W(F_1, F_0)$.*

Proof. Due to [20, Proposition 1.33] and Corollary 5 we have

$$\deg_F \Phi_N^W(F) = [\Gamma_W : \Gamma_W \cap \Gamma_0(N)] = [\mathrm{SL}_2(\mathbb{Z}) : \Gamma_0(N)] = \deg_J \Phi_N(J),$$

and the product formula for $\Phi_N(F)$ follows directly from the fact that this product is Γ_W-invariant, monic of the correct degree and has $\mathfrak{f}(N\tau)$ as a root. The fact that $\Phi_N^W(F)$ has coefficients in $\mathbb{Z}[j(\tau)]$ follows via analysis of the q-expansion of $\mathfrak{f}(\tau)$ analogously to [38, §5.2] and [24, Theorem 11.18(i)][7], and the symmetry follows from the fact that $\mathfrak{f}(N\tau) = \omega_N^* \mathfrak{f}(\tau)$ due to $\left(\begin{smallmatrix} 0 & -1 \\ 1 & 0 \end{smallmatrix}\right) \in \Gamma_W$ (see also [38, Theorem 5.2.3]). $\qquad\square$

Remark 6. The above highlights the first advantage of the Weber modular function $\mathfrak{f}(\tau)$ over $\mathfrak{f}_\pm(\tau)$: Since $\left(\begin{smallmatrix} 0 & -1 \\ 1 & 0 \end{smallmatrix}\right) \in \Gamma_W$, which would not hold for the invariance subgroups of $\mathfrak{f}_\pm(\tau)$ by Lemma 4, we can simply compute $\omega_N^* \mathfrak{f}(\tau)$ as $\mathfrak{f}(N\tau)$.

4.1   The Weber Multiplicity Theorem

To simplify formulas, we restrict to primes $N = \ell$ with $\gcd(N, 48) = 1$, i.e. $\ell \geq 5$, from now on. We again use resultant theory to relate the Weber modular polynomial to the classical modular polynomial; our motivation comes from Corollary 5 and Theorem 5, which indicate that Φ_ℓ^W plays the role of the classical modular polynomial for $\mathfrak{f}$-invariants above the j-invariants. The proof of the following result can be found in the full version of this article [34, Proposition 25].

---

[7] For our purposes it will be enough to know this for a few small prime degrees $N = \ell$; for $\ell < 5000$ these polynomials can be found on Sutherland's website https://math. mit.edu/~drew/WeberModPolys.html.

Proposition 9 (Weber resultant equation). *Let $\ell \geq 5$ be a prime. Then we have*

$$\operatorname{res}_{F_1}\left(\Phi_\ell^W(F_0, F_1), \Psi^W(F_1, J_1)\right) = \operatorname{res}_{J_0}\left(\Phi_\ell(J_0, J_1), \Psi^W(F_0, J_0)\right),$$

or, equivalently,

$$\operatorname{res}_{F_1}\left(\Phi_\ell^W(F_0, F_1), \Psi^W(F_1, J_1)\right) = F_0^{24\cdot(\ell+1)}\Phi_\ell(\mathcal{W}(F_0), J_1)$$

where $\mathcal{W}(F) = \dfrac{\left(F^{24}-16\right)^3}{F^{24}}$ defines the cover $\mathcal{W}\colon X(\Gamma_W) \to X(1)$.

With our tool for derivatives of resultants, we can now connect the Weber modular polynomial to ℓ-isogenies:

Weber Multiplicity Theorem *Let $\ell \geq 5$ be a prime, let K be a field with $\operatorname{char}(K) \notin [\ell]$ and let $\mathfrak{f}_0, j_1 \in K$. Then the number of (non-equivalent) ℓ-isogenies $j_0 := \mathcal{W}(\mathfrak{f}_0) \to j_1$ is equal to the cardinality of the multiset*

$$\left\{\!\!\left\{ \text{Roots } \mathfrak{f}_1 \in \overline{K}^\times \text{ of } \Phi_\ell^W(\mathfrak{f}_0, F_1) \text{ such that } \Psi^W(\mathfrak{f}_1, j_1) = 0 \right\}\!\!\right\}$$

In particular, j_0 and j_1 are ℓ-isogenous if and only if there exists an $\mathfrak{f}$-invariant above j_1 that is ℓ-isogenous to $\mathfrak{f}_0$, i.e. an $\mathfrak{f}_1 \in \overline{K}^\times$ such that

$$\mathcal{W}(\mathfrak{f}_1) = \frac{\left(\mathfrak{f}_1^{24}-16\right)^3}{\mathfrak{f}_1^{24}} = j_1 \quad and \quad \Phi_\ell^W(\mathfrak{f}_0, \mathfrak{f}_1) = 0. \tag{WM}$$

Proof. As both $\Psi^W(F_0, J_0)$ and $\Phi_\ell^W(F_0, F_1)$ are monic in F_0, Propositions 1 and 9 yield

$$\operatorname{res}_{F_1}\left(\Phi_\ell^W(\mathfrak{f}_0, F_1), \Psi^W(F_1, J_1)\right) = \mathfrak{f}_0^{24\cdot(\ell+1)}\Phi_\ell(\mathcal{W}(\mathfrak{f}_0), J_1).$$

Applying Theorem 1 to the K-linear evaluation $J_1 \mapsto j_1$ thus shows that, due to $\mathfrak{f}_0 \neq 0$, the multiplicity of j_1 as a root of $\Phi_\ell(j_0, J_1)$ is an upper bound for the number of roots of $\Phi_\ell^W(\mathfrak{f}_0, F_1)$, counted with multiplicity, that also solve $\Psi^W(F_1, j_1) = 0$. Since both $\Phi_\ell^W(\mathfrak{f}_0, F_1)$ and $\Phi_\ell(j_0, J_1)$ have degree $\ell + 1$, we hence obtain the claim as in the proof of the Atkin Multiplicity Theorem. $\qquad\square$

Remark 7. Note that the above result extends to any congruence subgroup $\Gamma \subseteq \mathrm{SL}_2(\mathbb{Z})$ of level N with Hauptmodul $f(\tau)$ and any integer $\ell \in \mathbb{N}$ such that $\gcd(\ell, N) = 1$, as long as one only considers cyclic ℓ-isogenies and the minimal polynomials $\Phi_\ell^\Gamma(f(\tau), F_1) \in \mathbb{C}(f(\tau))[F_1]$ and $\Psi^\Gamma(F, j(\tau)) \in \mathbb{C}(j(\tau))[F]$ have coefficients in $\mathbb{Z}[f(\tau)]$ and $\mathbb{Z}[j(\tau)]$, respectively. However, there are some additional technicalities when $\left(\begin{smallmatrix} 0 & -1 \\ 1 & 0 \end{smallmatrix}\right) \in \mathrm{SL}_2(\mathbb{Z})$ does not lie in the subgroup Γ; see also [13, §6.8].

4.2 Weber Root Computation

As in Sect. 3.2 we take the greatest common divisor of our two equations to find a low-degree equation with which we can lift Weber invariants.

Corollary 6. *Let $\ell \geq 5$ be a prime, let $\mathfrak{f}_0, j_1 \in \overline{\mathbb{F}_p}$ for a prime $p > \ell$, and consider the gcd-polynomial*

$$\Omega_\ell(\mathfrak{f}_0, j_1) := \gcd(\Phi_\ell^W(\mathfrak{f}_0, F), \Psi^W(F, j_1)) \in \mathbb{F}_p(\mathfrak{f}_0, j_1)[F].$$

Writing $\nu_\ell(j, j')$ for the number of non-equivalent ℓ-isogenies $j \to j'$, we then have

$$\deg \Omega_\ell(\mathfrak{f}_0, j_1) \leq \nu_\ell(\mathcal{W}(\mathfrak{f}_0), j_1).$$

Moreover:

(a) $\deg \Omega_\ell(\mathfrak{f}_0, j_1) \geq 1$ *if and only if $\mathcal{W}(\mathfrak{f}_0)$ and j_1 are ℓ-isogenous.*
(b) *If $\mathcal{W}(\mathfrak{f}_0)$ is ordinary or $p > 4\ell^3$, then $\deg \Omega_\ell(\mathfrak{f}_0, j_1) \leq 3$, where the case $\deg \Omega_\ell(\mathfrak{f}_0, j_1) = 3$ can only occur if $\mathcal{W}(\mathfrak{f}_0) = 0$.*

Proof. As in the proof of Corollary 3, the general inequality and claim (a) follow directly from the Weber Multiplicity Theorem. Moreover, claim (b) follows from [12, Corollary 16], [42, Theorem 2(2)] and the structure of ordinary isogeny volcanoes (cf. [12, Corollary 27]). $\qquad\square$

In contrast to the Atkin modular polynomial, we can get a degree 3 equation even above the bound $p > 4\ell^3$:

Example 2. For $p = 509$ and $\ell = 5$ we have $\Phi_\ell(0, J) = (J - 151)^3 \cdot (J - 191)^3$, $\Psi^W(116, 0) = 0$ and $\Omega_5(116, 191) = F^3 - 118F^2 + 188F + 207$.

Moreover, the modular polynomial can again have multi-roots away from (lifts of) the special j-invariants 0 and 1728:

Example 3. For $p = 41$ and $\ell = 11$ we have $\Psi^W(8, j) = 4 \cdot (j - 32)$ and $\Phi_{11}^W(8, F)$ has a root of multiplicity 2 at $F = -10$.

As the $\mathfrak{f}$-invariants encode j-invariants with additional level structure, the number and occurrence of multi-roots of $\Phi_\ell^W(\mathfrak{f}_0, F_1)$ is limited by the behavior of $\Phi_\ell(\mathcal{W}(\mathfrak{f}_0), J_1)$. Any analysis beyond that is specific to the primes ℓ and p, but at least we can characterize when Ψ^W has roots of higher multiplicity.

Proposition 10. *We have*

$$\mathrm{disc}_F(\Psi^W(F, j)) = \mathrm{res}_F(\Psi^W(F, j), \tfrac{\partial}{\partial F}\Psi^W(F, j)) = -2^{540} \cdot 3^{72} \cdot (j - 1728)^{24} \cdot j^{48}.$$

In particular, for $j_0 \in \overline{\mathbb{F}_p}$ with $p \geq 5$:

$$\Psi^W(F, j_0) \text{ has multi-roots} \iff j_0 \in \{0, 1728\}.$$

Moreover,

$$\Psi^W(F, 0) = (F^6 - 2F^3 + 2)^3 \cdot (F^6 - 2)^3 \cdot (F^6 + 2)^3 \cdot (F^6 + 2F^3 + 2)^3$$

and

$$\Psi^W(F, 1728) = (F^8 - 4) \cdot (F^8 - 2F^4 + 4) \cdot (F^8 + 2F^4 + 4) \cdot (F^8 + 2)^2 \cdot (F^{16} - 2F^8 + 4)^2.$$

Proof. The claimed discriminant formula is a straightforward resultant computation. Moreover, as $\Psi^W(F, j)$ is monic in F, Proposition 1 shows that we can compute

$$\mathrm{disc}_F(\Psi^W(F, j_0)) = -2^{540} \cdot 3^{72} \cdot (j_0 - 1728)^{24} \cdot j_0^{48}$$

via evaluation of the above formula, and the claim on multi-roots follows from Proposition 1 as well. Finally, the two specific factorizations are also verified easily. $\qquad\square$

4.3 The (Supersingular) Splitting Behavior of $\Psi^W(F, j)$

Since we want to investigate the use of the Weber modular polynomials for R1CS-based proofs of knowledge, we need to study the splitting behavior of $\Psi^W(F, j_0) \in \mathbb{F}_{p^2}[F]$ for a supersingular j-invariant $j_0 \in \mathbb{F}_{p^2}$. While [23, §3.5] discusses how to efficiently lift j_0 to an $\mathfrak{f}$-invariant, the following theoretical result will be sufficient for us:

Theorem 6 ([20, **Theorem 5.38**]). *Let p be a prime and let $j_0 \in \mathbb{F}_{p^2}$ be a supersingular j-invariant. Then $\Psi^W(F, j_0)$ splits over $\mathbb{F}_{p^2}$.*

Remark 8. The discussion in [20, p. 111] highlights the main reason for the choice of the Weber modular function $\mathfrak{f}(\tau)$ over the other two functions $\mathfrak{f}_\pm(\tau)$: Due to Lemma 4 the 72 roots of $\Phi^{W,j}(F, j(\tau))$ are given by

$$\left\{ e^{2\pi \mathrm{i} \cdot k/24} \mathfrak{f}(\tau),\, e^{2\pi \mathrm{i} \cdot k/24} e^{\pm 2\pi \mathrm{i}/16} \mathfrak{f}_\pm(\tau) \mid k \in \{0, \ldots, 23\} \right\},$$

i.e. the functions $\mathfrak{f}_\pm(\tau)$ are first shifted by primitive 16th roots of unity. Due to this relation and the above result their minimal equation $(F^{24} + 16)^3 - F^{24} j_0$ has a root over $\mathbb{F}_{p^2}$ if and only if $\mathbb{F}_{p^2}$ contains a primitive 16th root of unity, which happens if and only if $p \equiv \pm 1 \bmod 8$. In fact, for $p \equiv \pm 3 \bmod 8$ the equation has to split into irreducible quadratic factors since $\mathbb{F}_{p^4}$ contains a primitive 16th root of unity.

5 Optimizing R1CS-Based Isogeny Proofs of Knowledge

5.1 Atkin Modular Polynomials

We will now arithmetize the Atkin modular polynomials by converting them into an R1CS. It will be crucial for efficiency that $\Phi_\ell^A(Y, j)$ only has one term linear in j as well as the term j^2. Interestingly, we can define four different arithmetization strategies, each with a different domain where it is optimal.

Lemma 5. *The condition $\Phi_\ell^A(Y, j_0) = \delta_\ell(Y, j_0, j_1) = 0$ can be arithmetized over $\mathbb{F}_{p^2}$ using*

ℓ	2	3	5	7	11	13	17	19	23	29	31	41	47	59	71
Constraints over $\mathbb{F}_{p^2}$	2	3	5	6	8	9	10	11	11	13	14	16	17	20	23
Constraints over $\mathbb{F}_p$	5	8	12	13	17	20	23	25	24	29	31	36	36	43	48

Proof. We describe 4 different approaches, all linear in ℓ, with a decreasing factor at the cost of an increased constant term.

1st *approach.* The first approach is to compute all powers of Y up to Y^ℓ, in $\ell - 1$ constraints. We can check $\delta_\ell(Y, j_0, j_1) = 0$ with a linear combination without any additional constraints. To compute $\Phi_\ell^A(Y, j_0)$, we can use the fact that

$$\Psi_\ell^A(Y, j_0) = (j_0 - Y)\left(j_0 - \sum_{i=0}^{\ell} a_i Y^i + Y\right) + \sum_{i=0}^{\ell+1} b_i Y^i - \sum_{i=1}^{\ell+1} a_{i-1} Y^i + Y^2$$

$$= -(j_0 - Y)(j_1 - Y) + \sum_{i=1}^{\ell} (b_i - a_{i-1}) Y^i + Y^2 + b_0$$

where the second equality follows from $\delta_\ell(Y, j_0, j_1) = 0$. Note that the term $Y^{\ell+1}$ term disappears from the sum. The result is a linear combination and a single additional product, using ℓ constraints in total for each step.

Working over $\mathbb{F}_p$, we can make use of the fact that even powers can be created using a square, and odd powers can be created through

$$Y^{2a+1} = \frac{1}{2}\left((Y^a + Y^{a+1})^2 - Y^{2a} - Y^{2a+2}\right)$$

Since computing Y^{2a+1} requires knowledge of Y^{2a+2}, this approach cannot be used for the highest power if it is odd. This means that over $\mathbb{F}_p$, $\ell = 2$ requires $2\ell + 1$ constraints, while for $\ell \geq 3$, we use $2\ell + 2$ constraints instead, 2 for $\ell - 2$ squares and 3 to compute Y^ℓ and $\Phi_\ell^A(Y, j_0)$.

2nd *approach.* Alternatively, the equations from Lemma 3 can be used to arithmetize these constraints more efficiently, by requiring fewer powers of Y. In particular,

$$\Phi_\ell^A(Y, j) = j^2 - 1728j + (1 - 1728^{-1}j)\Phi_\ell^A(Y, 0) + 1728^{-1}j\Phi_\ell^A(Y, 1728)$$

and

$$\delta_\ell(Y, j_0, j_1) = j_0 + j_1 - 1728 - 1728^{-1}\Phi_\ell^A(Y, 0) + 1728^{-1}\Phi_\ell^A(Y, 1728).$$

This gives rise to the following equivalent system:

$$\begin{bmatrix} 0 \\ 0 \end{bmatrix} = \begin{bmatrix} 1 & -j_0 \\ 0 & 1 \end{bmatrix} \begin{bmatrix} j_0^2 - 1728j_0 & 1 - 1728^{-1}j_0 & 1728^{-1}j_0 \\ j_0 + j_1 - 1728 & -1728^{-1} & 1728^{-1} \end{bmatrix} \begin{bmatrix} 1 \\ \Phi_\ell^A(Y, 0) \\ \Phi_\ell^A(Y, 1728) \end{bmatrix}$$

$$= \begin{bmatrix} -j_0 j_1 & 1 & 0 \\ j_0 + j_1 - 1728 & -1728^{-1} & 1728^{-1} \end{bmatrix} \begin{bmatrix} 1 \\ \Phi_\ell^A(Y, 0) \\ \Phi_\ell^A(Y, 1728) \end{bmatrix}.$$

To see that this is true, note that $\begin{bmatrix} 1 & -j_0 \\ 0 & 1 \end{bmatrix}$ is well-defined and invertible.

For arithmetization over $\mathbb{F}_{p^2}$, first compute powers of Y to $\frac{\ell+1}{2}$ (assume $\ell > 2$) in $\frac{\ell-1}{2}$ constraints. We can now use Lemma 3 to compute $\Phi_\ell^A(Y, 1728)$ using a single square. $\Phi_\ell^A(Y,0)$ can also be created using a square and taking a linear combination, using

$$\sum_{i=0}^{\ell+1} c_i Y^i = \left(\sum_{i=0}^{\frac{\ell+1}{2}} d_i Y^i\right)^2 + \sum_{i=0}^{\frac{\ell+1}{2}-1} e_i Y^i$$

$$= \sum_{k=0}^{\ell+1}\left(\sum_{i=\max\left(0,k-\frac{\ell+1}{2}\right)}^{\min\left(k,\frac{\ell+1}{2}\right)} d_i d_{k-i}\right) Y^k + \sum_{i=0}^{\frac{\ell+1}{2}-1} e_i Y^i. \tag{6}$$

Here the coefficients $d_0,\ldots,d_{\frac{\ell+1}{2}}$ can be used to create all powers $i \geq \frac{\ell+1}{2}$ with the right coefficient c_i, while $e_0,\ldots,e_{\frac{\ell-1}{2}}$ is used to fix the lower values.

Finally, for the first constraint we need to compute the product $j_0 j_1$ while the second constraint can be checked for free in a linear combination when computing $\Phi_\ell^A(Y,1728)$. In total, this method requires $\frac{\ell+1}{2} + 2$ constraints.

Over $\mathbb{F}_p$, if $\ell = 3 \mod 4$, the powers $Y^2,\ldots Y^{\frac{\ell+1}{2}}$ can be computed as squares, after which two squares and a product are needed to check the constraints, for $\ell + 6$ constraints in total. For $\ell = 1 \mod 4$, we need one additional constraint, since computing $Y^{\frac{\ell+1}{2}}$ now requires a product instead of a square, for $\ell + 7$ constraints in total.

3rd approach. Continuing, by building the powers up to just $Y^{\lceil\frac{\ell+1}{3}\rceil}$, we need $\lceil\frac{\ell+1}{3}\rceil - 1$ constraints. If $\ell \equiv 3 \mod 4$, two squarings are sufficient to compute $\Phi_\ell^A(Y,1728)$ through the technique of Eq. (6) and then using Lemma 3. If $\ell \equiv 1 \mod 4$, the method from Eq. (6) cannot be used and a product is necessary instead. The term $\Phi_\ell^A(Y,0)$ can be computed with a product and a square through Lemma 3, after which another product computes $j_0 j_1$. This process requires $\lceil\frac{\ell+1}{3}\rceil + 4$ constraints.

Over $\mathbb{F}_p$, if $\ell \equiv 11 \mod 12$, a square can be used for $Y^{\lceil\frac{\ell+1}{3}\rceil}$, and two squares can be used to build $\Phi_\ell^A(Y,1728)$, for a total of $2\lceil\frac{\ell+1}{3}\rceil + 10$ constraints. If $\ell \equiv 5 \mod 12$ or $\ell \equiv 7 \mod 12$, we require $2\lceil\frac{\ell+1}{3}\rceil + 11$ constraints instead, and for other ℓ, we need $2\lceil\frac{\ell+1}{3}\rceil + 12$ constraints.

4th approach. Finally, we may construct powers up to $Y^{\lceil\frac{\ell+1}{4}\rceil}$. If $\ell = 2 \mod 3$, we can compute h_0 as a square and $\Phi_\ell^A(Y,0)$ using a square and a product. Otherwise, if $\ell = 1 \mod 3$, either h_0 or $(Y - t_0^+)h_0$ has an even degree, we can use Eq. (6) to build one using a square and use a product for the other. Again a square and a product suffices for $\Phi_\ell^A(Y,0)$. If $\ell \equiv 3 \mod 4$, $(Y - t_{1728}^+)^{e_{1728}/2} \cdot h_{1728}$ may be constructed using a square, or using a product if $\ell \equiv 1 \mod 4$. Like before, we need one additional square for $\Phi_\ell^A(Y,1728)$ and one product for $j_0 j_1$. This requires $\lceil\frac{\ell+1}{4}\rceil + 5$ constraints if $\ell = 2 \mod 3$ and $\lceil\frac{\ell+1}{4}\rceil + 6$ constraints otherwise.

Over $\mathbb{F}_p$, if $\ell \equiv 7 \mod 8$, a square can be used for all powers of Y as well as for $(Y - t_{1728}^+)^{e_{1728}/2} \cdot h_{1728}$, and so $2\lceil\frac{\ell+1}{4}\rceil + 15$ constraints are necessary. If

$\ell \equiv 3 \mod 8$ or $\ell \equiv 5 \mod 8$, one square becomes a product for $2\left\lceil\frac{\ell+1}{4}\right\rceil + 16$ constraints in total. If $\ell \equiv 1 \mod 8$, another square becomes a product for $2\left\lceil\frac{\ell+1}{4}\right\rceil + 17$ constraints in total. $\qquad\square$

5.2   Weber Modular Polynomials

Unlike the Atkin modular polynomials, the Weber modular polynomials do not have a general structure that is easily exploitable to obtain an optimized constraint system. For smaller ℓ however, the Weber polynomials are very sparse, leading to similarly sparse constraint matrices. We will therefore focus on these cases.

Theorem 7. *A path of length k built from the Weber modular polynomial $\Phi_\ell^W(X, Y)$ for $\ell \in \{5, 7, 11\}$ can be arithmetized in $5k + 3$, $8k + 3$ and $10k + 4$ constraints over $\mathbb{F}_p$ and $12k + 4$, $19k + 6$ and $24k + 9$ over $\mathbb{F}_{p^2}$, respectively.*
Proof. We consider separately: $\ell = 5$. The Weber modular polynomial for $\ell = 5$ is

$$\Phi_5^W(X, Y) = X^6 + Y^6 - X^5Y^5 + 4XY.$$

Squaring each input twice and then taking a product, we obtain powers X^2, Y^2, X^4, Y^4, X^5 and Y^5 in $2k + 2$ squarings and $1k + 1$ multiplications. We can compute

$$XY = \frac{1}{2}\left((X + Y)^2 - X^2 - Y^2\right)$$

using one squaring (or use a product over $\mathbb{F}_{p^2}$) and finish by encoding the polynomial as

$$\Phi_5^W(X, Y) = -(X - Y^5)(Y - X^5) + 5XY = 0.$$

This gives a total of $5k + 3$ constraints over $\mathbb{F}_{p^2}$ and $12k + 7$ over $\mathbb{F}_p$. $\ell = 7$. The Weber modular polynomial for $\ell = 7$ is

$$\Phi_7^W(X, Y) = X^8 + Y^8 - X^7Y^7 + 7X^4Y^4 - 8XY,$$

and can be arithmetized as follows. First, we build the powers X^2, X^4 and X^8 in $3k + 3$ squarings. We then compute XY and X^2Y^2, X^3Y^3, X^4Y^4 and X^7Y^7 in $2k$ squares and $2k$ products. In the last product, the constraint can be tested for free. This takes $8k + 3$ constraints over $\mathbb{F}_{p^2}$ and $19k + 6$ over $\mathbb{F}_p$. $\ell = 11$. Finally, the Weber modular polynomial $\Phi_{11}^W(X, Y)$ is given by

$$X^{12} + Y^{12} - X^{11}Y^{11} + 11X^9Y^9 - 44X^7Y^7 + 88X^5Y^5 - 88X^3Y^3 + 32XY.$$

We first square three times to obtain X^2, X^4 and X^8. From this, X^{12} can be obtained using a product. We do the same for the cross terms, building first XY and then X^2Y^2, X^4Y^4 and X^8Y^8. We can now finish by using two constraints: First we compute $X^2Y^2(X^8Y^8 + 44X^4Y^4)$ and finally we test that

$$0 = X^{12} + Y^{12} + 32XY$$
$$+ XY\left(-\left(X^{10}Y^{10} + 44X^6Y^6\right) + 11X^8Y^8 + 88X^4Y^4 - 88X^2Y^2\right).$$

This takes $10k + 4$ constraints over $\mathbb{F}_{p^2}$ and $24k + 9$ constraints over $\mathbb{F}_p$. $\qquad\square$

5.3 Automatic R1CS Non-zero Entry Optimization

We have created a Rust library[8] to describe the constraint systems provided in this paper and count the number of constraints, variables and non-zero entries. Such a systematic approach is beneficial due the many subtle embedding choices that impact the final R1CS. For example, variables over $\mathbb{F}_{p^2}$ may be embedded into a R1CS using two elements of $\mathbb{F}_p$. A square over $\mathbb{F}_{p^2}$ may then be represented in two constraints, and a product in three. The variable $x \in \mathbb{F}_{p^2}$ itself may be represented as (a, b), with $x = a + b\alpha$ and α^2 a non-square residue in $\mathbb{F}_p$, but also as $(a, a + b)$, which in most cases results in sparser constraint matrices.

This optimization is one of the optimizations described in [33, Section 4]. Another is a change of variables: If multiple variables appear often in the same linear combination in the constraint system, it may be beneficial to redefine one of the variables in terms of this linear combination. The representation $(a, a + b)$ may in fact be described as a special case of variable redefinition over the resulting R1CS over $\mathbb{F}_p$, after transforming squares and products over $\mathbb{F}_{p^2}$ into constraints over $\mathbb{F}_p$. Our library captures and generalizes these optimizations.

Formally, a constraint system (A, B, C) can be transformed into an equivalent system (AV, BV, CV) for invertible matrix V. After this, a valid assignment $\boldsymbol{a}$ may be transformed into $V^{-1}\boldsymbol{a}$, since

$$A\boldsymbol{a} \circ B\boldsymbol{a} - C\boldsymbol{a} = AV(V^{-1}\boldsymbol{a}) \circ BV(V^{-1}\boldsymbol{a}) - CV(V^{-1}\boldsymbol{a}).$$

Minimizing the number of non-zero entries then involves finding an invertible $W = V^T$ such that $W\left(A^T \; B^T \; C^T\right)$ has the most zeros.

Instead of considering the full system, we can exploit the repetitive nature of the isogeny path and optimize each step individually, where we should take care to handle repeated variables correctly. To be precise, there are three categories of variables: A single variable representing '1', 'step' variables such as the roots t_i^+ that appear only in one step, and 'curve' variables such as the j-invariants that appear in two consecutive steps. These should be treated as follows:

- We should always keep the variable representing '1' intact, i.e. the left column and top row of W should consist of a 1 followed by zeros.
- Curve variables may be substituted, but only for linear combinations of '1' and of other variables of the same curve. For example, $j_i \to j_i + 100$ is allowed, while $j_i \to j_i + 100j_{i+1}$ is not, since this would now require us to compensate for $100j_{i+1}$ at index $i - 1$.
- Variables at steps may be substituted for linear combinations of any other variable used in the step. For example, root Y of $\Phi_\ell^A(Y, j_i)$ and $\Phi_\ell^A(Y, j_{i+1})$ may be substituted for $t_i^+ + j_0 + 3j_i + 50$.

Constructing the matrix W then consists of invertible column operations under the above restrictions. We use two approaches to this problem: First, an exact approach, based on the combinatorial search method from [28]. Since

---

[8] Available at https://github.com/QuSAC/isogeny-walk-constraint-counter.

it finds W in the case where it is unrestricted, we call this algorithm three times on a transformed problem, corresponding to only the step variables, the curve variables and the variable 1, respectively. Since the exact algorithm is too inefficient for large instances, there we use a heuristic approach, where we use pairwise linear combinations of columns to incrementally make the constraint matrices sparser[9].

6   Evaluation

Figure 1 shows the number of constraints required to express an isogeny walk using the different arithmetizations, normalized by dividing by $\log_2(\ell)$ to give the number of constraints per λ that is needed for a k-step walk such that $\ell^k \geq 2^\lambda$.

Table 1 shows the number of necessary constraints in table form, whereas Table 2 shows the number of non-zero entries in the constraint matrices. Because the constraint-minimizing approach may not necessarily be optimal in terms of the non-zero entries, the approach that optimizes the latter is also specified.

Table 1. The number of constraints required to arithmetize a walk for security level λ, i.e. a walk such that $\ell^k > 2^\lambda$. We compare the classical [21], canonical [33] and radical [41] approach to ours. In our approach, the number of variables is always equal to the number of constraints, plus one additional variable in $\mathbb{F}_{p^2}$ or two in $\mathbb{F}_p$. The number in brackets indicates which approach is used.

ℓ	$\mathbb{F}_{p^2}$					$\mathbb{F}_p$				
	Classical	Canonical	Radical	Atkin	Weber	Classical	Canonical	Radical	Atkin	Weber
2	$4\lambda + 2$	3λ	2λ	2λ (1)		$11\lambda + 7$	7λ	5λ	5λ (1)	
3		2.52λ		1.89λ (1)			6.94λ		5.05λ (1)	
5		2.58λ		2.15λ (1)	$2.15\lambda + 3$		6.46λ		5.17λ (2)	$5.17\lambda + 7$
7		2.49λ		2.14λ (2)	$2.85\lambda + 3$		6.06λ		4.63λ (2)	$6.77\lambda + 6$
11				2.31λ (4)	$2.89\lambda + 4$				4.91λ (2)	$6.94\lambda + 9$
13		2.70λ		2.43λ (3)			6.49λ		5.41λ (2)	
17				2.45λ (4)					5.63λ (3)	
19				2.59λ (4)					5.89λ (3)	
23				2.43λ (4)					5.31λ (4)	
29				2.68λ (4)					5.97λ (4)	
31				2.83λ (4)					6.26λ (4)	
41				2.99λ (4)					6.72λ (4)	
47				3.06λ (4)					6.48λ (4)	
59				3.40λ (4)					7.31λ (4)	
71				3.74λ (4)					7.81λ (4)	

We can see that switching to the Atkin and Weber polynomials has a threefold benefit. Firstly, the use of the Atkin polynomials allows for more isogeny degrees

---

[9] For more detail on both approaches, see the `Readme.md` file of the Rust library.

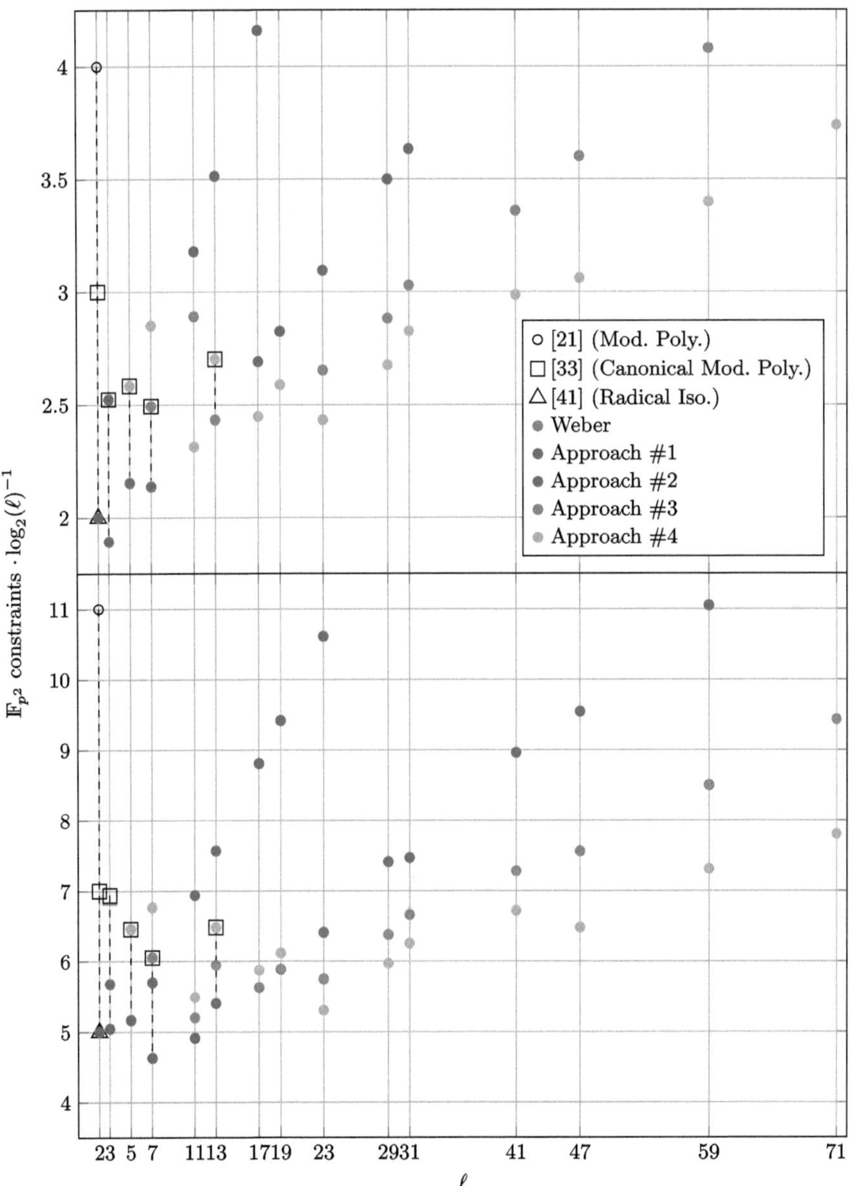

Fig. 1. A comparison of the number of constraints for an isogeny of degree ℓ^k between [21][33][41], and this work, with k such that $\ell^k \geq 2^\lambda$. The result is divided by λ. The top plot shows the results for $\mathbb{F}_{p^2}$, and the bottom for $\mathbb{F}_p$.

ℓ than previous approaches, while the Weber modular polynomials even give, in theory, an approach that works for every prime degree $\ell \geq 5$ and that should be more practical than using the classical modular polynomial.

Secondly, the Atkin modular polynomials provide more efficient constraint systems for all ℓ for which previous approaches *do* exist, with the exception of $\ell = 2$, where it is on par with the radical isogeny approach pursued in [41]. The biggest improvement is for $\ell = 3$ over $\mathbb{F}_p$, with a 27% reduction in the number of constraints. Our arithmetizations for $\ell = 3$ over $\mathbb{F}_{p^2}$ and for $\ell \in \{7, 11\}$ over $\mathbb{F}_p$ achieve a lower normalized constraint count than any existing approach and degree, reducing the number of constraints by 5% over the previous best.

The third improvement comes from the use of the Weber polynomials. These allow us to lower the number of non-zero entries by up to 39% in the case of $\ell = 5$ over $\mathbb{F}_{p^2}$. This approach also improves the normalized number of non-zero entries by 27% compared to the radical approach, which was the previous best.

Table 2. The number of non-zero entries required to arithmetize a walk for security level λ, i.e. a walk such that $\ell^k > 2^\lambda$. We compare the classical [21], canonical [33] and radical [41] approach to ours. We use the same approach for the Atkin polynomials as in Table 1. There are three cases where another approach is optimal over $\mathbb{F}_p$: approach 3 uses 48.37λ non-zero entries and 5.95λ constraints for $\ell = 13$, and approach 4 uses 43.06λ non-zero entries and 5.87λ constraints for $\ell = 17$ and 53.44λ non-zero entries with 6.12λ constraints for $\ell = 19$.

ℓ	$\mathbb{F}_{p^2}$					$\mathbb{F}_p$				
	Classical	Canonical	Radical	Atkin	Weber	Classical	Canonical	Radical	Atkin	Weber
2	$21\lambda + 6$	13λ	10λ	12λ		$79\lambda + 23$	41λ	36λ	46λ	
3		11.36λ		10.10λ			41.01λ		37.86λ	
5		12.06λ		11.20λ	$7.32\lambda + 9$		41.78λ		42.21λ	$31.01\lambda + 31$
7		12.47λ		15.67λ	$9.26\lambda + 9$		43.81λ		45.95λ	$31.70\lambda + 28$
11				11.85λ	$10.41\lambda + 12$				45.95λ	$35.27\lambda + 40$
13		15.13λ		14.59λ			52.43λ		55.67λ	
17				13.21λ					52.85λ	
19				17.19λ					57.68λ	
23				16.14λ					48.41λ	
29				17.09λ					53.93λ	
31				22.00λ					66.81λ	
41				19.60λ					62.34λ	
47				23.24λ					69.67λ	
59				26.01λ					78.88λ	
71				30.08λ					90.25λ	

We also note that, while the Weber modular polynomials are competitive in the number of constraints for $\ell = 5$, for increasing ℓ this number seems to grow much faster than for the Atkin modular polynomials. Conceptually, this comes from the fact that, being of degree $\ell + 1$ in both of its variables, the Weber modular polynomial has asymptotically $O(\ell)$ times as many monomial terms as the Atkin modular polynomial, even though it is noticeably sparser than the classical modular polynomial. For this reason we expect the Weber modular polynomial to not outperform the Atkin modular polynomial for larger ℓ.

Table 3. An evaluation of our results compared to the classical [21] and canonical approach [33] for walks with $\ell = 2$. The results from $\mathbb{F}_{p^2}$ correspond to the identification protocol with parameter set p434, with path length $k = 216$ and security level $\lambda = 128$, while $\mathbb{F}_p$ corresponds to p441+. The timings and proof sizes are projected based on the number of constraints, from timings in [21] and the methodology of [33]. We expect our results for $\ell = 2$ to be on par with [41].

		Aurora			Ligero		
		Classical	Canonical	Ours	Classical	Canonical	Ours
$\mathbb{F}_{p^2}$	Proof time (ms)	934	669	418	587	420	263
	Verif. time (ms)	99	74	49	847	634	423
	Proof size (kB)	194	178	156	1849	1599	1306
$\mathbb{F}_p$	Proof time (ms)	1216	727	495	427	255	174
	Verif. time (ms)	98	62	44	493	313	224
	Proof size (kB)	166	147	134	1733	1381	1167

All results that perform optimally according to one metric or more can be found in the full version of this article [34, Appendix C]. The provided Rust code produces all results.

To give an indication of practical measurements, Table 3 contains the projected prover and verifier time as well as the proof size for a 2-isogeny walk in comparison to prior work.

Finally, let us give a more detailed comparison to the radical isogeny approach of [41]: We achieve the same number of constraints for $\ell = 2$ as described in Table 1, but our approach does not automatically prevent backtracking. Such backtracking prevention can be added at the cost of $\log_\ell(2) \cdot \lambda$ constraints both over $\mathbb{F}_{p^2}$ and over $\mathbb{F}_p$ using the technique of [33, Section 4.4], making our approach less competitive in practice. While radical isogeny formulas are available for primes $\ell \leq 37$ [16], their use for proving knowledge of odd degree isogenies has not been thoroughly explored in the literature yet. We expect them to also be very competitive with our approach for these larger degrees, though for a fair comparison one would need to analyze how much the equation system coming from these formulas can be optimized.

Acknowledgements. We would like to thank Marc Houben for pointing us to Weber polynomials and for several valuable insights. We also thank Eugenio Paracucchi for a helpful preliminary discussion, and the anonymous reviewers for their feedback.

References

1. Adj, G., Ahmadi, O., Menezes, A.: On isogeny graphs of supersingular elliptic curves over finite fields. Finite Fields Appl. **55**, 268–283 (2019). https://doi.org/10.1016/j.ffa.2018.10.002

2. Ames, S., Hazay, C., Ishai, Y., Venkitasubramaniam, M.: Ligero: lightweight sublinear arguments without a trusted setup. In: Thuraisingham, B.M., Evans, D., Malkin, T., Xu, D. (eds.) ACM CCS 2017: 24th Conference on Computer and Communications Security. pp. 2087–2104. ACM Press, Dallas, TX, USA (Oct 31 – Nov 2, (2017). https://doi.org/10.1145/3133956.3134104

3. Atkin, A.O.L.: The number of points on an elliptic curve modulo a prime (1991). https://www.lix.polytechnique.fr/Labo/Francois.Morain/AtkinEmails/19910614. txt. Email on the Number Theory Mailing List

4. Basso, A., et al.: PRISM: simple and compact identification and signatures from large prime degree isogenies. In: Jager, T., Pan, J. (eds.) PKC 2025: 28th International Conference on Theory and Practice of Public Key Cryptography, Part III. Lecture Notes in Computer Science, vol. 15676, pp. 300–332. Springer, Cham, Switzerland, Røros, Norway (2025). https://doi.org/10.1007/978-3-031-91826-1_10

5. Basso, A., et al.: Supersingular curves you can trust. In: Hazay, C., Stam, M. (eds.) Advances in Cryptology – EUROCRYPT 2023, Part II. Lecture Notes in Computer Science, vol. 14005, pp. 405–437. Springer, Cham, Switzerland, Lyon, France (2023). https://doi.org/10.1007/978-3-031-30617-4_14

6. Ben-Sasson, E., Chiesa, A., Riabzev, M., Spooner, N., Virza, M., Ward, N.P.: Aurora: transparent succinct arguments for R1CS. In: Ishai, Y., Rijmen, V. (eds.) Advances in Cryptology – EUROCRYPT 2019, Part I. Lecture Notes in Computer Science, vol. 11476, pp. 103–128. Springer, Cham, Switzerland, Darmstadt, Germany (2019). https://doi.org/10.1007/978-3-030-17653-2_4

7. Beullens, W., De Feo, L., Galbraith, S.D., Petit, C.: Proving knowledge of isogenies: a survey. Designs, Codes Cryptography **91**(11), 3425–3456 (2023). https://doi.org/ 10.1007/s10623-023-01243-3

8. Beullens, W., Kleinjung, T., Vercauteren, F.: CSI-FiSh: efficient isogeny based signatures through class group computations. In: Galbraith, S.D., Moriai, S. (eds.) Advances in Cryptology – ASIACRYPT 2019, Part I. Lecture Notes in Computer Science, vol. 11921, pp. 227–247. Springer, Cham, Switzerland, Kobe, Japan (2019). https://doi.org/10.1007/978-3-030-34578-5_9

9. Birch, B.J.: Weber's class invariants. Mathematika **16**(2), 283–294 (1969). https:// doi.org/10.1112/S0025579300008251

10. Boneh, D., Chen, B.: LatticeFold+: Faster, simpler, shorter lattice-based folding for succinct proof systems. In: Kalai, Y.T., Kamara, S.F. (eds.) Advances in Cryptology – CRYPTO 2025, Part VII. Lecture Notes in Computer Science, vol. 16006, pp. 327–361. Springer, Cham, Switzerland, Santa Barbara, CA, USA (2025). https:// doi.org/10.1007/978-3-032-01907-3_11

11. Borcherds, R.E.: Monstrous moonshine and monstrous lie superalgebras. Invent. Math. **109**(1), 405–444 (1992)

12. Boscardin, S., Spindler, S.A.: Exploring Kaneko's bound: on multi-edges, loops and the diameter of the supersingular ℓ-isogeny graph. Cryptology ePrint Archive, Paper 2025/1361 (2025). https://eprint.iacr.org/2025/1361

13. Bröker, R.: Constructing elliptic curves of prescribed order. Ph.D. thesis, Leiden University (2006). https://hdl.handle.net/1887/4425

14. Bröker, R., Lauter, K., Sutherland, A.V.: Modular polynomials via isogeny volcanoes. Math. Comput. **81**(278), 1201–1231 (2012)

15. Castryck, W., Decru, T.: CSIDH on the surface. In: Ding, J., Tillich, J.P. (eds.) Post-Quantum Cryptography - 11th International Conference, PQCrypto 2020, pp. 111–129. Springer, Cham, Switzerland, Paris, France (2020). https://doi.org/ 10.1007/978-3-030-44223-1_7

16. Castryck, W., Decru, T., Houben, M., Vercauteren, F.: Horizontal racewalking using radical isogenies. In: Agrawal, S., Lin, D. (eds.) Advances in Cryptology – ASIACRYPT 2022, Part II. Lecture Notes in Computer Science, vol. 13792, pp. 67–96. Springer, Cham, Switzerland, Taipei, Taiwan (2022). https://doi.org/10.1007/978-3-031-22966-4_3

17. Castryck, W., Decru, T., Vercauteren, F.: Radical isogenies. In: Moriai, S., Wang, H. (eds.) Advances in Cryptology – ASIACRYPT 2020, Part II. Lecture Notes in Computer Science, vol. 12492, pp. 493–519. Springer, Cham, Switzerland, Daejeon, South Korea (2020). https://doi.org/10.1007/978-3-030-64834-3_17

18. Chávez-Saab, J., Rodríguez-Henríquez, F., Tibouchi, M.: Verifiable isogeny walks: Towards an isogeny-based postquantum VDF. In: AlTawy, R., Hülsing, A. (eds.) SAC 2021: 28th Annual International Workshop on Selected Areas in Cryptography. Lecture Notes in Computer Science, vol. 13203, pp. 441–460. Springer, Cham, Switzerland, Virtual Event (2022). https://doi.org/10.1007/978-3-030-99277-4_21

19. Chiang-Hsieh, H.J., Yang, Y.: Determination of hauptmoduls and construction of abelian extensions of quadratic number fields. Canadian Math. Bull. **50**(3), 334—-346 (2007). https://doi.org/10.4153/CMB-2007-032-1

20. Colò, L.: Oriented supersingular elliptic curves and class group actions. Ph.D. thesis, Aix-Marseille Université (2022). https://leonardocolo.com/documents/thesis/PhD_Thesis.pdf

21. Cong, K., Lai, Y.F., Levin, S.: Efficient isogeny proofs using generic techniques. In: Tibouchi, M., Wang, X. (eds.) ACNS 2023: 21st International Conference on Applied Cryptography and Network Security, Part II. Lecture Notes in Computer Science, vol. 13906, pp. 248–275. Springer, Cham, Switzerland, Kyoto, Japan (2023). https://doi.org/10.1007/978-3-031-33491-7_10

22. Conway, J.H., Norton, S.P.: Monstrous moonshine. Bull. Lond. Math. Soc. **11**(3), 308–339 (1979). https://doi.org/10.1112/blms/11.3.308

23. Corte-Real Santos, M., Eriksen, J.K., Leroux, A., Meyer, M., Panny, L.: Evaluation of modular polynomials from supersingular elliptic curves. Cryptology ePrint Archive, Paper 2025/1154 (2025). https://eprint.iacr.org/2025/1154

24. Cox, D.A.: Primes of the Form $x^2 + ny^2$. Fermat, Class Field Theory, and Complex Multiplication. Pure and Applied Mathematics: A Wiley Series of Texts, Monographs and Tracts, John Wiley & Sons, 2nd edn. (2013). https://doi.org/10.1002/9781118400722

25. De Feo, L., Kohel, D., Leroux, A., Petit, C., Wesolowski, B.: SQISign: compact post-quantum signatures from quaternions and isogenies. In: Moriai, S., Wang, H. (eds.) Advances in Cryptology – ASIACRYPT 2020, Part I. Lecture Notes in Computer Science, vol. 12491, pp. 64–93. Springer, Cham, Switzerland, Daejeon, South Korea (2020). https://doi.org/10.1007/978-3-030-64837-4_3

26. Delpech de Saint Guilhem, C., Orsini, E., Tanguy, T.: Limbo: efficient zero-knowledge MPCitH-based arguments. In: Vigna, G., Shi, E. (eds.) ACM CCS 2021: 28th Conference on Computer and Communications Security, pp. 3022–3036. ACM Press, Virtual Event, Republic of Korea (2021). https://doi.org/10.1145/3460120.3484595

27. Diamond, F., Shurman, J.: A First Course in Modular Forms, Graduate Texts in Mathematics, vol. 228. Springer New York, NY (2005). https://doi.org/10.1007/978-0-387-27226-9

28. Egner, S., Minkwitz, T.: Sparsification of rectangular matrices. J. Symb. Comput. **26**(2), 135–149 (1998)

29. Elkies, N.D.: Elliptic and modular curves over finite fields and related computational issues. In: Buell, D.A., Teitelbaum, J.T. (eds.) Computational Perspectives on Number Theory: Proceedings of a Conference in Honor of A. O. L. Atkin. AMS/IP Studies in Advanced Mathematics, vol. 7, pp. 21–76. American Mathematical Society, International Press (1998)

30. Galbraith, S.D., Petit, C., Silva, J.: Identification protocols and signature schemes based on supersingular isogeny problems. In: Takagi, T., Peyrin, T. (eds.) Advances in Cryptology – ASIACRYPT 2017, Part I. Lecture Notes in Computer Science, vol. 10624, pp. 3–33. Springer, Cham, Switzerland, Hong Kong, China (2017). https://doi.org/10.1007/978-3-319-70694-8_1

31. Gow, R.: Some properties and uses of the discriminant of a polynomial. In: Ryan, R., Hurley, T., Rippon, P. (eds.) Irish Mathematical Society Bulletin. vol. 24, pp. 12–19. Irish Mathematical Society (March 1990)

32. Hajouji, N.: Supersingular isogeny graphs from algebraic modular curves. arXiV:2303.09096v3 [math.NT] (2023)

33. den Hollander, T., Kleine, S., Mula, M., Slamanig, D., Spindler, S.A.: More efficient isogeny proofs of knowledge via canonical modular polynomials. In: Kalai, Y.T., Kamara, S.F. (eds.) Advances in Cryptology – CRYPTO 2025, Part I. Lecture Notes in Computer Science, vol. 16000, pp. 131–166. Springer, Cham, Switzerland, Santa Barbara, CA, USA (2025). https://doi.org/10.1007/978-3-032-01855-7_5

34. den Hollander, T., Mula, M., Slamanig, D., Spindler, S.A.: On the use of Atkin and Weber modular polynomials in isogeny proofs of knowledge. Cryptology ePrint Archive, Paper 2026/XXXX (2026). https://eprint.iacr.org/2026/XXXX, full ePrint version

35. Houben, M., Streng, M.: Generalized class polynomials. Res. Number Theory $8(4)$, 103 (2022). https://doi.org/10.1007/s40993-022-00400-2

36. Igusa, J.I.: Fibre systems of Jacobian varieties: (III. Fibre systems of elliptic curves). American J. Math. $81(2)$, 453–476 (1959). https://doi.org/10.2307/2372751

37. Kothapalli, A., Setty, S., Tzialla, I.: Nova: recursive zero-knowledge arguments from folding schemes. In: Dodis, Y., Shrimpton, T. (eds.) Advances in Cryptology – CRYPTO 2022, Part IV. Lecture Notes in Computer Science, vol. 13510, pp. 359–388. Springer, Cham, Switzerland, Santa Barbara, CA, USA (2022). https://doi.org/10.1007/978-3-031-15985-5_13

38. Lang, S.: Elliptic Functions. Springer, New York, New York, NY (1987)

39. Lehner, J., Newman, M.: Weierstrass points of $\gamma_0(n)$. Ann. Math. $79(2)$, 360–368 (1964). http://www.jstor.org/stable/1970550

40. Lercier, R.: Algorithmique des courbes elliptiques dans les corps finis. Ph.D. thesis, Ecole Polytechnique (1997). https://univ-rennes.hal.science/tel-01101949

41. Levin, S., Pedersen, R.: Faster proofs and VRFs from isogenies. In: Hanaoka, G., Yang, B.Y. (eds.) Advances in Cryptology – ASIACRYPT 2025, Part IV. Lecture Notes in Computer Science, vol. 16248, pp. 307–340. Springer, Singapore, Singapore, Melbourne, VIC, Australia (2025). https://doi.org/10.1007/978-981-95-5113-2_10

42. Li, S., Ouyang, Y., Xu, Z.: Neighborhood of the supersingular elliptic curve isogeny graph at $j = 0$ and 1728. Finite Fields Their Appl. 61, 101600 (2020). https://doi.org/10.1016/j.ffa.2019.101600

43. Li, Y., Yang, T.: On a conjecture of Yui and Zagier. Algebra & Number Theory (2019)

44. The LMFDB Collaboration: The L-functions and modular forms database (beta version) (2025). https://beta.lmfdb.xyz

45. Maughan, K., Near, J.P., Vincent, C.: Foldable, recursive proofs of isogeny computation with reduced time complexity. In: Osinski, M., Cour, B.L., Yeh, L. (eds.) IEEE International Conference on Quantum Computing and Engineering, QCE 2024, Montreal, QC, Canada, September 15-20, 2024, pp. 1304–1308. IEEE (2024). https://doi.org/10.1109/QCE60285.2024.00155
46. Milne, J.S.: Modular functions and modular forms (elliptic modular curves) (2017). https://www.jmilne.org/math/CourseNotes/MF.pdf, V1.31
47. Morain, F.: Calcul du nombre de points sur une courbe elliptique dans un corps fini: aspects algorithmiques. Journal de Théorie des Nombres de Bordeaux **7**(1), 255–282 (1995). http://www.jstor.org/stable/43972443
48. Müller, V.: Ein Algorithmus zur Bestimmung der Punktanzahl elliptischer Kurven über endlichen Körpern der Charakteristik größer drei. Ph.D. thesis, Universität des Saarlandes (1995). https://publikationen.sulb.uni-saarland.de/handle/20.500.11880/25777
49. Ogg, A.P.: Hyperelliptic modular curves. Bulletin de la Société Mathématique de France **102**, 449–462 (1974). https://doi.org/10.24033/bsmf.1789
50. Schoof, R.: Elliptic curves over finite fields and the computation of square roots mod p. Math. Comput. **44**(170), 483–494 (1985)
51. Silverman, J.H.: The arithmetic of elliptic curves, Grad. Texts Math., vol. 106. Springer New York, NY, 2nd edn. (2009). https://doi.org/10.1007/978-0-387-09494-6
52. Weber, H.: Lehrbuch der Algebra, vol. 3. F. Vieweg und Sohn, Braunschweig, 2nd edn. (1898), dritter Band: Elliptische Funktionen und algebraische Zahlen
53. Yui, N., Zagier, D.: On the singular values of weber modular functions. Math. Comput. **66**(220), 1645–1662 (1997). https://doi.org/10.1090/S0025-5718-97-00854-5

On the Active Security of the PEARL-SCALLOP Group Action

Tako Boris Fouotsa[1], Marc Houben[2,3(✉)], Gioella Lorenzon[4], Ryan Rueger[5,6], and Parsa Tasbihgou[7]

[1] University of Manchester, Manchester M13 9PL, UK
`research@borisfouotsa.com`
[2] Inria Bordeaux, Bordeaux, France
[3] Institut de Mathématiques de Bordeaux, Bordeaux, France
`marc.houben@math.u-bordeaux.fr`
[4] COSIC, KU Leuven, Leuven, Belgium
`gioella.lorenzon@esat.kuleuven.be`
[5] IBM Research Europe, Zurich, Switzerland
[6] Technische Universität München, Munich, Germany
`ryan@rueg.re`
[7] Ecole Polytechnique Federal de Lausanne, Lausanne, Switzerland
`parsa.tasbihgou@epfl.ch`

Abstract. We present an active attack against the PEARL-SCALLOP group action. Modelling Alice as an oracle that outputs the action by a secret ideal class on suitably chosen oriented elliptic curves, we show how to recover the secret using a handful of oracle calls (four for the parameter set targeting a security level equivalent to CSIDH-1024), by reducing to the computation of moderately-sized group action discrete logarithms. The key ingredient to the attack is to employ curves with non-primitive orientations inherent to the PEARL-SCALLOP construction. We provide methods for public-key validation—that is, for deciding whether a given orientation is primitive—and discuss their practicality.

Keywords: Isogeny-based cryptography · class group actions · active attacks

1 Introduction

Class group actions on elliptic curves were introduced as a building block for post-quantum cryptography by Couveignes, Rostovtsev, and Stolbunov [35,90]. The resulting key exchange protocol, colloquially known as CRS, was the first cryptographic scheme to base its security on the hardness of finding isogenies between elliptic curves over finite fields, marking the origin of the field of isogeny-based cryptography. CSIDH [25] is an amendment to CRS that employs super-singular elliptic curves instead of ordinary ones, giving rise to the first practical

Authors listed alphabetically ams.org/profession/leaders/CultureStatement04.pdf.

© The Author(s), under exclusive license to Springer Nature Switzerland AG 2026
M. Bardet and R. Niederhagen (Eds.): PQCrypto 2026, LNCS 16492, pp. 74–104, 2026.
https://doi.org/10.1007/978-3-032-22698-3_3

variant of the protocol. Based on the more general theory of class group actions on oriented supersingular elliptic curves, several alternatives have since emerged, such as OSIDH [33] (no longer considered viable [39]), (d, ϵ)-structures [31], the SCALLOP family [4,30,43], and large discriminant instantiations [24,62].

To this date, class group actions on elliptic curves are the only known approach instantiate *commutative* post-quantum group actions. Although commutativity of the action exposes a vulnerability to subexponential quantum attacks [66,67,87], it is also the most compelling attribute: commutative group actions give rise to the closest existing analogue of classical Diffie–Hellman (in fact, a natural generalization thereof) in a post-quantum scenario.[1] One of the major selling points is that this allows to instantiate a non-interactive key exchange (NIKE), for which few (post-quantum) alternatives are known [52,88]. Most notably, however, commutative group actions are especially powerful building block for constructing advanced cryptographic primitives. This includes blind signatures [59,63], threshold schemes [5,37,45], oblivious transfer [68], ID protocols [6], oblivious pseudorandom functions [15,46,60], verifiable random functions [73], zero-knowledge proofs [29], public key encryption [80], password authenticated key exchange [2], updatable encryption [72,75], and quantum money [78].

The precise features desired of the class group action depend on the targeted primitive. For instance, it is often desirable for the underlying class group to be known. Indeed, this is one approach for instantiating an *effective* group action, which is crucial for e.g. signature schemes [11–13] (although more recently, other methods for obtaining effective class group actions have been developed [41,84, 85]). Moreover, some threshold schemes [45, Sec. 3] crucially rely on a known class group structure as a necessary ingredient for the protocol. The SCALLOP family [4,30,43], of which PEARL-SCALLOP [4] is the most efficient candidate, specifically targets parameter sets where the class group structure is efficiently computable.

To the best of our knowledge—apart from some particularly dubious parameter choices [53]—no attacks specific to the SCALLOP constructions have appeared in the literature. Cryptanalysis of class group actions is largely centered around CSIDH, and involves cost analysis of quantum attacks [10,16,28,86], side-channel analysis [20]—with a particular focus on constant time implementations [7,17,18,27,32,61,76,77], fault injections [8,19,69–71], and pairing-based attacks [22,23,26,53].

An avenue that remains largely unstudied in the general context of class group actions is that of *active attacks*, by which we mean an attacker model in which adversaries may deviate from an honest execution of the protocol in an attempt to extract secret information.[2] Such attacks—sometimes referred to as *adaptive* attacks—have been considered in isogeny-based cryptography

---

[1] Classical Diffie–Hellman can be viewed as relying on a commutative group action $(\mathbf{Z}/q\mathbf{Z})^{\times} \circlearrowright G$, where G is a cyclic group of order q.

[2] We do not consider fault injections and side channel analysis as part of the attacker model.

mainly in the setting of SIDH-like protocols [9,47,48,50,51,56,57,65], although other isogeny-based schemes (not based on class group actions) have also been considered [74,79,81,95].

Our Contributions

- We present an active attack against instances of the isogeny class group action in which the conductor of the orientation is a product of medium-sized primes; this is precisely the setting of PEARL-SCALLOP.

  The efficacy of our attack crucially relies on access to a *static CDH oracle* (sometimes also called the *strong oracle* [57,65] in the context of active attacks). More concretely, we model Alice as an oracle that, on input of an oriented elliptic curve (E, ι), returns $(E', \iota') = [\mathfrak{a}] * (E, \iota)$, where $[\mathfrak{a}]$ is her secret ideal class.

  Contrary to other active attacks in the isogeny-based literature, this attack is *not* "adaptive"; indeed, all inputs to the oracle calls are precomputed, and in particular independent of the secret $[\mathfrak{a}]$. Moreover, the attack does not rely on side-channel information.
- We show that our attack significantly affects the security of PEARL-SCALLOP for all proposed parameter sets. For example, for the CSIDH-1024 equivalent, we can recover the secret using four oracle calls together with four group action inversions for groups of size ~ 128 bits.
- We describe public-key validation algorithms to mitigate the attack, and discuss their efficiency. We show that they significantly impact the practicality of PEARL-SCALLOP.

Technical Overview. We now present the main idea of our attack. Let $\mathcal{O}_K$ be the maximal order of an imaginary quadratic number field K, and suppose that $\mathcal{O} \subseteq \mathcal{O}_K$ is a suborder of conductor $f_1 \cdots f_r$, where $f_1, \ldots, f_r$ are primes, each roughly of size 2^{128}. This gives rise to a sequence of suborders $\mathcal{O}_K = \mathcal{O}^{(0)} \supsetneq \ldots \supsetneq \mathcal{O}^{(r)} = \mathcal{O}$, where, say, $\mathcal{O}^{(i)}$ has conductor $f_1 \cdots f_i$.

We think of curves primitively oriented by one of these orders as sitting inside of an isogeny volcano[3] [92], where the curves at the top are (primitively) oriented by $\mathcal{O}_K$ and the curves at the bottom are primitively oriented by $\mathcal{O}$.[4] Adjacent levels of the volcano are connected by oriented isogenies of large prime degree; the *ascending* isogeny from a curve oriented by $\mathcal{O}^{(i)}$ to one oriented by $\mathcal{O}^{(i-1)}$ is of degree f_i.

In (a simplified version of) PEARL-SCALLOP, one acts by the class group $\mathrm{Cl}(\mathcal{O})$ on curves that are primitively oriented by $\mathcal{O}$, *i.e.* curves at the bottom of the volcano.[5] For this to be a cryptographically useful group action, PEARL-

---

[3] One difference with the usual isogeny volcano, whose edges correspond to ℓ-isogenies for a fixed prime ℓ, is that our descending/ascending isogenies have various different degrees.

[4] We recall that curves sitting "at level i" in the volcano, namely curves that are primitively oriented by $\mathcal{O}^{(i)}$, are also (non-primitively) oriented by $\mathcal{O}^{(i+1)}, \ldots, \mathcal{O}^{(r)}$.

[5] In reality, the conductor of $\mathcal{O}$ also has some small smooth divisor.

SCALLOP sets parameters so that (a) the class group $Cl(\mathcal{O})$ is sufficiently large, so solving vectorization (*i.e.* finding an ideal class connecting two given curves at the bottom of the volcano) is hard; and (b) computing ascending isogenies is infeasible, because their degree is a large prime.

Now suppose that we are trying to recover a secret ideal class $[\mathfrak{a}] \in Cl(\mathcal{O})$, given access to an oracle that, on input of an $\mathcal{O}$-oriented elliptic curve (E, ι), returns $(E', \iota') = [\mathfrak{a}] * (E, \iota)$. The crucial subtlety to exploit here is that the $\mathcal{O}$-orientation is *not* assumed to be primitive. Indeed, as it will turn out, the group action underlying the PEARL-SCALLOP protocol is well defined on any $\mathcal{O}$-oriented curve. On input of a primitively $\mathcal{O}'$-oriented curve (E, ι), where $\mathcal{O}' \supseteq \mathcal{O}$, one naturally obtains $[\mathfrak{a}\mathcal{O}'] * (E, \iota)$, where $[\mathfrak{a}\mathcal{O}'] \in Cl(\mathcal{O}')$. Now, by calling the oracle on curves that are higher up in the volcano—*i.e.* where the vectorization problem is easier—and subsequently finding a connecting ideal class, we obtain non-trivial information about the secret ideal class.

A more precise description of the attack is as follows. We first call the oracle on a curve (E_0, ι_0) that is at the top of the isogeny volcano: it will return $(E_0^{\mathfrak{a}}, \iota_0^{\mathfrak{a}}) = [\mathfrak{a}\mathcal{O}_K] * (E, \iota)$. Then, given that $Cl(\mathcal{O}_K)$ is not too large (say of size $\sim 2^{128}$), we can compute an $\mathcal{O}_K$-ideal $\mathfrak{a}_0$ such that $[\mathfrak{a}_0\mathcal{O}_K] = [\mathfrak{a}\mathcal{O}_K]$ by solving the vectorization problem (*i.e.* finding a connecting ideal class) between (E_0, ι_0) and $(E_0^{\mathfrak{a}}, \iota_0^{\mathfrak{a}})$, using either a classical or a quantum algorithm.

Next, we call the oracle on a curve (E_1, ι_1) that is one level down in the volcano, *i.e.* primitively oriented by the order $\mathcal{O}^{(1)}$ of conductor f_1, obtaining $(E_1^{\mathfrak{a}}, \iota_1^{\mathfrak{a}}) = [\mathfrak{a}\mathcal{O}^{(1)}] * (E_1, \iota_1)$. Applying $[\mathfrak{a}_0 \cap \mathcal{O}^{(1)}]$ to (E_1, ι_1), we obtain a curve (E_1', ι_1'). Crucially, since $[\mathfrak{a}_0\mathcal{O}_K] = [\mathfrak{a}\mathcal{O}_K]$, we now have that the ascending f_1-isogenies from (E_1', ι_1') and $(E_1^{\mathfrak{a}}, \iota_1^{\mathfrak{a}})$ map to a common curve at the top of the volcano. This implies that the connecting ideal class $[\mathfrak{c}_i]$ between the two curves lies in the kernel κ_1 of the projection $Cl(\mathcal{O}^{(1)}) \to Cl(\mathcal{O}_K)$, which is roughly of size $\#\kappa_1 \approx f_1$. Given that f_1 is not too large, we can again solve the vectorization problem, this time inside the group κ_1. From this, we can obtain an $\mathcal{O}^{(1)}$-ideal $\mathfrak{a}_1$ such that $[\mathfrak{a}_1\mathcal{O}^{(1)}] = [\mathfrak{a}\mathcal{O}^{(1)}]$. Continuing this process down the isogeny volcano, we eventually obtain an $\mathcal{O}^{(r)}$-ideal (*i.e.* an $\mathcal{O}$-ideal) $\mathfrak{a}_r$ such that $[\mathfrak{a}_r] = [\mathfrak{a}]$ (Fig. 1).

Outline. In Sect. 2, we compile preliminary results; in particular, we show that the PEARL-SCALLOP class group action is well defined in case of a non-primitively oriented curve, and that known algorithms already compute this action without modification. In Sect. 3, we describe our attack in the context of various active attacker models, and discuss the security implications. Finally, in Sect. 4, we describe methods to validate public keys and discuss their practicality.

2 Preliminaries

2.1 The Class Group Action on Oriented Elliptic Curves

Throughout this subsection, all elliptic curves are assumed to be defined over a perfect field k of characteristic $p > 0$. By $End(E)$ we mean the endomorphism

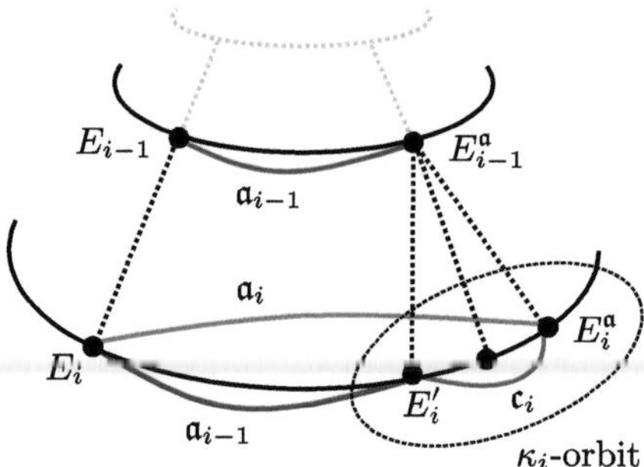

Fig. 1. A simplified sketch of the attack. We have omitted the orientations for visual clarity, and used representatives $\mathfrak{a}$ instead of classes $[\mathfrak{a}]$. We translate the information $\mathfrak{a}_{i-1}$ down one level by acting on E_i. Then we solve a vectorisation problem within the κ_i-orbit, to obtain the "correction" $\mathfrak{c}_i$ which delivers $\mathfrak{a}_i$. Note that we never evaluate the descending isogenies.

ring over $\overline{k}$ and by $\mathrm{End}^0(E) := \mathrm{End}(E) \otimes \mathbf{Q}$ the (full) endomorphism algebra. Our main references are [83,93]. For cryptographic applications of the isogeny class group action, we refer to [3].

Imaginary Quadratic Orders. An imaginary quadratic order $\mathcal{O}$ is an order in an imaginary quadratic number field K. It can always be written as $\mathcal{O} = \mathbf{Z}[\sigma] = \{a + b\sigma \mid a, b \in \mathbf{Z}\}$ for some algebraic integer $\sigma \in K$. The *discriminant* $\mathrm{Disc}(\mathcal{O}) \in \mathbf{Z}_{<0}$ of $\mathcal{O}$ is the discriminant of σ; it defines $\mathcal{O}$ uniquely up to ring isomorphism. An imaginary *fundamental discriminant* d is a negative integer that is either (i) squarefree and $d \equiv 1 \pmod 4$, or (ii) of the form $d = 4 \cdot d'$, where d' is squarefree and $d' \equiv 2, 3 \pmod 4$. An imaginary quadratic order is maximal with respect to inclusion, *i.e.* equal to the ring of integers of its fraction field, if and only if its discriminant is fundamental. The *class group* $\mathrm{Cl}(\mathcal{O})$ of $\mathcal{O}$ is the group of invertible fractional $\mathcal{O}$-ideals modulo its subgroup of principal fractional $\mathcal{O}$-ideals.

Inclusions of Orders. If $\mathcal{O}_1 \supseteq \mathcal{O}_2$, then $\mathrm{Disc}(\mathcal{O}_1) = f^2 \mathrm{Disc}(\mathcal{O}_2)$ for some integer $f \in \mathbf{Z}_{>0}$, called the *relative conductor* of $\mathcal{O}_2$ in $\mathcal{O}_1$. The ideal $f\mathcal{O}_1$ is the largest ideal (with respect to inclusion) of $\mathcal{O}_1$ that is contained in $\mathcal{O}_2$ [34, Thm. 1.3] and is called the *conductor ideal*. If $\mathcal{O}_1 = \mathbf{Z}[\sigma]$ then $\mathcal{O}_2 = \mathbf{Z}[f\sigma]$. If $\mathcal{O}_1 \supseteq \mathcal{O}_2 \supseteq \mathcal{O}_3$, then the relative conductor of $\mathcal{O}_3$ in $\mathcal{O}_1$ is the product of the relative conductors of $\mathcal{O}_2$ in $\mathcal{O}_1$ and of $\mathcal{O}_3$ in $\mathcal{O}_2$. There is an exact sequence relating the class groups of $\mathcal{O}_1 \supseteq \mathcal{O}_2$ [64, Theorem 5.4]:

$$1 \to \frac{\mathcal{O}_1^\times}{\mathcal{O}_2^\times} \to \frac{(\mathcal{O}_1/f\mathcal{O}_1)^\times}{(\mathcal{O}_2/f\mathcal{O}_1)^\times} \to \mathrm{Cl}(\mathcal{O}_2) \to \mathrm{Cl}(\mathcal{O}_1) \to 1. \tag{1}$$

Orientations. With K still being an imaginary quadratic number field, we define a K-*orientation* on an elliptic curve E to be (necessarily injective) ring homomorphism $\iota\colon K \to \mathrm{End}^0(E)$. If $\mathcal{O} \subseteq K$ is an imaginary quadratic order, then ι is called an $\mathcal{O}$-*orientation* if $\iota(\mathcal{O}) \subseteq \mathrm{End}(E)$. If an $\mathcal{O}$-orientation does not extend to a strictly larger imaginary quadratic order $\mathcal{O}' \subseteq K$, then it is called *primitive*.

Definition 2.1. A K-orientation $\iota\colon K \to \mathrm{End}^0(E)$ is primitive for a unique order $\mathcal{O}^{\mathrm{pr}}(\iota) \subseteq K$, called the *primitive order (of ι)*. It is given by $\mathcal{O}^{\mathrm{pr}}(\iota) = \iota^{-1}(\mathrm{End}(E))$. The *absolute conductor of ι*, denoted $f^{\mathrm{pr}}(\iota)$, is the conductor of $\mathcal{O}^{\mathrm{pr}}(\iota)$ in the ring of integers $\mathcal{O}_K$.

If (E, ι) is a K-oriented elliptic curve and $\varphi\colon E \to E'$ is an isogeny, then the *induced K-orientation* $\varphi_*(\iota)$ on E' is given by

$$\varphi_*(\iota)(\alpha) := \frac{1}{\deg \varphi}\varphi \circ \iota(\alpha) \circ \hat{\varphi}$$

for all $\alpha \in K$. Let $\mathfrak{O} := \mathcal{O}^{\mathrm{pr}}(\iota), \mathfrak{O}' := \mathcal{O}^{\mathrm{pr}}(\varphi_*(\iota))$ denote the primitive orders of ι and $\varphi_*(\iota)$ respectively. If $\deg \varphi = \ell$ is prime, then either

  (i) $\mathfrak{O} = \mathfrak{O}'$ and we call φ *horizontal*; or
 (ii) $\mathfrak{O} \subsetneq \mathfrak{O}'$ and we call φ *ascending*; or
(iii) $\mathfrak{O} \supsetneq \mathfrak{O}'$ and we call φ *descending*.

In the last two cases, the relative conductor is ℓ. We will use the same terminologies (horizontal, ascending, descending) for isogenies whose degree is not prime, if the primitive orders of the domain and codomain are comparable, in the sense that one is contained in the other.

Class Group Actions. Let (E, ι) be an $\mathcal{O}$-oriented elliptic curve, and denote by $\mathcal{O}^{\mathrm{pr}}$ the associated primitive order. Write $f_{\mathcal{O}^{\mathrm{pr}}/\mathcal{O}}$ for the relative conductor of $\mathcal{O}$ in $\mathcal{O}^{\mathrm{pr}}$. To an ideal $\mathfrak{a} \subseteq \mathcal{O}$ of norm coprime to $p, f_{\mathcal{O}^{\mathrm{pr}}/\mathcal{O}}$, we associate a separable isogeny $\varphi_{\mathfrak{a}}\colon E \to \mathfrak{a} * E$ of degree $N(\mathfrak{a})$ with kernel

$$E[\mathfrak{a}] := \bigcap_{\alpha \in \mathfrak{a}} E[\iota(\alpha)].$$

The isogeny $\varphi_{\mathfrak{a}}$ is horizontal if and only if $\mathfrak{a}$ is invertible. In that case, the oriented curve $(\mathfrak{a} * E, (\varphi_{\mathfrak{a}})_*(\iota))$ depends—up to K-oriented isomorphism—only on the ideal class of $\mathfrak{a}$. This induces a well-defined group action

$$\mathrm{Cl}(\mathcal{O}) \circlearrowright \{(E, \iota) \mid E/\overline{k} \text{ an elliptic curve}, \iota \text{ an } \mathcal{O}\text{-orientation}\}/ \cong . \tag{2}$$

If $f_{\mathcal{O}^{\mathrm{pr}}/\mathcal{O}} = 1$ (*i.e.* if the orientation is primitive) then this action is free, and the number of orbits is at most two [94, Thm. 1].

Acting by Exponent Vectors. Let K be an imaginary quadratic number field and let $\ell_1, \ldots, \ell_n$ be a collection of (distinct) primes that split in $\mathcal{O}_K$. Suppose σ generates $\mathcal{O}_K = \mathbf{Z}[\sigma]$. Since each prime ℓ_j split, the reduction modulo ℓ_j of the minimal polynomial of σ has two distinct eigenvalues $\lambda_j, \mu_j \in \mathbf{Z}/\ell_j\mathbf{Z}$. This corresponds to a factorization of the principal ideal generated by ℓ_j into prime ideals of norm ℓ_j, as

$$(\ell_j) = (\ell_j, \sigma - \lambda_j)(\ell_j, \sigma - \mu_j).$$

Let us choose, for each $1 \le j \le n$, one of the two eigenvalues. That is, we fix a choice of prime ideal $\mathfrak{l}_j \subseteq \mathcal{O}_K$ above ℓ_j, say $\mathfrak{l}_j = (\ell_j, \sigma - \lambda_j)$. Then we obtain a well-defined group homomorphism

$$\varpi \colon \mathbf{Z}^n \to \mathrm{Cl}(\mathcal{O}_K), \ (s_1, \ldots, s_n) \mapsto [\mathfrak{l}_1]^{s_1} \cdots [\mathfrak{l}_n]^{s_n}.$$

In the context of class group actions, once a map ϖ has been defined, elements $(s_1, \ldots, s_n) \in \mathbf{Z}^n$ are also referred to as *exponent vectors*. Our choice of $\mathfrak{l}_j$ essentially amounts to determining which ideal of norm ℓ_j is considered *positive* (*i.e.* corresponding to $s_j = 1$). Using ϖ, we can extend (2) to an action

$$\mathbf{Z}^n \circlearrowright \{(E, \iota) \mid E/\overline{k} \text{ an elliptic curve}, \iota \text{ an } \mathcal{O}_K\text{-orientation}\}/ \cong .$$

Since the action (2) on primitively oriented elliptic curves is free, the stabilizer of every point is the kernel of ϖ. If $\mathcal{O} \subseteq \mathcal{O}_K$ is an order of absolute conductor coprime to ℓ_j, then ℓ_j splits in $\mathcal{O}$, and $\mathfrak{l}_j \cap \mathcal{O}$ is an invertible $\mathcal{O}$-ideal of norm ℓ_j. Choosing $\mathfrak{l}_j \cap \mathcal{O}$ as the "positive" ideal, we can further extend to a group action

$$\mathbf{Z}^n \circlearrowright \left\{(E, \iota)\,\middle|\, E/\overline{k}, \iota \text{ a } K\text{-orientation}, \gcd\left(\textstyle\prod_j \ell_j, f^{\mathrm{pr}}(\iota)\right) = 1\right\}/ \cong, \tag{3}$$

where, explicitly,

$$(s_1, \cdots, s_n) * (E, \iota) := \left([\mathfrak{l}_1 \cap \mathcal{O}^{\mathrm{pr}}(\iota)]^{s_1} \ldots [\mathfrak{l}_n \cap \mathcal{O}^{\mathrm{pr}}(\iota)]^{s_n}\right) * (E, \iota).$$

Here, the stabilizer of (E, ι) is the kernel Λ of the map $\varpi^{\mathrm{pr}} \colon \mathbf{Z}^n \to \mathrm{Cl}(\mathcal{O}^{\mathrm{pr}}(\iota))$. If ϖ^{pr} is surjective, then we have $\mathrm{Cl}(\mathcal{O}^{\mathrm{pr}}(\iota)) \cong \mathbf{Z}^n/\Lambda$, and we call Λ the *relation lattice* of $\mathcal{O}^{\mathrm{pr}}(\iota)$.

Compatibility of the Action Between Levels. Let $\mathcal{O}' \subseteq \mathcal{O} \subseteq \mathcal{O}_K$ be orders of absolute conductor f', f respectively. We recall that the $\mathcal{O}$-ideals prime to f are in bijection with the $\mathcal{O}_K$-ideals prime to f via the norm-preserving maps of extension $(I \mapsto I\mathcal{O}_K)$ and restriction $(J \mapsto J \cap \mathcal{O})$ [36, Prop. 7.20]; and because an ideal $I \subseteq \mathcal{O}$ is prime to an integer m if and only if its norm $\mathrm{N}(I)$ is [36, Lem. 7.18][6], this bijection restricts to a bijection between $\mathcal{O}$-ideals prime to f' and $\mathcal{O}_K$-ideals prime to f'. Together, we conclude that restriction and extension deliver a bijection between $\mathcal{O}$-ideals prime to f' and $\mathcal{O}'$-ideals prime to f'.

---

[6] Cox proves this for $m = f$, but the statement still holds for any integer m.

Consider now a prime $\mathcal{O}_K$-ideal $\mathfrak{l} = (\ell, \sigma - \lambda)$ above ℓ. Then

$$\mathfrak{l} \cap \mathcal{O} = \ell\mathcal{O} + f(\sigma - \lambda)\mathcal{O} = (\ell, f(\sigma - \lambda)),$$

and similarly for $\mathfrak{l} \cap \mathcal{O}'$.

Lemma 2.2. *If $f, f' \in \mathbf{Z}_{>0}$ are coprime to ℓ, then $(\ell, f(\sigma - \lambda)) = (\ell, f'(\sigma - \lambda))$ as $\mathcal{O}$-ideals.*

Proof. This is exactly the statement that the extension of $\mathfrak{l} \cap \mathcal{O}'$ to $\mathcal{O}$ is $\mathfrak{l} \cap \mathcal{O}$, which follows from the fact that extension and restriction of ideals coprime to the conductor is bijective. $\qquad\square$

Corollary 2.3. *Let (E, ι) be a K-oriented elliptic curve. Let $\mathbf{Z}[\sigma] = \mathcal{O}^{\mathrm{pr}}(\iota)$ and $f = f^{\mathrm{pr}}(\iota)$. Let $\omega \in K$ be any element such that $\iota(\omega) \in \mathrm{End}(E)$. Denote by f' the relative conductor of $\mathbf{Z}[\omega]$ in $\mathbf{Z}[\sigma]$, and assume that $\gcd(\ell, f') = 1$ for a prime ℓ. Write $\omega = c + f'\sigma$ for some $c \in \mathbf{Z}$. Then, if $\mathfrak{l} = (\ell, \sigma - \lambda)$ is a prime $\mathcal{O}_K$-ideal above ℓ,*

$$E[(\ell, \omega - c - f'\lambda)] = E[\mathfrak{l} \cap \mathcal{O}^{\mathrm{pr}}(\iota)].$$

Proof. We have

$$E[(\ell, \omega - c - f'\lambda)] = E[(\ell, f'\sigma - f'\lambda)] = E[(\ell, f\sigma - f\lambda)] = E[\mathfrak{l} \cap \mathcal{O}^{\mathrm{pr}}(\iota)],$$

where the second equality follows from Lemma 2.2. $\qquad\square$

This result is essentially [4, Prop. 3.1]; it implies that we can evaluate the group action (3) using the image under ι of *any* element $\omega \in \mathcal{O}^{\mathrm{pr}}(\iota)$ (not necessarily a generator for the primitive order), as long as the absolute conductor of $\mathbf{Z}[\omega]$ is coprime to all primes $\ell_1, \ldots, \ell_n$.

2.2 PEARL-SCALLOP

PEARL-SCALLOP is a group action based on oriented isogenies of supersingular elliptic curves, which was proposed in [4] as a variant of SCALLOP [43]. The orienting imaginary quadratic order is a suborder of a maximal order with a class number that is large but efficiently computable, and the conductor is taken to be a product of a few large primes, rather than a single large prime.

PEARL-SCALLOP features a representation of the orientation by an endomorphism whose degree is a power of 2. This avoids higher-dimensional isogeny representations, in contrast to SCALLOP-HD [30], and simplifies a constraint on the norm of the acting ideal. We give here a brief summary of PEARL-SCALLOP.

The Orientation. Let $f, d \in \mathbf{Z}_{>0}$, $\mathcal{O} = \mathbf{Z}[f\sqrt{-d}]$ be an order inside the imaginary quadratic number field K, ω an element of smooth norm inside $\mathcal{O}$, and g the relative conductor of $\mathbf{Z}[\omega]$ in $\mathbf{Z}[f\sqrt{-d}]$. Given a (maximal supersingular) $\mathcal{O}$-oriented elliptic curve (E, ι) along with an efficient representation of the endomorphism $\iota(\omega)$, one can efficiently compute the action of any prime-normed $\mathcal{O}$-ideal I so long its norm is prime to g and polynomially sized in the input. This is shown in [4, Prop. 3.1], and also follows from Corollary 2.3.

For completeness, we give a self-contained description here. If δ is a generator of $\mathbf{Z}[f\sqrt{-d}]$, then $g\delta$ is a generator of $\mathbf{Z}[\omega]$, hence $g\delta = c + \omega$ for some $c \in \mathbf{Z}$. Let $\mathfrak{l} = (\ell, a + \delta)$ be an ideal of $\mathbf{Z}[\delta]$ with prime norm ℓ, coprime to g. Then $\mathfrak{l} = (\ell, g(a + \delta)) = (\ell, ga + c + \omega)$, and computing the isogeny corresponding to the action of $[\mathfrak{l}]$ amounts to computing the isogeny with kernel $E[\ell] \cap E[\iota(\omega) + [ga + c]] = (\widehat{\iota(\omega)} + [c + ga])(E[\ell])$. In other words, to compute the action of $\mathfrak{l}$ on E one essentially needs to compute eigenvectors of $\widehat{\iota(\omega)}$ on $E[\ell]$.

The endomorphism $\iota(\omega)$ is represented by a pair cyclic isogenies φ_P, φ_Q which compose to $\iota(\omega) = \widehat{\varphi_Q}\varphi_P$, and these isogenies are in turn represented by generators P, Q of their kernels. From now on, we will drop the orientation ι in the notation, and write for example ω for $\iota(\omega)$.

In practice, $\deg(\omega) = 2^{2e} \mid (p+1)^2$ for some $e \in \mathbf{Z}_{>0}$, and $\{P, Q\}$ is a basis of $E[2^e]$. The prime p is taken to be of the form $p = c2^e \prod_{i=1}^n \ell_i - 1$, where $\ell_1, \ldots \ell_n$ are split odd primes not dividing the relative conductor g, and c is a small cofactor such that p satisfies $(\mathrm{Disc}(\mathcal{O}) \mid p) = -1$. This last condition ensures that the set of $\mathcal{O}$-oriented supersingular elliptic curves in characteristic p is nonempty [83, Prop. 3.2]).

Evaluating the Action. When evaluating the action of an ideal of $\mathcal{O}$, one first finds a smooth normed representative $\mathfrak{a} = \prod_{i=1}^n \mathfrak{l}_i^{e_i}$ of its class in $\mathrm{Cl}(\mathcal{O})$ using the pre-computed class group structure (see [4, Sec. 4] for more details); then one repeatedly applies Algorithm 1 ([4, Algorithm 2]) to ideals of the form $\prod_{i=1}^n \mathfrak{l}_i^{b_i}$ with $b_i \in \{0, 1\}$ until the action by $\mathfrak{a}$ has been computed. The evaluation procedure is standard, and has a standard optimization obtained by using a different point sampling method (see [4, Algorithm 3]), but the core idea remains the same.

Generating a Starting Curve. A starting elliptic curve, together with a representation of an $\mathcal{O}$-orientation, is computed in the following way. First, one considers a definite quaternion algebra $\mathcal{B}_{p,\infty}$, ramified at p and infinity, and a special p-extremal maximal quaternion order $\mathcal{O}_0 \subseteq \mathcal{B}_{p,\infty}$ where the quaternion embedding problem is easily solvable. Then, one tries different smooth values h until a (primitive) embedding of $\mathbf{Z} + h\mathcal{O}$ in $\mathcal{O}_0$ is found (this is done using the heuristic algorithm GenericOrderEmbeddingFactorisation, see [49, Algorithm 3]).

From a curve E_0 such that $\mathrm{End}(E_0) \cong \mathcal{O}_0$, it is then easy to compute an ascending h-isogeny to a curve E, which will be oriented by $\mathcal{O}$. Finally, one needs to find points P, Q representing the smooth element $\omega \in \mathcal{O}$. This is done by

---

Algorithm 1. GroupAction($\mathfrak{a}, E, P, Q$)

Input: A smooth $\mathcal{O}$-ideal $\mathfrak{a} = \prod_{i=1}^{N} \mathfrak{l}_i$, an $\mathcal{O}$-oriented elliptic curve E, points $P, Q \in E$ generating isogenies such that $\hat{\varphi}_Q \circ \varphi_P$ is an endomorphism corresponding to an element of $\mathcal{O}$ of norm 2^{2e}.

Output: An $\mathcal{O}$-oriented curve $(E_\mathfrak{a}, P_\mathfrak{a}, Q_\mathfrak{a}) = \mathfrak{a} * (E, P, Q)$.

1: Let B_1, B_2 be a basis of $E[L]$ where $L = \prod_{i=1}^{N} \ell_i$.
2: Let $\hat{\omega} = \hat{\varphi}_P \circ \varphi_Q$.
3: Compute $B_1' = \hat{\omega}(B_1)$, $B_2' = \hat{\omega}(B_2)$.
4: **for** $i \in \{1, \ldots n\}$ **do**
5:     Compute $K_i = [L/\ell_i]([\lambda_i]B_1 + B_1')$ where $\mathfrak{l}_i = (\ell_i, \lambda_i + \omega)$.
6:     **if** $K_i = 0_E$ **then**
7:         Compute $K_i = [L/\ell_i]([\lambda_i]B_2 + B_2')$.
8:     **end if**
9: **end for**
10: Compute $\varphi_\mathfrak{a} \colon E \to E_\mathfrak{a}$ from its kernel $K = \langle K_1, \ldots K_n \rangle$.
11: **return** $(E_\mathfrak{a}, \varphi_\mathfrak{a}(P), \varphi_\mathfrak{a}(Q))$.

---

factoring the ideal generated by ω in $\mathcal{O}_E \cong \mathrm{End}(E)$ as a product of smooth-norm ideals, pulling back these ideals through the ideal corresponding to the ascending h-isogeny, and eventually obtaining the corresponding kernel generators. This is a standard technique used also in SQIsign [44], from which PEARL-SCALLOP takes algorithms IdealToIsogeny and IdealToKernel. The procedure is summarised in [4, Algorithm 1], which we do not report here as it will not be needed for the rest of the paper.

Parameters. The two key properties of PEARL-SCALLOP are that its orientation is by an order $\mathcal{O} = \mathbf{Z}[d\sqrt{-d}]$ with f a product of a few medium-sized primes, and that this orientation can be encoded by an element of smooth norm. These properties respectively make the class group computation feasible, whilst allowing for efficient evaluation.

To find such f and ω, the idea is to consider powers m of a generic element $a + \sqrt{-d} \in \mathbf{Z}[\sqrt{-d}]$ satisfying the norm equation $a + d^2 = 2N^2$ with N smooth, until the coefficient of $\sqrt{-d}$ in $(a + \sqrt{-d})^m$ is divided by a few large primes.

For parameters targeting a security level equivalent to CSIDH-1024, the authors set $N = 2^{129}$, and consider $(a + \sqrt{-d})^4$ so that the coefficient of $\sqrt{-d}$ equals $24a(a - N)(N + a)/3$. They pick a and $d = 2N^2 - a^2$ so that a, $N - a$ and $(N + a)/3$ are 128-bit primes that split in $\mathbf{Q}(\sqrt{-d})$, in order to ensure easier discrete logarithms in the class group computation. Thanks to [4, Lemma 3.3], the splitting condition is achieved when the above three factors are prime, and $a < N$ satisfies $a \equiv 19 \bmod 24$.

A similar approach is taken for parameters equivalent to CSIDH-$\{2048, 4096\}$, obtaining a conductor divided by seven primes of size 299 bits and 640 bits, respectively. Finally, the authors propose an intermediate set of parameters achieving a discriminant of $\mathbf{Q}(f\sqrt{-d})$ of size roughly 1500 bits. We refer to the original paper [4, Section 3] for more details.

2.3   Interpolating and Dividing Isogenies

In this subsection we briefly cover isogeny representations by embedding into higher dimensional isogenies and an algorithm to test whether a given isogeny factors through multiplication by an integer, with [89] as our main reference. This content will be relevant for Sect. 4, where we will discuss how to validate PEARL-SCALLOP public keys, in particular how to verify whether a given orientation is primitive.

Embedding Isogenies. Robert's *embedding lemma* [89, Ex. 5.16] tells us that every n-isogeny $\varphi\colon (A, \lambda_A) \to (B, \lambda_B)$ between g-dimensional principally polarised Abelian varieties can be embedded into a $2ug$-dimensional N-isogeny

$$\Phi = (\alpha, (\widetilde{\varphi}\,\mathrm{id}_u); -(\varphi\,\mathrm{id}_u), \widetilde{\alpha}) : A^u \times B^u \to A^u \times B^u,$$

for any $N > n$, when $N - n$ is the sum of $u \in \{1, 2, 4\}$ integer squares. Here, $\widetilde{\varphi} = \lambda_A^{-1}\widehat{\varphi}\lambda_B$ denotes the *polarised dual*[7] of φ; $(\varphi\,\mathrm{id}_u)\colon A^u \to B^u$ denotes the $u \times u$ matrix with φ on the diagonal; and α is a $u \times u$ integer matrix which induces a polarised endomorphism on both A^u, B^u and has determinant $N - n$ [89, Prop. 5.15][8]. Moreover, if N is prime to n and to the characteristic of the base field, we have

$$\ker(\Phi) = \{((N - n)P, (\mathrm{id}_u\,\varphi) \circ \alpha(P)) \mid P \in A^u[N]\}. \tag{4}$$

Interpolating Isogenies. Given *interpolation data* $\{(P_i, \varphi(P_i), Q_i, \varphi(Q_i))\}_i$ of an n-isogeny φ on a *CRT basis* $\{(P_i, Q_i)\}_i$[9] of $A[N]$ and a decomposition of $N - n$ as the sum of u squares[10], one can one can write down the corresponding matrix α and generators of $\ker(\Phi)$ as described by (4).

With $\ker(\Phi)$ computed this way, one can evaluate Φ (and therefore φ) on points R in $A \times B$ in time $\widetilde{O}(aed(m\ell)^g \log(q))$, where $\mathbb{F}_q$ is the field of definition of A, B; $N = \ell_1^{e_1} \cdots \ell_a^{e_a}$; $e = \max_i(e_i)$; $\ell = \max_i(\ell_i)$; d is such that all $R + P_i, R + Q_i$ live in $A(\mathbb{F}_{q^d})$; and m is the level of theta coordinates describing A, B [89, Lem. 5.7]. With the N-torsion *accessible*[11] this justifies calling such interpolation data an *HD-representation* of φ, because it gives rise to an efficient representation of φ.

We remark that it is possible to efficiently evaluate Φ (and therefore φ) if φ is only known on $A[N_1] \cup A[N_2] \subseteq A[N]$ where $N = N_1 N_2$ by *splitting the HD-representation* [89, Sec. B.2]. Informally, this is because it is possible to decompose $\Phi = \Phi_2 \Phi_1$ into N_i-isogenies which satisfy $\ker(\Phi_1) \subseteq A[N_1]$ and

---

[7] Robert calls this the *contragredient* in [89].

[8] For example, when $N - n = x^2 + y^2$, then $\alpha = (x, y; -y, x)$ is a polarisation-respecting endomorphism on A^2, B^2.

[9] *i.e.* $\{P_i, Q_i\}$ is a basis of $A[\ell_i^{e_i}]$ where $N = \ell_1^{e_1} \cdots \ell_a^{e_a}$ and $\ell_1, \ldots, \ell_a$ are coprime.

[10] which requires factoring $N - n$ in general.

[11] *i.e.* is defined over an extension of degree polynomial in $\log(p)$ [89, Def. A.1].

$\ker(\widetilde{\Phi_2}) \subseteq B[N_2]$. We remark this does not require N_1 coprime to N_2 and is in particular true for $N_1 = N_2$.

More precisely, $\ker(\Phi_1) = \ker(\Phi) \cap (A^u \times B^u)[N_1]$ [42, Prop. 13], and so we have $\ker(\Phi_1) = \{((N-n)P, (\mathrm{id}_u\,\varphi) \circ \alpha(P)) \mid P \in (A^u \times B^u)[N_1]\}$.[12] Likewise for the polarised dual, $\ker(\widetilde{\Phi_2}) = \{((N-n)P, (\mathrm{id}_u\,\varphi) \circ \alpha(P)) \mid P \in (A^u \times B^u)[N_2]\}$, where the values $\widetilde{\varphi}(P)$ are recovered from knowing $\varphi(P)$ by computing discrete logarithms in μ_N. Indeed, by properties of the Weil pairing, $e_{B,N}(\varphi(P), Q) = e_{A,N}(P, \widetilde{\varphi}(Q))$.

Testing for Division. To test whether a given n-isogeny φ factors through scalar multiplication by m, one can produce apparent interpolation data for $\psi = \varphi/m$ by computing $\{(P_i, \varphi(P_i)/m, Q_i, \varphi(Q_i)/m\}_i^j$ on some CRT bases of the d_j-torsion, with $N = d_1 d_2 > n/m^2$ prime to m.

From this interpolation data, one obtains a maximally isotropic subgroup of $E_1^u \times E_2^u$ by selecting a powersmooth polarised degree N, finding a $u \times u$ matrix α which induces a polarised endomorphism on $E_1^u \times E_2^u$ with determinant $N - n/m^2$ and writing down the subgroup as in (4). This subgroup is the kernel of *some* N-isogeny $\Phi \colon E_1^u \times E_2^u \to A$ and because N is powersmooth, it is possible to compute the codomain A of Φ in polynomial time.

If $A \not\cong E_1^u \times E_2^u$, then Φ does not encode one-dimensional isogenies, hence φ certainly does not factor through multiplication by m; if $A \cong E_1^u \times E_2^u$, then Φ is a $u \times u$ matrix of n_{ij}-isogenies Φ_{ij} which need to further investigation. Using pairing computations on the images of Φ_{ij}, the degree n_{ij} of Φ_{ij} can be recovered, and the isogeny $\Phi_{i'j'}$ of degree $n_{i'j'} = n/m^2$ can be identified [89, Lem. 6.2]. Evaluating on a point P of order $N \geq 4n/m^2 + 1$, and testing for equality $\varphi(P)/m = \Phi_{i'j'}(P)$, one can conclude whether m divides φ or not.

3   An Active Attack

We now present a powerful active attack against the PEARL-SCALLOP group action, which uses a *static action-CDH* oracle to model the party being attacked. We also demonstrate two less effective attacks using the weaker *hashed static action-CDH* and *static action-DDH* oracles. Whilst the attacks do not impact the conjectured security of the currently proposed parameter sets, the corresponding oracles have much stronger cryptographic motivation (*c.f.* Subsect. 3.3), and so we discuss their use for completeness.

3.1   Notation

Let K be an imaginary quadratic number field and let $\mathcal{O}_K = \mathbf{Z}[\sigma]$ be its ring of integers. Let $f \in \mathbf{Z}_{>0}$ be a square-free integer and write $f = \prod_{i=1}^{r} f_i$ for its prime factorization. Denote by $\mathcal{O}$ the order of conductor f in $\mathcal{O}_K$. For $0 \leq i \leq r$, we will also write $\mathcal{O}^{(i)}$ for the order of conductor $f_1 \cdots f_i$ in $\mathcal{O}_K$, so that $\mathcal{O}^{(0)} = \mathcal{O}_K$

---

[12] under the continued assumption that N is prime to n.

and $\mathcal{O}^{(r)} = \mathcal{O}$. Let $n \in \mathbf{Z}_{>0}$ and let $\ell_1, \ldots, \ell_n$ denote prime numbers that split in $\mathcal{O}$ (in particular, they are all coprime to the conductor f). For every ℓ_j, fix one of the two prime ideals $\mathfrak{l}_j \subseteq \mathcal{O}$ that lies above it, and write $\mathfrak{l}_j^{(i)} = \mathfrak{l}_j \mathcal{O}^{(i)}$ for its extension to $\mathcal{O}^{(i)}$. Define

$$\varpi^{(i)} \colon \mathbf{Z}^n \to \mathrm{Cl}(\mathcal{O}^{(i)}), \quad (s_1, \ldots, s_n) \mapsto \left[\mathfrak{l}_1^{(i)}\right]^{s_1} \cdots \left[\mathfrak{l}_n^{(i)}\right]^{s_n}.$$

Assume that every $\varpi^{(i)}$ is surjective. The i-th *relation lattice* $\Lambda^{(i)}$ is defined to be the kernel of $\varpi^{(i)}$. We also write $\Lambda^{(-1)} = \mathbf{Z}^n$. Note that the relationship between the orders and the relation lattices is strictly inclusion preserving That is, $\mathcal{O}^{(i)} \subsetneq \mathcal{O}^{(j)}$ implies $\Lambda^{(i)} \subsetneq \Lambda^{(j)}$.

We say that an $\mathcal{O}$-oriented curve (E, ι) is *at level i* if $\mathcal{O}^{\mathrm{pr}}(\iota) = \mathcal{O}^{(i)}$. In particular, if (E, ι) is at level i, then its stabilizer for the action in (3) is $\Lambda^{(i)}$. Moreover, we say that two curves $(E, \iota), (E', \iota')$ at level i are *siblings* if they lie below the same curve on level $i - 1$, i.e. there exists a vector $\mathbf{v_i}$ in $\Lambda^{(i-1)}$ such that $\mathbf{v_i} * (E, \iota) = (E', \iota')$.

3.2   The Attacks

We describe our attacks using the language of exponent vectors. That is, we consider the class group action as given by (3). This agrees with the usual method for evaluating the group action in practice (cf. Algorithm 1). Assume that all lattices of relations $\Lambda^{(i)}$ have been computed. Moreover, assume that a precomputed list of $\mathcal{O}$-oriented curves $(E_0, \iota_0), \ldots, (E_r, \iota_r)$ with (E_i, ι_i) at level i is known. Note that we do not assume knowledge of isogenies between different (E_i, ι_i) levels. Write $\kappa_i = \Lambda^{(i-1)}/\Lambda^{(i)}$ for the kernel of the surjective map $\mathrm{Cl}(\mathcal{O}^{(i)}) \to \mathrm{Cl}(\mathcal{O}^{(i-1)})$. Recall that $\#\kappa_0 = \#\mathrm{Cl}(\mathcal{O}^{(0)}) = h(D_K) \approx \sqrt{-D_K}$ [91] and $\#\kappa_i = f_i - (D_K \mid f_i) = f_i \pm 1$ [36, Th. 7.24], where $D_K = \mathrm{Disc}(\mathcal{O}_K)$.

Suppose now that Alice has secret key $\mathbf{a}$ in $\mathbf{Z}^n$. We describe three active attacks to recover $\mathbf{a}$ by modelling the interaction with Alice through one of the following three oracles. We discuss the cryptographic motivation of these oracles later.

(i)   *Static action-CDH oracle* $\mathcal{A}^{\mathbf{a}}$. On input an $\mathcal{O}$-oriented curve (E, ι), the oracle returns $\mathbf{a} * (E, \iota)$.

(ii) *Hashed static action-CDH oracle* $\mathcal{A}_{\mathsf{H}}^{\mathbf{a}}$. On input an $\mathcal{O}$-oriented curve (E, ι), the oracle returns the hash $\mathsf{H}(\mathbf{a} * (E, \iota))$.

(iii) *Static action-DDH oracle* $\mathcal{A}_?^{\mathbf{a}}$. On input an $\mathcal{O}$-oriented curve (E, ι) and a bitstring h, the oracle returns the bit $b = 1$ if $\mathsf{H}(\mathbf{a} * (E, \iota)) = \mathsf{h}$, else $b = 0$.

The corresponding attacks are as follows.

Attack 3.1 (Using the static action-CDH oracle). Query $\mathcal{A}^{\mathbf{a}}$ on the curves (E_i, ι_i) to obtain $(E_i^{\mathbf{a}}, \iota_i^{\mathbf{a}})$. Then inductively proceed as follows.

(i)   *Base case.* Solve the vectorisation problem between (E_0, ι_0) and $(E_0^{\mathbf{a}}, \iota_0^{\mathbf{a}})$ to obtain $[\mathbf{c_0}]$ in $\mathbf{Z}^n/\Lambda^{(0)}$. Then $\mathbf{a_0} := \mathbf{c_0}$ is equal to $\mathbf{a}$ modulo $\Lambda^{(0)}$.

(ii) *Inductive step.* Assume that $\mathbf{a}_{i-1} = \mathbf{a}$ modulo $\Lambda^{(i-1)}$ is known. Compute $(E_i', \iota_i') = \mathbf{a}_{i-1} * (E_i, \iota_i)$ using any polynomial-time algorithm for evaluating the class group action (e.g. using [84]). Solve the vectorisation problem between the sibling curves (E_i', ι_i') and $(E_i^{\mathbf{a}}, \iota_i^{\mathbf{a}})$ to obtain $[\mathbf{c}_i]$ in $\Lambda^{(i-1)}/\Lambda^{(i)}$. Then $\mathbf{a}_i := \mathbf{a}_{i-1} + \mathbf{c}_i$ is equal to $\mathbf{a}$ modulo $\Lambda^{(i)}$.

Attack 3.2 (Using the hashed static action-CDH oracle). Query $\mathcal{A}_{\mathsf{H}}^{\mathbf{a}}$ on the curves (E_i, ι_i) to obtain $\mathsf{h}_i = \mathsf{H}((E_i^{\mathbf{a}}, \iota_i^{\mathbf{a}}))$. Then inductively proceed as follows.

(i) *Base case.* Compute $\mathbf{a}_0$ such that $\mathsf{H}(\mathbf{a}_0 * (E_0, \iota_0)) = \mathsf{h}_0$ using brute force, by acting by (representatives of) elements in $\mathbf{Z}^n/\Lambda^{(0)}$. Note that we then obtain $\mathbf{a}_0 = \mathbf{a}$ modulo $\Lambda^{(0)}$.

(ii) *Inductive step.* Assume that $\mathbf{a}_{i-1} = \mathbf{a}$ modulo $\Lambda^{(i-1)}$ is known. Compute $(E_i', \iota_i') = \mathbf{a}_{i-1} * (E_i, \iota_i)$ using any polynomial-time algorithm for evaluating the class group action (e.g. using [84]). Compute $\mathbf{a}_i$ such that $\mathsf{H}(\mathbf{a}_i * (E_i, \iota_i)) = \mathsf{h}_i$ using brute force, by acting by (representatives of) elements in $\Lambda^{(i)}/\Lambda^{(i-1)}$. We obtain $\mathbf{a}_i = \mathbf{a}$ modulo Λ^i.

Attack 3.3 (Using the static action-DDH oracle). Query $\mathcal{A}_?^{\mathbf{a}}$ on the curves (E_i, ι_i), together with a guess $\mathsf{h}_{g,i} = \mathsf{H}(\mathbf{g}_i * (E_i, \iota_i))$ obtained from $\mathbf{g}_i$ in $\Lambda^{(i-1)}/\Lambda^{(i)}$ until $\mathsf{h}_{g,i} = \mathsf{h}_i = \mathsf{H}((E_i^{\mathbf{a}}, \iota_i^{\mathbf{a}}))$ is found. Then proceed with the hashed static action-CDH attack, Attack 3.2.

We remark that in each of the attacks, the queries to the $\mathcal{A}^{\mathbf{a}}, \mathcal{A}_{\mathsf{H}}^{\mathbf{a}}, \mathcal{A}_?^{\mathbf{a}}$ oracles are independent to the secret $\mathbf{a}$, making these attacks non-adaptive; in particular allowing for the expensive computation to be offline. This is a small detail of Attack 3.3: it really makes all (independent) $\mathcal{A}_?^{\mathbf{a}}$ queries first, before proceeding to the inductive loop; this does not affect the overall complexity and avoids a more analogous strategy to Attack 3.2, with guesses submitted to the oracle at every level, which would result in an adaptive attack.

We now proceed with a precise analysis of the attacks' complexities.

Lemma 3.4. *Attack 3.1 makes $r + 1$ $\mathcal{A}^{\mathbf{a}}$-oracle queries and can be implemented classically using $\widetilde{O}(\max(\{f_i\}_i, |D_K|^{1/2})^{1/2})$ group action computations, and quantumly using $\exp(O(\log(\max(\{f_i\}_i, |D_K|^{1/2}))^{1/2}))$ group action computations. Note that group action computations (i.e. computing $\mathbf{s} * (E, \iota)$ for some known vector $\mathbf{s}$ in $\mathbf{Z}^n$) are done without querying the $\mathcal{A}^{\mathbf{a}}$ oracle.*

Proof. We immediately see that, crucially, the attack performs vectorisation successively at every level, not simultaneously; hence costs are added, not multiplied.

The initial vectorisation in the base case (at the *crater* of the isogeny volcano), occurs in the class group of $\mathcal{O}_K$ which is of size $\widetilde{O}(|D_K|^{1/2})$. The vectorisation problem at level i between (E_i', ι_i') and $(E_i^{\mathbf{a}}, \iota_i^{\mathbf{a}})$ is within the same $\Lambda^{(i-1)}$-orbit precisely because $\mathbf{a}_i = \mathbf{a}$ modulo $\Lambda^{(i-1)}$. Each of these $\Lambda^{(i-1)}$-orbits is simply acted on by $\kappa_i = \Lambda^{(i-1)}/\Lambda^{(i)}$, where we recall that $\#\kappa_i = f_i \pm 1$.

Having identified the sizes of the groups in which vectorisation occurs, we obtain the stated complexities by employing meet-in-the-middle search [55] in the classical case and Kuperberg's linear hidden shift algorithm [66] in the quantum setting. $\square$

Lemma 3.5. *Attack 3.2 makes $r+1$ $\mathcal{A}_{\mathsf{H}}^{\mathsf{a}}$-oracle queries; and can be implemented classically using $\widetilde{O}(\max(\{f_i\}_i, |D_K|^{1/2}))$ hashed group action computations, and quantumly using $\widetilde{O}(\max(\{f_i\}_i, |D_K|^{1/2})^{1/2})$ hashed group action computations. Note that hashed group action computations (i.e. computing $\mathsf{H}(\mathbf{s} * (E, \iota))$ for some known vector $\mathbf{s}$ in $\mathbf{Z}^n$) are done without using the $\mathcal{A}_{\mathsf{H}}^{\mathsf{a}}$ oracle.*

Proof. As in Attack 3.1, the vectorisation problems can be solved successively at every level. The main computational cost is brute-force pre-image search in the sets $\kappa_i = \Lambda^{(i-1)}/\Lambda^{(i)}$. Classically, this can be done using $\widetilde{O}(|D_K|^{1/2})$ hashed group action computations at the crater, and with $O(f_i)$ hashed group action computations at lower levels. Quantumly, we get a quadratic speedup using Grover's search algorithm [58] over the classical brute force search to obtain the stated complexity. $\qquad\square$

Lemma 3.6. *Attack 3.3 can be implemented using $\widetilde{O}(\max(\{f_i\}, |D_K|^{1/2}))$ classical $\mathcal{A}_?^{\mathsf{a}}$-oracle queries and hashed group action computations; and quantumly implemented making $\widetilde{O}(\max(\{f_i\}_i, |D_K|^{1/2})^{1/2})$ $\mathcal{A}_?^{\mathsf{a}}$-oracle queries and hashed group action computations.* $\qquad\square$

Proof. As in the previous two attacks, the vectorisation problems can be solved successively at every level. Classically, to obtain the correct guess $\mathbf{g}_i$, one must first compute $\widetilde{O}(|D_K|^{1/2})$ group actions and then submit these as queries to the $\mathcal{A}_?^{\mathsf{a}}$ oracle at the crater, and $O(f_i)$ queries at lower levels; quantumly we may use Grover search to reduce this to $\widetilde{O}(|D_K|^{1/4})$ action computations and queries at the crater, and to $O(f_i^{1/2})$ action computations and queries at levels below. $\quad\square$

Implications for Concrete PEARL-SCALLOP Parameters. Using the parameter sets targeting a security level equivalent to CSIDH-$\{1024, 2048, 4096\}$, we see that — classically — Attack 3.1 (which assumes access to the *static action-CDH oracle*) requires $\approx 2^{64}$, 2^{150}, 2^{320} group action evaluations respectively. Since PEARL-SCALLOP targets 128 classical bits of security, this constitutes a significant classical security reduction for the CSIDH-1024 case.

The quantum security, however, is substantially affected for all parameter sets. Indeed, Kuperberg's algorithm [66] is a generic algorithm for solving discrete logarithms for commutative group actions, that is subexponential in the size of the group. Compared to $\mathrm{Cl}(\mathcal{O})$, which is of size $\approx 512, 1024, 2048$ bits for the CSIDH-$\{1024, 2048, 4096\}$ parameter sets respectively, the relative vectorization groups $\kappa_i := \ker\left(\mathrm{Cl}(\mathcal{O}^{(i)}) \to \mathrm{Cl}(\mathcal{O}^{(i-1)})\right)$ are significantly smaller; of (maximal) size $128, 300$, and 640 bits respectively. Moreover, since $\Lambda^{(i)} \supseteq \Lambda^{(r)}$ for all i, the quantum cost of the group action evaluation oracle (cf. [10]) is at most as large as the one for $\mathrm{Cl}(\mathcal{O}) = \mathrm{Cl}(\mathcal{O}^{(r)})$-vectorization (on which the proposed quantum security is based).

The *hashed static action-CDH oracle* (Attack 3.2) and *static action-DDH oracle* (Attack 3.3) versions of the attack do not directly compromise the conjectured classical or quantum security. Indeed, we note that the quantum versions of the attacks likely do not outperform solving the full vectorization problem for $\mathrm{Cl}(\mathcal{O})$ using Kuperberg's algorithm.

3.3   Motivating the Oracles

We discuss the motivation of all three oracles in descending strength.

The Static Action-CDH Oracle $\mathcal{A}^{\mathbf{a}}$. First, we emphasize that the $\mathcal{A}^{\mathbf{a}}$ oracle truly gives rise to a *static* action-CDH oracle, and not a full action-CDH oracle. This is an important distinction, because action-CDH and action-DLOG are quantumly equivalent [54]. The cost for evaluating $(t\mathbf{a})*E$ is t $\mathcal{A}^{\mathbf{a}}$ calls, whereas a full action-CDH oracle would only require $O(\log(t))$ calls, by double-and-adding. Efficient computation of $(t\mathbf{a}) * E$ is a crucial ingredient in the quantum action-CDH to action-DLOG reduction.

Still, the $\mathcal{A}^{\mathbf{a}}$ oracle is very powerful, because it fully impersonates Alice: any interaction in any cryptographic protocol that defines Alice through knowing $\mathbf{a}$ can be performed by the oracle $\mathcal{A}^{\mathbf{a}}$. However, it is still meaningful to speak of key recovery from such an oracle because versions of this oracle appear in some threshold settings.

For example, a naive implementation of the threshold ElGamal decryption scheme described in [45, Sec. 3.2] exposes the $\mathcal{A}^{\mathbf{a}}$ oracle. Indeed, during decapsulation, the first user will apply their secret to an adversarially chosen curve and relay the result to the next user in the threshold group. Since the parties are assumed to communicate publicly, this value can be extracted by the same adversary that submitted the curve. Even if the parties used secure channels for communication, the adversary could be part of the threshold group, which is a common threat model in the threshold setting.

The Hashed Static Action-CDH Oracle $\mathcal{A}^{\mathbf{a}}_{\mathsf{H}}$. This oracle is akin to obtaining the session key obtained through a key exchange, where the hash function is replaced with a key-derivation function.

The query complexity $r+1$ of our attack is dictated by the number r of (large) prime divisors of the conductor f, *i.e.* logarithmic in f. Concretely though, to make the ascending isogenies computationally infeasible, the conductor is usually particularly non-smooth, with only a handful of large factors *e.g.* 3 for PEARL-SCALLOP's CSIDH-1024 parameters set. As such, just 4 leaked session keys would give sufficient information to mount the offline attack.

The Static Action-DDH Oracle $\mathcal{A}^{\mathbf{a}}_{?}$. This oracle is naturally instantiated in many internet communication protocols. An adversary may initiate communications with a server by submitting many non-primitively oriented curves, and if they can decrypt the responses, meaning they have correctly guessed the session keys, they can proceed with the inductive phase of the attack.

4   Validating Primitive Orientations

One method to thwart these active "class group downgrade" attacks is to *validate* the orientation of the curves before continuing with the protocol. In the language of cryptographic group actions [3] (with G acting on X), validation means that parties simply ensure that a proposed element x, *e.g.* given as a bitstring, actually encodes an element in the set X before acting with their secrets g in G. In the context of a NIKE, this is referred to as *public-key validation*, since parties act by their secrets on (potentially adversarially generated) *public keys*.

We note that every orientation $\iota\colon K \to \mathrm{End}^0(E)$ is uniquely defined by the image $\gamma = \iota(\omega)$ of a generator ω of $\mathcal{O}^{\mathrm{pr}}(\iota)$. Conversely, every non-scalar endomorphism γ of E defines a $\mathbf{Q}(\sqrt{\mathrm{disc}(\gamma)})$-orientation ι_γ characterised by $(\mathrm{tr}(\gamma) - \sqrt{\mathrm{disc}(\gamma)})/2 \mapsto \gamma$. In practice, orientations are usually explicitly encoded through an endomorphism. Indeed, the only family of isogeny class group computations that do *not* do this are the CSIDH/CSURF families [21,25], for there the orientation is implicitly given by the Frobenius endomorphism.

Hence, we assume that the orientation is given as an endomorphism ω on E. To verify that (E, ι_ω) is in fact a primitive $\mathcal{O}$-orientation for the desired order $\mathcal{O}$, one must verify that $\mathbf{Z}[\omega]$ has the correct discriminant, which establishes that $\mathbf{Z}[\omega] \simeq \mathcal{O}$, and that ι_ω is a *primitive* $\mathbf{Z}[\omega]$-orientation. We treat these two challenges in the next two subsections.

4.1   Verifying the Discriminant

The general setting of an oriented group action requires that the orientation ω is given by an *efficient representation* [89, Sec. 2.1]. In particular, this means that the degree of ω is (implicitly or explicitly) given.

Concretely in PEARL-SCALLOP we recall that, ω is represented as a pair of points $P, Q \in E$ of order 2^e which generate the kernels of the isogenies φ_P, φ_Q respectively and satisfy $\widehat{\varphi_Q}\varphi_P = \omega$. The order $\mathcal{O}$ by which E should be primitively oriented by has discriminant $f^2 D_K$, and the degree of ω should be 2^{2e}, both values supplied in the public parameters of the scheme. To verify the degree of ω, one checks that P and Q have order 2^e and that $\widehat{\varphi_Q}\varphi_P$ is a cyclic endomorphism. Since $\widehat{\varphi_Q}\varphi_P$ has degree 2^{2e}, its cyclicity could be checked by verifying that $\widehat{\varphi_Q}\varphi_P(E[2]) \neq \{0\}$. Nevertheless, we postpone the cyclicity check to the primitivity check, as the orientation being primitive implies that $\widehat{\varphi_Q}\varphi_P$ is cyclic.

Then, to verify the that discriminant satisfies $\mathrm{disc}(\omega) = \mathrm{tr}(\omega)^2 - 4\deg(\omega) = \mathrm{disc}(\mathcal{O})$, it remains to verify that the trace satisfies $\mathrm{tr}(\omega)^2 = \mathrm{disc}(\mathcal{O}) + 4\deg(\omega)$. Whilst one can *compute* the trace in polynomial time, with reasonable runtimes in practice [82]; we must merely *verify* that the (square of the) trace of the given endomorphism matches what we expect. This distinction allows to avoid potentially expensive discrete logarithm computations.

In general, a natural way to check the trace is to evaluate ω and its dual $\hat\omega$ on one of the points of a basis $\{S_1, S_2\}$ of $E[N]$ for some integer N, compute the Weil pairing

$$e_N(S_1, (\omega + \hat\omega)(S_2)) = e_N(S_1, S_2)^{\mathrm{tr}(\omega)}$$

and check whether it matches $e_N(S_1, S_2)^{\pm\sqrt{\mathrm{disc}(\mathcal{O})+4\deg(\omega)}}$ for the expected value of the discriminant $\mathrm{disc}(\mathcal{O})$.

This test only verifies the value of $\mathrm{tr}(\omega)$ modulo N, hence only becomes sufficient when $N \geq 2\sqrt{\deg(\omega)}$. Indeed, assuming ω is not (multiplication by) an integer, the order it generates $\mathbf{Z}[\omega]$ has negative discriminant $\mathrm{Disc}(\mathbf{Z}[\omega]) = \mathrm{tr}(\omega)^2 - 4\deg(\omega)$ and so $\mathrm{tr}(\omega)^2 < 4\deg(\omega)$. Note that verifying the correct sign of $\mathrm{tr}(\omega)$ is not needed, since only the square is relevant for the discriminant. In fact, we can always assume that the parameters are chosen such that $\mathrm{tr}(\omega)$ is positive, as one can always replace ω by $-\omega$.

In the rest of this subsection, we improve on this idea to design a trace validation method to validate the trace t of any supersingular endomorphism θ in $\mathrm{End}(E)$ of known degree d satisfying $4\sqrt{d}+1 \le p+1$, by evaluating exclusively $\hat{\omega}$. This is especially relevant for PEARL-SCALLOP, because we see that the group-action evaluation algorithm (Algorithm 1) already evaluates $\hat{\omega}$ on a large torsion basis. We note that an early rejection due to an incorrect orientation does not leak any secret information, because the values of $\hat{\omega}$ do not depend on secrets, even if they are re-used later in conjunction with the secret key to compute the action. Finally, we note that when validating the trace up to sign one can relax the requirement on d to $2\sqrt{d} + 1 \le p + 1$.

Recall that the field characteristic p has the shape $p + 1 = c2^e \prod_{i=1}^{n} \ell_i$ where the ideals lying above the primes ℓ_i are used to evaluate the group action; and the concrete parameter choices enforce that $p \ge 2^{2e} = \deg(\omega)$.

Lemma 4.1. *Let E be a supersingular curve and let $\theta \in \mathrm{End}(E)$ be an endomorphism of degree d and of positive trace. Let t be an integer such that $0 \le t \le 2\sqrt{d}$ and let R be a point of order $N \ge 2\sqrt{d} + 1$. If $\theta^2(R) - [t]\theta(R) + [d]R = 0$, then $\mathrm{tr}(\theta) = t$.*

Proof. Let $u > 0$ be the trace of θ. Then $\theta^2(R) - [u]\theta(R) + [d]R = 0$. Hence, we have that $\theta^2(R) - [u]\theta(R) + [d]R = \theta^2(R) - [t]\theta(R) + [d]R$, that is $[u]\theta(R) = [t]\theta(R)$, implying that $u \equiv t \mod N$. Since $0 \le u, t \le 2\sqrt{d} < N$, we conclude $u = t$. $\square$

To verify the trace of a given ω using Lemma 4.1, we only need to check that the (purported) minimal polynomial of ω holds on a single point R of order $N \ge 2\sqrt{\deg(\omega)} + 1 = 2^{e+1} + 1$.

We now describe how to check that $\hat{\omega}^2(R) - [t]\hat{\omega}(R) + [\deg(\omega)]R = 0$. Let S_1, S_2 be a basis of $E[N]$, let $S_1' = \hat{\omega}(S_1)$ and $S_2' = \hat{\omega}(S_2)$. Write $\hat{\omega}(R) = [x]S_1 + [y]S_2$, then

$$e_N(\hat{\omega}(R), S_2) = e_N(S_1, S_2)^x, \quad e_N(S_1, \hat{\omega}(R)) = e_N(S_1, S_2)^y, \text{ and}$$

$$\hat{\omega}^2(R) = \hat{\omega}([x]S_1 + [y]S_2) = [x]\hat{\omega}(S_1) + [y]\hat{\omega}(S_2) = [x]S_1' + [y]S_2'.$$

Hence, we obtain that $\hat{\omega}^2(R) - [t]\hat{\omega}(R) + [\deg(\omega)]R = 0$ if and only if $\hat{\omega}^2(R) = [t]\hat{\omega}(R) - [\deg(\omega)]R$, which holds if and only if $[t]\hat{\omega}(R) - [\deg(\omega)]R = [x]S_1' + [y]S_2'$. Setting $R_2 = [t]\hat{\omega}(R) - [\deg(\omega)]R$, the last equality holds if and only if

$$e_N(R_2, S_2') = e_N(S_1', S_2')^x = e_N(S_1, S_2)^{x \deg(\omega)} = e_N(\hat{\omega}(R), S_2)^{\deg(\omega)} \text{ and}$$

$$e_N(S_1', R_2) = e_N(S_1', S_2')^y = e_N(S_1, S_2)^{y \deg(\omega)} = e_N(S_1, \hat{\omega}(R))^{\deg(\omega)}.$$

Notice that if one chooses $R = S_1$, then $\hat{\omega}(R) = S_1'$ and

$$e_N(S_1', R_2) = e_N(S_1', [t]S_1' - [\deg(\omega)]S_1) = e_N(S_1, S_1')^{\deg(\omega)} = e_N(S_1, \hat{\omega}(R))^{\deg(\omega)},$$

meaning that the second check always passes. We are hence left with only one pairing equality to be tested.

To summarize, let S_1, S_2 be a basis of $E[N]$, let $S_1' = \hat{\omega}(S_1)$ and $S_2' = \hat{\omega}(S_2)$. The trace check is done by setting $R_2 = [t]\hat{\omega}(S_1) - [\deg(\omega)]S_1$, and checking whether the following equality holds

$$e_N(R_2, S_2') = e_N(S_1', S_2)^{\deg(\omega)}.$$

In the summary (Sect. 4.3) of our orientation validation, we will be using a point $R = S_1$ of order a (small) multiple of $p + 1$.

4.2   Testing for Primitivity

We now present two different algorithms to test for primitivity: the first method follows a more folklore approach to verify primitivity by computing a handful of group actions on carefully selected ideals; the second method applies more recently developed techniques, employing higher-dimensional isogenies to test the orienting endomorphism for divisibility by primes dividing the conductor.

The only requirement of the first method is that the class group structure is known, which is exactly the setting which all SCALLOP variants target. Conversely, the second method always runs in polynomial time for all isogeny class group actions, and when the discriminant of the orienting endomorphism is sufficiently small in comparison to the available 2-torsion, can be concretely implemented with very performant algorithms.

On balance, the PEARL-SCALLOP parameters allow for concrete instantiations in which the second method to likely outperform the first.

Using the Group Action. If a given $\mathcal{O}$-orientation (E, ι) is contained in a primitive order $\mathcal{O}' \supsetneq \mathcal{O}$, then the action on (E, ι) by any ideal $\mathfrak{a} \subseteq \mathcal{O}$ such that $\mathfrak{a}\mathcal{O}'$ represents a trivial element in $\mathrm{Cl}(\mathcal{O}')$ is trivial, even if $\mathfrak{a}$ represents a non-trivial class in $\mathrm{Cl}(\mathcal{O})$. As a consequence, testing triviality of the action by such an ideal for every superorder $\mathcal{O}'$ of $\mathcal{O}$ allows one to test whether (E, ι) is primitive or not.

Moreover, if (E, ι) cannot be extended to an intermediate order $\mathcal{O} \subsetneq \mathcal{O}'' \subseteq \mathcal{O}'$, then clearly it cannot be extended to $\mathcal{O}'$. Consequently, to verify whether (E, ι) is primitively oriented by $\mathcal{O}$, it suffices to perform this action-triviality test for all orders $\mathcal{O}''$ in which $\mathcal{O}$ has prime relative conductor. In other words, if $\mathcal{O}$ has conductor $f = \prod_{i=1}^{r} f_i$ in $\mathcal{O}_K$, then it suffices to test orders $\mathcal{O}_{f_i}$ with conductor f/f_i on $\mathcal{O}_K$, for all $1 \leq i \leq r$.

To carry out this check, one is faced with the problem of finding non-principal ideals of $\mathcal{O}$ that become principal when lifted to $\mathcal{O}_{f_i}$, namely ideals whose class is in the kernel of the map $\mathrm{Cl}(\mathcal{O}) \to \mathrm{Cl}(\mathcal{O}_{f_i})$ from (1). We sketch here how one can compute such ideals, provided that the structure of $\mathrm{Cl}(\mathcal{O})$ and $\mathrm{Cl}(\mathcal{O}_{f_i})$ is known.

Remark 4.2. The outlined strategy is reminiscent of [14, Sec. 3.2], in which the purported conductor u of the endomorphism ring of an *ordinary* curve is verified. Our situation is different, because the parameters of our isogeny volcano allow us to compute the class group structure at every level $\mathcal{O}^{(i)}$, and so we do not need to FINDRELATIONS during certification.

In PEARL-SCALLOP, the group structure of $\mathrm{Cl}(\mathcal{O})$ is computed in the parameter generation phase, and public (see [4, Section 2.3] on how it is computed in practice). It is given as a set of $\mathcal{O}$-ideals $\{\mathfrak{l}_j\}_{1 \le j \le n}$ whose classes generate the whole class group, and a basis of the relation lattice $\Lambda_{\mathcal{O}}$ (equal to $\Lambda^{(r)}$ in the notation of Sect. 3.1). Similarly, one can compute $\mathrm{Cl}(\mathcal{O}_{f_i})$ by computing its relation lattice Λ_{f_i}. A way to find ideals in $\ker(\mathrm{Cl}(\mathcal{O}) \to \mathrm{Cl}(\mathcal{O}_{f_i}))$ and express them in terms of a given set of generators of $\mathrm{Cl}(\mathcal{O})$ is described in [39, Section 3.3], in a context where $\mathcal{O}$ has absolute conductor which is a power of a small prime, and hence $\mathrm{Cl}(\mathcal{O})$ is cyclic or almost cyclic. Nevertheless, we can use a similar approach for a conductor which is a product of distinct primes that split in $\mathcal{O}_K$, as is the case for PEARL-SCALLOP.

First of all, we show that $\ker(\mathrm{Cl}(\mathcal{O}) \to \mathrm{Cl}(\mathcal{O}_{f_i})) \cong \mathbf{F}_{f_i}^{\times}$ for any prime f_i that splits in $\mathcal{O}_K$, in particular it is a cyclic subgroup of order $f_i - 1$ in $\mathrm{Cl}(\mathcal{O})$.

Lemma 4.3. *Let K be an imaginary quadratic field and let ℓ be a prime that splits in K. Let $\mathcal{O}_1 \supseteq \mathcal{O}_2$ be orders of K with relative conductor $[\mathcal{O}_1 : \mathcal{O}_2] = \ell$. Assuming that $(\mathcal{O}_1)^{\times} = \{\pm 1\}$, then*

$$\ker(\mathrm{Cl}(\mathcal{O}_2) \to \mathrm{Cl}(\mathcal{O}_1)) \cong \mathbf{F}_{\ell}^{\times}.$$

Before proving the lemma, we remark that the requirement $(\mathcal{O}_1)^{\times} = \{\pm 1\}$ only excludes $\mathcal{O}_1$ being the maximal order of $K = \mathbf{Q}(\sqrt{-1})$ or of $K = \mathbf{Q}(\sqrt{-3})$.

Proof. If $(\mathcal{O}_1)^{\times} = \{\pm 1\}$ then $(\mathcal{O}_2)^{\times} = \{\pm 1\}$, and the exact sequence (1) becomes

$$1 \to \frac{(\mathcal{O}_1/\ell\mathcal{O}_1)^{\times}}{(\mathcal{O}_2/\ell\mathcal{O}_1)^{\times}} \to \mathrm{Cl}(\mathcal{O}_2) \to \mathrm{Cl}(\mathcal{O}_1) \to 1.$$

In particular, $\ker(\mathrm{Cl}(\mathcal{O}_2) \to \mathrm{Cl}(\mathcal{O}_1)) \cong \frac{(\mathcal{O}_1/\ell\mathcal{O}_1)^{\times}}{(\mathcal{O}_2/\ell\mathcal{O}_1)^{\times}}$. Assume without loss of generality that $K \cong \mathbf{Q}(X)/(X^2 + D)$ for some square-free integer D. Let L be the absolute conductor of $\mathcal{O}_2$, then ℓ divides L and L/ℓ is the absolute conductor of $\mathcal{O}_1$. Then,

$$\mathcal{O}_1/\ell\mathcal{O}_1 \cong \frac{\mathbf{Z}[X]/(X^2 + DL^2/\ell^2)}{\ell(\mathbf{Z}[X]/(X^2 + DL^2/\ell^2))} \cong \frac{\mathbf{F}_{\ell}[X]}{(X^2 + DL^2/\ell^2)}.$$

Since ℓ splits in K, it holds that $\left(\frac{-D}{\ell}\right) = 1$, hence

$$\frac{\mathbf{F}_{\ell}[X]}{(X^2 + DL^2/\ell^2)} \cong \mathbf{F}_{\ell} \times \mathbf{F}_{\ell}.$$

Since $\mathcal{O}_2/\ell\mathcal{O}_1$ is a subring of $\mathcal{O}_1/\ell\mathcal{O}_1$, and $[\mathcal{O}_1/\ell\mathcal{O}_1 : \mathcal{O}_2/\ell\mathcal{O}_1] = \ell$, it follows that $\mathcal{O}_2/\ell\mathcal{O}_1 \cong \mathbf{F}_\ell$, embedding diagonally into $\mathcal{O}_1/\ell\mathcal{O}_1 \cong \mathbf{F}_\ell \times \mathbf{F}_\ell$. Finally,

$$\frac{(\mathcal{O}_1/\ell\mathcal{O}_1)^\times}{(\mathcal{O}_2/\ell\mathcal{O}_1)^\times} \cong \frac{\mathbf{F}_\ell^\times \times \mathbf{F}_\ell^\times}{\mathbf{F}_\ell^\times} \cong \mathbf{F}_\ell^\times,$$

where the last isomorphism is given by $(x, y) \mapsto xy^{-1}$. $\qquad\square$

Once we know that $\ker(\mathrm{Cl}(\mathcal{O}) \to \mathrm{Cl}(\mathcal{O}_{f_i}))$ is a cyclic group of order $f_i - 1$, we are left with finding an element in that group. Since

$$\ker(\mathrm{Cl}(\mathcal{O}) \to \mathrm{Cl}(\mathcal{O}_{f_i}) \cong \Lambda_{\mathcal{O}_{f_i}}/\Lambda_{\mathcal{O}},$$

upon computing the orders of the classes corresponding to each $\mathfrak{l}_i$ in $\mathrm{Cl}(\mathcal{O})$, we can sample vectors $(e_1, \ldots e_n) \in \Lambda_{\mathcal{O}_{f_i}}$ that are not zero modulo $\Lambda_{\mathcal{O}}$, until a product $\mathfrak{g} = \prod_{i=1}^n \mathfrak{l}_i^{e_i}$ has order dividing $f_i - 1$, yielding an element of $\ker(\mathrm{Cl}(\mathcal{O}) \to \mathrm{Cl}(\mathcal{O}_{f_i}))$.

Notice that in this approach, computing the special test ideals is done once for each parameter set during the parameter generation stage and can be published as part of public parameters. As such, computing the test ideals themselves does not need to be done during protocol execution; however, before computing any group action by a secret ideal, one must first compute the action of the test ideals on the given curve to validate its orientation. In PEARL-SCALLOP, this amounts to r additional group action computations. Concretely, for the CSIDH-1024 parameters, $r = 3$, yielding a slowdown factor of 4.

We leave it as an open question to investigate whether it is possible to find particularly cheap test ideals to compute $e.g.$ whose exponent vectors have low ℓ_1-norm.

Using a Division Algorithm. We now present another approach for validating whether a given orientation is primitive. In essence, we only need to check whether a well-chosen endomorphism coming from the orientation is cyclic.

Lemma 4.4. *Let E be an elliptic curve and γ an endomorphism of discriminant $f^2 d_0$, where d_0 is a fundamental discriminant. Then ι_γ is a primitive $\mathbf{Z}[\gamma]$-orientation on E if and only if $\gamma_0 = 2\gamma - \mathrm{tr}(\gamma)$ is not divisible by 2ρ for any prime factor $\rho > 1$ of f.*

Proof. Viewing γ as an algebraic integer, we see that $(2\gamma - \mathrm{tr}(\gamma))/(2\rho)$ generates the index-ρ superorder of $\mathbf{Z}[\gamma]$ for any prime divisor ρ of f. As such, if the endomorphism $2\gamma - \mathrm{tr}(\gamma)$ factors through scalar multiplication by 2ρ for a divisor ρ of f, the orientation ι_γ is not $\mathbf{Z}[\gamma]$-primitive. $\qquad\square$

This lemma delivers us a primitivity testing algorithm. Indeed, the current instantiations of the isogeny class group action encode the orientations of curves E by endomorphisms γ in efficient isogeny representation with a discriminant df^2. Because it is given in efficient isogeny representation, the degree of γ is known and its trace can be verified as a function of degree and supposed discriminant. Once the discriminant is known to be $\mathrm{tr}(\gamma)^2 - 4\deg(\gamma) = f^2 d$, it remains to verify whether $2\gamma - \mathrm{tr}(\gamma)$ is divisible by 2ρ for any prime divisor ρ of f.

The general problem of testing whether an isogeny $\varphi\colon E_1 \to E_2$ is divisible by an integer can be solved in asymptotic polynomial time [89, Prop. 6.6]. However, we realize that the case of PEARL-SCALLOP is particularly tame, resulting in the computation of 4-dimensional 2-isogenies instead of 8-dimensional N-isogenies (which would be necessary general). Indeed, computing 4-dimensional 2-isogenies can be done efficiently in practice [38, 41].

We note that in the setting of PEARL-SCALLOP the conductor f is the product of a few large primes, the fundamental discriminant D_K is 1 modulo 4, and the endomorphism $\omega_0 = 2\omega - \mathrm{tr}(\omega)$ has degree $4\deg(\omega) - \mathrm{tr}(\omega)^2 = -f^2 D_K$. Picking $N = 2^\bullet$, one sees that the quantity $N - \deg(\varphi) = 2^\bullet + f^2 D_K$ is 1 modulo 4, and so there is hope that concrete parameters can be chosen so that it is a sum of two squares. Robert's *embedding lemma* and the subsequent *division algorithm* then would tell us that ω_0 can be tested for division by computing 4-dimensional 2-isogenies.

By tweaking the parameter generation of PEARL-SCALLOP and rejecting early by using bounded trial divisions whilst testing whether $2^{e_i} - (f/f_i)^2 D_K$ is a sum of two squares, we found the following CSIDH-1024 parameters within $\approx 2^{25}$ re-randomisations, taking ≈ 6 Core-GHz-Hours[13]. The parameters are defined through the seeds

$$a = 2713922031919385646100431219044428032251, \quad N = 2^{129},$$

and derived from the expressions $d = 2N^2 - a^2$, $f_1 = a, f_2 = (a + N)/3, f_3 = N - a, f = f_1 f_2 f_3$, ensuring that the quantities $2^{e_i} + (f/f_i)^2 D_K$ are sums of two squares with $e_1 = 1039, e_2 = 1036, e_3 = 1037$. We recall that the e_i determine the length of the 4-dimensional 2-isogeny chains, and so play a role in the cost of computing them.

The "unofficial" CSIDH-512 parameters provided with the PEARL-SCALLOP implementation on GitHub[14] have $f = f_1$ of 128 bits and $d = 1$ (mod 4) of 256 bits. Their concrete choices lead to $2^{256} - d$ being a perfect square, in which case a 2-dimensional 2-isogeny chain suffices for validation. Such isogenies have been implemented in the context of SQISign [1] and take mere milliseconds for the NIST-V parameters (which also correspond to a field of characteristic 2^{500}).

We note that for the CSIDH-$\{1024, 2048, 4096\}$ parameters, the large factors m of f are of size $\{128, 299, 640\}$ bits and so $\deg((2\omega - \mathrm{tr}(\omega))/m) = (4\deg(\omega) - \mathrm{tr}(\omega)^2)/m^2 = (f/m)^2 D_K \approx \{2^{768}, 2^{1450}, 2^{2816}\}$, but the available $2^\bullet$-torsion is $2^e \approx \{2^{512}, 2^{1024}, 2^{2048}\}$. This necessitates *splitting the HD-*

---

[13] Or, more precisely, about 40 seconds on a server with 255 cores and a clock speed of 2.2 GHz.

[14] https://github.com/biasse/SCALLOP-params.

representation; a technical endeavour, but with very little overhead since the two isogeny chains one computes are half as long.

Remark 4.5. We remark that in the precise setting of PEARL-SCALLOP, ω generates an order of conductor gf, where g is a small smooth number. To verify (non-)divisibility by these small factors, we evaluate on the respective torsion subgroups, instead of invoking the expensive higher-dimensional test.

Performance Comparison. To give a rough estimate of the cost of the 4-dimensional isogenies in the second primitivity test for the CSIDH-1024 parameter set, we compare to the qt-PEGASIS implementation of [40, Tab. 1].

Their C implementation takes 146 milliseconds to compute one chain of 4-dimensional 2-isogenies of length roughly 1024 steps over a *prime* field $\mathbb{F}_p$ of characteristic roughly 2^{1024}. Since the isogenies of PEARL-SCALLOP are defined over $\mathbb{F}_{p^2}$, and the arithmetic in 4-dimensional isogeny computation is mostly addition and multiplication [38, Table 1], a rough figure of 0.5 ($\approx 3 \cdot 0.15$) seconds can be used to estimate the cost of the corresponding 4-dimensional 2-isogeny chain over $\mathbb{F}_{p^2}$. Repeating for all 3 factors of the conductor $f = f_1 f_2 f_3$, this gives a total overhead of around 1.5 seconds.

This very favourably compares to the PEARL-SCALLOP, whose C++ implementation which takes $58\,\mathrm{s}$ to evaluate one action at the CSIDH-1024 parameters, and would require an additional $r = 3$ group action computations.

Remark 4.6. We remind that PEARL-SCALLOP is exactly constructed to allow for computing the class group structure, something which appears to be out of reach for the parameters in qt-PEGASIS, which [40] implements. So even though [40] can be used to implement a much faster class group action, we note it has less features.

4.3   Summary of the Key Validation

We now summarize our key validation. Recall that the base prime is of the form $p = c2^e \prod_{i=1}^n \ell_i - 1$. Let $f = f_0 \cdot f_1 \cdots \cdot f_k$ be the conductor of $\mathcal{O}$, where f_i for $1 \le i \le k$ are the large prime factors and f_0 the (very) small smooth factor of f. Let $q = q_1 \cdots q_r$ be the product of the prime factors of f_0. Let (E, P, Q) be a PEARL-SCALLOP public key that we want to validate and act upon with an ideal $\mathfrak{a} = \prod_{i=1}^N \mathfrak{l}_i$ of norm $L = \prod_{i=1}^N \ell_i = N(\mathfrak{a})$.

For evaluating the group action, we need to compute $\hat{\omega}(E[L])$, while for the primitivity test with respect to the large prime factors f_i for $1 \le i \le k$ of the conductor f, we need to evaluate $2\hat{\omega} - \mathrm{tr}(\hat{\omega})$ on $E[2^e]$ before running the divisibility test discussed in Sects. 2.3 and 4.2. When checking the primitivity of the orientation with respect to the small prime factors q_i for $1 \le i \le r$ of f_0, one can directly evaluate $2\omega - \mathrm{tr}(w)$ on $E[q_i]$ and check that $(2\hat{\omega} - \mathrm{tr}(\hat{\omega}))(E[q_i]) \ne \{0\}$. We hence need the evaluation of $2\hat{\omega} - \mathrm{tr}(\hat{\omega})$ on $E[q2^e]$, which can be derived from that of $\hat{\omega}$ on $E[q2^e]$. To batch all these evaluations, we set $q = 2q_1 \cdots q_r$ and $M = (p+1)q'$ where $q' = q/\gcd(p+1, q)$ and evaluate $\hat{\omega}$ on $E[M]$. This evaluation allows to check whether $\hat{\omega}$ is an endomorphism on E by rejecting if the image points do not lie on E. Moreover, it is used to check the trace as described in Sect. 4.1. One then retrieves the evaluation of $2\hat{\omega} - \mathrm{tr}(\hat{\omega})$ on $E[q_i]$ or $E[2q_i]$ if $q_i = 2$, and (relying on Lemma 4.4) uses it to check whether the orientation is primitive with respect to the small prime factors q_i of f_0. One also retrieves the evaluation of $2\hat{\omega} - \mathrm{tr}(\hat{\omega})$ on $E[2^e]$, and uses it to check whether the

---

Algorithm 2. GroupActionWithKeyValidation$(\mathfrak{a}, E, P, Q)$

Input: A smooth $\mathcal{O}$-ideal $\mathfrak{a} = \prod_{i=1}^{n} \mathfrak{l}_i$, an $\mathcal{O}$-oriented elliptic curve E, points $P, Q \in E$ generating isogenies such that $\hat{\varphi}_Q \circ \varphi_P$ is an endomorphism corresponding to an element of $\mathcal{O}$ of norm 2^{2e} and of trace t. The large prime factors f_i $(1 \le i \le k)$ and the very small smooth factor f_0 of the conductor $f = f_0 \cdot f_1 \cdots f_k$ of $\mathcal{O}$. Let $q = 2q_1 \cdots q_r$ be the product of the prime factors of f_0.

Output: An $\mathcal{O}$-oriented curve $(E_{\mathfrak{a}}, P_{\mathfrak{a}}, Q_{\mathfrak{a}}) = \mathfrak{a} * (E, P, Q)$, or Invalid.

 1: Let $q' = q/\gcd(p+1, q)$ and let $M = (p+1)q'$.
 2: Let S_1, S_2 be a basis of $E[M]$.
 3: Compute $\hat{\omega} = \hat{\varphi}_P \circ \varphi_Q$ together with $S_1' = \hat{\omega}(S_1)$, $S_2' = \hat{\omega}(S_2)$.
 4: **if** $\hat{\omega}$ is not an endomorphism of E **then**
 5:     **return** Invalid. $\triangleright$ ω is not an endomorphism
 6: **end if**
 7: Let $R_2 = [t]S_1' - [\deg(\omega)]S_1$.
 8: **if** $e_M(R_2, S_2') \ne e_M(S_1', S_2)^{\deg(\omega)}$ **then**
 9:     **return** Invalid. $\triangleright$ Trace is incorrect
10: **end if**
11: Let $U_1 = [2]S_1' - [\mathrm{tr}(\omega)]S_1$, $U_2 = [2]S_2' - [\mathrm{tr}(\omega)]S_2$. $\triangleright$ Evaluating $2\hat{\omega} - \mathrm{tr}(\hat{\omega})$
12: Let $Q_1 = [M/q]U_1$, $Q_2 = [M/q]U_2$
13: **for** $i \in \{1, \ldots r\}$ **do**
14:     **if** $q_i = 2$ **then**
15:         **if** $[q/4]Q_1 = 0 - [q/4]Q_2$ **then**
16:             **return** Invalid. $\triangleright$ Non primitive orientation WRT 2
17:         **end if**
18:     **else**
19:         **if** $[q/q_i]Q_1 = 0 = [q/q_i]Q_2$ **then**
20:             **return** Invalid. $\triangleright$ Non primitive orientation WRT q_i
21:         **end if**
22:     **end if**
23: **end for**
24: Let $T_1 = [M/2^e]S_1$, $T_1' = [M/2^e]U_1$, $T_2 = [M/2^e]S_2$, $T_2' = [M/2^e]U_2$
25: **for** $i \in \{1, \ldots k\}$ **do**
26:     **if** $\{(T_j, [f_i^{-1}]T_j'), j \in \{1,2\}\}$ represents an isogeny of degree $f^2 D_K / f_i^2$ **then**
27:         **return** Invalid. $\triangleright$ Non primitive orientation WRT f_i
28:     **end if**
29: **end for** $\triangleright$ End of the key validation
30: Let $L = \prod_{i=1}^{N} \ell_i = N(\mathfrak{a})$.
31: Compute $B_1 = [M/L]S_1$, $B_2 = [M/L]S_2$, $B_1' = [M/L]S_1'$, $B_2' = [M/L]S_2'$.
32: Use B_1, B_1', B_2 and B_2' to compute $(E_{\mathfrak{a}}, \varphi_{\mathfrak{a}}(P), \varphi_{\mathfrak{a}}(Q)) = \mathfrak{a} * (E, P, Q)$. $\triangleright$ Alg.1.
33: **return** $(E_{\mathfrak{a}}, \varphi_{\mathfrak{a}}(P), \varphi_{\mathfrak{a}}(Q))$.

---

orientation is primitive with respect to the large prime factors f_i for $1 \le i \le k$ of f. If all the checks pass, one retrieves $\hat{\omega}(E[L])$ from $\hat{\omega}(E[M])$ and proceeds to the computation of the group action. This full process is summarized in Algorithm 2.

Remark 4.7. In Algorithm 2, step 1–29 constitute the key validation, while step 30–33 constitute the group action evaluation—these are the only steps where the secret key is used. Consequently, whether key validation succeeds or fails reveals no information about the secret key.

Acknowledgments. We would like to thank the organisers of the Isogeny Club Brainstorm Days at Eurocrypt 2025, where this project was started. We also thank Jonathan Komada Eriksen and Lorenz Panny for useful discussions.

Marc Houben was supported by the France 2030 program, managed by the French National Research Agency under grant agreement No. ANR-22-PETQ-0008 PQ-TLS. Gioella Lorenzon was supported by the Fonds voor Wetenschappelijk Onderzoek (FWO) under grant number 1139225N, by the European Research Council (ERC) under the European Union's Horizon 2020 research and innovation programme (grant agreement ISOCRYPT – No. 101020788), by the Research Council KU Leuven grant C14/24/099, and by CyberSecurity Research Flanders with reference number VOEWICS02. Ryan Rueger was supported by SNSF Consolidator Grant CryptonIs 213766.

References

1. Aardal, M.A., et al.: SQIsign. Tech. Rep., National Institute of Standards and Technology (2024), available at https://csrc.nist.gov/Projects/pqc-dig-sig/round-2-additional-signatures
2. Abdalla, M., Eisenhofer, T., Kiltz, E., Kunzweiler, S., Riepel, D.: Password-authenticated key exchange from group actions. In: Dodis, Y., Shrimpton, T. (eds.) CRYPTO 2022, Part II. LNCS, vol. 13508, pp. 699–728. Springer, Cham (Aug 2022). https://doi.org/10.1007/978-3-031-15979-4_24
3. Alamati, N., De Feo, L., Montgomery, H., Patranabis, S.: Cryptographic group actions and applications. In: Moriai, S., Wang, H. (eds.) ASIACRYPT 2020, Part II. LNCS, vol. 12492, pp. 411–439. Springer, Cham (Dec 2020). https://doi.org/10.1007/978-3-030-64834-3_14
4. Allombert, B., et al.: Faster SCALLOP from non-prime conductor suborders in medium sized quadratic fields. In: Jager, T., Pan, J. (eds.) PKC 2025, Part III. LNCS, vol. 15676, pp. 333–363. Springer, Cham (May 2025). https://doi.org/10.1007/978-3-031-91826-1_11
5. Atapoor, S., Baghery, K., Cozzo, D., Pedersen, R.: CSI-SharK: CSI-FiSh with sharing-friendly keys. In: Simpson, L., Baee, M.A.R. (eds.) ACISP 23. LNCS, vol. 13915, pp. 471–502. Springer, Cham (Jul 2023). https://doi.org/10.1007/978-3-031-35486-1_21
6. Baghery, K., Cozzo, D., Pedersen, R.: An isogeny-based id protocol using structured public keys. In: Paterson, M.B. (ed.) Cryptography and Coding, pp. 179–197. Springer International Publishing, Cham (2021)
7. Banegas, G., et al.: CTIDH: faster constant-time CSIDH. IACR TCHES **2021**(4), 351–387 (2021). https://doi.org/10.46586/tches.v2021.i4.351-387, https://tches.iacr.org/index.php/TCHES/article/view/9069

8. Banegas, G., et al.: Disorientation faults in CSIDH. In: Hazay, C., Stam, M. (eds.) EUROCRYPT 2023, Part V. LNCS, vol. 14008, pp. 310–342. Springer, Cham (Apr 2023). https://doi.org/10.1007/978-3-031-30589-4_11

9. Basso, A., Kutas, P., Merz, S.P., Petit, C., Weitkämper, C.: On adaptive attacks against jao-urbanik's isogeny-based protocol. In: Nitaj, A., Youssef, A.M. (eds.) AFRICACRYPT 20. LNCS, vol. 12174, pp. 195–213. Springer, Cham (Jul 2020). https://doi.org/10.1007/978-3-030-51938-4_10

10. Bernstein, D.J., Lange, T., Martindale, C., Panny, L.: Quantum circuits for the CSIDH: Optimizing quantum evaluation of isogenies. In: Ishai, Y., Rijmen, V. (eds.) EUROCRYPT 2019, Part II. LNCS, vol. 11477, pp. 409–441. Springer, Cham (May 2019). https://doi.org/10.1007/978-3-030-17656-3_15

11. Beullens, W., Dobson, S., Katsumata, S., Lai, Y.F., Pintore, F.: Group signatures and more from isogenies and lattices: Generic, simple, and efficient. In: Dunkelman, O., Dziembowski, S. (eds.) EUROCRYPT 2022, Part II. LNCS, vol. 13276, pp. 95–126. Springer, Cham (May/Jun 2022). https://doi.org/10.1007/978-3-031-07085-3_4

12. Beullens, W., Katsumata, S., Pintore, F.: Calamari and Falafl: logarithmic (linkable) ring signatures from isogenies and lattices. In: Moriai, S., Wang, H. (eds.) ASIACRYPT 2020, Part II. LNCS, vol. 12492, pp. 464–492. Springer, Cham (Dec 2020). https://doi.org/10.1007/978-3-030-64834-3_16

13. Beullens, W., Kleinjung, T., Vercauteren, F.: CSI-FiSh: efficient isogeny based signatures through class group computations. In: Galbraith, S.D., Moriai, S. (eds.) ASIACRYPT 2019, Part I. LNCS, vol. 11921, pp. 227–247. Springer, Cham (Dec 2019). https://doi.org/10.1007/978-3-030-34578-5_9

14. Bisson, G., Sutherland, A.V.: Computing the endomorphism ring of an ordinary elliptic curve over a finite field. Cryptology ePrint Archive, Report 2009/100 (2009). https://eprint.iacr.org/2009/100

15. Boneh, D., Kogan, D., Woo, K.: Oblivious pseudorandom functions from isogenies. In: Moriai, S., Wang, H. (eds.) ASIACRYPT 2020, Part II. LNCS, vol. 12492, pp. 520–550. Springer, Cham (Dec 2020).https://doi.org/10.1007/978-3-030-64834-3_18

16. Bonnetain, X., Schrottenloher, A.: Quantum security analysis of CSIDH. In: Canteaut, A., Ishai, Y. (eds.) EUROCRYPT 2020, Part II. LNCS, vol. 12106, pp. 493–522. Springer, Cham (May 2020). https://doi.org/10.1007/978-3-030-45724-2_17

17. Campos, F., et al.: Optimizations and practicality of high-security CSIDH. CiC 1(1), 5 (2024). https://doi.org/10.62056/anjbksdja

18. Campos, F., Hellenbrand, A., Meyer, M., Reijnders, K.: dCTIDH: Fast and deterministic CTIDH. Cryptology ePrint Archive, Report 2025/107 (2025). https://eprint.iacr.org/2025/107

19. Campos, F., Kannwischer, M.J., Meyer, M., Onuki, H., Stöttinger, M.: Trouble at the CSIDH: protecting CSIDH with dummy-operations against fault injection attacks. Cryptology ePrint Archive, Report 2020/1005 (2020). https://eprint.iacr.org/2020/1005

20. Campos, F., Meyer, M., Reijnders, K., Stöttinger, M.: Patient zero and patient six: zero-value and correlation attacks on CSIDH and SIKE. In: Smith, B., Wu, H. (eds.) SAC 2022. LNCS, vol. 13742, pp. 234–262. Springer, Cham (Aug 2024). https://doi.org/10.1007/978-3-031-58411-4_11

21. Castryck, W., Decru, T.: CSIDH on the surface. In: Ding, J., Tillich, J.P. (eds.) Post-Quantum Cryptography - 11th International Conference, PQCrypto 2020. pp. 111–129. Springer, Cham (2020). https://doi.org/10.1007/978-3-030-44223-1_7

22. Castryck, W., Houben, M., Merz, S.P., Mula, M., van Buuren, S., Vercauteren, F.: Weak instances of class group action based cryptography via self-pairings. In: Handschuh, H., Lysyanskaya, A. (eds.) CRYPTO 2023, Part III. LNCS, vol. 14083, pp. 762–792. Springer, Cham (Aug 2023). https://doi.org/10.1007/978-3-031-38548-3_25

23. Castryck, W., Houben, M., Vercauteren, F., Wesolowski, B.: On the decisional Diffie-Hellman problem for class group actions on oriented elliptic curves. Res. Number Theor. **8**(4), 99 (2022). https://doi.org/10.1007/s40993-022-00399-6

24. Castryck, W., Invernizzi, R., Lorenzon, G., Meers, J., Vercauteren, F.: Orient express: using frobenius to express oriented isogenies. Cryptology ePrint Archive, Paper 2025/1047 (2025). https://eprint.iacr.org/2025/1047

25. Castryck, W., Lange, T., Martindale, C., Panny, L., Renes, J.: CSIDH: an efficient post-quantum commutative group action. In: Peyrin, T., Galbraith, S. (eds.) ASIACRYPT 2018, Part III. LNCS, vol. 11274, pp. 395–427. Springer, Cham (Dec 2018). https://doi.org/10.1007/978-3-030-03332-3_15

26. Castryck, W., Sotáková, J., Vercauteren, F.: Breaking the decisional Diffie-Hellman problem for class group actions using genus theory: Extended version. J. Cryptol. **35**(4), 24 (2022). https://doi.org/10.1007/s00145-022-09435-1

27. Cervantes-Vázquez, D., et al.: Stronger and faster side-channel protections for CSIDH. In: Schwabe, P., Thériault, N. (eds.) LATINCRYPT 2019. LNCS, vol. 11774, pp. 173–193. Springer, Cham (Oct 2019). https://doi.org/10.1007/978-3-030-30530-7_9

28. Chávez-Saab, J., Chi-Domínguez, J.J., Jaques, S., Rodríguez-Henríquez, F.: The SQALE of CSIDH: sublinear Vélu quantum-resistant isogeny action with low exponents. J. Cryptogr. Eng. **12**(3), 349–368 (2022). https://doi.org/10.1007/s13389-021-00271-w

29. Chen, M., Lai, Y.F., Laval, A., Marco, L., Petit, C.: Malleable commitments from group actions and zero-knowledge proofs for circuits based on isogenies. In: Chattopadhyay, A., Bhasin, S., Picek, S., Rebeiro, C. (eds.) INDOCRYPT 2023, Part I. LNCS, vol. 14459, pp. 221–243. Springer, Cham (Dec 2023). https://doi.org/10.1007/978-3-031-56232-7_11

30. Chen, M., Leroux, A., Panny, L.: SCALLOP-HD: group action from 2-dimensional isogenies. In: Tang, Q., Teague, V. (eds.) PKC 2024, Part II. LNCS, vol. 14603, pp. 190–216. Springer, Cham (Apr 2024). https://doi.org/10.1007/978-3-031-57725-3_7

31. Chenu, M., Smith, B.: Higher-degree supersingular group actions. Cryptology ePrint Archive, Report 2021/955 (2021). https://eprint.iacr.org/2021/955

32. Chi-Domínguez, J.J., Reijnders, K.: Fully projective radical isogenies in constant-time. In: Galbraith, S.D. (ed.) CT-RSA 2022. LNCS, vol. 13161, pp. 73–95. Springer, Cham (Mar 2022). https://doi.org/10.1007/978-3-030-95312-6_4

33. Colò, L., Kohel, D.: Orienting supersingular isogeny graphs. J. Math. Cryptol. **14**, 414–437 (2020). https://doi.org/10.1515/jmc-2019-0034

34. Conrad, K.: The conductor ideal of an order. https://kconrad.math.uconn.edu/blurbs/gradnumthy/conductor.pdf

35. Couveignes, J.M.: Hard homogeneous spaces. Cryptology ePrint Archive, Report 2006/291 (2006). https://eprint.iacr.org/2006/291

36. Cox, D.A.: Primes of the form $x^2 + ny^2$: Fermat, Class Field Theory, and Complex Multiplication, Pure and Applied Mathematics, vol. 116. Wiley, 2nd edn. (2013)

37. Cozzo, D., Smart, N.P.: Sashimi: cutting up CSI-FiSh secret keys to produce an actively secure distributed signing protocol. In: Ding, J., Tillich, J.P. (eds.) Post-

Quantum Cryptography - 11th International Conference, PQCrypto 2020, pp. 169–186. Springer, Cham (2020). https://doi.org/10.1007/978-3-030-44223-1_10

38. Dartois, P.: Fast computation of 2-isogenies in dimension 4 and cryptographic applications. Cryptology ePrint Archive, Report 2024/1180 (2024). https://eprint.iacr.org/2024/1180

39. Dartois, P., De Feo, L.: On the security of OSIDH. In: Hanaoka, G., Shikata, J., Watanabe, Y. (eds.) PKC 2022, Part I. LNCS, vol. 13177, pp. 52–81. Springer, Cham (Mar 2022). https://doi.org/10.1007/978-3-030-97121-2_3

40. Dartois, P., Duparc, M.: Chasing rabbits through hypercubes: better algorithms for higher dimensional 2-isogeny computations. Cryptology ePrint Archive, Paper 2026/114 (2026). https://eprint.iacr.org/2026/114

41. Dartois, P., et al.: PEGASIS: practical effective class group action using 4-dimensional isogenies. In: Kalai, Y.T., Kamara, S.F. (eds.) CRYPTO 2025, Part I. LNCS, vol. 16000, pp. 67–99. Springer, Cham (Aug 2025). https://doi.org/10.1007/978-3-032-01855-7_3

42. Dartois, P., Leroux, A., Robert, D., Wesolowski, B.: SQISignHD: new dimensions in cryptography. Cryptology ePrint Archive, Report 2023/436 (2023). https://eprint.iacr.org/2023/436

43. De Feo, L., et al.: SCALLOP: scaling the CSI-FiSh. In: Boldyreva, A., Kolesnikov, V. (eds.) PKC 2023, Part I. LNCS, vol. 13940, pp. 345–375. Springer, Cham (May 2023). https://doi.org/10.1007/978-3-031-31368-4_13

44. De Feo, L., Leroux, A., Longa, P., Wesolowski, B.: New algorithms for the deuring correspondence - towards practical and secure SQISign signatures. In: Hazay, C., Stam, M. (eds.) EUROCRYPT 2023, Part V. LNCS, vol. 14008, pp. 659–690. Springer, Cham (Apr 2023). https://doi.org/10.1007/978-3-031-30589-4_23

45. De Feo, L., Meyer, M.: Threshold schemes from isogeny assumptions. In: Kiayias, A., Kohlweiss, M., Wallden, P., Zikas, V. (eds.) PKC 2020, Part II. LNCS, vol. 12111, pp. 187–212. Springer, Cham (May 2020). https://doi.org/10.1007/978-3-030-45388-6_7

46. Delpech de Saint Guilhem, C., Pedersen, R.: New proof systems and an OPRF from CSIDH. In: Tang, Q., Teague, V. (eds.) PKC 2024, Part II. LNCS, vol. 14603, pp. 217–251. Springer, Cham (Apr 2024). https://doi.org/10.1007/978-3-031-57725-3_8

47. Dobson, S., Galbraith, S.D., LeGrow, J., Ti, Y.B., Zobernig, L.: An adaptive attack on 2-SIDH. Int. J. Comput. Math. Comput. Syst. Theor. 6(4), 387–404 (2021). https://doi.org/10.1080/23799927.2021.2018115

48. Dobson, S., Li, T., Zobernig, L.: A note on a static SIDH protocol. Cryptology ePrint Archive, Report 2019/1244 (2019). https://eprint.iacr.org/2019/1244

49. Eriksen, J.K., Leroux, A.: Computing orientations from the endomorphism ring of supersingular curves and applications. CiC 1(3), 5 (2024). https://doi.org/10.62056/ae0fhbmo

50. Fouotsa, T.B., Petit, C.: SHealS and HealS: isogeny-based PKEs from a key validation method for SIDH. In: Tibouchi, M., Wang, H. (eds.) ASIACRYPT 2021, Part IV. LNCS, vol. 13093, pp. 279–307. Springer, Cham (Dec 2021). https://doi.org/10.1007/978-3-030-92068-5_10

51. Fouotsa, T.B., Petit, C.: A new adaptive attack on SIDH. In: Galbraith, S.D. (ed.) CT-RSA 2022. LNCS, vol. 13161, pp. 322–344. Springer, Cham (Mar 2022). https://doi.org/10.1007/978-3-030-95312-6_14

52. Gajland, P., de Kock, B., Quaresma, M., Malavolta, G., Schwabe, P.: SWOOSH: efficient lattice-based non-interactive key exchange. In: Balzarotti, D., Xu, W.

(eds.) USENIX Security 2024. USENIX Association (Aug 2024). https://www.usenix.org/conference/usenixsecurity24/presentation/gajland

53. Galbraith, S., Gilchrist, V., Robert, D.: Improved algorithms for ascending isogeny volcanoes, and applications. Cryptology ePrint Archive, Paper 2025/1243 (2025). https://eprint.iacr.org/2025/1243

54. Galbraith, S., Panny, L., Smith, B., Vercauteren, F.: Quantum equivalence of the DLP and CDHP for group actions. Cryptology ePrint Archive, Report 2018/1199 (2018). https://eprint.iacr.org/2018/1199

55. Galbraith, S.D., Hess, F., Smart, N.P.: Extending the GHS Weil descent attack. In: Knudsen, L.R. (ed.) EUROCRYPT 2002. LNCS, vol. 2332, pp. 29–44. Springer, Berlin, Heidelberg (Apr/May 2002). https://doi.org/10.1007/3-540-46035-7_3

56. Galbraith, S.D., Lai, Y.F.: Attack on SHealS and HealS: the second wave of GPST. In: Cheon, J.H., Johansson, T. (eds.) Post-Quantum Cryptography - 13th International Workshop, PQCrypto 2022. pp. 399–421. Springer, Cham (Sep 2022). https://doi.org/10.1007/978-3-031-17234-2_19

57. Galbraith, S.D., Petit, C., Shani, B., Ti, Y.B.: On the security of supersingular isogeny cryptosystems. In: Cheon, J.H., Takagi, T. (eds.) ASIACRYPT 2016, Part I. LNCS, vol. 10031, pp. 63–91. Springer, Heidelberg (Dec 2016). https://doi.org/10.1007/978-3-662-53887-6_3

58. Grover, L.K.: A fast quantum mechanical algorithm for database search. In: 28th ACM STOC. pp. 212–219. ACM Press (May 1996). https://doi.org/10.1145/237814.237866

59. Hanzlik, L., Lai, Y.F., Mula, M., Paracucchi, E., Slamanig, D., Tang, G.: Tanuki: new frameworks for (concurrently secure) blind signatures from post-quantum groups actions. Cryptology ePrint Archive, Paper 2025/1100 (2025). https://eprint.iacr.org/2025/1100

60. Heimberger, L., Hennerbichler, T., Meisingseth, F., Ramacher, S., Rechberger, C.: OPRFs from isogenies: designs and analysis. In: Zhou, J., Quek, T.Q.S., Gao, D., Cárdenas, A.A. (eds.) ASIACCS 24. ACM Press (Jul 2024). https://doi.org/10.1145/3634737.3645010

61. Houben, M.: Deterministic algorithms for class group actions. In: Kalai, Y.T., Kamara, S.F. (eds.) CRYPTO 2025, Part I. LNCS, vol. 16000, pp. 100–130. Springer, Cham (Aug 2025). https://doi.org/10.1007/978-3-032-01855-7_4

62. Houben, M.: Efficient post-quantum commutative group actions from orientations of large discriminant. Cryptology ePrint Archive, Paper 2025/1098 (2025). https://eprint.iacr.org/2025/1098

63. Katsumata, S., Lai, Y.F., LeGrow, J.T., Qin, L.: CSI-Otter: isogeny-based (partially) blind signatures from the class group action with a twist. In: Handschuh, H., Lysyanskaya, A. (eds.) CRYPTO 2023, Part III. LNCS, vol. 14083, pp. 729–761. Springer, Cham (Aug 2023). https://doi.org/10.1007/978-3-031-38548-3_24

64. Kopp, G.S., Lagarias, J.C.: Class field theory for orders of number fields (2022). https://arxiv.org/abs/2212.09177

65. Kunzweiler, S., Ti, Y.B., Weitkämper, C.: Secret keys in genus-2 SIDH. In: AlTawy, R., Hülsing, A. (eds.) SAC 2021. LNCS, vol. 13203, pp. 483–507. Springer, Cham (Sep/Oct 2022). https://doi.org/10.1007/978-3-030-99277-4_23

66. Kuperberg, G.: A subexponential-time quantum algorithm for the dihedral hidden subgroup problem. SIAM J. Comput. **35**(1), 170–188 (2005)

67. Kuperberg, G.: Another subexponential-time quantum algorithm for the dihedral hidden subgroup problem. In: 8th Conference on the Theory of Quantum Computation, Communication and Cryptography (TQC 2013). Leibniz International

Proceedings in Informatics (LIPIcs), vol. 22, pp. 20–34. Schloss Dagstuhl–Leibniz-Zentrum fuer Informatik (2013). https://doi.org/10.4230/LIPIcs.TQC.2013.20, http://drops.dagstuhl.de/opus/volltexte/2013/4321

68. Lai, Y.F., Galbraith, S.D., Delpech de Saint Guilhem, C.: Compact, efficient and UC-secure isogeny-based oblivious transfer. In: Canteaut, A., Standaert, F.X. (eds.) EUROCRYPT 2021, Part I. LNCS, vol. 12696, pp. 213–241. Springer, Cham (Oct 2021). https://doi.org/10.1007/978-3-030-77870-5_8

69. LeGrow, J., Hutchinson, A.: An analysis of fault attacks on CSIDH. Cryptology ePrint Archive, Report 2020/1006 (2020). https://eprint.iacr.org/2020/1006

70. LeGrow, J.T.: A faster method for fault attack resistance in static/ephemeral CSIDH. J. Cryptogr. Eng. **13**(3), 283–294 (2023). https://doi.org/10.1007/s13389-023-00318-0

71. LeGrow, J.T., Hutchinson, A.: (Short paper) analysis of a strong fault attack on static/ephemeral CSIDH. In: Nakanishi, T., Nojima, R. (eds.) IWSEC 21. LNCS, vol. 12835, pp. 216–226. Springer, Cham (Sep 2021). https://doi.org/10.1007/978-3-030-85987-9_12

72. Leroux, A., Roméas, M.: Updatable encryption from group actions. In: Saarinen, M.J., Smith-Tone, D. (eds.) Post-Quantum Cryptography - 15th International Workshop, PQCrypto 2024, Part II. pp. 20–53. Springer, Cham (Jun 2024). https://doi.org/10.1007/978-3-031-62746-0_2

73. Levin, S., Pedersen, R.: Faster proofs and VRFs from isogenies. Cryptology ePrint Archive, Report 2024/1626 (2024). https://eprint.iacr.org/2024/1626

74. Lim, D., Ti, Y.B.: Adaptive attack on static POKÉ keys. Cryptology ePrint Archive, Paper 2025/1541 (2025). https://eprint.iacr.org/2025/1541

75. Meers, J., Riepel, D.: CCA secure updatable encryption from non-mappable group actions. In: Saarinen, M.J., Smith-Tone, D. (eds.) Post-Quantum Cryptography - 15th International Workshop, PQCrypto 2024, Part I. pp. 137–169. Springer, Cham (Jun 2024). https://doi.org/10.1007/978-3-031-62743-9_5

76. Meyer, M., Campos, F., Reith, S.: On lions and elligators: an efficient constant-time implementation of CSIDH. In: Ding, J., Steinwandt, R. (eds.) Post-Quantum Cryptography - 10th International Conference, PQCrypto 2019. pp. 307–325. Springer, Cham (2019). https://doi.org/10.1007/978-3-030-25510-7_17

77. Meyer, M., Reith, S.: A faster way to the CSIDH. In: Chakraborty, D., Iwata, T. (eds.) INDOCRYPT 2018. LNCS, vol. 11356, pp. 137–152. Springer, Cham (Dec 2018). https://doi.org/10.1007/978-3-030-05378-9_8

78. Montgomery, H., Sharif, S.: Quantum money from class group actions on elliptic curves. In: Chung, K.M., Sasaki, Y. (eds.) ASIACRYPT 2024, Part IX. LNCS, vol. 15492, pp. 33–64. Springer, Singapore (Dec 2024). https://doi.org/10.1007/978-981-96-0947-5_2

79. Moriya, T., Onuki, H.: The wrong use of FESTA trapdoor functions leads to an adaptive attack. Cryptology ePrint Archive, Report 2023/1092 (2023). https://eprint.iacr.org/2023/1092

80. Moriya, T., Onuki, H., Takagi, T.: SiGamal: a supersingular isogeny-based PKE and its application to a PRF. In: Moriai, S., Wang, H. (eds.) ASIACRYPT 2020, Part II. LNCS, vol. 12492, pp. 551–580. Springer, Cham (Dec 2020). https://doi.org/10.1007/978-3-030-64834-3_19

81. Moriya, T., Onuki, H., Xu, M., Zhou, G.: Adaptive attacks against FESTA without input validation or constant-time implementation. In: Saarinen, M.J., Smith-Tone, D. (eds.) Post-Quantum Cryptography - 15th International Workshop, PQCrypto 2024, Part II. pp. 3–19. Springer, Cham (Jun 2024). https://doi.org/10.1007/978-3-031-62746-0_1

82. Morrison, T., Panny, L., Sotáková, J., Wills, M.: The sea algorithm for endomorphisms of supersingular elliptic curves (2025). https://arxiv.org/abs/2501.16321
83. Onuki, H.: On oriented supersingular elliptic curves. Finite Fields Appl. **69**, 101777 (2021). https://doi.org/10.1016/j.ffa.2020.101777
84. Page, A., Robert, D.: Introducing clapoti(s): evaluating the isogeny class group action in polynomial time. Cryptology ePrint Archive, Report 2023/1766 (2023). https://eprint.iacr.org/2023/1766
85. Panny, L., Petit, C., Stopar, M.: KLaPoTi: an asymptotically efficient isogeny group action from 2-dimensional isogenies. Cryptology ePrint Archive, Report 2024/1844 (2024). https://eprint.iacr.org/2024/1844
86. Peikert, C.: He gives C-sieves on the CSIDH. In: Canteaut, A., Ishai, Y. (eds.) EUROCRYPT 2020, Part II. LNCS, vol. 12106, pp. 463–492. Springer, Cham (May 2020). https://doi.org/10.1007/978-3-030-45724-2_16
87. Regev, O.: A subexponential time algorithm for the dihedral hidden subgroup problem with polynomial space (2004). https://arxiv.org/pdf/quant-ph/0406151
88. Robert, D.: The module action for isogeny based cryptography. Cryptology ePrint Archive, Report 2024/1556 (2024). https://eprint.iacr.org/2024/1556
89. Robert, D.: On the efficient representation of isogenies (a survey). Cryptology ePrint Archive, Report 2024/1071 (2024). https://eprint.iacr.org/2024/1071
90. Rostovtsev, A., Stolbunov, A.: Public-key cryptosystem based on isogenies. Cryptology ePrint Archive, Report 2006/145 (2006). https://eprint.iacr.org/2006/145
91. Siegel, C.: Über die classenzahl quadratischer zahlkörper. Acta Arith **1**(1), 83–86 (1935). https://doi.org/eudml.org/doc/205054
92. Sutherland, A.: Isogeny volcanoes. Open Book Ser. **1**(1), 507–530 (2013). https://doi.org/10.2140/obs.2013.1.507
93. Sutherland, A.: Lecture notes for MIT course 18.783: Elliptic Curves (2023). https://math.mit.edu/classes/18.783/2023/LectureNotes17.pdf
94. Wesolowski, B.: Orientations and the supersingular endomorphism ring problem. In: Dunkelman, O., Dziembowski, S. (eds.) EUROCRYPT 2022, Part III. LNCS, vol. 13277, pp. 345–371. Springer, Cham (May / Jun 2022). https://doi.org/10.1007/978-3-031-07082-2_13
95. Zhou, G., Xu, M.: An efficient adaptive attack against FESTA. Cryptology ePrint Archive, Report 2024/345 (2024). https://eprint.iacr.org/2024/345

Cryptographic Protocols and PQC Transition

A Practical Framework for Lattice-Based Non-interactive Publicly Verifiable Secret Sharing

Behzad Abdolmaleki[1(✉)], John Clark[1], Mohammad Foroutani[2], Shahram Khazaei[2], and Sajjad Nasirzadeh[2]

[1] University of Sheffield, Sheffield, UK
{behzad.abdolmaleki,john.clark}@sheffield.ac.uk
[2] Sharif University of Technology, Tehran, Iran
shahram.khazaei@sharif.edu

Abstract. Non-interactive publicly verifiable secret sharing (PVSS) schemes enable the decentralized (re-)sharing of secrets in adversarial environments, allowing anyone to verify the correctness of distributed shares. Such schemes are essential for large-scale decentralized applications, including committee-based systems that require both transparency and robustness. However, existing PVSS schemes rely on group-based cryptography, making them vulnerable to quantum attacks and limiting their suitability for post-quantum applications.

In this work, we propose the first practical, fully lattice-based, non-interactive PVSS scheme, grounded on standard lattice assumptions for post-quantum security. At the heart of our design lies a generic framework that transforms vector commitments and linear encryption schemes into practical PVSS protocols. We enhance vector commitments by incorporating proof of smallness, ensuring that encrypted shares are both verifiable and privacy-preserving. Our scheme introduces two tailored lattice-based encryption schemes, each supporting efficient proofs of decryption correctness. This framework provides strong verifiability guarantees while maintaining low proof sizes and computational efficiency.

Keywords: PVSS · Lattice-Based Cryptography · Post-Quantum Cryptography · Vector Commitment

1 Introduction

Publicly verifiable secret sharing (PVSS) schemes enable a dealer to distribute a secret among multiple participants, in such a way that anyone – not only the participants – can verify the correctness of the distributed shares [25]. PVSS protocols are foundational components in decentralized cryptographic systems, including distributed key generation, threshold signatures, and committee-based consensus protocols [3,8]. As decentralized systems continue to scale, efficient

© The Author(s), under exclusive license to Springer Nature Switzerland AG 2026
M. Bardet and R. Niederhagen (Eds.): PQCrypto 2026, LNCS 16492, pp. 107–142, 2026.
https://doi.org/10.1007/978-3-032-22698-3_4

PVSS schemes become critical to maintain transparency, robustness against malicious dealers, and scalability to large committees.

A fundamental property of PVSS is *public verifiability*. This ensures that any party, not just the participants, can audit the distribution process and detect any misbehavior by the dealer. Public verifiability is particularly crucial in open, decentralized environments where trust assumptions are minimal, and external observers must independently verify the integrity of the secret sharing process. However, many existing constructions rely heavily on pairing-based cryptography or group-based assumptions to achieve this property, which leads to substantial computational costs and large proof sizes [4,5,7,10,11,13,23,24]. These inefficiencies hinder scalability, especially in systems with large committees.

Another critical requirement is *compactness of proofs*. In decentralized networks involving thousands of participants, the size of the proofs associated with each share directly impacts communication overhead and verification efficiency. Most recently, there have been efforts to design more efficient and compact PVSS schemes [3,8]. However, these constructions still rely on group-based primitives and discrete logarithm assumptions, leaving them vulnerable to quantum attacks and limiting their suitability for post-quantum applications.

Post-quantum security is increasingly vital in the era of quantum computing. Cryptographic schemes based on traditional hardness assumptions, such as the discrete logarithm or factoring problems, are rendered insecure against quantum adversaries. Unfortunately, most PVSS constructions to date rely on these vulnerable foundations, leaving future decentralized systems exposed to potential quantum attacks. Lattice-based cryptography, founded on hard problems such as the Learning With Errors (LWE) and Short Integer Solution (SIS) problems [1,6,16,18,20,21], provides a promising post-quantum secure alternative. However, designing efficient, publicly verifiable, and compact PVSS schemes based solely on lattice assumptions remains an open challenge. An important step towards lattice-based PVSS was made by Gentry *et al.* [11], who proposed a PVSS construction at EUROCRYPT 2022 that partially incorporates lattice-based primitives. Their scheme combines LWE-based encryption with a discrete-logarithm-based proof system. While this hybrid design improves efficiency and introduces lattice techniques into PVSS, it falls short of achieving full post-quantum security. Specifically, because the underlying proof system relies on DL-based assumptions, the security of the overall scheme is compromised in the presence of quantum adversaries. In their work, Gentry *et al.* explicitly identified the construction of an efficient, fully lattice-based PVSS scheme as an open problem.

Finally, *modularity and flexibility* of the construction are highly desirable features for PVSS schemes. A modular design enables flexible instantiation of building blocks, allowing protocol designers to adapt the scheme for varying performance and security requirements. Yet, achieving such modularity in the lattice setting while preserving efficiency and strong security properties poses significant technical difficulties.

With all of this in mind, it is interesting to ask the following question:

Can we design a non-interactive, PVSS scheme that simultaneously achieves post-quantum security, compact and efficient proofs, and modularity to support large-scale decentralized systems?

In this work, we answer this question affirmatively by introducing the first fully *lattice-based*, practical, non-interactive PVSS scheme. Our design departs from traditional group-based approaches and instead builds a modular framework that composes vector commitments with linear encryption schemes. At the core of our framework lies a *generic framework* that transforms any compatible vector commitment and encryption scheme into a PVSS protocol, providing both correctness and public verifiability. We enhance vector commitments by adopting *proof of smallness* property. Proof of smallness guarantees that the committed values remain within prescribed bounds, that is essential for verifiability in the lattice setting. To instantiate our framework concretely, we also propose two lattice-based encryption schemes, each supporting efficient zero-knowledge proofs of decryption correctness and public key validity.

1.1   Our Contributions

We make several contributions towards constructing a practical, fully lattice-based PVSS scheme. Our results advance the state of the art in both the theoretical understanding and practical deployment of PVSS protocols, particularly in the post-quantum setting. Our contributions are summarized as follows:

- **A generic framework for PVSS construction.** We develop a modular framework that generically composes vector commitments and linear encryption schemes into a PVSS protocol. Our framework requires the encryption scheme to support efficient proofs of correct decryption and public key validity, and the vector commitment to satisfy linear opening, functional hiding, and proof of smallness properties. This modularity allows our scheme to flexibly accommodate different cryptographic primitives, making it adaptable to a variety of performance and security trade-offs.
- **Two adopted lattice-based encryption schemes.** To instantiate our framework, we design and adapt two lattice-based linear encryption schemes that fit efficiently within our PVSS framework. In one scheme, the structural form of the public key inherently guarantees its validity under the SIS assumption, removing the explicit key verification step and its proof overhead. It represents a novel simplification that replaces key verification with inherent validity derived from lattice structure, improving efficiency without weakening verifiability. The second, ring-based encryption scheme employs lattice identification protocols for key generation and decryption proofs, achieving greater computational efficiency in the random oracle model.
- **Enhanced linear vector commitment with proof of smallness.** We introduce a new definition of *Linear Vector Commitment with Proof of Smallness (LVC-PoS)*. This definition enables vector commitment schemes to support linear evaluations together with proofs of smallness that is degree-2

relation. Specifically, we adapt the existing VC construction to fit this new formulation by incorporating a proof of smallness mechanism that enables the prover to efficiently demonstrate that the committed values lie within a bounded range. This enhancement is essential for ensuring both correctness and soundness in our lattice-based PVSS construction.

- **Fully lattice-based, practical PVSS instantiations.** Using our proposed framework, we instantiate the *first fully lattice-based* PVSS constructions, achieving post-quantum security under standard (Ring) − LWE and SIS assumptions. These instantiations combine our enhanced vector commitment and the adapted linear encryption schemes to form complete, publicly verifiable secret sharing protocols. The first instantiation operates entirely in the standard model without relying on any random oracle, demonstrating that full verifiability and correctness can be achieved purely from structural validity and lattice hardness. To further enhance efficiency, we also instantiate a second PVSS in the random oracle model, leveraging identification-based proofs to achieve lower computational and communication overhead. Together, these results show that our framework unifies theoretical soundness and practical efficiency, marking the first instantiation of fully lattice-based PVSS schemes across both cryptographic models.

1.2   Our Technical Overview

Our central contribution is the design of the *first PVSS construction based entirely on standard lattice assumptions*, achieved through a *generic framework* that transforms any suitable combination of a *Vector Commitment (VC)* scheme and a *linear encryption scheme* into a secure and publicly verifiable secret sharing protocol. This framework enables instantiations fully grounded on standard lattice assumptions, providing a post-quantum secure solution for decentralized secret sharing. Below, we describe the essential components and technical choices underlying our construction, detailing both the cryptographic primitives and the intuition behind their integration.

Vector Commitments with Proof of Smallness. At the heart of our design lies on enhanced *vector commitment* scheme, which the dealer uses to commit to a vector $\mathbf{x}$ containing: (i) The secret-sharing polynomial coefficients $\mathbf{a}$, (ii) The computed shares s_i, (iii) The encryption randomness values r_i.

The commitment ensures that the dealer cannot alter these values post-commitment (binding), and the opening proof attests that all entries of $\mathbf{x}$ satisfy a consistency function M, verifying both the correct computation of shares and the encryption of these shares under participants' public keys. The details of the polynomial interpolation used in Shamir's scheme are recalled in Appendix A.3

To reinforce this commitment, we extend linear VC definition with *Proof of Smallness* property. In lattice-based setting, bounding the norm of committed values is crucial. The proof of smallness is used to verify that the dealer has encrypted the shares correctly. We incorporate efficient proof that all secret entries of $\mathbf{x}$, notably share values s_i and randomness r_i, are bounded by a parameter β, ensuring: $\|\mathbf{x}_s\| \leq \beta \ \ \forall s \in$ S, where S is the index set of sensitive components. Our instantiation built upon the VC of Albrecht *et al.* [2], which inherently satisfies functional hiding for linear function families precisely matching the requirement of our framework. We extend this scheme to additionally support the proof-of-smallness property efficiently within our construction.

Linear Encryption with Proof of Decryption Correctness. Next, we employ a family of *linear encryption scheme* based on Regev encryption, see Appendix A.2, that is fully compatible with our vector commitment structure and support efficient zero-knowledge proofs of correct decryption. For any message m, randomness r, and public key pk, encryption takes the form:

$$\mathcal{E}.\mathsf{Encrypt}(\mathcal{E}.\mathsf{pp}, \mathsf{pk}, m, r) = m \cdot \mathbf{G} + r \cdot \mathbf{A}$$

where $\mathbf{G}$ is a fixed public gadget matrix (or ring element in the polynomial setting), and $\mathbf{A}$ is part of the public parameters or public key. To enable public verification of decryption correctness, the scheme provides:

- $\mathcal{E}.\mathsf{ProveDecrypt}(\mathsf{sk}; (\mathsf{pk}, m, C))$ – the decryptor generates a non-interactive proof that C decrypts to message m, without revealing the secret key sk.
- $\mathcal{E}.\mathsf{VerifyDecrypt}(\mathsf{pk}, m, C, \mathsf{pf})$ – any verifier can efficiently check the validity of this decryption proof pf.

Correctness requires that honestly generated proofs always verify, while soundness ensures no adversary can produce valid (m, pf_{Dec}) inconsistent with any secret key. We instantiate this encryption component using two adapted lattice-based schemes described in Sects. 4.2 and 4.3:

- For the scheme in Algorithm 4, the decryptor reveals r to prove decryption correctness via: $C - m \cdot \mathbf{G} = r \cdot \mathbf{A}$., More precisely encryption produces $(\mathbf{U}, \mathbf{h}, \mathbf{C})$, and the decryptor uses the lattice trapdoor td , for more details see Appendix A.1, to sample a short preimage consistent with $\mathbf{A}$:

$$\mathbf{B}' = \mathsf{SampPre}(\mathrm{td}, \mathbf{U}, \alpha), \qquad \mathbf{e} = \mathbf{h}^\top \cdot \mathbf{B}' + \mathrm{m} \cdot \mathbf{g}^\top - \mathbf{C}.$$

The decryption proof is $\mathsf{pf}_{Dec} = (\mathbf{B}', \mathbf{e})$, demonstrating that all relations from the encryption step are satisfied. Any verifier checks:

$$\mathbf{A} \cdot \mathbf{B} = \mathbf{U}, \quad \mathbf{h}^\top \cdot \mathbf{B}' + \mathbf{e}^\top + m \cdot \mathbf{g}^\top = \mathbf{C}, \quad \|\mathbf{B}'\|, \|\mathbf{e}\| < \alpha.$$

If all tests hold, C decrypts correctly.
- For the scheme in Algorithm 5, the linear structure is preserved in the polynomial ring $R = \mathbb{Z}[x]/(x^k + 1)$. Encryption outputs (c, c') with

$$c = r \cdot a + e, \qquad c' = r \cdot \mathsf{pk} + e' + \hat{m}\lfloor q/2 \rfloor,$$

where $\hat{m}$ encodes the message in polynomial form. During decryption, the decryptor computes $b = c \cdot s$ and derives the residual noise $e = b + \hat{m}\lfloor q/2 \rfloor - c'$.

To prove correctness publicly, the decryptor invokes the lattice identification protocol [16]: $\mathsf{pf}_{Dec} = \mathrm{id.prove}(c, b, s)$, for more detail see Appendix A.4. Verification checks relational validity through

$$b + e + \hat{m}\lfloor q/2 \rfloor = c', \quad \|e\| < \alpha, \quad \mathrm{id.verify}(c, b, \mathsf{pf}_{\mathrm{Dec}}).$$

The completeness, soundness, and zero-knowledge properties of the identification protocol ensure that every accepted proof corresponds to a genuine short secret s, establishing both key and decryption verifiability.

Both schemes balance compactness, efficiency, and post-quantum security, while supporting public verifiability.

SIS Based Structural Validity of Public Keys. A notable innovation in our framework appears in the first linear encryption instantiation (Algorithm 4), where we eliminate the key verification proof used in PVSS. When public keys follow the SIS form $\mathsf{pk} = \mathbf{A} \cdot \mathsf{sk}$ with sk sampled from a bounded domain, or as in this case for decryption we just need to sample a short preimage all we need in key verification is that public key fulfills the SIS conditions that from theorem 3.6 of [14] and so we just need to check properties of matrix $\mathbf{A}$.

Theorem 1.1 ([14]). *For any $d \geq 1$ and $\varepsilon(N) = N^{-\omega(1)}$, there is a probabilistic polynomial-time reduction from solving $\mathsf{ModGIVP}_\gamma^\infty$ in polynomial-time (in the worst case, with high probability) to solving $\mathsf{MSIS}_{q,n,m,\beta}$ in polynomial-time with non-negligible probability, for any $m(N), q(N), \beta(N), \gamma(N)$ such that*

$$\gamma \geq \beta\sqrt{N} \cdot \omega(\sqrt{\log N}), \quad q \geq \beta\sqrt{N} \cdot \omega(\log N), \quad n, \log q \leq poly(N).$$

This theorem guarantees the existence of a short preimage for any $\mathbf{A}$ and its finding hardness to achieve soundness. Thus, any syntactically valid $(\mathbf{A}, \mathsf{pk})$ pair inherently satisfies public key validity under the SIS assumption. This structural argument replaces key verification with correctness derived from lattice hardness itself, reducing setup communication and computation while preserving full public verifiability.

Our Generic framework: From Building Blocks to PVSS. We combine these primitives into a complete PVSS protocol through our generic framework. The workflow is as follows:

1. *Setup:* Initialize public parameters for Shamir secret sharing, vector commitments, and encryption schemes.
2. *Key Generation:* Each participant generates $(\mathsf{pk}_i, \mathsf{sk}_i)$ along with a proof $\mathsf{pf}_{\mathsf{Key},i}$ of valid key generation.
3. *Distribution:*
   - The dealer defines a polynomial $f(x)$ of degree t such that $f(0) = s$.
   - Compute shares $s_i = f(i)$ and encrypt them:

$$C_i = \mathcal{E}.\mathsf{Encrypt}(\mathcal{E}.\mathsf{pp}, \mathsf{pk}_i, s_i, r_i)$$

- Form the vector $\mathbf{x} = (\mathbf{a}, s_1, \ldots, s_n, r_1, \ldots, r_n)$, commit to $\mathbf{x}$, and generate an opening proof for:
  - Correctness of shares $s_i = f(i)$
  - Correctness of ciphertexts $C_i = \mathcal{E}.\mathsf{Encrypt}(\mathcal{E}.\mathsf{pp}, \mathsf{pk}_i, s_i, r_i)$
  - Proof of smallness for validation of encryption.

Notice that both f and $\mathcal{E}.\mathsf{Encrypt}$ are linear functions on vector $\mathbf{x}$ that fits our linear VC.

4. *Distribution Verification:* Any party verifies the dealer's commitment and opening proof, ensuring correct distribution.
5. *Decryption:* Each participant decrypts their ciphertext and produces a proof $\mathsf{pf}_{\mathsf{Dec},i}$ of correct decryption.
6. *Reconstruction:* Using Lagrange interpolation on decrypted shares s_i, any set of at least t participants can reconstruct the secret s.

1.3 Comparison

We present two PVSS instantiations within the same framework, each combining a VC scheme with a lattice-based encryption scheme. **Ours 1** uses the plain LWE encryption of Sect. 4.2 with the VC from Sect. 3.1, relying on the standard LWE assumption. **Ours 2** uses the compact ring-based encryption of Sect. 4.3 under $(\mathsf{Ring}) - \mathsf{LWE}$, yielding faster computation; for efficiency we use an identification protocol (in the random oracle model) for both key generation and decryption proofs.

Comparison with Prior Work. Let $\mathbb{G}$ be a cyclic group of order q (elements have $\log q$ bits); $\mathsf{op}_{\mathbb{G}}$ counts exponentiations in $\mathbb{G}$ and $\mathsf{op}_{\mathbb{Z}_q}$ counts arithmetic in $\mathbb{Z}_q$. Table 1 compares communication, computation, and assumptions against [7–9,11]. Our communication is $O(n \log q)$ (matching the best known), while computation is $O(n^2 \log q \cdot \mathsf{op}_{R_q})$ via a tight integration of lattice-based VCs, linear encryption, and efficient decryption-correctness proofs. Unlike group-based or hybrid-assumption schemes, ours relies only on standard lattice assumptions (notably $(\mathsf{Ring}) - \mathsf{LWE}$ and $\mathsf{k} - \mathsf{R} - \mathsf{ISIS}$) and the random oracle model, yielding post-quantum security.

Table 1. Comparisons.

Work	Communication	Computation	Secret	Assumptions
[7]	$O((n + \ell) \cdot \log q)$	$O((n^2 + n\ell + n \log^2 n) \cdot \mathsf{op}_{\mathbb{Z}_q})$	$\mathbb{G}^\ell$	DLOG+ROM
[11]	$O(n \cdot (u + v) \cdot \log q)$	$O(n \cdot (u + v) \log q)$	$\mathbb{Z}_q$	LWE+DLOG+ROM
[9]	$O(n \cdot \log q)$	$O(n \cdot \mathsf{op}_G + n \log^2 n \cdot \mathsf{op}_{\mathbb{Z}_q})$	G	DLOG+ROM
[8]	$O(n \cdot \log q)$	$O(n \cdot \mathsf{op}_G + n \log^2 n \cdot \mathsf{op}_{\mathbb{Z}_q})$	$\mathbb{Z}_q$	DLOG+ROM
Ours 1	$O(n \cdot \log^2 q)$	$O(n^2 \log^3 q \cdot \mathsf{op}_{R_q})$	$\mathbb{Z}_q$	LWE+k-R-ISIS
Ours 2	$O(n \cdot \log q)$	$O(n^2 \log q \cdot \mathsf{op}_{R_q})$	$\mathbb{Z}_q$	R-LWE+k-R-ISIS + ROM

Concurrent Work. In a concurrent work, Minh *et al.* [19] introduce a post-quantum secure PVSS framework based on the LWE assumption and trapdoor Σ-protocols, with security proven in the standard model. While achieving these desirable properties, their construction exhibits significant computational and communication overheads. Specifically, as indicated in their work (cf. Table 1), the communication complexity is $\Omega(n\lambda(u + v)\log q)$, and the total computational cost is $\Omega(\lambda(n^2 + nuv)) \cdot op_{\mathbb{Z}_q}$, where λ denotes the security parameter, q is the modulus, and u, v represent lattice dimensions. A further contributing factor to this high cost is the reliance on binary-challenge Σ-protocols, which necessitate λ parallel repetitions to achieve a negligible soundness error, thereby magnifying the overall expenses. Moreover, their parameterization, as detailed in Table 1 of their paper, suggests a modulus q on the order of $\lambda^{11}n$. Such a polynomial dependency of the modulus on the security parameter λ is uncharacteristic of typical cryptographic constructions and presents practical challenges. If λ is chosen towards the lower end of cryptographically secure values to maintain manageable costs, the λ^{11} scaling might result in a modulus q that offers insufficient concrete security, particularly against adversaries equipped with substantial computational power (e.g., supercomputers). Conversely, selecting a λ large enough to guarantee robust security would lead to an exceptionally large modulus, further exacerbating the already considerable communication and computation costs, likely rendering the protocol impractical for many applications.

Table 2. Notation.

n	Number of participants
t	Reconstruction threshold
pp	Public parameters generated by Setup
$\mathsf{pk}_i, \mathsf{sk}_i$	Public/secret key of participant i
s_i	Secret share of participant i
C_i	Ciphertext encrypting s_i
$\mathsf{pf}_{\mathsf{Dec},i}$	Proof of correct decryption for participant i
ρ	Linear function evaluated in the vector commitment

In contrast, our construction is non-interactive by design and leverages efficient lattice-based components. We achieve a much tighter communication complexity of $O(n \cdot \log q)$ and computation complexity $O(n^2 \cdot \log q \cdot op_{R_q})$, while supporting compact proofs and practical efficiency. Our design avoids λ-fold repetition and achieves negligible soundness error through direct integration of proof-of-smallness techniques within vector commitments and verifiable linear encryption. This makes our protocol better suited for deployment in real-world post-quantum settings.

2   Preliminaries

Notation. Throughout, bold lowercase letters (e.g., $\mathbf{x}$) denote vectors and bold uppercase letters (e.g., $\mathbf{A}$) denote matrices; $\langle \cdot, \cdot \rangle$ is the standard inner product and $\circ$ is component-wise multiplication. We write $\mathbb{Z}_q$ for integers modulo q, $R^{\times}$ for the unit group of a ring R, $\mathcal{R}$ for the ring used in our lattice-based construction (e.g., $\mathbb{Z}_q^n$), and $\mathcal{K}$ for the base field. All algorithms are PPT unless stated otherwise; $x \leftarrow \mathcal{D}$ means sampling from distribution $\mathcal{D}$. The security parameter is λ and negligibility is with respect to λ. Notation is summarized in Table 2.

2.1   Publicly Verifiable Secret Sharing

We first present the definitions of a PVSS and security properties, where we mainly adopt the definitions from [8].

Definition 2.1 (Publicly Verifiable Secret Sharing). *A PVSS scheme consists of the following algorithms.*

Setup:

- pp $\leftarrow$ Setup($1^{\lambda}, 1^n, 1^t$): *The setup algorithm generates the public parameters on input of the security parameter $\lambda \in \mathbb{N}$, number of parties $n \in \mathbb{N}$ and reconstruction thresholds $t \in \mathbb{N}$. The public parameters include a description of spaces of secrets and shares S and spaces of private and public keys SK and PK and the relation $R_{Key} \subseteq PK \times SK$ describing valid key pairs.*
- $(\mathsf{sk}_i, \mathsf{pk}_i, \mathsf{pf}_{Key,i}) \leftarrow$ KeyGen(pp, i): *The key generation algorithm generates $(\mathsf{pk}_i, \mathsf{sk}_i) \in R_{Key}$ and proof $\mathsf{pf}_{Key,i}$ for identification of pk_i.*
- $b \leftarrow$ VerifyKey(pp, i, pk_i, $\mathsf{pf}_{Key,i}$): *The key verification algorithm outputs a bit b deciding whether to accept or reject that pk_i is a valid identification.*

Distribution: $((C_i)_{i \in [n]}, \mathsf{pf}_D) \leftarrow$ Dist(pp, $(\mathsf{pk}_i)_{i \in [n]}, s$) *The distribution algorithm outputs encrypted shares C_i and a proof pf_D of sharing correctness on input the secret $s \in S$.*

Distribution Verification: $b \leftarrow$ VerifyDist(pp, $(\mathsf{pk}_i, C_i)_{i \in [n]}, \mathsf{pf}_D$): *The distribution verification algorithm outputs a bit b deciding whether to accept or reject that for each i share C_i is valid.*

Reconstruction:

- $(s_i, \mathsf{pf}_{Dec,i}) \leftarrow$ Decrypt(pp, i, pk_i, sk_i, C_i): *The decrypt share algorithm outputs a decrypted share s_i and a proof $\mathsf{pf}_{Dec,i}$ of correct decryption.*
- $s' \leftarrow$ Reconstruct(pp, $\{s_i : i \in T\}$): *The reconstruction algorithm for some $T \subseteq [n]$ outputs an element of the secret space $s' \in S$ or an error symbol $\perp$.*
- $b \leftarrow$ VerifyDecrypt(pp, i, pk_i, $s_i C_i$, $\mathsf{pf}_{Dec,i}$): *The decryption verification algorithm outputs a bit b deciding whether to accept or reject that s_i is a valid decryption of C_i.*

Security Properties. We require a PVSS to satisfy correctness, verifiability and IND2-secrecy. We briefly summarize these here and defer the formal definitions to Appendix A.5.

Correctness. If all parties behave honestly, the protocol guarantees that:

- All verification procedures succeed, including key verification VerifyKey, distribution verification VerifyDist, and decryption verification VerifyDecrypt.
- Any set of at least t honest participants can successfully reconstruct the secret from their decrypted shares.

Verifiability. Itensures that all cryptographic objects are publicly verifiable:

- *Key verifiability:* Any public key is certified to correspond to a valid secret key via VerifyKey.
- *Distribution verifiability:* The dealer's distribution of encrypted shares and proof pf_D certifies correct sharing of the secret using VerifyDist.
- *Decryption verifiability:* Each decrypted share is accompanied by a proof of correctness, verified using VerifyDecrypt.

Privacy. We define indistinguishability of secrets against an adversary corrupting t parties, following [2]. The adversary may compute the corrupted parties' public keys after seeing those of the honest parties; given chosen (s_0, s_1) and a sharing of s_b, it has negligible advantage in guessing b. We adopt IND2-privacy (adversary-chosen secrets), which is stronger than IND1-privacy where the challenger samples the secrets at random.

Definition 2.2. *The PVSS is t-IND2-private if for any $poly(1^\lambda)$-time adversary $\mathcal{A}$ corrupting t parties (w.l.o.g. $\mathcal{A}$ corrupts $[n - t + 1, n]$), we have*

$$\Pr[\mathrm{Game}_{\mathcal{A},\mathrm{PVSS}}^{\mathrm{ind-secrecy},0}(\lambda) = 1] - \Pr[\mathrm{Game}_{\mathcal{A},\mathrm{PVSS}}^{\mathrm{ind-secrecy},1}(\lambda) = 1] = \mathrm{negl}(\lambda)$$

where for $b = 0, 1$, $\mathrm{Game}_{\mathcal{A},\mathrm{PVSS}}^{\mathrm{ind-secrecy},\mathrm{b}}(\lambda)$ is the following game:

- *The challenger runs $\mathsf{pp} \leftarrow \mathsf{Setup}(1^\lambda, 1^n, 1^t)$ and sends pp to $\mathcal{A}$.*
- *For $i \in [n - t]$, the challenger runs $(\mathsf{sk}_i, \mathsf{pk}_i, \mathsf{pf}_{Key,i}) \leftarrow \mathsf{KeyGen}(\mathsf{pp}, i)$ and sends all created $(\mathsf{pk}_i, \mathsf{pf}_{Key,i})$ to $\mathcal{A}$.*
- *For the corrupted parties, $\mathcal{A}$ creates $(\mathsf{pk}_i, \mathsf{pf}_{Key,i})_{i \in [n-t+1,n]} \leftarrow \mathcal{A}(\mathsf{pp}, (\mathsf{pk}_i, \mathsf{pf}_{Key,i})_{i \in [n-t]})$ and sends them to the challenger, together with two values s_0, s_1 in S.*
- *The challenger runs $\mathsf{VerifyKey}(\mathsf{pp}, i, \mathsf{pk}_i, \mathsf{pf}_{Key,i})$ for $i \in [n - t + 1, n]$. If any of these output 0 (reject), the challenger sends $\perp$ to $\mathcal{A}$.*
- *Otherwise, if all key verifications accept, the challenger runs $(C_1, \ldots, C_n, \mathsf{pf}_D) \leftarrow \mathsf{Dist}(\mathsf{pp}, \{\mathsf{pk}_i : i \in [n]\}, s_b)$, and sends $(C_1, \ldots, C_n, \mathsf{pf}_D)$ to $\mathcal{A}$.*
- *$\mathcal{A}$ outputs a guess $b' \in \{0, 1\}$.*

2.2   Linear Public Key Encryption

We describe here explicitly the encryption scheme as we use it in our protocol. Let $\mathcal{E} = (\mathsf{Setup}, \mathsf{KeyGen}, \mathsf{VerifyKey}, \mathsf{Encrypt}, \mathsf{Decrypt})$ be a public key encryption scheme. The results in this paper require linear encryption schemes with proofs of decryption correctness.

Proofs of Decryption Correctness [9]. We need proofs of decryption correctness, where of, the prover wants to keep its secret key hidden, i.e., proofs for the relation.

$$R_{\mathcal{E},\mathsf{Decrypt}} = \{(\mathsf{sk}; (\mathsf{pk}, m, c)) :$$

$$(\mathsf{pk}, \mathsf{sk}) \text{ is a valid key-pair for } \mathsf{Encrypt} \text{ and } m = \mathsf{Decrypt}(\mathsf{sk}, c)\}$$

Definition 2.3. *These algorithms are added to $\mathcal{E}$:*

- $\mathsf{pf}_{Dec} \leftarrow \mathsf{ProveDecrypt}(\mathsf{sk}; (\mathsf{pk}, m, C))$: *The proof of decryption correctness algorithm generates a proof* pf_{Dec}.
- $b \leftarrow \mathsf{VerifyDecrypt}(\mathsf{pk}, m, C, \mathsf{pf}_{Dec})$: *The decryption verification algorithm outputs a bit b deciding whether to accept or reject that m is a valid decryption of C.*

Definition 2.4. *The public key encryption scheme $\mathcal{E}$ satisfies verifiability of decryption if the following is satisfied: For every PPT $\mathcal{A}$,*

$$\Pr\left[\mathcal{E}.\mathsf{VerifyDecrypt}(\mathsf{pk}, m, C_i, \mathsf{pf}_{Dec}) = 1 \right.$$

$$\wedge \; \nexists \mathsf{sk} \in SK \; s.t. \; (m, \cdot) \leftarrow \mathcal{E}.\mathsf{Decrypt}(\mathsf{pp}, \mathsf{pk}, \mathsf{sk}, C)$$

$$\left. \Big| \; \mathsf{pp} \leftarrow \mathcal{E}.\mathsf{Setup}(1^\lambda, p), (\mathsf{pk}, m, C, \mathsf{pf}_{Dec}) \leftarrow \mathcal{A}(\mathsf{pp})\right] \; \text{is negligible in } \lambda.$$

If the prover knows the randomness under which the message was encrypted or recovers a valid randomness, the proving algorithm $\mathsf{ProveDecrypt}(\mathsf{sk}; (\mathsf{pk}, m, C))$ can simply output that randomness as pf_{Dec}; the verification $\mathsf{VerifyDecrypt}(\mathsf{pk}, m, C, \mathsf{pf}_{Dec})$ accepts if $\mathsf{Encrypt}(\mathsf{pk}, m; \mathsf{pf}_{Dec}) = C$. Alternatively, we leverage the identification protocol to prove the validity of decrypted shares. This ensures decrypted shares remain consistent with ciphertexts and the corresponding secret key, providing an additional layer of verifiability.

2.3   Vector Commitments

A vector commitment (VC) lets a committer bind to a vector and later prove correct openings at chosen indices. Formally, it consists of four PPT algorithms:

- $\mathsf{Setup}(1^\lambda, 1^v, 1^w, 1^o)$: A setup algorithm that generates public parameters pp given the security parameter λ and the dimensions of the function family.
- $\mathsf{Com}(\mathsf{pp}, \mathbf{x})$: A commitment algorithm that outputs a commitment c to a vector $\mathbf{x}$ along with auxiliary information aux.

- Open(pp, f, **z**, aux): It generates a proof π that the committed vector **x** satisfies $f(\mathbf{z}, \mathbf{x}) = \mathbf{y}$ for a given public input **z** and function f.
- Verify(pp, f, **z**, **y**, c, π): A verification algorithm that checks whether the proof π correctly certifies the claimed evaluation result.

A VC scheme must satisfy the following security properties:

- *Correctness:* Any honest commitment and proof must pass verification for correctly computed evaluations.
- *Binding:* An adversary must not be able to produce two valid openings of the same commitment to different outputs for the same function.
- *Functional Hiding:* The commitment and proof should reveal no more about the committed vector than what is implied by the evaluation outputs.

We defer to Appendix A.6 for the full formal definition.

3   New Framework: A Framework from VC to PVSS

In this section, we introduce a modular framework that builds publicly verifiable PVSS from a suitably structured vector commitment and a linear encryption scheme. We first formalize *Linear Vector Commitments with Proof of Smallness (LVC-PoS)*, a VC variant that supports proving smallness of designated vector components, which is essential for our construction. We then present the generic transformation from any LVC-PoS and compatible linear encryption to a PVSS protocol guaranteeing correctness, public verifiability, and privacy, specified in Algorithm 1 and analyzed in the following subsections. Finally, we discuss lattice-based instantiations in Sect. 4.

3.1   Linear Vector Commitments with Proof of Smallness

We now define our extended vector commitment scheme, *LVC-PoS*. This primitive extends conventional vector commitments by enforcing linearity of the supported function family and providing explicit proofs of smallness for specific components of the input vector. The smallness proofs are essential in scenarios where certain quadratic relations, such as ensuring the binary nature or bounded norm of vector components, must be enforced alongside linear function correctness. By embedding these proofs within the VC structure, we ensure that our framework preserves both soundness and efficiency. We formally define the LVC-PoS scheme and its security properties below.

Definition 3.1 (LVC-PoS). *A LVC-PoS scheme is parameterized by the families of linear functions over $\mathcal{R}$ and an input alphabet $\mathcal{X} \subseteq \mathcal{R}$:*

$$\mathcal{F} = \{\mathcal{F}_{v,w,o} \subseteq \{f : \mathcal{R}^v \times \mathcal{R}^w \to \mathcal{R}^o\}\}_{v,w,o \in \mathbb{N}}$$

$$and \quad \mathcal{Y} = \{\mathcal{Y}_{v,o} \subseteq \{y : \mathcal{R}^v \to \mathcal{R}^o\}\}_{v,o \in \mathbb{N}}$$

The parameters v, w, and o represent the dimensions of public inputs, secret inputs, and outputs of the function f, respectively. Here, $\mathcal{Y}$ defines the family of valid right-hand side functions (which may simply be constant functions representing a target vector). The LVC-PoS scheme consists of the PPT algorithms ($\mathsf{Setup}, \mathsf{Com}, \mathsf{Open}, \mathsf{Verify}$) *defined as follows:*

- $\mathsf{pp} \leftarrow \mathsf{Setup}(1^\lambda, 1^v, 1^w, 1^o, S, \beta_S)$: *Generate public parameters given the security parameter $\lambda \in \mathbb{N}$, dimensions $v, w, o \in \mathbb{N}$, a smallness bound β_S, and an index set $S = \{s_1, s_2, ..., s_k\}$ indicating the positions in the input vector $\mathbf{x}$ for which smallness proofs are required.*
- $(c, \mathsf{aux}) \leftarrow \mathsf{Com}(\mathsf{pp}, \mathbf{x})$: *Compute a commitment c to the vector $\mathbf{x} \in \mathcal{X}^w$, along with auxiliary opening information aux.*
- $\pi \leftarrow \mathsf{Open}(\mathsf{pp}, f, \mathbf{z}, \mathsf{aux})$: *Generate a proof π for function $f \in \mathcal{F}_{v,w,o}$ evaluated at public input $\mathbf{z} \in \mathcal{X}^v$, together with proofs that each indexed subvector $\mathbf{x}_s$ satisfies $\|\mathbf{x}_s\| \leq \beta_S$ for all $s \in S$.*
- $b \leftarrow \mathsf{Verify}(\mathsf{pp}, f, \mathbf{z}, y, c, \pi)$: *Given public parameters, function $f \in \mathcal{F}_{v,w,o}$, public input $\mathbf{z} \in \mathcal{X}^v$, a target function $y \in \mathcal{Y}_{v,o}$ (defining the claimed relationship), commitment c, and proof π, output a bit b that decides whether:*

$$f(\mathbf{z}, \mathbf{x}) = y(\mathbf{z}) \quad and \quad \forall s \in S, \ \|\mathbf{x}_s\| \leq \beta_S$$

Remark on Proof Structure. The proof π generated by the Open algorithm can be conceptually partitioned into two components:

- π_f: proof of correctness of the linear function evaluation.
- $\{\pi_s\}$: individual proofs of smallness for each subvector in S.

Thus, the proof can be expressed as $\pi = (\pi_f, \{\pi_s\})$. For efficiency, aggregation techniques can be employed to compress multiple proofs into a single compact proof, which is beneficial for reducing communication and verification overhead.

Definition 3.2 (Correctness). *An LVC-PoS scheme is* correct *if for any $\lambda, v, w, o \in \mathbb{N}$, any $\mathsf{pp} \in \mathsf{Setup}(1^\lambda, 1^v, 1^w, 1^o, S, \beta_S)$, any $(f, \mathbf{z}, \mathbf{x}, \mathbf{y}) \in \mathcal{F}_{v,w,o} \times \mathcal{X}^v \times \mathcal{X}^w \times \mathcal{Y}_{v,o}$ s.t.: $f(\mathbf{z}, \mathbf{x}) = \mathbf{y}(\mathbf{z})$ and $\forall s \in S, \ \|\mathbf{x}_s\| \leq \beta_S$ and for any $(c, \mathsf{aux}) \leftarrow \mathsf{Com}(\mathsf{pp}, \mathbf{x})$ and $\pi \leftarrow \mathsf{Open}(\mathsf{pp}, f, \mathbf{z}, \mathsf{aux})$, it holds that:*

$$\mathsf{Verify}(\mathsf{pp}, f, \mathbf{z}, \mathbf{y}, c, \pi) = 1$$

The notions of weak binding and functional hiding closely follow the standard definitions for vector commitments, which we recall in Appendix A.6. For clarity and self-containment, we also define them explicitly here.

Definition 3.3 (Weak Binding). *Let $\rho : \mathbb{N}^3 \to [0, 1]$. A LVC-PoS scheme for $(\mathcal{F}, \mathcal{X}, \mathcal{Y})$ is said to be* weakly binding *if for any pair of PPT adversary $\mathcal{A}$ and any $s, w \in poly(\lambda)$ it holds that $\rho(\lambda, v, w)$ is negligible in λ and the following expression is upper-bounded by $\rho(\lambda, v, w)$:*

$$\Pr\left[\begin{array}{l} \forall i \in \{0,1\}, \mathsf{Verify}(\mathsf{pp}, f_i, \mathbf{z}_i, \mathbf{y}_i, c, \pi_i) = 1, \\[2mm] \wedge f_0(\mathbf{z}_0, \cdot) = f_1(\mathbf{z}_1, \cdot) \wedge \mathbf{y}_0(\mathbf{z}_0) \neq \mathbf{y}_1(\mathbf{z}_0) \end{array} \,\middle|\, \begin{array}{l} \mathsf{pp} \leftarrow \mathsf{Setup}(1^\lambda, 1^v, 1^w, 1^o) \\[2mm] (c, (f_i, \mathbf{z}_i, \mathbf{y}_i, \pi_i)_{i=0}^1) \leftarrow \mathcal{A}(\mathsf{pp}) \end{array}\right]$$

Definition 3.4 (Functional Hiding). *An LVC-PoS scheme satisfies functional hiding if, given a commitment c and an opening proof π_f for a function f, no adversary can distinguish between commitments to different vectors $\mathbf{x}, \mathbf{x}' \in \mathcal{X}^w$, beyond what is revealed by $f(\mathbf{z}, \mathbf{x})$ and the smallness proofs.*

3.2   Framework from Vector Commitment to PVSS

Our framework transforms a VC scheme and a linear encryption into a PVSS protocol. The central idea is to commit to the dealer's secret shares, the associated encryption randomness, and the polynomial coefficients used for secret sharing, all within a single vector. This commitment, together with an opening proof, serves as a verifiable certificate of correct share generation and encryption.

Setup fixes the PVSS parameters: choose a prime p for Shamir sharing, instantiate the encryption to support plaintexts up to p^3, and set the vector dimension w to cover the secret, polynomial coefficients, shares, and encryption randomness. The output size o is chosen to enable verification of share and ciphertext correctness. Finally, generate the VC parameters for vectors of size w with corresponding proofs.

Key Generation. In this step, each participant generates their own encryption key pair along with a corresponding proof of correct key generation. These proofs ensure that the public keys are correctly formed and trustworthy, allowing all parties to verify the validity of the public encryption keys before they are used in the distribution of shares.

In this phase, the dealer samples a degree-t polynomial with secret as the constant term, computes shares by evaluation at each index, and encrypts each share under the corresponding public key using fresh randomness. The dealer then commits to a vector containing the polynomial coefficients, shares, and encryption randomness. The opening map $M(\mathbf{x})$ enforces consistency of (i) share correctness w.r.t. the polynomial and (ii) ciphertext correctness w.r.t. the encrypted share, and the dealer outputs the commitment together with an opening proof, yielding a publicly verifiable distribution proof.

Distribution Verification. Here, anyone recomputes $M(\mathbf{x})$ and checks the commitment and opening proof against the published ciphertexts and public parameters, ensuring the dealer correctly formed and encrypted the shares without trusting the dealer.

Decrypt Share. After distribution, each participant decrypts their ciphertext using the Decrypt Share procedure to recover their individual share. In addition to recovering the share, participants generate a decryption proof that certifies the correctness of their decryption relative to the original ciphertext. This decryption proof is crucial for ensuring the integrity of the reconstruction process, allowing other parties to verify that decrypted shares are valid.

Decryption Verification. The validity of each participant's decryption is checked using the Decryption Verification procedure. Verifiers use this step to confirm that the decrypted share corresponds correctly to the ciphertext and the participant's

---

Algorithm 1. PVSS Framework

---

procedure SETUP($1^\lambda, 1^n, 1^t$)

    Let $p = \text{poly}(\lambda)$ such that $n < p$, $\mathcal{E}.\text{pp} \leftarrow \mathcal{E}.\text{Setup}(1^\lambda, p^3)$, $w \leftarrow n(r+1) + t + 1$

    $o \leftarrow n(m+1)$, $\mathcal{VC}.\text{pp} \leftarrow \mathcal{VC}.\text{Setup}(1^\lambda, 1^v, 1^w, 1^o, \{n+t+2, \dots, w\}, \mathcal{E}.\text{pp}.\mathcal{R})$

    return $\text{pp} = (n, t, p, \mathcal{E}.\text{pp}, \mathcal{VC}.\text{pp})$

procedure KEY GENERATION(pp, i)

    $(\text{pk}_i, \text{sk}_i, \text{pf}_{Key,i}) \leftarrow \mathcal{E}.\text{KeyGen}(\mathcal{E}.\text{pp})$

    return $\text{sk}_i, \text{pk}_i, \text{pf}_{Key,i}$

procedure KEY VERIFICATION($\text{pp}, i, \text{pk}_i, \text{pf}_{Key,i}$)

    return $\mathcal{E}.\text{VerifyKey}(\mathcal{E}.\text{pp}, \text{pk}_i, \text{pf}_{Key,i})$

procedure DISTRIBUTION($\text{pp}, (\text{pk}_i), s$)

    $(a_1, \dots, a_t) \leftarrow \mathbb{Z}_p^t$ ▷ Coefficients of the secret-sharing polynomial

    $\mathbf{a} \leftarrow (s, a_1, \dots, a_t)$

    for $i = 1$ to n **do**

        $\mathbf{b}_i \leftarrow (1, i^1 \bmod p, \dots, i^t \bmod p)$ ▷ Vandermonde vector for evaluation at point i

        $s_i \leftarrow \langle \mathbf{b}_i, \mathbf{a} \rangle$ ▷ Share of participant i (polynomial evaluation at i)

        $r_i \leftarrow \mathcal{R}$

        $C_i \leftarrow \mathcal{E}.\text{Encrypt}(\mathcal{E}.\text{pp}, \text{pk}_i, s_i, r_i)$

    $\mathbf{x} \leftarrow (\mathbf{a}, s_1, \dots, s_n, r_1, \dots, r_n)$

    Define opening function:

$$M(\mathbf{x}) = \begin{cases} s_i = \langle \mathbf{b}_i, \mathbf{a} \rangle & \forall i \in [n] \\ \mathcal{E}.\text{Encrypt}(\mathcal{E}.\text{pp}, \text{pk}_i, s_i, r_i) = C_i & \forall i \in [n] \end{cases}$$

    $(c, \text{aux}) \leftarrow \mathcal{VC}.\text{Com}(\mathcal{VC}.\text{pp}, \mathbf{x})$

    $\text{pf} \leftarrow \mathcal{VC}.\text{Open}(\mathcal{VC}.\text{pp}, M, \bot, \text{aux})$ ▷ As mapping to the definition of $\mathcal{VC}$ we set $f = M$, $z = \bot$, and $y = M(x)$

    return Encrypted shares: $(C_1, \dots, C_n)$

    return Distribution proof: $\text{pf}_D = (c, \text{pf})$

procedure DISTRIBUTION VERIFICATION($\text{pp}, (C_i), \text{pf}_D, (\text{pk}_i)$)

    Recompute M as in Distribution

    $\mathbf{y} \leftarrow ([0]^n, C_1, \dots, C_n)$

    return $\mathcal{VC}.\text{Verify}(\mathcal{VC}.\text{pp}, M, \bot, \mathbf{y}, c, \text{pf})$

procedure DECRYPT SHARE($\text{pp}, i, \text{pk}_i, \text{sk}_i, C_i$)

    $s_i \leftarrow \mathcal{E}.\text{Decrypt}(\mathcal{E}.\text{pp}, \text{sk}_i, C_i)$

    $\text{pf}_{Dec,i} \leftarrow \mathcal{E}.\text{ProveDecrypt}(\text{sk}_i; (\text{pk}_i, s_i, C_i))$

    return $s_i, \text{pf}_{Dec,i}$

procedure RECONSTRUCTION($\text{pp}, (s_i)$)

    return Lagrange interpolation over $(s_i \bmod p)$

procedure DECRYPTION VERIFICATION($\text{pp}, i, \text{pk}_i, s_i, C_i, \text{pf}_{Dec,i}$)

    return $\mathcal{E}.\text{VerifyDecrypt}(\text{pk}_i, s_i, C_i, \text{pf}_{Dec,i})$

---

public key. This verification ensures that dishonest participants cannot inject invalid shares into the reconstruction process.

<u>Reconstruction.</u> Finally, once a sufficient number of correct decrypted shares have been collected, the secret is reconstructed using the Reconstruction proce-

dure. Standard Lagrange interpolation is applied over the finite field defined by modulus p, recovering the original secret without interaction between participants.

Overall, our framework makes distribution, encryption, decryption, and reconstruction publicly verifiable by combining binding/hiding vector commitments with efficient encryption, ensuring correctness and robustness. Next, we instantiate the framework with lattice-based primitives to obtain practical post-quantum PVSS schemes.

3.3 Security Proofs

Now, we prove security of the generic PVSS framework: correctness, verifiable key generation, verifiable distribution, verifiable share decryption, and IND2-privacy, under standard assumptions on the underlying encryption and vector commitment schemes. By modularity, these guarantees are inherited directly from the primitives.

Theorem 3.5 (Correctness). *The PVSS framework described in Algorithm 1 satisfies correctness with t-reconstruction, provided that the VC scheme is complete and the encryption scheme is correct.*

Proof. Assuming all participants honestly generate their keys, each public key pk_i is associated with a valid secret key sk_i, and the corresponding proof $\mathsf{pf}_{Key,i}$ validates successfully.

If the dealer is honest, the shares are computed as $s_i = \langle \mathbf{b}_i, \mathbf{a} \rangle = a'(i) \mod p$, where $a'(x)$ is the dealer's polynomial of degree t with constant term $a'(0) = s$, the secret. Each ciphertext is computed as $C_i = \mathcal{E}.\mathsf{Encrypt}(\mathcal{E}.\mathsf{pp}, \mathsf{pk}_i, s_i, r_i)$ for freshly sampled randomness r_i. The dealer commits to the vector $\mathbf{x}$ containing $(\mathbf{a}, s_1, \ldots, s_n, r_1, \ldots, r_n)$, and the opening proof pf_D with commitment c guarantees that $M(\mathbf{x}) = \mathbf{y}$ holds as defined in the algorithm. Given valid decryption keys sk_i, participants can correctly decrypt their ciphertexts to obtain $s_i = \mathcal{E}.\mathsf{Decrypt}(\mathcal{E}.\mathsf{pp}, \mathsf{sk}_i, C_i)$. Finally, any subset of at least t correctly decrypted shares suffices to reconstruct the secret $s = a'(0)$ via Lagrange interpolation. Therefore, correctness holds.

Theorem 3.6 (Verifiability of Key Generation). *The PVSS framework satisfies verifiability of key generation, provided the underlying encryption supports verifiable key generation.*

Proof. The Key Verification procedure in Algorithm 1 directly corresponds to the key verification mechanism of the underlying encryption scheme. Since we assume the encryption scheme provides verifiable key generation, correctness of this verification implies that any participant's public key is valid only if the associated proof $\mathsf{pf}_{Key,i}$ verifies successfully.

Theorem 3.7 (Verifiability of Distribution). *The PVSS framework satisfies verifiability of distribution, provided that the underlying vector commitment scheme is sound.*

Proof. The Distribution Verification procedure in Algorithm 1 leverages the verification mechanism of the vector commitment scheme. If the commitment is sound, then the verification procedure guarantees that the shares and ciphertexts are consistent with the committed data. Therefore, verifiability of distribution follows from the soundness of the vector commitment.

Theorem 3.8 (Verifiability of Share Decryption). *The PVSS framework satisfies verifiability of share decryption, provided that the underlying encryption scheme supports proofs of correct decryption.*

Proof. The Decryption Verification procedure in Algorithm 1 corresponds to the verification algorithm for the decryption correctness proof provided by the encryption scheme. Thus, assuming the encryption scheme correctly supports proof of decryption, this procedure ensures that only valid decrypted shares will be accepted.

Theorem 3.9 (Privacy). *The PVSS framework achieves t-IND2-privacy, provided that the vector commitment scheme satisfies functional hiding and the encryption scheme is semantically secure.*

Proof. Let $\mathcal{A}$ be a PPT adversary corrupting up to t parties. We will show that $\mathcal{A}$'s advantage in the t-IND2-privacy game is negligible by a sequence of hybrid games. Let $\mathrm{Adv}_{\mathcal{A}}^{\mathrm{priv}}(\lambda)$ be the advantage of $\mathcal{A}$.

Game 0: This is the original $\mathrm{Game}_{\mathcal{A},\mathrm{PVSS}}^{\mathrm{ind\text{-}secrecy},0}(\lambda)$ as defined. The challenger uses the challenge secret s^0. The commitment c and proof pf are generated honestly.

Game 1: This game is identical to Game 0, except that the commitment-proof pair (c, pf) is generated using the VC scheme's simulator $\mathcal{S} = (\mathcal{S}_0, \mathcal{S}_1)$ instead of the real VC scheme's algorithms. For this reason, the challenger computes $(\mathsf{pp}', \mathsf{td}) \leftarrow \mathcal{S}_0(1^\lambda, 1^w, 1^o, \{n+t+2, \ldots, w\}, \mathcal{E}.\mathsf{pp}.\mathcal{R})$ and, in the Setup phase, sets $\mathcal{VC}.\mathsf{pp} = \mathsf{pp}'$. Then, letting $y = (C_1, \ldots, C_n)$ be the public outputs (ciphertexts), the challenger computes $(c, \mathsf{pf}) \leftarrow \mathcal{S}_1(\mathsf{pp}', \mathsf{td}, M, y)$. Due to the *functional hiding* property of the vector commitment scheme, an adversary cannot distinguish between a real proof and a simulated one. Therefore, the adversary's view in Game 0 and Game 1 are computationally indistinguishable. We have:

$$|\Pr[\mathcal{A} \text{ outputs } 1 \text{ in Game } 0] - \Pr[\mathcal{A} \text{ outputs } 1 \text{ in Game } 1]| \leq \mathrm{negl}(\lambda)$$

Game 2: This game is identical to Game 1, but the challenger switches from using the secret s^0 to s^1. The shares are computed based on s^1 and then encrypted to get $(C_1', \ldots, C_n')$. The commitment-proof pair (c', pf') is still generated by the simulator $\mathcal{S}_1$, but now using the new public outputs $y' = (C_1', \ldots, C_n')$. In this game, the proof part is simulated and thus reveals nothing about the underlying secret shares (beyond the public ciphertexts). The only difference in the adversary's view between Game 1 and Game 2 is the set of ciphertexts. Due to the *IND-CPA security* of the underlying encryption scheme, the adversary cannot distinguish between the encryption of shares derived from s^0 and those from s^1. Thus:

$$|\Pr[\mathcal{A} \text{ outputs } 1 \text{ in Game } 1] - \Pr[\mathcal{A} \text{ outputs } 1 \text{ in Game } 2]| \leq \mathrm{negl}(\lambda)$$

Game 3: This game is identical to Game 2, but the commitment-proof pair (c', pf') is now generated honestly using the real Com and Open algorithms with the secret s^1. This game is equivalent to the original $\mathrm{Game}_{\mathcal{A},\mathrm{PVSS}}^{\mathrm{ind\ secrecy},1}(\lambda)$. Similar to the transition between Game 0 and Game 1, the switch from a simulated proof (Game 2) to a real one (Game 3) is indistinguishable due to the *functional hiding* property of the VC scheme.

$$|\Pr[\mathcal{A} \text{ outputs } 1 \text{ in Game } 2] - \Pr[\mathcal{A} \text{ outputs } 1 \text{ in Game } 3]| \leq \mathrm{negl}(\lambda)$$

Thus, by combining the steps via the triangle inequality, the total advantage of the adversary in distinguishing Game 0 (with s^0) from Game 3 (with s^1) is negligible:

$$\mathrm{Adv}_{\mathcal{A}}^{\mathrm{priv}}(\lambda) = \Big| \Pr[\mathcal{A} \text{ outputs } 1 \text{ in Game } 0]$$
$$- \Pr[\mathcal{A} \text{ outputs } 1 \text{ in Game } 3] \Big| \leq \mathrm{negl}(\lambda)$$

This concludes the proof of t-IND2-privacy.

3.4   Computation Cost of Our PVSS Framework

The computational cost of our PVSS protocol is analyzed by considering each procedure defined in Algorithm 1. We express these costs in terms of operations performed by the underlying cryptographic primitives: a linear encryption scheme $\mathcal{E}$ and a vector commitment scheme $\mathcal{VC}$. Let n be the number of participants and t be the threshold. The vector $\mathbf{x} = (\mathbf{a}, s_1, \ldots, s_n, r_1, \ldots, r_n)$ contains the $t + 1$ coefficients of the polynomial $\mathbf{a} = (s, a_1, \ldots, a_t)$, the n shares $(s_1, \ldots, s_n)$, and the n randomness values $(r_1, \ldots, r_n)$ used for encryption. Assuming that each randomness r_i is treated as r elements for length counting purposes, the total length of the committed vector $\mathbf{x}$ is $t + 1 + n + nr = O(nr)$.

The subscript p^3 associated with the $\mathcal{E}$ operations indicates that the scheme is instantiated to support a message space of size p^3, where p is the modulus for Shamir's secret sharing. This ensures that inner products used to compute shares $s_i = \langle \mathbf{b}_i, \mathbf{a} \rangle$ do not overflow, i.e., $s_i < p^3$. The parameters p^3, nr, n for the $\mathcal{VC}$ operations refer to characteristics related to the bound of the elements involved, the length of the committed vector, and the number of outputs, respectively. The $2n$ relations checked by the opening function $M(\mathbf{x})$ are implicitly handled by the $\mathcal{VC}$ operations, whose costs depend primarily on nr and n.

Setup. This procedure is run once, typically by a trusted party or as a distributed process, to establish the common parameters. It involves initializing the encryption scheme parameters via $\mathcal{E}.\mathsf{Setup}(1^\lambda, p^3)$; this has a computational cost of

$\text{op}_{\mathcal{E}.\mathsf{Setup}_{p3}}$. Additionally, it sets up the vector commitment public parameters through $\mathcal{VC}.\mathsf{Setup}(1^\lambda, 1^v, 1^w, 1^o, \ldots)$. The crucial parameters for the VC scheme derived from our framework are the vector length nr, and the number of relations $2n$. The cost of this VC setup is denoted as $\text{op}_{\mathcal{VC}.\mathsf{Setup}_{p3,nr,n}}$. The total computational cost for the Setup procedure is therefore $\text{op}_{\mathcal{E}.\mathsf{Setup}_{p3}} + \text{op}_{\mathcal{VC}.\mathsf{Setup}_{p3,nr,n}}$.

Key Generation. Each of the n participants executes this procedure once to generate their individual encryption key pair $(\mathsf{pk}_i, \mathsf{sk}_i)$ and a corresponding proof of correct key generation $\mathsf{pf}_{Key,i}$. This is performed by calling $\mathcal{E}.\mathsf{KeyGen}(\mathcal{E}.\mathsf{pp})$. The computational cost incurred by each participant for Key Generation is $\text{op}_{\mathcal{E}.\mathsf{KeyGen}_{p3}}$.

Key Verification. To verify a participant's public key pk_i using its associated proof $\mathsf{pf}_{Key,i}$, any interested party (e.g., the dealer, other participants) invokes $\mathcal{E}.\mathsf{VerifyKey}(\mathcal{E}.\mathsf{pp}, \mathsf{pk}_i, \mathsf{pf}_{Key,i})$. The computational cost for verifying a single public key is $\text{op}_{\mathcal{E}.\mathsf{VerifyKey}_{p3}}$.

Distribution. This procedure is executed once by the dealer to share the secret s.

1. *Polynomial definition and evaluation*: The dealer defines a degree-t polynomial $P(X) = s + a_1 X + \cdots + a_t X^t$ with $a_0 = s$. Then, n shares $s_i = P(i)$ are computed. Each evaluation $s_i = \langle \mathbf{b}_i, \mathbf{a} \rangle$ (where $\mathbf{b}_i = (i^0, \ldots, i^t)$) requires $O(t)$ arithmetic operations in $\mathbb{Z}_p$. This step totals $n \cdot O(t)$ operations.
2. *Encryption of shares*: Each share s_i is encrypted under the respective participant's public key pk_i using fresh randomness r_i: $C_i \leftarrow \mathcal{E}.\mathsf{Encrypt}(\mathcal{E}.\mathsf{pp}, \mathsf{pk}_i, s_i, r_i)$. This involves n encryptions, leading to a total cost of $n \cdot \text{op}\mathcal{E}.\mathsf{Encrypt}_{p3}$.
3. *Vector Commitment*: The dealer commits to the vector $\mathbf{x} = (\mathbf{a}, s_1, \ldots, s_n, r_1, \ldots, r_n)$ of length nr. This operation, $(c, \mathsf{aux}) \leftarrow \mathcal{VC}.\mathsf{Com}(\mathcal{VC}.\mathsf{pp}, \mathbf{x})$, has a cost of $\text{op}_{\mathcal{VC}.\mathsf{Com}_{p3,nr,n}}$.
4. *Opening Proof Generation*: An opening proof pf is generated for the relations defined in $M(\mathbf{x})$. These relations ensure that $s_i = \langle \mathbf{b}_i, \mathbf{a} \rangle$ and $\mathcal{E}.\mathsf{Encrypt}(\mathcal{E}.\mathsf{pp}, \mathsf{pk}_i, s_i, r_i) = C_i$ for all $i \in [n]$. This step, $\mathsf{pf} \leftarrow \mathcal{VC}.\mathsf{Open}(\mathcal{VC}.\mathsf{pp}, M, \bot, \mathsf{aux})$, costs $\text{op}_{\mathcal{VC}.\mathsf{Open}(p3,nr,n)}$.

Overall computational cost for the Distribution phase, approximating the $n \cdot O(t)$ term as n^2 (as $t = O(n)$ is typical), is:

$$n(n + \text{op}_{\mathcal{E}.\mathsf{Encrypt}_{p3}}) + \text{op}_{\mathcal{VC}.\mathsf{Com}_{p3,nr,n}} + \text{op}_{\mathcal{VC}.\mathsf{Open}(p3,nr,n)}$$

Distribution Verification. This procedure can be performed by any party to verify the integrity of the dealer's actions using the public ciphertexts $(C_1, \ldots, C_n)$ and the distribution proof $\mathsf{pf}_D = (c, \mathsf{pf})$. It involves reconstructing the opening function M (which is a specification and has negligible computational cost) and then executing $\mathcal{VC}.\mathsf{Verify}(\mathcal{VC}.\mathsf{pp}, M, \bot, \mathbf{y}, c, \mathsf{pf})$, where $\mathbf{y} = ([0]^n, C_1, \ldots, C_n)$. The dominant computational cost for Distribution Verification is $\text{op}_{\mathcal{VC}.\mathsf{Verify}_{p3,nr,n}}$.

Decrypt Share. Each participant P_i who has received an encrypted share C_i performs this procedure.

1. *Decryption*: The participant decrypts C_i using their secret key sk_i to obtain the share $s_i \leftarrow \mathcal{E}.\mathsf{Decrypt}(\mathcal{E}.\mathsf{pp}, \mathsf{sk}_i, C_i)$. This costs $\mathrm{op}_{\mathcal{E}.\mathsf{Decrypt}_{p^3}}$.
2. *Proof of Decryption*: A proof $\mathsf{pf}_{Dec,i}$ is generated certifying that s_i is the correct decryption of C_i with respect to pk_i. This is done via $\mathcal{E}.\mathsf{ProveDecrypt}(\mathsf{sk}_i; (\mathsf{pk}_i, s_i, C_i))$, costing $\mathrm{op}_{\mathcal{E}.\mathsf{ProveDecrypt}_{p^3}}$.

The total computational cost for a participant to decrypt their share and generate the accompanying proof is $\mathrm{op}_{\mathcal{E}.\mathsf{Decrypt}_{p^3}} + \mathrm{op}_{\mathcal{E}.\mathsf{ProveDecrypt}_{p^3}}$.

Decryption Verification. To confirm the validity of a decrypted share s_i (provided by participant P_i along with C_i and $\mathsf{pf}_{Dec,i}$), any party can perform this verification. It involves calling $\mathcal{E}.\mathsf{VerifyDecrypt}(\mathsf{pk}_i, s_i, C_i, \mathsf{pf}_{Dec,i})$. This step is crucial before using the share s_i in the reconstruction phase. The computational cost for verifying one decrypted share is $\mathrm{op}_{\mathcal{E}.\mathsf{VerifyDecrypt}_{p^3}}$.

Reconstruction. Once a threshold of at least $t + 1$ valid decrypted shares (i, s_i) are collected, the original secret s (i.e., $P(0)$) is recovered using Lagrange interpolation over the field $\mathbb{Z}_p$. The computational cost for Reconstruction using standard interpolation algorithms is $O(t^2)$ arithmetic operations in $\mathbb{Z}_p$. More advanced techniques (e.g., FFT-based algorithms) can reduce this to $O(t \log^2 t)$ or $O(t \log t)$; we conservatively state $O(t^2)$.

Table 3 below summarizes the computational cost for each procedure.

Table 3. Computation costs for the core procedures in our PVSS protocol. All encryption-related costs are parameterized by the message space size p^3. VC costs are driven by the committed vector length $O(nr)$ and output size n.

Procedure	Computation Cost
Setup	$\mathrm{op}_{\mathcal{E}.\mathsf{Setup}_{p^3}} + \mathrm{op}_{\mathcal{VC}.\mathsf{Setup}_{p^3, nr, n}}$
Key Generation	$\mathrm{op}_{\mathcal{E}.\mathsf{KeyGen}_{p^3}}$
Key Verification	$\mathrm{op}_{\mathcal{E}.\mathsf{VerifyKey}_{p^3}}$
Distribution	$n(n + \mathrm{op}_{\mathcal{E}.\mathsf{Encrypt}_{p^3}}) + \mathrm{op}_{\mathcal{VC}.\mathsf{Com}_{p^3, nr, n}} + \mathrm{op}_{\mathcal{VC}.\mathsf{Open}_{p^3, nr, n}}$
Dist. Verification	$\mathrm{op}_{\mathcal{VC}.\mathsf{Verify}_{p^3, nr, n}}$
Decrypt Share	$\mathrm{op}_{\mathcal{E}.\mathsf{Decrypt}_{p^3}} + \mathrm{op}_{\mathcal{E}.\mathsf{ProveDecrypt}_{p^3}}$
Dec. Verification	$\mathrm{op}_{\mathcal{E}.\mathsf{VerifyDecrypt}_{p^3}}$
Reconstruction	$O(t^2)$ operations in $\mathbb{Z}_p$

4 Instantiations: PVSS Constructions

We provide two instantiations of our framework: we realize LVC-PoS using the VC of [2], and instantiate the linear encryption with two schemes inspired

---

Algorithm 2. Vector Commitment [2]

> **procedure** $\text{SETUP}(1^\lambda, 1^v, 1^w, 1^o)$
>
> $\quad \mathbf{v} \leftarrow (R_q^\times)^w,\ h \leftarrow R_p^o,\ (\mathbf{A}, td) = \mathsf{TrapGen}(1^n, 1^l, q, R, \beta)$
>
> $\quad t \leftarrow T$ where T is set of generators for R_q (from definition of MSIS in [2])
>
> $\quad \mathbf{u}_{\frac{v_i}{v_j}} = \mathsf{SampPre}(td, \frac{v_i}{v_j} t, \beta),\ \forall i, j \in \mathbb{Z}_w \mid i \neq j$
>
> $\quad$ **return** $(\mathbf{A}, t, \{\mathbf{u}_{v_i/v_j}\}, \mathbf{v}, h)$
>
> **procedure** $\text{COM}(\mathsf{pp}, \mathbf{x}) : c = \langle \mathbf{v}, \mathbf{x} \rangle \mod q$
>
> $\quad$ **for** $i = 1$ to w **do** $: \mathbf{u}_i = \sum_{j \neq i} x_j \cdot \mathbf{u}_{\frac{v_j}{v_i}}$
>
> $\quad \mathsf{aux} = (\mathbf{u}_i)_{i \in \mathbb{Z}_w}$
>
> $\quad$ **return** (c, aux)
>
> **procedure** $\text{OPEN}(\mathsf{pp}, f, \mathbf{z}, \mathsf{aux}) : \pi = \sum_{i \in \mathbb{Z}_o} \sum_{j \in \mathbb{Z}_w} h_i f_{i,j}(\mathbf{z}) \mathbf{u}_j$
>
> $\quad$ **return** π
>
> **procedure** $\text{VERIFY}(\mathsf{pp}, f, \mathbf{z}, \mathbf{y}, c, \pi)$
>
> $\quad a_1 = \left(\mathbf{A} \cdot \mathbf{u} \overset{?}{=} \left(\sum_{k \in \mathbb{Z}_o} h_k \left(\sum_{j \in \mathbb{Z}_w} f_{k,j}(\mathbf{z}) \frac{c}{v_j} - y_k\right)\right) \cdot t \mod q\right),\ a_2 = \left(\|\mathbf{u}\| \overset{?}{\leq} \delta_0\right)$
>
> $\quad$ **return** $a_1 \wedge a_2$

---

by [16, 22] supporting publicly verifiable decryption. We also give a ring-based instantiation via the compact scheme of Lyubashevsky *et al.* [17]. Combined with our framework, these yield three fully lattice-based PVSS constructions.

4.1 Instantiation of LVC-PoS

In this section, we present our extended vector commitment, *LVC-PoS*, which is a core component of our PVSS. Starting from the VC of Albrecht *et al.* [2], we (i) restrict evaluations to linear and multi-output linear functions and (ii) add proofs of smallness, including *binary satisfiability* of committed vectors. This is essential since our commitments contain sharing coefficients, shares, and encryption randomness that must be shown well-formed and small; in our setting the vectors are fixed-length binary, so smallness is immediate, while larger domains can use techniques such as [15]. We proceed in two steps: recall the base VC (Algorithm 2) and then define LVC-PoS (Algorithm 3).

Base Vector Commitment (Algorithm 2). The goal of the VC scheme is to allow a dealer to commit to a vector $\mathbf{x}$ and later provide succinct, non-interactive proofs that linear relations over $\mathbf{x}$ hold, without revealing $\mathbf{x}$ itself. We recall the VC scheme [2] in Algorithm 2. For more details see Appendix A.7.

LVC-PoS Scheme (Algorithm 3). We now extend the VC scheme to support proof of smallness and binary satisfiability.

Setup: The setup is similar to the base VC but with a refined commitment key:

$$\mathbf{v}' \leftarrow (R_p^\times)^w, \quad \mathbf{v} = \frac{1}{\mathbf{v}'} \mod q$$

Algorithm 3. LVC-PoS

---

procedure $\textsc{Setup}(1^\lambda, 1^v, 1^w, 1^o, S, \beta_S)$

    Let $\mathbf{v}' \leftarrow (R_p^\times)^w$ and $\mathbf{v} = \dfrac{1}{\mathbf{v}'} \mod q$, $h \leftarrow R_p^o$, $(\mathbf{A}, td) = \mathsf{TrapGen}(1^\eta, 1^l, q, R, \beta)$

    $t \leftarrow T$, $\mathbf{u}_g = \mathsf{SampPre}(td, g(v)t, \beta), \forall g \in G$ $\triangleright$ Where $G = \left\{ \frac{v_i}{v_j} \big| i \neq j \right\}$

    return Public Parameters: $(\mathbf{A}, t, (\mathbf{u}_g)_{g \in G}, v, h, S, \beta_S)$

procedure $\overline{\textsc{Com}}(\mathsf{pp}, \mathbf{x})$ $\triangleright$ Inner function

    Let $c = <\dfrac{1}{\mathbf{v}}, \mathbf{x}> \mod q$

    for $i \in \{1, \ldots, w\}$ **do** : Let $\mathbf{u}_i = \sum_{i \neq j=1}^{w} x_j \mathbf{u}_{\frac{v_i}{v_j}}$

    Let $\mathsf{aux} = (\mathbf{u}_i)_{i \in \{1, \ldots, w\}}$

    return Commitment: (c, aux)

procedure $\textsc{Com}(\mathsf{pp}, \mathbf{x})$

    return Commitment: $\mathcal{VC}.\mathsf{Com}(\mathsf{pp}, \mathbf{x})$

procedure $\textsc{Open}(\mathsf{pp}, f, \mathbf{z}, \mathsf{aux})$

    Let $\pi = \mathcal{VC}.\mathsf{Open}(\mathsf{pp}, f, \mathbf{z}, \mathsf{aux})$

    Let $\bar{c}_{\mathsf{hox}}, \mathsf{aux}_{\mathsf{hox}} = \overline{\mathsf{Com}}(\chi_S(\mathbf{h}) \circ \mathbf{x})$ $\triangleright$ Where χ_S is indicator function of S

    Let $\pi_{eq} = \mathcal{VC}.\mathsf{Open}(\mathsf{pp}, \dfrac{\chi_S(\mathbf{h})}{\mathbf{v}}, \mathbf{z}, \mathsf{aux}_{\mathsf{hox}})$

    Let $\pi_{ip} = \sum_{i,j \in \mathbb{Z}_w : i \neq j} x_i((\chi_S(h))_j (x_j - 1)) \mathbf{u}_{\frac{v_i}{v_j}}$

    return Proof: $(\pi, \bar{c}_{\mathsf{hox}}, \pi_{eq}, \pi_{ip})$

procedure $\textsc{Verify}(\mathsf{pp}, f, \mathbf{z}, \mathbf{y}, c, \pi)$

    Let $b_1 = \mathcal{VC}.\mathsf{Verify}(\mathsf{pp}, f, \mathbf{z}, \mathbf{y}, c, \pi)$, and $b_2 = \mathcal{VC}.\mathsf{Verify}(\mathsf{pp}, \dfrac{\mathbf{h}}{\mathbf{v}}, \mathbf{z}, \bar{c}_{\mathsf{hox}}, c_{\mathbf{x}}, \pi_{eq})$

    Let $\bar{c}_{\mathsf{ho}(\mathbf{x}-1)} = \bar{c}_{\mathsf{hox}} - <\mathbf{h}, \dfrac{1}{\mathbf{v}}>$, and $b_3 = (c_{\mathbf{x}} \times \bar{c}_{\mathsf{ho}(\mathbf{x}-1)} \times t \overset{?}{=} <\mathbf{A}, \pi_{ip}>)$

    return $\bigwedge_{i=1}^{3} b_i$

This transformation simplifies the commitments required for verifying quadratic relations in the binary proof.

<u>Commit</u>: Commitment is delegated to the base VC. Additionally, we define an internal function $\overline{\mathsf{Com}}$ for auxiliary commitments: $\bar{c} = \langle \mathbf{x}, \frac{1}{\mathbf{v}} \rangle \mod q$.

<u>Open and Verify</u>: We combine three proof components:

- Base proof π (as in VC).
- Proof π_{eq} ensuring consistency of auxiliary commitment $\bar{c}_{\mathsf{hox}}$ with $h \circ \mathbf{x}$.
- Inner product proof π_{ip} verifying the binary relation.

The final verification checking $c_{\mathbf{x}} \cdot \bar{c}_{\mathsf{ho}(\mathbf{x}-1)} \cdot t \overset{?}{=} \langle \mathbf{A}, \pi_{ip} \rangle$ confirms that the committed vector $\mathbf{x}$ is binary.

Binary Satisfiability Proof. Finally, we prove that a committed vector $\mathbf{x}$ is binary. The prover constructs: $\pi_{ip} = \sum_{i,j \in \mathbb{Z}_w, i \neq j} x_i (h_j(x_j - 1)) \mathbf{u}_{v_i/v_j}$ The verifier reconstructs $\bar{c}_{\mathsf{ho}(\mathbf{x}-1)} = \bar{c}_{\mathsf{hox}} - \langle h, \frac{1}{\mathbf{v}} \rangle$ and checks $c_{\mathbf{x}} \cdot \bar{c}_{\mathsf{ho}(\mathbf{x}-1)} \cdot t \overset{?}{=} \langle \mathbf{A}, \pi_{ip} \rangle$. Thus, we conclude that $\mathbf{x}$ is a binary vector.

Theorem 4.1 (Security Properties of LVC-PoS). *Assuming the correctness, functional hiding, and binding properties of the underlying VC scheme (Algorithm 2), the LVC-PoS (Algorithm 3) achieves the following properties:*

- *Correctness: Algorithm 3 correctly verifies both the evaluation of linear functions and the smallness of specified indices in the committed vector.*
- *Functional Hiding: Algorithm 3 preserves functional hiding for linear function openings, meaning that the commitment and proof reveal no information about the committed vector beyond the output of the opened function and smallness verification.*
- *Weak Binding: Algorithm 3 satisfies weak binding, ensuring that after committing to a vector, it is computationally infeasible to produce two distinct valid openings.*

We defer the proof to Appendix B.1.

4.2   Instantiation of Linear Encryption Scheme I

In this section, we present our first instantiation of the linear encryption scheme, which we refer to as *Linear Encryption Scheme I*. This scheme is built upon lattice-based assumptions and is designed to work seamlessly with our vector commitment construction and PVSS framework. It supports both encryption of messages (shares in our setting) and efficient public proofs of correct decryption, an essential feature for enabling verifiability in distributed systems. A critical aspect of this design lies in its treatment of key generation and verification, where validity is derived structurally from SIS hardness, thereby eliminating the need for explicit key proofs and ensuring public keys are valid by construction.

We detail the design of this scheme in Algorithm 4, and we now explain each component of the construction, step by step, highlighting the technical rationale and the role of each operation.

Setup: The scheme begins with the parameter setup, as specified in the **Setup** procedure of Algorithm 4. We select the appropriate cryptographic parameters:

- Define $k = \lceil \log(p) \rceil$ to represent the bit length of the modulus.
- Choose dimensions: l (rows of public keys), $m = 2lk$ (columns of public keys), and gadget dimension d.
- Set the error bound parameter $\alpha = \frac{\sqrt{p}}{4}$, which controls noise size during encryption and decryption and ensures correctness of proofs.

These parameters jointly balance security and efficiency and establish the environment for trapdoor generation and gadget operations.

Key Generation: During **Key Generation**, both the public and secret keys are sampled using lattice trapdoor techniques [12]:

- Invoke the trapdoor generation function to sample a public matrix $\mathbf{A} \in \mathbb{Z}_p^{l \times m}$ and its associated trapdoor td: $(\mathbf{A}, td) = \mathrm{TrapGen}(1^l, 1^m, 1^p, \alpha)$.

Algorithm 4. Linear Encryption Scheme I

---

procedure SETUP$(1^\lambda, p)$
$\quad k = \lceil \log(p) \rceil$. Select $l \in \mathbb{N}$, $m = 2lk$, $d \in \mathbb{N}$, and $\alpha = \frac{\sqrt{p}}{4}$
$\quad$**return** (p, l, m, d, α)
procedure KEY GENERATION(p, l, m, d, α)
$\quad (\mathbf{A}, td) = \text{TrapGen}(1^l, 1^m, 1^P, \alpha)$ $\qquad\qquad\qquad\qquad$ ▷ Drived from [12]
$\quad \mathsf{pf} = \varnothing$ $\qquad\qquad\qquad\qquad\qquad\qquad\qquad\qquad\qquad\qquad\qquad$ ▷ Placeholder
$\quad$**return** Secret Key: td, Public Key: $\mathbf{A}$, Key Proof: pf
procedure KEY VERIFICATION$(\mathbf{A}, \mathsf{pf})$
$\quad$**return** SIS structural validity and syntactic check
procedure ENCRYPTION$(\mathbf{A}, m, (\mathbf{B}, \mathbf{f}, \mathbf{e}, \mathbf{e}'))$
$\quad \mathbf{U} = \mathbf{A} \cdot \mathbf{B}$, $\mathbf{h}^\top = \mathbf{f}^\top \cdot \mathbf{A} + \mathbf{e}^\top$, $\mathbf{C}^\top = \mathbf{f}^\top \cdot \mathbf{U} + \mathbf{e}'^\top + m \cdot \mathbf{g}^\top$
$\quad$**return** $(\mathbf{U}, \mathbf{h}, \mathbf{C})$
procedure DECRYPTION$(td, (\mathbf{U}, \mathbf{h}, \mathbf{C}))$
$\quad \mathbf{B}' = \text{SampPre}(td, \mathbf{U}, \alpha)$, $m = \text{GadgetSolve}(\mathbf{C} - \mathbf{h}^\top \cdot \mathbf{B}')$
$\quad$**return** m
procedure PROVE DECRYPTION$(td, \mathbf{A}, m, (\mathbf{U}, \mathbf{h}, \mathbf{C}))$
$\quad \mathbf{B}' = \text{SampPre}(td, \mathbf{U}, \alpha)$, $\mathbf{e} = \mathbf{h}^\top \cdot \mathbf{B}' + m \cdot \mathbf{g}^\top - \mathbf{C}$
$\quad$**return** $(\mathbf{e}, \mathbf{B}')$
procedure VERIFY DECRYPTION$(\mathbf{A}, m, (\mathbf{U}, \mathbf{h}, \mathbf{C}), (\mathbf{e}, \mathbf{B}'))$
$\quad a_1 = \mathbf{A} \cdot \mathbf{B}'$, $b_1 = \mathbf{U}$; $a_2 = \mathbf{h}^\top \cdot \mathbf{B}' + \mathbf{e}^\top + m \cdot \mathbf{g}^\top$, $b_2 = \mathbf{C}$
$\quad$**return** $a_1 \stackrel{?}{=} b_1$ and $a_2 \stackrel{?}{=} b_2$ and $\|\mathbf{e}\| \stackrel{?}{<} \alpha$ and $\|\mathbf{B}'\| \stackrel{?}{<} \alpha$

- Define a placeholder for the key proof: $\mathsf{pf} = \varnothing$.

Following Theorem 1.1, the matrix $\mathbf{A}$ generated by TrapGen already defines a valid SIS instance that guarantees the existence of short preimages. Thus, public key validity is ensured *structurally by construction*, and no explicit proof of key generation is required. The placeholder pf is included solely to preserve interface consistency with the generic PVSS framework.

Key Verification. In this simplified design, key verification is purely structural: since $\mathbf{A}$ is generated through a statistically correct SIS procedure, its validity automatically follows from the hardness assumptions. The verifier accepts any syntactically valid $(\mathbf{A}, \mathsf{pf})$ instance, where $\mathsf{pf} = \varnothing$.

Encryption: To encrypt a message m, as described in `Encryption`, the sender performs:

- Sample randomness: $\mathbf{B} \in \mathbb{Z}_p^{m \times d}$, $\mathbf{f} \in \mathbb{Z}_p^l$, $\mathbf{e} \in \mathbb{Z}_p^m$ (with $\|\mathbf{e}\| < \alpha$), and $\mathbf{e}' \in \mathbb{Z}_p^d$ (with $\|\mathbf{e}'\| < \alpha$).
- Compute $\mathbf{U} = \mathbf{A} \cdot \mathbf{B}$, $\mathbf{h}^\top = \mathbf{f}^\top \cdot \mathbf{A} + \mathbf{e}^\top$, and $\mathbf{C}^\top = \mathbf{f}^\top \cdot \mathbf{U} + \mathbf{e}'^\top + m \cdot \mathbf{g}^\top$. Where $\mathbf{g}$ is the public gadget vector.

The ciphertext $(\mathbf{U}, \mathbf{h}, \mathbf{C})$ encapsulates both the randomized encryption and the structured form enabling efficient decryption and proof generation.

<u>Decryption</u>: As shown in the `Decryption` procedure, the decryptor uses the trapdoor td to recover a short preimage: $\mathbf{B}' = \text{SampPre}(td, \mathbf{U}, \alpha)$. The message is reconstructed by solving: $m = \text{GadgetSolve}(\mathbf{C} - \mathbf{h}^\top \cdot \mathbf{B}')$. Correctness follows directly from the SIS-structured design of $\mathbf{A}$ and the bounded error terms.

<u>Prove Decryption</u>: To provide public verifiability of decryption, the decryptor runs `Prove Decryption`. Using td, the decryptor computes: $\mathbf{B}' = \text{SampPre}(td, \mathbf{U}, \alpha)$ and $\mathbf{e} = \mathbf{h}^\top \cdot \mathbf{B}' + m \cdot \mathbf{g}^\top - \mathbf{C}$. The proof consists of the tuple $(\mathbf{e}, \mathbf{B}')$, which shows that the ciphertext decrypts to m correctly.

<u>Verify Decryption</u>: Any verifier can confirm correctness of the decryption proof by checking::

1. Consistency of $\mathbf{B}'$ with $\mathbf{U}$: $\mathbf{A} \cdot \mathbf{B}' \overset{?}{=} \mathbf{U}$.
2. Consistency of $\mathbf{e}$ with ciphertext $\mathbf{C}$: $\mathbf{h}^\top \cdot \mathbf{B}' + \mathbf{e}^\top + m \cdot \mathbf{g}^\top \overset{?}{=} \mathbf{C}$.
3. Norm bounds: $\|\mathbf{e}\| \overset{?}{<} \alpha, \quad \|\mathbf{B}'\| \overset{?}{<} \alpha$.

If all conditions are satisfied, the decryption proof is accepted.

Lemma 4.2. *Let the Regev encryption scheme be IND-CPA secure, then the encryption scheme I in Algorithm 4 also satisfies IND-CPA security.*

Proof. The Regev scheme achieves IND-CPA security under the LWE assumption. Algorithm 4 presents a variant of Regev's scheme where:

- The key generation outputs $(\mathbf{A}, td) = \text{TrapGen}(1^l, 1^m, 1^P, \alpha)$ and $\mathsf{pf} = \varnothing$. The view of the attacker is $(\mathbf{A}, \varnothing)$ which is pseudorandom due to the properties of TrapGen and SIS hardness [12].
- The encryption algorithm outputs $\mathbf{U} = \mathbf{A} \cdot \mathbf{B}$ and $\mathbf{h}^\top = \mathbf{f}^\top \cdot \mathbf{A} + \mathbf{e}^\top$ and $\mathbf{C}^\top = \mathbf{f}^\top \cdot \mathbf{U} + \mathbf{e}'^\top + m \cdot \mathbf{g}^\top$. The view of the attacker is $(\mathbf{U}, \mathbf{h}, \mathbf{C})$, where $\mathbf{U}$ is pseudorandom under the SIS assumption and $(\mathbf{h}, \mathbf{C})$ is pseudorandom under the LWE assumption.

Consequently, Algorithm 4 satisfies IND-CPA security.

Lemma 4.3. *The encryption scheme 4 satisfies verifiability of key generation and verifiability of decryption.*

Proof. Verifiability of key generation is guaranteed structurally by Theorem 1.1, which ensures that any $\mathbf{A}$ produced by TrapGen defines a valid SIS instance with short preimages. The verifiability of decryption follows from the fact that the ProveDecrypt outputs randomness as pf_{Dec}, and the verification algorithm checks consistency of the Encrypt algorithm.

Theorem 4.4 (Security of PVSS Instantiation with Linear Encryption Scheme I). *Assuming the security of the LVC-PoS and Linear Encryption Scheme I, our instantiated PVSS construction achieves correctness, verifiability, and t-IND2 privacy.*

Proof (Proof Sketch). Follows from the security of the generic framework established in Sect. 3, together with the properties of Linear Encryption Scheme I.

Algorithm 5. Linear Encryption Scheme

---

procedure $\text{SETUP}(1^\lambda, p)$
    $k = \lceil \log(p) \rceil$. Select λ-bit prime q s.t. $q = 1 \mod k$.
    Let $R = \mathbb{Z}[x]/(x^k + 1)$, $a \leftarrow R_q$
    return (a, k, p, q, R)

procedure $\text{KEY GENERATION}(a, k, p, q, R)$
    Let $\mathsf{sk}, e \leftarrow R$ be small and $\mathsf{pk} = a \cdot \mathsf{sk} + e$
    $\mathsf{pf}_{Key} = \text{id.prove}((a, 1), \mathsf{pk}, (\mathsf{sk}, e))$ [16]
    return Secret Key: sk, Public Key: pk, Key Proof: pf_{Key}

procedure $\text{KEY VERIFICATION}(a, \mathsf{pk}, \mathsf{pf})$
    return $\text{id.verify}((a, 1), \mathsf{pk}, \mathsf{pf}_{Key})$ [16]

procedure $\text{ENCRYPTION}(a, \mathsf{pk}, m, (r, e, e'))$
    Let $\hat{m}$ be a polynomial such that its i-th coefficient is m's i-th bit
    $c = r \cdot a + e$; $c' = r \cdot \mathsf{pk} + e' + \hat{m} \lfloor \frac{q}{2} \rfloor$
    return (c, c')

procedure $\text{DECRYPTION}(\mathsf{sk}, (c, c'))$
    $b = c \cdot \mathsf{sk}$; $m' = \lceil \frac{c' - b}{q/2} \rceil \mod 2$
    return $m = m'(2)$

procedure $\text{PROVE DECRYPTION}(\mathsf{sk}, \mathsf{pk}, m, (c, c'))$
    $b = c \cdot \mathsf{sk}$; $e = b + \hat{m} \lfloor \frac{q}{2} \rfloor - c'$; $\mathsf{pf}_{Dec} = \text{id.prove}(c, b, \mathsf{sk})$ [16]
    return $(e, b, \mathsf{pf}_{Dec})$

procedure $\text{DECRYPTION VERIFICATION}(\mathsf{pk}, m, c, c', e, b, \mathsf{pf}_{Dec})$
    $a = b + e + \hat{m} \lfloor \frac{q}{2} \rfloor$
    return $a \stackrel{?}{=} c'$ and $\|e\| \stackrel{?}{<} \alpha$ and $\text{id.verify}(c, b, \mathsf{pf}_{Dec})$ [16]

4.3 Instantiation Linear Encryption Scheme II

We now present our second instantiation, *Linear Encryption Scheme II*, based on the compact ring-based construction of Lyubashevsky *et al.* [17], which is IND-CPA secure under MLWE. It operates over polynomial rings for compactness and compatibility with our framework, and supports public-key and decryption verifiability via lattice-based identification protocols [16]. Algorithm 5 gives the full specification.

Setup. The **Setup** procedure generates the public parameters. Given security parameter λ and modulus p, set $k = \lceil \log(p) \rceil$, and q a λ-bit prime such that $q \equiv 1 \mod k$, and define the polynomial ring $R = \mathbb{Z}_q[x]/(x^k + 1)$. Sample $a \leftarrow R_q$ uniformly at random; the tuple (a, k, p, q, R) constitutes the public parameters.

Key Generation. The **Key Generation** procedure samples a short secret $s \leftarrow R$ and error $e \leftarrow R$ with small norm. The public key is computed as $\mathsf{pk} = a \cdot s + e \in R_q$, and the key proof is obtained using the lattice-based identification protocol [16]: $\mathsf{pf}_{Key} = \text{id.prove}((a, 1), \mathsf{pk}, (s, e))$. The output consists of the secret key s, public key pk, and proof pf_{Key}, enabling public verification of key validity.

Key Verification. Anyone can verify the correctness of a public key by executing $\mathsf{id.verify}((a,1), \mathsf{pk}, \mathsf{pf}_{\mathsf{Key}})$, ensuring structural trust in pk without revealing secret information.

Encryption. Given public key pk and message m, the sender samples randomness $r, e, e' \leftarrow R$ (each with small norm) and computes: $c = r \cdot a + e$, and $c' = r \cdot \mathsf{pk} + e' + \hat{m}\lfloor q/2 \rfloor$, where $\hat{m}$ denotes the bitwise polynomial encoding of m. The ciphertext (c, c') retains the linearity necessary for public verifiability.

Decryption. It executed by the holder of s, computes $b = c \cdot s$, and recovers the message as $m' = \left[\frac{c' - b}{q/2} \right] \bmod 2$, returning $m = m'(2)$. Correctness follows since $\hat{m}\lfloor q/2 \rfloor$ dominates the noise term under the prescribed bound.

Prove Decryption. To enable public verification, the decryptor computes

$$b = c \cdot s, \qquad e = b + \hat{m}\lfloor q/2 \rfloor - c',$$

and generates a proof of correct relation using [16]: $\mathsf{pf}_{\mathsf{Dec}} = \mathsf{id.prove}(c, b, s)$. The tuple $(e, b, \mathsf{pf}_{\mathsf{Dec}})$ forms the decryption proof.

Decryption Verification. Any verifier checks the correctness by confirming:

$$b + e + \hat{m}\lfloor q/2 \rfloor \stackrel{?}{=} c', \quad \|e\| \stackrel{?}{<} \alpha, \quad \mathsf{id.verify}(c, b, \mathsf{pf}_{\mathsf{Dec}}).$$

If all conditions hold, the ciphertext is correctly decrypted and publicly verifiable.

Lemma 4.5. *If the Regev encryption scheme is IND-CPA secure, then the Linear Encryption Scheme in Algorithm 5 also satisfies IND-CPA security.*

Proof. The construction mirrors Regev's scheme within the ring setting. Key generation produces (s, e) small in R, with $\mathsf{pk} = a \cdot s + e$. The adversary's view $(\mathsf{pk}, \mathsf{pf}_{\mathsf{Key}})$ is pseudorandom due to the MSIS hardness of recovering short preimages and the zero-knowledge properties of [16]. Encryption outputs (c, c') where c is pseudorandom under SIS and (c', m) is pseudorandom under LWE. Hence IND-CPA security follows directly.

Table 4. Computation costs for the core procedures in our PVSS instantiations.

Procedure	Computation Cost (Number of Operations)	
	Ours 1 (LWE-based)	Ours 2 ((Ring) − LWE based)
Setup	$1 \cdot \mathrm{op}_{\mathsf{TrapGen}} + w(w-1) \cdot \mathrm{op}_{\mathsf{SampPre}}$	
Key Generation	$1 \cdot \mathrm{op}_{\mathrm{MV\text{-}Mult}} + 1 \cdot \mathrm{op}_{\mathrm{ID\text{-}P}}$	$1 \cdot \mathrm{op}_{\mathrm{Poly\text{-}Mult}} + 1 \cdot \mathrm{op}_{\mathrm{ID\text{-}P}}$
Key Verification	0	$1 \cdot \mathrm{op}_{\mathrm{ID\text{-}V}}$
Distribution	$\approx 2w^2 \cdot \mathrm{op}_{\mathrm{vec\text{-}scalar\ mult}} + n \cdot \mathrm{op}_{\mathrm{Enc1}}$	$\approx 2w^2 \cdot \mathrm{op}_{\mathrm{poly\text{-}scalar\ mult}} + n \cdot \mathrm{op}_{\mathrm{Enc3}}$
Distribution Verification	$\approx 2nw \cdot \mathrm{op}_{\mathrm{mult}}$	$\approx 2nw \cdot \mathrm{op}_{\mathrm{Poly\text{-}Mult}}$
Decrypt Share	$1 \cdot \mathrm{op}_{\mathrm{MV\text{-}Mult}} + 1 \cdot \mathrm{op}_{\mathrm{ID\text{-}P}}$	$1 \cdot \mathrm{op}_{\mathrm{Poly\text{-}Mult}} + 1 \cdot \mathrm{op}_{\mathrm{ID\text{-}P}}$
Decryption Verification	$1 \cdot \mathrm{op}_{\mathrm{ID\text{-}V}}$	$1 \cdot \mathrm{op}_{\mathrm{ID\text{-}V}}$
Reconstruction	$(t+1)^2$ multiplications in $\mathbb{Z}_p$	

Lemma 4.6. *The scheme in Algorithm 5 satisfies verifiability of key generation and decryption.*

Proof. Both follow from the completeness, soundness and zero-knowledge of the identification protocol [16], which guarantees that any accepted proof corresponds to a correct relation on short secrets, ensuring structural verifiability of (s, e) and correctness of decryption proofs.

Theorem 4.7 (Security of PVSS Instantiation with Linear Encryption Scheme II). *Assuming the hardness of the* MLWE *and* SIS *problems, and the security of the LVC-PoS and Linear Encryption Scheme II, our PVSS instantiation achieves correctness, verifiability, and t-IND2 privacy.*

Proof (Proof Sketch). Follows from the security of the generic framework established in Sect. 3, together with the properties of Linear Encryption Scheme II.

5   Implementation Cost of Core Procedures

Table 4 evaluates the computational cost of our PVSS core procedures for two instantiations: *Ours 1* (standard LWE) and *Ours 2* (efficient (Ring) $-$ LWE), corresponding to Sect. 4. The table reports dominant operations per procedure, where $\mathrm{op}_{\mathsf{TrapGen}}$ is trapdoor generation, $\mathrm{op}_{\mathsf{SampPre}}$ is preimage sampling, $\mathrm{op}_{\mathrm{MV\text{-}Mult}}/\mathrm{op}_{\mathrm{Poly\text{-}Mult}}$ are matrix–vector/polynomial multiplications, $\mathrm{op}_{\mathrm{ID\text{-}P}}/\mathrm{op}_{\mathrm{ID\text{-}V}}$ are identification steps, and distribution/decryption costs are driven by scalar multiplications and encryption routines $(\mathrm{op}_{\mathrm{vec\text{-}scalar\ mult}}, \mathrm{op}_{\mathrm{Enc1}}, \mathrm{op}_{\mathrm{Enc3}})$. We also account for CRS size (not shown in the table): it scales as $w(w-1) \cdot m \cdot \log q$ for *Ours 1* versus $w(w-1) \cdot k \cdot \log q$ for *Ours 2*. Since typically $m \gg k$, the (Ring) $-$ LWE instantiation yields a substantially more compact CRS due to its ring structure. Our implementation results are reported to capture relative costs and scalability trends rather than absolute timings.

A   Omitted Preliminaries

A.1   Lattice Trapdoors and Sampling Algorithms

Our constructions build on lattice trapdoors and Gaussian sampling, following GPV and Micciancio–Peikert.

-   **TrapGen**: It samples a random matrix $\mathbf{A} \in \mathbb{Z}_q^{n \times m}$ with a trapdoor $\mathbf{T_A}$ (a short basis for $\Lambda^\perp(\mathbf{A})$): $(\mathbf{A}, \mathbf{T_A}) \leftarrow \mathsf{TrapGen}(1^n, q, m)$. The trapdoor enables efficient sampling of short lattice vectors associated with $\mathbf{A}$.
    Given the trapdoor $\mathbf{T_A}$, a target $\mathbf{u} \in \mathbb{Z}_q^n$, and Gaussian parameter σ, this algorithm samples a short $\mathbf{e}$ from a discrete Gaussian over the appropriate coset such that $\mathbf{Ae} = \mathbf{u} \bmod q$: $\mathbf{e} \leftarrow \mathsf{SampPre}(\mathbf{A}, \mathbf{T_A}, \mathbf{u}, \sigma)$.
-   **GadgetSolve**: This is a deterministic algorithm operating on the gadget matrix $\mathbf{G}$ (often defined as powers of 2). Given a target $\mathbf{u}$, it outputs a short vector $\mathbf{x}$ such that $\mathbf{Gx} = \mathbf{u} \pmod q$. Unlike $\mathsf{SampPre}$, this does not require a trapdoor but relies on the special structure of $\mathbf{G}$: $\mathbf{x} \leftarrow \mathsf{GadgetSolve}(\mathbf{u})$

A.2   Regev Encryption Scheme

The Regev encryption scheme consists of three algorithms:

- KeyGen(1^n): Choose a secret key $\mathbf{s} \in \mathbb{Z}_q^n$. Choose a random matrix $\mathbf{A} \in \mathbb{Z}_q^{n \times m}$ and an error vector $\mathbf{e}$ from a noise distribution χ. Calculate $\mathbf{b} = \mathbf{A}^T \mathbf{s} + \mathbf{e}$. The public key is $(\mathbf{A}, \mathbf{b})$ and the secret key is $\mathbf{s}$.
- Enc($\mathbf{pk}, \mu$): To encrypt a bit $\mu \in \{0,1\}$, choose a random binary vector $\mathbf{r} \in \{0,1\}^m$. The ciphertext is: $\mathbf{c} = (\mathbf{u}, v) = (\mathbf{Ar}, \mathbf{b}^T \mathbf{r} + \mu \cdot \lfloor q/2 \rfloor)$
- Dec($\mathbf{sk}, \mathbf{c}$): Compute $v - \mathbf{s}^T \mathbf{u} \approx \mu \cdot \lfloor q/2 \rfloor + \text{noise}$. The message is recovered by rounding to the nearest multiple of $\lfloor q/2 \rfloor$.

A.3   Shamir Secret Sharing

We utilize Shamir's Secret Sharing to distribute a secret S among n participants such that any t participants can reconstruct it.

1. **Distribution**: The dealer chooses a random polynomial $P(x)$ of degree $t-1$ such that $P(0) = S$. The shares are $y_i = P(i)$ for $i = 1, \ldots, n$.
2. **Reconstruction**: Given any subset of t shares $\{(x_i, y_i)\}$, the secret S is recovered using Lagrange interpolation: $S = P(0) = \sum_{j=1}^{t} y_{i_j} \left(\prod_{k=1, k \neq j}^{t} \frac{-x_{i_k}}{x_{i_j} - x_{i_k}} \right)$

A.4   Lattice-Based Identification Protocols

We refer to interactive identification protocols denoted by procedures id.prove and id.verify. These are typically Sigma-protocols (Σ-protocols) adapted for lattice settings (e.g., based on Lyubashevsky's framework or Stern's protocol).

- id.prove($\mathbf{sk}$, public inputs): The prover (holding the secret key $\mathbf{sk}$) engages in a 3-move interaction:
    1. **Commitment**: Prover sends a commitment $\mathbf{w}$ based on random noise.
    2. **Challenge**: Verifier sends a random challenge c.
    3. **Response**: Prover computes a response $\mathbf{z}$ using $\mathbf{sk}$ and c, ensuring $\mathbf{z}$ does not leak information about $\mathbf{sk}$ (often using rejection sampling).
- id.verify($\mathbf{pk}$, transcript): The verifier checks if the response $\mathbf{z}$ is short (has small norm) and satisfies the algebraic relation linking the commitment, challenge, and public key (e.g., $\mathbf{Az} = \mathbf{w} + c \cdot \mathbf{t}$).

A.5   Security Definitions of PVSS

A PVSS scheme should satisfy correctness, verifiability and IND2-secrecy.

Correctness. Correctness with r-reconstruction means that with all parties honest, all proofs verify and any set of at least r participants can recover the secret by decrypting their shares and running Reconstruct.

Definition A.1. *For a set $T \subseteq [n]$, and a probability distribution $\mathcal{D}_s$ over the secret space, define the following experiment* $\mathrm{ExpCorr}_{T,\mathcal{D}_s}(1^\lambda)$.

- $\mathsf{pp} \leftarrow \mathsf{Setup}(1^\lambda, 1^n, 1^t)$
- $\forall i \in [n],\ (\mathsf{sk}_i, \mathsf{pk}_i, \mathsf{pf}_{Key,i}) \leftarrow \mathsf{KeyGen}(\mathsf{pp}, i)$
- $s \leftarrow \mathcal{D}_s\ ,\ ((C_i)_{i \in [n]}, \mathsf{pf}_D) \leftarrow \mathsf{Dist}(\mathsf{pp}, \{\mathsf{pk}_i : i \in [n]\}, s)$
- $\forall i \in T,\ (s_i, \mathsf{pf}_{Dec,i}) \leftarrow \mathsf{Decrypt}(\mathsf{pp}, \mathsf{pk}_i, \mathsf{sk}_i, C_i)$
- $s' \leftarrow \mathsf{Reconstruct}(\mathsf{pp}, \{s_i : i \in T\})$, *where* $s' \in S \cup \{\bot\}$
- *Output* $(\mathsf{pp}, (\mathsf{pk}_i, \mathsf{pf}_{Key,i}, C_i)_{i \in [n]}, \mathsf{pf}_D, (\mathsf{pf}_{Dec,i})_{i \in T}, s, s')$

We say that the PVSS is correct with r-reconstruction if for all $T \subseteq [n]$ of size at least r, any probability distribution $\mathcal{D}_s$ over the secret space,

$$\Pr\Big[\mathsf{VerifyKey}(\mathsf{pp}, i, \mathsf{pk}_i, \mathsf{pf}_{Key,i}) = 1\, \forall i \in [n] \wedge \mathsf{VerifyDist}(\mathsf{pp}, (C_i)_{i \in [n]}, \mathsf{pf}_D, (\mathsf{pk}_i)_{i \in [n]}) = 1$$

$$\wedge\, \mathsf{VerifyDecrypt}(\mathsf{pp}, i, \mathsf{pk}_i, s_i, C_i, \mathsf{pf}_{Dec,i}) = 1\, \forall i \in T$$

$$\wedge\, s' = s \,\Big|\, (\mathsf{pp}, (\mathsf{pk}_i, \mathsf{pf}_{Key,i}, C_i)_{i \in [n]}, \mathsf{pf}_D, (\mathsf{pf}_{Dec,i})_{i \in T}, s, s') \leftarrow \mathrm{ExpCorr}_{T,\mathcal{D}_s}(1^\lambda)\Big] = 1$$

Verifiability. Verifiability means that acceptance by VerifyKey, VerifyDist, and VerifyDecrypt guaranties, respectively, well-formed keys, a correct secret sharing encoded in the ciphertexts, and correct decryption of the shares.

Definition A.2. *The PVSS satisfies verifiability of key generation if underlying encryption scheme satisfies verifiability of key generation.*

Definition A.3. *The PVSS satisfies verifiability of sharing distribution if for every PPT $\mathcal{A}$,*

$$\Pr\Big[\mathsf{VerifyDist}(\mathsf{pp}, (C_i)_{i \in [n]}, \mathsf{pf}_D, (\mathsf{pk}_i)_{i \in [n]}) = 1$$

$$\wedge\, \nexists s \in S \text{ s.t. } ((C_i)_{i \in [n]}, \cdot) \leftarrow \mathsf{Dist}(\mathsf{pp}, \{\mathsf{pk}_i : i \in [n]\}, s)$$

$$\Big|\, \mathsf{pp} \leftarrow \mathsf{Setup}(1^\lambda, 1^n, 1^t), ((C_i)_{i \in [n]}, \mathsf{pf}_D) \leftarrow \mathcal{A}(\mathsf{pp})\Big] \text{ is negligible in } \lambda.$$

Definition A.4. *The PVSS satisfies verifiability of share decryption if the underlying encryption scheme satisfies verifiability of decryption 2.4.*

Privacy. We define secret indistinguishability against an adversary corrupting t parties, following [2]: after seeing honest public keys, the adversary may derive corrupted ones, yet given (s_0, s_1) and a sharing of s_b it has negligible advantage in guessing b. We use IND2-privacy (adversary-chosen secrets), stronger than IND1 where the challenger samples the secrets.

Definition A.5. *The PVSS is t-IND2-private if for any poly(1^λ)-time adversary $\mathcal{A}$ corrupting t parties (w.l.o.g. $\mathcal{A}$ corrupts $[n-t+1,n]$), we have*

$$\Pr[\mathrm{Game}_{\mathcal{A},\mathrm{PVSS}}^{\mathrm{ind-secrecy},0}(\lambda) = 1] - \Pr[\mathrm{Game}_{\mathcal{A},\mathrm{PVSS}}^{\mathrm{ind-secrecy},1}(\lambda) = 1] = \mathrm{negl}(\lambda)$$

where for $b = 0, 1$, $\mathrm{Game}_{\mathcal{A},\mathrm{PVSS}}^{\mathrm{ind-secrecy},b}(\lambda)$ is below game against a challenger:

- *The challenger runs $\mathsf{pp} \leftarrow \mathsf{Setup}(1^\lambda, 1^n, 1^t)$ and sends pp to $\mathcal{A}$.*
- *For $i \in [n-t]$, the challenger runs $(\mathsf{sk}_i, \mathsf{pk}_i, \mathsf{pf}_{Key,i}) \leftarrow \mathsf{KeyGen}(\mathsf{pp}, i)$ and sends all created $(\mathsf{pk}_i, \mathsf{pf}_{Key,i})$ to $\mathcal{A}$.*
- *For the corrupted parties, $\mathcal{A}$ creates $(\mathsf{pk}_i, \mathsf{pf}_{Key,i})_{i \in [n-t+1,n]} \leftarrow \mathcal{A}(\mathsf{pp}, (\mathsf{pk}_i, \mathsf{pf}_{Key,i})_{i \in [n-t]})$ and sends them to the challenger, together with two values s_0, s_1 in S.*
- *The challenger runs $\mathsf{VerifyKey}(\mathsf{pp}, i, \mathsf{pk}_i, \mathsf{pf}_{Key,i})$ for $i \in [n-t+1,n]$. If any of these output 0 (reject), the challenger sends $\perp$ to $\mathcal{A}$.*
- *Otherwise, if all key verification proofs accept, it runs $(C_1, \ldots, C_n, \mathsf{pf}_D) \leftarrow \mathsf{Dist}(\mathsf{pp}, \{\mathsf{pk}_i : i \in [n]\}, s_b)$, and sends $(C_1, \ldots, C_n, \mathsf{pf}_D)$ to $\mathcal{A}$.*
- *$\mathcal{A}$ outputs a guess $b' \in \{0, 1\}$.*

A.6   Vector Commitments

Definition A.6 (Vector Commitments (VC)) [2]. *A VC scheme is parameterized by the families of functions over $\mathcal{R}$ and an input alphabet $\mathcal{X} \subseteq \mathcal{R}$*

$$\mathcal{F} = \{\mathcal{F}_{v,w,o} \subseteq \{f : \mathcal{R}^v \times \mathcal{R}^w \to \mathcal{R}^o\}\}_{v,w,o \in \mathbb{N}}$$
$$and \quad \mathcal{Y} = \{\mathcal{Y}_{v,o} \subseteq \{y : \mathcal{R}^v \to \mathcal{R}^o\}\}_{v,o \in \mathbb{N}}$$

The parameters v, w, and o are the dimensions of public inputs, secret inputs, and outputs of f respectively. Here, $\mathcal{Y}$ defines the family of valid right-hand side functions (which may simply be constant functions representing a target vector), The VC scheme consists of the PPT algorithms ($\mathsf{Setup}, \mathsf{Com}, \mathsf{Open}, \mathsf{Verify}$) defined as follows:

- $\mathsf{pp} \leftarrow \mathsf{Setup}(1^\lambda, 1^v, 1^w, 1^o)$: *The setup algorithm generates the public parameters on input of the security parameter $\lambda \in \mathbb{N}$, the size parameters $v, w, o \in \mathbb{N}$.*
- $(c, \mathsf{aux}) \leftarrow \mathsf{Com}(\mathsf{pp}, \mathbf{x})$: *The commitment algorithm generates a commitment c of a given vector $\mathbf{x} \in \mathcal{X}^w$ with some auxiliary opening information aux.*
- $\pi \leftarrow \mathsf{Open}(\mathsf{pp}, f, \mathbf{z}, \mathsf{aux})$: *The opening algorithm generates a proof π for $f(\mathbf{z}, \cdot)$ for the public input $\mathbf{z}$ and function $f \in \mathcal{F}_{v,w,o}$.*
- $b \leftarrow \mathsf{Verify}(\mathsf{pp}, f, \mathbf{z}, \mathbf{y}, c, \pi)$: *The verification algorithm inputs public parameters pp, linear function $f \in \mathcal{F}_{v,w,o}$, $\mathbf{z} \in \mathcal{X}^v$, $\mathbf{y} \in \mathcal{X}^o$ and a commitment c, and an opening proof π. It outputs a bit b deciding whether to accept or reject that the vector $\mathbf{x}$ committed in c satisfies $f(\mathbf{z}, \mathbf{x}) = y(\mathbf{z})$*

Definition A.7 (Correctness). *A VC scheme for $(\mathcal{F}, \mathcal{X})$ is said to be correct if for any $\lambda, v, w, o \in \mathbb{N}$, any $\mathsf{pp} \in \mathsf{Setup}(1^\lambda, 1^v, 1^w, 1^o)$, any $(f, \mathbf{z}, \mathbf{x}, \mathbf{y}) \in \mathcal{F}_{v,w,o} \times \mathcal{X}^v \times \mathcal{X}^w \times \mathcal{Y}_{v,o}$ satisfying $f(\mathbf{z}, \mathbf{x}) = y(\mathbf{z})$, any $(c, \mathsf{aux}) \leftarrow \mathsf{Com}(\mathsf{pp}, \mathbf{x})$, any $\pi \in \mathsf{Open}(\mathsf{pp}, f, \mathbf{z}, \mathbf{y}, \mathsf{aux})$, it holds that:* $\mathsf{Verify}(\mathsf{pp}, \mathbf{z}, \mathbf{y}, c, \pi) = 1$.

Definition A.8 (Binding). *Let $\rho : \mathbb{N}^3 \to [0,1]$. A VC scheme for $(\mathcal{F}, \mathcal{X}, \mathcal{Y})$ is said to be* weakly ρ-binding *if for any pair of PPT adversary $\mathcal{A}$ and any $v, w \in \mathrm{poly}(\lambda)$ it holds that the following expression is upper-bounded by $\rho(\lambda, v, w)$:*

$$\Pr\left[\begin{array}{l} \forall i \in \{0,1\}, \mathsf{Verify}(\mathsf{pp}, f_i, \mathbf{z}_i, \mathbf{y}_i, c, \pi_i) = 1 \\ \wedge f_0(\mathbf{z}_0, \cdot) = f_1(\mathbf{z}_1, \cdot) \wedge \mathbf{y}_0(\mathbf{z}_0) \neq \mathbf{y}_1(\mathbf{z}_1) \end{array} \middle| \begin{array}{l} \mathsf{pp} \leftarrow \mathsf{Setup}(1^\lambda, 1^v, 1^w, 1^o) \\ (c, (f_i, \mathbf{z}_i, \mathbf{y}_i, \pi_i)_{i=0}^1) \leftarrow \mathcal{A}(\mathsf{pp}) \end{array}\right]$$

We say that the scheme is weakly binding *if it is weakly ρ-binding and $\rho(\lambda, v, w)$ is negligible in λ for any $v, w \in \mathrm{poly}(\lambda)$.*

The scheme is said to be ρ-binding if for any PPT adversary $\mathcal{A}$ and $w, t = \mathrm{poly}(\lambda)$ it holds that the following expression is upper-bounded by $\rho(\lambda)$:

$$\Pr\left[\begin{array}{l} \forall i \in I; \mathsf{Verify}(\mathsf{pp}, f_i, \mathbf{z}_i, \mathbf{y}_i, c, \pi_i) = 1, \\ \wedge \neg(\exists x \in \mathcal{K}^w, \forall i \in I, f_i(\mathbf{z}_i, x) = \mathbf{y}_i(\mathbf{z}_i) \end{array} \middle| \begin{array}{l} \mathsf{pp} \leftarrow \mathsf{Setup}(1^\lambda, 1^v, 1^w, 1^o) \\ (c, I, (f_i, \mathbf{z}_i, \mathbf{y}_i, \pi_i)_{i \in \mathbb{Z}_t}) \leftarrow \mathcal{A}(\mathsf{pp}) \end{array}\right]$$

We say that the scheme is binding *if it is ρ-binding and $\rho(\lambda, v, w)$ is negligible in λ for any $v, w \in \mathrm{poly}(\lambda)$.*

Note that binding quantifies $\mathbf{x}$ over the base field $\mathcal{K}$ (not the ring $\mathcal{R}$); this choice is motivated by our binding proof. We discuss potential approaches to modify the VC scheme to achieve hiding and functional hiding.

Definition A.9 ((Functional) Hiding)). *A VC scheme for $(\mathcal{F}, \mathcal{X}, \mathcal{Y})$ is said to be statistically/computationally hiding if for any $\lambda, w, o \in \mathbb{N}$, any $\mathsf{pp} \in \mathsf{Setup}(1^\lambda, 1^w, 1^o)$, and any $\mathbf{x}, \mathbf{x}' \in \mathcal{X}^w$, the distributions*

$$\{c : (c, \mathsf{aux}) \leftarrow \mathsf{Com}(\mathsf{pp}, \mathbf{x})\} \quad \text{and} \quad \{c : (c, \mathsf{aux}) \leftarrow \mathsf{Com}(\mathsf{pp}, \mathbf{x}')\}$$

are statistically/computationally indistinguishable.

A VC scheme for $(\mathcal{F}, \mathcal{X}, \mathcal{Y})$ is said to be statistically/computationally functional hiding if there exists a tuple of PPT simulators $\mathcal{S} = (\mathcal{S}_0, \mathcal{S}_1)$ such that, for any $\lambda, v, w, o \in \mathbb{N}$ and any $(f, \mathbf{z}, \mathbf{x}, \mathbf{y}) \in \mathcal{F}_{v,w,o} \times \mathcal{X}^v \times \mathcal{X}^w \times \mathcal{Y}_{v,o}$ satisfying $f(\mathbf{z}, \mathbf{x}) = \mathbf{y}(\mathbf{z})$, the distributions

$$\left\{(c, \pi) : \begin{array}{l} \mathsf{pp} \leftarrow \mathsf{Setup}(1^\lambda, 1^w, 1^o), \\ (c, \mathsf{aux}) \leftarrow \mathsf{Com}(\mathsf{pp}, \mathbf{x}) \\ \pi \leftarrow \mathsf{Open}(\mathsf{pp}, f, \mathbf{z}, \mathsf{aux}) \end{array}\right\} \quad \text{and} \quad \left\{(c, \pi) : \begin{array}{l} (\mathsf{pp}, \mathsf{td}) \leftarrow \mathcal{S}_0(1^\lambda, 1^w, 1^o) \\ \\ (c, \pi) \leftarrow \mathcal{S}_1(\mathsf{pp}, \mathsf{td}, f, \mathbf{z}, y(\mathbf{z})) \end{array}\right\}$$

are statistically/computationally indistinguishable.

A.7   Base VC of Albrecht *et al.* [2]

A VC scheme lets a dealer commit to a vector $\mathbf{x}$ and later give succinct non-interactive proofs that linear relations on $\mathbf{x}$ hold, without revealing $\mathbf{x}$. We recall the VC scheme of [2] in Algorithm 6.

<u>Setup</u>: In Setup, the public parameters are generated as follows:

- Sample $\mathbf{v} \in (R_q^{\times})^w$ to act as the commitment key.
- Sample a vector $h \in R_p^o$ for random linear combinations in proofs.
- Generate a trapdoor matrix A and auxiliary data td.
- Precompute vectors $\mathbf{u}_g = \mathsf{SampPre}(td, g(\mathbf{v})t, \beta)$ for all $g = \frac{v_i}{v_j}$ in the set G.

The vectors $\mathbf{u}_g$ enable efficient proofs of linear relations by acting as compressed witnesses for relations between components of $\mathbf{x}$.

<u>Commit</u>: In Com, to commit to vector $\mathbf{x} \in R_q^w$, compute: $c = \langle \mathbf{v}, \mathbf{x} \rangle \mod q$. Additionally, compute auxiliary vectors $\mathbf{u}_i = \sum_{j \neq i} x_j \cdot \mathbf{u}_{\frac{v_j}{v_i}}$. These are stored in aux for future proof generation.

<u>Open</u>: Given a linear function f and the vector $\mathbf{x}$, the dealer computes the opening proof: $\pi = \sum_{i=1}^{o} \sum_{j=1}^{w} h_i f_{ij}(\mathbf{x}) \mathbf{u}_j$. This proves that $f(\mathbf{x})$ evaluates to the claimed value without revealing $\mathbf{x}$.

<u>Verify</u>: The verifier checks two properties:

1. Correctness of the proof π: $A \cdot \mathbf{u} \stackrel{?}{=} \left(\sum_{k=1}^{o} h_k \left(\sum_{j=1}^{w} f_{kj} \frac{c}{v_j} - y_k \right) \right) \cdot t \mod q$.
2. Smallness of auxiliary vector $\mathbf{u}$: $\|\mathbf{u}\| \leq \delta_0$.

B   Omitted Proofs

B.1   Security Proof of LVC-PoS

Proof Correctness. The proof consists of three components: $(\pi, \pi_{eq}, \pi_{ip})$.

- π: This is the opening proof from Algorithm 6 for standard linear function evaluation. Since the correctness of Algorithm 6 is established in [2], correctness of this component follows directly.
- π_{eq}: This component verifies the auxiliary commitment consistency. Specifically, we use a commitment with parameter vector $\mathbf{v} = \frac{1}{\mathbf{v}}$. Since we possess the trapdoor for all ratios $\frac{\frac{1}{v_i}}{\frac{1}{v_j}}$, and this commitment operates over the same algebraic structure as the underlying VC, the correctness of π_{eq} follows from the correctness of Algorithm 6.

Algorithm 6. Vector Commitment [2]

---

procedure $\text{SETUP}(1^\lambda, 1^v, 1^w, 1^o)$
   $\mathbf{v} \leftarrow (R_q^\times)^w \ , h \leftarrow R_p^o, t \leftarrow T,$
   $(A, td) = \text{TrapGen}(1^\eta, 1^l, q, R, \beta)$
   $\mathbf{u}_{\frac{v_i}{v_j}} = \text{SampPre}(td, \frac{v_i}{v_j}t, \beta), \forall i, j \in \mathbb{Z}_w | i \neq j$
   return $(A, t, \{\mathbf{u}_{v_i/v_j}\}, \mathbf{v}, h)$

procedure $\text{COM}(\mathsf{pp}, \mathbf{x})$
   $c = \langle \mathbf{v}, \mathbf{x} \rangle \mod q$
   for $i = 1$ **to** w **do**
      $\mathbf{u}_i = \sum_{j \neq i} x_j \cdot \mathbf{u}_{\frac{v_j}{v_i}}.$
   $\mathsf{aux} = (\mathbf{u}_i)_{i \in \mathbb{Z}_w}.$
   return (c, aux)

procedure $\text{OPEN}(\mathsf{pp}, f, \mathbf{z}, \mathsf{aux})$
   $\pi = \sum_{i \in \mathbb{Z}_o} \sum_{j \in \mathbb{Z}_w} h_i f_{i,j}(\mathbf{z}) \mathbf{u}_j$
   return π

procedure $\text{VERIFY}(\mathsf{pp}, f, \mathbf{z}, \mathbf{y}, c, \pi)$
   $a_1 = \left(\mathbf{A} \cdot \mathbf{u} \stackrel{?}{=} \left(\sum_{k \in \mathbb{Z}_o} h_k \left(\sum_{j \in \mathbb{Z}_w} f_{k,j}(\mathbf{z})\frac{c}{v_j} - y_k\right)\right) \cdot t \mod q\right), \ a_2 = \left(\|\mathbf{u}\| \stackrel{?}{\leq} \delta_0\right)$
   return $a_1 \wedge a_2$

π_{ip}: This component proves the smallness (binary property) of the committed vector. The validity is demonstrated by the following relation:

$$c_{\mathbf{x}} \cdot \bar{c}_{\mathbf{h} \circ (\mathbf{x}-1)} = \left(\sum_{i \in w} x_i v_i\right) \cdot \left(\sum_{i \in w} h_i(x_i - 1)\frac{1}{v_i}\right)$$

$$= \sum_{i,j \in \mathbb{Z}_w : i \neq j} x_i(h_j(x_j - 1))\frac{v_i}{v_j} + \langle \mathbf{h} \circ (\mathbf{x} - 1), \mathbf{x} \rangle = \langle \mathbf{a}, \pi_{ip} \rangle + 0$$

Therefore, the correctness of π_{ip} is established.

Functional Hiding. Functional hiding of Algorithm 3 follows from functional hiding of Algorithm 6 in [2], since our commitments and proofs are obtained via homomorphic evaluations and the auxiliary openings are linear functions of the committed vector. Moreover, using the Gaussian Leftover Hash Lemma (cf. [2]), the joint distribution of commitments and proofs is statistically close to uniform given only the revealed function value and smallness check, so no extra information about $\mathbf{x}$ leaks. *Weak Binding.* The binding property of Algorithm 3 similarly follows from the binding of the underlying VC (Algorithm 6) as established in [2]. Specifically, the commitments in Algorithm 3 are homomorphic transformations of the base commitments in Algorithm 6.

The binding property of [2] ensures that a fixed commitment cannot be opened to two different vectors yielding different function outputs or smallness witnesses. Since π_{eq} and π_{ip} are linear openings for the same commitment and use the VC trapdoor structure, Algorithm 3 inherits weak binding.

References

1. Ajtai, M.: Determinism versus non-determinism for linear time RAMs (extended abstract). In: 31st ACM STOC, pp. 632–641. ACM Press (1999). https://doi.org/10.1145/301250.301424
2. Albrecht, M.R., Cini, V., Lai, R.W.F., Malavolta, G., Thyagarajan, S.A.K.: Lattice-based SNARKs: publicly verifiable, preprocessing, and recursively composable - (extended abstract). In: Dodis, Y., Shrimpton, T. (eds.) CRYPTO 2022, Part II. LNCS, vol. 13508, pp. 102–132. Springer, Cham (2022). https://doi.org/10.1007/978-3-031-15979-4_4
3. Bacho, R., Loss, J.: Adaptively secure (aggregatable) PVSS and application to distributed randomness beacons. In: Meng, W., Jensen, C.D., Cremers, C., Kirda, E. (eds.) ACM CCS 2023, pp. 1791–1804. ACM Press (2023). https://doi.org/10.1145/3576915.3623106
4. Baghery, K.: π: a unified framework for verifiable secret sharing. Cryptology ePrint Archive (2023)
5. Boudot, F., Traoré, J.: Efficient publicly verifiable secret sharing schemes with fast or delayed recovery. In: Information and Communication Security: Second International Conference, ICICS 1999, Sydney, Australia, November 9–11, 1999. Proceedings 2, pp. 87–102. Springer (1999). https://doi.org/10.1007/978-3-540-47942-0_8
6. Brakerski, Z., Langlois, A., Peikert, C., Regev, O., Stehlé, D.: Classical hardness of learning with errors. In: Boneh, D., Roughgarden, T., Feigenbaum, J. (eds.) 45th ACM STOC, pp. 575–584. ACM Press (2013). https://doi.org/10.1145/2488608.2488680
7. Cascudo, I., David, B.: ALBATROSS: publicly attestable batched randomness based on secret sharing. In: Moriai, S., Wang, H. (eds.) ASIACRYPT 2020, Part III. LNCS, vol. 12493, pp. 311–341. Springer, Cham (2020). https://doi.org/10.1007/978-3-030-64840-4_11
8. Cascudo, I., David, B.: Publicly verifiable secret sharing over class groups and applications to DKG and YOSO. In: Joye, M., Leander, G. (eds.) EUROCRYPT 2024, Part V. LNCS, vol. 14655, pp. 216–248. Springer, Cham (2024). https://doi.org/10.1007/978-3-031-58740-5_8
9. Cascudo, I., David, B., Garms, L., Konring, A.: YOLO YOSO: fast and simple encryption and secret sharing in the YOSO model. In: Agrawal, S., Lin, D. (eds.) ASIACRYPT 2022, Part I. LNCS, vol. 13791, pp. 651–680. Springer, Cham (2022). https://doi.org/10.1007/978-3-031-22963-3_22
10. Fujisaki, E., Okamoto, T.: A practical and provably secure scheme for publicly verifiable secret sharing and its applications. In: Nyberg, K. (ed.) EUROCRYPT 1998. LNCS, vol. 1403, pp. 32–46. Springer, Berlin, Heidelberg (1998). https://doi.org/10.1007/BFb0054115
11. Gentry, C., Halevi, S., Lyubashevsky, V.: Practical non-interactive publicly verifiable secret sharing with thousands of parties. In: Dunkelman, O., Dziembowski, S. (eds.) EUROCRYPT 2022, Part I. LNCS, vol. 13275, pp. 458–487. Springer, Cham (2022). https://doi.org/10.1007/978-3-031-06944-4_16
12. Gentry, C., Peikert, C., Vaikuntanathan, V.: Trapdoors for hard lattices and new cryptographic constructions. In: STOC 2008, Proceedings of the Fortieth Annual ACM Symposium on Theory of Computing, pp. 197–206. Association for Computing Machinery, New York, NY, USA (2008). https://doi.org/10.1145/1374376.1374407

13. Heidarvand, S., Villar, J.L.: Public verifiability from pairings in secret sharing schemes. In: International Workshop on Selected Areas in Cryptography, pp. 294–308. Springer (2008). https://doi.org/10.1007/978-3-642-04159-4_19

14. Langlois, A., Stehlé, D.: Worst-case to average-case reductions for module lattices. Des. Codes Crypt. **75**(3), 565–599 (2015)

15. Libert, B.: Vector commitments with proofs of smallness: short range proofs and more. In: Tang, Q., Teague, V. (eds.) Public-Key Cryptography - PKC 2024, pp. 36–67. Springer Nature Switzerland, Cham (2024). https://doi.org/10.1007/978-3-031-57722-2_2

16. Lyubashevsky, V.: Lattice-based identification schemes secure under active attacks. In: Cramer, R. (ed.) PKC 2008. LNCS, vol. 4939, pp. 162–179. Springer, Berlin, Heidelberg (2008). https://doi.org/10.1007/978-3-540-78440-1_10

17. Lyubashevsky, V., Peikert, C., Regev, O.: A toolkit for ring-LWE cryptography. In: Johansson, T., Nguyen, P.Q. (eds.) EUROCRYPT 2013. LNCS, vol. 7881, pp. 35–54. Springer, Berlin, Heidelberg (2013). https://doi.org/10.1007/978-3-642-38348-9_3

18. Micciancio, D., Regev, O.: Lattice-based cryptography. In: Post-quantum Cryptography, pp. 147–191. Springer (2009). https://doi.org/10.1007/11818175_8

19. Minh, P.N., Nguyen, K., Susilo, W., Nguyen-An, K.: Publicly verifiable secret sharing: generic constructions and lattice-based instantiations in the standard model. arXiv preprint arXiv:2504.14381 (2025)

20. Peikert, C., et al.: A decade of lattice cryptography. Found. Trends Theor. Comput. Sci. **10**(4), 283–424 (2016)

21. Regev, O.: On lattices, learning with errors, random linear codes, and cryptography. In: Gabow, H.N., Fagin, R. (eds.) 37th ACM STOC, pp. 84–93. ACM Press (2005). https://doi.org/10.1145/1060590.1060603

22. Regev, O.: On lattices, learning with errors, random linear codes, and cryptography. J. ACM **56**(6) (2009). https://doi.org/10.1145/1568318.1568324

23. Ruiz, A., Villar, J.L.: Publicly verifiable secret sharing from paillier's cryptosystem. In: WEWoRC 2005-Western European Workshop on Research in Cryptology, pp. 98–108. Gesellschaft für Informatik eV (2005)

24. Schoenmakers, B.: A simple publicly verifiable secret sharing scheme and its application to electronic. In: Wiener, M.J. (ed.) CRYPTO 1999. LNCS, vol. 1666, pp. 148–164. Springer, Berlin, Heidelberg (1999). https://doi.org/10.1007/3-540-48405-1_10

25. Stadler, M.: Publicly verifiable secret sharing. In: Maurer, U.M. (ed.) EUROCRYPT 1996. LNCS, vol. 1070, pp. 190–199. Springer, Berlin, Heidelberg (1996). https://doi.org/10.1007/3-540-68339-9_17

Compact, Efficient and Non-separable Hybrid Signatures

Julien Devevey[1(✉)], Morgane Guerreau[2], and Maxime Roméas[1]

[1] ANSSI, Paris, France
`julien.devevey@ssi.gouv.fr`
[2] PQShield, Oxford, UK

Abstract. The transition to post-quantum cryptography involves balancing the long-term threat of quantum adversaries with the need for post-quantum algorithms and their implementations to gain maturity safely. Hybridization, *i.e.* combining classical and post-quantum schemes, offers a practical and safe solution.

We introduce a new security notion for hybrid signatures, Hybrid EU-CMA, which captures cross-protocol, separability, and recombination attacks that may occur during the post-quantum transition, while encompassing standard unforgeability guarantees. Using this framework, we adapt the Fiat-Shamir (with or without aborts) transform to build hybrid signature schemes that satisfy our notion from two identification schemes. Compared to simple concatenation of signatures, our construction (i) has no separability issues, (ii) reduces signature size, (iii) runs faster, and (iv) remains easily implementable.

As a concrete application, we propose Silithium, a hybrid signature combining the identification schemes underlying EC-Schnorr and ML-DSA. Implementing Silithium requires only an ML-DSA implementation supporting the "external μ" option during verification and an elliptic curve library. In the security analysis, we show that our scheme can be safely used along with ML-DSA and either EC-Schnorr or ECDSA. A proof-of-concept OpenSSL implementation demonstrates its practicality, simplicity, and performance.

Keywords: Post-Quantum Transition · Hybrid Signatures · Fiat-Shamir

1 Introduction

The ongoing transition to post-quantum cryptography presents one of the most delicate challenges in modern security engineering. While post-quantum algorithms are progressively being standardized, their deployment in real-world infrastructures requires careful planning to mitigate security risks. Although these newly standardized algorithms have undergone at least a decade of analysis, the confidence and maturity gained through cryptanalysis, implementation, and deployment cannot yet compare to that accumulated for classical factorization-

M. Bardet and R. Niederhagen (Eds.): PQCrypto 2026, LNCS 16492, pp. 143–177, 2026.
https://doi.org/10.1007/978-3-032-22698-3_5

and discrete logarithm-based algorithms. This creates a tension between the long-term threat posed by cryptographically relevant quantum computers and the need for post-quantum algorithms to gain maturity through large-scale deployment, all while maintaining the robust security assurances of established classical schemes. For these reasons, several European security agencies—such as ANSSI [1], BSI [9], and NLNCSA [26]—strongly recommend an intermediate state known as *hybridization*: combining classical and post-quantum algorithms in such a way that overall security is preserved as long as at least one algorithm remains secure.

In the case of digital signatures, the most straightforward approach to hybridization is *concatenation*—that is, forming a hybrid verification key, signing key, and signature by concatenating the respective values of at least two schemes, with verification checking both signatures independently and accepting only if both succeed. This method guarantees unforgeability (EU-CMA security) of the hybrid as long as one component remains unforgeable. However, it fails to ensure strong unforgeability (sEU-CMA) whenever one component is probabilistic, due to attacks that exploit the independence of the component signatures. This distinction is critical in practice, as sEU-CMA security is required in applications such as authenticated key exchange [2,18], SSH [4], and cryptocurrencies [21].

As Table 1 illustrates, different transition strategies require distinct patterns of key updates. A purely post-quantum transition involves a single key update, whereas a "hygienic" hybridization approach requires two updates to ensure strict separation between key lifecycles. In practice, however, users and systems are more likely to adopt a minimal-overhead strategy, adding a post-quantum key to an existing pre-quantum key and later phasing out the pre-quantum component. In this scenario, achieving only EU-CMA security for the hybrid signature is insufficient. Indeed, a concatenated signature can be stripped to yield a valid component signature or recombined from independent component signatures to form a valid hybrid. Such separability makes the scheme vulnerable to upgrade, downgrade, and cross-protocol attacks, undermining the security guarantees of the hybrid approach.

Table 1. Key usage during the post-quantum transition.

Strategy	Key Updates
Post-Quantum only	$vk_1 \longrightarrow vk_2$
Hygienic Hybridization	$vk_1 \rightarrow (vk_1', vk_2') \rightarrow vk_2$
Expected Hybridization	$vk_1 \rightarrow (vk_1, vk_2) \rightarrow vk_2$

Non-separability. Previous works introduced the notion of *non-separability* to capture the idea that access to a hybrid signature oracle should not facilitate forgery against any of its components [5,7]. More concretely, a non-separable hybrid scheme prevents an adversary from extracting valid component signatures—or generating them for related messages—based on hybrid signatures obtained for messages of their choice. As definitions evolved, it became clear that non-separability is not a single property but rather a spectrum: from separability, to *weak non-separability* (WNS), which ensures that producing a component signature from hybrid ones leaves recognizable artifacts, and *strong non-separability* (SNS), which unconditionally prohibits the reconstruction of any valid component signature from hybrid ones.

These refinements, along with the broader design and security goals for hybrid signatures, are discussed in two recent IETF PQC drafts [6,28]. The latter also introduces *simultaneous verification* (SV), an informal property which ensures that an honest but sloppy verifier cannot prematurely terminate the verification process after validating only one component. Together, SNS and SV represent the most stringent design objectives for hybrid signatures, ensuring that the hybrid behaves as a single, indivisible algorithm rather than two independent ones. As discussed above, simple concatenation of signatures does not satisfy these requirements.

Following the guidance of [6,28], an ideal hybrid signature scheme should achieve the following goals:

Hybrid security. Its EU-CMA security should be at least as hard to break as the strongest security assumption it relies on.

Transition security. SNS, SV, and resistance to cross-protocol attacks in the transition scenario of Fig. 1.

Advanced security. sEU-CMA security and Beyond UnForgeability Features (BUFF) [11,13,14] to ensure usability across a wide range of real-world applications.

Efficiency. Computational and space requirements no worse than concatenation, minimizing the operational cost of hybridization.

Implementation simplicity. Reusing existing standardized implementations whenever possible to facilitate adoption and increase trust.

Generality. Instantiable with all schemes within a broad family, such as Fiat-Shamir-based signatures, supporting cryptographic agility.

Proof composability. Leveraging the existing security proofs and cryptanalysis of standardized components wherever possible.

Existing Constructions. Several generic approaches to constructing hybrid signature schemes have been explored in the literature. The most straightforward one is concatenation, in which component signatures are computed independently and then concatenated. While this approach ensures unforgeability of the hybrid as long as at least one component remains secure, it fails to preserve strong unforgeability whenever any of the component is probabilistic. Moreover, it does not satisfy SNS or SV. A concrete example is the Composite ML-DSA construction defined in the IETF draft [28] which specifies concatenation between ML-DSA and pre-quantum signature algorithms. In this design, a fixed prefix is prepended to each message before both components sign it, a modification that allows the scheme to achieve WNS, since the prefix serves as a recognizable artifact of hybridization. However, SNS remains out of reach for this design.

To overcome these limitations, several works have proposed more sophisticated hybrid constructions. A first line of research [7,16] investigates *nested* hybrids, where a message is first signed by one component, and the resulting pair consisting of the message and its signature is then signed by the second component. This design preserves the strong unforgeability of the outer (second) component. However, if the outer scheme is broken, the security of the construction collapses to that of simple concatenation. Furthermore, nested hybrids do not achieve SNS—a limitation that is typical for hybrid schemes making black-box use of one of their components. Indeed, the hybrid verification algorithm can be executed by anyone and it needs to verify the signature of the black-box component at some point.

Bindel and Hale [5] propose a family of generic and semi-generic hybrid constructions based on the Fiat-Shamir (FS) paradigm. Their FS-FS hybrid combines two FS signatures using a single hash computation, thereby improving efficiency compared to concatenation while maintaining comparable signature sizes. They also present semi-generic hybrids involving RSA [29], DSA, or Falcon [15]. All of their constructions are claimed EU-CMA secure in the Random Oracle Model (ROM), but proofs are not available. Their FS-FS approach cannot be instantiated with ML-DSA as it uses the Fiat-Shamir *with aborts* (FSwA) framework, and it is unclear how to make sure that the two identification schemes have the same challenge space, required by the construction. Moreover, they observe that hybridization of signatures whose verification ends with a digest comparison allows for means of mixing the two components to ensure SV.

A recent eprint by Janneck [19] introduces three new hybrids that use their post-quantum component in black-box—aiming for FIPS compliance—and preserve strong unforgeability if it holds for at least one component. However, as discussed previously, this black-box constraint makes their hybrids separable with respect to the post-quantum component, thus preventing them from achieving SNS. In addition, [19] formalizes a new security property called Random-Message Validity, which serves to analyze the BUFF security properties of their schemes.

Despite these advances, the literature still exhibits gaps. Most hybrid signature constructions either fail to ensure strong non-separability for all components, lack simultaneous verification, or do not provide proof composability and generality across different signature families. Furthermore, existing works do not consider adversaries in the Quantum Random Oracle Model (QROM), limiting the relevance of their security guarantees in post-quantum settings. To date, no existing construction simultaneously achieves strong non-separability for both components, simultaneous verification, proof composability, and generality across signature families—while maintaining efficiency and ease of implementation comparable to concatenation. In addition, the ongoing evolution of formal definitions for non-separability, the lack of formal proofs for schemes targeting these notions, and the insufficient consideration of cross-protocol attacks highlight the need for a more rigorous and unified framework for hybrid signature security. Such a framework should accurately capture the operational reality of hybrid deployments during the post-quantum transition and facilitate the writing of rigorous security proofs.

1.1   Contributions and Technical Overview

We take the following steps to address the challenges identified in the literature.

Formalization. To accurately capture cross-protocol, separability, and recombination attacks that may arise during the post-quantum transition, we introduce in Sect. 3 a new hybrid unforgeability notion, denoted H-EU-CMA^{X}, together with its *strong* variant. Given signature oracles for a hybrid signature scheme Σ_{H} as well as for its two component schemes Σ_1 and Σ_2, the adversary must forge a signature for Σ_{X}, where $\mathsf{X} \in \{1, 2, \mathsf{H}\}$. We illustrate this new notion in Fig. 1.

If the target scheme is one of the two components, *i.e.* $\mathsf{X} \in \{1, 2\}$, security under this notion ensures that no adversary can separate hybrid signatures to create a forgery against that component. When the target scheme is the hybrid one, *i.e.* $\mathsf{X} = \mathsf{H}$, the notion guarantees that no adversary can recombine component signatures into a valid hybrid signature. Our notion goes even further, allowing the adversary to mix and match multiple signatures across all oracles.

Finally, we observe that our notion subsumes the standard (s)EU-CMA notions: disabling the components oracles yields the traditional unforgeability game for the hybrid scheme, while disabling the hybrid oracle and one component oracle recovers the standard unforgeability notions for the remaining component. As such, the H-EU-CMA security notion appears as the *de facto* definition for hybrid signature schemes that simultaneously achieve goals Hybrid security and Transition security, except for SV. This unified definition provides the foundation for the formal security proofs of our hybrid construction presented in Sect. 4.

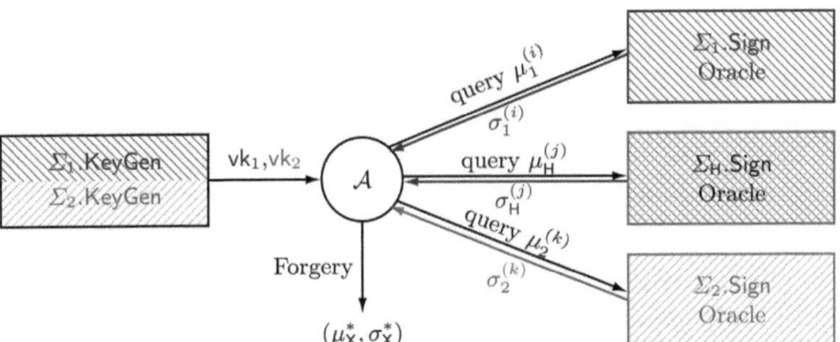

Fig. 1. H-EU-CMA^{X} security game for $\mathsf{X} \in \{1, 2, \mathsf{H}\}$. Adversary $\mathcal{A}$ wins if Σ_{X} verifies σ^* correctly for message μ^*, and μ^* was never queried to Σ_{X}.Sign.

Construction. Throughout this section, the reader may keep in mind the examples of the Schnorr [31] identification scheme[1] and that underlying ML-DSA. Our construction, presented in Sect. 4, begins with two identification schemes that share the same challenge space, where the second one may involve aborts. We start with the following idea: concatenate the identification schemes, by merging all prover messages while using a single challenge from the verifier, and then convert the resulting protocol into a signature scheme using the Fiat-Shamir with aborts framework—an approach reminiscent of the hybrid construction of [5]. However, we account for potential aborts and adopt the BUFF transform, in which the message is first hashed together with a hash of the verification key to achieve the related security notions.

Since only one protocol may abort, modifying the commitment of the other one seems unnecessary. Therefore, we take this commitment out of the while loop and generate it only once. We put it as a prefix to the message before the BUFF hashing step, thereby minimizing the size of the hash input inside the loop and improving efficiency. The resulting scheme is formally described in Fig. 5 of Sect. 4 and satisfies the following properties.

Hybrid security and Transition security. We study the security of our hybrid scheme with respect to the BUFF variant of the component signature schemes, as these are the versions typically deployed in practice, particularly for post-quantum schemes. We prove that our hybrid scheme is H-EU-CMA^H-secure in the ROM as long as one of the two underlying assumptions remains hard. Similarly, it is H-EU-CMA^1- and H-EU-CMA^2-secure in the ROM as long as the corresponding underlying assumption holds. Simultaneous verification is achieved because the verification of the second component inherently requires recovering the commitment of the first scheme. Since the second scheme recomputes the challenge, part of the verification for the first scheme is also performed in this step. A lazy verifier may, at most, omit the final portion of the first scheme's verification if one exists, but simultaneous verification is otherwise ensured.

Advanced security: sEU-CMA. The aforementioned proofs can be extended to the sH-EU-CMA setting. Moreover, since we can extract valid signatures for the non-BUFF version of the second component, our scheme is sEU-CMA-secure in the QROM as long as its second component is. However, the sEU-CMA security of the scheme is as weak as the weakest out of the following three: breaking the EU-CMA security of the hybrid scheme or breaking the sEU-CMA security of any of the two components without breaking its EU-CMA security, *i.e.* being able to produce new signatures for already signed messages but not for new messages.

Advanced security: BUFF. We prove that our construction satisfies the three usual BUFF notions: exclusive ownership and message-bound signature result from the collision resistance of the hash function used. Non-resignability is trickier to prove, but the proof follows from standard arguments [13].

---

[1] An identification scheme is a three-message interactive proof, where a prover first *commits* to a value, then *responds* to a *challenge* issued by the verifier, with the goal of convincing the verifier of knowledge of a secret.

Efficiency. Our scheme is efficient: compared to the concatenation of the two BUFF FS(wA) signature schemes, it saves one hash computation without increasing the input sizes for the remaining hash computations. Other operations remain unchanged.

Implementation simplicity. As noted earlier, our scheme essentially makes calls to the non-BUFF FS(wA) component signature scheme. In practice, this allows us to use, for example, an "external μ" implementation of ML-DSA as a black-box.

Generality. Our construction can hybridize any post-quantum FS(wA) signature with EC-Schnorr. This includes the NIST standard ML-DSA [27], nine of the fourteen candidates from the NIST round 2 additional digital signature schemes standardization process [24] as well as the South Korean standard Haetae [10], demonstrating the flexibility and broad applicability of our construction. Sharing a common challenge space is the case in practice: implementations convert the output of a cryptographic hash function into the challenge with post-processing (*e.g.*, SampleInBall in ML-DSA). In Appendices A and B, we demonstrate how to adapt the underlying protocols of ML-DSA and Schnorr to use the output set of the hash function as their challenge space. While this adaptation must be done for each scheme, it represents the only part that needs modification when applying our hybridization technique.

Proof composability. Our proof strategy for H-EU-CMA security closely follows existing proofs of EU-CMA security for FS(wA) signature schemes. Our QROM proof is a direct reduction from the hybrid signature to the non-BUFF component signature scheme, providing strong assurance that our hybrid scheme is at least as secure as its components.

Comparison with previous schemes. While similar to [5], our scheme incorporates the BUFF transform and accounts for potential aborts, resulting in stronger security guarantees and greater flexibility in instantiation. Compared to the BoP2 construction from [19], our approach slightly opens the black-box of the second signature component, achieving SNS for both components rather than just one. Additionally, our design computes one less hash for the second signature, which could be costly depending on the instantiation. We give a comparison between existing hybrid signatures constructions in Table 2.

Instantiation. In Sect. 5, we instantiate our construction with EC-Schnorr and ML-DSA, yielding the Silithium signature scheme. The different challenge space issue is solved in Appendices A and B, with a negligible security loss. Our construction satisfies all security notions introduced above, though these guarantees are stated with respect to the BUFF EC-Schnorr signature scheme, which is not standard. We outline how our generic proofs can be adapted to the case where Silithium is defined as a hybrid between ML-DSA and ECDSA. Since ECDSA employs a different hash function than ML-DSA and Silithium, access to an ECDSA oracle does not interfere with the random oracle management in our proofs, yielding comparable security guarantees.

Table 2. Comparison of existing generic hybrid signatures constructions. For (s)EU-CMA, a mark indicates that the property holds as long as one component remains secure, while an asterisk indicates that the property holds only if the post-quantum component remains secure. Our stronger H-EU-CMA notion captures attacks linked to the transition scenarios of Fig. 1.

Hybrid construction	EU-CMA	sEU-CMA	SNS w.r.t.	H-EU-CMA	BUFF	SV
Concatenation [28]	✓	✗	none	✗	?	✗
Nested [7,16]	✓	✓*	none	✗	✗	✗
FS-FS [5]	✓†	✓*†	all†	?	✗	✓
BoP2 [19]	✓	✓	only one	✗	✓	✓
This work	✓	✓*	all	✓	✓	✓

†: no proof given.

To demonstrate the simplicity of our approach, we implemented Silithium within a fork of the popular OpenSSL open-source library. This integration leverages OpenSSL's support for both elliptic curve operations and the "external μ" variant of ML-DSA. Our source code is available online[2].

2   Preliminaries

Notations. Given a set X, we denote by $U(\mathsf{X})$ the uniform distribution over X. For any integer η, we let S_η denote the set $\{-\eta, \ldots, 0, \ldots \eta\}$. The statistical distance between two distributions A and B is denoted by $\Delta(A, B)$. For two random variables X and Y, let $\mathsf{Supp}(X) = \{x \mid \Pr(X = x) > 0\}$. We define the conditional min-entropy of X given Y as $H_\infty(X|Y) = -\log(\max_{x,y} \Pr(X = x|Y = y))$.

We let $\mathcal{R}$ (resp. $\mathcal{R}_q$) denote the ring $\mathbb{Z}[x]/(x^n + 1)$ (resp. $\mathbb{Z}_q[x]/(x^n + 1)$) for n a power of two. For any integers r and α, we define $r \bmod {}^+\alpha$ (resp. $r \bmod {}^\pm\alpha$) as the unique integer r' in $[0, \alpha - 1]$ (resp. $(-\alpha/2, \alpha/2]$) such that $r = r' \bmod \alpha$.

An algorithm $\mathcal{A}$ with oracle access to $\mathcal{O}$ is denoted $\mathcal{A}^\mathcal{O}$. In the ROM (resp. QROM), a hash function $H : \{0,1\}^* \to \{0,1\}^n$ is modeled as a random oracle if its outputs are independently sampled from $U(\{0,1\}^n)$ and an adversary $\mathcal{A}$ can query (resp. in superposition) an oracle to have access to H. For a probabilistic algorithm f, we write $f(\cdot; x)$ to explicitly denote its random coins x.

2.1   Probabilities

Lemma 1. *Let $q > 0$ be an integer. Let $X_1, \ldots, X_q$ be i.i.d. discrete random variables. For any probabilistic function $f : \mathsf{Supp}(X_1)^q \to [0, q - 1] \cap \mathbb{Z}$ with random coins R, let $Y = X_{f(X_1,\ldots,X_q;R)}$. It holds:*

$$H_\infty(Y|R) \geq H_\infty(X_1) - \log(q).$$

---

[2] At https://github.com/mguerrea/openssl-silithium.

Proof. For any $k \in \mathsf{Supp}(X_1)$ and $r \in \mathsf{Supp}(R)$, we have

$$\Pr(Y = k | R = r) \le \Pr(\exists i, X_i = k) \le \sum_{i=1}^{q} \Pr(X_i = k) = q \Pr(X_1 = k).$$

We recall the general forking lemma from [3] in a way such that the reprogrammed value may not be chosen by the forking algorithm, which does not change the probability computations from [3, Lemma 1]. We also note that it can be applied in presence of oracles that are unrelated to the random oracle.

Lemma 2 (General Forking Lemma [3, Lemma 1]). *For any algorithm* A *making at most q queries to a random oracle $H : \{0,1\}^* \to \mathcal{C}$ and outputting a pair (i, σ), where $0 \le i \le q$, we define the algorithm pair $\mathcal{F} = (\mathcal{F}_1, \mathcal{F}_2)$ in Fig. 2. Then, for any distribution D, the following holds:*

$$\Pr_{x \hookleftarrow D}(\mathsf{A}(x) \to (i, \sigma) \wedge i > 0) \le \frac{q}{|\mathcal{C}|} + \sqrt{q \cdot \Pr_{x \hookleftarrow D}(\mathsf{F}(x) \to 1)} \ .$$

If A *also needs an access to an oracle that is independent of its random oracle, the above still holds by assuming that $\mathcal{F}$ also has access to this oracle.*

<table>
<tr><td>

Game F(x):

1: $st = (i, \sigma, \mathcal{S}) \leftarrow \mathcal{F}_1(x)$
2: $(\star, c) \leftarrow \mathcal{S}[i-1]$
3: $c' \hookleftarrow U(\mathcal{C} \setminus \{c\})$
4: $(b, \star, \star) \leftarrow \mathcal{F}_2(x, c', st)$
5: **return** b

$\mathcal{F}_1(x)$:

1: Pick random coins ρ for A
2: $\mathcal{S} \leftarrow []$
3: $(i, \sigma) \leftarrow \mathsf{A}^H(x; \rho)$
4: **return** $(i, \sigma, \mathcal{S})$

</td><td>

$\mathcal{F}_2(x, c', (i, \sigma, \mathcal{S}))$:

1: **if** $i = 0$ **then**
2:     **return** $(0, \varepsilon, \varepsilon)$
3: $(y, c) \leftarrow \mathcal{S}[i-1]$
4: $\mathcal{S}[i] \leftarrow (y, c')$
5: $\mathcal{S} \leftarrow \mathcal{S}[: i]$
6: $(i', \sigma') \leftarrow \mathsf{A}^H(x; \rho)$
7: **if** $i = i'$ **then**
8:     **return** $(1, \sigma, \sigma')$
9: **return** $(0, \varepsilon, \varepsilon)$

</td><td>

$H(y)$:

1: **if** $\exists k, \mathcal{S}[k] = (y, c')$
    then
2:     $c \leftarrow c'$
3: **else**
4:     $c \hookleftarrow U(\mathcal{C})$
5: $\mathcal{S}.\mathsf{append}((y, c))$
6: **return** c

</td></tr>
</table>

Fig. 2. Forking algorithm $\mathcal{F} = (\mathcal{F}_1, \mathcal{F}_2)$ and its random oracle. We use Python syntax for list manipulations.

2.2 Security Assumptions

We recall the definitions of the collision game for hash functions [30], the Discrete Logarithm problem (DL) [12], and the Module-Short Integer Solution (MSIS) and the Module-Learning with Errors (MLWE) problems [23].

Definition 1 (Collision Game). *Let $H : \{0,1\}^* \to \{0,1\}^n$. For any adversary $\mathcal{A}$, we define $\mathsf{Adv}_H^{\mathsf{col}}(\mathcal{A}) = \Pr(\mathcal{A}() \to (x, x') | H(x) = H(x') \wedge x \ne x')$.*

Definition 2 (DL). *Let $\mathbb{G}$ be a group with generator g and order p. For any adversary $\mathcal{A}$, its advantage in the DL problem is defined as:*

$$\mathsf{Adv}^{\mathsf{DL}}_{\mathbb{G},g}(\mathcal{A}) = \Pr_{k \hookleftarrow U(\mathbb{Z}_p)}(k \leftarrow \mathcal{A}(g^k)).$$

Definition 3 (MSIS). *Let q, k, ℓ, B be four integers. For any adversary $\mathcal{A}$, its advantage in the $\mathsf{MSIS}_{n,q,k,\ell,B}$ problem is defined as:*

$$\mathsf{Adv}^{\mathsf{MSIS}}_{n,q,k,\ell,B}(\mathcal{A}) = \Pr_{\mathbf{A} \hookleftarrow U(\mathcal{R}_q^{k \times \ell})}(\mathbf{Ax} = 0 \bmod q \wedge \|\mathbf{x}\|_\infty \leq B | \mathbf{x} \leftarrow \mathcal{A}(\mathbf{A})).$$

Definition 4 (MLWE). *Let q, k, ℓ be three integers and let χ be a distribution over $\mathbb{Z}$, extended over $\mathcal{R}$ where each coefficient is i.i.d. following χ. For any distinguisher $\mathcal{A}$, its advantage in the $\mathsf{MLWE}_{n,q,k,\ell,\chi}$ problem is defined as:*

$$\mathsf{Adv}^{\mathsf{MLWE}}_{n,q,k,\ell,\chi}(\mathcal{A}) = \left| \Pr_{\substack{\mathbf{A} \hookleftarrow U(\mathcal{R}_q^{k \times \ell}) \\ \mathbf{b} \hookleftarrow U(\mathcal{R}_q^k)}}(1 \leftarrow \mathcal{A}(\mathbf{A}, \mathbf{b})) - \Pr_{\substack{\mathbf{A} \hookleftarrow U(\mathcal{R}_q^{k \times \ell}) \\ \mathbf{s},\mathbf{e} \hookleftarrow \chi^\ell \otimes \chi^k}}(1 \leftarrow \mathcal{A}(\mathbf{A}, \mathbf{As} + \mathbf{e})) \right|.$$

2.3 Signature Schemes

We now briefly recall the formalism of digital signatures.

Definition 5. *A signature scheme Σ is a tuple $(\Sigma.\mathsf{KeyGen}, \Sigma.\mathsf{Sign}, \Sigma.\mathsf{Verify})$ of probabilistic polynomial time (PPT) algorithms with the following specifications:*

- *$\Sigma.\mathsf{KeyGen} : 1^\lambda \to (\mathsf{vk}, \mathsf{sk})$ takes as input a security parameter λ and outputs a verification key vk and a signing key sk.*
- *$\Sigma.\mathsf{Sign} : (\mathsf{sk}, \mu) \to \sigma$ takes as inputs a signing key sk and a message μ and outputs a signature σ.*
- *$\Sigma.\mathsf{Verify} : (\mathsf{vk}, \mu, \sigma) \to b \in \{0,1\}$ takes as inputs a verification key vk, a message μ and a signature σ and accepts $(b = 1)$ or rejects $(b = 0)$.*

Σ is correct if for any μ and $(\mathsf{vk}, \mathsf{sk})$ in the range of $\Sigma.\mathsf{KeyGen}$ it always holds:

$$\Sigma.\mathsf{Verify}(\mathsf{vk}, \mu, \Sigma.\mathsf{Sign}(\mathsf{sk}, \mu)) = 1.$$

Definition 6 (EU-CMA). *Let Σ be a signature scheme. For any adversary $\mathcal{A}$ making at most Q_s queries to a $\Sigma.\mathsf{Sign}(\mathsf{sk}, \cdot)$ oracle $\mathcal{O}$, its advantage against the EU-CMA game is defined as:*

$$\mathsf{Adv}^{\mathsf{EU\text{-}CMA}}(\mathcal{A}) = \Pr_{\substack{(\mathsf{vk},\mathsf{sk}) \leftarrow \Sigma.\mathsf{KeyGen}(1^\lambda) \\ (\sigma^*,\mu^*) \leftarrow \mathcal{A}^{\mathcal{O}}(\mathsf{vk})}} \left(\begin{array}{c} \Sigma.\mathsf{Verify}(\mathsf{vk}, \sigma^*, \mu^*) = 1 \wedge \\ \mu^* \text{ was not queried to } \mathcal{O} \end{array} \right).$$

If $Q_s = 0$, the game is called EU-NMA instead. If the second condition is replaced with "σ^* is not a reply from $\mathcal{O}$ to a query for μ^*", we call it sEU-CMA instead.

"BUFF-ing" signature schemes ensures security properties that go beyond unforgeability. We recall the Fiat-Shamir version of this transform.

Definition 7 (BUFF *transform*)**.** *Let Σ be a signature scheme and $\mathcal{H}$ be a collision-resistant hash function. We define* $\mathsf{BUFF}(\Sigma)$ *as:*

- $\mathsf{BUFF}(\Sigma).\mathsf{KeyGen}$ *is exactly* $\Sigma.\mathsf{KeyGen}$ *(*sk *may optionally include* $\mathcal{H}(\mathsf{vk})$*).*
- $\mathsf{BUFF}(\Sigma).\mathsf{Sign}$, *on input a signing key* sk *and a message* M, *first computes* $\mu = \mathcal{H}(\mathcal{H}(\mathsf{vk}), M)$ *and returns* $\Sigma.\mathsf{Sign}(\mathsf{sk}, \mu)$.
- $\mathsf{BUFF}(\Sigma).\mathsf{Verify}$, *on input a verification key* vk, *a signature* σ *and a message* M, *first computes* $\mu = \mathcal{H}(\mathcal{H}(\mathsf{vk}), M)$ *and returns* $\Sigma.\mathsf{Verify}(\mathsf{vk}, \sigma, \mu)$.

We recall the properties targeted by this transform: *exclusive ownership* prevents reusing a signature under a different key; *message binding* ensures a signature cannot be valid for two messages; and *non-resignability* prevents producing a valid key and signature pair for an unknown signed message.

Definition 8 (Exclusive Ownership [8]). *The advantage of an adversary* $\mathcal{A}$ *against the* malicious strong universal exclusive ownership *property of a signature scheme* Σ *is defined as:*

$$\mathsf{Adv}_{\Sigma}^{\mathsf{EO}}(\mathcal{A}) = \Pr_{(\mathsf{vk},\mathsf{vk}',m,m',\sigma)\leftarrow\mathcal{A}} (\Sigma.\mathsf{Verify}(\mathsf{vk}, m, \sigma) = \Sigma.\mathsf{Verify}(\mathsf{vk}', m', \sigma) = 1 \wedge \mathsf{vk} \neq \mathsf{vk}').$$

Definition 9 (Message Bound Signatures [8]). *The advantage of an adversary* $\mathcal{A}$ *against the* message bound signatures *property of a signature scheme* Σ *is defined as:*

$$\mathsf{Adv}_{\Sigma}^{\mathsf{MBS}}(\mathcal{A}) = \Pr_{(\mathsf{vk},m,m',\sigma)\leftarrow\mathcal{A}} (\Sigma.\mathsf{Verify}(\mathsf{vk}, m, \sigma) = \Sigma.\mathsf{Verify}(\mathsf{vk}, m', \sigma) = 1 \wedge m \neq m').$$

Definition 10 (Non-Resignability [13]). *The advantage of adversaries* $\mathcal{A}, \mathcal{B}$ *against the* non-resignability *property of a signature scheme* Σ *and a randomized algorithm* aux *that, on input a message and a signing key, returns a so-called hint is defined as:*

$$\mathsf{Adv}_{\Sigma,\mathsf{aux}}^{\mathsf{NR}}(\mathcal{A}, \mathcal{B}) = \Pr_{\substack{(\mathsf{vk},\mathsf{sk})\leftarrow\Sigma.\mathsf{KeyGen}(1^{\lambda})\\ m\leftarrow\mathcal{B}(\mathsf{sk})\\ \sigma\leftarrow\Sigma.\mathsf{Sign}(\mathsf{sk},m)\\ (\mathsf{vk}^*,\sigma^*)\leftarrow\mathcal{A}(\mathsf{sk},\sigma,\mathsf{aux}(m,\mathsf{sk}))}} (\Sigma.\mathsf{Verify}(\mathsf{vk}^*, \sigma^*, m) = 1 \wedge \mathsf{vk}^* \neq \mathsf{vk}).$$

2.4   Identification Schemes

We recall the definition of an identification scheme as they lie at the core of the Fiat-Shamir transform, which we recall in the next section.

Definition 11 (Identification Scheme). *An identification scheme is a tuple of PPT algorithms* $\mathsf{ID} = (\mathsf{Igen}, \mathsf{P}, \mathsf{V})$ *such that:*

- Igen: *On input the security parameter* 1^{λ}, *algorithm* Igen *outputs a verification key* vk *and a secret key* sk. *We assume that* vk *defines the challenge space* $\mathcal{C}$.

- P*: The prover* $P = (P_1, P_2)$ *is split into two algorithms: given* sk*, algorithm* P_1 *produces a* commitment w *(first message sent to the verifier) and a state* st*; algorithm* P_2*, on input* (sk, w, st) *and a uniformly random* challenge $c \in C$ *sent by the verifier in response to commitment* w*, outputs an* answer z.
- V*: On input* (vk, w, c, z)*, the deterministic verifier* V *outputs 1 or 0.*

We let $P(sk, vk) \leftrightarrow V(vk)$ *denote the transcript* (w, c, z) *of an interaction between the prover and the verifier, as illustrated in Fig. 3.*

P_2 *may output* $z = \perp$*, in which case we say that the identification scheme aborts. The probability this happens is called the aborting probability of* ID.

We say that ID *has* unique response *if for any* (w, c)*, there is at most one value for* z *such that* (w, c, z) *is a valid transcript.*

<table>
<tr><td align="center">P(sk, vk)</td><td align="center">V(vk)</td></tr>
<tr><td>$(w, st) \leftarrow ID.P_1(sk) \quad \xrightarrow{\ w\ }$</td><td></td></tr>
<tr><td>$\xleftarrow{\ c\ } \qquad c \hookleftarrow U(\mathcal{C})$</td><td></td></tr>
<tr><td>$z \leftarrow ID.P_2(sk, w, st, c) \xrightarrow{\ z\ }$ Accept or Reject</td><td></td></tr>
</table>

Fig. 3. Interaction between P and V

We start by recalling *completeness* and *commitment-recoverability*, two properties which allow to define and prove the correctness of $FS[ID, H]$.

Definition 12 (Completeness and commitment-recoverability). *An identification scheme* ID $= (Igen, P, V)$ *is* complete *if for any* $(vk, sk) \leftarrow Igen(1^\lambda)$*, for any challenge* $c \in C$*, we have:*

$$\Pr\left[V(vk, (w, c, z)) = 1 \mid (w, c, z) \leftarrow (P(sk, vk) \leftrightarrow V(vk)) \wedge z \neq \perp \right] = 1,$$

where the randomness is taken over the random coins of P.

In addition, ID *satisfies* commitment-recoverability *if for any public key* vk*, challenge* $c \in C$*, and answer* z*, there is at most one commitment* w *such that the transcript* (w, c, z) *is valid, and there exists a PPT algorithm* ID.Rec *such that* $w = ID.Rec(vk, c, z)$.

Unless otherwise specified, we only consider identification schemes satisfying commitment-recoverability. The notions of *honest-verifier zero-knowledge* and *commitment min-entropy* allow to reduce the EU-CMA game of $FS[ID, H]$ to its EU-NMA one.

Definition 13 (HVZK and commitment min-entropy). *An identification scheme* ID $= (Igen, P, V)$ *is* Honest-Verifier Zero-Knowledge *(HVZK) if there exists a PPT simulator* Sim *such that, conditioned on* $z \neq \perp$:

$$\Delta\Big((w, c, z) \leftarrow (P(sk, vk) \leftrightarrow V(vk)) \, , \, Sim(c, vk) \Big) = 0.$$

ID *has α bits of commitment min-entropy* if for any $(\mathsf{vk}, \mathsf{sk})$ *in the range of* IGen*:*

$$H_\infty\Big(w|(w,c,z) \leftarrow (\mathsf{P}(\mathsf{sk},\mathsf{vk}) \leftrightarrow \mathsf{V}(\mathsf{vk}))\Big) \geq \alpha.$$

The EU-NMA problem is linked via the Forking Lemma to the 2-special-soundness of the identification scheme, which asks an adversary to find two valid transcripts starting with the same commitment. In the context of lattice-based schemes, it is useful to introduce a lossy key generation algorithm, giving rise to the lossy-2-special-soundness property. In this work, we actually use a weaker notion: the adversary does not choose the second challenge. Looking ahead, this relaxation allows our modified identification schemes in Appendices A and B to satisfy this notion, while still allowing reductions to use the Forking Lemma.

Definition 14 (Soundness). *Let* ID *be an identification scheme with challenge space $\mathcal{C}$ and let* LossyIGen *be an algorithm that on input 1^λ returns* vk*.*

- *For any distinguisher $\mathcal{B}$, its advantage in the* key-indistinguishability *with respect to* LossyIGen *game is defined as:*

$$\mathsf{Adv}_{\mathsf{ID}}^{\mathsf{key\text{-}ind}}(\mathcal{B}) = \left| \Pr_{\mathsf{vk}\leftarrow\mathsf{LossyIGen}(1^\lambda)}(\mathcal{B}(\mathsf{vk}) \to 1) - \Pr_{(\mathsf{vk},\mathsf{sk})\leftarrow\mathsf{ID}.\mathsf{IGen}(1^\lambda)}(\mathcal{B}(\mathsf{vk}) \to 1) \right|.$$

- *For any adversary $\mathcal{A} = (\mathcal{A}_1, \mathcal{A}_2)$, its advantage in the* lossy-2-special-soundness *with respect to* LossyIGen *game is defined as:*

$$\mathsf{Adv}_{\mathsf{ID}}^{\mathsf{lossy\text{-}2\text{-}ss}}(\mathcal{A}) = \Pr_{\substack{\mathsf{vk}\leftarrow\mathsf{LossyIGen}(1^\lambda)\\(w,c_1,z_1,st)\leftarrow\mathcal{A}_1(\mathsf{vk})\\c_2\hookleftarrow U(\mathcal{C}\backslash\{c_1\})\\z_2\leftarrow\mathcal{A}_2(st,z_2)}}(\mathsf{V}(\mathsf{vk},w,c_1,z_1) = \mathsf{V}(\mathsf{vk},w,c_2,z_2) = 1).$$

If LossyIGen *calls* ID.IGen *and returns* vk*, we call this game* 2-special-soundness*.*

Finally, the notion of computational unique response (CUR) is necessary to achieve strong unforgeability.

Definition 15 (CUR). *Let* ID *be an identification scheme. For any adversary $\mathcal{A}$, its advantage in the* CUR *game is defined as:*

$$\mathsf{Adv}_{\mathsf{ID}}^{\mathsf{CUR}}(\mathcal{A}) = \Pr_{\substack{(\mathsf{sk},\mathsf{vk})\leftarrow\mathsf{ID}.\mathsf{IGen}(1^\lambda)\\(w,c,z,z')\leftarrow\mathcal{A}(\mathsf{vk})}}(\mathsf{V}(\mathsf{vk},w,c,z) = \mathsf{V}(\mathsf{vk},w,c,z') = 1 \;\wedge\; z \neq z').$$

2.5 Fiat-Shamir with Aborts Transform

We now recall the Fiat-Shamir with Aborts (FSwA) transform in Fig. 4, which allows to transform a commitment-recoverable identification scheme into a digital signature, even when the identification scheme has a nonzero aborting probability. Essentially, it asks the signer to run as many times as necessary a non-interactive version of the identification scheme, where the challenge is sampled

KeyGen(1^λ) :	Sign(sk, μ) :	Verify$(\mathsf{vk}, (c, z), \mu)$:
1: $(\mathsf{vk}, \mathsf{sk}) \leftarrow \mathsf{ID.IGen}(1^\lambda)$	1: $z \leftarrow \perp$	1: $w \leftarrow \mathsf{ID.Rec}(\mathsf{vk}, c, z)$
2: **return** $(\mathsf{vk}, \mathsf{sk})$	2: **while** $z = \perp$ **do**	2: **if** $c \neq H(w, \mu)$ **then**
	3: $(w, \mathsf{st}) \leftarrow \mathsf{ID.P_1}(\mathsf{sk})$	3: **return** 0
	4: $c \leftarrow H(w, \mu)$	4: $b \leftarrow \mathsf{ID.V}(\mathsf{vk}, (w, c, z))$
	5: $z \leftarrow \mathsf{ID.P_2}(\mathsf{sk}, \mathsf{st}, w, c)$	5: **return** b
	6: **return** (c, z)	

Fig. 4. Fiat-Shamir with Aborts Signature $\mathsf{FSwA}[\mathsf{ID}, H]$.

as the hash of the commitment w and the message to sign μ. The signature is the first pair (c, z) such that $z \neq \perp$, which is verified by first recovering $w = \mathsf{ID.Rec}(\mathsf{vk}, c, z)$ and then by checking that $c = H(w, \mu)$. Finally, the validity of the transcript (w, c, z) is verified.

The resulting signature is correct as long as ID is complete, and its HVZK property allows to reduce the EU-CMA game to the EU-NMA game, as long as ID has sufficiently high commitment min-entropy.

3   Hybrid Security for Signature Schemes

In practice, the usual EU-CMA notion or its strong variant are not sufficient for hybrid signatures in the wild, as highlighted by existing non-separability notions. We therefore introduce a new security notion, called *Hybrid Unforgeability*, for hybrid signature schemes where an adversary is given access to signature oracles for the hybrid signature and its two components, and must forge a signature for a target scheme out of the three. The goal of this new notion is to capture the various attack vectors enabled by the post-quantum transition scenarios illustrated in Fig. 1 where a hybrid signature scheme coexists with its components.

Definition 16 (Hybrid Unforgeability). *Let $\Sigma_\mathsf{H}, \Sigma_1, \Sigma_2$ be three signature schemes such that $\Sigma_\mathsf{H}.\mathsf{KeyGen}(1^\lambda)$ calls $(\mathsf{vk}_i, \mathsf{sk}_i) \leftarrow \Sigma_i.\mathsf{KeyGen}(1^\lambda)$ for $i \in \{1, 2\}$ and then returns $\mathsf{vk}_\mathsf{H} = (\mathsf{vk}_1, \mathsf{vk}_2)$ and $\mathsf{sk}_\mathsf{H} = (\mathsf{sk}_1, \mathsf{sk}_2)$*[3].

Let $\mathsf{X} \in \{\mathsf{H}, 1, 2\}$. For any $\mathsf{Y} \in \{\mathsf{H}, 1, 2\}$, let $\mathcal{O}_\mathsf{Y}(\mathsf{sk}_\mathsf{Y})$ denote the oracle that, on input μ, returns $\Sigma_\mathsf{Y}.\mathsf{Sign}(\mathsf{sk}_\mathsf{Y}, \mu)$. We define the $\mathsf{H\text{-}EU\text{-}CMA}^\mathsf{X}_{Q_1, Q_2, Q_\mathsf{H}}$ advantage of an adversary $\mathcal{A}$ making Q_Y queries to $\mathcal{O}_\mathsf{Y}(\mathsf{sk}_\mathsf{Y})$, for any $\mathsf{Y} \in \{\mathsf{H}, 1, 2\}$ as:

$$\mathsf{Adv}^{\mathsf{H\text{-}EU\text{-}CMA}^\mathsf{X}}_{Q_1, Q_2, Q_\mathsf{H}}(\mathcal{A}) = \Pr_{\substack{(\mathsf{vk}_1, \mathsf{sk}_1) \leftarrow \Sigma_1.\mathsf{KeyGen}(1^\lambda) \\ (\mathsf{vk}_2, \mathsf{sk}_2) \leftarrow \Sigma_2.\mathsf{KeyGen}(1^\lambda) \\ (\sigma^*, \mu^*) \leftarrow \mathcal{A}^{\mathcal{O}_\mathsf{H}(\mathsf{sk}_\mathsf{H}), \mathcal{O}_1(\mathsf{sk}_1), \mathcal{O}_2(\mathsf{sk}_2)}(\mathsf{vk}_1, \mathsf{vk}_2)}} \left(\begin{array}{c} \Sigma_\mathsf{X}.\mathsf{Verify}(\mathsf{vk}_\mathsf{X}, \sigma^*, \mu^*) = 1 \\ \wedge \\ \mu^* \text{ was not queried to } \mathcal{O}_\mathsf{X} \end{array} \right).$$

---

[3] In general, one may consider vk_H and sk_H to be deterministically derived from $(\mathsf{vk}_1, \mathsf{vk}_2)$ and $(\mathsf{sk}_1, \mathsf{sk}_2)$ respectively, as long as the derivation is reversible.

We omit Q_1, Q_2, Q_H from the name of the game whenever clear from context. If we replace the condition on μ^* with "σ^* was not $\mathcal{O}_X$'s answer to a signature query for μ^*", we instead denote the game with sH-EU-CMA^X, *standing for strong hybrid unforgeability.*

Remark 1. Conveniently, our new hybrid unforgeability notion subsumes several existing ones. In particular, the H-EU-CMA^H (resp. sH-EU-CMA^H) game coincides with the standard EU-CMA (resp. sEU-CMA) game of Σ_H when $Q_1 = Q_2 = 0$.

Similarly, when $Q_1 = Q_2 = Q_H = 0$, the H-EU-CMA^H game coincides with the EU-NMA one for Σ_H.

4 Fiat-Shamir with *Partial* Aborts and Identification Schemes Concatenation

Assuming that we have two identification schemes, of which at most one may have aborts, we exhibit in Fig. 5 a variant of the BUFF Fiat-Shamir transform to turn them into a hybrid signature scheme satisfying all three H-EU-CMA^X security notions, $X \in \{1, 2, H\}$. It can be seen as an application of the Fiat-Shamir transform over the concatenation of the two identification schemes, with the following tweaks. First, the commitment of the non-aborting protocol is not resampled during the rejection phase of the aborting protocol. Second, it is included in the BUFF hash of the message and not in the rejection loop to save time during signing. Last, the two protocols share the raw output of the hash function, and it is up to them to use it to deduce their respective challenge. Note that during key generation, we restart if the verification keys are identical, which should never happen in practice as different identification schemes usually have different verification key sizes and verification keys have large entropy.

4.1 Description and Correctness of the Signature Scheme

Our main construction, denoted H-FSwA[$ID_1 \| ID_2, H$], is presented in Fig. 5. The two signing algorithms shown are functionally identical and differ only in the way they are written, see Fig. 4 for further details. The signature scheme relies on two hash functions $H : \{0,1\}^* \rightarrow \{0,1\}^\ell$ and $\mathcal{H} : \{0,1\}^* \rightarrow \{0,1\}^\alpha$. The former is modeled as a random oracle in the proofs, while the security of the scheme relies on the collision resistance of the latter.

Theorem 1 (Correctness). *Let $\ell > 0$. Let ID_1 and ID_2 be two complete identification schemes with ID_1 (resp. ID_2) having aborting probability 0 (resp. β), and challenge space $\{0,1\}^\ell$ for both. The scheme* H-FSwA[$ID_1 \| ID_2, H$] *defined in Fig. 5 is a correct signature scheme. Moreover, the runtime of* Sign *is at most the sum of those of* FS[ID_1, H].Sign *and* BUFF(FSwA[ID_2, H]).Sign.

Proof. For any $i \in \{1, 2\}$ and genuine transcripts (w_i, c, z_i) such that $z_2 \neq \bot$ and $w_i = ID_i.\text{Rec}(vk_i, c, z_i)$, it holds that $ID_i.V$ accepts this transcript, by completeness. In particular, the distribution of c does not matter. The runtime of Sign is most easily analyzed using the second description of the algorithm, which makes calls to FSwA[ID_2, H].Sign. All remaining operations either correspond to a call to $\mathcal{H}$, included in BUFF, or are already present in FS[ID_1, H].Sign. $\square$

<table>
<tr><td>

$\mathsf{KeyGen}(1^\lambda)$:

1: **repeat**
2:     $(\mathsf{vk}_1, \mathsf{sk}_1) \leftarrow \mathsf{ID}_1.\mathsf{IGen}(1^\lambda)$
3:     $(\mathsf{vk}_2, \mathsf{sk}_2) \leftarrow \mathsf{ID}_2.\mathsf{IGen}(1^\lambda)$
4: **until** $\mathsf{vk}_1 \neq \mathsf{vk}_2$
5: $tr \leftarrow \mathcal{H}(\mathsf{vk}_1 \| \mathsf{vk}_2)$
6: **return** $((\mathsf{vk}_1, \mathsf{vk}_2), (tr, \mathsf{sk}_1, \mathsf{sk}_2))$

$\mathsf{Sign}((tr, \mathsf{sk}_1, \mathsf{sk}_2), M)$:

1: $(w_1, st_1) \leftarrow \mathsf{ID}_1.\mathsf{P}_1(\mathsf{sk}_1)$
2: $\mu \leftarrow \mathcal{H}(tr \| w_1 \| M)$
3: $z_2 \leftarrow \perp$
4: **while** $z_2 = \perp$ **do**
5:     $(w_2, st_2) \leftarrow \mathsf{ID}_2.\mathsf{P}_1(\mathsf{sk}_2)$
6:     $c = H(w_2 \| \mu)$
7:     $z_2 \leftarrow \mathsf{ID}_2.\mathsf{P}_2(\mathsf{sk}_2, c, st_2)$
8: $z_1 \leftarrow \mathsf{ID}_1.\mathsf{P}_2(\mathsf{sk}_1, c, st_1)$
9: **return** (z_1, z_2, c)

</td><td>

$\mathsf{Verify}((\mathsf{vk}_1, \mathsf{vk}_2), (z_1, z_2, c), M)$:

1: $w_1 \leftarrow \mathsf{ID}_1.\mathsf{Rec}(\mathsf{vk}_1, c, z_1)$
2: $\mu \leftarrow \mathcal{H}(\mathcal{H}(\mathsf{vk}_1 \| \mathsf{vk}_2) \| w_1 \| M)$
3: $w_2 \leftarrow \mathsf{ID}_2.\mathsf{Rec}(\mathsf{vk}_2, c, z_2)$
4: **if** $H(w_2 \| \mu) \neq c$ **then**
5:     **return** 0
6: **else if not** $\mathsf{ID}_1.\mathsf{V}(w_1, c, z_1)$ **then**
7:     **return** 0
8: **else if not** $\mathsf{ID}_2.\mathsf{V}(w_2, c, z_2)$ **then**
9:     **return** 0
10: **return** 1

$\mathsf{Sign}((tr, \mathsf{sk}_1, \mathsf{sk}_2), M)$:

1: $(w_1, st_1) \leftarrow \mathsf{ID}_1.\mathsf{P}_1(\mathsf{sk}_1)$
2: $\mu \leftarrow \mathcal{H}(tr \| w_1 \| M)$
3: $(z_2, c) \leftarrow \mathsf{FSwA}[\mathsf{ID}_2, H].\mathsf{Sign}(\mathsf{sk}_2, \mu)$
4: $z_1 \leftarrow \mathsf{ID}_1.\mathsf{P}_2(\mathsf{sk}_1, c, st_1)$
5: **return** (z_1, z_2, c)

</td></tr>
</table>

Fig. 5. Hybrid Fiat-Shamir Transform H-FSwA[$\mathsf{ID}_1 \| \mathsf{ID}_2, H$]. The two formulations of Sign are functionally equivalent.

4.2 (s)H-EU-CMA^{H} Security in the QROM

As a warm-up, we show that H-FSwA[$\mathsf{ID}_1 \| \mathsf{ID}_2, H$] is at least as secure as the signature scheme FSwA[ID_2, H] in the QROM, even in the presence of additional oracles for its components, whatever choice for Σ_1 we make.

Theorem 2 (QROM Security). *Let $\ell > 0$. Let ID_1 (resp. ID_2) be an identification scheme satisfying HVZK, with aborting probability 0 (resp. β), α_1 (resp. α_2) bits of commitment min-entropy and challenge space $\{0,1\}^\ell$. Let Σ_1 be a signature scheme such that $\Sigma_1.\mathsf{KeyGen} = \mathsf{ID}_1.\mathsf{IGen}$, up to bijection. Let $\Sigma_\mathsf{H} = $ H-FSwA[$\mathsf{ID}_1 \| \mathsf{ID}_2, H$] as defined in Fig. 5 and $\Sigma_2 = \mathsf{BUFF}(\mathsf{FSwA}[\mathsf{ID}_2, H])$.*

In the QROM, by modeling H as a random oracle, there exist adversaries $\mathcal{B}_1$ and $\mathcal{B}_2$, explicitly given in the proof of this theorem, such that for any hash function $\mathcal{H} : \{0,1\}^* \to \{0,1\}^\alpha$, and adversary $\mathcal{A}$, we have that:

$$\mathsf{Adv}_{Q_2, Q_2, Q_\mathsf{H}}^{\mathsf{H\text{-}EU\text{-}CMA}^{\mathsf{H}}} (\mathcal{A}) \leq \mathsf{Adv}_{\mathsf{FSwA}[\mathsf{ID}_2, H]}^{\mathsf{EU\text{-}CMA}}(\mathcal{B}_1) + \mathsf{Adv}_{\mathcal{H}}^{\mathsf{col}}(\mathcal{B}_2) \ .$$

where $\mathcal{B}_1$ and $\mathcal{B}_2$ make the same amount of quantum random oracle queries as $\mathcal{A}$, make $Q_2 + Q_\mathsf{H}$ classical signature queries and have essentially the same runtime as $\mathcal{A}$. Assuming that ID_1 has unique response, we moreover have

$$\mathsf{Adv}_{Q_1, Q_2, Q_\mathsf{H}}^{\mathsf{sH\text{-}EU\text{-}CMA}^{\mathsf{H}}} (\mathcal{A}) \leq \mathsf{Adv}_{\mathsf{FSwA}[\mathsf{ID}_2, H]}^{\mathsf{sEU\text{-}CMA}}(\mathcal{B}_1) + \mathsf{Adv}_{\mathcal{H}}^{\mathsf{col}}(\mathcal{B}_2) \ .$$

Proof. The adversary $\mathcal{B}_1$, on input vk_2, runs $\mathsf{ID}_1.\mathsf{IGen}$ to get $\mathsf{sk}_1, \mathsf{vk}_1$. It is then able to run the rest of H-FSwA[$\mathsf{ID}_1 \| \mathsf{ID}_2, H$].$\mathsf{KeyGen}(1^\lambda)$ and calls $\mathcal{A}$ on $(\mathsf{vk}_1, \mathsf{vk}_2)$. It answers $\mathcal{A}$'s queries in the following manner.

Hash queries. $\mathcal{B}_1$ forwards the query to its own random oracle and forwards back the answer to $\mathcal{A}$.

Σ_1 **signature.** On input M, $\mathcal{B}_1$ is able to run $\Sigma_1.\mathsf{Sign}(\mathsf{sk}_1, \mathcal{H}(\mathcal{H}(\mathsf{vk}_1)\|M))$ and returns the answer to $\mathcal{A}$.

Σ_2 **signature.** On input M, $\mathcal{B}_1$ computes $\mu = \mathcal{H}(\mathcal{H}(\mathsf{vk}_2)\|M)$ and calls its signature oracle on μ. It returns the answer of its oracle to $\mathcal{A}$.

Σ_H **signature.** On input M, $\mathcal{B}_1$ first runs $(w_1, st_1) \leftarrow \mathsf{ID}_1.\mathsf{P}_1(\mathsf{sk}_1)$, then computes $\mu = \mathcal{H}(tr\|w_1\|M)$ and calls its signature oracle on μ to get (z_2, c). It then computes $z_1 \leftarrow \mathsf{ID}_1.\mathsf{P}_2(\mathsf{sk}_1, c, st_1)$ and returns (z_1, z_2, c) to $\mathcal{A}$.

When $\mathcal{A}$ outputs a forgery (z_1^*, z_2^*, c^*) for message M^*, $\mathcal{B}_1$ outputs (z_2^*, c^*) as its forgery, for the message $\mu^* = \mathcal{H}(tr\|\mathsf{ID}_1.\mathsf{Rec}(\mathsf{vk}_1, z_1^*, c^*)\|M^*)$.

We study the implications of the existence of a signature query for μ_i made by $\mathcal{B}_1$ such that $\mu^* = \mu_i$. This signature query was made in response to a signature query made by $\mathcal{A}$, for some message M. Let (z_2, c) be the answer to the query made by $\mathcal{B}_1$ and $w_1^* = \mathsf{ID}_1.\mathsf{Rec}(\mathsf{vk}_1, z_1^*, c^*)$. Two cases arise.

(i) $\mu_i = \mathcal{H}(tr\|w_1\|M)$, *i.e.* $\mathcal{B}_1$ was responding to a Σ_H signature query. There are two subcases.
  (a) $w_1\|M = w_1^*\|M^*$. In particular, $w_1 = w_1^*$. Assuming that (z_1^*, z_2^*, c^*) is accepted by $\Sigma_\mathsf{H}.\mathsf{Verify}$, due to the unique response of ID_1, either $c \neq c^*$ or (z_1^*, z_2, c^*) was the signature returned to $\mathcal{A}$ after its query for M.
  (b) $w_1\|M \neq w_1^*\|M^*$. As $\mu^* = \mu_i$, we have two preimages for μ^* with different suffixes for $\mathcal{H}$.
(ii) $\mu_i = \mathcal{H}(\mathcal{H}(\mathsf{vk}_2)\|M)$, *i.e.* $\mathcal{B}_1$ was responding to a Σ_2 signature query. There are again two subcases.
  (a) $tr = \mathcal{H}(\mathsf{vk}_2)$. As $\mathsf{vk}_2 \neq \mathsf{vk}_1\|\mathsf{vk}_2$, we have two preimages for tr for $\mathcal{H}$.
  (b) $tr \neq \mathcal{H}(\mathsf{vk}_2)$. As $\mu^* = \mu_i$, we have two preimages, with different prefixes, for μ^* for $\mathcal{H}$.

In the H-EU-CMA$^\mathsf{H}$ contexts, $\mathcal{B}_1$ wins only if (z_2^*, c^*) is a valid signature for μ^* for $\mathsf{FSwA}[\mathsf{ID}_2, H]$ and μ^* was not queried by $\mathcal{B}_1$. If $\mathcal{A}$ wins, then (z_1^*, z_2^*, c^*) is a valid signature for M^* for Σ_H and M^* was not queried to its Σ_H oracle. Then, if $\mathcal{A}$ wins, (z_2^*, c^*) is a valid signature for μ^* for $\mathsf{FSwA}[\mathsf{ID}_2, H]$, and $\mathcal{B}_1$ wins if it did not query μ^*. Moreover, if $\mathcal{A}$ wins and μ^* was queried, then we are in one of the above cases, with the exception of case (i)a, as $\mathcal{A}$ did not make a query for M^* to its Σ_H oracle. In all of those cases, we found a collision for $\mathcal{H}$, and $\mathcal{B}_2$ is defined as running $\mathcal{B}_1$ and its challenger, and checking whether one of those cases is realized. Then, if $\mathcal{A}$ wins, either $\mathcal{B}_1$ wins too or $\mathcal{B}_2$ finds a collision for $\mathcal{H}$.

The sH-EU-CMA$^\mathsf{H}$ context is identical with the exception of the case (i)a. If $\mathcal{A}$ wins and case (i)a happens, we must have $(z_1^*, z_2^*, c^*) \neq (z_1, z_2, c)$. It is then impossible to have $(z_2^*, c^*) = (z_2, c)$ as it implies that $z_1 = z_1^*$, as shown above. Hence, if $\mathcal{A}$ wins the sH-EU-CMA$^\mathsf{H}$ game and we are in case (i)a, then $\mathcal{B}_1$ wins the sEU-CMA game too, yielding the same conclusion.

$\square$

4.3   (s)H-EU-CMA Security in the ROM

We now show that our construction satisfies all H-EU-CMA security flavors in the ROM. Our proof strategy follows from standard Fiat-Shamir security arguments: we simulate the three signature oracles using the HVZK property of ID_1 and ID_2, while reprogramming the random oracle as needed. The main technical challenge lies in bounding the probability that an input is reprogrammed more than once, since all three signature oracles share the same random oracle—making this step more intricate than in the standard EU-CMA setting. Once this issue is handled, we can get rid of the signature oracles, and reduce the H-EU-CMA^{X} security to the EU-NMA security of Σ_{X}.

Extending the proof to the strong variant adds an adversary against the CUR property of ID_1 and ID_2, as is also the case for standard Fiat-Shamir signatures.

Lemma 3. *Let $\ell > 0$. Let ID_1 (resp. ID_2) be an identification scheme satisfying HVZK, with aborting probability 0 (resp. β), α_1 (resp. α_2) bits of commitment min-entropy and challenge space $\{0,1\}^\ell$.*

Let $\Sigma_{\mathsf{H}} = \mathsf{H\text{-}FSwA}[\mathsf{ID}_1\|\mathsf{ID}_2, H]$ as in Fig. 5. Let $\Sigma_1 = \mathsf{BUFF}(\mathsf{FS}[\mathsf{ID}_1, H])$ and $\Sigma_2 = \mathsf{BUFF}(\mathsf{FSwA}[\mathsf{ID}_2, H])$. Let $\mathcal{O}_i(\mathsf{sk}_i)$ be the oracle that on input M answers with $\Sigma_i.\mathsf{Sign}(\mathsf{sk}_i, M)$ for $i \in \{\mathsf{H}, 1, 2\}$.

In the ROM, by modeling H as a random oracle, there exist PPT classical adversaries $\mathcal{B}_0$ and $\mathcal{B}_1$, explicitly given in the proof of this theorem, such that for any $\mathsf{X} \in \{\mathsf{H}, 1, 2\}$ and hash function $\mathcal{H} : \{0,1\}^* \to \{0,1\}^\alpha$, and PPT classical adversary $\mathcal{A}$ making Q_i queries to oracle $\mathcal{O}_i(\mathsf{sk}_i)$ for $i \in \{\mathsf{H}, 1, 2\}$ and Q_h queries to the random oracle, we have that

$$\mathsf{Adv}^{\mathsf{H\text{-}EU\text{-}CMA}^{\mathsf{X}}}_{Q_1, Q_2, Q_{\mathsf{H}}}(\mathcal{A}) \leq \frac{\beta}{(1-\beta)^2} \cdot \left(Q_{\mathsf{H}} \cdot 2^{-\alpha_1-\alpha_2} + Q_2 \cdot 2^{-\alpha_2}\right)$$

$$+ \left(Q_h + Q_1 + \frac{Q_2 + Q_{\mathsf{H}}}{1-\beta}\right)\left(\frac{Q_{\mathsf{H}} \cdot 2^{-\alpha_1-\alpha_2}}{1-\beta} + Q_1 \cdot 2^{-\alpha_1} + \frac{Q_2 \cdot 2^{-\alpha_2}}{1-\beta}\right)$$

$$+ \mathsf{Adv}^{\mathsf{EU\text{-}NMA}}_{\Sigma_{\mathsf{X}}}(\mathcal{B}_0) + \mathsf{Adv}^{\mathsf{col}}_{\mathcal{H}}(\mathcal{B}_1) \ . \tag{1}$$

If $\mathcal{A}$ plays the $\mathsf{sH\text{-}EU\text{-}CMA}^{\mathsf{X}}$ game, there exist two more adversaries $\mathcal{B}_2$ and $\mathcal{B}_3$ explicitly given in the proof such that Eq. 1 holds by adding $\mathsf{Adv}^{\mathsf{CUR}}_{\mathsf{ID}_{\mathsf{X}}}(\mathcal{B}_{1+\mathsf{X}})$ if $\mathsf{X} \neq \mathsf{H}$, otherwise $\mathsf{Adv}^{\mathsf{CUR}}_{\mathsf{ID}_1}(\mathcal{B}_2) + \mathsf{Adv}^{\mathsf{CUR}}_{\mathsf{ID}_2}(\mathcal{B}_3)$ to the right-hand side.

Proof. First, we introduce intermediate oracles in Fig. 6, where oracles $\mathcal{O}^u_{\mathsf{X}}$ for $\mathsf{X} \in \{1, 2, \mathsf{H}\}$ replace the generation of the challenge c with a uniformly sampled one. They patch accordingly the random oracle afterwards. The oracle $\mathcal{O}^{s_2}_{\mathsf{H}}$ moreover simulates the ID_2 transcript using its HVZK simulator.

We consider the difference when $\mathcal{A}$ is given access to $\mathcal{O}_{\mathsf{H}}, \mathcal{O}_1, \mathcal{O}_2, H$, *i.e.* the H-EU-CMA^{X} game and when it is given access to $\mathcal{O}^u_{\mathsf{H}}, \mathcal{O}^u_1, \mathcal{O}^u_2, H$, which we dub the $\mathsf{Game}^{\mathsf{X}}_1$ game. Let $\{s_i\}_i$ be the set of all bit strings of the form $w_1\|\mu$ or $w_2\|\mu$ generated during oracle calls to $\mathcal{O}_1, \mathcal{O}_2$ or $\mathcal{O}_{\mathsf{H}}$ (resp. $\mathcal{O}^u_1, \mathcal{O}^u_2$ or $\mathcal{O}^u_{\mathsf{H}}$), even the ones that are rejected, as well as bit strings sent by $\mathcal{A}$ to the random oracle H. We consider the following event Bad: "$\exists i < j, s_i = s_j$ and s_j was not a

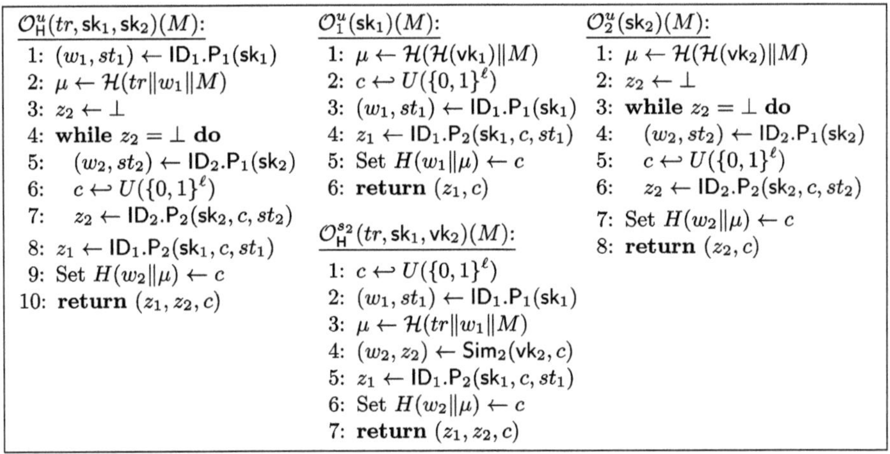

$\mathcal{O}_{\mathsf{H}}^{u}(tr, \mathsf{sk}_1, \mathsf{sk}_2)(M):$
1: $(w_1, st_1) \leftarrow \mathsf{ID}_1.\mathsf{P}_1(\mathsf{sk}_1)$
2: $\mu \leftarrow \mathcal{H}(tr \| w_1 \| M)$
3: $z_2 \leftarrow \bot$
4: **while** $z_2 = \bot$ **do**
5: $\quad (w_2, st_2) \leftarrow \mathsf{ID}_2.\mathsf{P}_1(\mathsf{sk}_2)$
6: $\quad c \hookleftarrow U(\{0,1\}^{\ell})$
7: $\quad z_2 \leftarrow \mathsf{ID}_2.\mathsf{P}_2(\mathsf{sk}_2, c, st_2)$
8: $z_1 \leftarrow \mathsf{ID}_1.\mathsf{P}_2(\mathsf{sk}_1, c, st_1)$
9: Set $H(w_2 \| \mu) \leftarrow c$
10: **return** (z_1, z_2, c)

$\mathcal{O}_1^{u}(\mathsf{sk}_1)(M):$
1: $\mu \leftarrow \mathcal{H}(\mathcal{H}(\mathsf{vk}_1) \| M)$
2: $c \hookleftarrow U(\{0,1\}^{\ell})$
3: $(w_1, st_1) \leftarrow \mathsf{ID}_1.\mathsf{P}_1(\mathsf{sk}_1)$
4: $z_1 \leftarrow \mathsf{ID}_1.\mathsf{P}_2(\mathsf{sk}_1, c, st_1)$
5: Set $H(w_1 \| \mu) \leftarrow c$
6: **return** (z_1, c)

$\mathcal{O}_{\mathsf{H}}^{s_2}(tr, \mathsf{sk}_1, \mathsf{vk}_2)(M):$
1: $c \hookleftarrow U(\{0,1\}^{\ell})$
2: $(w_1, st_1) \leftarrow \mathsf{ID}_1.\mathsf{P}_1(\mathsf{sk}_1)$
3: $\mu \leftarrow \mathcal{H}(tr \| w_1 \| M)$
4: $(w_2, z_2) \leftarrow \mathsf{Sim}_2(\mathsf{vk}_2, c)$
5: $z_1 \leftarrow \mathsf{ID}_1.\mathsf{P}_2(\mathsf{sk}_1, c, st_1)$
6: Set $H(w_2 \| \mu) \leftarrow c$
7: **return** (z_1, z_2, c)

$\mathcal{O}_2^{u}(\mathsf{sk}_2)(M):$
1: $\mu \leftarrow \mathcal{H}(\mathcal{H}(\mathsf{vk}_2) \| M)$
2: $z_2 \leftarrow \bot$
3: **while** $z_2 = \bot$ **do**
4: $\quad (w_2, st_2) \leftarrow \mathsf{ID}_2.\mathsf{P}_1(\mathsf{sk}_2)$
5: $\quad c \hookleftarrow U(\{0,1\}^{\ell})$
6: $\quad z_2 \leftarrow \mathsf{ID}_2.\mathsf{P}_2(\mathsf{sk}_2, c, st_2)$
7: Set $H(w_2 \| \mu) \leftarrow c$
8: **return** (z_2, c)

Fig. 6. Intermediary signature oracles.

query from $\mathcal{A}$ to the random oracle". Conditioned on this event not happening, the oracles are strictly identical in both cases: no random oracle output is overwritten, all of them are chosen uniformly, and values that are not programmed during rejected iterations are not accessed afterwards. As such, we have

$$\mathsf{Adv}_{Q_1, Q_2, Q_{\mathsf{H}}}^{\mathsf{H\text{-}EU\text{-}CMA}^{\mathsf{X}}}(\mathcal{A}) \leq \mathsf{Adv}_{Q_1, Q_2, Q_{\mathsf{H}}}^{\mathsf{Game}_1^{\mathsf{X}}}(\mathcal{A}) + \Pr(\mathsf{Bad}).$$

We assess the probability of Bad happening in $\mathsf{Game}_1^{\mathsf{X}}$ by letting $B_i^{(\mathsf{H})}$ (resp. $B_i^{(2)}$) denote the number of iterations necessary to answer the i-th $\mathcal{O}_{\mathsf{H}}^{u}$ (resp. $\mathcal{O}_2^{u}$) query for $i \leq Q_{\mathsf{H}}$ (resp. Q_2). Note that $B_i^{(\mathsf{H})}$ and $B_i^{(2)}$ are identically and independently distributed and follow the geometrical law with parameter $1 - \beta$.

As oracle $\mathcal{O}_1^{u}$ (resp. $\mathcal{O}_2^{u}$ and $\mathcal{O}_{\mathsf{H}}^{u}$) sample a commitment for ID_1 (resp. ID_2) and as this commitment has to match the begin of any recorded bit string, using the union bound and the commitment min-entropy of ID_1 and ID_2, we end up with the following upper bound:

$$\Pr\left(\mathsf{Bad} \,\middle|\, \begin{matrix} B_1^{(\mathsf{H})}, \ldots, B_{Q_{\mathsf{H}}}^{(\mathsf{H})} \\ B_1^{(2)}, \ldots, B_{Q_2}^{(2)} \end{matrix}\right) \leq Q \cdot \left(Q_1 \cdot 2^{-\alpha_1} + \sum_{i=1}^{Q_2} B_i^{(2)} \cdot 2^{-\alpha_2} + \sum_{i=1}^{Q_{\mathsf{H}}} B_i^{(\mathsf{H})} \cdot 2^{-\alpha_2}\right),$$

where we let $Q = Q_1 + \sum_{i=1}^{Q_2} B_i^{(2)} + \sum_{i=1}^{Q_\mathsf{H}} B_i^{(\mathsf{H})} + Q_h$ be the number of elements in $\{s_i\}_i$. The law of total probabilities with this bound gives:

$$
\Pr(\mathsf{Bad}) \leq \mathbb{E}\left(\sum_{i=1}^{Q_\mathsf{H}} B_i^{(\mathsf{H})}\right) \cdot \left(Q_h + Q_1 + \mathbb{E}\left(\sum_{j=1}^{Q_2} B_j^{(2)}\right)\right) \cdot 2^{-\alpha_2}
$$

$$
+ Q_1 \cdot \left(Q_h + \mathbb{E}\left(\sum_{j=1}^{Q_\mathsf{H}} B_j^{(\mathsf{H})}\right) + Q_1 + \mathbb{E}\left(\sum_{j=1}^{Q_2} B_j^{(2)}\right)\right) \cdot 2^{-\alpha_1}
$$

$$
+ \mathbb{E}\left(\sum_{i=1}^{Q_2} B_i^{(2)}\right) \cdot \left(Q_h + \mathbb{E}\left(\sum_{j=1}^{Q_\mathsf{H}} B_j^{(\mathsf{H})}\right) + Q_1\right) \cdot 2^{-\alpha_2}
$$

$$
+ \mathbb{E}\left(\left(\sum_{i=1}^{Q_\mathsf{H}} B_i^{(\mathsf{H})}\right)^2\right) \cdot 2^{-\alpha_2} + \mathbb{E}\left(\left(\sum_{i=1}^{Q_2} B_i^{(2)}\right)^2\right) \cdot 2^{-\alpha_2}.
$$

We identify the mean and 2nd order moment of a sum of geometrical laws, thus $\mathbb{E}(\sum_{i=1}^{Q_\mathsf{H}} B_i^{(\mathsf{H})}) = Q_\mathsf{H}/(1 - \beta)$, $\mathbb{E}(\sum_{i=1}^{Q_2} B_i^{(2)}) = Q_2/(1 - \beta)$, and

$$
\mathbb{E}\left(\left(\sum_{i=1}^{Q_\mathsf{Y}} B_i^{(\mathsf{Y})}\right)^2\right) = \frac{(Q_\mathsf{Y})^2}{(1 - \beta)^2} + \frac{\beta \cdot Q_\mathsf{Y}}{(1 - \beta)^2}, \forall \mathsf{Y} \in \{2, \mathsf{H}\}.
$$

This gives the bound:

$$
\Pr(\mathsf{Bad}) \leq \frac{Q_\mathsf{H}}{1 - \beta} \cdot \left(Q_h + Q_1 + \frac{Q_2}{1 - \beta}\right) \cdot 2^{-\alpha_2}
$$

$$
+ Q_1 \left(Q_h + \frac{Q_\mathsf{H}}{1 - \beta} + Q_1 + \frac{Q_2}{1 - \beta}\right) 2^{-\alpha_1} + \frac{Q_2}{1 - \beta}\left(Q_h + Q_1 + \frac{Q_\mathsf{H}}{1 - \beta}\right) 2^{-\alpha_2}
$$

$$
+ \left(\frac{(Q_\mathsf{H})^2}{(1 - \beta)^2} + \frac{\beta \cdot Q_\mathsf{H}}{(1 - \beta)^2}\right) \cdot 2^{-\alpha_2} + \left(\frac{(Q_2)^2}{(1 - \beta)^2} + \frac{\beta \cdot Q_2}{(1 - \beta)^2}\right) \cdot 2^{-\alpha_2}
$$

$$
= \left(Q_h + Q_1 + \frac{Q_2 + Q_\mathsf{H}}{1 - \beta}\right)\left(\frac{Q_\mathsf{H} \cdot 2^{-\alpha_2}}{1 - \beta} + Q_1 \cdot 2^{-\alpha_1} + \frac{Q_2 \cdot 2^{-\alpha_2}}{1 - \beta}\right)
$$

$$
+ \frac{\beta}{(1 - \beta)^2} \cdot \left(Q_\mathsf{H} \cdot 2^{-\alpha_2} + Q_2 \cdot 2^{-\alpha_2}\right).
$$

Next, we replace the $\mathcal{O}_\mathsf{H}^u$ oracle with $\mathcal{O}_\mathsf{H}^{s_2}$, and the $\mathcal{O}_2^u$ oracle with $\mathcal{O}_2^s$ from Fig. 7. By the HVZK property of ID_2, the resulting game $\mathsf{Game}_2^\mathsf{X}$ is such that

$$
\mathsf{Adv}_{Q_1, Q_2, Q_\mathsf{H}}^{\mathsf{Game}_1^\mathsf{X}}(\mathcal{A}) = \mathsf{Adv}_{Q_1, Q_2, Q_\mathsf{H}}^{\mathsf{Game}_2^\mathsf{X}}(\mathcal{A}).
$$

Similarly, we use the HVZK property of ID_1, allowing us to replace $\mathcal{O}_\mathsf{H}^{s_2}$ with $\mathcal{O}_\mathsf{H}^s$, and $\mathcal{O}_1^u$ with $\mathcal{O}_1^s$. The resulting game $\mathsf{Game}_3^\mathsf{X}$ is such that

$$
\mathsf{Adv}_{Q_1, Q_2, Q_\mathsf{H}}^{\mathsf{Game}_2^\mathsf{X}}(\mathcal{A}) = \mathsf{Adv}_{Q_1, Q_2, Q_\mathsf{H}}^{\mathsf{Game}_3^\mathsf{X}}(\mathcal{A}).
$$

$\mathcal{O}_\mathsf{H}^s(\mathsf{vk}_1,\mathsf{vk}_2)(M):$	$\mathcal{O}_1^s(\mathsf{vk}_1)(M):$	$\mathcal{O}_2^s(\mathsf{vk}_2)(M):$
$c \hookleftarrow U(\{0,1\}^\ell)$	$\mu \leftarrow \mathcal{H}(\mathcal{H}(\mathsf{vk}_1)\|M)$	$\mu \leftarrow \mathcal{H}(\mathcal{H}(\mathsf{vk}_2)\|M)$
$(w_1,z_1) \leftarrow \mathsf{Sim}_1(\mathsf{vk}_1,c)$	$c \hookleftarrow U(\{0,1\}^\ell)$	$c \hookleftarrow U(\{0,1\}^\ell)$
$\mu \leftarrow \mathcal{H}(\mathcal{H}(\mathsf{vk}_1\|\mathsf{vk}_2)\|w_1\|M)$	$(w_1,z_1) \leftarrow \mathsf{Sim}_1(\mathsf{vk}_1,c)$	$(w_2,z_2) \leftarrow \mathsf{Sim}_2(\mathsf{vk}_2,c)$
$(w_2,z_2) \leftarrow \mathsf{Sim}_2(\mathsf{vk}_2,c)$	Set $H(w_1\|\mu) \leftarrow c$	Set $H(w_2\|\mu) \leftarrow c$
Set $H(w_2\|\mu) \leftarrow c$	**return** (z_1,c)	**return** (z_2,c)
return (z_1,z_2,c)		

Fig. 7. Simulation oracles.

Finally, we note that the three simulated oracles do not use the signing key. As such, we define an adversary $\mathcal{B}_0$ that only queries the random oracle H, and that calls $\mathcal{A}$ by simulating the three oracles $\mathcal{O}_\mathsf{Y}^s$ and random oracle H' which is H except on inputs that were reprogrammed by the other oracles. When $\mathcal{A}$ outputs a forgery σ^*, M^*, the reduction $\mathcal{B}_0$ outputs it as its own. It wins if $\mathcal{A}$ wins, and it did not patch the random oracle on any input used during the verification process. Reprogramming only happens whenever a call to an oracle is made. Since $\mathcal{A}$ must output a message M^* for which it did not query a signature for Σ_X, its forgery was either on an input not reprogrammed, or it found a collision for the hash function $\mathcal{H}$, as it implies that the associated μ^* is identical to some μ_i that appeared during some query to oracle $\mathcal{O}_\mathsf{Y}$ with message M_i. We have:

$\mathsf{Y} = \mathsf{X}$. As $M_i \neq M^*$, we have two preimages for μ^* by $\mathcal{H}$.

$\mathsf{Y} \neq \mathsf{X}$. There are two subcases.

    $tr_\mathsf{X} = tr_\mathsf{Y}$. As $\mathsf{vk}_\mathsf{X} \neq \mathsf{vk}_\mathsf{Y}$, where $\mathsf{vk}_\mathsf{H} = \mathsf{vk}_1\|\mathsf{vk}_2$, we have two preimages for tr_X by $\mathcal{H}$.

    $tr_\mathsf{X} \neq tr_\mathsf{Y}$. As $\mu^* = \mu_i$, we have two preimages for μ^* by $\mathcal{H}$.

The adversary $\mathcal{B}_1$ is defined as running $\mathcal{B}_0$ and its challenger, and returning such a collision, if one is found. This gives the final bound.

In the strong unforgeability setting, we furthermore look into what happens when $M^* = M_i$. If the forgery is not on an input that was reprogrammed, then this forgery is valid for the reduction $\mathcal{B}$. Otherwise, there is a signature σ_i generated by $\mathcal{O}_\mathsf{X}$ for M_i such that the challenges contained in σ^* and σ_i are identical, as well as the inputs of the random oracle recovered during verification. We then have:

- If $\mathsf{X} = 1$ or 2, then we extract an adversary $\mathcal{B}_{\mathsf{X}+1}$ against the CUR property of ID_X, as we have two transcripts having common commitment and challenge, but different answers, as the forgery differs from the signature.
- If $\mathsf{X} = \mathsf{H}$, we may have found a collision for $\mathcal{H}$ in the case where $\mu^* = \mu_i$ but the ID_1 commitments are different for the signature and the forgery. Otherwise, we extract an adversary $\mathcal{B}_2$ or $\mathcal{B}_3$ against the CUR property of either ID_1 or ID_2, as both the signature and forgery contain a valid transcript for both ID_1 and ID_2, where those transcripts have common commitments and challenges, and either the ID_1 or ID_2 transcripts have different answers.

This concludes the extension of the proof to the sH-EU-CMA setting.   □

We show that one can swap Σ_1 with any signature scheme not using H.

Corollary 1. *Let everything as in Lemma 3, except that Σ_1 is any signature scheme such that $\Sigma_1.\mathsf{KeyGen} = \mathsf{ID}_1.\mathsf{IGen}$ and Σ_1 does not use H.*

In the ROM, by modeling H as a random oracle, there exist PPT classical adversaries $\mathcal{B}_0$ and $\mathcal{B}_1$, explicitly given in the proof of this theorem, such that for any $\mathsf{X} \in \{\mathsf{H}, 1, 2\}$ and hash function $\mathcal{H} : \{0,1\}^* \to \{0,1\}^\alpha$, and PPT classical adversary $\mathcal{A}$ making Q_i queries to oracle $\mathcal{O}_i(\mathsf{sk}_i)$ for $i \in \{\mathsf{H}, 1, 2\}$ and Q_h queries to the random oracle, we have that

$$\mathsf{Adv}^{\mathsf{H\text{-}EU\text{-}CMA}^{\mathsf{X}}}_{Q_1, Q_2, Q_{\mathsf{H}}}(\mathcal{A}) \le \mathsf{Adv}^{\mathsf{game}}_{\Sigma_{\mathsf{X}}}(\mathcal{B}_0) + \frac{\beta}{(1-\beta)^2} \cdot \left(Q_{\mathsf{H}} \cdot 2^{-\alpha_1 - \alpha_2} + Q_2 \cdot 2^{-\alpha_2}\right)$$

$$+ \left(Q_h + \frac{Q_2 + Q_{\mathsf{H}}}{1-\beta}\right)\left(\frac{Q_{\mathsf{H}} \cdot 2^{-\alpha_1 - \alpha_2}}{1-\beta} + \frac{Q_2 \cdot 2^{-\alpha_2}}{1-\beta}\right) + \mathsf{Adv}^{\mathsf{col}}_{\mathcal{H}}(\mathcal{B}_1) , \qquad (2)$$

where game *is EU-NMA for $\mathsf{X} = 2$, EU-CMA for $\mathsf{X} = 1$ or $\mathsf{H\text{-}EU\text{-}CMA}^{\mathsf{H}}_{Q_1,0,0}$ for $\mathsf{X} = \mathsf{H}$. If $\mathcal{A}$ plays the $\mathsf{sH\text{-}EU\text{-}CMA}^{\mathsf{X}}$ game, there exist two more adversaries $\mathcal{B}_2$ and $\mathcal{B}_3$ explicitly given in the proof such that Eq. 2 holds by changing* game *to sEU-CMA if $\mathsf{X} = 1$, or adding $\mathsf{Adv}^{\mathsf{CUR}}_{\mathsf{ID}_2}(\mathcal{B}_3)$ if $\mathsf{X} = 2$, otherwise adding $\mathsf{Adv}^{\mathsf{CUR}}_{\mathsf{ID}_1}(\mathcal{B}_2) + \mathsf{Adv}^{\mathsf{CUR}}_{\mathsf{ID}_2}(\mathcal{B}_3)$ to the right-hand side.*

Proof. Consider the same sequence of hybrid games as in the proof of Lemma 3, with the difference that $\mathcal{O}_1$ is never replaced and we do not consider $\mathcal{O}_1^u$ nor $\mathcal{O}_1^s$. The bounds computed in the above proof are still valid, with $Q_1 = 0$ as Σ_1 does not use H. This reduces the $\mathsf{H\text{-}EU\text{-}CMA}^{\mathsf{X}}_{Q_1, Q_2, Q_{\mathsf{H}}}$ game to the $\mathsf{H\text{-}EU\text{-}CMA}^{\mathsf{X}}_{Q_1, 0, 0}$ game. If $\mathsf{X} = 1$, this is the EU-CMA game of Σ_1. If $\mathsf{X} = 2$, this game reduces to the EU-NMA one of Σ_2, by sampling $(\mathsf{vk}_1, \mathsf{sk}_2) \leftarrow \mathsf{ID}_1.\mathsf{IGen}(1^\lambda)$ and managing the Σ_1 signature oracle.   □

We conclude by showing that the EU-NMA security of $\mathsf{H\text{-}FSwA}[\mathsf{ID}_1\|\mathsf{ID}_2, H]$ reduces to the special soundness of ID_1 and ID_2, which are also the base assumptions for $\mathsf{FS}[\mathsf{ID}_1, H]$ and $\mathsf{FSwA}[\mathsf{ID}_2, H]$. In the proof, we show that the identification scheme ID, that concatenates ID_1 and ID_2, has a Fiat-Shamir transform whose EU-NMA game is equivalent to that of $\mathsf{H\text{-}FSwA}[\mathsf{ID}_1\|\mathsf{ID}_2, H]$, allowing us to conclude using standard arguments, in particular Lemma 2.

Theorem 3 (EU-NMA Security of $\mathsf{H\text{-}FSwA}[\mathsf{ID}_1\|\mathsf{ID}_2, H]$). *Let everything as in Lemma 3. Let two algorithms $\mathsf{LossyIGen}_i$, $i \in \{1, 2\}$. In the ROM, there exist three adversaries explicitly given in the proof, $\mathcal{B}_1$ and $\mathcal{B}_2$ against the lossy-2-special-soundness of ID_1 and ID_2 and $\mathcal{B}_3$ against the collision game of $\mathcal{H}$, and two distinguishers $\mathcal{D}_1$ and $\mathcal{D}_2$ against the key-indistinguishability of ID_1 and ID_2 such that for any adversary $\mathcal{A}$ against the EU-NMA security of $\mathsf{H\text{-}FSwA}[\mathsf{ID}_1\|\mathsf{ID}_2, H]$*

making at most Q_h random oracle queries:

$$\mathsf{Adv}^{\mathsf{EU\text{-}NMA}}_{\mathsf{H\text{-}FSwA}[\mathsf{ID}_1\|\mathsf{ID}_2,H]}(\mathcal{A}) \leq \min_{i\in\{1,2\}} \left(\mathsf{Adv}^{\mathsf{key\text{-}ind}}_{\mathsf{ID}_i}(\mathcal{D}_i) + \frac{Q_h+1}{2^\ell} \right.$$

$$\left. + \sqrt{(Q_h+1)\left(\mathsf{Adv}^{\mathsf{lossy\text{-}2\text{-}ss}}_{\mathsf{ID}_i}(\mathcal{B}_i) + (2-i)\cdot\mathsf{Adv}^{\mathsf{col}}_{\mathcal{H}}(\mathcal{B}_3)\right)} \right).$$

Proof. We first consider the following three games.

Game$_0$. This is the standard EU-NMA game.

Game$_i$, $i \in \{1,2\}$. This is Game$_0$ except that LossyIGen$_i$ replaces ID_i.IGen. $\mathcal{D}_i$ is defined as taking vk_i as input, running $\mathsf{vk}_{3-i} \leftarrow \mathsf{ID}_{3-i}.\mathsf{IGen}(1^\lambda)$ and calling $\mathcal{A}$ on $\mathsf{vk} = (\mathsf{vk}_1, \mathsf{vk}_2)$. If $\mathcal{A}$ wins, $\mathcal{D}_i$ returns 1, else it returns 0. We have

$$\forall i \in \{1,2\}, \mathsf{Adv}^{\mathsf{key\text{-}ind}}_{\mathsf{ID}_i}(\mathcal{D}_i) = \left| \mathsf{Adv}^{\mathsf{EU\text{-}NMA}}(\mathcal{A}) - \mathsf{Adv}^{\mathsf{Game}_i}(\mathcal{A}) \right|.$$

Before defining the reductions to the lossy-2-special-soundness, we define the algorithm A, that on input $\mathsf{vk} = (\mathsf{vk}_1, \mathsf{vk}_2)$ and access to the random oracle H runs $\mathcal{A}^H(\mathsf{vk})$ and records all random oracle queries made by it. When $\mathcal{A}$ outputs a forgery $(\sigma^* = (z_1^*, z_2^*, c^*), M^*)$, let $w_i^* = \mathsf{ID}_1.\mathsf{Rec}(\mathsf{vk}_i, z_i^*, c^*), i \in \{1,2\}$ as well as $\mu^* = \mathcal{H}(\mathcal{H}(\mathsf{vk}), w_1^*, M^*)$. Algorithm A checks whether $\mathcal{A}$ wins by computing $\mathsf{H\text{-}FSwA}[\mathsf{ID}_1\|\mathsf{ID}_2, H].\mathsf{Verify}(\mathsf{vk}, \sigma^*, M^*)$, which entails querying once more the random oracle. Algorithm A finally outputs $(i, (\sigma^*, M^*))$, where i is the rank of the first random oracle query it made for $w_2^*\|\mu^*$, if $\mathcal{A}$ wins, otherwise $(0, \varepsilon)$.

Applying Lemma 2 on A, we get an algorithm $\mathcal{F} = (\mathcal{F}_1, \mathcal{F}_2)$ that on input vk may return $(1, ((z_1^*, z_2^*, c^*), M^*), ((z_1' z_2', c'), M'))$ with $c' \neq c^*$ chosen externally. Letting $w_i' = \mathsf{ID}_i.\mathsf{Rec}(\mathsf{vk}_i, z_i', c'), i \in \{1,2\}$ and $\mu' = \mathcal{H}(\mathcal{H}(\mathsf{vk}), w_1', M')$, we have $w_2^* = w_2'$ and $\mu^* = \mu'$.

Adversary $\mathcal{B}_i, i \in \{1,2\}$, playing the lossy-2-special-soudness of ID_i, on input vk_i, runs $(\mathsf{vk}_{3-i}, \mathsf{sk}_{3-i}) \leftarrow \mathsf{ID}_{3-i}.\mathsf{IGen}(1^\lambda)$ and runs $\mathcal{F}_1$ on $\mathsf{vk} = (\mathsf{vk}_1, \mathsf{vk}_2)$. When it returns $(i^*, (z_1^*, z_2^*, c^*, M^*))$, $\mathcal{B}_i$ returns (w_i^*, c^*, z_i^*) and gets $c' \neq c^*$. It then runs $\mathcal{F}_2(c', st)$. Assuming it returns $(1, (z_1^*, z_2^*, c^*, M^*), (z_1', z_2', c', M'))$, if $i = 1$ and $w_1' = w_1^*$ or if $i = 2$, $\mathcal{B}_i$ returns z_i'. Otherwise, it aborts.

Adversary $\mathcal{B}_i$ then wins if and only if it did not abort, which is equivalent to $\mathcal{F}_2$ returning something starting with 1 for $\mathcal{B}_2$. It is equivalent to $\mathcal{F}_2$ returning something starting with 1 and $w_1' = w_1^*$ for $\mathcal{B}_1$. However, if $w_1' \neq w_1^*$ we have found a collision for $\mathcal{H}$ as we have two preimages for $\mu^* = \mu'$, and we define $\mathcal{B}_3$ as running everything, and returning this collision, if found. We have the bound:

$$\mathsf{Adv}^{\mathsf{Game}_i}(\mathcal{A}) \leq \frac{Q_h+1}{2^\ell} + \sqrt{(Q_h+1)\cdot\left(\mathsf{Adv}^{\mathsf{lossy\text{-}2\text{-}ss}}_{\mathsf{ID}_i}(\mathcal{B}_i) + (2-i)\cdot\mathsf{Adv}^{\mathsf{col}}_{\mathcal{H}}(\mathcal{B}_3)\right)}.$$

$\square$

Remark 2. If Σ_1 is instead a signature scheme that does not use H, by considering LossyIGen$_1 = \mathsf{ID}_1.\mathsf{IGen}$, the same proof allows to reduce the H-EU-CMA$^H_{Q_1,0,0}$ game to a "2-special-soundness for ID_1 with a Σ_1 signature oracle" game. As the signature oracle is independent from H, the forking lemma still applies.

4.4 BUFF Properties

We now turn to proving the BUFF properties of our construction.

Theorem 4 (EO Security of H-FSwA[$\mathsf{ID}_1\|\mathsf{ID}_2, H$]). *In the standard model, there exist adversaries $\mathcal{B}_0$ and $\mathcal{B}_1$, explicitly given in the proof of this theorem, such that for any hash functions $\mathcal{H} : \{0,1\}^* \to \{0,1\}^\alpha$ and $H : \{0,1\}^* \to \{0,1\}^\ell$, and any adversary $\mathcal{A}$ against the EO security of H-FSwA[$\mathsf{ID}_1\|\mathsf{ID}_2, H$], we have*

$$\mathsf{Adv}^{\mathsf{EO}}_{\mathsf{H\text{-}FSwA}[\mathsf{ID}_1\|\mathsf{ID}_2, H]}(\mathcal{A}) \le \mathsf{Adv}^{\mathsf{Col}}_{\mathcal{H}}(\mathcal{B}_0) + \mathsf{Adv}^{\mathsf{Col}}_{H}(\mathcal{B}_1).$$

Proof. We use the notations of Fig. 5. Let $(\mathsf{vk}, \mathsf{vk}', m, m', \sigma)$ be $\mathcal{A}$'s output. If $\mathcal{A}$ wins the EO game, then σ is a valid signature for m (resp. m') under vk (resp. vk'). From line 4 of the verification algorithm in Fig. 5, it follows that $c = H(w_2\|\mu) = H(w_2'\|\mu')$ where μ and μ' are both α-bit strings. If $\mu \ne \mu'$, this directly yields a collision for H. Otherwise, by line 2, we have

$$\mathcal{H}(\mathcal{H}(\mathsf{vk}_1\|\mathsf{vk}_2)\|w_1\|m) = \mathcal{H}(\mathcal{H}(\mathsf{vk}_1'\|\mathsf{vk}_2')\|w_1'\|m'). \tag{3}$$

By the EO definition, $\mathcal{A}$ can only win if $(\mathsf{vk}_1, \mathsf{vk}_2) \ne (\mathsf{vk}_1', \mathsf{vk}_2')$. We directly obtain a collision for $\mathcal{H}$ if $\mathcal{H}(\mathsf{vk}_1\|\mathsf{vk}_2) = \mathcal{H}(\mathsf{vk}_1'\|\mathsf{vk}_2')$. Else, Eq. 3 yields a collision for $\mathcal{H}$ since both inputs have distinct α-bit prefixes. Finally, adversary $\mathcal{B}_0$ (resp. $\mathcal{B}_1$) runs $\mathcal{A}$ and outputs the corresponding collision on H (resp. $\mathcal{H}$), if any. $\qquad\square$

Theorem 5 (MBS Security of H-FSwA[$\mathsf{ID}_1\|\mathsf{ID}_2, H$]). *In the standard model, there exist adversaries $\mathcal{B}_0$ and $\mathcal{B}_1$, explicitly given in the proof of this theorem, such that for any hash functions $\mathcal{H} : \{0,1\}^* \to \{0,1\}^\alpha$ and $H : \{0,1\}^* \to \{0,1\}^\ell$, and any adversary $\mathcal{A}$ against the MBS security of H-FSwA[$\mathsf{ID}_1\|\mathsf{ID}_2, H$], we have*

$$\mathsf{Adv}^{\mathsf{MBS}}_{\mathsf{H\text{-}FSwA}[\mathsf{ID}_1\|\mathsf{ID}_2, H]}(\mathcal{A}) \le \mathsf{Adv}^{\mathsf{Col}}_{\mathcal{H}}(\mathcal{B}_0) + \mathsf{Adv}^{\mathsf{Col}}_{H}(\mathcal{B}_1).$$

Proof. We use the notations of Fig. 5. Let $(\mathsf{vk}, m, m', \sigma)$ be $\mathcal{A}$'s output. If $\mathcal{A}$ wins the MBS game, then σ is a valid signature for both m and m' under vk. The proof proceeds identically to that of Theorem 4 except that Eq. 3 now becomes

$$\mathcal{H}(\mathcal{H}(\mathsf{vk}_1\|\mathsf{vk}_2)\|w_1\|m) = \mathcal{H}(\mathcal{H}(\mathsf{vk}_1\|\mathsf{vk}_2)\|w_1\|m'). \tag{4}$$

Since $\mathcal{A}$ can only win if $m \ne m'$, we immediately obtain a collision for $\mathcal{H}$ if one was not already found for H. Finally, both adversaries $\mathcal{B}_0$ and $\mathcal{B}_1$ run $\mathcal{A}$ and output their respective collisions for H or $\mathcal{H}$, if any. $\qquad\square$

Analyzing the non-resignability of our construction requires introducing the Hide-and-Seek game from [13].

Definition 17 (Hide-and-Seek). *Let H be a random oracle. For any adversaries $\mathcal{A}$ and $\mathcal{D}$, we define* $\mathsf{Adv}^{\mathsf{HnS}}_{H}(\mathcal{A}, \mathcal{D}) := \Pr_{\substack{(x,z)\leftarrow\mathcal{D}^H \\ x^*\leftarrow\mathcal{A}^H(H(x),z)}} (x = x^*).$

Theorem 6 (NR Security of $\mathsf{H\text{-}FSwA}[\mathsf{ID}_1\|\mathsf{ID}_2, H]$). *In the ROM, where $\mathcal{H}:\{0,1\}^* \to \{0,1\}^\alpha$ and $H:\{0,1\}^* \to \{0,1\}^\ell$ are modeled as random oracles, for any adversaries $\mathcal{A}$ and $\mathcal{D}$ against the NR security of $\mathsf{H\text{-}FSwA}[\mathsf{ID}_1\|\mathsf{ID}_2, H]$, there exist adversaries $\bar{\mathcal{A}}$, $\bar{\mathcal{D}}$, such that*

$$\mathsf{Adv}^{\mathsf{NR}}_{\mathsf{H\text{-}FSwA}[\mathsf{ID}_1\|\mathsf{ID}_2,H],\mathsf{aux}}(\mathcal{A},\mathcal{D}) \leq Q_A \cdot \mathsf{Adv}^{\mathsf{HnS}}_{\mathcal{H}}(\bar{\mathcal{A}},\bar{\mathcal{D}}) + \frac{1}{2^\ell} + Q_h \cdot Q_D \cdot 2^{-\alpha},$$

where $\mathcal{A}$ and $\bar{\mathcal{A}}$ make at most Q_A queries to $\mathcal{H}$, $\mathcal{A}$ makes at most Q_h queries to H and $\mathcal{D}$ makes at most Q_D queries to $\mathcal{H}$.

Proof. We follow the first game hop of [13,19] as defined in Fig. 8.

Games Game_0 to Game_1:
1: $(\mathsf{vk}, tr, \mathsf{sk}) \leftarrow \varSigma.\mathsf{KeyGen}(1^\lambda)$
2: $m \leftarrow \mathcal{D}^{H,\mathcal{H}}(\mathsf{sk})$
3: $\sigma \leftarrow \varSigma.\mathsf{Sign}(\mathsf{sk}, m)$
4: $(z_1, z_2, c) \leftarrow \sigma$
5: $(\mathsf{vk}^*, \sigma^*) \leftarrow \mathcal{A}^{H,\bar{\mathcal{H}}}(\mathsf{sk}, \sigma, \mathsf{aux}(\mathsf{sk}, m))$
6: **if** $\mathsf{vk}^* = \mathsf{vk}$ **then return** $\perp$
7: **if** $\varSigma.\mathsf{Verify}(\mathsf{vk}^*, \sigma^*, m) = 1$ **then**
8:     **return** 1
9: **return** $\perp$

Oracle $H(y)$:
1: **return** $H(y)$

Oracle $\bar{\mathcal{H}}(y)$:
1: **if** $y = \cdot \| m$ **then**   // Game_1
2:     **abort**   // Game_1
3: **return** $\mathcal{H}(y)$

Fig. 8. Games Game_0 to Game_1 for the proof of Theorem 6.

Game Game_0 is the NR game for $\varSigma := \mathsf{H\text{-}FSwA}[\mathsf{ID}_1\|\mathsf{ID}_2, H]$. We define Game_1 as Game_0, except that $\mathcal{H}$ aborts whenever queried by $\mathcal{A}$ on an input with suffix m (the message produced by $\mathcal{D}$). Let $\bar{\mathcal{H}}$ denote this new oracle. There exist adversaries $\bar{\mathcal{A}}$, $\mathcal{B}$, and $\bar{\mathcal{D}}$, described in Fig. 9, against the HnS property of $\mathcal{H}$, such that

$$\begin{cases} \displaystyle\operatorname*{H_\infty}_{\substack{(\mathsf{vk},tr,\mathsf{sk})\leftarrow\varSigma.\mathsf{KeyGen} \\ m\leftarrow\mathcal{D}^{H,\mathcal{H}}(\mathsf{sk})}} (m \mid \mathcal{H}, \mathsf{sk}, \mathsf{aux}(\mathsf{sk}, m)) \leq \operatorname*{H_\infty}_{(x,z)\leftarrow\bar{D}^{H,\mathcal{H}}} (x \mid \mathcal{H}, z) \\[6pt] \left| \Pr(1 \leftarrow \mathsf{Game}_0^{\mathcal{A}}) - \Pr(1 \leftarrow \mathsf{Game}_1^{\mathcal{A}}) \right| \leq Q_A \cdot \mathsf{Adv}^{\mathsf{HnS}}_{\mathcal{H}}(\bar{\mathcal{A}}, \bar{\mathcal{D}}) \end{cases}$$

Specifically, $\bar{\mathcal{D}}$ returns $x = tr\|w_1\|m$ and $z = (\mathsf{sk}, \mathsf{vk}, \mathsf{st}_1, w_1, \mathsf{aux}(\mathsf{sk}, m))$.
On input $\nu = \mathcal{H}(x) = \mathcal{H}(tr\|w_1\|m)$ and z, $\bar{\mathcal{A}}$ samples a random index $i \in [1, Q_A]$, runs $\mathcal{B}^H(\nu, z)$ internally, inspects its i-th query to obtain $(tr^*\|w_1^*\|m_i^*)$, and outputs $(tr\|w_1\|m_i^*)$. Moreover,

$$\operatorname*{H_\infty}_{(x,z)\leftarrow\bar{D}^{\mathcal{H}}}(x \mid \mathcal{H}, z) = \operatorname*{H_\infty}_{\substack{(\mathsf{vk},tr,\mathsf{sk}_1\|\mathsf{sk}_2)\leftarrow\varSigma.\mathsf{KeyGen} \\ m\leftarrow\mathcal{D}^{H,\mathcal{H}}(\mathsf{sk}) \\ (w_1,\mathsf{st}_1)\leftarrow\mathsf{ID}_1.\mathsf{P1}(\mathsf{sk}_1)}}(\mathsf{vk}, m, w_1 \mid \mathcal{H}, \mathsf{sk}, \mathsf{st}_1, w_1, \mathsf{aux}(\mathsf{sk}, m))$$

$$\geq H_\infty(m \mid \mathcal{H}, \mathsf{sk}, \mathsf{st}_1, w_1, \mathsf{aux}(\mathsf{sk}, m))$$
$$[\dots]$$

$$\geq \operatorname*{H_\infty}_{\substack{(\mathsf{vk},tr,\mathsf{sk})\leftarrow\varSigma.\mathsf{KeyGen} \\ m\leftarrow\mathcal{D}^{H,\mathcal{H}}(\mathsf{sk})}}(m \mid \mathcal{H}, \mathsf{sk}, \mathsf{aux}(\mathsf{sk}, m))$$

where the first inequality holds because min-entropy can only decrease when fewer random variables are considered, and the second follows from independence of m and (st_1, w_1). By construction, both $\bar{\mathcal{D}}$ and $\bar{\mathcal{A}}$ preserve the efficiency of $\mathcal{D}$ and $\mathcal{A}$. Furthermore, $\bar{\mathcal{A}}$ makes at most Q_A queries to $\mathcal{H}$. Since $\mathcal{A}$ makes only classical queries, the two games differ only if $\mathcal{B}$ queries an input on which $\mathcal{H}$ and $\bar{\mathcal{H}}$ disagree. Hence,

$$\left| \Pr(1 \leftarrow \mathsf{Game}_0^{\mathcal{A}}) - \Pr(1 \leftarrow \mathsf{Game}_1^{\mathcal{A}}) \right| \leq \Pr(\exists i \in [1, Q_A] : m_i^* = m)$$

$$\leq Q_A \cdot \mathsf{Adv}_{\mathcal{H}}^{\mathsf{HnS}}(\bar{\mathcal{A}}, \bar{\mathcal{D}})$$

<table>
<tr><td valign="top">

$\underline{\bar{\mathcal{D}}^{H,\mathcal{H}}:}$

1: $(\mathsf{vk}, tr, \mathsf{sk}) \leftarrow \Sigma.\mathsf{KeyGen}(1^\lambda)$
2: $m \leftarrow \mathcal{D}^{H,\mathcal{H}}(\mathsf{sk})$
3: $\mathsf{sk}_1 \| \mathsf{sk}_2 \leftarrow \mathsf{sk}$
4: $(w_1, st_1) \leftarrow \mathsf{ID}_1.\mathsf{P}_1(\mathsf{sk}_1)$
5: $x \leftarrow tr \| w_1 \| m$
6: $z \leftarrow (\mathsf{sk}, \mathsf{vk}, \mathsf{st}_1, w_1, \mathsf{aux}(\mathsf{sk}, m))$
7: **return** (x, z)

</td><td valign="top">

$\underline{\mathcal{B}^H(\nu, z):}$

1: $(\mathsf{sk}, \mathsf{vk}, \mathsf{st}_1, w_1, h) \leftarrow z$
2: $\mathsf{sk}_1 \| \mathsf{sk}_2, \mathsf{vk}_1 \| \mathsf{vk}_2 \leftarrow \mathsf{sk}, \mathsf{vk}$
3: $(z_2, c) \leftarrow \mathsf{FSwA}[\mathsf{ID}_2, H].\mathsf{Sign}(\mathsf{sk}_2, \nu)$
4: $z_1 \leftarrow \mathsf{ID}_1.\mathsf{P}_2(\mathsf{sk}_1, c, st_1)$
5: $\sigma \leftarrow (z_1, z_2, c)$
6: $(\mathsf{vk}^*, \sigma^*) \leftarrow \mathcal{A}^{H,\bar{\mathcal{H}}}(\mathsf{sk}, \sigma, h)$
7: **return** $\perp$

</td></tr>
</table>

Fig. 9. Reductions $\mathcal{B}$ and $\bar{\mathcal{D}}$ against the Hide-and-Seek property of $\mathcal{H}$.

In Game_1, we have the following inequality:

$$\Pr(\mathcal{A} \text{ wins}) = \Pr\left(\begin{array}{c} \mathcal{A} \text{ wins} \wedge \\ \mathcal{A} \text{ queried } H \text{ on } w_2^* \| \mu^* \end{array} \right) + \Pr\left(\begin{array}{c} \mathcal{A} \text{ wins } \wedge \mathcal{A} \text{ did not} \\ \text{query } H \text{ on } w_2^* \| \mu^* \end{array} \right)$$

$$\leq \Pr(\mathcal{A} \text{ queried } H \text{ on } w_2^* \| \mu^*) + \frac{1}{2^\ell}$$

$$\leq Q_h \cdot 2^{-H_\infty(\mu^* | \mathsf{view}(\mathcal{A}))} + \frac{1}{2^\ell} \;,$$

as $H(w_2^* \| \mu^*) \hookleftarrow (\{0,1\}^\ell)$ and where $\mathsf{view}(\mathcal{A}) = (H, \bar{\mathcal{H}}, \mathsf{sk}, \sigma, \mathsf{aux}(\mathsf{sk}, m), \mathsf{vk}^*, \sigma^*)$. Conditioned on $\mathcal{D}$ not querying $\mathcal{H}$ on $\mathcal{H}(\mathsf{vk}^*) \| w_2^* \| m$, the value μ^* is independent from $\mathsf{view}(\mathcal{A})$ and its min-entropy is α. Conditioned on $\mathcal{D}$ querying $\mathcal{H}$ on $\mathcal{H}(\mathsf{vk}^*) \| w_2^* \| m$, we apply Lemma 1, where the X_i are the outputs of the query of $\mathcal{D}$ to $\mathcal{H}$ and f runs the first five lines of Game_1, using X_i as the answer to $\mathcal{D}$'s i-th query to $\mathcal{H}$. It returns the index i such that the i-th query of $\mathcal{D}$ to $\mathcal{H}$ was on $\mathsf{vk}^* \| w_2^* \| m$. Lemma 1 gives the min-entropy on μ^* even with knowledge of all random coins of the procedure, which includes $\mathsf{view}(\mathcal{A})$. $\qquad\square$

Remark 3. While adapting this proof in the QROM is out of scope of this work, [13] already explains how to adapt the first game hop.

5 Silithium: Instantiation with **EC-Schnorr** and **ML-DSA**

We now propose our main instantiation of the H-FSwA$[\mathsf{ID}_1\|\mathsf{ID}_2, H]$ construction: the Silithium signature scheme. We use $\mathsf{ID}_1 = \mathsf{ID}_{\mathsf{Schnorr}}$ as defined in Fig. 11, in Appendix A and $\mathsf{ID}_2 = \mathsf{ID}_{\mathsf{ML\text{-}DSA}}$ as defined in Fig. 14, in Appendix B.

5.1 Specification

In our specification, we consider a cyclic subgroup $\mathbb{G}$ of an elliptic curve with generator point G of order n. We assume access to a function ECCLib.RandomPoint that outputs a pair (k, R), with an integer $0 < k < n$ and curve point R such that $k.G = R$ and $k \hookleftarrow U(\mathbb{Z}_n)$. We also assume access to an ML-DSA implementation supporting the "external μ" variant described in FIPS 204 [27]. Finally, following the specification of ML-DSA, $\mathcal{H}$ is instantiated as SHAKE256$(\cdot, 512)$ and H as SHAKE256$(\cdot, 2\lambda)$, and we also require an implementation of SHAKE256, where λ is the security parameter. The resulting scheme is described in Fig. 10.

These aforementioned ingredients are enough to implement Silithium: they allow to generate key pairs, and to update the hash of the verification key contained in the signing key. During signing, the Schnorr commitment R is embedded into the μ computation and then ML-DSA.Sign_mu is used as a black-box. The verification procedure is performed in a similar way.

Note that it is also possible to embed R in the ML-DSA context string during the signature, thus removing the need to compute μ externally. However, this cannot be applied to verification due to our modification of tr.

On Simultaneous Verification. Verifying the $\mathsf{ID}_{\mathsf{ML\text{-}DSA}}$ part of the signature implies first recovering the $\mathsf{ID}_{\mathsf{Schnorr}}$ commitment. As the hash verification is common to the two schemes, this implies verifying the $\mathsf{ID}_{\mathsf{Schnorr}}$ component. Moreover, to verify the $\mathsf{ID}_{\mathsf{Schnorr}}$ part, one must first recover the $\mathsf{ID}_{\mathsf{ML\text{-}DSA}}$ commitment. One could however ignore the norm bound check for $\mathsf{ID}_{\mathsf{ML\text{-}DSA}}$. As this implies rewriting an incomplete implementation of ML-DSA.Verify, we believe that a lazy developer would not choose to go down this path.

5.2 Theoretical Analysis

Section 4, when instantiated with $\mathsf{ID}_1 = \mathsf{ID}_{\mathsf{Schnorr}}$ and $\mathsf{ID}_2 = \mathsf{ID}_{\mathsf{ML\text{-}DSA}}$, gives the following results, that see Silithium as a hybrid between BUFF(FS$[\mathsf{ID}_{\mathsf{Schnorr}}, H]$) and ML-DSA.

Corollary 2 (EC-Schnorr+ML-DSA hybrid). *Let* $\Sigma_1 = $ BUFF(FS$[\mathsf{ID}_{\mathsf{Schnorr}}, H]$) *and* $\Sigma_2 = $ BUFF(FSwA$[\mathsf{ID}_{\mathsf{ML\text{-}DSA}}, H]$) $= $ ML-DSA. *The scheme* $\Sigma_{\mathsf{H}} = $ Silithium *defined in Fig. 10 is correct and:*

- H-EU-CMA^{H} *(resp.* sH-EU-CMA^{H}*) secure in the QROM as long as* ML-DSA *is* EU-CMA *(resp.* sEU-CMA*) secure in the QROM,*
- sH-EU-CMA^1 *secure in the ROM under the* DL *assumption in* $\mathbb{G}$,

```
KeyGen():                                      Sign((sk₁, sk₂), M): (external μ)
 1: (vk₁, sk₁) ← ECCLib.RandomPoint()           1: (r, R) ← ECCLib.RandomPoint()
 2: (vk₂, sk₂) ← ML-DSA.KeyGen()                 2: μ ← H(tr‖R‖M)
 3: (ρ, K, tr, s₁, s₂, t₀) ← sk₂                 3: (z, c̃, h) ← ML-DSA.Sign_mu(sk₂, μ)
 4: tr ← H(vk₁‖vk₂)                              4: x ← r + sk₁ · c̃ mod n
 5: sk₂ ← (ρ, K, tr, s₁, s₂, t₀)                 5: return (c̃, z, h, x)
 6: return ((vk₁, vk₂), (sk₁, sk₂))

Verify((vk₁, vk₂), (c̃, z, h, x), M):           Sign((sk₁, sk₂), M): (context)
 1: if x < 0 or x ≥ n then                       1: (r, R) ← ECCLib.RandomPoint()
 2:     return 0                                 2: (z, c̃, h) ← ML-DSA.Sign(sk₂, M, R)
 3: R ← x.G − c̃.vk₁                             3: x ← r + sk₁ · c̃ mod n
 4: μ ← H(H(vk₁‖vk₂)‖R‖M)                        4: return (c̃, z, h, x)
 5: b ← ML-DSA.Verify_mu(vk₂, μ, (z, c̃, h))
 6: return b
```

Fig. 10. Silithium specification. Key generation updates the hash of vk_2 in sk_2.

- H-EU-CMA^2 *(resp.* sH-EU-CMA^2*) secure in the ROM under both (resp. all three)* MLWE$_{n,q,k,\ell,U(S_\eta)}$ *and* MSIS$_{n,q,k,\ell+1,2\zeta}$ *(resp. and* MSIS$_{n,q,k,\ell,2\zeta'}$*) assumptions,*
- H-EU-CMA$^\mathsf{H}$ *secure in the ROM under the* DL *assumption in* $\mathbb{G}$ *or both the* MLWE$_{n,q,k,\ell,U(S_\eta)}$ *and* MSIS$_{n,q,k,\ell+1,2\zeta}$ *assumptions,*
- sH-EU-CMA$^\mathsf{H}$ *secure under both the same assumptions as its* H-EU-CMA$^\mathsf{H}$ *security and the* MSIS$_{n,q,k,\ell,2\zeta'}$ *assumption,*

where ζ and ζ' are defined in Lemma 7 and Lemma 6, respectively.

The above result seems artificial on the classical signature side. Indeed, while EC-Schnorr is standard [17], it does not use SHAKE256 as its hash function. We are interested in the case where Σ_1 is chosen as ECDSA [25], as it is likely to be the classical signature used in tandem with Silithium and ML-DSA.

Theorem 7 (ECDSA+ML-DSA hybrid). *Let $\Sigma_1 =$ ECDSA and $\Sigma_2 =$ ML-DSA. The signature scheme $\Sigma_\mathsf{H} =$ Silithium defined in Fig. 10 is correct and:*

- H-EU-CMA$^\mathsf{H}$ *(resp.* sH-EU-CMA$^\mathsf{H}$*) secure in the QROM as long as* ML-DSA *is* EU-CMA *(resp.* sEU-CMA*) secure in the QROM,*
- (s)H-EU-CMA^1 *secure in the ROM as long as* ECDSA *is* EU-CMA *secure,*
- H-EU-CMA^2 *(resp.* sH-EU-CMA^2*) secure in the ROM under both (resp. all three)* MLWE$_{n,q,k,\ell,U(S_\eta)}$ *and* MSIS$_{n,q,k,\ell+1,2\zeta}$ *(resp. and* MSIS$_{n,q,k,\ell,2\zeta'}$*) assumptions,*
- H-EU-CMA$^\mathsf{H}$ *secure in the ROM under the hardness of* ECDSA *key-recovery or both the* MLWE$_{n,q,k,\ell,U(S_\eta)}$ *and* MSIS$_{n,q,k,\ell+1,2\zeta}$ *assumptions,*
- sH-EU-CMA$^\mathsf{H}$ *secure under both the same assumptions as its* H-EU-CMA$^\mathsf{H}$ *security and the* MSIS$_{n,q,k,\ell,2\zeta'}$ *assumption,*

where ζ and ζ' are defined in Lemma 7 and Lemma 6, respectively.

Proof. The correctness follows from Theorem 1. The first point is a direct application of Theorem 2. The rest is an application of Corollary 1 and Remark 2. Note that breaking the "2-special-soundness for ID_1 with a Σ_1 signature oracle" implies recovering the signing key used by ECDSA.

5.3 Implementation Considerations

One of our claims is the relative simplicity of implementing Silithium, providing that the following requirements are met:

- availability of an elliptic curve library;
- availability of an ML-DSA implementation supporting the "external μ" feature described in FIPS 204 [27];
- familiarity with elliptic curve operations.

Note that familiarity with ML-DSA is not required, as the ML-DSA functions are used in a black-box approach. Thus, our scheme is intended to be easy to implement for software engineers with prior experience in implementing classical (elliptic curve) cryptography.

Implementation approach. To meet the above requirements, we implemented Silithium within (a fork of) OpenSSL's default provider. The OpenSSL library already includes both an ML-DSA implementation supporting "external μ" computation and built-in elliptic curve operations. Silithium was implemented directly inside OpenSSL codebase, as access to internal elliptic curve functions was required. While it could have been implemented as a third party provider, embedding it within the default provider significantly sped up development. We provide three Silithium instantiations, described in Table 3.

Table 3. Silithium instantiations.

Variant	ML-DSA	Curve	Signature Size
Silithium-44	ML-DSA-44	P-256	2420 + 32
Silithium-65	ML-DSA-65	P-384	3309 + 48
Silithium-87	ML-DSA-87	P-521	4627 + 66

Implementation Effort. The implementation was carried out by a developer familiar with OpenSSL internals and its elliptic curve API. The majority of the effort was divided between implementing elliptic curve operations and integrating the resulting code into OpenSSL. The Silithium implementation itself boils down to less than 500 lines of codes (excluding OpenSSL-related logic). The total workload to produce a functional proof-of-concept amounted to roughly one week. We emphasize that, although functionally correct, the provided code is not production-ready and should not be used as-is. The workload estimate is given only as an indication of the expected development cost of Silithium for an average cryptography software engineer.

Performances. When comparing a single execution of Silithium to the successive execution of ECDSA (or EC-S-DSA) and ML-DSA, it can be observed that Silithium performs one fewer call to the underlying hash function, which is SHA-256 in our instanciation. This optimization yields only a marginal performance gain for short messages, as the cost of SHA-256 (especially when accelerated via the sha-ni instruction set) is negligible compared to that of ML-DSA. However, the benefit becomes more noticeable when signing larger messages. Our experiments confirmed that Silithium is as fast as the hybrid concatenation scheme, although we do not report detailed benchmark results here, as precise hash benchmarking is out of scope of this work. Since our implementation is fully integrated within OpenSSL, one can easily measure performance under various conditions. Compared to the BoP-2 construction from [19], Silithium saves two hash computations, and is therefore theoretically faster—though the lack of published code does not allow for direct experimental comparisons. From a code-size perspective, Silithium employs a single hash function and is thus more compact than the hybrid concatenation scheme.

A Note on Masking. Although a masked implementation is beyond the scope of this work, we note that masking Silithium is neither harder nor easier than masking its components, namely ML-DSA and the relevant elliptic curve operations. In other words, if a developer has access to a masked implementation of ML-DSA and a masked elliptic curve library, then masking Silithium is straightforward. In particular, we emphasize that the computation of μ relies solely on public data.

A   Schnorr Identification Scheme with Tweaked Challenge

Let $\mathbb{G}$ be a cyclic group with generator g and prime order p. We describe a modification of Schnorr's identification scheme, where the challenge is a bit-string $c \in \{0,1\}^{\ell}$. It is then up to the prover and the verifier to interpret it as an integer in $[0, 2^{\ell} - 1]$ and reduce it mod p to get the "real" challenge.

$\mathsf{IGen}(1^{\lambda})$:	$\mathsf{P}_1(\mathsf{sk})$:	$\mathsf{V}(\mathsf{vk}, w, c, z)$:
1: $\mathsf{sk} \leftarrow U(\mathbb{Z}_p)$	1: $y \leftarrow U(\mathbb{Z}_p)$	1: $c' \leftarrow \sum_{i=0}^{\ell-1} c_i 2^i \bmod p$
2: $\mathsf{vk} \leftarrow g^{\mathsf{sk}}$	2: $w \leftarrow g^y$	2: **if** $w \neq g^z \mathsf{vk}^{-c'}$ **then**
3: **return** $(\mathsf{vk}, \mathsf{sk})$	3: **return** $(w, st = y)$	3: **return** 0
		4: **return** 1
$\mathsf{Rec}(\mathsf{vk}, z, c)$:	$\mathsf{P}_2(\mathsf{sk}, w, c, st)$:	
1: $c' \leftarrow \sum_{i=0}^{\ell-1} c_i 2^i \bmod p$	1: $c' \leftarrow \sum_{i=0}^{\ell-1} c_i 2^i \bmod p$	
2: **return** $g^z \mathsf{vk}^{-c'}$	2: $z = y + c' \mathsf{sk}$	
	3: **return** z	

Fig. 11. Schnorr identification scheme with ℓ bits challenge $\mathsf{ID}_{\mathsf{Schnorr}}$.

Lemma 4 (Adapted from [31]). *Let ℓ be an integer such that $2^\ell > p$. The scheme from Fig. 11 is complete, commitment-recoverable, HVZK, has unique response and for any adversary $\mathcal{A}$ against its 2-special-soundness, there exists an adversary $\mathcal{B}$ against the discrete logarithm in $\mathbb{G}$ such that:*

$$\mathsf{Adv}^{2-\mathsf{ss}}_{\mathsf{ID}_{\mathsf{Schnorr}}}(\mathcal{A}) \le \mathsf{Adv}^{\mathsf{DL}}_{\mathbb{G},g}(\mathcal{B}) + \frac{1}{p}.$$

Proof. The completeness, commitment-recoverability and HVZK proofs are identical to the original description of the Schnorr identification scheme. Concerning the 2-special-soundness property, we recall that given (w, c_1, c_2, z_1, z_2) such that $g^{z_1}\mathsf{vk}^{-c_1'} = w = g^{z_2}\mathsf{vk}^{-c_2'}$, the discrete log of vk is $(z_1 - z_2) \cdot (c_1' - c_2')^{-1} \bmod p$ as long as $(c_1' - c_2')$ is nonzero. For any $c_1 \in [0, 2^\ell - 1]$ and $c_2 \hookleftarrow U([0, 2^\ell - 1]$, the probability that $c_1 = c_2 \bmod p$ while $c_1 \ne c_2$ is such that:

$$\Pr_{c_1 \ne c_2}(c_1 = c_2 \bmod p) = \Pr(c_1 = c_2 \bmod p) - \Pr(c_1 = c_2)$$

$$\le \frac{\lfloor (2^\ell - 1)/p \rfloor + 1}{2^\ell} - \frac{1}{2^\ell} \le \frac{1}{p} \; ,$$

as at most $\lfloor (2^\ell - 1)/p \rfloor + 1$ values in $[0, 2^\ell - 1]$ are sent to k when reduced mod p.

Finally, given four elements (w, c, z, z') such that $g^z\mathsf{vk}^{-c} = w = g^{z'}\mathsf{vk}^{-c}$, it implies $g^z = g^{z'}$ thus $z = z' \bmod p$, showing the scheme has unique response. $\square$

B   ML-DSA Identification Scheme with Tweaked Challenge

We recall supporting algorithms for ML-DSA in Fig. 12. These algorithms are extended on vectors by applying them coefficient-wise.

Power2Round$_q(r, d)$:
1: $r = r \bmod {}^+q$
2: $r_0 = r \bmod {}^\pm 2^d$
3: **return** $((r - r_0)/2^d, 2)$

MakeHint$_q(z, r, \alpha)$:
1: $r_1 \leftarrow \mathsf{HighBits}_q(r, \alpha)$
2: $v_1 \leftarrow \mathsf{HighBits}(r + z, \alpha)$
3: **return** $|r_1 - v_1|$

Decompose$_q(r, \alpha)$:
1: $r \leftarrow r \bmod {}^+q$
2: $r_0 \leftarrow r \bmod {}^\pm \alpha$
3: **if** $r - r_0 = q - 1$ **then**
4: $\quad (r_1, r_0) \leftarrow (0, r_0 - 1)$
5: **else**
6: $\quad r_1 \leftarrow (r - r_0)/\alpha$
7: **return** (r_1, r_0)

UseHint$_q(h, r, \alpha)$:
1: $m \leftarrow (q - 1)/\alpha$
2: $(r_1, r_0) \leftarrow \mathsf{Decompose}_q(r, \alpha)$
3: **return** $r_1 + h \cdot \mathsf{sgn}(r_0) \bmod {}^+m$

HighBits$_q(r, \alpha)$:
1: $(r_1, r_0) \leftarrow \mathsf{Decompose}_q(r, \alpha)$
2: **return** r_1

LowBits$_q(r, \alpha)$:
1: $(r_1, r_0) \leftarrow \mathsf{Decompose}_q(r, \alpha)$
2: **return** r_0

Fig. 12. Supporting Algorithms for ML-DSA.

The inside-out Fisher-Yates shuffling algorithm is used in ML-DSA to sample the challenge polynomial. We recall it in Fig. 13.

$$\begin{array}{|ll|}
\hline
\textbf{SampleInBall}(\tau, (j_i, s_i)_{i=n-\tau}^{n-1}): & \text{Inputs: } \tau \le n,\ s_i \in \{0,1\}, j_i \le i, \forall i \le n-1 \\
\hline
\end{array}$$

SampleInBall$(\tau, (j_i, s_i)_{i=n-\tau}^{n-1})$:

Inputs: $\tau \le n$, $s_i \in \{0,1\}$, $j_i \le i, \forall i \le n-1$

Outputs: ternary polynomial c with τ nonzero elements.

1: $\mathbf{c} \leftarrow 0^n$
2: **for** $i = n - \tau$ to $n - 1$ **do**
3:     $c_i \leftarrow c_{j_i}$
4:     $c_{j_i} \leftarrow (-1)^{s_i}$
5: **return** $\sum_{i=0}^{n-1} c_i x^i$

Fig. 13. SampleInBall description.

Lemma 5 (Adapted from [22]). *Let $0 < \tau \le n$ be two integers. For all integers $i \in [n - \tau, n - 1]$, let $s_i \hookleftarrow U(\{0,1\})$ and $j_i \hookleftarrow U(\{0,1,\ldots,i\})$, then the output of* SampleInBall$(\tau, (j_i, s_i)_{i=n-\tau}^{n-1}$ *follows* $U(\{x \in \mathcal{R} | \|x\|_\infty = 1 \wedge \|x\|_1 = \tau\})$.

We propose the following tweak to the ML-DSA identification scheme, as described in [20, Section 4]. Instead of using a challenge c that is a ternary polynomial with fixed Hamming weight, we use a bitstring of length ℓ, the one that is used to derive the inputs of SampleInBall in the ML-DSA signature scheme. Turning the bitstring into a polynomial is left to both P_2 and V.

IGen(1^λ):

1: $\mathbf{A} \hookleftarrow U(\mathcal{R}_q^{k \times \ell})$
2: $\mathbf{s}_1, \mathbf{s}_2 \hookleftarrow S_\eta^k \times S_\eta^\ell$
3: $\mathbf{t} = \mathbf{A}\mathbf{s}_1 + \mathbf{s}_2 \bmod q$
4: $(\mathbf{t}_1, \mathbf{t}_0) = \mathsf{Power2Round}_q(\mathbf{t}, d)$
5: **return** $\mathsf{vk} = (\mathbf{A}, \mathbf{t}_1), \mathsf{sk} = (\mathbf{A}, \mathbf{s}_1, \mathbf{s}_2)$

V$(\mathsf{vk}, \mathbf{w}_1, c, \mathbf{z}, \mathbf{h})$:

1: $c' \leftarrow \mathsf{SampleInBall}(\tau, H(c))$
2: **if** $\|\mathbf{z}\|_\infty \ge \gamma_1 - \beta$ **then**
3:     **return** 0
4: **if** $\mathbf{w}_1 \ne \mathsf{UseHint}(\mathbf{h}, \mathbf{A}\mathbf{z} - c'\mathbf{t}_1 \cdot 2^d, 2\gamma_2)$ **then**
5:     **return** 0
6: **return** 1

P$_1(\mathsf{sk})$:

1: $\mathbf{y} \hookleftarrow \tilde{S}_{\gamma_1}^\ell$
2: $\mathbf{w} = \mathbf{A}\mathbf{y} \bmod q$
3: $\mathbf{w}_1 = \mathsf{HighBits}(\mathbf{w}, 2\gamma_2)$
4: **return** $w = \mathbf{w}_1, st = \mathbf{y}$

P$_2(\mathsf{vk}, c, \mathbf{y})$:

1: $c' \leftarrow \mathsf{SampleInBall}(\tau, H(c))$
2: $\mathbf{z} \leftarrow \mathbf{y} + c\mathbf{s}_1$
3: $\mathbf{r}_0 \leftarrow \mathsf{LowBits}(\mathbf{w} - c\mathbf{s}_2, 2\gamma_2)$
4: **if** $\|\mathbf{z}\|_\infty \ge \gamma_1 - \beta$ or $\|\mathbf{r}_0\|_\infty \ge \gamma_2 - \beta$ **then**
5:     **return** $\bot$
6: $\mathbf{h} \leftarrow \mathsf{MakeHint}(-c\mathbf{t}_0, \mathbf{w} - c\mathbf{s}_2 + c\mathbf{t}_0, 2\gamma_2)$
7: **if** $\|c\mathbf{t}_0\|_\infty \ge \gamma_2$ or $\|\mathbf{h}\|_1 \ge \omega$ **then**
8:     **return** $\bot$
9: **return** $(\mathbf{z}, \mathbf{h})$

Fig. 14. ML-DSA identification scheme with $\{0,1\}^\ell$ challenge space $\mathsf{ID}_{\mathsf{ML\text{-}DSA}}$.

This change does not modify the following properties of the scheme.

Lemma 6 (Adapted from [20, Section 4.3]). *The scheme from Fig. 14 is complete, HVZK and commitment recoverable. Let $\zeta' = \max(2(\gamma_1 - \beta), 4\gamma_2 + 2)$. For any adversary playing the key-indistinguishability game, there exists an adversary against the* $\mathsf{MLWE}_{n,q,k,\ell,U(S_\eta)}$ *problem with the same advantage, with*

respect to the LossyIGen *algorithm that samples* $(\mathbf{A}, \mathbf{t}) \hookleftarrow U(\mathcal{R}_q^{k \times \ell} \times \mathcal{R}_q^k)$ *and outputs* $\mathsf{vk} = (\mathbf{A}, \mathbf{t}_1)$ *with* $(\mathbf{t}_1, \mathbf{t}_0) = \mathsf{Power2Round}(\mathbf{t}, d)$.
For any adversary playing the CUR *game, there exists an adversary against the* $\mathsf{MSIS}_{n,q,k,\ell+1,\zeta'}$ *problem with the same advantage.*

However, the change in the challenge space means that we have to adapt the proof of the folklore lossy-2-special-soundness property.

Lemma 7 (Lossy-2-Special-Soundness). *Let* $\mathsf{ID}_{\mathsf{ML\text{-}DSA}}$ *be the identification scheme from Fig. 14. Let* $H : \{0,1\}^\ell \to \mathcal{X}$ *be a hash function modeled as a random oracle and where* $\mathcal{X}$ *is the input set of* $\mathsf{SampleInBall}(\tau, \cdot)$. *Let* $\mathcal{A}$ *be an adversary against the lossy-2-special-soundness of the scheme from Fig. 14. Let* $\zeta = \max(\gamma_1 - \beta, 2\gamma_2 + 1 + \tau 2^{d-1})$. *There exists an adversary* $\mathcal{B}$ *against the* $\mathsf{MSIS}_{n,q,k,\ell+1,2\zeta}$ *problem such that:*

$$\mathsf{Adv}_{\mathsf{ID}_{\mathsf{ML\text{-}DSA}}}^{\mathsf{lossy\text{-}2\text{-}ss}}(\mathcal{A}) \leq \mathsf{Adv}_{n,q,k,\ell+1,2\zeta}^{\mathsf{MSIS}}(\mathcal{B}) + \frac{1}{2^\tau \binom{n}{\tau}} \ .$$

Proof. Let $(\mathbf{w}_1, c_1, c_2, \mathbf{z}_1, \mathbf{z}_2, \mathbf{h}_1, \mathbf{h}_2)$ with $c_1 \neq c_2$ such that:

- $\max(\|\mathbf{z}_1\|_\infty, \|\mathbf{z}_2\|_\infty) < \gamma_1 - \beta$,
- $\mathsf{UseHint}_q(\mathbf{h}_1, \mathbf{A}\mathbf{z}_1 - c_1'\mathbf{t}_1 \cdot 2^d, 2\gamma_2) = \mathbf{w}_1 = \mathsf{UseHint}_q(\mathbf{h}_2, \mathbf{A}\mathbf{z}_2 - c_2'\mathbf{t}_1 \cdot 2^d, 2\gamma_2)$,

where $c_b' = \mathsf{SampleInBall}(\tau, H(c_b)), b \in \{1, 2\}$. For $b \in \{1, 2\}$, there exists $\mathbf{u}_b \in \mathcal{R}_q^k$ such that $2\gamma_2 \cdot \mathsf{UseHint}_q(\mathbf{h}_2, \mathbf{A}\mathbf{z}_b - c_b'\mathbf{t}_1 \cdot 2^d, 2\gamma_2) = \mathbf{A}\mathbf{z}_b - c_b'\mathbf{t}_1 2^d + \mathbf{u}_b$ and $\|\mathbf{u}_b\|_\infty \leq 2\gamma_2 + 1$. We can thus rewrite $\mathbf{A}\mathbf{z}_1 - c_1'\mathbf{t} + \mathbf{u}_1 + c_1'\mathbf{t}_0 = \mathbf{A}\mathbf{z}_2 - c_2'\mathbf{t} + \mathbf{u}_2 + c_2'\mathbf{t}_0$. Letting $\mathbf{u}_b' = \mathbf{u}_b + c_b'\mathbf{t}_0$, we get:

$$(\mathbf{A}|\mathbf{t}|\mathbf{I}) \cdot \begin{pmatrix} \mathbf{z}_1 - \mathbf{z}_2 \\ c_2' - c_1' \\ \mathbf{u}_1' - \mathbf{u}_2' \end{pmatrix} = 0 \bmod q \quad \text{and} \quad \|\mathbf{u}_b'\|_\infty \leq \tau 2^{d-1} + 2\gamma_2 + 1 \ .$$

Thus, we have a candidate solution for a $\mathsf{MSIS}_{n,q,k,\ell+1,2\zeta}$ instance. This is indeed a solution if it is nonzero, which is the case if $c_1' \neq c_2'$. As H is a random oracle, we use Lemma 5 to conclude that for fixed $c_1 \in \{0,1\}^\ell$ and $c_2 \hookleftarrow U(\{0,1\}^\ell)$, this happens with probability at least $1 - 1/2^\tau \binom{n}{\tau}$. $\qquad\square$

References

1. ANSSI. ANSSI views on the post-quantum cryptography transition (2023). follow up
2. Bader, C., Hofheinz, D., Jager, T., Kiltz, E., Li, Y.: Tightly-secure authenticated key exchange. In: Dodis, Y., Nielsen, J.B. (eds.) TCC 2015, Part I, volume 9014 of LNCS, pp. 629–658. Springer, Berlin, Heidelberg (2015)
3. Bellare, M., Neven, G.: Multi-signatures in the plain public-key model and a general forking lemma. In: Juels, A., Wright, R.N., De Capitani di Vimercati, S. (ed.) ACM CCS 2006, pp. 390–399. ACM Press (2006)

4. Bergsma, F., Dowling, B., Kohlar, F., Schwenk, J., Stebila, D.: Multi-ciphersuite security of the Secure Shell (SSH) protocol. In: Ahn, G.-J., Yung, M., Li, N. (eds.) ACM CCS 2014, pp. 369–381. ACM Press (2014)

5. Bindel, N., Hale, B.: A note on hybrid signature schemes. Cryptology ePrint Archive, Report 2023/423 (2023)

6. Bindel, N., Hale, B., Connolly, D., Driscoll, F.: Hybrid signature spectrums. Internet-Draft draft-ietf-pquip-hybrid-signature-spectrums-07, IETF (2025)

7. Bindel, N., Herath, U., McKague, M., Stebila, D.: Transitioning to a quantum-resistant public key infrastructure. In: Lange, T., Takagi, T. (eds.) Post-Quantum Cryptography - 8th International Workshop. PQCrypto 2017, pp. 384–405. Springer, Cham (2017)

8. Brendel, J., Cremers, C., Jackson, D., Zhao, M.: The provable security of Ed25519: Theory and practice. In: 2021 IEEE Symposium on Security and Privacy, pp. 1659–1676. IEEE Computer Society Press (2021)

9. BSI. Cryptographic mechanisms: Recommendations and key lengths - BSI tr-02102-1 (2024)

10. Cheon, J.H., et al.: HAETAE: shorter lattice-based fiat-shamir signatures. IACR TCHES **2024**(3), 25–75 (2024)

11. Cremers, C., Düzlü, S., Fiedler, R., Fischlin, M., Janson, C.: BUFFing signature schemes beyond unforgeability and the case of post-quantum signatures. In: 2021 IEEE Symposium on Security and Privacy, pp. 1696–1714. IEEE Computer Society Press (2021)

12. Diffie, W., Hellman, M.E.: New directions in cryptography. IEEE Trans. Inf. Theory **22**(6), 644–654 (1976)

13. Don, J., Fehr, S., Huang, Y.-H., Liao, J.-J., Struck, P.: Hide-and-seek and the non-resignability of the BUFF transform. In: Boyle, E., Mahmoody, M. (eds.) TCC 2024. Part III, volume 15366 of LNCS, pp. 347–370. Springer, Cham (2024)

14. Don, J., Fehr, S., Huang, Y.-H., Struck, P.: On the (in)security of the BUFF transform. In: Reyzin, L., Stebila, D. (eds.) CRYPTO 2024. Part I, volume 14920 of LNCS, pp. 246–275. Springer, Cham (2024)

15. Fouque, P.-A., et al.: Falcon: Fast-Fourier Lattice-based Compact Signatures over NTRU. Submission to the NIST Post-Quantum Cryptography Standardization Project (2020)

16. Ghinea, D., et al.: Hybrid post-quantum signatures in hardware security keys. In: Applied Cryptography and Network Security Workshops: ACNS 2023 Satellite Workshops, ADSC, AIBlock, AIHWS, AIoTS, CIMSS, Cloud S&P, SCI, SecMT, SiMLA, Kyoto, Japan, June 19–22, 2023, Proceedings, pp. 480–499. Springer-Verlag (2023)

17. International Organization for Standardization. It security techniques — digital signatures with appendix — part 3: Discrete logarithm based mechanisms (2018). Standard number 76382 on ISO website

18. Jager, T., Kiltz, E., Riepel, D., Schäge, S.: Tightly-secure authenticated key exchange, revisited. In: Canteaut, A., Standaert, F.-X. (eds.) EUROCRYPT 2021. Part I, volume 12696 of LNCS, pp. 117–146. Springer, Cham (2021)

19. Janneck, J.: Bird of prey: Practical signature combiners preserving strong unforgeability. Cryptology ePrint Archive, Paper 2025/1844 (2025)

20. Kiltz, E., Lyubashevsky, V., Schaffner, C.: A concrete treatment of Fiat-Shamir signatures in the quantum random-oracle model. In: Nielsen, J.B., Rijmen, V. (eds.) EUROCRYPT 2018, Part III, volume 10822 of LNCS, pp. 552–586. Springer, Cham (2018)

21. Klitzke, E.: Bitcoin transaction malleability (2017)
22. Knuth, D.: The Art of Computer Programming. Addison-Wesley (1997)
23. Langlois, A., Stehlé, D.: Worst-case to average-case reductions for module lattices. DCC **75**(3), 565–599 (2015)
24. National Institute of Standards and Technology. Post-Quantum Cryptography: Additional Digital Signature Schemes — Round 2. https://csrc.nist.gov/projects/pqc-dig-sig/round-2-additional-signatures (2022)
25. National Institute of Standards and Technology. Digital signature standard (DSS): Federal information processing standards publication 186-5. Technical Report FIPS 186-5, U.S. Department of Commerce, National Institute of Standards and Technology, Gaithersburg, MD, USA (2023)
26. NLNCSA. Bereid je voor op de dreiging van quantumcomputers (2021)
27. National Institute of Standards and Technology. Module-lattice-based digital signature standard. Technical Report Federal Information Processing Standards Publications (FIPS) 204, 2024, U.S. Department of Commerce, Washington, D.C. (2024)
28. Ounsworth, M., Gray, J., Pala, M., Klaußner, J., Fluhrer, S.: Composite ML-DSA for use in X.509 Public Key Infrastructure. Internet-Draft draft-ietf-lamps-pq-composite-sigs-12, IETF (2025)
29. Rivest, R.L., Shamir, A., Adleman, L.: A method for obtaining digital signatures and public-key cryptosystems. Commun. ACM **21**(2), 120–126 (1978)
30. Rogaway, P.: Formalizing human ignorance. In: Nguyen, P.Q. (ed.) Progress in Cryptology - VIETCRYPT 06. LNCS, vol. 4341, pp. 211–228. Springer, Berlin, Heidelberg (2006)
31. Schnorr, C.-P.: Efficient identification and signatures for smart cards. In: Brassard, G. (ed.) CRYPTO'89. LNCS, vol. 435, pp. 239–252. Springer, New York (1990)

PETCHA: Post-quantum Efficient Transciphering with ChaCha

Antonio Guimarães[1], Gabriela M. Jacob[2], and Hilder V. L. Pereira[2(✉)]

[1] IMDEA Software Institute, Madrid, Spain
antonio.guimaraes@imdea.org
[2] University of Campinas, Campinas, Brazil
g186087@dac.unicamp.br, hilder@unicamp.br

Abstract. Fully Homomorphic Encryption (FHE) is a powerful primitive which allows a computationally weak client to outsource computation to a powerful server while maintaining privacy. However, FHE typically suffers from high ciphertext expansion, meaning that the amount of data the client has to send to the server increases by many orders of magnitude after it is encrypted. To solve this problem, the approach known as transciphering consists in combining symmetric encryption with FHE. The most common choice of cipher in this context is the AES, which has been used as a benchmark for transciphering. However, although FHE is typically post-quantum secure, existing transciphering protocols only use AES-128, failing thus to offer security against quantum adversaries. In this work, we construct transciphering protocols based on standard ciphers and offering post-quantum security. For this, we propose algorithms to efficiently evaluate the ChaCha cipher with FHE. We notice that ChaCha is a well-established cipher which even has a standardized version in TLS offering 256 bits of security against classic attackers, thus, 128 bits of security in the quantum world. We show that our solutions have both better latency and throughput than the state-of-the-art transciphering protocol based on AES. Namely, compared with an extended (128-bit PQ secure) version of Hippogryph (Belaïd et al., IACR CiC 2025), in single-core experiments, our running times are up to 11.7 times faster while our throughput is more than 50 times higher.

1 Introduction

Fully homomorphic encryption (FHE) [35] is a very powerful and general cryptographic primitive that simultaneously offers data secrecy and the possibility of computing on encrypted data. Thus, it is the standard tool to obtain *secure outsourced computation*, where a computationally strong server receives encrypted data from a client, performs computation, and sends back to the client the encrypted result. In this scenario, the server does not know the client's input data or the output, thus, the privacy is preserved.

Although having many applications, like electronic voting [15], federated learning [64], and privacy-preserving machine learning as a service [22,28,65],

M. Bardet and R. Niederhagen (Eds.): PQCrypto 2026, LNCS 16492, pp. 178–203, 2026.
https://doi.org/10.1007/978-3-032-22698-3_6

FHE still faces many practical challenges. Those include, for example, the difficulty in using existing FHE libraries to write applications; the computational overhead that FHE brings, increasing by many orders of magnitude the running times; the memory usage in the server side; and the communication cost, especially the amount of data sent from the client to the server.

Trying to solve one of those limitations, *transciphering* (or hybrid homomorphic encryption) has been proposed [54]. The main idea is to allow the client to encrypt its data with a regular symmetric cipher, which does not increase the amount of data sent through the network, then, the server has to use FHE to execute the decryption circuit of the symmetric cipher, obtaining then FHE ciphertexts, which can then be processed normally. This idea represents a communication-time tradeoff that is usually very worthwhile. For instance, imagine a scenario where a client has a data set m of 1 GB. Then, to allow the server to compute some function f on m using FHE, the client would encrypt m under FHE, obtaining a set of ciphertexts c. However, because FHE's ciphertext expansion can at the order of 10^3 for some schemes [25], the size of the value c sent to the server would be at least 1 TB. This represents a huge cost and would even be very slow considering common network speeds. On the other hand, if m were encrypted with, say, AES, then the c would still have 1 GB, thus, the amount of data the client would send to the server would not increase. The cost we have to pay with this solution is the transformation of the AES-encrypted data into FHE-encrypted data, in other words, the homomorphic evaluation of the AES decryption function.

In more detail, transciphering is done in two phases. The first one is the setup, which is executed one single time. In this phase, the client sends to the server both the key of the homomorphic encryption scheme pk and the key k of the traditional cipher, but encrypted under FHE. After the setup, the client can send any data encrypted under k. Then, the server evaluates the decryption circuit of the block cipher using FHE, that is, it homomorphically decrypts the data, obtaining it reencrypted under pk, the key of the FHE scheme. After that, the server can evaluate any function on the data and send the result to the client. This step can be repeated as much as needed. We illustrate this process in Fig. 1.

To further optimize this trade-off between communication and computation, it is important to minimize the time spent by the server on the homomorphic decryption. Aiming on this, several works [3, 19, 29, 30, 43] have proposed ciphers whose decryption circuit can be evaluated homomorphically using little memory and time. We call them FHE-friendly ciphers. The main downside to these ciphers is the lack of extensive cryptanalysis, meaning that we are less sure about the existence of weaknesses in their designs. In fact, there are attacks showing that some of those ciphers are indeed insecure [46, 48, 49]. Moreover, none of them has been standardized, therefore, it may not even be clear to the clients how to implement them to attain desired security levels and guarantee interoperability with other applications.

A different approach to solve this problem is trying to minimize the homomorphic evaluation time of standardized ciphers, such as AES, which were

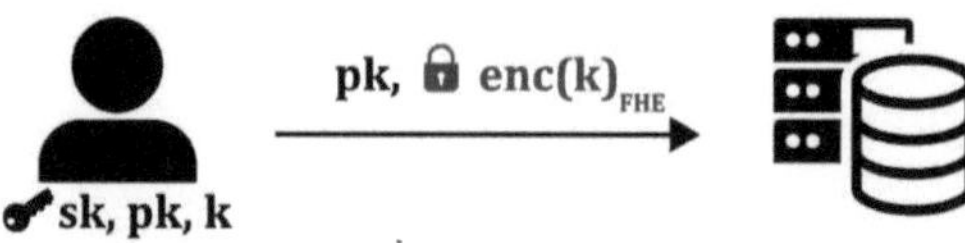

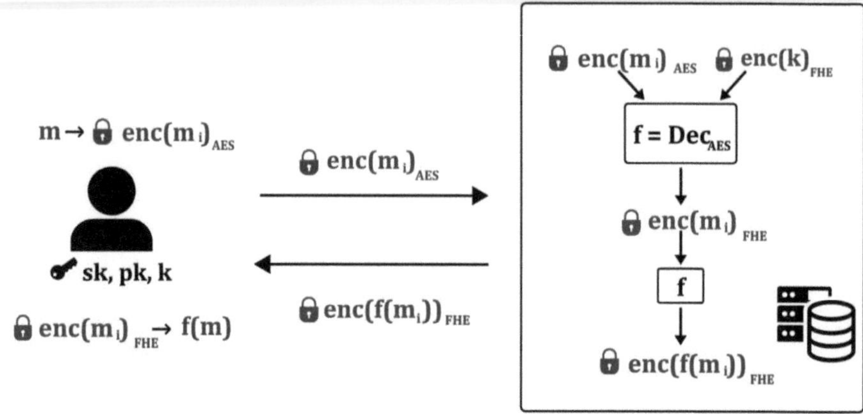

Fig. 1. Example of a typical transciphering protocol using AES as the block cipher. During the setup (top) the client only sends the FHE public key and the AES key encrypted under FHE. During the online phase (bottom), AES-encrypted data is homomorphically decrypted in the server.

not created to be FHE-friendly, but are well-established, well-studied and offer stronger security guarantees. For a long time, AES has been considered the reference benchmark when it comes to transciphering based on standard ciphers, with many studies improving its execution times over the years [9,36,62]. Only recently other standard ciphers, such as the stream cipher Trivium [7], have started to gain attention and to be used in transciphering protocols.

Although the security of standard ciphers is better understood, current works on transciphering have neglected the threat imposed by quantum computers. Namely, works usually only try to achieve classic security and fail to achieve acceptable post-quantum (PQ) security levels. For instance, [9,36,62] only implement transciphering using AES-128, which means 64 bits of PQ security due to Grover's algorithm. Even worse, Trivium [7] only offers 80 bits of classic security, thus, 40 bits of PQ security. For the best of our knowledge, no previous work has implemented transciphering protocols based on standard ciphers targeting 128 bits of PQ security. This is possibly due to the fact that standard ciphers are already somehow slow to evaluate homomorphically even at 128 bits of classic security. Then, since achieving 256 bits of security usually requires increasing the number of rounds, the existing solutions would be even slower. Additionally, since transciphering also involves FHE, both the standard cipher and the FHE scheme would have to be instantiated at 128-bit PQ security. As FHE is typically based on lattice problems, one can make it post-quantum secure by simply choosing slightly larger parameters, but this also implies another slowdown.

In other words, to be considered quantum-safe, these protocols should be adapted to AES-256, which will increase execution times. This transition offers an opportunity to reevaluate the efficiency of AES on transciphering protocols and, especially, to study and analyze the behavior of other symmetric ciphers, which offer the same level of security, when applied to transciphering protocols. This brings us to ChaCha, a standard cipher [56] designed by Bernstein [10] that is even used in the TLS protocol [59]. ChaCha has a simple design, using only ordinary 32-bit integer operations, like addition, bitwise exclusive or, and bit shifts, instead of finite field operations, as AES. More importantly, it was already designed to offer 256 bits of (classic) security, therefore, it naturally achieves 128 bits of PQ security. Finally, it has a wider state when compared to AES, namely, 512 bits instead of 128, which helps us to obtain a transciphering protocol with higher throughput, as one homomorphic execution of ChaCha produces 512 encrypted bits, 4 times more than AES. Thus, this works focus on constructing post-quantum secure transciphering using ChaCha.

Our Contributions

We propose different algorithms to evaluate ChaCha with FHE and construct the first transciphering protocol based on standard ciphers and secure against quantum computers, offering 128 bits of post-quantum (PQ) security. To obtain efficient implementations of ChaCha, we propose new ways to evaluate the 32-bit adder and XOR operations, which allow us to instantiate FHE schemes with message spaces smaller than what natural homomorphic versions of ChaCha would require. We then instantiate the TFHE scheme with 128 bits of security against quantum adversaries and execute ChaCha homomorphically.

We also provide a public proof-of-concept implementation[1] using the MOSFHET library [41] and show that our algorithms are very competitive in practice. Comparing them with transciphering with AES, which is the state-of-art in transciphering protocols based in standard ciphers, our running times for ChaCha20 on a single core are up to 11.7 times faster and our throughput, that is, the number of encrypted bits produced per second, is more than 50 times higher. We also provide a multi-threaded implementation, which homomorphically evaluates ChaCha8, ChaCha12, and ChaCha20 on 4 threads in 13.4, 17.5, and 25.8 s, respectively. This is a significant improvement even over the fastest homomorphic evaluation of the AES-128 [9], which takes 42.3 s using 32 threads on the same machine.

---

[1] GitLab repository with our C code: https://gitlab.ic.unicamp.br/hilder/transciphering-with-chacha.

2   Preliminaries

2.1   Vectors, Matrices, Distributions

Notation: We use lower-case bold letters for vectors and upper-case bold letters for matrices. The inner product of two vectors $\mathbf{a}$ and $\mathbf{b}$ is denoted by $\mathbf{a} \cdot \mathbf{b}$. For any vector $\mathbf{u}$, $\|\mathbf{u}\|$ denotes the infinity norm. In some cases, we may also use the Euclidean norm, which we denote by $\|\mathbf{u}\|_2$. For a vector $\mathbf{x}$, $\mathbf{x}[i]$ or x_i denotes the i-th entry of $\mathbf{x}$. We use the Euclidean norm as a default norm for a vector $\mathbf{x}$. The power-of-two cyclotomic ring is represented by $\mathcal{R} := \mathbb{Z}[X]/\langle X^N + 1 \rangle$. All its elements can be seen as polynomials of degree up to $N - 1$. Then, for any $g \in \mathcal{R}$, the norm of g is defined as the norm of the vector consisting of the coefficients of g. For $Q \in \mathbb{N}^*$, $\mathcal{R}_Q$ denotes $\mathbb{Z}_Q[X]/\langle X^N + 1 \rangle$.

Subgaussian Distribution. A random variable X over $\mathbb{R}$ is σ-subgaussian if for all $t \in \mathbb{R}$, it holds that $\mathbb{E}[\exp(t \cdot V)] \leq \frac{1}{2}\exp(\sigma^2 \cdot t^2)$. This implies that the variance of V, denoted by $\mathsf{Var}(X)$ is bounded by σ^2, i.e. $\mathsf{Var}(V) \leq \sigma^2$. Informally, the tails of V are dominated by a Gaussian function with standard deviation σ. A vector (or a polynomial) is subgaussian with parameter σ with all its entries (respec. coefficients) are subgaussians with parameter less than or equal to σ. Given a α-subgaussian X and an independent β-subgaussian Y, and $a, b \in \mathbb{Z}$, the random variable $a \cdot X + b \cdot Y$ is $\sqrt{a^2 \cdot \alpha^2 + b^2 \cdot \beta^2}$-subgaussian (this is known as Pythagorean additivity). If X is α-subgaussian, then for any positivie $t \in \mathbb{R}$, we can bound $|X|$ as $\Pr[|X| \geq t] \leq 2 \cdot e^{-t^2/(2\sigma^2)}$.

2.2   Fully Homomorphic Encryption

Since our construction can be instantiated with basically any of the so-called *3rd-generation* FHE schemes, such as FHEW [32], TFHE [24], FHE over the integers [58], and FINAL [14], as long as they are implemented supporting functional bootstrappings [16]. In the following, we present an abstract definition of this type of scheme, adapted from [52].

Consider three types of ciphertexts:

- *Integer ciphertext*: for a ciphertext modulus q, a secret key $\mathbf{z}$, and a plaintext modulus p, $\mathsf{IntCtxt}_{\mathbf{z}}^{q/p}(m, E)$ is the set of integer ciphertexts encrypting $m \in \mathbb{Z}_p$, under key $\mathbf{s}$, and with E-subgaussian noise.
- *Ring ciphertext*: for $Q, N \in \mathbb{N}$, where N is a power of two, a ring ciphertext is a pair or a single element of $\mathcal{R}_Q := \mathbb{Z}_Q[X]/\langle X^N + 1 \rangle$. We denote by $\mathsf{RingCtxt}_s^{Q/p}(m, E)$ the set of ring ciphertexts encrypting $m \in \mathcal{R}_p$, under key s, and with E-subgaussian noise.
- *Gadget ciphertext*: for integers Q, N, ℓ, we define $\mathsf{GadgetCtxt}_s^{Q,\ell}(m, E)$ as the set of gadget ciphertexts encrypting $m \in \mathcal{R}$, under key $s \in \mathcal{R}$, and with E-subgaussian noise. An element of $\mathsf{GadgetCtxt}_s^{Q,\ell}(m, E)$ is typically a matrix with ℓ rows or a vector of dimension ℓ where each entry is an element of $\mathcal{R}_Q$.

We may omit the noise (subgaussian) parameter if it is clear from the context. This abstract scheme can then be defined by the following algorithms:

- FHE.ParamGen($1^\lambda, p$): generate parameters achieving λ bits of security and allowing us to work with plaintext space $\mathbb{Z}_p$. The parameters also include the ring $\mathcal{R}$ an integer B_g, called the decomposition base, and $\ell := \lceil \log Q \rceil$, which defines the dimension of the gadget ciphertexts. The parameters are denoted by params.
- FHE.KeyGen(params): generate the secret key $\mathsf{sk} := (\mathbf{z}, s)$, a key-switching key ksk from $\mathbf{s}$ to $\mathbf{z}$, where $\mathbf{s}$ is the vector of coefficients of s, and the bootstrapping key bk.
- FHE.EncInt($\mathbf{z}, m$): using params, output $c \in \mathsf{IntCtxt}_{\mathbf{z}}^{q/p}(m, E_{in})$ with small noise, typically $E_{in} = O(q/p)$.
- FHE.DecInt($\mathbf{z}, \mathbf{c}$): output the message $m \in \mathbb{Z}_p$ encrypted by $\mathbf{c}$ under the secret key $\mathbf{z}$.
- FHE.EncRing(s, m): using params, output $\mathbf{c} \in \mathsf{RingCtxt}_s^{Q/p}(m, E_{in})$ for some $E_{in} = O(q/p)$.
- FHE.EncGadget(s, m): using params, output $\mathbf{C} \in \mathsf{GadgetCtxt}_s^{Q,\ell}(m, E_{in})$ for some $E_{in} = O(q/p)$.

We define a trivial-noiseless ciphertext as an FHE ciphertext (of any of the 3 types defined above) where the secret key and the noise are set to 0. Moreover, we can perform the following operations over ciphertexts.

- FHE.Add: homomorphically add two ciphertexts of the same type, e.g., maps $\mathsf{RingCtxt}_s^{Q/p}(m_0, E_0)$ $\times$ $\mathsf{RingCtxt}_s^{Q/p}(m_1, E_1)$ to $\mathsf{RingCtxt}_s^{Q/p}\left(m_0 + m_1, \sqrt{E_0^2 + E_1^2}\right)$.
- FHE.AddPtxt: given a plaintext $m_1 \in \mathbb{Z}_p$ and a ciphertext of any type encrypting some message $m_0 \in \mathbb{Z}_p$, this operation outputs a ciphertext of the same type encrypting $m_0 + m_1 \bmod p$. The noise is unchanged, i.e., both input and output have the same noise.
- FHE.MultPtxt: given a message $m_0 \in \mathcal{R}_p$ and a ciphertext $\mathbf{c}_1 \in \mathsf{RingCtxt}_s^{Q/p}(m_1, E_1)$, outputs $\mathbf{c} \in \mathsf{RingCtxt}_s^{Q/p}(m_0 \cdot m_1, E)$. If instead of a ring ciphertext, we have $\mathbf{C}_1 \in \mathsf{GadgetCtxt}_s^{Q,\ell}(m_1, E_1)$, it outputs $\mathbf{C} \in \mathsf{GadgetCtxt}_s^{Q,\ell}(m_0 \cdot m_1, E)$. In both cases, $E = \|m_0\|_2 \cdot E_1$.
- FHE.ExtProd: given ciphertexts $\mathbf{c}_0 \in \mathsf{RingCtxt}_s^{Q/p}(m_0, E_0)$ and $\mathbf{C}_1 \in \mathsf{GadgetCtxt}_s^{Q,\ell}(m_1, E_1)$, it outputs $\mathbf{c} \in \mathsf{RingCtxt}_s^{Q/p}(m_0 \cdot m_1, E)$ where $E \leq \sqrt{\ell N \cdot \mathsf{B}_g^2 \cdot E_1^2 + \|m_1\|_2^2 \cdot E_0^2}$, where B_g is the decomposition base. For succinctness, we can write $\mathbf{c}_0 \boxdot_{i=1}^k \mathbf{C}_i$ to denote FHE.ExtProd(...(FHE.ExtProd($\mathbf{c}_0, \mathbf{C}_1$), $\mathbf{C}_2$), ..., $\mathbf{C}_k$). In this case, assuming that $\|m_i\|_2 = 1$ for $1 \leq i \leq k$, the resulting ciphertext has E-gaussian noise with $E \leq \sqrt{\sum_{i=1}^k \ell \cdot N \cdot \mathsf{B}_g^2 \cdot E_i^2 + E_0^2}$,
- FHE.ModSwt: Given $\hat{c} \in \mathsf{IntCtxt}_{\mathbf{s}}^{q/p}(m, \hat{E})$ and $q \in \mathbb{N}$, output $c \in \mathsf{IntCtxt}_{\mathbf{s}}^{q/p}(m, E)$, with $E \leq \sqrt{(\hat{E} \cdot (q/Q))^2 + (\|\mathbf{s}\|_2 / 2)^2}$.

- FHE.KeySwt: Given $\hat{c} \in \mathsf{IntCtxt}_{\mathbf{s}}^{q/p}(m, \hat{E})$, and a key-switching key ksk from $\mathbf{s} \in \mathbb{Z}^N$ to $\mathbf{z} \in \mathbb{Z}^n$, output $c \in \mathsf{IntCtxt}_{\mathbf{z}}^{q/p}(m, E)$, with $E \leq \sqrt{\hat{E}^2 + N \cdot \log_{\mathsf{B}_{\mathsf{ksk}}} q \cdot \mathsf{B}_{\mathsf{ksk}}^2 \cdot E_k^2}$, where $\mathsf{B}_{\mathsf{ksk}}$ is the decomposition base used during the key-switching.
- FHE.Bootstrap: Given $c' \in \mathsf{IntCtxt}_{\mathbf{z}}^{q/p}(m, E')$, and a function $f : \mathbb{Z}_p \to \mathbb{Z}_p$, output, $c \in \mathsf{IntCtxt}_{\mathbf{z}}^{q/p}(f(m), E_{in})$ where $E_{in} < E'$.
- FHE.MultValBoot: Given $c \in \mathsf{IntCtxt}_{\mathbf{z}}^{q/p}(m, E)$ and functions $f_1, ..., f_L$ from $\mathbb{Z}_p$ to $\mathbb{Z}_p$, output, $c_1, ..., c_L$ where $c_i \in \mathsf{IntCtxt}_{\mathbf{z}}^{q/p}(f_i(m), E_{in})$ and $E_{in} < E$. Executing FHE.MultValBoot for L functions runs in essentially the same time as executing FHE.Bootstrap one single time.

2.3   Homomorphic Evaluation of Look-up-Tables (k-LUT)

The plaintext space $\mathbb{Z}_p$ is typically defined during the parameter and key generation. Usually, p is a power of two, that is, $p = 2^k$ for some k and, hence, the message space is composed by k bits, i.e., $\{0, 1\}^k$. This means that with the functional bootstrapping [16] and the multivalue bootstrapping [20], we can evaluate arbitrary functions from $\{0, 1\}^k$ to $\{0, 1\}^k$. In this case, we say that the bootstrapping evaluates a k-LUT, which stands for look-up-table on k bits.

In 3rd-generation FHE schemes, the running time of the bootstrapping is typically exponential in k, thus, one can only work directly with messages having very few bits. For k ranging from 2 to 4, the bootstrapping typically becomes only slightly slower, but for $k \geq 5$, as we increase k, costs quickly become prohibitive. For instance, the OpenFHE library [1] typically handles $k \leq 4$ and Zama's TFHE-rs [63] provides bootstrapping for messages of up to 8 bits. For larger messages, for example, 32-bit integers, one has to decompose them in k-bit words and operate with them separately [17, 26, 40].

2.4   ChaCha

ChaCha [10, 56] is a stream cipher designed to offer 256 bits of (classic) security. It is a variant of Salsa20, but with extra diffusion, and it is built around a 512-bit state, which initially is composed of a 128-bit constant, a 256-bit key, a 64-bit counter, and a 64-bit nonce, in this order. The state is then represented as a sequence of 16 integers (with 32 bits each). The core function of ChaCha is the *quarter-round* (QR), consisting of 3 operations: 32-bit integer addition, bitwise XOR, and circular left shift. ChaCha20 is a standardized cipher used in Transport Layer Security (TLS [59]), consisting of 20 rounds, each of which applies the quarter-round function four times. Every execution of the QR function operates on distinct portions of the internal state to ensure thorough diffusion. By seeing the state as a 4×4 matrix, the odd rounds apply the QR function to the columns and the even rounds apply the QR function to the diagonals. Given four 32-bit words of the state, denoted as $a, b, c,$ and d, a single iteration of $\mathsf{QR}(a, b, c, d)$ is

---

Algorithm 1: $QR(a, b, c, d)$ — ChaCha's quarter round

Input: 32-bit integers a, b, c, and d

Output: Updated values of a, b, c, and d

1   $a = (a + b)$; $d = \mathsf{XOR}(d, a)$; $d = (d \lll 16)$;

2   $c = (c + d)$; $b = \mathsf{XOR}(b, c)$; $b = (b \lll 12)$;

3   $a = (a + b)$; $d = \mathsf{XOR}(d, a)$ $d = (d \lll 8)$;

4   $c = (c + d)$; $b = \mathsf{XOR}(b, c)$; $b = (b \lll 7)$;

---

composed of 4 lines, each one performing one addition, one bitwise XOR, and one circular shift, as shown in Algoritm 1.

To obtain the final state, one last step is performed: the diffused state, obtained after all the executions of QR, is added to the initial state. This is shown in detail in Algorithm 2.

Algorithm 2: $\mathsf{ChaCha}(E)$ — ChaCha block

Input: State $E \in \mathbb{Z}_{2^{32}}^{16}$ composed of 16 integers of 32 bits each

Output: Updated state E

1   $T = E$ ▷ Copy the state

2   **for** $1 \leq j \leq \texttt{ROUNDS}$ **do**

3   **if** j *is odd* **then**

      ▷ **Odd round (columns of the state)**

4      $QR(T[0], T[4], T[8], \ T[12])$;

5      $QR(T[1], T[5], T[9], \ T[13])$;

6      $QR(T[2], T[6], T[10], T[14])$;

7      $QR(T[3], T[7], T[11], T[15])$;

8   **else**

      ▷ **Even round (diagonals of the state)**

9      $QR(T[0], T[5], T[10], T[15])$;

10     $QR(T[1], T[6], T[11], T[12])$;

11     $QR(T[2], T[7], T[8], \ T[13])$;

12     $QR(T[3], T[4], T[9], \ T[14])$;

13   **for** $0 \leq i < 16$ **do**

14     $E[i] = E[i] + T[i]$;

Then, to encrypt any message, one needs to XOR the plaintext to the final state, obtaining the ciphertext. The same is done to decrypt messages, by XOR'ring the ciphertext to the final state, obtaining the original message.

Since we use 3rd-generation FHE schemes to evaluate ChaCha, we operate with bits, thus, the 32-bit addition used in the QR function was implemented using a Ripple Carry Adder. This adder performs a sequential bitwise addition, where each stage depends on the carry propagated from the previous one. Given input bits x_i, y_i, and the carry input carry_i, the output sum bit sum_i and the output carry bit carry_{i+1} are computed as specified in Equation (1), where $\oplus$ denotes the XOR operation.

$$\mathsf{sum}_i = x_i \oplus y_i \oplus \mathsf{carry}_i \quad \text{and} \quad \mathsf{carry}_{i+1} = (x_i \wedge y_i) \vee (\mathsf{carry}_i \wedge (x_i \oplus y_i)) \tag{1}$$

ChaCha's Cryptanalysis. ChaCha was designed already considering a quantum attacker, thus, it offers 128 bits of PQ security, or, equivalently, 256 bits of classic security. Soon after its appearance, researchers started to analyze it and a first attack against a *round-reduced* version of ChaCha, i.e., ChaCha considering less rounds that what is recommended, appeared. Namely, in [6], it was proposed an attack against ChaCha with 6 rounds running in about 2^{139} operations and against ChaCha with 7 rounds (ChaCha7) costing about 2^{248} operations, thus, less than 2^{256}, which is the expected cost of attacking the full-round ChaCha. After that, new attacks against ChaCha7 started to appear, each one reducing a little the security level, culminating in [37] claiming a distinguisher attack on ChaCha7 with time 2^{135}. However, it seems that attacking ChaCha with 8 rounds (ChaCha8) is much harder. Indeed, there is no known attack against ChaCha8 running in less than 2^{256} operations, that is, better than brute forcing it. Instead, there are some attacks considering fractions of the eighth round. For example, [34] shows an attack against ChaCha with 7.25 rounds running in time 2^{236} and [33] attacks ChaCha with 7.5 rounds in time 2^{250}, i.e., degrading ChaCha's security in just 6 bits.

It is worth noticing that many of those attacks need more pairs of plaintext/ciphertext than a normal user would ever be able to produce. For instance, this attack on ChaCha with 7.5 rounds requires around 2^{127} pairs [33], but producing this amount of ciphertexts is far above the computational power available for anyone (for example, if one could execute that amount of operations, then one could even break AES-128 by brute forcing it).

In summary, ChaCha has been the target of a lot of cryptanalysis, but there are still no realistic attacks. Even with only 8 rounds, it already offers 256 bits of security. And indeed, Aumasson argues that we should use ChaCha8 for this security level [5]. Nevertheless, the authors of the post-quantum signature scheme SPHINCS were more conservative and used ChaCha with 12 rounds (ChaCha12) targeting 256 bits of security. Even more conservative, TLS 1.3 standardized ChaCha20 (with 20 rounds) for 256 bits of security [59].

3   Our Transciphering Protocols

In this section, we propose two ways of evaluating ChaCha homomorphically using very small message space in FHE, that is, by instantiating FHE schemes with small parameters so that each ciphertext only encrypt 2 or 3 bits. It is worth noticing that increasing the message space in 3rd-generation FHE schemes can bring severe slowdowns to the homomorphic computation, since the running time of the bootstrapping in these schemes is exponential in the bit length of the encrypted messages. Basically, to evaluate ChaCha homomorphically, one can choose to perform the additions then perform the XOR gates separately, or one can try to perform them together. The first strategy is more natural and, at first glance, would require a message space of 3 bits, since computing the i-th bit of the sum requires two input bits and one carry bit. However, we show how to do it using a message space of only 2 bits instead of 3.

The second strategy, namely, evaluating the full-adder and the bitwise XOR simultaneously is less natural, but by analyzing the output bits of the QR, we see that it is possible to evaluate them together with a message space of 4 bits. We go beyond that and propose a way to evaluate them using only 3 bits. Thus, this allows us to save all the bootstrappings that would be used to evaluate the XOR gates at the cost of increasing a little the running time of each bootstrapping, since bootstrappings over $\{0,1\}^3$ are not much slower than over $\{0,1\}^2$.

3.1 Evaluating ChaCha Using 2-LUT

The natural way to use k-LUTs to evaluate a function $f(x_1, ..., x_k)$ where each $x_i \in \{0,1\}$ is as follows. Firstly, given ciphertexts $\mathbf{c}_0, ..., \mathbf{c}_{k-1}$ encrypting bits $m_0, ..., m_{k-1}$, respectively, one multiplies the i-th ciphertext by 2^i, then adds all of them together, that is, one computes

$$\mathbf{c} := \sum_{i=0}^{k-1} \mathsf{FHE.MultPtxt}(\mathbf{c}_i, 2^i)$$

Then, given $\mathbf{c}$ encrypting $m := \sum_{i=0}^{k-1} m_i \cdot 2^i$, one defines the function $g : \{0,1\}^k \to \{0,1\}^k$ as a function which firstly computes the binary decomposition of x, that is, $x_0 = x \bmod 2$, $x_1 = (x - x_0) \bmod 2$, $x_2 = (x - x_0 - 2 \cdot x_1) \bmod 2$, etc., then outputs $f(x_1, ..., x_{k-1})$. Finally, one uses the bootstrapping to evaluate the k-LUT on $\mathbf{c}$, obtaining $\mathbf{c}' \in \mathsf{IntCtxt}_{\mathbf{z}}^{q/p}(g(m)) = \mathsf{IntCtxt}_{\mathbf{z}}^{q/p}(f(m_1, ..., m_{k-1}))$.

Applying this natural strategy to the ripple carry adder to compute the i-th sum bit and the $(i+1)$-th carry bit, as given by Equation (1), one would need to aggregate 3 bits, that is, to compute an encryption of $x_i + 2 \cdot y_i + 4 \cdot \mathsf{carry}_i$, then use the multivalue bootstrapping to extract encryptions of $f_1(x_i, y_i, \mathsf{carry}_i) := \mathsf{sum}_i$ and $f_2(x_i, y_i, \mathsf{carry}_i) := \mathsf{carry}_{i+1}$. Of course, that means that we would need to instantiate FHE with a message space of 3 bits. Instead, we propose to aggregate the bits by simply adding them together, which just requires 2-bit message space, and show that it is still possible to extract sum_i and carry_{i+1}. In more detail, let $S = x_i + y_i + \mathsf{carry}_i$, then we notice that $\mathsf{sum}_i = S \bmod 2$, $\mathsf{carry}_{i+1} = 0$ if $S < 2$, and $\mathsf{carry}_{i+1} = 1$ if $S \geq 2$. Therefore, we can firstly generate an encryption of S, then use the multivalue bootstrapping to extract the sum bit and the next carry. This is shown formally in Lemma 1.

Lemma 1. *Define two functions f_1 and f_2 from $\mathbb{N}$ to $\{0,1\}$ as*

$$f_1(x) = x \bmod 2 \quad \text{and} \quad f_2(x) = \begin{cases} 0 & \text{if } 0 \leq x < 2 \\ 1 & \text{if } x \geq 2 \end{cases}$$

Algorithm 3: 2-LUT-FullAdder

Input: Functions f_1 and f_2 as defined in Lemma 1. A bootstrapping key bk for 2-LUTs. For $0 \leq i < 32$, $\mathbf{x}_i \in \mathsf{IntCtxt}_\mathbf{s}^{q/p}(x_i)$, $\mathbf{y}_i \in \mathsf{IntCtxt}_\mathbf{s}^{q/p}(y_i)$.

Output: For $0 \leq i \leq 31$, $\mathbf{u}_i \in \mathsf{IntCtxt}_\mathbf{s}^{q/p}(\mathsf{sum}_i)$

1 Let $\mathbf{c}^{\mathsf{carry}_0}$ be a trivial and noiseless encryption of 0

2 **for** $0 \leq i \leq 31$ **do**

3 $\quad \mathbf{c} \leftarrow \mathsf{FHE.Add}(\mathbf{x}_i, \mathbf{y}_i)$

4 $\quad \mathbf{c} \leftarrow \mathsf{FHE.Add}(\mathbf{c}, \mathbf{c}^{\mathsf{carry}_i})$; $\qquad\qquad\qquad \triangleright \mathsf{IntCtxt}_\mathbf{s}^{q/p}(x_i + y_i + \mathsf{carry}_i)$

5 $\quad \mathbf{u}_i, \mathbf{c}^{\mathsf{carry}_{i+1}} \leftarrow \mathsf{FHE.MultValBoot}(\mathbf{c}, f_1, f_2)$

6 **return** $\mathbf{u}_0, \mathbf{u}_1, ..., \mathbf{u}_{31}$; $\qquad\qquad\qquad\qquad\qquad \triangleright \mathbf{u}_i \in \mathsf{IntCtxt}_\mathbf{s}^{q/p}(\mathsf{sum}_i)$

Let $x_i, y_i, \mathsf{carry}_i \in \{0, 1\}$, and $S = x_i + y_i + \mathsf{carry}_i$. Then, $f_1(S)$ and $f_2(S)$ give us the sum bit and the next carry bit, as described in Equation (1), that is, $f_1(S) = x_i \oplus y_i \oplus \mathsf{carry}_i$ and $f_2(S) = (x_i \wedge y_i) \vee (\mathsf{carry}_i \wedge (x_i \oplus y_i))$.

Proof. Since the XOR operation is equivalent to addition in $\mathbb{Z}_2$, it is trivial that $x_i \oplus y_i \oplus \mathsf{carry}_i = f_1(S) = (x_i + y_i + \mathsf{carry}_i \bmod 2)$.

Also, let $\mathsf{carry}_{i+1} = (x_i \wedge y_i) \vee (\mathsf{carry}_i \wedge (x_i \oplus y_i))$. Let's check that $f_2(S) = \mathsf{carry}_{i+1}$ in the two following cases.

– When $\mathsf{carry}_i = 0$: Then $\mathsf{carry}_{i+1} = 1$ if, and only if, $x_i = y_i = 1$. In other words, $\mathsf{carry}_{i+1} = 1 \Leftrightarrow S = 2$. Thus, if $0 \leq S < 1$, then $\mathsf{carry}_{i+1} = 0$. Since $S < 3$ in this case, we have that $f_2(S) = \mathsf{carry}_{i+1}$.

– When $\mathsf{carry}_i = 1$: Then $\mathsf{carry}_{i+1} = 0$ if, and only if $x_i = y_i = 0$. In other words, $\mathsf{carry}_{i+1} = 0 \Leftrightarrow S = 1$. Thus, for other values of x_i and y_i, we have $\mathsf{carry}_{i+1} = 1$ and $S \geq 2$. Therefore, $f_2(S) = \mathsf{carry}_{i+1}$.

$\qquad\qquad\qquad\qquad\qquad\qquad\qquad\qquad\qquad\qquad\qquad\qquad\qquad\qquad\qquad \square$

By using Lemma 1, we design Algorithm 3, which homomorphically evaluates a 32-bit full adder using FHE with only 2-bit message space. We prove its correctness in Lemma 2.

Lemma 2. *Let x and y be two 32-bit integers with binary representation $(x_0, ..., x_{31})$ and $(y_0, ..., y_{31})$, with x_0 and y_0 being the least significant bits. Let $z = x + y \bmod 2^{32}$, that is, the 32-bit integer resulting from adding x and y. Finally, let $(z_0, ..., z_{31}) \in \{0, 1\}^{32}$ be the binary representation of z, i.e., $z = \sum_{i=0}^{31} z_i \cdot 2^i$. Then, Algorithm 3 returns encryptions of $z_0, ..., z_{31}$.*

Proof. Let $S_i = x_i + y_i + \mathsf{carry}_i$. By the correctness of the homomorphic addition, $\mathbf{c} \in \mathsf{IntCtxt}_\mathbf{s}^{q/p}(x_i + y_i + \mathsf{carry}_i)$. By the correctness of the multivalue bootstrapping, $\mathbf{u}_i \in \mathsf{IntCtxt}_\mathbf{s}^{q/p}(f_1(S_i))$ and $\mathbf{c}^{\mathsf{carry}_{i+1}} \in \mathsf{IntCtxt}_\mathbf{s}^{q/p}(f_2(S_i))$. By Lemma 1, $f_1(S_i) = z_i$ and $f_2(S_i) = \mathsf{carry}_{i+1}$, thus, $\mathbf{u}_i$ encrypts the correct value and the next iteration happens with correct carry. Therefore, at the end of the algorithm, for all $i \in [\![0, 31]\!]$, $\mathbf{u}_i \in \mathsf{IntCtxt}_\mathbf{s}^{q/p}(z_i)$. $\qquad\qquad \square$

Once we have a homomorphic 32-bit full adder using 2-LUTs, it is straightforward to implement the whole ChaCha. We start by Algorithm 4, which homomorphically evaluates one single line of the QR function. To do so, it firstly calls the homomorphic full adder, then it uses the programmable bootstrapping to perform the bitwise XOR, executing thus the bootstrapping 32 times, and finally, it applies the rotations essentially for free, by simply relabeling the ciphertexts.

Algorithm 4: 2-LUT-QRLine

Input: Functions f_1 and f_2 as defined in Lemma 1. A bootstrapping key bk for 2-LUTs. A rotation index $r \in \{7, 8, 12, 16\}$. For $0 \leq i < 32$, $\mathbf{a}_i \in \mathsf{IntCtxt}_\mathbf{s}^{q/p}(a_i)$, $\mathbf{b}_i \in \mathsf{IntCtxt}_\mathbf{s}^{q/p}(b_i)$, and $\mathbf{c}_i \in \mathsf{IntCtxt}_\mathbf{s}^{q/p}(c_i)$, where $a_i, b_i, c_i \in \{0, 1\}$.

Output: For $0 \leq i < 32$, $\mathbf{a}_i \in \mathsf{IntCtxt}_\mathbf{s}^{q/p}(a_i')$, and $\mathbf{c}_i \in \mathsf{IntCtxt}_\mathbf{s}^{q/p}(c_i')$, where $a_i', c_i' \in \{0, 1\}$.

1 $\mathbf{a}_0, ..., \mathbf{a}_{31} \leftarrow$ 2-LUT-FullAdder$(\mathbf{a}_0, ..., \mathbf{a}_{31}, \mathbf{b}_0, ..., \mathbf{b}_{31}, f_1, f_2, \mathsf{bk})$

2   **for** $0 \leq i \leq 31$ **do**

3 $\hat{\mathbf{c}}_i = \mathsf{FHE.Add}(\mathbf{c}_i, \mathbf{a}_i)$

4 $\hat{\mathbf{c}}_i \leftarrow \mathsf{FHE.Bootstrap}(\hat{\mathbf{c}}_i, f_1)$; $\triangleright \mathsf{IntCtxt}_\mathbf{s}^{q/p}(\mathsf{XOR}(a_i', c_i))$

5   **for** $0 \leq i \leq 31$ **do**

6 $\mathbf{c}_i \leftarrow \hat{\mathbf{c}}_{(i+r) \bmod 32}$

7   **return** $\mathbf{a}_0, ..., \mathbf{a}_{31}, \mathbf{c}_0, ..., \mathbf{c}_{31}$

To implement the QR function, one just has to execute Algorithm 4 four times, with r assuming the values $16, 12, 8$, and 7, as in the description of the plaintext QR function in Algorithm 1. Finally, after R rounds which execute the QR function $4 \cdot R$ times in total, we just execute one more time the homomorphic full adder, Algorithm 3.

Computational Cost of ChaCha Using 2-LUT. The running time of the homomorphic evaluation of ChaCha is dominated by the executions of the programmable and multivalue bootstrappings. As they run in basically the same time, we count them as the same. Hence, we obtain the following. To execute one line of the QR function, we need 64 bootstrappings, 32 for the adder and 32 for the bitwise XOR. Therefore, one execution of the QR function requires $4 \cdot 64 = 256$ bootstrappings. Considering ChaCha with R rounds, the QR function is executed $4 \cdot R$, which gives us then $4 \cdot R \cdot 256 = 1024 \cdot R$ bootstrappings. Finally, the updated state is added to the initial state, thus, in total, we have $1024 \cdot R + 32$ bootstrappings evaluating LUTs on 2-bit messages.

3.2   Evaluating ChaCha Using 3-LUT

The main advantage of instantiating FHE with 3-bit message space instead of just using 2 bits is that it allows us to merge the computation of the XORs in each line of the QR function into the full adder, that is, with one single MVB we can extract the i-th sum bit, the next carry, and the i-th bit of the subsequent XOR. This means that we can save half of bootstrappings per line of the QR function, evaluating it with 32 bootstrappings instead of 64.

For this, first notice that the QR always stores the sum into a variable, then uses this same variable to compute the XOR with a third variable. In the binary level, this means that we can look at the bits x_i, y_i, and carry_i, which are used to compute the i-th sum bit, say, sum_i, and the bit that will be XORed, say, z_i. Thus, given $(x_i, y_i, \mathsf{carry}_i, z_i)$, we want to compute sum_i, carry_{i+1}, and $w_i :=\mathsf{sum}_i \oplus z_i$. Of course, we could easily compute it using 4-LUTs by accumulating the four input bits in the natural way and using the MVB to extract each of the three output bits. However, as in Sect. 3.1, we want to gain one bit and perform this computation with 3-LUTs. To do so, we compute $S = x_i + y_i + \mathsf{carry}_i + 4 \cdot z_i$. Notice that $0 \leq S \leq 7$, hence, it can be encrypted with 3 bits. Then, we define three functions f_1, f_2, and f_3, where the first two reduce S modulo 4, then compute the sum and the next carry bits as described in Sect. 3.1, while $f_3(S)$ firstly extracts the most significant bit of S, then computes its XOR with $f_1(S)$. We present it in detail in Lemma 3

Lemma 3. *Define three functions f_1, f_2, and f_3 from $\mathbb{N}$ to $\{0, 1\}$ as*

- *$f_1(x) = x \bmod 2$*
- *$f_2(x) = \begin{cases} 0 & \text{if } 0 \leq (x \bmod 4) < 2 \\ 1 & \text{if } (x \bmod 4) \geq 2 \end{cases}$*
- *$f_3(x) = (f_1(x) + \lfloor x/4 \rfloor) \bmod 2$*

Let $x_i, y_i, \mathsf{carry}_i, z_i \in \{0, 1\}$, and $S = x_i + y_i + \mathsf{carry}_i + 4 \cdot z_i$. Then, $f_1(S)$ and $f_2(S)$ give us the sum bit and the next carry bit, as described in Equation (1), that is, $f_1(S) = x_i \oplus y_i \oplus \mathsf{carry}_i$ and $f_2(S) = (x_i \wedge y_i) \vee (\mathsf{carry}_i \wedge (x_i \oplus y_i))$. Moreover, $f_3(S) = f_1(S) \oplus z_i$.

Proof. We have $f_1(S) = (x_i + y_i + \mathsf{carry}_i + 4 \cdot z_i) \bmod 2 = (x_i + y_i + \mathsf{carry}_i) \bmod 2 = x_i \oplus y_i \oplus \mathsf{carry}_i$.

Also, notice that $(S \bmod 4) = x_i + y_i + \mathsf{carry}_i$, thus, by the same argument used in the proof of Lemma 1, we have $f_2(S) = \mathsf{carry}_{i+1}$.

Finally, since $f_1(S) = \mathsf{sum}_i$ and $\lfloor S/4 \rfloor = z_i + \lfloor (x_i + y_i + \mathsf{carry}_i)/4 \rfloor = z_i + 0$, it holds that $f_3(S) = \mathsf{sum}_i \oplus z_i$, as expected. $\qquad\square$

Finally, evaluating one line of the QR function boils down to using the multivalue bootstrapping (MVB) to apply the three functions defined in Lemma 3. Namely, for each triple of encrypted bits a_i, b_i and c_i, and the current encrypted carry carry_i, we just use the cheap homomorphic addition to generate an encryption of $S = a_i + b_i + \mathsf{carry}_i + 4 \cdot c_i$, then apply the MVB to obtain encryptions of $f_1(S), f_2(S)$, and $f_3(S)$, which are the i-th sum bit, the $(i+1)$-th carry bit, and the sum bit xored with c_i, respectively. We describe this in detail in Algorithm 5.

As for the 2-LUT case, once we have Algorithm 5 to evaluate one line of the QR function, we just need to execute it four times, with r assuming the values

---

Algorithm 5: 3-LUT-QRLine

Input: Functions f_1, f_2, and f_3 as defined in Lemma 3. A bootstrapping key bk for 3-LUTs. A rotation index $r \in \{7, 8, 12, 16\}$. For $0 \le i < 32$, $\mathbf{a}_i \in \mathsf{IntCtxt}_\mathbf{s}^{q/p}(a_i)$, $\mathbf{b}_i \in \mathsf{IntCtxt}_\mathbf{s}^{q/p}(b_i)$, and $\mathbf{c}_i \in \mathsf{IntCtxt}_\mathbf{s}^{q/p}(c_i)$, where $a_i, b_i, c_i \in \{0, 1\}$.

Output: For $0 \le i < 32$, $\mathbf{u}_i \in \mathsf{IntCtxt}_\mathbf{s}^{q/p}(u_i')$, and $\mathbf{x}_i \in \mathsf{IntCtxt}_\mathbf{s}^{q/p}(x_i')$, where $u_i', x_i' \in \{0, 1\}$.

1   Let $\mathbf{c}^{\mathsf{carry}_0}$ be a trivial and noiseless encryption of 0

2   **for** $0 \le i \le 31$ **do**

3      $\mathbf{w} \leftarrow \mathsf{FHE.Add}(\mathbf{c}_i, \mathbf{c}_i)$

4      $\mathbf{w} \leftarrow \mathsf{FHE.Add}(\mathbf{w}, \mathbf{w})$; $\triangleright$ $\mathsf{IntCtxt}_\mathbf{s}^{q/p}(4 \cdot c_i)$

5      $\mathbf{w} \leftarrow \mathsf{FHE.Add}(\mathbf{w}, \mathbf{a}_i)$

6      $\mathbf{w} \leftarrow \mathsf{FHE.Add}(\mathbf{w}, \mathbf{b}_i)$

7      $\mathbf{w} \leftarrow \mathsf{FHE.Add}(\mathbf{w}, \mathbf{c}^{\mathsf{carry}_i})$; $\triangleright$ $\mathsf{IntCtxt}_\mathbf{s}^{q/p}(a_i + b_i + \mathsf{carry}_i + 4 \cdot c_i)$

8      $\mathbf{u}_i, \mathbf{c}^{\mathsf{carry}_{i+1}}, \hat{\mathbf{x}}_i \leftarrow \mathsf{FHE.MultValBoot}(\mathbf{c}, f_1, f_2, f_3)$

9   **for** $0 \le i \le 31$ **do**

10     $\mathbf{x}_i \leftarrow \hat{\mathbf{x}}_{(i+r) \bmod 32}$; $\triangleright$ **Apply the rotation to the xored bits**

11   **return** $\mathbf{u}_0, ..., \mathbf{u}_{31}, \mathbf{x}_0, ..., \mathbf{x}_{31}$

$16, 12, 8$, and 7, to execute the full QR. And to evaluate one block of ChaCha with R rounds, we just have to call the QR function 4 times per round and, at the very end, use the same adder as Algorithm 3, which, of course, also works with 3-bit instead of 2-bit message space.

Computational Cost of 3-LUT ChaCha. As for ChaCha with 2-LUTs, the running time is dominated by the executions of the multivalue bootstrapping (MVB), as it is orders of magnitude slower than the homomorphic additions and the bit rotations. One execution of the QR function requires 128 bootstrappings, being 32 for each line, which are evaluated with Algorithm 5. Therefore, to evaluate ChaCha with R rounds, we need $4 \cdot R \cdot 128 = 512 \cdot R$, as each round makes 4 calls to the quarter round. Counting the final addition on the state, we have then a total of $512 \cdot R + 32$ bootstrappings on 3-bit messages to completely evaluate ChaCha with R rounds producing one block of 512 encrypted bits.

4   Related Work

To the best of our knowledge, this is the first paper to consider and implement post-quantum secure transciphering based on standard ciphers. Even among works that proposed FHE-friendly ciphers for transciphering, most of them do not consider post-quantum security and some of them discuss 256-bit secure versions of their ad hoc ciphers, but end up focusing on transciphering with 128 bits of security.

Among works that studied non-standard ciphers, designed specifically to be FHE-friendly, Rasta [30] raised the discussion on 256-bit security transciphering, but almost all their implementations used the FHE scheme BGV [18] with security level 128 or less, sometimes even together with Rasta-256, which shows that providing quantum security was not in the scope of the paper. Moreover, the only instantiation of Rasta together with BGV both with 128 bits of PQ security is much slower than the other instantiations, running in about 23 min in their experiments. Dasta [44], a variation of Rasta, only implements its transciphering protocol with 80 and 128 bits of security. LowMC [3] also only shows implementation using 128 bits of classic security both for their symmetric cipher and for BVG. Kreyvium [19] was designed with only 128-bit security. There are many other examples of recent studies that propose the efficient evaluation of FHE-friendly ciphers but do not discuss post-quantum security [4,8,27,52]. For example, [50] and [43] only present parameters for their ciphers achieving 80 or 128 bits of security, while [29] only presents a 128-bit secure version of its cipher.

Considering works that studied transciphering with standard ciphers, we could not find any offering at least 256 bits of security. Gentry, Halevi and Smart used the BGV scheme to evaluate AES-128 homomorphically [36]. Later, Mella and Susella [53] discussed the homomorphic evaluation of different families of ciphers (AES-128, SHA-256 [55], Salsa20 [11] and Keccak [12]) using BGV, but all of their implementations used a security level equivalent to AES-128. Wei *et al.* [62] optimized the homomorphic evaluation of AES with TFHE, but instantiating both AES and TFHE with only 128 bits of security. In a follow-up work, Wei *et al.* proposed Thunderbird [61], an evaluation framework, but only implemented the evaluation of SNOW 3G, ZUC, and AES-128, all providing 128-bit security. Finally, Hippogryph [9] only discusses AES-128.

This reveals the growing academic interest in transciphering and in the optimization of this method, but also the lack of works that consider post-quantum security.

5   Experimental Results and Comparisons

We implement our homomorphic evaluation approach using the MOSFHET library [41] and benchmarked it on an `r7i.metal-24xl` instance on AWS (Intel Xeon Platinum 8488C at 2.4 GHz/3.8 GHz-boost and 768GB of memory, supporting up to with 96 threads). For multithreaded results, we parallelized our implementation using OpenMP with 4 threads. Our main comparison baselines are the state-of-the-art homomorphic evaluations of the AES from [13] and [9], which we run in the same environment described above. Since these works originally only provide AES-128, we extend them to evaluate the AES-256 by increasing the number of rounds from 10 to 14. As an additional result, in Appendix A, we also provide a comparison between ChaCha8 and the original (AES-128) implementations from [9,13]. We defer comparisons with FHE-friendly ciphers to Sect. 5.4.

5.1   Parameters

We selected 4 sets of parameters which are provided by the TFHE-rs library [63][2] for evaluating bootstrappings with 2 and 3 bits of precision, as required by our two evaluations approaches (2-LUT and 3-LUT). For each case, we experiment with parameters that provide both negligible ($\approx 2^{-128}$) and nonnegligible ($2^{-34} \sim 2^{-40}$) probabilities of failure (FP) for the homomorphic evaluation. All parameters achieve around 128-bit PQ security according to the Lattice Estimator [2]. Table 1 presents them.

Table 1. TFHE parameters. The ciphertext modulus q is always 2^{64}. n and $N \cdot k$ are the dimension of the LWE and the module-LWE problems, respectively. The parameters of the noise distributions are σ_{LWE} and σ_{RLWE}. As explained in Sect. 2.2), the decomposition base and dimension of the GSW ciphertexts are B_g and ℓ_g, while the ones of the key-switching key are $\mathsf{B}_{\mathsf{ksk}}$ and ℓ_{ksk}.

	n	σ_{LWE}	N	k	σ_{RLWE}	$\mathsf{B}_{\mathsf{ksk}}$	ℓ_{ksk}	B_g	ℓ_g
2-LUT$_{\mathsf{FP}=2^{-40}}$	779	$2^{47.27}$	512	3	$2^{28.42}$	2^3	4	2^{17}	1
2-LUT$_{\mathsf{FP}=2^{-128}}$	837	$2^{45.82}$	512	4	$2^{15.68}$	2^3	5	2^{23}	1
3-LUT$_{\mathsf{FP}=2^{-34}}$	837	$2^{45.82}$	512	4	$2^{15.68}$	2^3	5	2^{23}	1
3-LUT$_{\mathsf{FP}=2^{-128}}$	885	$2^{44.63}$	1024	2	$2^{15.68}$	2^3	5	2^{23}	1

5.2   Results

Table 2 presents our main results and compares them with the extended (AES-256) version of Hippogryph [9]. As discussed in Sect. 2.4, current state-of-the-art cryptanalysis on ChaCha considers 8 rounds to be enough for 128-bit post-quantum security. Nevertheless, we focus on more conservative choices and present results for ChaCha20 and ChaCha12 (ChaCha8 is presented in Appendix A and compared with AES-128). On a single thread, our implementation of ChaCha20 is 11.7 times faster than Hippogryph in latency while providing a more than 50 times higher throughput. For ChaCha12, the latency improvement goes up to 18.3 times while throughput is 86 times higher. Hippogryph's latency improves significantly in the multi-threaded experiment, since their code is highly parallelizable, and we are using a very large machine (with 96 virtual cores). Their throughput, however, is still more than 10 times smaller than what our evaluation of ChaCha12 provides. Furthermore, our implementation is parallelized to use only 4 threads, which would allows us to run several instances in parallel to further increase throughput. In all cases, we note that our 3-LUT evaluation approach was significantly faster than 2-LUT, which was expected

---

[2] We consider parameters from commit 4cc2df42ed8a617a49da8797b1f2f9de88c11e2d for negligible and nonnegligible FP.

based on our cost analysis and typical bootstrapping performance. Nonetheless, the results for 2-LUT remain relevant, as future bootstrapping performance improvements may favor different bit lengths.

Table 2. Homomorphic evaluation results with negligible ($\approx 2^{-128}$) probability of failure. Latency in seconds; Throughput in bits per second. Multi-thread version of Hippogryph uses 32 threads while ChaCha20 and ChaCha12 uses 4 threads.

Cipher	Single-thread		Multi-thread	
	Latency	Throughput	Latency	Throughput
AES-256 (Hippogryph [9])	1087.7	0.1	59.3	2.2
ChaCha20 (2-LUT)	179.2	2.9	54.2	9.4
ChaCha20 (3-LUT)	92.7	5.5	25.8	19.9
ChaCha12 (2-LUT)	117.2	4.4	33.5	15.3
ChaCha12 (3-LUT)	59.5	8.6	17.5	29.2

5.3   Results for Higher Probability of Failure

Although it is generally accepted that a negligible probability of failure (FP) is required [23], higher probabilities of failure are still acceptable in some scenarios, particularly if one can bound the number of allowed decryptions. Considering that, and the fact that several previous work used FP about 2^{-40}, we also benchmark our implementation for this higher probability of failure (FP $\approx 2^{-40}$). In this case, we compare with the work of Bon $et\ al.$ [13], which has the lowest monothread latency among the AES-based transciphering protocols with similar failure probability.[3] Table 3 presents our results. In this case, our best monothreaded latency with ChaCha20 is about 4 times smaller while our throughout is about 19 times higher. When considering ChaCha12, the latency is approximately 6.5 times lower while the throughput is about 30 times higher. Interestingly, notice that while we can observe small improvements in our single-threaded performance, our multi-threaded results for 3-LUT become worse than what we previously achieved. This is likely explained by the fact that the parameter set for 3-LUT with higher FP (See Table 1) enables improvements in computation, but it also increases the size of bootstrapping keys (which takes $8n\ell(k+1)^2N$ bytes), which increases the memory bottleneck for the multi-threaded evaluation.

---

[3] We note that Hippogryph also provides HE parameters for FP $\approx 2^{-40}$ ($P_{err} = 2^{-40}$ in Table 2 of [9]), but we do not compare to this specific parameter set because they seem to offer less than 128 bits of security. Indeed, by checking those parameters in the Lattice Estimator [2], we could only obtain around 70 bits of security. It is also not possible to update it to 128-bit security without affecting their performance or claimed probability of failure.

Table 3. Homomorphic evaluation results with higher probability of failure ($\approx 2^{-40}$). Latency in seconds; Throughput in bits per second.

Cipher	Single-thread		Multi-thread	
	Latency	Throughput	Latency	Throughput
AES-256 [13]	371.8	0.3	178.8	0.7
ChaCha20 (2-LUT)	117.7	4.4	35.2	14.5
ChaCha20 (3-LUT)	86.2	5.9	27.6	18.5
ChaCha12 (2-LUT)	74.1	6.9	22.3	23.0
ChaCha12 (3-LUT)	56.7	9.0	19.1	26.8

5.4   Comparison with Transciphering Protocols Based on FHE-Friendly Ciphers

Traditional ciphers such as ChaCha and AES follow well-established design principals to guarantee security. On the other hand, FHE-friendly ciphers are designed to be efficiently evaluated by FHE and it is not uncommon that vulnerabilities are found after some independent cryptanalysis [38, 39, 47, 49]. Therefore, comparing those two types of transciphering protocols is complicated, as ad hoc ciphers tend to perform much better, but they lack extensive cryptanalysis. Despite that, we present a comparison between the main transciphering based on ad hoc ciphers and our solutions with ChaCha.

To select the ciphers we are comparing to, we proceeded as follows: firstly notice that FHE-friendly ciphers can be subdivided in two categories, the ones designed to be efficiently evaluated with TFHE-like schemes (which we call latency-oriented), and the ones designed for BGV, FV, and CKKS, that is, FHE schemes that use SIMD techniques (we call this category of transciphering throughput-oriented). Thus, we analyzed recent surveys and SoKs, such as [57, 60], and selected the ones with either lowest latency or the highest throughput in each of the two categories, of course, only considering the ones that are still secure, as many of them have already been broken. Finally, we also searched for FHE-friendly ciphers published after those surveys to make sure we are not missing any secure and competitive cipher. Hence, we selected five ad hoc ciphers: we compare with the *Latency-oriented* Margrethe [45], Transistor [8], and Nostalgia [21], and with the *Throughput-oriented* Pasta [31] and Rubato [43]. We briefly describe those five ciphers below.

– Margrethe [45] is an FHE-friendly designed to take advantage of the LUT-evaluations possible with 3rd-generation FHE schemes. It is based on filter permutations (FP), a stream cipher design introduced together with the ad hoc cipher FiLIP [51], where a stream is generated by applying to the key a non-linear function f whose domain consists of several bits but the output has only few bits (hence, f is called a filtering function). At each cycle, the key is updated with simple operations, such as, permutations, and it is given as input to f. Aiming to improve FiLIP's efficiency, a new FP-based cipher was proposed, Elisabeth [29]. However, about one year later, a key-recovery attack against Elisabeth appeared, lowering its security from 128 to 88 bits [38]. Finally, Margrethe was proposed as a secure variant of Elisabeth, where the filter function f is defined in a way that avoids the weaknesses found in [38]. In our comparison, we use the only public implementation of Margrethe we are aware of, which was presented in [4].

- Transistor [8] is another ad hoc cipher designed to be compatible with 3rd-generation FHE schemes. Its design mixes classic stream ciphers with classic block ciphers. Namely, it uses two LSFRs, one that generates whitening strings with 4 elements of $\mathbb{F}_{17}$ each and another acting as the key schedule and outputting strings with 16 elements of $\mathbb{F}_{17}$ each. The output of the key schedule is added to the previous state and it is processed by AES-like operations, that is, the 16 elements are represented as a matrix in $\mathbb{F}_{17}^{4\times 4}$ which is processed by a S-box, a MixColumns and a ShiftRows. The resulting 16 elements are then filtered by a function that outputs only 4 elements, which are finally added to the current whitening string and then output as the result keystream. To argue that Transistor is secure, the authors firstly present an information-theoretic argument showing that it is not possible to recover information about the output of the key schedule LSFR if one only has access to 3 or less consecutive keystream outputs. Using this, they can find upper-bounds on the linear relation of the LSFR output and the output of the whole cipher, arguing thus that Transistor is secure against linear distinguishing attacks and other correlation attacks.

- Nostalgia [21] is based on filtered LFSRs, arguing that this is a well-studied design choice and it is suitable to obtain secure ciphers. Moreover, LFSRs can be evaluated efficiently with 3rd-generation FHE schemes, as they typically only uses simple operations, such as shifts and XORs. The remaining obstacle is the filtering function, but Nostalgia chooses one that can be computed as an inner-product. Therefore, at the end, Nostalgia can be completely evaluated only with external products and so-called internal products (multiplications of GSW ciphertexts), without even using bootstrapping, which makes its running time very competitive with other latency-oriented ciphers while having an apparently more conservative design.

- Pasta [31] is a cipher designed specifically to schemes like BGV and FV, as those schemes can encrypt a vector of messages in a single ciphertext (instead of a single message, as in 3rd-gen schemes) and can operate on each entry of that vector in parallel with a single homomorphic operation (this is known as SIMD). Also, using SIMD and homomorphic rotations, one can use BGV/FV to perform more efficient matrix operations, such as multiplication. With that in mind, Pasta (and the previous works in the same line, Rasta [30] and Masta [42]) uses matrix operations over $\mathbb{F}_p$ to update the internal state. Each round in Pasta applies an affine layer where the state is multiplied by random matrices added to random vectors (sampled using an XOF), then a non-linear operation that multiplies the values and mix them using a Feistel-like structure is performed.

– Rubato [43] takes advantage of the efficiency of CKKS, an FHE scheme that encrypts real numbers up to some precision and offers homomorphic operations with approximate results. Thus, it is suitable for applications where the client's data is composed of floating-point values instead of exact values, like integers or strings. Inspired by the FHE schemes themselves and by the LWE problem, at the end of the encryption process, Rubato adds Gaussian noise to its ciphertexts, aiming to increase its non-linearity. As a result, the authors of Rubato argue that they can use low-degree non-linear functions, reducing thus the multiplicative depth, and therefore making the cipher more efficient to evaluate with FHE. This novelty in its design also makes it an approximate cipher, where encrypting then decrypting a message m yields m' that is close but not equal to m. Just like in many FHE schemes, ciphertexts produced by Rubato are composed by elements of $\mathbb{Z}_q$. While the hardness of the LWE problem only depends on the size of q, but not on its format, Rubato was shown to be insecure if it uses composite q [39].

We measure execution time for the selected ciphers in the same environment described at the beginning of Sect. 5, using the benchmarking tools provided by the respective implementations. Table 4 shows the results.

Table 4. Comparison with HE-friendly ciphers. We indicate multithreaded executions with "$(n\mathrm{T})$", where n is the number of threads.

Cipher	Latency (ms)	Throughput (bits/s)
Margrethe $[4, 45]$ (14T)	2.9	1398.6
Margrethe $[4, 45]$	20.4	196.0
Nostalgia [21]	41.0	24.4
Transistor [8]	207.0	82.1
Pasta 4 [31] (HELib)	8178.0	62.6
Pasta 4 [31] (Seal)	2495.0	205.2
Rubato 128S [43]	15042.7	9208.4
ChaCha12	59538.0	8.6
ChaCha12 (4T)	17511.0	29.2
ChaCha20	92660.7	5.5
ChaCha20 (4T)	25780.7	19.9

6   Conclusion

In this article, we presented a new transciphering method using ChaCha, a standard and well-established cipher. We developed optimizations to lower the execution times of the homomorphic evaluation, proposing techniques to use message space with less bits than natural implementations would require, thus reducing the number of bootstrappings by nearly half. This led to a major reduction in execution times, and a substancial increase in throughput. With this work, we intended to raise the discussion on studying and implementing transciphering methods that are post-quantum secure, since almost all previous literature on this topic seeks to improve execution times of existing implementations or to implement new methods, but none considering the rising importance of using constructions that are post-quantum secure.

A   Results for ChaCha8 and Comparison with AES-128

While the focus of this work is to show the performance of quantum resistant transciphering protocols, we consider that it is also beneficial for academic community to know how ChaCha would compare with transciphering based on AES-128, thus, not quantum secure, since that is the scenario considered in all previous works. For this, we used ChaCha8, i.e., ChaCha with 256-bit key but reduced to 8 rounds. Although, as discussed in Sect. 2.4, ChaCha8 still offers 256 bits of security, thus, giving us a large security margin compared to 128 bits.

As in Sect. 5, we run all the experiments on a `r7i.metal-24xl` instance on AWS (Intel Xeon Platinum 8488C at 2.4 GHz/3.8 GHz-boost and 768 GB of memory, supporting up to with 96 threads). Our multi-thread versions of homomorphic ChaCha8 use 4 threads. We compare our results to previous works in the tables below. One can see that considering negligible failure probability (FP), around 2^{-128}, our best single thread latency is about 19 times lower and our best throughput is about 62 times higher. For higher FP, about 2^{-40}, our best single thread latency is about 6.6 times lower and our best throughput is about 26 times higher (Table 5 and 6).

Table 5. Homomorphic evaluation results for 128-bit security and negligible ($\approx 2^{-128}$) probability of failure. Latency in seconds; Throughput in bits per second.

Cipher	Single-thread		Multi-thread	
	Latency	Throughput	Latency	Throughput
AES-128 (Hippogryph [9])	784.4	0.2	42.3	3.0
ChaCha8 (2 LUT)	76.7	6.7	24.6	20.8
ChaCha8 (3 LUT)	41.0	12.5	13.4	38.3

Table 6. Homomorphic evaluation results for higher probability of failure ($\approx 2^{-40}$). Latency in seconds; Throughput in bits per second.

Cipher	Single-thread		Multi-thread	
	Latency	Throughput	Latency	Throughput
AES-128 [13]	259.9	0.5	126.2	1.0
ChaCha8 (2 LUT)	50.4	10.2	15.6	32.8
ChaCha8 (3 LUT)	39.4	13.0	14.1	36.4

References

1. Al Badawi, A., et al.: OpenFHE: open-source fully homomorphic encryption library. In: Proceedings of the 10th Workshop on Encrypted Computing & Applied Homomorphic Cryptography, pp. 53–63. WAHC'22, New York, NY, USA. Association for Computing Machinery (2022). https://doi.org/10.1145/3560827.3563379
2. Albrecht, M.R., Player, R., Scott, S.: On the concrete hardness of learning with errors. J. Math. Cryptol. **9**(3), 169–203 (2015). https://doi.org/10.1515/jmc-2015-0016
3. Albrecht, M.R., Rechberger, C., Schneider, T., Tiessen, T., Zohner, M.: Ciphers for MPC and FHE. In: Oswald, E., Fischlin, M. (eds.) Advances in Cryptology – EUROCRYPT 2015, Part I. LNCS, vol. 9056, pp. 430–454. Springer, Heidelberg (2015). https://doi.org/10.1007/978-3-662-46800-5_17
4. Aranha, D.F., Guimarães, A., Hoffmann, C., Méaux, P.: Secure and efficient transciphering for FHE-based MPC. IACR Trans. Cryptographic Hardware Embedded Syst. **2025**(3), 745–780 (2025). https://doi.org/10.46586/tches.v2025.i3.745-780
5. Aumasson, J.P.: Too much crypto. Cryptology ePrint Archive, Report 2019/1492 (2019), https://eprint.iacr.org/2019/1492
6. Aumasson, J.P., Fischer, S., Khazaei, S., Meier, W., Rechberger, C.: New features of Latin dances: analysis of Salsa, ChaCha, and Rumba. In: Nyberg, K. (ed.) FSE 2008. LNCS, vol. 5086, pp. 470–488. Springer, Heidelberg (2008). https://doi.org/10.1007/978-3-540-71039-4_30
7. Balenbois, T., Orfila, J.B., Smart, N.: Trivial transciphering with trivium and TFHE. In: Proceedings of the 11th Workshop on Encrypted Computing & Applied Homomorphic Cryptography. WAHC '23, New York, NY, USA, pp. 69–78. Association for Computing Machinery (2023). https://doi.org/10.1145/3605759.3625255
8. Baudrin, J., et al.: Transistor: a TFHE-friendly stream cipher. In: Kalai, Y.T., Kamara, S.F. (eds.) Advances in Cryptology – CRYPTO 2025, Part V. LNCS, vol. 16004, pp. 530–565. Springer, Cham (2025). https://doi.org/10.1007/978-3-032-01901-1_17
9. Belaïd, S., Bon, N., Boudguiga, A., Sirdey, R., Trama, D., Ye, N.: Further improvements in AES execution over TFHE. IACR Commun. Cryptol. (CiC) **2**(1), 39 (2025). https://doi.org/10.62056/ahmp-4tw9
10. Bernstein, D.J.: ChaCha, a variant of Salsa20. Workshop Record of SASC 2008: The State of the Art of Stream Ciphers (2008). https://cr.yp.to/chacha/chacha-20080128.pdf
11. Bernstein, D.J.: The Salsa20 family of stream ciphers. In: Robshaw, M., Billet, O. (eds.) New Stream Cipher Designs, LNCS, vol. 4986, pp. 84–97. Springer, Heidelberg (2008). https://doi.org/10.1007/978-3-540-68351-3_7

12. Bertoni, G., Daemen, J., Peeters, M., Assche, G.V.: Keccak. In: Advances in Cryptology - EUROCRYPT 2013. LNCS, vol. 7881, pp. 313–314. Springer, Heidelberg (2013). https://doi.org/10.1007/978-3-642-38348-9_19, https://www.iacr.org/archive/eurocrypt2013/78810311/78810311.pdf, invited paper

13. Bon, N., Pointcheval, D., Rivain, M.: Optimized homomorphic evaluation of Boolean functions. IACR Trans. Cryptographic Hardware Embedded Syst. **2024**(3), 302–341 (2024). https://doi.org/10.46586/tches.v2024.i3.302-341

14. Bonte, C., Iliashenko, I., Park, J., Pereira, H.V.L., Smart, N.P.: FINAL: faster FHE instantiated with NTRU and LWE. In: Agrawal, S., Lin, D. (eds.) ASIACRYPT 2022, Part II. LNCS, vol. 13792, pp. 188–215. Springer, Cham (2022). https://doi.org/10.1007/978-3-031-22966-4_7

15. Bonte, C., Nicolas, G., Smart, N.P.: Complex elections via threshold (fully) homomorphic encryption. Cryptology ePrint Archive, Paper 2025/1482 (2025). https://eprint.iacr.org/2025/1482

16. Boura, C., Gama, N., Georgieva, M., Jetchev, D.: Simulating homomorphic evaluation of deep learning predictions. Cryptology ePrint Archive, Report 2019/591 (2019). https://eprint.iacr.org/2019/591

17. Bourse, F., Sanders, O., Traoré, J.: Improved secure integer comparison via homomorphic encryption. In: Jarecki, S. (ed.) CT-RSA 2020. LNCS, vol. 12006, pp. 391–416. Springer, Cham (2020). https://doi.org/10.1007/978-3-030-40186-3_17

18. Brakerski, Z., Gentry, C., Vaikuntanathan, V.: (Leveled) fully homomorphic encryption without bootstrapping. In: Goldwasser, S. (ed.) ITCS 2012: 3rd Innovations in Theoretical Computer Science, Cambridge, MA, USA, pp. 309–325. Association for Computing Machinery (2012). https://doi.org/10.1145/2090236.2090262

19. Canteaut, A., et al.: Stream ciphers: a practical solution for efficient homomorphic-ciphertext compression. In: Peyrin, T. (ed.) FSE 2016. LNCS, vol. 9783, pp. 313–333. Springer, Heidelberg (2016). https://doi.org/10.1007/978-3-662-52993-5_16

20. Carpov, S., Izabachène, M., Mollimard, V.: New techniques for multi-value input homomorphic evaluation and applications. In: Matsui, M. (ed.) CT-RSA 2019. LNCS, vol. 11405, pp. 106–126. Springer, Cham (2019). https://doi.org/10.1007/978-3-030-12612-4_6

21. Chacal, N., Guimarães, A., Martinelli, A., Méaux, P., Poussier, R.: Nostalgia cipher: can filtered LFSRs be secure again? An application to hybrid homomorphic encryption with Sub-50 ms Latency. IACR Trans. Symmetric Cryptol. **2025**(4), 1–30 (Dec 2025). https://doi.org/10.46586/tosc.v2025.i4.1-30, https://tosc.iacr.org/index.php/ToSC/article/view/12609

22. Chen, H., Dai, W., Kim, M., Song, Y.: Efficient multi-key homomorphic encryption with packed ciphertexts with application to oblivious neural network inference. In: Cavallaro, L., Kinder, J., Wang, X., Katz, J. (eds.) ACM CCS 2019: 26th Conference on Computer and Communications Security, London, UK, pp. 395–412. ACM Press (2019). https://doi.org/10.1145/3319535.3363207

23. Cheon, J.H., Choe, H., Passelègue, A., Stehlé, D., Suvanto, E.: Attacks against the IND-CPA^{D} security of exact FHE schemes. In: Luo, B., Liao, X., Xu, J., Kirda, E., Lie, D. (eds.) ACM CCS 2024: 31st Conference on Computer and Communications Security, Salt Lake City, UT, USA, pp. 2505–2519. ACM Press (2024). https://doi.org/10.1145/3658644.3690341

24. Chillotti, I., Gama, N., Georgieva, M., Izabachène, M.: Faster fully homomorphic encryption: Bootstrapping in less than 0.1 seconds. In: Cheon, J.H., Takagi, T. (eds.) Advances in Cryptology – ASIACRYPT 2016, Part I. LNCS, vol. 10031, pp. 3–33. Springer Heidelberg (2016). https://doi.org/10.1007/978-3-662-53887-6_1

25. Chillotti, I., Gama, N., Georgieva, M., Izabachène, M.: TFHE: Fast fully homomorphic encryption over the torus. J. Cryptol. **33**(1), 34–91 (2020). https://doi.org/10.1007/s00145-019-09319-x

26. Chillotti, I., Ligier, D., Orfila, J.B., Tap, S.: Improved programmable bootstrapping with larger precision and efficient arithmetic circuits for TFHE. In: Tibouchi, M., Wang, H. (eds.) Advances in Cryptology – ASIACRYPT 2021, Part III. LNCS, vol. 13092, pp. 670–699. Springer, Cham (2021). https://doi.org/10.1007/978-3-030-92078-4_23

27. Cho, M., Chung, W., Ha, J., Lee, J., Oh, E.G., Son, M.: FRAST: TFHE-friendly cipher based on random S-boxes. IACR Trans. Symmetric Cryptol. **2024**(3), 1–43 (2024). https://doi.org/10.46586/tosc.v2024.i3.1-43

28. Cong, K., Das, D., Park, J., Pereira, H.V.: Sortinghat: Efficient private decision tree evaluation via homomorphic encryption and transciphering. In: Proceedings of the 2022 ACM SIGSAC Conference on Computer and Communications Security. CCS '22, New York, NY, USA, pp. 563–577. Association for Computing Machinery (2022). https://doi.org/10.1145/3548606.3560702

29. Cosseron, O., Hoffmann, C., Méaux, P., Standaert, F.X.: Towards case-optimized hybrid homomorphic encryption - featuring the Elisabeth stream cipher. In: Agrawal, S., Lin, D. (eds.) ASIACRYPT 2022, Part III. LNCS, vol. 13793, pp. 32–67. Springer, Cham (2022). https://doi.org/10.1007/978-3-031-22969-5_2

30. Dobraunig, C., et al.: Rasta: a cipher with low ANDdepth and few ANDs per bit. In: Shacham, H., Boldyreva, A. (eds.) CRYPTO 2018, Part I. LNCS, vol. 10991, pp. 662–692. Springer, Cham (2018). https://doi.org/10.1007/978-3-319-96884-1_22

31. Dobraunig, C., Grassi, L., Helminger, L., Rechberger, C., Schofnegger, M., Walch, R.: Pasta: a case for hybrid homomorphic encryption. IACR Trans. Cryptographic Hardware Embedded Syst. **2023**(3), 30–73 (2023). https://doi.org/10.46586/tches.v2023.i3.30-73

32. Ducas, L., Micciancio, D.: FHEW: bootstrapping homomorphic encryption in less than a second. In: Oswald, E., Fischlin, M. (eds.) EUROCRYPT 2015, Part I. LNCS, vol. 9056, pp. 617–640. Springer, Heidelberg (2015). https://doi.org/10.1007/978-3-662-46800-5_24

33. Flórez-Gutiérrez, A., Todo, Y.: Improved cryptanalysis of ChaCha: beating PNBs with bit puncturing. In: Fehr, S., Fouque, P.A. (eds.) EUROCRYPT 2025, Part I. LNCS, vol. 15601, pp. 427–457. Springer, Cham (2024). https://doi.org/10.1007/978-3-031-91107-1_15

34. Gao, Y., Wang, J., Hu, H., He, B.: Attacking ECDSA with nonce leakage by lattice sieving: bridging the gap with Fourier analysis-based attacks. In: Chung, K.M., Sasaki, Y. (eds.) ASIACRYPT 2024, Part VIII. LNCS, vol. 15491, pp. 3–34. Springer, Singapore (2024). https://doi.org/10.1007/978-981-96-0944-4_1

35. Gentry, C.: A fully homomorphic encryption scheme. Ph.D. thesis, Stanford University (2009). crypto.stanford.edu/craig

36. Gentry, C., Halevi, S., Smart, N.P.: Homomorphic evaluation of the AES circuit. In: Safavi-Naini, R., Canetti, R. (eds.) CRYPTO 2012. LNCS, vol. 7417, pp. 850–867. Springer, Heidelberg (2012). https://doi.org/10.1007/978-3-642-32009-5_49

37. Ghafoori, N., Miyaji, A.: Higher-order differential-linear cryptanalysis of ChaCha stream cipher. IEEE Access **12**, 13386–13399 (2024). https://doi.org/10.1109/ACCESS.2024.3356868

38. Gilbert, H., Boissier, R.H., Jean, J., Reinhard, J.R.: Cryptanalysis of Elisabeth-4. In: Guo, J., Steinfeld, R. (eds.) ASIACRYPT 2023, Part III. LNCS, vol. 14440, pp. 256–284. Springer, Singapore (2023). https://doi.org/10.1007/978-981-99-8727-6_9

39. Grassi, L., Ayala, I.M., Hovd, M.N., Øygarden, M., Raddum, H., Wang, Q.: Cryptanalysis of symmetric primitives over rings and a key recovery attack on rubato. In: Handschuh, H., Lysyanskaya, A. (eds.) CRYPTO 2023, Part III. LNCS, vol. 14083, pp. 305–339. Springer, Cham (2023). https://doi.org/10.1007/978-3-031-38548-3_11
40. Guimarães, A., Borin, E., Aranha, D.F.: Revisiting the functional bootstrap in TFHE. IACR Trans. Cryptographic Hardware Embedded Syst. **2021**(2), 229–253 (2021). https://doi.org/10.46586/tches.v2021.i2.229-253, https://tches.iacr.org/index.php/TCHES/article/view/8793
41. Guimarães, A., Borin, E., Aranha, D.F.: MOSFHET: optimized software for FHE over the Torus. J. Cryptographic Eng. (2024). https://doi.org/10.1007/s13389-024-00359-z
42. Ha, J., et al.: Masta: an he-friendly cipher using modular arithmetic. IEEE Access **8**, 194741–194751 (2020). https://doi.org/10.1109/ACCESS.2020.3033564
43. Ha, J., Kim, S., Lee, B., Lee, J., Son, M.: Rubato: noisy ciphers for approximate homomorphic encryption. In: Dunkelman, O., Dziembowski, S. (eds.) EUROCRYPT 2022, Part I. LNCS, vol. 13275, pp. 581–610. Springer, Cham (2022). https://doi.org/10.1007/978-3-031-06944-4_20
44. Hebborn, P., Leander, G.: Dasta – alternative linear layer for Rasta. IACR Transactions on Symmetric Cryptology **2020**(3), 46–86 (2020). https://doi.org/10.13154/tosc.v2020.i3.46-86
45. Hoffmann, C., Méaux, P., Standaert, F.X.: The patching landscape of elisabeth-4 and the mixed filter permutator paradigm. In: Chattopadhyay, A., Bhasin, S., Picek, S., Rebeiro, C. (eds.) INDOCRYPT 2023, Part I. LNCS, vol. 14459, pp. 134–156. Springer, Cham (2023). https://doi.org/10.1007/978-3-031-56232-7_7
46. Liu, F., Anand, R., Wang, L., Meier, W., Isobe, T.: Coefficient grouping: Breaking chaghri and more. In: Hazay, C., Stam, M. (eds.) EUROCRYPT 2023, Part IV. LNCS, vol. 14007, pp. 287–317. Springer, Cham (2023). https://doi.org/10.1007/978-3-031-30634-1_10
47. Liu, F., Isobe, T., Meier, W.: Cryptanalysis of full LowMC and LowMC-M with algebraic techniques. In: Malkin, T., Peikert, C. (eds.) Advances in Cryptology – CRYPTO 2021, Part III. LNCS, vol. 12827, pp. 368–401. Springer, Cham (2021). https://doi.org/10.1007/978-3-030-84252-9_13
48. Liu, F., Meier, W., Sarkar, S., Isobe, T.: New low-memory algebraic attacks on LowMC in the Picnic setting. IACR Transactions on Symmetric Cryptology **2022**(3), 102–122 (2022). https://doi.org/10.46586/tosc.v2022.i3.102-122
49. Liu, F., Sarkar, S., Meier, W., Isobe, T.: Algebraic attacks on RASTA and DASTA using low-degree equations. In: Tibouchi, M., Wang, H. (eds.) ASIACRYPT 2021, Part I. LNCS, vol. 13090, pp. 214–240. Springer, Cham (2021). https://doi.org/10.1007/978-3-030-92062-3_8
50. Méaux, P., Carlet, C., Journault, A., Standaert, F.X.: Improved filter permutators for efficient FHE: better instances and implementations. In: Hao, F., Ruj, S., Sen Gupta, S. (eds.) Progress in Cryptology - INDOCRYPT 2019. LNCS, vol. 11898, pp. 68–91. Springer, Cham (2019). https://doi.org/10.1007/978-3-030-35423-7_4
51. Méaux, P., Journault, A., Standaert, F.X., Carlet, C.: Towards stream ciphers for efficient FHE with low-noise ciphertexts. In: Fischlin, M., Coron, J.S. (eds.) EUROCRYPT 2016, Part I. LNCS, vol. 9665, pp. 311–343. Springer, Heidelberg (2016). https://doi.org/10.1007/978-3-662-49890-3_13
52. Méaux, P., Park, J., Pereira, H.V.L.: Towards practical transciphering for FHE with setup independent of the plaintext space. IACR Commun. Cryptol. (CiC) **1**(1), 20 (2024). https://doi.org/10.62056/anxrxrxqi

53. Mella, S., Susella, R.: On the homomorphic computation of symmetric cryptographic primitives. In: Stam, M. (ed.) IMACC 2013. LNCS, vol. 8308, pp. 28–44. Springer, Heidelberg (2013). https://doi.org/10.1007/978-3-642-45239-0_3

54. Naehrig, M., Lauter, K., Vaikuntanathan, V.: Can homomorphic encryption be practical? In: Proceedings of the 3rd ACM Workshop on Cloud Computing Security Workshop. CCSW '11, New York, NY, USA, pp. 113–124. Association for Computing Machinery (2011). https://doi.org/10.1145/2046660.2046682, https://doi.org/10.1145/2046660.2046682

55. National Institute of Standards and Technology: Secure hash standard (shs). Technical report FIPS PUB 180-4, U.S. Department of Commerce, Gaithersburg, MD (2015). https://nvlpubs.nist.gov/nistpubs/FIPS/NIST.FIPS.180-4.pdf. Accessed 11 Jul 2025

56. Nir, Y., Langley, A.: ChaCha20 and Poly1305 for IETF Protocols. RFC 7539 (2015). https://doi.org/10.17487/RFC7539. https://www.rfc-editor.org/info/rfc7539

57. Niu, C., et al.: SoK: FHE-friendly symmetric ciphers and transciphering. IACR Trans. Cryptographic Hardware Embedded Syst. **2025**(3), 583–613 (2025). https://doi.org/10.46586/tches.v2025.i3.583-613, https://tches.iacr.org/index.php/TCHES/article/view/12228

58. Pereira, H.V.L.: Bootstrapping fully homomorphic encryption over the integers in less than one second. In: Garay, J. (ed.) PKC 2021, Part I. LNCS, vol. 12710, pp. 331–359. Springer, Cham (2021). https://doi.org/10.1007/978-3-030-75245-3_13

59. Rescorla, E.: The Transport Layer Security (TLS) Protocol Version 1.3. RFC 8446 (2018). https://doi.org/10.17487/RFC8446, https://www.rfc-editor.org/info/rfc8446

60. Thakur, I., Karmakar, A., Li, C., Preneel, B.: A survey on transciphering and symmetric ciphers for homomorphic encryption. Cryptology ePrint Archive, Report 2025/093 (2025). https://eprint.iacr.org/2025/093

61. Wei, B., Lu, X., Wang, R., Liu, K., Li, Z., Wang, K.: Thunderbird: efficient homomorphic evaluation of symmetric ciphers in 3GPP by combining two modes of TFHE. IACR Trans. Cryptographic Hardware Embedded Syst. **2024**(3), 530–573 (2024). https://doi.org/10.46586/tches.v2024.i3.530-573

62. Wei, B., Wang, R., Li, Z., Liu, Q., Lu, X.: Fregata: faster homomorphic evaluation of AES via TFHE. In: Athanasopoulos, E., Mennink, B. (eds.) ISC 2023. LNCS, vol. 14411, pp. 392–412. Springer, Cham (2023). https://doi.org/10.1007/978-3-031-49187-0_20

63. Zama: TFHE-rs: A Pure Rust Implementation of the TFHE Scheme for Boolean and Integer Arithmetics Over Encrypted Data (2022). https://github.com/zama-ai/tfhe-rs

64. Zhang, C., Li, S., Xia, J., Wang, W., Yan, F., Liu, Y.: BatchCrypt: efficient homomorphic encryption for Cross-Silo federated learning. In: 2020 USENIX Annual Technical Conference (USENIX ATC 20), pp. 493–506. USENIX Association (2020). https://www.usenix.org/conference/atc20/presentation/zhang-chengliang

65. Zuber, M., Sirdey, R.: Efficient homomorphic evaluation of k-NN classifiers. In: Proceedings on Privacy Enhancing Technologies 2021, pp. 111–129 (2021)

Code-Based Attacks

Recursion Enabled: Improved Cryptanalysis of the Permuted Kernel Problem

Alessandro Budroni[1]($\boxtimes$) , Marco Defranceschi[1,2] , and Federico Pintore[2]

[1] Technology Innovation Institute, Abu Dhabi, UAE
`{alessandro.budroni,marco.defranceschi}@tii.ae`
[2] University of Trento, Trento, Italy
`federico.pintore@unitn.it`

Abstract. The Permuted Kernel Problem (PKP) is a computational problem for linear codes over finite fields that has emerged as a promising hard problem for constructing post-quantum cryptographic schemes, with its main application found in the digital signature scheme PERK, submitted to the NIST standardization process for quantum-secure additional signatures. Upon reviewing the first version of PERK, NIST recommended further research on the concrete complexity of PKP. In this work, we follow this recommendation and investigate algorithmic improvements to the known methods for solving PKP. Specifically, we build upon the state-of-the-art work of Santini, Baldi, and Chiaraluce (IEEE Trans. Inf. Theory, 2024), and introduce a new algorithm that outperforms it over a wide range of parameters, yielding double-digit bit reductions in estimated complexity on representative instances. Nevertheless, our analysis shows that these improvements do not affect the parameter-set choices in PERK, thereby reinforcing confidence in its security.

Keywords: Permuted Kernel Problem · Code-based Cryptography · Post-quantum Cryptography · PERK

1 Introduction

Following Shor's seminal work [27], which introduced a quantum algorithm capable of solving the hard mathematical problems underlying much of classical cryptography in polynomial time, the cryptographic community began to seek alternative hardness assumptions that would withstand quantum adversaries. This effort gave birth to the field of Post-quantum Cryptography.

In 2017, the National Institute of Standards and Technology (NIST) launched a call for post-quantum schemes [18]. Three out of the five schemes selected

This work was conducted during Marco Defranceschi's internship at the Technology Innovation Institute, Abu Dhabi.

M. Bardet and R. Niederhagen (Eds.): PQCrypto 2026, LNCS 16492, pp. 207–241, 2026.
https://doi.org/10.1007/978-3-032-22698-3_7

for standardization are based on assumptions on algebraic lattices [17,21,25], reflecting the maturity reached by cryptosystems based on this family of problems. However, with the subsequent NIST "on-ramp" call for additional digital signature [19], NIST emphasized the importance of diversifying beyond lattices, encouraging the study of alternative quantum-resistant assumptions. In this context, the Permuted Kernel Problem (PKP), originally introduced by Shamir in 1989 [26] to construct an identification scheme, has resurfaced as a promising candidate for building digital signatures. Among the proposals submitted to the NIST "on-ramp" call for additional signatures, PERK [1] is a digital signature scheme built on the hardness of PKP. PERK successfully advanced through the first evaluation phase and is now in the second round of the NIST process for the selection of additional signatures to standardize.

Motivation and Contribution. In its report on the first round of the additional signatures selection process, where candidates advancing to the second round are enumerated [3, Sec. 3.6], NIST explicitly highlighted the need for further research on the concrete complexity of PKP, underlining the importance of assessing the long-term security of the parameter choice in PERK. In this work, we take up this challenge and present new advances in the cryptanalysis of PKP, focusing on its concrete complexity. Specifically, we introduce a new algorithm that improves upon the state of the art across several parameter sets.

Related Work. Shamir was the first one to construct a cryptographic scheme based on PKP [26]. More recently, a series of digital signature schemes relying on the hardness of PKP have been proposed [4,7,8,10,11]. However, the most prominent instantiation is represented by PERK [1]. Specifically, PERK version 1.0, submitted to the first round of the NIST process for additional signatures, relies on a variant of PKP that can nonetheless be solved by any algorithm solving the standard PKP. More recently, version 2.1 of PERK has been made public [2], this time relying on the pure PKP over a finite field of characteristic two.

Shamir was also the first one to provide some considerations on the security of PKP [26]. In particular, he observed that a reduction from the 3-Partition problem implies that the mono-dimensional version of PKP is NP-complete [12]. The NP-completeness of the multi-dimensional case was later proved in [6]. Since Shamir's original work, several works have examined the hardness of PKP [5,13,14,16,20], progressively refining the understanding of the computational complexity of the problem. More recently, Koussa, Macario-Rat and Patarin (KMP) [15] proposed a *meet-in-the-middle* algorithm, which was subsequently improved by Santini, Baldi, and Chiaraluce (SBC) [23,24] through the introduction of a preprocessing (*filtering*) step. The latter currently represents the state of the art in solving PKP.

1.1 Overview of the Contribution

The Permuted Kernel Problem. Informally, the Permuted Kernel Problem (PKP) consists in finding a permutation π such that

$$\pi(\vec{V})\vec{H}^\top = \vec{0},$$

where $\vec{H} \in \mathbb{F}_q^{r\times n}$ and $\vec{V} \in \mathbb{F}_q^{\ell\times n}$ are public matrices. An equivalent inhomogeneous version of the problem, denoted by IPKP, asks for a permutation π satisfying

$$\pi(\vec{V})\vec{H}^\top = \vec{E}, \tag{1}$$

where $\vec{E} \in \mathbb{F}_q^{\ell\times r}$ is also public. Typically, the parameters n, r, ℓ, and q are chosen so that the permutation π is unique with high probability.

Key Contributions. In one of its subroutines, the SBC algorithm employs an Information Set Decoding (ISD) procedure to find a subcode of the code generated by $\vec{H}$ having dimension $d \leq r$ and small support $w \leq n$, that is, a subcode with a generator matrix with $n-w$ zero columns. The algorithm then performs a *meet-in-the-middle* style routine over this subcode to filter potential candidates for the permutation π.

Our first algorithmic improvement stems from the observation that, by disregarding the zero columns in the generator matrix of the subcode with support size w, one obtains a subinstance of IPKP where the corresponding public matrix $\vec{\bar{H}}$ has size $d \times w$. In other words, the *filtering* subroutine of SBC can be interpreted as solving smaller IPKP instances. This suggests that SBC could be applied recursively, since SBC solves IPKP (and not only PKP). However, this recursive approach is generally inefficient or inapplicable unless one considers another key observation of this work, that is, the dual form of Eq. (1). Indeed, we notice that

$$\pi^{-1}(\vec{H})\vec{V}^\top = \vec{E}^\top,$$

can be seen as an instance of IPKP with secret permutation π^{-1} (the inverse of π), and we find that applying SBC recursively leads to improvements only when the subinstance is considered in its dual version. Moreover, enabling such recursion is non-trivial as the subinstance may admit no solution or multiple solutions. To address this, we revisited and extended SBC, introducing several subtle modifications to make recursive application feasible.

Building on the observations above, we introduce a new algorithm that either outperforms or matches SBC. Specifically, we find improvements for parameter sets where q is relatively small. Most importantly, depending on the code rate $R := r/n$, our algorithm is faster also for very small values of ℓ, that is the typical setting in cryptographic applications. As an example, for $(n, r, \ell, q) = (112, 54, 3, 16)$, our algorithm reduces the estimated complexity from 255 to 243 bits, corresponding to an improvement of 12 bits. Similarly, for $(n, r, \ell, q) = (118, 83, 1, 223)$, we observe a reduction from 199 to 189 bits, i.e., an improvement of 10 bits.

Implications for PERK. Despite significantly improving upon SBC for a wide range of parameters, our newly proposed algorithm does not affect the security estimates of either PERK 1.0 or PERK 2.1. In the former case, the parameter sets employ a very large field size q, which prevents our algorithmic improvements from being effective. In the latter, the combination of the code rate R and the choice $\ell = 1$ places the parameters in a regime where SBC remains the optimal solving algorithm.

Artifacts. We make our scripts used to compute the complexities publicly available [9].

Organization. In Sect. 2, we provide the necessary preliminaries and background. Section 3 reviews the KMP and SBC algorithms, serving as essential background for introducing our contribution in Sect. 4. Finally, we analyze our results and evaluate their impact on PERK in Sect. 5.

2   Preliminaries

Notation. Let $n \in \mathbb{N}^*$. We define $[n] := \{1, \ldots, n\}$. If $I \subseteq [n]$, we denote by $\neg_n I$ its complementary $[n] \setminus I$. We use capital bold letters for matrices and lowercase bold letters for vectors. When the base field is clear from the context, the $n \times n$ identity matrix is denoted by $\vec{I}_n$. All vectors are row-vectors if not stated otherwise. Given a vector $\vec{v}$ we denote by $\vec{v}_i$ its i-th entry. Similarly, for an $m \times n$ matrix $\vec{A}$, with $m \in \mathbb{N}^*$, we denote its j-th column by $\vec{a}_j$ and its entry in the i-th row and j-th column by $\vec{a}_{i,j}$. Given a set of indices $I \subseteq [n]$, $\vec{v}_I$ is the projection of the length-n vector $\vec{v}$ onto the indices in I, i.e. $\vec{v}_I = (\vec{v}_i)_{i \in I}$. We extend this to matrices by letting $\vec{A}_I$ be the submatrix formed by the columns of $\vec{A}$ indexed by I. Similarly, we denote by $\vec{A}^J$ the submatrix obtained by taking the rows of $\vec{A}$ indexed by J, if $J \subseteq [m]$. The transpose of a matrix $\vec{A}$ is denoted by $\vec{A}^\top$.

Let $\mathbb{F}_q$ be a finite field of size q, with q a prime power. We denote by $\mathsf{GL}_n(\mathbb{F}_q)$ the linear group of invertible $n \times n$ matrices over $\mathbb{F}_q$ and by $\mathsf{GL}_{k,n}(\mathbb{F}_q)$ the set of $k \times n$ (with $k \leq n$) matrices over $\mathbb{F}_q$ with full rank k.

We denote by $\mathsf{Sym}(n)$ the set of all permutations of $[n]$. For a permutation $\pi \in \mathsf{Sym}(n)$ and $\vec{A} \in \mathbb{F}_q^{m \times n}$, we write $\pi(\vec{A})$ to denote the matrix obtained by permuting the columns of $\vec{A}$ according to π, that is the matrix $\vec{A}\vec{P}$ where $\vec{P} \in \mathbb{F}_q^{n \times n}$ is the permutation matrix associated to π.

Given a matrix $\vec{A} \in \mathsf{GL}_{k,n}(\mathbb{F}_q)$ we say that a set of indices $I \subseteq [n]$ with cardinality k is an information set for $\vec{A}$ if $\vec{A}_I$ is invertible. When this is the case, we denote by $\mathsf{RREF}_I(\vec{A})$ the *Row Reduced Echelon Form* of $\vec{A}$ w.r.t. to the set I, that is $\vec{A}_I^{-1}\vec{A}$. In addition, we denote by $\mathsf{RREF}^*_I(\vec{A})$ the pair composed of $\mathsf{RREF}_I(\vec{A})$ and the matrix $\vec{A}_I^{-1}$.

For a matrix $\vec{A}$ with n columns and a non-zero natural number $x \leq n$, we define $\mathcal{S}_x(\vec{A})$ as the set of all matrices with x columns, each of them picked from those of $\vec{A}$. It is easy to see that, if $\vec{A}$ has no repeated columns (we show in

Sect. 4.2 that this might not be always the case), $|\mathcal{S}_x(\vec{A})| = \frac{n!}{(n-x)!}$. We call $\bar{\mathcal{S}}_x(\vec{A})$ the set obtained by identifying elements in $\mathcal{S}_x(\vec{A})$ up to column permutation, that is, the set of all the subsets of x columns of $\vec{A}$. Therefore, $|\bar{\mathcal{S}}_x(\vec{A})| = \frac{|\mathcal{S}_x(\vec{A})|}{x!} = \binom{n}{x}$.

With an abuse of notation, for two matrices $\vec{A} \in \mathbb{F}_q^{m \times n}$ and $\vec{B} \in \mathbb{F}_q^{n \times \ell}$ we say that $\vec{B} \in \mathsf{ker}(\vec{A})$ if $\vec{A}\vec{B} = \vec{0}$.

Finally, we say that an event occurs with "high probability" if it happens with probability $1 - o(1)$.

Linear Codes. An $[n, k]$-linear code $\mathcal{C}$ over a finite field $\mathbb{F}_q$ is a subspace, of dimension k, of $\mathbb{F}_q^n$. $\mathcal{C}$ can be represented via a basis $\vec{G} \in \mathbb{F}_q^{k \times n}$, called *generator matrix*, or by a *parity-check matrix* $\vec{H} \in \mathbb{F}_q^{n-k \times n}$ satisfying $\vec{H}\vec{c}^\top = \vec{0} \Leftrightarrow \vec{c} \in \mathcal{C}$. The linear code generated by (the rows of) $\vec{H}$ is called the dual code of $\mathcal{C}$ and is denoted by $\mathcal{C}^\perp$. We refer to n as the *length* of $\mathcal{C}$ and to the quantity $R := k/n$ as the *code rate*. Given a codeword $\vec{c} \in \mathcal{C}$, we define its support as the set of indices of its nonzero entries, i.e. $\mathrm{Supp}(\vec{c}) := \{i \in [n] : \vec{c}_i \neq 0\}$. We also define the support of a linear code $\mathcal{C}$ as the union of the supports of its codewords, that is $\mathrm{Supp}(\mathcal{C}) := \{i \in [n] : \exists\, \vec{c} \in \mathcal{C} \text{ s.t. } \vec{c}_i \neq 0\}$. The Hamming weight $\mathrm{wt}(\vec{c}) := |\mathrm{Supp}(\vec{c})|$ of $\vec{c}$ is the size of its support.
A subspace $\mathcal{C}'$ of a linear code $\mathcal{C}$ over $\mathbb{F}_q$ is said to be a subcode of $\mathcal{C}$. If $\mathcal{C}$ has dimension k, the number of its subcodes having dimension $k' \leq k$ is given by $\begin{bmatrix} k \\ k' \end{bmatrix}_q = \prod_{i=0}^{k'-1} \frac{1-q^{k-1}}{1-q^{i+1}}$. In our complexity estimates, we make use of the approximation used in [24], i.e.

$$\frac{\begin{bmatrix} \omega n \\ d \end{bmatrix}_q}{\begin{bmatrix} n \\ d \end{bmatrix}_q} \approx q^{-d(1-\omega)n} \tag{2}$$

for $d \in \mathbb{N}$ and $\omega \in [0, 1]$.

Counting the Number of Operations. Coherently with the PKP literature, in our complexity analysis we consider as elementary operations both matrix multiplications and list operations. Therefore, when we say "operations", we refer to such operations and not to finite-field additions/multiplications.

Subcodes with Small Support. Given a $[n, k]$-linear code over $\mathbb{F}_q$, we follow [23, Thm. IV.1] and estimate the number of subcodes with support size $w \leq n$ and dimension $d \leq k$ with

$$N_{n,k}(w, d) = \binom{n}{w}(q^d - 1)^{w-d} \frac{\begin{bmatrix} k \\ d \end{bmatrix}_q}{\begin{bmatrix} n \\ d \end{bmatrix}_q}.$$

In [24, Prop. 2], it is shown the existence of an adaptation of Prange's ISD algorithm ([24, Alg. 3]) that takes in input a linear code $\mathcal{C} \subseteq \mathbb{F}_q^n$ of dimension k and two other integers $w, d \in \mathbb{N}$ such that $w \leq n + d - k$ and returns a subcode of $\mathcal{C}$ with dimension d and support size w. The average running time of the algorithm is

$$T_{\mathsf{ISD}}^{(d)}(n, k, w) = \mathcal{O}\left(\frac{k^3 + \binom{k}{d}}{p^{(d)}(n, k, w)} \right) \tag{3}$$

with $p^{(d)}(n,k,w) = \min\left\{ \frac{\binom{w}{d}\binom{n-w}{k-d}}{\binom{n}{k}} N_{n,k}(w,d),\ 1 \right\}$.

2.1   The Permuted Kernel Problem

We now introduce the Permuted Kernel Problem (PKP), the central object of our study. We consider it directly in its search version, that is, under the assumption that a solution exists, as is the case in the setting of PERK [1].

Definition 1 (Permuted Kernel Problem). *Let $\vec{H} \in \mathbb{F}_q^{m\times n}$ be a random matrix and $\vec{V} \in \mathbb{F}_q^{\ell\times n}$, with $\ell \leq n - m$, be a random matrix for which there exists a permutation $\pi \in \mathsf{Sym}(n)$ such that $\pi(\vec{V})\vec{H}^\top = \vec{0}$. The* Permuted Kernel Problem (PKP) *is to recover π from $\vec{H}$ and $\vec{V}$.*

With this notation, we say that a PKP instance has parameters (n, m, q, ℓ). Note that in Definition 1 a solution exists by construction. However, in the following sections, we also consider instances that may not admit any solution. In such cases, we rely on an exhaustive search approach for solving them, which allows to detect whenever no solution exists. We nevertheless continue to refer to these as "PKP instances," even if they admit no solutions.

Remark 1. In contrast to [24], we restrict from the beginning to the case $\ell \leq n - m$. We show that this is actually not a restriction. First, notice that we can consider the matrices $\vec{V}$ and $\vec{H}$ to be full rank, since if that is not the case we can obtain an equivalent instance (i.e. they admit the same solutions) by removing the redundant rows. Such instance is equivalent to the starting one because the redundant rows introduce equations that are always verified (the other direction is easy). Under the assumption of full-rank matrices, the case $\ell > n - m$ is not possible. This can be easily seen considering the kernel dimension: consider $\vec{H} \in \mathsf{GL}_{m,n}(\mathbb{F}_q)$, $\vec{V} \in \mathsf{GL}_{\ell,n}(\mathbb{F}_q)$ and $\pi \in \mathsf{Sym}(n)$ such that

$$\pi(\vec{V})\vec{H}^\top = \vec{0},$$

which is equivalent to requiring that $\vec{H}^\top \in \mathsf{ker}(\pi(\vec{V}))$. If the matrices are full-rank, we have that $\dim(\mathsf{ker}(\pi(\vec{V}))) = n - \mathsf{rank}(\pi(\vec{V})) = n - \ell$, which implies that $m \leq n - \ell$.

On the Expected Number of Solutions. If π is a solution to the instance, its corresponding subspace must be orthogonal to the one generated by the rows of $\vec{H}$. Thus, the space generated by the rows of $\pi(\vec{V})$ must lie in the orthogonal complement of the subspace generated by the rows of $\vec{H}$, which has dimension $n - m$. Therefore, the probability that a random ℓ-dimensional subspace of $\mathbb{F}_q^n$ is orthogonal to the space generated by $\vec{H}$ is $\frac{\left[\begin{smallmatrix}n-m\\\ell\end{smallmatrix}\right]_q}{\left[\begin{smallmatrix}n\\\ell\end{smallmatrix}\right]_q}$. The expected number of solutions is $n!\frac{\left[\begin{smallmatrix}n-m\\\ell\end{smallmatrix}\right]_q}{\left[\begin{smallmatrix}n\\\ell\end{smallmatrix}\right]_q}$. By putting $\omega = (1 - \frac{m}{n})$ and $d = \ell$ in Eq. (2), we can approximate this quantity with $n!q^{-\ell m}$. Coherently with the literature on PKP [15,24], we consider instances where only one solution is expected, which is guaranteed by the following conditions (see [24]):

i) $\mathsf{rank}(\vec{V}) = \ell$ and $\mathsf{rank}(\vec{H}) = m$;

ii) $\vec{V}$ and $\vec{H}$ have no repeated columns;

iii) $q^\ell \geq n$ and $q^m \geq n$;

iv) $n!\dfrac{\left[\begin{smallmatrix} n-m \\ \ell \end{smallmatrix}\right]_q}{\left[\begin{smallmatrix} n \\ \ell \end{smallmatrix}\right]_q} < 1.$

Condition iii) is necessary because, for every column of $\vec{V}$ and $\vec{H}$, there are q^ℓ and q^m possible choices, respectively. If this condition does not hold, then either $\vec{V}$ or $\vec{H}$ must contain repeated columns. Condition iv) ensures that, in expectation, there exists only one solution—namely, the one introduced by construction. We remark that, from a purely brute-force approach point of view, instances admitting a unique solution are the hardest to solve. However, this is not necessarily the case for more advanced algorithms [15,24], whose complexity might grow with the expected number of solutions. Nevertheless, this choice is conservative in our case, since our algorithm introduced in Sect. 4 significantly benefits from having smaller field sizes q, which typically occurs when multiple solutions are expected. An in-depth analysis of the number of solutions to a random PKP instance was recently given in [22].

2.2   Basic Approach to Solve PKP

We show now how to exploit the kernel dimension to reduce the computational complexity of a brute force attack on PKP, which in principle is $n!$. Before doing that, we introduce the following variant of the problem.

Definition 2 (Inhomogeneous PKP). *Let $\vec{H} \in \mathbb{F}_q^{r \times n}$ be a random matrix. Let $\vec{V} \in \mathbb{F}_q^{\ell \times n}$ and $\vec{E} \in \mathbb{F}_q^{\ell \times r}$, with $\ell \leq n - r$, be random matrices for which there exists a permutation $\pi \in \mathsf{Sym}(n)$ such that $\pi(\vec{V})\vec{H}^\top = \vec{E}$. The Inhomogeneous Permuted Kernel Problem (IPKP) is to recover π from $\vec{H}$, $\vec{V}$ and $\vec{E}$.*

Analogously as for PKP, we say that an IPKP instance has parameters (n, r, q, ℓ) and we refer to IPKP instances even in cases that may not admit any solution. For the sake of easy presentation, we also denote by $\pi(\vec{V})\vec{H}^\top = \vec{E}$ an IPKP instance defined by the matrices $\vec{H}$, $\vec{V}$ and $\vec{E}$. Moreover, we refer to IPKP instances even in cases in which the matrices are not completely random, as we will deal with instances in which the matrix $\vec{E}$ and the last row of $\vec{H}$ are fixed. We do this because our original goal is to solve a (homogeneous) PKP instance, which we show now to be equivalent to an IPKP instance with such properties.

If $\vec{H} \in \mathbb{F}_q^{m \times n}$, $\vec{V} \in \mathbb{F}_q^{\ell \times n}$ and $\pi(\vec{V})\vec{H}^\top = \vec{0}$ for some $\pi \in \mathsf{Sym}(n)$, then if we define $\vec{H}^{\mathrm{ext}} = \begin{bmatrix} \vec{H} \\ (1, \ldots, 1) \end{bmatrix}$, $\vec{E} = [\vec{0}_{\ell \times m} \ \sum_{i=1}^n \vec{v}_i]$ and $\vec{\tilde{V}} = \pi(\vec{V})$, we have that

$$\vec{\tilde{V}}\vec{H}^{\mathrm{ext}\,\top} = \left[\vec{\tilde{V}}\vec{H}^\top \ \vec{\tilde{V}} \cdot (1, \ldots, 1)^\top\right] = [\vec{0}_{\ell \times m} \ \textstyle\sum_{i=1}^n \vec{\tilde{v}}_i] = \vec{E}. \tag{4}$$

This means that $\pi \in \mathsf{Sym}(n)$ also solves the IPKP instance defined by the matrices $\vec{H}^{\mathsf{ext}}$, $\vec{V}$ and $\vec{E}$. The other direction follows because, if $\pi \in \mathsf{Sym}(n)$ satisfies Eq. (4), then it holds that $\vec{V}(\vec{H}^{\mathsf{ext}}\{1,\ldots,m\})^{\top} = \vec{E}_{\{1,\ldots,m\}} = \vec{0}_{\ell \times m}$, which is the equation defining the starting PKP instance. This is useful because we now show that to solve an $(n,r,q,\ell) - $ IPKP instance it suffices to guess the action of π on $n - r$ coordinates. The same applies to PKP. However, if we want to solve an $(n,m,q,\ell) - $ PKP instance, it is more convenient to solve the equivalent $(n,m+1,q,\ell) - $ IPKP instance, since we need to guess the action of π on one coordinate less.

From now on, we refer to $\vec{H}$ as the extended parity check matrix.

Remark 2. In the same way as above, it is also possible to extend the parity check matrix in IPKP instances. In our newly-proposed algorithm we make use of this, see, for example, Line 7 and Line 15 in Algorithm 7. Notice, however, that we can not extend the same parity check matrix more than once, since doing this would not increase the rank.

Basic Solver for IPKP. Let us consider now an (n,r,q,ℓ)-IPKP instance $(\vec{H},\vec{V},\vec{E})$ for which there exists $\pi \in \mathsf{Sym}(n)$ such that $\pi(\vec{V})\vec{H}^{\top} = \vec{E}$. If we suppose that $J = \{n - r + 1,\ldots,n\}$ is an information set for $\vec{H}$ and let $[\vec{U}\ \vec{I}_r]$, $\vec{S} = \mathsf{RREF}^*_J(\vec{H})$, then $\left[\tilde{\vec{V}}_{\neg_n J}\ \tilde{\vec{V}}_J\right](S\vec{H})^{\top} = E\vec{S}^{\top}$. This is equivalent to

$$\tilde{\vec{V}}_{\neg_n J}\vec{U}^{\top} + \tilde{\vec{V}}_J = E\vec{S}^{\top} \quad \Leftrightarrow \quad \tilde{\vec{V}}_J = E\vec{S}^{\top} - \tilde{\vec{V}}_{\neg_n J}\vec{U}^{\top}.$$

Finally, note that if J' is another information set for $\vec{H}$, it holds that

$$\tilde{\vec{V}}_{J'} = (\vec{E} - \tilde{\vec{V}}_{\neg_n J'}(\vec{H}_{\neg_n J'})^{\top})(\vec{H}_{J'})^{-\top}, \tag{5}$$

where $^{-\top}$ denotes the inverse transposal operator. The relation above provides an improved brute-force solver: the columns with indices in $\neg_n J'$ are guessed, while the others are deduced from Eq. (5). This method to solve IPKP is formalized in Algorithm 1 and has a time complexity of $\mathcal{O}(\frac{n!}{r!})$. This is obtained because the *Row-Reduced-Echelon-Form* can be computed with one elementary operation, since computing it has the same cost as a matrix multiplication (that is $\mathcal{O}(n^3)$ field operations). Therefore the cost of computing the RREF is absorbed by the $\mathcal{O}$-notation. In Algorithm 1, for the sake of easy presentation, we assume that $\{n - r + 1,\ldots,n\}$ is an information set for $\vec{H}$, but the reasoning works for every information set J by using Eq. (5).

Algorithm 1 SolveIPKP$(\vec{H}, \vec{V}, \vec{E})$

Input: $\vec{H} \in \mathbb{F}_q^{r \times n}$, $\vec{V} \in \mathbb{F}_q^{\ell \times n}$, $\vec{E} \in \mathbb{F}_q^{\ell \times r}$

Output: $\pi \in \mathsf{Sym}(n)$ s.t. $\pi(\vec{V})\vec{H}^\top = \vec{E}$

1: $[\vec{U} \ \vec{I}_r], \vec{S} \leftarrow \mathsf{RREF}^*_{\{n-r+1,\dots,n\}}(\vec{H})$
2: Initialize an empty list $\mathcal{L}$
3: **for** $\tilde{\vec{V}}_1 \in \mathcal{S}_{n-r}(\vec{V})$ **do**
4:     $\tilde{\vec{V}}_2 \leftarrow \vec{E}\vec{S}^\top - \tilde{\vec{V}}_1\vec{U}^\top$
5:     **if** $\left[\tilde{\vec{V}}_1 \ \tilde{\vec{V}}_2\right] \in \mathcal{S}_n(\vec{V})$ **then**
6:         Compute $\pi \in \mathsf{Sym}(n)$ s.t. $\left[\tilde{\vec{V}}_1 \ \tilde{\vec{V}}_2\right] = \pi(\vec{V})$
7:         **Return:** π

2.3 Working with the Dual

Consider now the following (n, r, q, ℓ)-IPKP instance.

$$\pi(\vec{V})\vec{H}^\top = \vec{E}.$$

If we take the transpose we obtain the *dual* version of the problem (notice that, if $\vec{E} = \vec{0}$, the *dual* denomination becomes proper)

$$\pi^{-1}(\vec{H})\vec{V}^\top = \vec{E}^\top. \tag{6}$$

This can be seen as an IPKP instance with parameters (n, ℓ, q, r). By means of Algorithm 1, we can solve this problem instance by guessing the action of π^{-1} on $n - \ell$ coordinates, that is with $\mathcal{O}(\frac{n!}{\ell!})$ operations. Finally note that we can extend $\vec{V}$ by adding a row of ones in the same way as for $\vec{H}$ and so the number of operations needed is $\mathcal{O}(\frac{n!}{(\ell+1)!})$.

Remark 3. As explained above, Algorithm 1 terminates in either $\mathcal{O}(\frac{n!}{r!})$ (here we consider $\vec{H}$ to have already been extended) operations or in $\mathcal{O}(\frac{n!}{(\ell+1)!})$ operations when considering the dual problem. Considering the dual problem shows that IPKP (the same applies to PKP) becomes easier as ℓ grows, since Algorithm 1 becomes faster.

The existing algorithms, that are presented in the next section, also become faster as ℓ grows, but for different reasons (their time complexity depends on ℓ in a different way). In this paper we show how increasing ℓ can affect the hardness of the problem in a more impactful way than in the existing algorithms.

3 Review of the Known Attacks to PKP

In this section, we review the main known algorithms to solve PKP. We focus in particular on the algorithms by Koussa, Macario-Rat and Patarin (KMP) [15], and Santini, Baldi and Chiaraluce (SBC) [24]. More precisely, for the KMP algorithm, we review its generalization to the multi-dimensional (i.e. $\ell > 1$) setting given in [24].

3.1 KMP Algorithm

We focus on solving an IPKP instance defined by the matrices $\vec{H} \in \mathbb{F}_q^{r \times n}$, $\vec{V} \in \mathbb{F}_q^{\ell \times n}$, $\vec{E} \in \mathbb{F}_q^{\ell \times r}$, that is, we want to find $\pi \in \mathsf{Sym}(n)$ such that $\pi(\vec{V})\vec{H}^\top = \vec{E}$. As in Sect. 2, let $\tilde{\vec{V}} = \pi(\vec{V})$. In a nutshell, the KMP algorithm performs a brute-force attack to guess the action of π on $n - r$ columns, but it does it by adopting a *meet-in-the-middle* approach, which leads to significant time-complexity improvements. More specifically, the algorithm aims at guessing the action of π on v columns, with $v > n - r$, by guessing the action on u_1 and u_2 (with $v = u_1 + u_2$) columns separately and then matching the guessed columns. Notice that this matching can be seen as a sieving phase. The optimal values for u_1, u_2 depend on the instance and so they will be two parameters of the algorithm.

Outline of the Algorithm. As in Algorithm 1, $\vec{H}$ is put in systematic form with the identity matrix on the right, that is, we are assuming that $\{n-r+1, \ldots n\}$ is an information set for $\vec{H}$, but the reasoning works for every information set. Let $\vec{H}', \vec{M} = \mathsf{RREF}^*_{\{n-r+1, \ldots n\}}(\vec{H})$. Then $\tilde{\vec{V}}\vec{H}^\top = \vec{E}$ if and only if $\tilde{\vec{V}}\vec{H}'^\top = \vec{E}\vec{M}^\top$. Let $\bar{\vec{H}} = \vec{H}'^{\{1,\ldots,\tilde{r}\}}_{\{1,\ldots,u_1+u_2\}}$ be the matrix obtained by taking the first $\tilde{r}$ rows and the first $u_1 + u_2$ columns of $\vec{H}'$, with $\tilde{r} = u_1 + u_2 - (n - r) \geq 1$. Let $\vec{M}' = \vec{M}^{\{1,\ldots,\tilde{r}\}}$ (notice that $\vec{M}' \in \mathsf{GL}_{\tilde{r},r}(\mathbb{F}_q)$), so that $\bar{\vec{H}} = \vec{M}'\vec{H}_{\{1,\ldots,u_1+u_2\}}$. Then, it holds that $\tilde{\vec{V}}_{\{1,\ldots,u_1+u_2\}}\bar{\vec{H}}^\top = \vec{E}\vec{M}'^\top$. Indeed, $\tilde{\vec{V}}\vec{H}'^\top = \vec{E}\vec{M}^\top$ and $\vec{H}'$ can be written as

$$\vec{H}' = \begin{bmatrix} \bar{\vec{H}} & \vec{0}_{\tilde{r} \times n-(u_1+u_2)} \\ \vec{A} & \vec{I}_{n-(u_1+u_2)} \end{bmatrix} \text{ with } \vec{A} \in \mathbb{F}_q^{(r-\tilde{r}) \times (u_1+u_2)}, \text{ so that}$$

$$\tilde{\vec{V}}\vec{H}'^\top = \begin{bmatrix} \tilde{\vec{V}}_{\{1,\ldots,u_1+u_2\}} & \tilde{\vec{V}}_{\{u_1+u_2+1,\ldots,n\}} \end{bmatrix} \begin{bmatrix} \bar{\vec{H}} & \vec{0}_{\tilde{r} \times n-(u_1+u_2)} \\ \vec{A} & \vec{I}_{n-(u_1+u_2)} \end{bmatrix}^\top =$$

$$= \begin{bmatrix} \tilde{\vec{V}}_{\{1,\ldots,u_1+u_2\}}\bar{\vec{H}}^\top & \tilde{\vec{V}}_{\{1,\ldots,u_1+u_2\}}\vec{A}^\top + \tilde{\vec{V}}_{\{u_1+u_2+1,\ldots,n\}} \end{bmatrix} = \vec{E}\vec{M}^\top.$$

By definition of $\vec{M}'$, $(\vec{E}\vec{M}^\top)_{\{1,\ldots,\tilde{r}\}} = \vec{E}\vec{M}'^\top$. We define $\bar{\vec{E}} = \vec{E}\vec{M}'^\top$ and so we have

$$\tilde{\vec{V}}_{\{1,\ldots,u_1+u_2\}}\bar{\vec{H}}^\top = \bar{\vec{E}}. \tag{7}$$

Then, we call $\bar{\vec{H}}_1 = \bar{\vec{H}}_{\{1,\ldots,u_1\}}$ and $\bar{\vec{H}}_2 = \bar{\vec{H}}_{\{u_1+1,\ldots,u_1+u_2\}}$ and search for candidates for $\tilde{\vec{V}}_{\{1,\ldots,u_1+u_2\}}$. For a visualization of these matrices see Fig. 1.

Such candidates are found by building the following lists:

$$\mathcal{L}_1 = \left\{ (\vec{X}, \vec{X}\bar{\vec{H}}_1^\top) \mid \vec{X} \in \mathcal{S}_{u_1}(\vec{V}) \right\},$$

$$\mathcal{L}_2 = \left\{ (\vec{Y}, \bar{\vec{E}} - \vec{Y}\bar{\vec{H}}_2^\top) \mid \vec{Y} \in \mathcal{S}_{u_2}(\vec{V}) \right\}. \tag{8}$$

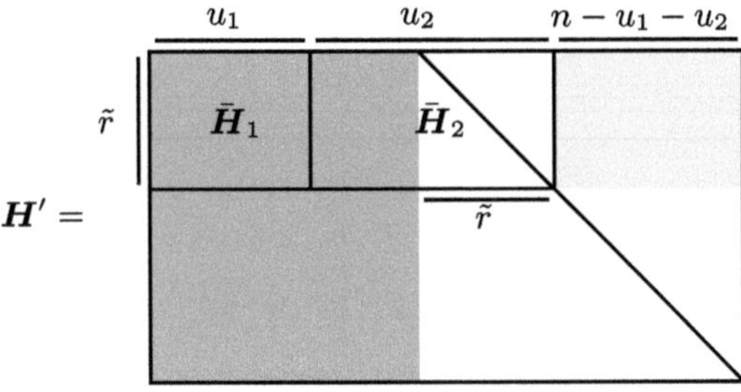

Fig. 1. Representation of the considered matrices, the yellow area is the zero matrix (Color figure online)

The algorithm proceeds by finding all *valid* collisions between $\mathcal{L}_1$ and $\mathcal{L}_2$, that is, finding pairs $(\vec{X}, \bar{\vec{X}}) \in \mathcal{L}_1$ and $(\vec{Y}, \bar{\vec{Y}}) \in \mathcal{L}_2$ s.t. $\bar{\vec{X}} = \bar{\vec{Y}}$ and $[\vec{X}\ \vec{Y}] \in \mathcal{S}_{u_1+u_2}(\vec{V})$ (therefore $[\vec{X}\ \vec{Y}]$ is a *valid* candidate for $\tilde{\vec{V}}_{\{1,\ldots,u_1+u_2\}}$). We denote this operation of selecting all *valid* candidates by $\bowtie$, and call $\mathcal{L}$ the resulting list for $\tilde{\vec{V}}_{\{1,\ldots,u_1+u_2\}}$, that is,

$$\mathcal{L} = \mathcal{L}_1 \bowtie \mathcal{L}_2 = \left\{ \vec{Z} \in \mathcal{S}_{u_1+u_2}(\vec{V}) \mid \vec{Z}\bar{\vec{H}}^{\top} = \bar{\vec{E}} \right\}.$$

From Eq. (7) we have that $\tilde{\vec{V}}_{\{1,\ldots,u_1+u_2\}} \in \mathcal{L}$ so, for every element in $\mathcal{L}$, we truncate it of $\tilde{r}$ columns and proceed as in Algorithm 1, and eventually find $\tilde{\vec{V}}$. Finally note that the requirement $u_1 + u_2 \geq n - r + 1$ is needed to have $\tilde{r} \geq 1$, so that it makes sense to look for collisions among matrices that have $\tilde{r}$ columns. The full algorithm is formalized in Algorithm 2.

Complexity of KMP. For the asymptotic analysis of the complexity of KMP we refer to [24]; here we are only interested in the finite regime, where its running time, measured in the number of matrix multiplications and list operations, is given by the following proposition.

Proposition 1 (Complexity of KMP [24, Prop. 5]). *Let $u_1, u_2 \in \mathbb{N}^*$ such that $n - r + 1 \leq u_1 + u_2 \leq n$. Then the KMP algorithm runs in average time*

$$T_{\mathsf{KMP}}(u_1, u_2) = |\mathcal{L}_1| + |\mathcal{L}_2| + N_{\mathcal{L}_1 \bowtie \mathcal{L}_2} + |\mathcal{L}|$$

where

$$|\mathcal{L}_i| = \frac{n!}{(n-u_i)!}, \quad N_{\mathcal{L}_1 \bowtie \mathcal{L}_2} = \frac{(n!)^2 q^{\ell(n-r-u_1-u_2)}}{(n-u_1)!(n-u_2)!},$$

$$|\mathcal{L}| = \frac{n!}{(n-u_1-u_2)!} q^{\ell(n-r-u_1-u_2)}.$$

Remark 4. We note that $N_{\mathcal{L}_1 \bowtie \mathcal{L}_2}$ is the estimated number of collisions between $\mathcal{L}_1$ and $\mathcal{L}_2$. Indeed we are searching for collisions between $\ell \times \tilde{r}$ matrices, so the

---

Algorithm 2 $\mathrm{KMP}(\vec{H}, \vec{V}, \vec{E})$

Parameters: $u_1, u_2 \in \mathbb{N}^*$ s.t. $n - r + 1 \leq u_1 + u_2 \leq n$

Input: $\vec{H} \in \mathbb{F}_q^{r \times n}$, $\vec{V} \in \mathbb{F}_q^{\ell \times n}$, $\vec{E} \in \mathbb{F}_q^{\ell \times r}$

Output: $\pi \in \mathsf{Sym}(n)$ such that $\pi(\vec{V})\vec{H}^\top = \vec{E}$

1: $\tilde{r} \leftarrow u_1 + u_2 - (n - r)$

2: $\vec{H}', \vec{M} \leftarrow \mathsf{RREF}^*_{\{n-r+1,\ldots,n\}}(\vec{H})$, $[\vec{U}\ \vec{I}_r] \leftarrow \vec{H}'$

3: $\bar{\vec{H}} \leftarrow \vec{H}'^{\{1,\ldots,\tilde{r}\}}_{\{1,\ldots,u_1+u_2\}}$, $\quad \vec{M}' \leftarrow \vec{M}^{\{1,\ldots,\tilde{r}\}}$

4: $\bar{\vec{E}} \leftarrow \vec{E}\vec{M}'^\top$, $\bar{\vec{H}}_1 \leftarrow \bar{\vec{H}}_{\{1,\ldots,u_1\}}$, $\bar{\vec{H}}_2 \leftarrow \bar{\vec{H}}_{\{u_1+1,\ldots,u_1+u_2\}}$

5: $\mathcal{L}_1 \leftarrow \left\{ (\vec{X}, \vec{X}\bar{\vec{H}}_1^\top) \mid \vec{X} \in \mathcal{S}_{u_1}(\vec{V}) \right\},$

6: $\mathcal{L}_2 \leftarrow \left\{ (\vec{X}, \bar{\vec{E}} - \vec{Y}\bar{\vec{H}}_2^\top) \mid \vec{Y} \in \mathcal{S}_{u_2}(\vec{V}) \right\}$

7: $\mathcal{L} \leftarrow \mathcal{L}_1 \bowtie \mathcal{L}_2$

8: **for** $\tilde{\vec{V}}_1 \in \mathcal{L}$ **do**

9: $\quad \tilde{\vec{V}}_2 \leftarrow \vec{E}\vec{M}^\top - \tilde{\vec{V}}_{1\{1\ldots,n-r\}}\vec{U}^\top$

10: $\quad$ **if** $\left[\tilde{\vec{V}}_1\ \tilde{\vec{V}}_2 \right] \in \mathcal{S}_n(\vec{V})$ **then**

11: $\quad\quad$ Compute $\pi \in \mathsf{Sym}(n)$ s.t. $\left[\tilde{\vec{V}}_1\ \tilde{\vec{V}}_2 \right] = \pi(\vec{V})$

12: $\quad\quad$ **Return:** π

---

average number of collisions can be estimated by the number of possible pairs (given by $|\mathcal{L}_1| \cdot |\mathcal{L}_2|$) multiplied by the probability of a pair to collide, that is $\frac{1}{q^{\ell \tilde{r}}}$. Since $|\mathcal{L}| \leq N_{\mathcal{L}_1 \bowtie \mathcal{L}_2}$ by construction (here the inequality is considered between the estimates), the complexity of the algorithm is dominated by $\max\{|\mathcal{L}_1|, |\mathcal{L}_2|, N_{\mathcal{L}_1 \bowtie \mathcal{L}_2}\}$ and the algorithm is optimized when $|\mathcal{L}_1| \approx |\mathcal{L}_2| \approx N_{\mathcal{L}_1 \bowtie \mathcal{L}_2}$, which implies that either $u_1 = u_2$ if $u_1 + u_2$ is even or $u_1 = u_2 \pm 1$ otherwise. For the sake of simplicity, let us consider from now on $u_1 = u_2 = u$ so that $|\mathcal{L}_1| = |\mathcal{L}_2| = \frac{n!}{(n-u)!}$. Then to optimize the algorithm it is necessary to require that $N_{\mathcal{L}_1 \bowtie \mathcal{L}_2} \leq \frac{n!}{(n-u)!}$, which is equivalent to

$$\frac{n!}{(n-u)!} \leq q^{\ell(2u+r-n)}.$$

Hence, u is chosen as the smallest integer which satisfies the above inequality.

Notice that increasing q allows us to choose a smaller u, which speeds up the algorithm; therefore, the hardest PKP instances are the ones in which q is chosen adaptively as the smallest prime or prime power that guarantees the uniqueness of the solution, that is, the smallest q, that satisfies Condition iv) in Sect. 2.1. Moreover, notice that choosing q as small as possible has other advantages when considering applications of PKP to cryptosystems, such as speeding up the encryption/decryption or sign/verify and reducing the bit-size of keys or witnesses in ZK-proofs (see [24]).

Finally, in [24] it was also shown that the complexity of KMP does not asymptotically depend on the value of ℓ and, even in the finite regime, increasing ℓ does not significantly change the running time (this will be examined in Sect. 5).

3.2 SBC Algorithm

The SBC algorithm works similarly to KMP, but with an additional *filtering step*. Instead of building the lists as in Eq. (8), here the idea is to choose the elements of the second list from a smaller set of matrices (that is why the algorithm can be considered as a version of KMP with an additional filtering step). Suppose that we want to solve an (n, r, q, ℓ)-IPKP instance $\pi(\vec{V})\vec{H}^{\top} = \vec{E}$. As usual, we denote $\pi(\vec{V})$ by $\tilde{\vec{V}}$. We now provide a description of the algorithm divided into 3 steps.

STEP 1 : Filtering Step. The first step of the algorithm is to find a subcode of the linear code generated by $\vec{H}$ with support size w and dimension d, where w and d will be two parameters taken as input by the algorithm (actually, instead of w, the algorithm will take in input $w_1, w_2 \in \mathbb{N}^*$ with $w_1 + w_2 = w$ since, again, a *meet-in-the-middle* approach is used). Notice that it is not possible to find such subcode for every $w \in [n]$ and for every $d \in [r]$, therefore a necessary condition for w, d to be valid parameters is that $N_{n,r}(w, d) > 1$. Assuming one subcode with the desired properties has been found, let $\vec{H}^* \in \mathbb{F}_q^{d \times n}$ be its generator matrix. We have that $\vec{H}^* = \vec{S}\vec{H}$ for some $\vec{S} \in \mathsf{GL}_{d,r}(\mathbb{F}_q)$. We will use the relation between $\vec{H}^*$ and $\vec{E}^* = \vec{E}\vec{S}^{\top}$ to filter the candidates for $\tilde{\vec{V}}_L$ where $L \subseteq [n]$ has size w. As in KMP, the idea is to guess $n - r + \tilde{r}$ columns with $\tilde{r} \geq 1$; however, this time $\tilde{r}$ is not fixed as in KMP, but it is a parameter itself that is taken as input by the algorithm with the condition $d \leq \tilde{r} \leq r$.

Remark 5. We now show why in the algorithm it is useful to consider another auxiliary permutation of the columns of $\vec{V}$ and why the condition $\tilde{r} \geq d$ arises. As in [24], we consider another permutation $\sigma \in \mathsf{Sym}(n)$ such that $\sigma(\vec{H}^*)$ has its w non-null columns in positions indexed by $J = \{n - r + \tilde{r} - w + 1, \ldots, n - r + \tilde{r}\}$. This choice simplifies the description of the algorithm because, at some point, $\sigma(\vec{H})$ will be brought into *Row Reduced Echelon Form* with respect to $\{n - r + 1, \ldots, n\}$, and this arrangement of σ ensures that this can be done (i.e. it guarantees that $\sigma(\vec{H})_{\{n-r+1,\ldots,n\}}$ is non-singular). To see this, assume, for example, that σ moves the non-null columns of $\vec{H}^*$ to the first w positions. Now let $\vec{S} \in \mathsf{GL}_{d,r}(\mathbb{F}_q)$ be such that $\vec{S}\sigma(\vec{H}) = \sigma(\vec{H}^*)$ (notice that this is the same matrix $\vec{S}$ defined before, so $\vec{H}^* = \vec{S}\vec{H}$), and define $\vec{N} = \begin{bmatrix} \vec{S}' \\ \vec{S} \end{bmatrix}$, where $\vec{S}' \in \mathbb{F}_q^{(r-d) \times r}$ is chosen so that $\vec{N}$ is non singular. Then $\vec{N}\sigma(\vec{H})$ has, in its bottom-rightmost part, a $d \times (n - w)$ null matrix. To have that $\vec{N}\sigma(\vec{H})_{\{n-r+1,\ldots,n\}}$ is non-singular (which means that it is possible to compute $\mathsf{RREF}_{\{n-r+1,\ldots,n\}}(\sigma(\vec{H}))$, since $\vec{N}\sigma(\vec{H})$ and $\sigma(\vec{H})$ share the same *Row Reduced Echelon Form*), it is necessary that it does not have linearly dependent rows. Since the last d of them have zeros in $n - w$ entries, this implies that $r - (n - w) \geq d$. This is equivalent to $w \geq n - r + d$. However, in this case, the *filtering step* would be as expensive as the KMP algorithm itself, since we are guessing $w \geq n - r + d \geq n - r + 1$ columns and in KMP we were guessing $v \geq n - r + 1$ columns. Instead, if $\sigma \in \mathsf{Sym}(n)$ moves the non-null columns of $\vec{H}^*$ in positions $\{n - r + \tilde{r} - w + 1, \ldots, n - r + \tilde{r}\}$, we have that $\vec{N}\sigma(\vec{H})$ has a $d \times (r - \tilde{r})$ null matrix in its bottom-rightmost matrix. Thus, for $\vec{N}\sigma(\vec{H})_{\{n-r+1,\ldots,n\}}$ to be non-singular, it is necessary that $r - (r - \tilde{r}) \geq d$, which is set by hypothesis.

Consider now $w_1, w_2 \in \mathbb{N}^*$ with $w_1 + w_2 = w$ and set $J_1 = \{n - r + \tilde{r} - w + 1, \ldots, n - r + \tilde{r} - w_2\}$ and $J_2 = \{n - r + \tilde{r} - w_2 + 1, \ldots, n - r + \tilde{r}\}$ (notice that $|J_1| = w - w_2 = w_1$ and $|J_2| = w_2$). Let $\vec{H}_1^* = \sigma(\vec{H}^*)_{J_1}$ and $\vec{H}_2^* = \sigma(\vec{H}^*)_{J_2}$. Then $\sigma(\vec{H}^*)$ can be visualized as follows.

$$\sigma(\vec{H}^*) = \quad d \left\| \begin{array}{|c|c|c|c|} \hline \overset{\overbrace{\hspace{2.5cm}}^{n - r + \tilde{r} - w}}{\vec{0}} & \overset{\overbrace{\hspace{1.5cm}}^{w_1}}{\vec{H}_1^*} & \overset{\overbrace{\hspace{1.5cm}}^{w_2}}{\vec{H}_2^*} & \vec{0} \\ \hline \end{array} \right.$$

We further define $J = J_1 \cup J_2 = \{n - r + \tilde{r} - w + 1, \ldots, n - r + \tilde{r}\}$ and $\vec{\tilde{H}} = \sigma(\vec{H}^*)_J = \begin{bmatrix} \vec{H}_1^* & \vec{H}_2^* \end{bmatrix}$. Then the algorithm proceeds by searching for candidates for $\sigma(\vec{\tilde{V}})_J$ in the list

$$\mathcal{K} = \left\{ \vec{X} \in \mathcal{S}_w(\vec{V}) \mid \vec{X}\vec{\tilde{H}}^{\top} = \vec{E}^* \right\}. \tag{9}$$

We will show now that $\sigma(\vec{\tilde{V}})_J \in \mathcal{K}$. As $\vec{\tilde{V}}\vec{H}^{\top} = \vec{E}$, then it is easy to see that

$$\vec{E}\vec{A}^{\top} = \sigma(\vec{\tilde{V}})(\vec{A}\sigma(\vec{H}))^{\top}, \quad \forall \vec{A} \in \mathbb{F}_q^{r' \times r}, \forall r' \leq r, \forall \sigma \in \mathsf{Sym}(n). \tag{10}$$

Since $\vec{H}^* = \vec{S}\vec{H}$ we have that $\vec{E}^* = \vec{E}\vec{S}^{\top} = \sigma(\vec{\tilde{V}})\sigma(\vec{H}^*)^{\top}$ and $\sigma(\vec{H}^*)$ has the structure showed in the figure above. Therefore, if we call $J' = \{1, \ldots, n - r + \tilde{r} - w\}$ and $J'' = \{n - r + \tilde{r} + 1, \ldots, n\}$, we have

$$\vec{E}^* = \sigma(\vec{\tilde{V}})\sigma(\vec{H}^*)^{\top} = \begin{bmatrix} \sigma(\vec{\tilde{V}})_{J'} & \sigma(\vec{\tilde{V}})_J & \sigma(\vec{\tilde{V}})_{J''} \end{bmatrix} \begin{bmatrix} \vec{0} \\ \vec{\tilde{H}}^{\top} \\ \vec{0} \end{bmatrix} = \sigma(\vec{\tilde{V}})_J\vec{\tilde{H}}^{\top}.$$

To build the list $\mathcal{K}$, a *meet-in-the-middle* approach is used, so instead of building it like in Eq. (9), we build $\mathcal{K}$ as $\mathcal{K}_1 \bowtie \mathcal{K}_2$, with

$$\mathcal{K}_1 = \left\{ (\vec{X}_1, \vec{X}_1\vec{H}_1^{*\top}) \mid \vec{X}_1 \in \mathcal{S}_{w_1}(\vec{V}) \right\},$$

$$\mathcal{K}_2 = \left\{ (\vec{X}_2, \vec{E}^* - \vec{X}_2\vec{H}_2^{*\top}) \mid \vec{X}_2 \in \mathcal{S}_{w_2}(\vec{V}) \right\}.$$

STEP 2 : Extra Guessing. From now on, we assume that $\{n-r+1,\ldots,n\}$ is an information set for $\sigma(\vec{H})$, but the reasoning works for every information set. After the *filtering step*, we obtain a list of candidates for $\sigma(\vec{\tilde{V}})_J$, with $|J| = w$. Because of the considerations made in Remark 5, if $w \geq n-r+d$ we know enough columns to reconstruct the whole solution by exploiting the kernel dimension (as in Lines 4–7 in Algorithm 1). As observed in the same remark, the interesting values of w are the ones for which $w < n - r + d$ (otherwise the complexity of the algorithm would be essentially the same as KMP). If this is the case, we need to guess $n - r - w + \tilde{r}$ more columns. Notice that guessing $n - r - w + d$ more columns would be sufficient, however since this guessing is done by using a *meet-in-the-middle* approach, the algorithm might be optimized when guessing more columns.

The algorithm proceeds by computing $\vec{H}', \vec{M} = \mathsf{RREF}^*_{\{n-r+1,\ldots,n\}}(\sigma(\vec{H}))$. Now we call $\hat{\vec{H}} = \vec{H}'^{\{d+1,\ldots,\tilde{r}\}}$, $\hat{\vec{E}} = (\vec{E}\vec{M}^\top)_{\{d+1,\ldots,\tilde{r}\}}$, $\hat{\vec{H}}_1 = \hat{\vec{H}}_{J'}$ and $\hat{\vec{H}}_2 = \hat{\vec{H}}_J$ and build the lists

$$\mathcal{L}_1 = \left\{ (\vec{Y}_1, \vec{Y}_1\hat{\vec{H}}_1^\top) \mid \vec{Y}_1 \in \mathcal{S}_{n-r+\tilde{r}-w}(\vec{V}) \right\},$$

$$\mathcal{L}_2 = \left\{ (\vec{Y}_2, \hat{\vec{E}} - \vec{Y}_2\hat{\vec{H}}_2^\top) \mid \vec{Y}_2 \in \mathcal{K} \right\},$$

$$\mathcal{L} = \mathcal{L}_1 \bowtie \mathcal{L}_2.$$

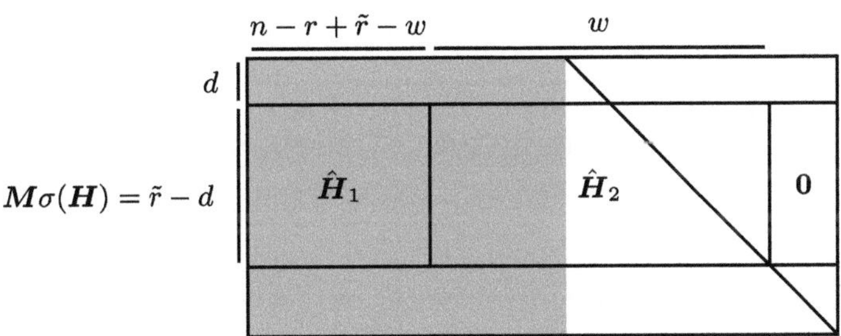

Fig. 2. Matrices employed in the SBC algorithm. The pink area is the matrix $\vec{U}$ defined in Algorithm 3 (Color figure online).

It is easy to see that $\sigma(\vec{V})_{J'\cup J} \in \mathcal{L}$. To visualize this, we refer to Fig. 2. Indeed, from Eq. (10) we have that $\vec{E}\vec{M}^\top = \sigma(\vec{\tilde{V}})(\vec{M}\sigma(\vec{H}))^\top$. This implies

$$(\vec{E}\vec{M}^\top)_{\{d+1,\ldots,\tilde{r}\}} = \left(\sigma(\vec{\tilde{V}})(\vec{M}\sigma(\vec{H}))^\top \right)_{\{d+1,\ldots,\tilde{r}\}} = \sigma(\vec{\tilde{V}}) \left((\vec{M}\sigma(\vec{H}))^\top \right)_{\{d+1,\ldots,\tilde{r}\}}.$$

Observing that selecting a set of columns of the transpose is the same as selecting that set of rows of the non-transpose, we obtain that:

$$\hat{\tilde{E}} = \sigma(\tilde{\vec{V}})\hat{\tilde{H}}^{\top} = \left[\sigma(\tilde{\vec{V}})_{J'} \ \sigma(\tilde{\vec{V}})_{J} \ \sigma(\tilde{\vec{V}})_{J''}\right] \begin{bmatrix} \hat{\tilde{H}}_1^{\top} \\ \hat{\tilde{H}}_2^{\top} \\ \vec{0} \end{bmatrix} = \left[\sigma(\tilde{\vec{V}})_{J'} \ \sigma(\tilde{\vec{V}})_{J}\right] \begin{bmatrix} \hat{\tilde{H}}_1^{\top} \\ \hat{\tilde{H}}_2^{\top} \end{bmatrix}.$$

Notice that the last columns $r - \tilde{r}$ of $\hat{\tilde{H}}$ are zero because they are obtained by taking a null submatrix of I_r. From the first step of the algorithm we have that $\sigma(\tilde{\vec{V}})_J \in \mathcal{K}$, so $\sigma(\tilde{\vec{V}})_{J' \cup J} \in \mathcal{L}$.

STEP 3 : Reconstruct the Solution. As said before, at the end of **STEP 2** we know enough columns of $\sigma(\pi(\vec{V}))$ to reconstruct the solution working as in Sect. 2.2 and in the last part of KMP (that is, by exploiting the kernel dimension).

Remark 6. In Algorithm 3, in **STEP 3**, the solution is reconstructed by considering the last $r - \tilde{r}$ rows of $\vec{U}$ and consequently the last $r - \tilde{r}$ columns of $\vec{E}\vec{M}^{\top}$. This is done because we are looking for $\vec{X}'$ such that $[\vec{X} \ \vec{X}'] \in \mathcal{S}_n(\vec{V})$ and $[\vec{X} \ \vec{X}'] \begin{bmatrix} \vec{U}^{\top} \\ I_r \end{bmatrix} = \vec{E}\vec{M}^{\top}$. However, we can just check the equality between the last $r - \tilde{r}$ columns of these matrices, because the equality between the first $n - r + \tilde{r}$ columns has already been checked in **STEP 2** (a similar reasoning also applies when discarding the first d columns after **STEP 1**).

Complexity of SBC. The next proposition provides the average running time of SBC.

Proposition 2 (Complexity of SBC [24, Prop. 9]). *Let d, w_1, w_2, $\tilde{r} \in \mathbb{N}^*$ be such that $w = w_1 + w_2 \leq n$, $d \leq \tilde{r} \leq r$ and $N_{n,r}(w,d) > 1$. Then Algorithm 3 runs in average time*

$$T_{\mathsf{SBC}}(n, r, q, \ell, w_1, w_2, d, \tilde{r}) = T_{\mathsf{ISD}}^{(d)}(n, r, w) + T_{\mathcal{K}} + T_{\mathcal{L}} + |\mathcal{L}| \tag{11}$$

where $T_{\mathsf{ISD}}^{(d)}(n, r, w)$ is defined as in Eq. (3) and

$$T_{\mathcal{K}} = \frac{n!}{(n - w_1)!} + \frac{n!}{(n - w_2)!} + \frac{(n!)^2 q^{-d\ell}}{(n - w_1)!(n - w_2)!},$$

$$T_{\mathcal{L}} = \frac{n!}{(r + w - \tilde{r})!} + |\mathcal{K}| + \frac{n!|\mathcal{K}|q^{-\ell(\tilde{r}-d)}}{(r + w - \tilde{r})!}, \tag{12}$$

$$|\mathcal{L}| = \frac{(n - w)!|\mathcal{K}|q^{-\ell(\tilde{r}-d)}}{(r - \tilde{r})!}, \quad |\mathcal{K}| = \max\left\{\frac{n!q^{-d\ell}}{(n - w)!}, 1\right\}. \tag{13}$$

Remark 7. In Proposition 2, $\tilde{r}$ is allowed to be equal to d. In this case, in **STEP 2**, one would build matrices with zero rows/columns. This is, in some sense, taken into account in Proposition 2, but in this case the complexity of the

---

Algorithm 3 SBC$(\vec{H}, \vec{V}, \vec{E})$

Parameters: w_1, w_2, $\tilde{r}$, $d \in \mathbb{N}$ with $w = w_1 + w_2 \leq n$, $d \leq \tilde{r} \leq r$ and
$N_{n,r}(w,d) > 1$

Input: $\vec{H} \in \mathsf{GL}_{r,n}(\mathbb{F}_q)$, $\vec{V} \in \mathsf{GL}_{\ell,n}(\mathbb{F}_q)$, $\vec{E} \in \mathbb{F}_q^{\ell \times r}$

Output: $\pi \in \mathsf{Sym}(n)$ such that $\pi(\vec{V})\vec{H}^\top = \vec{E}$

STEP 1: filtering step

1: Use ISD to find a subcode of the code generated by $\vec{H}$ with dimension d and
support size $w = w_1 + w_2$. Call $\mathcal{C}$ this subcode, $\vec{H}^*$ its generator matrix and
$\vec{S} \in \mathsf{GL}_{d,r}(\mathbb{F}_q)$ the matrix s.t. $\vec{H}^* = \vec{S}\vec{H}$.

2: Compute $\sigma \in \mathsf{Sym}(n)$ such that $\mathrm{Supp}(\sigma(\mathcal{C})) = \{n{-}r{+}\tilde{r}{-}w{+}1, \ldots, n{-}r{+}\tilde{r}\}$

3: $J_1 \leftarrow \{n{-}r{+}\tilde{r}{-}w{+}1, \ldots, n{-}r{+}\tilde{r}{-}w_2\}$, $J_2 \leftarrow \{n{-}r{+}\tilde{r}{-}w_2{+}1, \ldots, n{-}r{+}\tilde{r}\}$

4: $\vec{E}^* \leftarrow \vec{E}\vec{S}^\top$, $\vec{H}_1^* \leftarrow \sigma(\vec{H}^*)_{J_1}$, $\vec{H}_2^* \leftarrow \sigma(\vec{H}^*)_{J_2}$

5: $\mathcal{K}_1 \leftarrow \left\{ (\vec{X}_1, \vec{X}_1\vec{H}_1^{*\top}) \mid \vec{X}_1 \in \mathcal{S}_{w_1}(\vec{V}) \right\}$,

6: $\mathcal{K}_2 \leftarrow \left\{ (\vec{X}_2, \vec{E}^* - \vec{X}_2\vec{H}_2^{*\top}) \mid \vec{X}_2 \in \mathcal{S}_{w_2}(\vec{V}) \right\}$

7: $\mathcal{K} \leftarrow \mathcal{K}_1 \bowtie \mathcal{K}_2$

STEP 2: extra guessing

8: $\vec{H}', \vec{M} \leftarrow \mathsf{RREF}^*_{\{n-r+1,\ldots,n\}}(\sigma(\vec{H}))$, $\left[\vec{U}\ \vec{I}_r\right] \leftarrow \vec{H}'$

9: $\hat{\vec{H}} \leftarrow \vec{H}'^{\{d+1,\ldots,\tilde{r}\}}$, $\hat{\vec{E}} \leftarrow (\vec{E}\vec{M}^\top)_{\{d+1,\ldots,\tilde{r}\}}$

10: $J' \leftarrow \{1, \ldots, n-r+\tilde{r}-w\}$, $J \leftarrow J_1 \cup J_2$, $\hat{\vec{H}}_1 \leftarrow \hat{\vec{H}}_{J'}$, $\hat{\vec{H}}_2 \leftarrow \hat{\vec{H}}_J$

11: $\mathcal{L}_1 = \left\{ (\vec{Y}_1, \vec{Y}_1\hat{\vec{H}}_1^\top) \mid \vec{Y}_1 \in \mathcal{S}_{n-r+\tilde{r}-w}(\vec{V}) \right\}$

12: $\mathcal{L}_2 = \left\{ (\vec{Y}_2, \hat{\vec{E}} - \vec{Y}_2\hat{\vec{H}}_2^\top) \mid \vec{Y}_2 \in \mathcal{K} \right\}$

13: $\mathcal{L} = \mathcal{L}_1 \bowtie \mathcal{L}_2$

STEP 3: reconstruct the solution

14: $\vec{U} \leftarrow \vec{U}^{\{\tilde{r}+1,\ldots,r\}}$, $\vec{E} \leftarrow (\vec{E}\vec{M}^\top)_{\{\tilde{r}+1,\ldots,r\}}$

15: **for** $\vec{X} \in \mathcal{L}$ **do**

16: $\qquad \vec{X}' \leftarrow \vec{E} - \vec{X}_{\{1,\ldots,n-r\}}\vec{U}^\top$

17: $\qquad$ **if** $\left[\vec{X}\ \vec{X}'\right] \in \mathcal{S}_n(\vec{V})$ **then**

18: $\qquad\qquad$ Compute $\pi \in \mathsf{Sym}(n)$ s.t. $\sigma^{-1}\left(\left[\vec{X}\ \vec{X}'\right]\right) = \pi(\vec{V})$

19: $\qquad\qquad$ **Return:** π

---

algorithm is slightly overestimated. If $\tilde{r} = d$, then for every candidate $\vec{X} \in \mathcal{K}$,
one should try to reconstruct the solution for every possible way of choosing
$n - r + \tilde{r} - w$ columns of $\vec{V}$ (without checking for collisions as in **STEP 2**)
between the $n - w$ columns that do not appear in $\vec{X}$. This would lead to a
slightly smaller complexity than the one showed in Proposition 2, because the
complexity given by Eq. (11) assumes that for every candidate the extra guessing
is made between all the n columns of $\vec{V}$ instead of between the $n - w$ remaining
ones. Therefore, the term $T_\mathcal{L} + |\mathcal{L}|$ in Eq. (11) should be replaced by $\frac{(n-w)!|\mathcal{K}|}{(r-\tilde{r})!}$.

We point out that, based on our analysis, this does not lead to significant changes in the running time, but we report it for completeness.

4   New Algorithmic Improvements for Solving PKP

In this section, we introduce several improvements to SBC. These improvements apply to KMP as well, but since SBC outperforms KMP in the finite regime (see [24, Sec. 6.2]), that is of primary interest in this work, we focus on SBC. We introduce variants both for the *filtering step* (**STEP 1** in Algorithm 3) and for the *extra guessing* (**STEP 2** in Algorithm 3). Then, we outline our refined new algorithm which chooses the most convenient variant of these steps for each choice of parameters.

In the following, we consider an (n, r, q, ℓ)-IPKP instance $\pi(\vec{V})\vec{H}^\top = \vec{E}$ with $\mathsf{rank}(\vec{E}) = 1$ and in which the last row of $\vec{H}$ is a row of ones (this is the case of an IPKP-instance obtained by de-homogenizing a PKP instance) and use the same notation used in the previous section. Although the algorithm applies to arbitrary IPKP instances, we focus on instances with specific properties arising from the dehomogenization of a (homogeneous) PKP instance. Such IPKP instances cannot be treated as random in the complexity analysis, as dehomogenization introduces equations that hold for every permutation, which would otherwise lead to an underestimation of the number of solutions and hence of the complexity (see Remark 14).

4.1   Variant of STEP 2: Using the Dual to Guess More Columns

We begin introducing our proposed variant of **STEP 2** of SBC because this modification applies also to our variant of **STEP 1** that is presented in Sect. 4.2. In a nutshell, the variant exploits the RREF of $\vec{V}$ instead of the one of $\vec{H}$ by considering the dual version of the problem instance (see Sect. 2.3).

Recall that **STEP 2** starts with a list $\mathcal{K}$ containing all the candidates for $\sigma(\tilde{\vec{V}})_J$ (with $J = \{n - r + \tilde{r} - w + 1, \ldots, n - r + \tilde{r}\}$). By inverting σ, for each candidate $\vec{X}$ for $\sigma(\tilde{\vec{V}})_J$ (corresponding to a candidate permutation $\pi \in \mathsf{Sym}(n)$), it is possible to determine $i_1, \ldots, i_w$ s.t. $\pi(i_1) = j_1, \ldots, \pi(i_w) = j_w$ with $\sigma(j_1) = n - r + \tilde{r} - w + 1, \ldots, \sigma(j_w) = n - r + \tilde{r}$ and so we know $\pi^{-1}(j_1) = i_1, \ldots, \pi^{-1}(j_w) = i_w$. In the following, we call $\mathsf{InvCand}(\vec{X})$ the algorithm that takes in input a candidate $\vec{X}$ for $\sigma(\tilde{\vec{V}})_J$ and returns both the set $I_{\vec{X}} = \{i_1, \ldots, i_w\}$ and the corresponding candidate for $\pi^{-1}(\vec{H})_{I_{\vec{X}}}$. Notice that this candidate is unique only if $\vec{V}$ has no repeated columns, we clarify this in the next section but for now we assume this is the case.

Consider now the dual version of the problem

$$\pi^{-1}(\vec{H})\vec{V}^\top = \vec{E}^\top.$$

In this setting, for every $\vec{X} \in \mathcal{K}$, we know a candidate for $\pi^{-1}(\vec{H})_{I_{\vec{X}}}$, where in general the set $I_{\vec{X}}$ is different for every candidate $\vec{X}$. For this reason, it is not possible to build the list $\mathcal{L}$ with a *meet-in-the-middle* approach since for every candidate we need to compute the RREF w.r.t. a (possibly) different information set. In the original approach, we needed to guess the action of the permutation on $n - r - w + \tilde{r}$ more columns to have enough information to reconstruct the solution. Here, if we extend $\vec{V}$, we need to guess $n - (\ell+1) - w + \tilde{r}$ more columns of $\pi^{-1}(\vec{H})$. Thus, since we cannot use the *meet-in-the-middle* approach, for every element in $\mathcal{K}$ we try all the possible ways of choosing $n - (\ell+1) - w + \tilde{r}$ columns from the $n - w$ remaining ones.

Another difference with the original **STEP 2** in Algorithm 3 is that here we consider any $0 \leq \tilde{r} \leq \ell + 1$ instead of requiring $\tilde{r} \geq d$. The latter was required because of the considerations made in Remark 5 which are no longer valid in our case. In particular, the constraint was to avoid having a sub-matrix with zero columns in the positions indexed by the set used to compute the RREF, but since now we are computing the RREF of $\vec{V}$ instead of $\vec{H}$, no null sub-matrices are involved.

On the Probability of Failure. If we denote with $\vec{V}^{\text{ext}}$ the extended $\vec{V}$, we consider the probability of successfully computing $\mathsf{RREF}_{I'_{\vec{X}}}(\vec{V}^{\text{ext}})$ w.r.t. a fixed set $I'_{\vec{X}} \subseteq [n]$ with $|I'_{\vec{X}}| = \ell+1$ as the probability that a random $(\ell+1) \times (\ell+1)$ matrix is non-singular. However, we do not need to compute the RREF w.r.t. one fixed subset of indexes, as we usually have multiple possible choices. Indeed, we just need to compute the RREF w.r.t. a set $I'_{\vec{X}}$ that intersects the set $I_{\vec{X}}$ containing the indexes of the w known columns of $\pi^{-1}(\vec{H})$ in a set of cardinality $\tilde{r}$. This permits to use as much known columns as possible to reconstruct the solution. Since the possible choices of such $I'_{\vec{X}}$ are many, we can safely assume that the probability that every choice is not an information set for $\vec{V}^{\text{ext}}$ is negligible. We call $\mathsf{RecoverInfSet}(\vec{X})$ the procedure that takes in input a candidate $\vec{X}$ for $\sigma(\tilde{\vec{V}})_J$ and returns a "valid" information set in the sense we just explained.

By joining the above variant of **STEP 2** with the corresponding adaptation of **STEP 3**, we obtain Algorithm 4. Note that it is not necessary (more precisely, it is not useful) to introduce the auxiliary permutation σ, since it is inverted before having played any role. Nevertheless, we still consider it in order to be consistent with the original **STEP 2** in which σ is needed.

Remark 8. Notice that in Line 4 of Algorithm 4, we introduce an auxiliary permutation μ to simplify the description of the algorithm. This permutation is not required for the algorithm to function, but is introduced solely for clarity of exposition. Moreover, such a permutation exists because, by construction, $|\{i_1, \ldots, i_w\} \cap I'_{\vec{X}}| = \tilde{r}$.

Remark 9. Instead of taking $\vec{V}$ and $\vec{E}$ as inputs, Algorithm 4 takes the extended matrices, which we call $\vec{V}^{\text{ext}}$ and $\vec{E}^{\text{ext}}$ respectively. We explicitly build these matrices, for example, at Line 15 of Algorithm 7. Another observation is that Algorithm 4 could, in principle, terminate as soon as a solution is found. Nevertheless, we intentionally make it not terminate to account for instances with multiple solutions, which we encounter in the following section.

Algorithm 4 DualGuessSolve($\vec{H}, \vec{V}^{\text{ext}}, \vec{E}^{\text{ext}}, \mathcal{K}$)

Parameters: $w, \tilde{r}, d \in \mathbb{N}^*$ with $0 \leq \tilde{r} \leq \ell + 1$ and $N_{n,r}(w,d) > 1$

Input: $\vec{H} \in \mathsf{GL}_{r,n}(\mathbb{F}_q)$, $\vec{V}^{\text{ext}} \in \mathsf{GL}_{\ell+1,n}(\mathbb{F}_q)$, $\vec{E}^{\text{ext}} \in \mathbb{F}_q^{r \times (\ell+1)}$, $\mathcal{K}$ containing all
    candidates for $\sigma(\vec{V})_J$

Output: A list $\mathcal{L}$ containing $\tilde{\vec{H}} \in \mathcal{S}_n(\vec{H})$ such that $\tilde{\vec{H}}(\vec{V}^{\text{ext}})^\top = \vec{E}^{\text{ext}}$

1: Initialize an empty list $\mathcal{L}$

2: **for** $\vec{X} \in \mathcal{K}$ **do**

3:     $\{i_1 \ldots, i_w\}, \vec{Y} \leftarrow \mathsf{InvCand}(\vec{X})$, $I'_{\vec{X}} \leftarrow \mathsf{RecoverInfSet}(\vec{X})$

4:     Let $\mu \in \mathsf{Sym}(n)$ s.t. $\mu(I'_{\vec{X}}) = \{n - \ell, \ldots, n\}$ and

$$\mu(i_1) = n - (\ell + 1) - w + \tilde{r} + 1, \ldots, \mu(i_w) = n - (\ell + 1) + \tilde{r}$$

5:     $\vec{V}', \vec{M} \leftarrow \mathsf{RREF}^*_{\{n-\ell,\ldots,n\}}(\mu(\vec{V}^{\text{ext}}))$, $\vec{U} \leftarrow \vec{V}'_{\{1,\ldots,n-(\ell+1)\}}$

6:     $\vec{E}' \leftarrow (\vec{E}^{\text{ext}}\vec{M}^\top)_{\{1,\ldots,\tilde{r}\}}$

7:     **for** $\vec{Z} \in \mathcal{S}_{n-(\ell+1)-w+\tilde{r}}(\vec{H}_{\neg_n\{i_1,\ldots,i_w\}})$ **do**

8:         $\tilde{\vec{V}} \leftarrow \vec{V}'^{\{1,\ldots,\tilde{r}\}}_{\{1,\ldots,n-(\ell+1)+\tilde{r}\}}$

9:         $\vec{W} \leftarrow \left[\vec{Z}\ \vec{Y}\right]$

10:        **if** $\vec{W}\tilde{\vec{V}}^\top = \vec{E}'$ **then**

11:           $\vec{W}' \leftarrow (\vec{E}^{\text{ext}}\vec{M}^\top) - \vec{W}_{\{1,\ldots,n-(\ell+1)\}}\vec{U}^\top$

12:          **if** $\left[\vec{W}_{\{1,\ldots,n-(\ell+1)\}}\ \vec{W}'\right] \in \mathcal{S}_n(\vec{H}))$ **then**

13:             $\mathcal{L} \leftarrow \mathcal{L} \cup \left\{\mu^{-1}\left(\left[\vec{W}_{\{1,\ldots,n-(\ell+1)\}}\ \vec{W}'\right]\right)\right\}$

14: **Return:** $\mathcal{L}$

Proposition 3. *Let $\vec{H} \in \mathsf{GL}_{r,n}(\mathbb{F}_q)$, $\vec{V} \in \mathsf{GL}_{\ell+1,n}(\mathbb{F}_q)$ be matrices with no repeated columns and $\vec{E} \in \mathbb{F}_q^{r \times (\ell+1)}$. Let $w, d \in \mathbb{N}^*, \tilde{r} \in \mathbb{N}$ s.t. $w \leq n, 0 \leq \tilde{r} \leq \ell + 1$ and $N_{n,r}(w,d) > 1$. Let $\tilde{\vec{V}} = \pi(\vec{V})$ and let $\mathcal{K}$ be the list containing the candidates for $\sigma(\tilde{\vec{V}})_J$, with $J \subseteq [n]$ and $|J| = w$. Then the running time of Algorithm 4 is given by*

$$\bar{T}_{\mathcal{L}}(n, \ell, w, \tilde{r}, |\mathcal{K}|) = \begin{cases} |\mathcal{K}|\frac{(n-w)!}{(\ell+1-\tilde{r})!} & \text{if} \quad \ell + 1 - \tilde{r} \leq n - w, \\ |\mathcal{K}| & \text{otherwise.} \end{cases} \tag{14}$$

Proof. We first consider the case $\ell + 1 - \tilde{r} \leq n - w$. The cost of Line 3, because of the considerations above, can be assumed to be absorbed by the $\mathcal{O}$-notation. Therefore the overall complexity is given by $|\mathcal{K}| \cdot |\mathcal{S}_{n-(\ell+1)-w+\tilde{r}}(\vec{H}_{\neg_n\{i_1,\ldots,i_w\}})|$.

Finally, if $\ell + 1 - \tilde{r} > n - w$, then, after the *filtering step*, we know enough columns to directly reconstruct the solution (which means that in the for loop at Line 7 it is not needed to compute $\vec{W}$ since we already know it). $\qquad\square$

Remark 10. In Proposition 3 we allow $\tilde{r} = 0$, even if this means considering matrices with zero rows/columns. In this case, analogously to Remark 7, we try to reconstruct the solution directly from every candidate in $\mathcal{K}$. This observation does not affect the complexity of the algorithm given by Eq. (14).

Remark 11. Note that our variant of **STEP 2** is not always an improvement w.r.t. the original version. Depending on the parameters, it might be more convenient to choose one version or the other. The two variants are compared in Table 1. Note that the last row in the table, corresponding to the dimensions of the colliding matrices, does not affect directly the running time of the algorithm as it is proposed now. However, as shown in this section, it affects the number of expected solutions. This affects the running time of our newly proposed Algorithm 7, see Lemma 2.

Table 1. Comparison of the two variants. Red cells indicate the variant that results in higher complexity for each respective parameter.

	Original STEP 2	Our variant
Amount of extra guesses	$n - r + \tilde{r} - w$	$n - (\ell + 1) + \tilde{r} - w$
Constraint on $\tilde{r}$	$d \leq \tilde{r} \leq r$	$0 \leq \tilde{r} \leq \ell + 1$
Meet-in-the-middle	$\checkmark$	$\vec{\times}$
Dimensions of colliding matrices	$\ell \times (\tilde{r} - d)$	$\tilde{r} \times (r - 1)$

4.2 Variant of STEP 1: Recursive Filtering

We introduce here a variant for the *filtering step* of SBC (**STEP 1** in Algorithm 3). The idea is to replace the *meet-in-the-middle* approach by solving multiple IPKP (sub)instances. Recall that the goal of the *filtering step* is to have a list $\mathcal{K} = \left\{ \vec{X} \in \mathcal{S}_w(\vec{V}) \mid \vec{X}\vec{\tilde{H}}^\top = \vec{E}^* \right\}$ containing candidates for $\sigma(\vec{\tilde{V}})_J$ (see Eq. (9)). For every $W \subseteq [n]$, with $|W| = w$, we populate the list $\mathcal{K}$ with elements of the form $\tilde{\pi}(\vec{V}_W)$, for some $\tilde{\pi} \in \mathsf{Sym}(w)$, such that

$$\tilde{\pi}(\vec{V}_W)\vec{\tilde{H}}^\top = \vec{E}^*, \tag{15}$$

which is a (w, d, q, ℓ)-IPKP instance. In total, that are $\binom{n}{w}$ possible choices for W. Notice that, for simplicity, we abuse the terminology of Definition 2 and refer to IPKP instances also in cases they have no solution. This can occur when the chosen set W is not the one containing the columns of $\sigma(\vec{\tilde{V}})_J$.

We only consider IPKP instances in their dual form (see Eq. (6)), as our complexity analysis shows this to be consistently the best choice. To increase the row dimension of the instances by one, we extend $\vec{V}_W$, which in the considered dual instances plays the role of the parity-check, by adding an additional row of ones analogously to Sect. 2.2. This means that $\mathcal{K}$ collects solutions of IPKP instances with parameters $(w, \ell + 1, q, d)$. We highlight that these subinstances might also have multiple solutions. In order to solve them, we use a slightly modified version of SBC.

Remark 12. To be precise, the subinstances to solve (after having extended $\vec{V}_W$) have parameters $(w, \mathsf{rank}(\vec{V}_W) + 1, q, d)$. In the following, we assume that $\mathsf{rank}(\vec{V}_W) = \min\{\ell, w - d + 1\}$. We motivate this in Appendix A.

Dealing with Instances with Multiple Solutions. Let $\ell^* := \mathsf{rank}(\vec{V}_W)$. In most cases, the subinstances under consideration have multiple solutions that need to be found all. If $\tilde{\vec{H}}$ has no repeated columns, we expect multiple solutions to occur whenever condition iv) in Sect. 2.1 does not hold (that is, when $\frac{w!}{q^{\ell^* d}} \geq 1$). In this case, Algorithm 3 can be easily adapted to return all solutions: it suffices to output all valid permutations instead of terminating as soon as one is found (as in Lines 13–14 of Algorithm 4). We define SBC* (Algorithm 5) and SBC$^*_{\mathsf{dual}}$ (Algorithm 6) as the variants of SBC (Algorithm 3) that take this into account, performing respectively the original **STEP 2-3** of Algorithm 3 and Algorithm 4. Suppose we are solving the instance $\pi(\vec{V})\vec{H}^\top = \vec{E}$. Differently from Algorithm 3, Algorithm 5 and Algorithm 6 return lists containing, respectively, all $\tilde{\vec{V}} \in \mathcal{S}_n(\vec{V})$ such that $\tilde{\vec{V}}\vec{H}^\top = \vec{E}$, and all $\tilde{\vec{H}} \in \mathcal{S}_n(\vec{H})$ such that $\tilde{\vec{H}}(\vec{V}^{\mathsf{ext}})^\top = \vec{E}^{\mathsf{ext}}$, where $\vec{V}^{\mathsf{ext}}$ is the matrix obtained by extending $\vec{V}$ with a row of ones and $\vec{E}^{\mathsf{ext}}$ is the matrix obtained by extending $\vec{E}^\top$ accordingly. We explicit these algorithms in Algorithms 5 and 6.

Algorithm 5 SBC*$(\vec{H}, \vec{V}, \vec{E})$

Parameters: w_1, w_2, $\tilde{r}$, $d \in \mathbb{N}$ with $w = w_1 + w_2 \leq n$, $d \leq \tilde{r} \leq r$ and
  $N_{n,r}(w, d) > 1$
Input: $\vec{H} \in \mathsf{GL}_{r,n}(\mathbb{F}_q)$, $\vec{V} \in \mathsf{GL}_{\ell,n}(\mathbb{F}_q)$, $\vec{E} \in \mathbb{F}_q^{\ell \times r}$
Output: $\pi \in \mathsf{Sym}(n)$ such that $\pi(\vec{V})\vec{H}^\top = \vec{E}$
 1: Proceed as in Lines 1–14 of Algorithm 3
 2: Initialize an empty list $\mathcal{T}$
 3: **for** $\vec{X} \in \mathcal{L}$ **do**
 4:     $\vec{X}' \leftarrow \bar{\vec{E}} - \vec{X}_{\{1,\ldots,n-r\}}\vec{U}^\top$
 5:     **if** $\begin{bmatrix} \vec{X} & \vec{X}' \end{bmatrix} \in \mathcal{S}_n(\vec{V})$ **then**
 6:         $\mathcal{T} \leftarrow \mathcal{T} \cup \{\sigma^{-1}(\begin{bmatrix} \vec{X} & \vec{X}' \end{bmatrix})\}$
 7:     **Return:** $\mathcal{T}$

Allowing Matrices to have Repeated Columns. We must solve IPKP instances with parameters $(w, \ell^* + 1, q, d)$ obtained by considering the dual version of Eq. (15), that is

$$\tilde{\pi}^{-1}(\vec{\bar{H}})\vec{V}_W^\top = \vec{E}^{*\top}.$$

Algorithm 6 $\mathsf{SBC}^*_{\mathsf{dual}}(\vec{H}, \vec{V}, \vec{E})$

Parameters: w_1, w_2, $\tilde{r}$, $d \in \mathbb{N}$ with $w = w_1 + w_2 \leq n$, $d \leq \tilde{r} \leq r$ and
$\quad N_{n,r}(w,d) > 1$
Input: $\vec{H} \in \mathsf{GL}_{r,n}(\mathbb{F}_q)$, $\vec{V} \in \mathsf{GL}_{\ell,n}(\mathbb{F}_q)$, $\vec{E} \in \mathbb{F}_q^{\ell \times r}$
Output: $\pi \in \mathsf{Sym}(n)$ such that $\pi(\vec{V})\vec{H}^\top = \vec{E}$
 1: Proceed as in Lines 1–7 of Algorithm 3
 2: $\vec{V}^{\mathsf{ext}} \leftarrow \begin{bmatrix} \vec{V} \\ (1,\ldots,1) \end{bmatrix}$, $\vec{E}^{\mathsf{ext}} \leftarrow \begin{bmatrix} \vec{E}^\top & \sum_{i=1}^{n} \vec{h}_i \end{bmatrix}$
 3: **Return:** $\mathsf{DualGuessSolve}(\vec{H}, \vec{V}^{\mathsf{ext}}, \vec{E}^{\mathsf{ext}}, \mathcal{K})$

We recall that $\vec{\bar{H}}$ is the matrix formed by the nonzero columns of the generator matrix of a random subcode of the code generated by $\vec{H}$, with dimension d and support size w (so $d < w$). We model $\vec{\bar{H}}$ as a random element of $\mathsf{GL}_{d,w}(\mathbb{F}_q)$ with no zero columns, meaning that there might be repeated columns. If this is the case, multiple solutions to the instance necessarily exist. Let us suppose, for example, that $\vec{\bar{H}}$ has 2 identical columns and all the others are distinct. If this happens and $\tilde{\pi}^{-1} \in \mathsf{Sym}(w)$ is a solution, another solution $\tilde{\mu} \in \mathsf{Sym}(w)$ can be found by swapping the images under $\tilde{\pi}^{-1}$ of the indexes corresponding to the repeating columns in $\vec{\bar{H}}$.

Definition 3. *If $\vec{H} \in \mathbb{F}_q^{r \times n}$ is a matrix with no zero columns, we define* $\mathsf{COL}_{\mathsf{REP}}(\vec{H}) = (m_1, \ldots, m_{q^r-1}) \in \mathbb{N}^{q^r-1}$, *where m_j is the number of times that the j-th element of $(\mathbb{F}_q^r)^*$ (ordered w.r.t. any ordering) appears among the columns of $\vec{H}$. We define the integer $N_{\mathsf{swaps}}(\vec{H})$ as*

$$N_{\mathsf{swaps}}(\vec{H}) = \prod_{i=1}^{q^r-1} m_i! \tag{16}$$

Proposition 4. *If $\pi(\vec{V})\vec{H}^\top = \vec{E}$, then from $\pi \in \mathsf{Sym}(n)$ (or equivalently from $\pi(\vec{V})$) we can obtain, performing only swaps, $N_{\mathsf{swaps}}(\vec{H})$ solutions to the problem (including π).*

Proof. Every swap of the permutation indices corresponding to two repeating columns gives a new distinct solution. Equation (16) counts the number of all possible swaps combined. $\square$

Proposition 5. *Let $\vec{H} \in \mathbb{F}_q^{r \times n}$ be a matrix with no zero columns and with* $\mathsf{COL}_{\mathsf{REP}}(\vec{H}) = (m_1, \ldots, m_{q^r-1})$. *Let $x \leq n$ be a positive integer and let*

$$J_{n,r,q}^{(x)} = \left\{ (\mu_1, \ldots, \mu_{q^r-1}) \in \mathbb{N}^{q^r-1} \ \middle| \ \mu_1 + \cdots + \mu_{q^r-1} = x,\ 0 \leq \mu_i \leq m_i \right\}.$$

Then

$$|\mathcal{S}_x(\vec{H})| = \sum_{(\mu_1,\ldots,\mu_{q^r-1}) \in J_{n,r,q}^{(\ell)}} \frac{x!}{\mu_1! \cdots \mu_{q^r-1}!}. \tag{17}$$

Proof. $|\mathcal{S}_x(\vec{H})|$ is given by the possible ways of choosing ordered collections of x elements from n with no replacement, but some of them might be repeated. This follows the multinomial distribution, which gives us Eq. (17). Notice that if $\vec{H}$ has no repeated columns, $\mathsf{COL}_{\mathsf{REP}}(\vec{H})$ has n entries equal to 1 and the rest of them equal to 0, so $|J_{n,r,q}^{(x)}| = \binom{n}{x}$, which implies

$$\sum_{(\mu_1,\ldots,\mu_{q^r-1})\in J_{n,r,q}^{(x)}} \frac{x!}{\mu_1!\cdots\mu_{q^r-1}!} = \binom{n}{x} r! = \frac{n!}{(n-x)!},$$

which is what we expected. $\qquad\square$

Remark 13. Since $\vec{\vec{H}}$ is modeled as random, we assume that its columns are uniformly distributed over $(\mathbb{F}_q^d)^*$, that is $\mathsf{COL}_{\mathsf{REP}}(\vec{\vec{H}}) = (u_1,\ldots,u_{q^d-1})$, where $(u_1,\ldots,u_{q^d-1}) \in \mathbb{N}^{q^d-1}$ is an element that minimizes the Euclidean distance from $(\frac{w}{q^d-1},\ldots,\frac{w}{q^d-1})$ in the set $\{(v_1,\ldots,v_{q^d-1}) \in \mathbb{N}^{q^d-1} \mid \sum_{i=1}^{q^d-1} v_i = w\}$. Notice that this element is not unique: if $(u_1,\ldots,u_{q^d-1})$ satisfies these requirements, then any permutation of it does as well. To justify this assumption, we model the distribution of each entry of $\mathsf{COL}_{\mathsf{REP}}(\vec{\vec{H}})$ as a binomial random variable with parameters (w,p), where $p = \frac{1}{q^d-1}$ is the probability of selecting a specific column (the probability of "success"). Hence, each entry has expected value $w \cdot p = \frac{w}{q^d-1}$, and by requiring every entry to be an integer, we obtain the above estimate.

Let $\mathsf{COL}_{\mathsf{REP}}^{(u)}(n,r,q)$ denote the vector $(u_1,\ldots,u_{q^r-1}) \in \mathbb{N}^{q^r-1}$ as in Remark 13 and let $N_{\mathsf{swaps}}^{(u)}(n,r,q) := \prod_{i=1}^{q^r-1} u_i!$. We also define $\mathsf{M}_{\mathsf{REP}}(n,r,q,x)$ as $|\mathcal{S}_x(\vec{H})|$, where $\vec{H} \in \mathbb{F}_q^{r\times n}$ is random with no zero columns, and therefore $\mathsf{M}_{\mathsf{REP}}(n,r,q,x)$ is computed using *Proposition* 5 with $\mathsf{COL}_{\mathsf{REP}}(\vec{H}) = \mathsf{COL}_{\mathsf{REP}}^{(u)}(n,r,q)$.

The next proposition presents the average running time of SBC^* (Algorithm 5) and $\mathsf{SBC}_{\mathsf{dual}}^*$ (Algorithm 6) in the case where $\vec{V}$ may contain repeated columns. Notice that, in our setting, the matrix that may have repeated columns is $\vec{\vec{H}}$; however, since we are solving the dual instance, it plays the role of $\vec{V}$ in Algorithm 5 and Algorithm 6.

Proposition 6. *Let* $\vec{H} \in \mathsf{GL}_{r,n}(\mathbb{F}_q)$ *with no repeated columns and s.t. its last row is a vector of all ones,* $\vec{V} \in \mathsf{GL}_{\ell,n}(\mathbb{F}_q)$ *be a matrix that might have repeated columns but no zero columns (and* $\vec{H}$, $\vec{V}$ *can be modeled as a random matrix with these properties) and* $\vec{E} \in \mathbb{F}_q^{\ell\times r}$*. Let now* $w_1, w_2, d \in \mathbb{N}^*$ *be valid parameters for* SBC^**, that is* $w = w_1 + w_2 \le n$ *and* $N_{n,r}(w,d) > 1$*. Then Algorithm 5 runs for* $d \le \tilde{r} \le r$ *in average time*

$$T_{\mathsf{SBC}^*}(n,r,q,\ell,w_1,w_2,d,\tilde{r}) = T_{\mathsf{ISD}}^{(d)}(n,r,w) + T_{\mathcal{K}}^* + T_{\mathcal{L}}^* + |\mathcal{L}^*|, \tag{18}$$

and Algorithm 6 runs for $0 \le \tilde{r} \le \ell+1$ *in average time*

$$T_{\mathsf{SBC}_{\mathsf{dual}}^*}(n,r,q,\ell,w_1,w_2,d,\tilde{r}) = T_{\mathsf{ISD}}^{(d)}(n,r,w) + \bar{T}_{\mathcal{K}} + \bar{T}_{\mathcal{L}}, \tag{19}$$

with

$$T_{\mathcal{K}}^* := \sum_{\bar{w}\in\{w_1,w_2\}} \mathsf{M}_{\mathsf{REP}}(n,\ell,q,\bar{w}) + \frac{1}{q^{dl}} \cdot \prod_{\bar{w}\in\{w_1,w_2\}} \mathsf{M}_{\mathsf{REP}}(n,\ell,q,\bar{w}),$$

$$T_{\mathcal{L}}^* := \mathsf{M}_{\mathsf{REP}}(n,\ell,q,n-r-w+\tilde{r}) + |\mathcal{K}^*| + \frac{\mathsf{M}_{\mathsf{REP}}(n,\ell,q,n-r-w+\tilde{r}) \cdot |\mathcal{K}^*|}{q^{\ell(\tilde{r}-d)}},$$

$$\bar{T}_{\mathcal{L}} := \bar{T}_{\mathcal{L}}(n,\ell,w,\tilde{r},|\bar{\mathcal{K}}|) \text{ as in Equation (14)},$$

$$|\mathcal{K}^*| := \frac{\mathsf{M}_{\mathsf{REP}}(n,\ell,q,w)}{q^{d\ell}}, \qquad |\bar{\mathcal{K}}| := |\mathcal{K}^*| \cdot N^{(u)}_{\mathsf{swaps}}(w,\ell,q),$$

$$|\mathcal{L}^*| := \frac{\mathsf{M}_{\mathsf{REP}}(n-w,\ell,q,n-r-w+\tilde{r}) \cdot |\mathcal{K}^*|}{q^{\ell(\tilde{r}-d)}}.$$

Proof. The running time of Algorithm 5 is obtained in the same way as for Algorithm 3. Thus, we obtain Eq. (18) by adapting Proposition 2 to the case in which $\vec{V}$ has repeated columns. Indeed, we obtain $T_{\mathcal{K}}^*$, $T_{\mathcal{L}}^*$, $|\mathcal{K}^*|$ and $|\mathcal{L}^*|$ as in Proposition 2 but we estimate $\mathcal{S}_x(\vec{V})$ with Eq. (17) instead of $\frac{n!}{(n-x)!}$.

The same reasoning also applies to Algorithm 6, but to prove Eq. (19) we still need to clarify $|\bar{\mathcal{K}}|$. As already mentioned, if $\vec{V}$ has repeated columns, then InvCand returns more than one candidate. Since $\vec{V}$ is modeled as a random matrix, we have that every candidate $\vec{X} \in \mathcal{K}^*$ for $\sigma(\vec{V}_J)$ (with $|J| = w$), where $\mathcal{K}^*$ is the list obtained after the *filtering step*, generates $N^{(u)}_{\mathsf{swaps}}(w,l,q)$ candidates for $\pi^{-1}(\vec{H})_I$ (the set I is possibly different for every $\vec{X}$). Therefore, Lines 7–14 in Algorithm 4 are executed $|\mathcal{K}^*| \cdot N^{(u)}_{\mathsf{swaps}}(w,l,q)$ times, which gives the list cardinality. $\qquad\square$

Proposition 7. *Under the same hypothesis and notation as in Proposition 6, with $\vec{E} \in \mathbb{F}_q^{\ell \times r}$ being of the form $\vec{E} = [\vec{0}_{\ell\times(r-1)} \sum_{i=1}^n \vec{v}_i]$, we have that the average number of solutions returned respectively by Algorithm 5 and Algorithm 6 is given by*

$$N_{\mathsf{SBC}^*}(n,r,q,\ell,w_1,w_2,d,\tilde{r}) = |\mathcal{L}^*| \cdot \min\left\{\frac{(r-\tilde{r})!}{q^{\ell(r-\tilde{r})} N^{(u)}_{\mathsf{swaps}}(r-\tilde{r},\ell,q)}, 1\right\},$$

$$N_{\mathsf{SBC}^*_{\mathsf{dual}}}(n,r,q,\ell,w_1,w_2,d,\tilde{r}) = \frac{|\bar{\mathcal{K}}|(n-(w_1+w_2))!}{(\ell+1-\tilde{r})!q^{\tilde{r}(r-1)}} \cdot \min\left\{\frac{(\ell+1-\tilde{r})!}{q^{(r-1)(\ell+1-\tilde{r})}}, 1\right\}.$$

$$\tag{20}$$

Proof. The number of solutions returned by Algorithm 5 is given by the number of elements in the list $\mathcal{L}$ that satisfy the condition at Line 5. Since, with the same notation as in Algorithm 5, $\vec{X}'$ can be modeled as a random $\ell \times (r-\tilde{r})$ matrix, then such condition is met with probability $\min\left\{\frac{|\mathcal{S}_{r-\tilde{r}}(\vec{V}_U)|}{q^{\ell(r-\tilde{r})}}, 1\right\}$ where U is the set of the indexes of the columns of $\vec{V}$ that are not columns of $\vec{X}$ (so $|U| = r-\tilde{r}$), therefore $|\mathcal{S}_{r-\tilde{r}}(\vec{V}_U)| = \frac{(r-\tilde{r})!}{N^{(u)}_{\mathsf{swaps}}(r-\tilde{r},\ell,q)}$.

On the other hand, the number of solutions returned by $\mathsf{SBC}^*_{\mathsf{dual}}$ is given by the number of candidates $\vec{W}$ of the form given at Line 9 of Algorithm 4 that satisfy both the condition at Line 10 and the condition at Line 12. The probability of the first condition to be met is the probability of a collision between two random $(r-1)\times\tilde{r}$ matrices. Considering the notation of Algorithm 4, the equality at Line 10 is checked for the matrices $\vec{W}\vec{V}'^{\top}$ and $\vec{E}'$, which are actually $r\times\tilde{r}$. However, the last row of such matrices is not random at all and, indeed, it always collides. To see this, let us recall that the last row of $\vec{H}$, and so the last one of $\vec{W}$, is a row of ones. On the other hand, the matrix $\vec{E}'$ is of the form

$$\vec{E}' = \vec{E}^{\text{ext}}(\vec{M}^{\top})_{\{1,\dots,\tilde{r}\}} = \begin{bmatrix} \vec{0}_{(r-1)\times\ell} & \sum_{i=1}^{n}\vec{h}_i \\ (\sum_{i=1}^{n}\vec{v}_i)^{\top} & \end{bmatrix}(\vec{M}^{\top})_{\{1,\dots,\tilde{r}\}},$$

since $\vec{E}^{\text{ext}}$ is as in Line 2 of Algorithm 6. Notice that the last entry of the last row of $\vec{E}^{\text{ext}}$ is given by $n \bmod q$ (which we denote with n_q). If we denote $\mu(\vec{V}^{\text{ext}})$ with $\tilde{\vec{V}}_\mu^{\text{ext}}$, we have that $\vec{V}^{\top} = (\tilde{\vec{V}}_\mu^{\text{ext}\top})^{\{1,\dots,n-(\ell+1)+\tilde{r}\}}(\vec{M}^{\top})_{\{1,\dots,\tilde{r}\}}$ and, since the last row of $\vec{W}$ is a row of ones, the last row of $\vec{W}\vec{V}^{\top}$ is given by $\left(\sum_{i=1}^{n-(\ell+1)+\tilde{r}}(\tilde{\vec{v}}_\mu^{\text{ext}})_i\right)^{\top}(\vec{M}^{\top})_{\{1,\dots,\tilde{r}\}}$. On the other hand, the last row of $\vec{E}'$ is given by

$$\left[\sum_{i=1}^{n}\vec{v}_i\, n_q\right](\vec{M}^{\top})_{\{1,\dots,\tilde{r}\}} = \left(\sum_{i=1}^{n}(\tilde{\vec{v}}_\mu^{\text{ext}})_i\right)^{\top}(\vec{M}^{\top})_{\{1,\dots,\tilde{r}\}}$$

$$= \left(\sum_{i=1}^{n-(\ell+1)+\tilde{r}}(\tilde{\vec{v}}_\mu^{\text{ext}})_i\right)^{\top}(\vec{M}^{\top})_{\{1,\dots,\tilde{r}\}},$$

where the last equality follows from the fact that, by construction, $\left(\tilde{\vec{v}}_\mu^{\text{ext}}\right)_i^{\top}(\vec{M}^{\top})_{\{1,\dots,\tilde{r}\}} = \vec{0}$ for every i s.t. $n-(\ell+1)+\tilde{r}+1 \le i \le n$.

To prove Eq. (20), it remains to estimate the probability of the condition at Line 12 to be met. This is the probability of the matrix $\vec{W}'$ having as columns those of $\vec{H}$ that do not appear in $\vec{W}_{\{1,\dots,n-(\ell+1)\}}$. This event happens for sure for $\tilde{r}$ columns (because $\vec{W}$ satisfies the condition at Line 10), while the other $\ell+1-\tilde{r}$ columns can be considered random. Therefore, the probability is given by $\min\left\{\frac{|\mathcal{S}_{\ell+1-\tilde{r}}(\vec{H}_U)|}{q^{(r-1)(\ell+1-\tilde{r})}}, 1\right\}$, where U is the set of columns of $\vec{H}$ that don't appear in $\vec{W}$. Since $\vec{H}$ has no repeated columns, $|\mathcal{S}_{\ell+1-\tilde{r}}(\vec{H}_U)| = (\ell+1-\tilde{r})!$. Notice that again we consider collision between random matrices with $r-1$ rows, since, analogously as above, one can show that the last row of $\vec{W}'$ is always a row of ones. $\qquad\square$

Remark 14. We showed in Proposition 7 how extending the matrix $\vec{H}$ in Algorithm 6 does not help to reduce the number of collisions. The same reasoning applies to the matrix $\vec{V}$ in Algorithm 5, hence it is not useful to extend it. Moreover, one could observe that in Algorithm 5 and Algorithm 6 the matrices that are being checked for collisions have a column deriving from the extension of $\vec{H}$ and $\vec{V}$, respectively, but they are still considered random. Indeed, we consider the matrices at Line 5 in Algorithm 5 to be random $\ell \times (r - \tilde{r})$ matrices instead of $\ell \times (r - 1 - \tilde{r})$ (the same applies to Algorithm 6 with $(r - 1) \times (\ell + 1 - \tilde{r})$ instead of $(r - 1) \times (\ell - \tilde{r})$). We can do this because the "non-random" column appears in a matrix that is being multiplied on the right by another matrix, so the resulting product cannot be split as it was done Proposition 7 for the last row: roughly speaking, the "row-times-columns" multiplication scrambles the column-structure of the matrix on the left. Let us consider the matrix $\vec{X}'$ in Algorithm 5 (for Algorithm 6 the reasoning is analogous), which is obtained as $\bar{\bar{E}} - \vec{X}_{\{1,\dots,n-r\}}\bar{\bar{U}}^{\top}$. We have that

$$
\begin{aligned}
\vec{X}_{\{1,\dots,n-r\}}\bar{\bar{U}}^{\top} &= \vec{X}_{\{1,\dots,n-r\}} \left((\vec{M}\sigma(\vec{H}))_{\{1,\dots,n-r\}}^{\{\tilde{r}+1,\dots,r\}} \right)^{\top} \\
&= \vec{X}_{\{1,\dots,n-r\}} \left(\sigma(\vec{H})^{\top} \right)^{\{1,\dots,n-r\}} \vec{M}_{\{\tilde{r}+1,\dots r\}}^{\top} \\
&= \begin{bmatrix} \vec{A} & \sum_{i=1}^{n-r} \vec{x}_i \end{bmatrix} \vec{M}_{\{\tilde{r}+1,\dots r\}}^{\top},
\end{aligned}
$$

for some $\vec{A} \in \mathbb{F}_q^{\ell \times (r-1)}$. Since $\bar{\bar{E}} = \vec{E}\vec{M}_{\{\tilde{r}+1,\dots,r\}}^{\top}$, we have that

$$
\begin{aligned}
\vec{X}' = \bar{\bar{E}} - \vec{X}_{\{1,\dots,n-r\}}\bar{\bar{U}}^{\top} &= \left(\begin{bmatrix} \vec{0} & \sum_{i-1}^{n} \vec{v}_i \end{bmatrix} - \begin{bmatrix} \vec{A} & \sum_{i=1}^{n-r} \vec{x}_i \end{bmatrix} \right) \vec{M}_{\{\tilde{r}+1,\dots r\}}^{\top} \\
&= \begin{bmatrix} -\vec{A} & \sum_{i=1}^{r} \bar{\vec{x}}_i \end{bmatrix} \vec{M}_{\{\tilde{r}+1,\dots r\}}^{\top},
\end{aligned}
\tag{21}
$$

where $\left\{ \bar{\vec{x}}_i \right\}_{i=1,\dots r}$ is the set of the columns of $\vec{V}$ that do not appear in $\vec{X}$. Note that these are the columns of $\vec{X}'$ if $\vec{X}$ is the candidate that leads to the solution. However, we cannot express the matrix resulting from the product in Eq. (21) in term of the last column of the matrix on the left, which is the one that we just showed to be not random. Therefore, for the sake of our analysis, we consider this matrix to look random.

Finally, notice that a similar reasoning can be applied when checking for collisions at Line 13 of Algorithm 3 (when using Algorithm 5) and at Line 10 of Algorithm 4 (when using Algorithm 6), for the case in which, respectively, $\tilde{r} = r$ and $\tilde{r} = \ell+1$. Indeed, in these cases we consider collisions between random $\ell \times (r - d)$ and $(r - 1) \times (\ell + 1)$ matrices (instead of between $\ell \times (r - 1 - d)$ and $(r - 1) \times \ell$ matrices), respectively. Notice that the above considerations apply only when the IPKP instance arises from the dehomogenization of a PKP instance, which is why this assumption is required in Proposition 7. For generic IPKP instances, the algorithm behaves identically, but the number of solutions can be estimated without these considerations, resulting in slightly smaller complexity estimates.

Remark 15. In Proposition 6 we do not require the existence of a solution. We do this since we use this proposition to estimate the complexity of solving the subinstances, which are not required to have a solution, except for one of them. Therefore to estimate the running time of SBC^* and $\mathsf{SBC}^*_{\mathsf{dual}}$ applied on $\binom{n}{w} - 1$

234   A. Budroni et al.

subinstances we use respectively Eq. (18) and Eq. (19), while in one subinstance we use $T^{(1)}_{\mathsf{SBC}*}$ and $T^{(1)}_{\mathsf{SBC}*_{\mathrm{dual}}}$. These are obtained in the same way as in Proposition 7, but taking $|\mathcal{K}^*| = \max\left\{\frac{\mathsf{M}_{\mathsf{REP}}(n,\ell,q,w)}{q^{d\ell}}, 1\right\}$ instead of taking it as in Proposition 6. Analogously, we define $N^{(1)}_{\mathsf{SBC}*}$ and $N^{(1)}_{\mathsf{SBC}*_{\mathrm{dual}}}$.

4.3   New Algorithm

We can now define our complete algorithm for solving IPKP, which incorporates all the modifications described above. The algorithm takes two additional Boolean parameters, $\mathsf{v}_{\mathsf{inn}}$ and $\mathsf{v}_{\mathsf{out}}$, which specify whether Algorithm 4 is used respectively in the subinstances and in the outer instance. Here, the algorithm $\mathsf{InvCand}^*(\vec{X})$ takes as input $\vec{X} \in \mathcal{S}_w(\vec{\bar{H}})$, a solution to the subinstance (that is, using the notation of the algorithm, $\vec{X}(\vec{W}^{\mathsf{ext}})^\top = \vec{E}^{*\mathsf{ext}}$), and returns all corresponding candidates for $\vec{\tilde{W}}^{\mathsf{ext}}$. In general, there is more than one such candidate, since $\vec{\bar{H}}$ typically contains repeated columns.

Lemma 1. *Let $\vec{H} \in \mathsf{GL}_{r,n}$, $\vec{V} \in \mathsf{GL}_{\ell,n}$ and $\vec{E} \in \mathbb{F}_q^{\ell \times r}$ be matrices that define an IPKP-instance obtained by de-homogenizing an $(n, r-1, q, \ell) - \mathsf{PKP}$ instance that has a solution. Let $\mathsf{v}_{\mathsf{inn}} \in \{0,1\}$ be a boolean parameter that specifies whether to use Algorithm 6 or Algorithm 5 in the (inner) subinstances. Let $w, d \in \mathbb{N}^*$ be valid parameters for the outer instance, that is $w \leq n$ and $N_{n,r}(w,d) > 1$. Let $\ell^* = \min\{\ell, w - d + 1\}$ and let $w_1^*, w_2^*, d^*, \tilde{r}^*$ be valid parameters for the subinstances, that is $w^* = w_1^* + w_2^* \leq w$, $N_{w,\ell^*+1}((w^*, d^*) > 1$ and*

$$\begin{cases} 0 \leq \tilde{r}^* \leq d+1 & if\ \mathsf{v}_{\mathsf{inn}} \\ d^* \leq \tilde{r}^* \leq \ell^* + 1 & otherwise \end{cases}.$$

We denote the vector of the parameters used in the subinstances as $\mathsf{par}_{\mathsf{inn}} = (w, \ell^* + 1, q, d, w_1^*, w_2^*, d^*, \tilde{r}^*)$. Then the average running time of Lines 6–13 of Algorithm 7, that is the average running time of the modified filtering step, is given by

$$T_{\mathcal{K}}^{(\mathsf{v}_{\mathsf{inn}})} = \begin{cases} \left(\binom{n}{w} - 1\right) T_{\mathsf{SBC}*_{\mathrm{dual}}}(\mathsf{par}_{\mathsf{inn}}) + T^{(1)}_{\mathsf{SBC}*_{\mathrm{dual}}}(\mathsf{par}_{\mathsf{inn}}), & if\ \mathsf{v}_{\mathsf{inn}}, \\ \left(\binom{n}{w} - 1\right) T_{\mathsf{SBC}*}(\mathsf{par}_{\mathsf{inn}}) + T^{(1)}_{\mathsf{SBC}*}(\mathsf{par}_{\mathsf{inn}}), & otherwise. \end{cases}$$

Proof. $\underline{\mathsf{v}_{\mathsf{inn}} = 1}$: Since $\mathsf{v}_{\mathsf{inn}} = 1$, the cost of executing Lines 6–13, which is $T_{\mathcal{K}}^{(\mathsf{v}_{\mathsf{inn}})}$, is given by $|\bar{\mathcal{S}}_w(\vec{V})| = \binom{n}{w}$ multiplied by the running time of Algorithm 6 applied to the subinstances. However, as anticipated before, one of the subinstance is required to have one solution, therefore we estimate the running time of Algorithm 6 applied to this subinstance with $T^{(1)}_{\mathsf{SBC}*_{\mathrm{dual}}}(\mathsf{par}_{\mathsf{inn}})$, while for all the other subinstances we use $T_{\mathsf{SBC}*_{\mathrm{dual}}}(\mathsf{par}_{\mathsf{inn}})$.

$\underline{\mathsf{v}_{\mathsf{inn}} = 0}$: The proof is exactly the same as in the previous case with Algorithm 6 replaced by Algorithm 5.   □

Algorithm 7 NewAlgorithm($\vec{H}, \vec{V}, \vec{E}$)

Parameters: $\mathsf{v}_{\mathsf{inn}}, \mathsf{v}_{\mathsf{out}} \in \{0,1\}$, $w, \tilde{r}, d \in \mathbb{N}$ with $w \le n$, $N_{n,r}(w,d) > 1$ and
$\quad 0 \le \tilde{r} \le \ell + 1 \quad$ **if** $\mathsf{v}_{\mathsf{out}} \quad$ **else** $\quad d \le \tilde{r} \le r$.
Input: $\vec{H} \in \mathsf{GL}_{r,n}(\mathbb{F}_q)$, $\vec{V} \in \mathsf{GL}_{\ell,n}(\mathbb{F}_q)$, $\vec{E} \in \mathbb{F}_q^{\ell \times r}$,
Output: $\pi \in \mathsf{Sym}(n)$ such that $\pi(\vec{V})\vec{H}^\top = \vec{E}$

1: Use ISD to find a subcode of the code generated by $\vec{H}$ with dimension d and
$\quad$ support size $w = w_1 + w_2$. Call $\mathcal{C}$ this subcode, $\vec{H}^*$ its generator matrix and
$\quad \vec{S} \in \mathsf{GL}_{d,r}(\mathbb{F}_q)$ the matrix s.t. $\vec{H}^* = \vec{S}\vec{H}$.

2: Compute $\sigma \in \mathsf{Sym}(n)$ such that $\mathsf{Supp}(\sigma(\mathcal{C})) = \{n-r+\tilde{r}-w+1, \ldots, n-r+\tilde{r}\}$

3: $J \leftarrow \{n-r+\tilde{r}-w+1, \ldots, n-r+\tilde{r}\}$

4: $\vec{E}^* \leftarrow \vec{E}\vec{S}^\top$, $\vec{\tilde{H}} \leftarrow \sigma(\vec{H}^*)_J$

5: Initialize an empty list $\mathcal{K}$

6: **for** $\vec{W} \in \bar{\mathcal{S}}_w(\vec{V})$ **do**

7: $\qquad \vec{W}^{\mathsf{ext}} \leftarrow \begin{bmatrix} \vec{W} \\ (1,\ldots,1) \end{bmatrix}$, $\vec{E}^{*\mathsf{ext}} \leftarrow \begin{bmatrix} \vec{E}^{*\top} & \sum_{i=1}^{w} \vec{h}_i \end{bmatrix}$

8: $\qquad$ **if** $\mathsf{v}_{\mathsf{inn}}$ **then**

9: $\qquad\qquad \mathcal{K} \leftarrow \mathcal{K} \cup \mathsf{SBC}^*_{\mathsf{dual}}(\vec{W}^{\mathsf{ext}}, \vec{\tilde{H}}, \vec{E}^{*\mathsf{ext}})$

10: $\qquad$ **else**

11: $\qquad\qquad \mathcal{K}^* \leftarrow \mathsf{SBC}^*(\vec{W}^{\mathsf{ext}}, \vec{\tilde{H}}, \vec{E}^{*\mathsf{ext}})$

12: $\qquad\qquad$ **for** $\vec{X} \in \mathcal{K}^*$ **do**

13: $\qquad\qquad\qquad \mathcal{K} \leftarrow \mathcal{K} \cup \mathsf{InvCand}^*(\vec{X})$

14: **if** $\mathsf{v}_{\mathsf{out}}$ **then**

15: $\qquad \vec{V}^{\mathsf{ext}} \leftarrow \begin{bmatrix} \vec{V} \\ (1,\ldots,1) \end{bmatrix}$, $\vec{E}^{\mathsf{ext}} \leftarrow \begin{bmatrix} \vec{E}^\top & \sum_{i=1}^{n} \vec{h}_i \end{bmatrix}$

16: $\qquad \vec{\tilde{H}} \leftarrow \mathsf{DualGuessSolve}(\vec{H}, \vec{V}^{\mathsf{ext}}, \vec{E}^{\mathsf{ext}}, \mathcal{K})$

17: $\qquad$ Compute $\pi \in \mathsf{Sym}(n)$ s.t. $\pi(\vec{H}) = \vec{\tilde{H}}$

18: $\qquad$ **Return:** π^{-1}

19: **else**

20: $\qquad$ Proceed as in Lines 8–19 of Algorithm 3

Lemma 2. *Under the same hypothesis and notation as in Lemma 1, then the cardinality of the list $\mathcal{K}$ obtained after Line 13 of Algorithm 7 is given on average by*

$$|\mathcal{K}^{(\mathsf{v}_{\mathsf{inn}})}| = \begin{cases} \left(\binom{n}{w} - 1\right) N_{\mathsf{SBC}^*_{\mathsf{dual}}}(\mathsf{par}_{\mathsf{inn}}) + \max\left\{N^{(1)}_{\mathsf{SBC}^*_{\mathsf{dual}}}(\mathsf{par}_{\mathsf{inn}}), 1\right\}, & \text{if } \mathsf{v}_{\mathsf{inn}}, \\ \left(\left(\binom{n}{w} - 1\right) N_{\mathsf{SBC}^*}(\mathsf{par}_{\mathsf{inn}}) + \max\left\{N^{(1)}_{\mathsf{SBC}^*}(\mathsf{par}_{\mathsf{inn}}), 1\right\}\right) \cdot N^{(u)}_{\mathsf{swaps}}(w,d,q), & \text{otherwise.} \end{cases}$$

Proof. $\underline{\mathsf{v}_{\mathsf{inn}} = 0}$: $|\mathcal{K}^{(\mathsf{v}_{\mathsf{inn}})}|$ is the cardinality of the list $\mathcal{K}$ containing all the candidates for $\sigma(\vec{\tilde{V}})_J$. This is given by the cardinality of the list $\mathcal{K}^*$ defined at Line 11 containing all the permuted $\vec{\tilde{H}}$ that solve the subinstance multiplied by $N^{(u)}_{\mathsf{swaps}}(w,d,q)$, since, for every element $\vec{X} \in \mathcal{K}^*$, $\mathsf{InvCand}^*(\vec{X})$ returns

$N_{\mathsf{swaps}}^{(u)}(w, d, q)$ candidates for $\sigma(\vec{V})_J$. Because of Proposition 7, we estimate $|\mathcal{K}^*|$ with $N_{\mathsf{SBC}^*}(\mathsf{par_{inn}})$ in $\binom{n}{w} - 1$ subinstances, while we use $\max\{N_{\mathsf{SBC}^*}^{(1)}(\mathsf{par_{inn}}), 1\}$ for one subinstance.

$\underline{\mathsf{v_{inn}} = 1}$: The proof is obtained in the same way as in the previous case, but we don't have the factor $N_{\mathsf{swaps}}^{(u)}(w, d, q)$ because $\mathsf{SBC}_{\mathsf{dual}}^*$ already returns the candidates for $\sigma(\tilde{\vec{V}})_J$ (the swaps are handled internally). $\qquad\square$

Lemma 3. *Under the same hypothesis and notation as in Lemma 1 and Lemma 2. Moreover, let $\mathsf{v_{out}} \in \{0, 1\}$ be a boolean parameter that specifies whether to use Algorithm 4 or the original* **STEP 2-STEP 3** *in the outer instance and let $\tilde{r} \in \mathbb{N}$ be a valid parameter for the outer instance, that is*

$$\begin{cases} 0 \leq \tilde{r} \leq \ell + 1 & \textit{if } \mathsf{v_{out}} \\ d \leq \tilde{r} \leq r & \textit{otherwise} \end{cases}.$$

Then the average running time of Lines 14–20 is given by

$$T_{\mathcal{L}}^{(\mathsf{v_{inn}}, \mathsf{v_{out}})} = \begin{cases} \bar{T}_{\mathcal{L}}(n, \ell, w, \tilde{r}, |\mathcal{K}^{(\mathsf{v_{inn}})}|), & \textit{if } \mathsf{v_{out}} \\ \dfrac{n!}{(r+w-\tilde{r})!} + |\mathcal{K}^{(\mathsf{v_{inn}})}| + \dfrac{n!|\mathcal{K}^{(\mathsf{v_{inn}})}|}{(r+w-\tilde{r})!q^{\ell(\tilde{r}-d)}} + \dfrac{(n-w)!|\mathcal{K}^{(\mathsf{v_{inn}})}|}{(r-\tilde{r})!q^{\ell(\tilde{r}-d)}}, & \textit{otherwise.} \end{cases}$$

Proof. $\underline{\mathsf{v_{out}} = 0}$: In these cases the proof follows as in Proposition 2 by using the estimates for $|\mathcal{K}|$ given by Lemma 2: in both cases, the first three terms of the sum are obtained as in Eq. (12) by replacing $|\mathcal{K}|$ with $|\mathcal{K}^{(\mathsf{v_{inn}})}|$. The last term of both sums is obtained in the same way from Eq. (13).

$\underline{\mathsf{v_{out}} = 1}$: The proof follows from Proposition 3 and Lemma 2. $\qquad\square$

Theorem 1. *Under the same hypothesis and notation as in Lemma 1, Lemma 2 and Lemma 3, then the average running time of Algorithm 7 is given by*

$$T^{(4)}(n, r, q, \ell, w, d, \tilde{r}, w_1^*, w_2^*, d^*, \tilde{r}^*, \mathsf{v_{inn}}, \mathsf{v_{out}}) = T_{\mathsf{ISD}}^{(d)}(n, r, w) + T_{\mathcal{K}}^{(\mathsf{v_{inn}})} + T_{\mathcal{L}}^{(\mathsf{v_{inn}}, \mathsf{v_{out}})}.$$

Proof. The proof follows by combining Eq. (3), Lemma 1 and Lemma 3, since the cost of Lines 2–5 is negligible. $\qquad\square$

Remark 16. Actually, in Theorem 1 we consider n and r to be valid values for respectively w and d, since the code generated by $\vec{H}$ is a subcode of itself. We make this explicit since n and r might not satisfy $N_{n,r}(n, r) > 1$. In this case Algorithm 7 becomes, if $\mathsf{v_{out}} = 0$, the same as Algorithm 3, as we are applying SBC^* to a single instance (since $\binom{n}{n} = 1$) with parameters (n, r, q, ℓ), where $\vec{V}$ has no repeated columns. Consequently, in this setting, the running time of SBC^* coincides with that of SBC.

5 Discussion and Comparisons

In this section, we assess the impact of the algorithmic improvements introduced in Sect. 4 by comparing the complexity of Algorithm 7 with that of KMP and SBC.

Complexity for Adaptive Field Size. Figure 3 reports the complexities of the three algorithms for $n \in \{64, 92, 118\}$, rates $R = \frac{r}{n} \in \{0.3, 0.5, 0.7\}$, and varying values of ℓ. For each parameter set (n, R, ℓ), the field size q is chosen as the smallest power of a prime satisfying conditions i)–iv) in Sect. 2.1, following the same approach adopted by Santini *et al.* [24]. Notice that, for given n, R and ℓ, a smaller field size q generally leads to a higher estimated time complexity of the problem instance when solving it with KMP or SBC. Hence, this choice of considering the smallest q admissible is motivated by the fact that it allows the construction of instances with smaller public key sizes. Moreover, notice that these conditions i)–iv) in Sect. 2.1 have to be met by the parameters of the homogeneous instance, since by adding a row of ones to the parity check matrix and extending the zero matrix accordingly, we introduce equations that are verified by every permutation. For every n and R, we consider all values of ℓ such that the corresponding q is at least 3. In addition, for each parameter set analyzed, we consider the minimum complexity between the problem and its dual version, as defined in Eq. (6). As explained in Remark 16, Algorithm 7 automatically falls back to the SBC setting whenever this is the most convenient choice. Hence, as one can observe in the plots, its complexity is always smaller than or equal to that of SBC. In particular, for $R = 0.7$, we observe gains already from $\ell = 1$, whereas for $R = 0.5$ and $R = 0.3$, the improvement becomes evident only for $\ell = 2$ and $\ell = 4$, respectively. On the other hand, KMP is generally worse or equal than SBC and Algorithm 7.

Complexity for Large Fields and Implications for PERK 1.0. When q is larger than the smallest suitable power of a prime, we observe that Algorithm 7 quickly converges to SBC. This behavior is expected, since larger field sizes q prevent the existence of subcodes with small support size that are useful when solving the IPKP subinstances, as explained in Sect. 4.2. Consequently, our variant of **STEP 1** in SBC becomes ineffective in this regime. This trend is clearly visible when comparing the complexities of Algorithm 7 and SBC for the PERK 1.0 [1] parameter sets, as reported in Table 2. We observe that Algorithm 7 achieves improvements for minimal field sizes q, while it coincides with SBC for the PERK field size $q = 1021$. This choice of q, despite leading to larger public keys, was motivated by other constraints imposed by the MPC-in-the-Head framework used in PERK.

Discussion on PERK 2.1 Parameter Sets. We found that SBC remains optimal also for the parameter sets of the more recent PERK 2.1 [2]. Unlike in the previous version of PERK, the field size $q = 2048$ is close to the minimum admissible value according to conditions i)–iv) in Sect. 2.1. Specifically, the minimal field sizes satisfying these conditions are 1997, 2017, and 1993 for

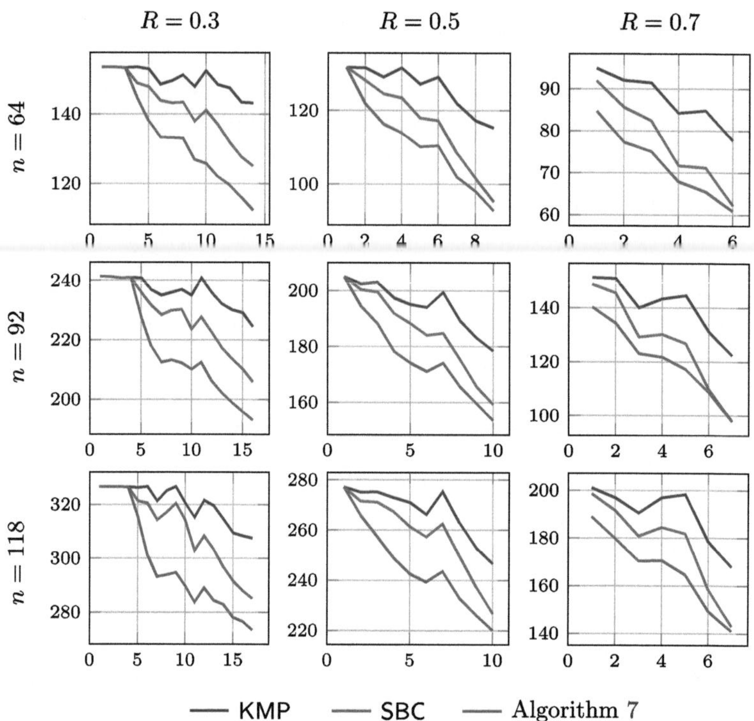

Fig. 3. Time complexity, expressed in $\log_2$ of the number of matrix and list operations, of KMP, SBC and Algorithm 7 for $n \in \{64, 92, 118\}$, $R \in \{0.3, 0.5, 0.7\}$ and different values of ℓ along the x-axis.

security levels I, III, and V, respectively. However, in this case, there is another reason supporting the optimality of SBC: across all parameter sets, we have $\ell = 1$ and $0.42 \leq R \leq 0.5$. From Fig. 3, which reports the same values of n as in the PERK 2.1 parameter sets, we indeed observe that for this range of code rates and $\ell = 1$, Algorithm 7 matches SBC in complexity.

Acknowledgments. We thank the anonymous reviewers for their insightful comments and suggestions that helped improving the manuscript. The third author acknowledges support from Ripple's University Blockchain Research Initiative and from the INDAM group GNSAGA.

A On the Rank of the Puncturings of V

We explain here why we can assume that $\ell^* = \mathsf{rank}(\vec{V}_W) = \min\{\ell, w - d + 1\}$. With the same notation as Sect. 4.2, we have that for W corresponding to the solution, $\mathsf{rank}(\vec{V}_W) \leq \min\{\ell, w - d + 1\}$. Indeed, $\vec{V}_W$ is $\ell \times w$ and there exists $\tilde{\pi} \in \mathsf{Sym}(w)$ such that

$$\tilde{\pi}(\vec{V}_W)\bar{\bar{H}}^{\top} = \vec{E}^*.$$

Table 2. Comparison of complexities for different PERK 1.0 parameter set and equivalent parameters but with minimal field size q.

	(n, r, ℓ)	q	KMP	SBC	Algorithm 7
perk-i-3	$(79, 35, 3)$	1021	146.7	145.6	145.6
minimum q		13	180.1	175.4	166.0
perk-i-5	$(83, 36, 5)$	1021	153.8	147.7	147.7
minimum q		5	191.3	185.2	171.2
perk-iii-3	$(112, 54, 3)$	1021	212.7	210.8	210.8
minimum q		16	257.6	254.7	242.6
perk-iii-5	$(116, 55, 5)$	1021	219.0	212.6	212.6
minimum q		5	276.8	270.1	248.6
perk-v-3	$(146, 75, 3)$	1021	280.0	275.2	275.2
minimum q		16	342.5	339.2	325.5
perk-v-5	$(150, 76, 5)$	1021	280.9	274.1	274.1
minimum q		5	363.6	358.0	329.0

Then, by rank-nullity theorem and by noting that $\mathsf{rank}(\tilde{\pi}(\vec{V}_W)) = \mathsf{rank}(\vec{V}_W)$ for any $\tilde{\pi} \in \mathsf{Sym}(w)$, we have that

$$\mathsf{rank}(\vec{V}_W) = \mathsf{rank}(\tilde{\pi}(\vec{V}_W)) \leq w - \mathsf{rank}(\bar{\vec{H}}) + \mathsf{rank}(\vec{E}^*) = w - d + 1. \qquad (22)$$

We can safely assume the equality in Eq. (22), that is $\mathsf{rank}(\vec{V}_W) = \min\{\ell, w - d + 1\}$. Indeed, for ℓ small enough (which corresponds to the cases of cryptographic interest), we have $\ell < w - d + 1 \leq w$. Then, Eq. (22) is satisfied, and $\vec{V}_W$ is a non-square submatrix of the full-rank matrix $\vec{V}$, and it is full rank with high probability. If, on the other hand, $\ell > w - d + 1$, we can obtain an equivalent instance after removing the redundant rows of $\vec{V}_W$, which are $\ell - (w - d + 1)$, and the resulting matrix is full-rank with high probability. It remains to consider the case $\ell = w - d + 1$. If $d > 1$, $\vec{V}_W$ is again non-square, so the previous considerations apply. Otherwise, if $d = 1$ and $\ell = w$, $\vec{V}_W$ is square, and the probability that it is not full rank is approximately $1/q$. In our estimates, however, we can safely assume that this never occurs. Indeed, when a square $\vec{V}_W$ is not full rank, solving such a subinstance requires an overhead of guessing $\tilde{\pi}$ on $w - \mathsf{rank}(\vec{V}_W)$ columns. With high probability, this overhead appears in few cases and, when it appears, it is absorbed by the overall complexity, so we assume it to be negligible.

References

1. Aaraj, N., et al.: PERK. Technical report, National Institute of Standards and Technology (2023). https://csrc.nist.gov/Projects/pqc-dig-sig/round-1-additional-signatures
2. Aaraj, N., et al.: PERK: a post-quantum signature scheme (version 2.1.0) (2025). https://pqc-perk.org/assets/downloads/perk-v2.1.0.pdf
3. Alagic, G., et al.: Status report on the first round of the additional digital signature schemes for the NIST post-quantum cryptography standardization process. NIST Interagency/Internal Report (NISTIR) 8528, National Institute of Standards and Technology (NIST), Gaithersburg, MD (2024). https://doi.org/10.6028/NIST.IR.8528
4. Baldi, M., Battagliola, M., Mechri, R.E., Santini, P., Schiavoni, R., Zuane, D.D.: SPECK: signatures from permutation equivalence of codes and kernels. Cryptology ePrint Archive, Paper 2025/923 (2025). https://eprint.iacr.org/2025/923
5. Baritaud, T., Campana, M., Chauvaud, P., Gilbert, H.: On the security of the permuted kernel identification scheme. In: Brickell, E.F. (ed.) CRYPTO'92. LNCS, vol. 740, pp. 305–311. Springer, Heidelberg (1993). https://doi.org/10.1007/3-540-48071-4_21
6. Berger, T.P., Gueye, C.T., Klamti, J.B.: A NP-complete problem in coding theory with application to code based cryptography. In: El Hajji, S., Nitaj, A., Souidi, E.M. (eds.) Codes, Cryptology and Information Security, pp. 230–237. Springer, Cham (2017)
7. Beullens, W.: Sigma protocols for MQ, PKP and SIS, and Fishy signature schemes. In: Canteaut, A., Ishai, Y. (eds.) EUROCRYPT 2020, Part III. LNCS, vol. 12107, pp. 183–211. Springer, Cham (2020). https://doi.org/10.1007/978-3-030-45727-3_7
8. Bidoux, L., Gaborit, P.: Compact post-quantum signatures from proofs of knowledge leveraging structure for the PKP, SD and RSD problems. In: El Hajji, S., Mesnager, S., Souidi, E.M. (eds.) Codes, Cryptology and Information Security, pp. 10–42. Springer, Cham (2023)
9. Budroni, A., Defranceschi, M., Pintore, F.: Accompanying repository (2025). https://github.com/Crypto-TII/pkp-complexity. Accessed 30 Oct 2025
10. Faugère, J.C., Koussa, E., Macario-Rat, G., Patarin, J., Perret, L.: PKP-based signature scheme. Cryptology ePrint Archive, Report 2018/714 (2018). https://eprint.iacr.org/2018/714
11. Feneuil, T.: Building MPCitH-based signatures from MQ, MinRank, rank SD and PKP. Cryptology ePrint Archive, Report 2022/1512 (2022). https://eprint.iacr.org/2022/1512
12. Garey, M.R., Johnson, D.S.: Computers and Intractability; A Guide to the Theory of NP-Completeness. W. H. Freeman & Co., USA (1990)
13. Georgiades, J.: Some remarks on the security of the identification scheme based on permuted kernels. J. Cryptol. 5(2), 133–137 (1992). https://doi.org/10.1007/BF00193565
14. Jaulmes, É., Joux, A.: Cryptanalysis of PKP: a new approach. In: Kim, K. (ed.) PKC 2001. LNCS, vol. 1992, pp. 165–172. Springer, Heidelberg (2001). https://doi.org/10.1007/3-540-44586-2_12
15. Koussa, E., Macario-Rat, G., Patarin, J.: On the complexity of the permuted kernel problem. Cryptology ePrint Archive, Report 2019/412 (2019). https://eprint.iacr.org/2019/412

16. Lampe, R., Patarin, J.: Analysis of some natural variants of the PKP algorithm. Cryptology ePrint Archive, Report 2011/686 (2011). https://eprint.iacr.org/2011/686

17. Lyubashevsky, V., et al.: CRYSTALS-DILITHIUM. Technical report, National Institute of Standards and Technology (2022). https://csrc.nist.gov/Projects/post-quantum-cryptography/selected-algorithms-2022

18. National Institute of Standards and Technology: Post-Quantum Cryptography Standardization (2017). https://csrc.nist.gov/projects/post-quantum-cryptography

19. National Institute of Standards and Technology: Post-quantum cryptography: Digital signature schemes. Round 2 Additional Signatures (2023). https://csrc.nist.gov/projects/pqc-dig-sig/round-2-additional-signatures

20. Patarin, J., Chauvaud, P.: Improved algorithms for the permuted kernel problem. In: Stinson, D.R. (ed.) CRYPTO'93. LNCS, vol. 773, pp. 391–402. Springer, Heidelberg (1994). https://doi.org/10.1007/3-540-48329-2_33

21. Prest, T., et al.: FALCON. Technical report, National Institute of Standards and Technology (2022). https://csrc.nist.gov/Projects/post-quantum-cryptography/selected-algorithms-2022

22. Sanna, C.: On the number of solutions to a random instance of the permuted kernel problem. J. Complex. **86**, 101898 (2025). https://doi.org/10.1016/j.jco.2024.101898. https://www.sciencedirect.com/science/article/pii/S0885064X2400075X

23. Santini, P., Baldi, M., Chiaraluce, F.: A novel attack to the permuted kernel problem. In: 2022 IEEE International Symposium on Information Theory (ISIT), pp. 1441–1446. IEEE Press (2022). https://doi.org/10.1109/ISIT50566.2022.9834867

24. Santini, P., Baldi, M., Chiaraluce, F.: Computational hardness of the permuted kernel and subcode equivalence problems. IEEE Trans. Inf. Theor. **70**(3), 2254–2270 (2024). https://doi.org/10.1109/TIT.2023.3323068

25. Schwabe, P., et al.: CRYSTALS-KYBER. Technical report, National Institute of Standards and Technology (2022). https://csrc.nist.gov/Projects/post-quantum-cryptography/selected-algorithms-2022

26. Shamir, A.: An efficient identification scheme based on permuted kernels (extended abstract) (rump session). In: Brassard, G. (ed.) CRYPTO'89. LNCS, vol. 435, pp. 606–609. Springer, New York (1990). https://doi.org/10.1007/0-387-34805-0_54

27. Shor, P.: Algorithms for quantum computation: discrete logarithms and factoring. In: Proceedings 35th Annual Symposium on Foundations of Computer Science, pp. 124–134 (1994). https://doi.org/10.1109/SFCS.1994.365700

Breaking RHQC's Post-Compromise Security

Philippe Gaborit, Philippe Krejčí[(✉)], and Cristina Onete

Université de Limoges/XLIM/CNRS 7252, Limoges, France
`{gaborit,philippe.krejci,maria-cristina.onete}@unilim.fr`

Abstract. Instant messaging applications, such as Signal or iMessage, are highly-popular, enabling users to communicate asynchronously in a secure manner. Asynchronous messaging protocols are particularly interesting since they allow the evolution of session keys through *ratcheting*. This evolution guarantees both Forward Secrecy (FS) —past session keys are protected even upon leakage— and Post-Compromise Secrecy (PCS) —following the compromise of a party's state, future session keys eventually become secure again.

Classical ratcheting algorithms, such as the Double Ratchet (proposed by Marlinspike and Perrin) rely on successive Diffie-Hellman key-exchange steps run asynchronously, which essentially amount to Non-Interactive Key-Exchange (NIKE). Yet, such algorithms are not quantum-secure. A recent proposal details RHQC: a double ratchet relying on the HQC Key-Encapsulation Mechanism —KEM— (with modified parameters). The RHQC scheme is optimized compared to a naïve quantum-secure ratchet, such as the one recently proposed in the context of Signal, and uses only two polynomials instead of three. This is possible since the first part of an HQC ciphertext is a syndrome and the public key is also a syndrome, with the same morphology. Unfortunately, we prove in this paper that RHQC is not PCS-secure, contradicting the claims made by the proposing work.

Our attack exploits the fact that compromising one of the two endpoints essentially allows the attacker to extract the private ratchet keys of following ratchets, which ensures that healing is never achieved. As, essentially, the ratchet public key is an Ouroboros-like ciphertext, we propose an extraction algorithm called `noisyBFmax` based on `BFmax`, as introduced by Baldelli *et al.*. This decoder allows us to break the PCS-security of RHQC with overwhelming probability. Additionally, we prove that it is impossible to fix RHQC with a lower complexity than the naïve approach.

Keywords: Ratchet · RHQC · Post-compromise security · HQC · BitFlip

1   Introduction

Instant Messaging applications allow users Alice and Bob to communicate securely and asynchronously over a long period of time. Typical asynchronous

M. Bardet and R. Niederhagen (Eds.): PQCrypto 2026, LNCS 16492, pp. 242–274, 2026.
https://doi.org/10.1007/978-3-032-22698-3_8

messaging runs in three main phases: an initial non-interactive key-exchange step allowing Alice and Bob to compute initial key material; ulterior, per-epoch key-evolution for that key material; and finally the actual secure messaging, using the current epoch's keys. The first step is usually achieved through a non-interactive key-exchange similar to asynchronous 0-Roundtrip Time (RTT) authenticated key-exchange (AKE), and relying on a summary public-key infrastructure (PKI) and some form of non-interactive key-exchange (NIKE) algorithm, while the third employs authenticated encryption.

In order to achieve key-evolution, modern asynchronous messaging protocols rely on mechanisms such as key-ratcheting, which enables two crucial, complementary properties upon the potential compromise of one of the peers:

FORWARD SECRECY: The compromise of long-term secrets does not impact the security of past epoch keys.

POST-COMPROMISE SECURITY: Even if an attacker compromises the (full or partial) state of a peer at some epoch t, the security of the session key is re-established starting from some ulterior epoch $t' \geq t$.

Applications such as Signal implement key-evolution through the double ratchet algorithm [18]. Subsequent work by Cohn-Gordon et al. [8] proved the fact that Signal's *symmetric*, HKDF-based ratchets guarantee Forward Secrecy, but not Post-Compromise Security (as defined by [9]), whereas its *asymmetric*, Diffie-Hellman (DH) based ratchets guarantee both properties.

Essentially, the double ratchet consists of a pair of asynchronous key-exchange steps, which are implemented here through two Non-Interactive DH key-exchange steps: first, Alice (who is assumed to be in possession of Bob's current ratchet public key rchpk_B, which is a public DH element) chooses a private/public ratcheting keypair $\mathsf{rchsk}_A = x, \mathsf{rchpk}_A = g^x$, sends this information to Bob, and refreshes the initial key-material with the DH product $(\mathsf{rchpk}_B)^x$; then, Bob does the reverse, refreshing the key material with his new ratchet key-material and Alice's rchpk_A. The double ratchet (and resulting protocol, Signal) were acclaimed as groundbreaking, and its authors, Moxie Marlinspike and Trevor Perrin, were awarded the Levchin prize in 2017.

Unfortunately, DH-based ratchets are vulnerable to quantum attacks against the Discrete Logarithm Problem. A naïve way of transposing the principle of the double ratchet by using quantum-secure Key-Encapsulation Mechanisms (KEMs) essentially doubles the communication complexity, as each ratchet requires two messages rather than a single one. Specifically, in order to achieve a single key-evolution, Bob first sends a public KEM key to Alice, she encapsulates a fresh secret (for instance the evolved secret) with this key, and finally sends this key to Bob (potentially together with a fresh public KEM key, allowing Bob to initiate the next evolution). Unfortunately, this approach is expensive. First, post-quantum KEMs like Kyber and HQC have larger key and ciphertext sizes compared to their classical counterparts for similar security levels. A second disadvantage is that, unlike in the DH-based double ratchet, which links the secrets used in consecutive epochs, this naïve approach does not permit such linking.

To address these shortcomings, a quantum-resistant ratchet based on the HQC KEM[1] was recently proposed by Juaneda et al. [16] at ISIT 2025. Specifically, in order to reduce complexity, RHQC reuses part of the ciphertext encapsulating the evolved secret at epoch t as the public ratchet key for epoch $t + 1$. This renders the RHQC approach highly interesting, and it is claimed in [16] that the scheme is forward- and post-compromise secure.

Our contribution. Unfortunately, in this paper, we show how to break the PCS-security of RHQC, assuming the attacker fully compromises the state of one of the two peers at some epoch t.

The weakness exploited here is that in RHQC, the ability to decrypt a ciphertext at epoch t allows the attacker to extract, from the KEM *public* key at epoch $t + 1$, the corresponding *private* key. In turn, this allows the adversary to then extract the private KEM key at the following epoch, and so on – ensuring that healing *never* occurs.

The key step in our attack is precisely this extraction. We observe that, given a key allowing the attacker to decapsulate the HQC ciphertext, the rest of the ciphertext is an Ouroboros encryption of the private key. Thus, the attacker uses an extractor relying on Ouroboros decapsulation, thus obtaining the private key. Even better, we do not need to decapsulate successfully the whole ciphertext, but only parts of it – which are enough to recover the private key.

As our second, essential contribution, we show that it is impossible to fix RHQC in order to both guarantee provable PCS-security, and achieve lower complexity than that of the naïve ratcheting method described above. In order to describe this impossibility result, we introduce a new decoding algorithm `noisyBFmax`. By studying its decoding failure rate (DFR), we are then able to reason on the impossibility of achieving correctness and PCS for RHQC-like schemes.

We also provide an implementation[2] of the new algorithm `noisyBFmax` and its theoretical DFR. We also give all the data that we have computed such as the heatmaps.

Related Work. A very recent proposal integrated in Signal proposes the *triple-ratchet protocol*, based on ML-KEM. The same paper proposing the triple ratchet also introduced an optimized version of it called Katana, which can be viewed as a lattice-based equivalent of RHQC. Interestingly, while our attack completely breaks the PCS-security of RHQC, the same does not hold for Katana. The main difference is that HQC is based on an underlying cipher, called Ouroboros, while for Katana, the lack of this underlying structure preserves its security, assuming Hint-Module-Learning-with-Errors (MLWE) is hard.

Our work follows the definition of Post-Compromise Security introduced and proved in the context of Signal by Cohn-Gordon et al. [8,9]. Following this

---

[1] The technical specifications of HQC can be found at https://pqc-hqc.org/doc/hqc_specifications_2025_08_22.pdf.

[2] The implementation can be found at https://gitlab.xlim.fr/krejci/implem-pcs-rhqc.

seminal work, several analyses focused on PCS-secure constructions in various settings, in 2-peer [1,13–15] and group settings [10], in mobile (5G) and identity-based settings [5–7]. Unfortunately, most security proofs somewhat limit either the type of information that can be learned by the adversary upon compromising, or the parties the attackers can corrupt. Very recently, Cremers et al. proved that PCS is unachievable in certain settings [11]. Our result here only underlines the difficulty of guaranteeing PCS in the post-quantum setting.

2 Preliminaries and Notations

We begin by recalling several cryptographic primitives and security assumptions, first in the classical, and then in the post-quantum settings.

2.1 Background in Classical Cryptography

In each of the following definitions, we suppose that p is a large prime, and g, a generator of a subgroup $\mathbb{G}$ of prime order q in $\mathbb{Z}_p^*$. We also consider a security parameter 1^λ (in unary).

Definition 1 (Hardness of the Discrete Logarithm Problem (DLOG)).
Given p, q, g as discussed above, let $\mathcal{A}$ be a probabilistic polynomial-time (PPT) adversary and let 1^λ be a security parameter (in unary).
The Discrete Logarithm Problem is hard *if, and only if, the following holds:*

$$\Pr\left[\mathcal{A}(g,p,q,X) = x \mid x \xleftarrow{\$} \mathbb{Z}_{q-1}^*, X \longleftarrow g^x \mod p\right] = \mathsf{negl}(\lambda).$$

Informally, given a randomly-chosen group element X, the adversary has a negligible probability of finding its discrete logarithm x.

Definition 2 (Hardness of the Decisional Diffie-Hellman Problem (DDH)). *Given p, q, g as discussed above, let $\mathcal{A}$ be a probabilistic polynomial-time (PPT) adversary and let 1^λ be a security parameter (in unary).*
The Decisional Diffie-Hellman Problem is hard *if, and only if, the following holds:*

$$\Pr\left[\mathcal{A}(g,p,q,X,Y,Z_b) = b \;\middle|\; \begin{array}{ll} x,y,z_0 \xleftarrow{\$} \mathbb{Z}_{q-1}^* & b \xleftarrow{\$} \{0,1\} \\ z_1 \leftarrow xy \bmod p, & X \longleftarrow g^x \\ Y \longleftarrow g^y \bmod p, & Z_0 \longleftarrow g^{z_0} \bmod p \\ Z_1 \longleftarrow g^{z_1} \bmod p, \end{array}\right] = \frac{1}{2} + \mathsf{negl}(\lambda).$$

Informally, an adversary cannot distinguish a random group element from the Diffie-Hellman product of two given values, with probability significantly better than $\frac{1}{2}$.

The double ratchet algorithm [18], which we present in more detail in Sect. 3, relies on successive runs of a DH-based Non-Interactive Key Exchange (NIKE) – which we briefly recall below.

Definition 3 (Diffie-Hellman Non-Interactive Key-Exchange (NIKE)).
Given p, q, g as discussed above, the DH-based NIKE consists of the following instantiated algorithms:

- $\mathbf{KGen}(1^\lambda) \to (\mathsf{sk}, \mathsf{pk})$ *with* $\mathsf{sk} \xleftarrow{\$} \mathbb{Z}^*_{q-1}$ *and* $\mathsf{pk} \leftarrow g^{\mathsf{sk}} \bmod p$
- $\mathbf{KShare}(\mathsf{sk}_a, \mathsf{pk}_b) \to k = \mathsf{pk}_b^{\mathsf{sk}_a} = g^{\mathsf{sk}_a \cdot \mathsf{sk}_b}$. *We notice that* $\mathbf{KShare}(\mathsf{sk}_a, \mathsf{pk}_b) = \mathbf{KShare}(\mathsf{sk}_b, \mathsf{pk}_a)$.

Finally, although it does not directly impact the double ratchet algorithm, we also present the ElGamal public-key encryption scheme (PKE), which will be handy to understand RHQC.

Definition 4 (The ElGamal cryptosystem). *Given p, q, g as discussed above, we instantiate the ElGamal PKE scheme as follows:*

- $\mathbf{KGen}(1^\lambda) \to (\mathsf{sk}, \mathsf{pk})$ *with* $\mathsf{sk} \xleftarrow{\$} \mathbb{Z}^*_{q-1}$ *and* $\mathsf{pk} \leftarrow g^{\mathsf{sk}} \bmod p$
- $\mathbf{Enc}(\mathsf{pk}, m) \to (c_1, c_2) = (g^r, m \cdot \mathsf{pk}^r)$ *with* $r \xleftarrow{\$} \mathbb{Z}^*_{q-1}$
- $\mathbf{Dec}(\mathsf{sk}, (c_1, c_2)) \to m = c_2 \cdot c_1^{-\mathsf{sk}}$

We note that the second component of an ElGamal ciphertext, c_2 masks the plaintext message by an implicit DH-based NIKE. More formally, we could express the encryption algorithm in the following manner, by using the DH NIKE above:

$$\mathbf{KGen}(1^\lambda) \to (\mathsf{sk}_{c_1}, c_1); \mathbf{KShare}(\mathsf{sk}_{c_1}, \mathsf{pk}) \to k; \mathbf{SE.SEnc}(k, m) \to c_2$$

Where SE (*i.e.* Symmetric Encryption) is a tuple of algorithms $(\mathbf{SEnc}, \mathbf{SDec})$, satisfying $\mathbf{SE.SDec}(k, \mathbf{SE.SEnc}(k, m)) = m$ for any $(k, m) \in \mathsf{SE}.\mathcal{K} \times \mathsf{SE}.\mathcal{M}$.

HQC has a similar structure, although the underlying structure is not veritably a NIKE. This is why we sometimes abuse language and state that "HQC is similar to ElGamal".

2.2 Post-Quantum Primitives and Problems

Throughout this paper, $\mathbb{Z}$ denotes the ring of integers and $\mathbb{F}_q$ (for a prime $q \in \mathbb{Z}$) a finite field, typically $\mathbb{F}_2$ for Hamming codes. Vectors and matrices are formatted in bold and italic, *e.g.* $\boldsymbol{a}$. Their representation in the polynomial ring $\mathcal{R} := \mathbb{F}_2/\langle X^n - 1 \rangle$ are written without specific formatting. The choosen n in ring $\mathcal{R}$ should be a prime integer and is said to be primitive if the polynomial $(X^n - 1)/(X - 1)$ is irreducible in $\mathcal{R}$. Vectors are not explicitly written as rows or columns; their orientation is inferred from the context. We define the matrix product in $\mathbb{N}$ as $\cdot_{\mathbb{N}}$ otherwise $\cdot$ is the matrix product in the appropriate field, it even can be implicit and $\cdot$ does not appear. We also use the symbole $\cdot$ to mean the polynomial multiplication in the ring $\mathcal{R}$.

We also define for $\boldsymbol{a} \in \mathbb{F}_2^n$ the supp$(\boldsymbol{a})$ as the indices of the coordinates that are set to 1. We denote the Hamming weight as $\omega_H(\cdot)$ and gives the number of coordinates set to 1 in a vector. Also we denote $\mathcal{R}_w := \{p \in \mathcal{R} : \omega_H(p) = w\}$. The matrix rot$(\boldsymbol{h}) \in \mathbb{F}_2^{n \times n}$ for $h \in \mathcal{R}$ denotes the circulant matrix whose i-th column is the vector corresponding to $hX^i \in \mathcal{R}$.

Property 1. Multiplication of polynomials $a \cdot b$ in $\mathcal{R}$ is equivalent to the matrix multiplication of the row vector a with the b's circulant matrix representation.

Most code-based primitives rely on the Syndrome Decoding (SD) problem, which has been proved NP-hard [4]. The problems used for HQC and Ouroboros, which rely on 2-*DQCSD* and 3-*DQCSD-PT*, respectively, are not proven to be NP-hard, nevertheless, these problems are considered hard by the community. We recall the Quasi-Cyclic Syndrome Decoding (QCSD) problems, and we specify that they are defined for binary codes in the Hamming metric.

Before continuing we introduce clearly the following notations. For $b_1 \in \{0, 1\}$, we define the finite set $\mathbb{F}_{2,b_1}^n := \{\boldsymbol{h} \in \mathbb{F}_2^n : h(1) = b_1 \mod 2\}$ *i.e.* binary vectors of length n and parity b_1. Similarly for matrices we define the finite sets:

$$\mathbb{F}_{2,b_1}^{n \times 2n} := \left\{ (\boldsymbol{I_n} \quad \text{rot}(\boldsymbol{h})) \in \mathbb{F}_2^{n \times 2n} : \boldsymbol{h} \in \mathbb{F}_{2,b_1}^n \right\}$$

$$\mathbb{F}_{2,b_1,b_2}^{2n \times 3n} := \left\{ \begin{pmatrix} \boldsymbol{I_n} & \boldsymbol{0} & \text{rot}(\boldsymbol{h_1}) \\ \boldsymbol{0} & \boldsymbol{I_n} & \text{rot}(\boldsymbol{h_2}) \end{pmatrix} \in \mathbb{F}_2^{2n \times 3n} : \boldsymbol{h_1} \in \mathbb{F}_{2,b_1}^n \wedge \boldsymbol{h_2} \in \mathbb{F}_{2,b_2}^n \right\}$$

Definition 5 (*s-QCSD* **Distribution**). *Let n, s, and w be positive integers. The s-**Quasi-Cyclic Syndrome Decoding Distribution** s-$QCSD(n, w)$ samples a parity-check matrix*

$$\boldsymbol{H} \xleftarrow{\$} \mathbb{F}_2^{(s-1)n \times sn}$$

of a systematic QC code $\mathfrak{C}$ of index s and rate $1/s$, and a vector $\boldsymbol{x} = (\boldsymbol{x_0}, \ldots, \boldsymbol{x_{s-1}}) \xleftarrow{\$} \mathbb{F}_2^{sn}$ such that $\forall i \in [0, s-1], \omega(\boldsymbol{x_i}) = w$. The value $\boldsymbol{y}^\top = \boldsymbol{H}\boldsymbol{x}^\top$ is computed and $(\boldsymbol{H}, \boldsymbol{y})$ is returned as output.

From this distribution we can define two problems on which HQC and Ouroboros rely on. The first one is 2-*QCSD* which guarantees mainly the strength of the public key, and 3-*QCSD* which guarantees the strength of the Ouroboros or HQC ciphertext.

Definition 6 (**Decisional** 2-*QCSD* **Problem with parity**). Let $\boldsymbol{h} \in \mathbb{F}_2^n$, $\boldsymbol{H} = (\boldsymbol{I_n}\text{rot}(\boldsymbol{h}))$, and $b' = w + bw \mod 2$. For $\boldsymbol{y} \in \mathbb{F}_{2,b'}^n$, the **Decisional 2-Quasi-Cyclic Syndrome Decoding Problem with parity** 2-$DQCSD(n, w, b)$ asks to decide with non-negligible advantage whether $(\boldsymbol{H}, \boldsymbol{y})$ follows the 2-$QCSD(n, wb)$ distribution with parity, or the uniform distribution over $\mathbb{F}_2^{n \times 2n} \times \mathbb{F}_{2,b'}^n$.

Definition 7 (3-*DQCSD-PT*). *Let n, w, b_1, b_2, l be positive integers and $b_3 = w + b_1 w \mod 2$. Given:*

$$\left(\boldsymbol{H}, (\boldsymbol{y_1}, \boldsymbol{y_2})\right) \in \mathbb{F}_{2,b_1,b_2}^{2n \times 3n} \times \left(\mathbb{F}_{2,b_3}^n \times \mathbb{F}_2^{n-l}\right),$$

where $\mathbb{F}_{2,b_1,b_2}^{2n\times 3n}$ is a set of matrices containing two circulant blocks, of dimension $n \times n$, one with Hamming weight b_1 and the other of Hamming weight b_2. The **Decisional 3–Quasi-Cyclic Syndrome Decoding with Parity and Truncation Problem** $3\text{-}DQCSD\text{-}PT(n, w, b_1, b_2, l)$ asks to decide with non-negligible advantage whether $(\boldsymbol{H}, (\boldsymbol{y}_1, \boldsymbol{y}_2))$ is distributed according to the:

$$3\text{-}DQCSD\text{-}PT(n, w, b_1, b_2, l)$$

distribution or the uniform distribution over:

$$\mathbb{F}_{2,b_1,b_2}^{2n\times 3n} \times \left(\mathbb{F}_{2,b_3}^{n} \times \mathbb{F}_{2}^{n-l}\right).$$

We state that the problems aforementioned are considered hard.

Assumption 1. *The Search 2-QCSD problem is hard on average.*

Assumption 2. *The Search 3-QCSD problem is hard on average.*

Although there is no general complexity result for quasi-cyclic codes, decoding these codes is considered hard by the community. The conclusion is that in practice, the best attacks are the same as those for non-circulant codes up to a small factor.

Now we present the two main KEMs that are involved in this paper. The first one is HQC, and the second one is Ouroboros, both are based on QC structures. For general notation we propose $\mathcal{M}$ and $\mathcal{C}$ to represent the message space and respectively the ciphertext space.

Definition 8 (HQC or Hamming-Quasi Cyclic). *HQC [17] uses two types of codes: a decodable $[n, k]$ code $\mathfrak{C}$, generated by $\boldsymbol{G} \in \mathbb{F}_2^{k\times n}$ and which can correct at least Δ errors via an efficient algorithm $\mathfrak{C}.\mathsf{Decode}(\cdot)$; and a random double circulant $[2n, n]$ code, of parity-check matrix $(\mathbf{1}|\boldsymbol{h})$. The four polynomial-time algorithms constituting the PKE version of the HQC cryptosystem are described as follows:*

- **Setup**(1^λ): *generates and outputs the global parameters* $param = (n, k, \Delta, w, w_r, w_e)$.
- **KGen**$(param)$: *samples* $h \xleftarrow{\$} \mathcal{R}$, *the generator matrix* $\boldsymbol{G} \in \mathbb{F}_2^{k\times n}$ *of* $\mathfrak{C}$, $sk := (x, y) \xleftarrow{\$} \mathcal{R}_w^2$, *sets* $pk := (h, s = x + h \cdot y)$, *and return* (pk, sk).
- **Encrypt**(pk, m): *generates* $e \xleftarrow{\$} \mathcal{R}_{w_e}$, $(r_1, r_2) \xleftarrow{\$} \mathcal{R}_{w_r}^2$, *sets* $u = r_1 + h \cdot r_2$ *and* $v = \boldsymbol{m}\boldsymbol{G}^\top + s \cdot r_2 + e$, *return* $c = (u, v)$.
- **Decrypt**(sk, c): *return* $\boldsymbol{m}' \leftarrow \mathfrak{C}.\mathsf{Decode}(v - u \cdot y)$.

HQC.PKE, with default parameters, satisfies both the correctness and the INDistinguishability under Chosen Plaintext Attack (IND-CPA) security properties under the assumption that both 2-DQCDSP and 3-DQCDSP are hard.

Definition 9 (Ouroboros). *Ouroboros [12] uses a random double circulant $[2n, n]$ Gallager code $\mathfrak{C}$, with parity-check matrix $(\mathbf{1}|\mathbf{h})$. The four polynomial-time algorithms constituting the KEM version of the Ouroboros cryptosystem are described as follows:*

- **Setup**(1^λ): *generates and outputs the global parameters* $param = (n, k, \Delta, w, w_r, w_e)$.
- **KGen**$(param)$: *samples* $h \xleftarrow{\$} \mathcal{R}$, $sk := (x, y) \xleftarrow{\$} \mathcal{R}_w^2$, *sets* $pk := (h, s = x + h \cdot y)$, *and return* (pk, sk).
- **Encaps**(pk): *generate* $(r_1, r_2) \xleftarrow{\$} \mathcal{R}_{w_r}^2$, *and* $e \leftarrow H(r_1\|r_2)$ *with* $H : \mathcal{R}_{w_r}^2 \to \mathcal{R}_{w_e}$, *set* $u = r_1 + h \cdot r_2$ *and* $v = s \cdot r_2 + e$, *return* $c = (u, v)$.
- **Decaps**(sk, c): *computes* $(r_1, r_2, e) \leftarrow \mathfrak{C}.\mathsf{Decode}(v - u \cdot y)$, *if* $H(r_1\|r_2) = e$ *then return* e *else* $\perp$.

Ouroboros.KEM, with default parameters, satisfies both the correctness and the INDistinguishability under Chosen Plaintext Attack (IND-CPA) security properties under the assumption that both 2-DQCSD and 3-DQCSD-PT are hard.

Since Ouroboros uses Gallager's code we give its definition:

Definition 10 (Gallager Code). *Let $n \in \mathbb{N}$ be the block length and let $H \in \{0, 1\}^{m \times n}$ be a binary matrix.*
A Gallager code $\mathcal{C} \subseteq \mathbb{F}_2^n$ is the linear block code defined by

$$\mathcal{C} = \left\{ \boldsymbol{x} \in \mathbb{F}_2^n \mid \boldsymbol{H}\boldsymbol{x}^\top = 0 \right\},$$

where the parity-check matrix $\boldsymbol{H}$ satisfies the following properties:

1. **Regularity:** *There exist integers $d_v \geq 2$ and $d_c \geq 2$ such that*
   - *each column of $\boldsymbol{H}$ has exactly d_v ones,*
   - *each row of $\boldsymbol{H}$ has exactly d_c ones.*
2. **Low density:** *The parameters satisfy $d_v \ll m$ and $d_c \ll n$.*
3. **Consistency condition:** *The dimensions satisfy $md_c = nd_v$, ensuring that the total number of ones counted by rows equals that counted by columns.*

2.3   BRKE Security Model

A **Bidirectional Ratcheted Key Exchange (BRKE)** [19] is a cryptographic protocol designed to provide secure communication by dynamically updating the long-term keys during an ongoing session; the bi-directionality implies that both participants can generate new keys independently of each other.

Definition 11 (BRKE). *Formally, a BRKE is defined for a finite key space $\mathcal{K}$ and an associated-data space $\mathcal{AD}$ as a triple $R = (\mathsf{init}, \mathsf{send}, \mathsf{receive})$ of algorithms together with a state space $\mathcal{S}$ and a ciphertext space $\mathcal{C}$.*

- *init: the randomized initialization algorithm returns a pair of states $(S_A, S_B) \in \mathcal{S} \times \mathcal{S}$.*

- *send(state$_i$, ad): the randomized sending algorithm takes a state **state**$_i$ and an associated-data string ad $\in \mathcal{AD}$, and produces an updated state **state**$_i' \in \mathcal{S}$, and a ciphertext c $\in \mathcal{C}$.*
- *receive(state$_i$, ad, c): the deterministic receiving algorithm takes a state **state**$_i \in \mathcal{S}$, an associated-data string ad $\in \mathcal{AD}$, and a ciphertext c $\in \mathcal{C}$, and either outputs an updated state **state**$_i' \in \mathcal{S}$ and a key k $\in \mathcal{K}$ or outputs the special symbol $\perp$ to indicate rejection.*

A BRKE scheme is secure if and only if it respects the properties of *correctness* and *key indistinguishability*. Both properties are formalized through two games FUNC and KIND$_{BR}$ in Fig. 11 in Sect. A.

We also provide a brief description of the *correctness* and *key indistinguishability*, core principles of BRKE model.

- **Correctness:** According to [19], the *correctness* property requires that as long as one party only accepts the output of the send function sent by the other (*i.e.*, accepts no forged messages from the attacker), the output keys m_i match those output by the receive function. In practice, this means that if both parties follow the protocol honestly, they will always derive the same shared key, even if an attacker attempts to interfere.
- **Key Indistinguishability:** The *key indistinguishability* property asks that an adversary cannot distinguish between two (or more) keys obtained with the send($\cdot$) algorithm. This means the final shared key is computationally indistinguishable from a random key, ensuring that an attacker gains no useful information about the key from observing the exchange.

2.4   Probability

Later in this paper we compute the decoding failure rate of decoding algorithms. To do so, we model them using probabilities. Here we present the basis of probabilities. We denote $\Pr[A]$ as the probability for an event A to happen, furthermore we denote $\Pr[A|B]$ the probability that event A happens knowing the event B.

Definition 12 (Binomial distribution). *We state that $X \sim$ Binomial(n, p), gives the* probability mass function

$$\forall x \in [\![0, n]\!], \Pr[X = x] = \binom{n}{x} p^x (1 - p)^{n-x}$$

We also give the following given cumulative distribution

$$\forall x \in [\![0, n]\!], \Pr[X \leq x] = \sum_{k=0}^{x} \binom{n}{k} p^x (1 - p)^{n-x}$$

Further in the article, the reader may see the use of a Markov chain. This helps mainly to study certain random walks, that we will need in order to compute later on a decoding failure rate.

Definition 13 (Markov process). *A process is a Markov process if and only if the future evolution of the process from time t_n only depends on the state at time t_n and not on any previous state, or more formally,*

$$\Pr\left[X(t_{n+1}) = x_{n+1} \mid X(t_n) = x_n, X(t_{n-1}) = x_{n-1}, \ldots, X(t_1) = x_1\right]$$
$$= \Pr\left[X(t_{n+1}) = x_{n+1} \mid X(t_n) = x_n\right]$$

2.5 Higher Order Functions

Definition 14 (High order function). *A higher-order function is a function that satisfies at least one of the following conditions:*

- *Takes one or more functions as arguments (i.e., it accepts functions as input).*
- *Returns a function as its result (i.e., it outputs a function).*

In other words, higher-order functions operate on other functions, either by consuming them, producing them, or both.

Definition 15 (left fold (foldl)). *A left fold is a higher-order function that processes a sequence of elements by applying a binary operation cumulatively from left to right.*
Given:

- *Two sets A and B*
- *A sequence of elements: $(b_1, b_2, \ldots, b_n) \in B^n$*
- *A binary function: $f : A \times B \longrightarrow A$*
- *An initial value (accumulator): $a \in A$*

We define a left fold as:

$$\mathsf{foldl} : (A \times B \longrightarrow A) \times A \times B^* \longrightarrow A$$
$$f, a, (b_1, b_2, \ldots, b_n) \longmapsto f(\ldots f(f(f(a, b_1), b_2), \ldots), b_n)$$

Remark 1. We state that a function f is left foldable if for any sets A and B, the function is defined as $f : A \times B \longrightarrow A$.

3 The Double Ratchet and RHQC

In this section, we briefly review the DH-based double-ratchet algorithm [18] and the corresponding RHQC ratchet [16]. Finally, we compare the two approaches.

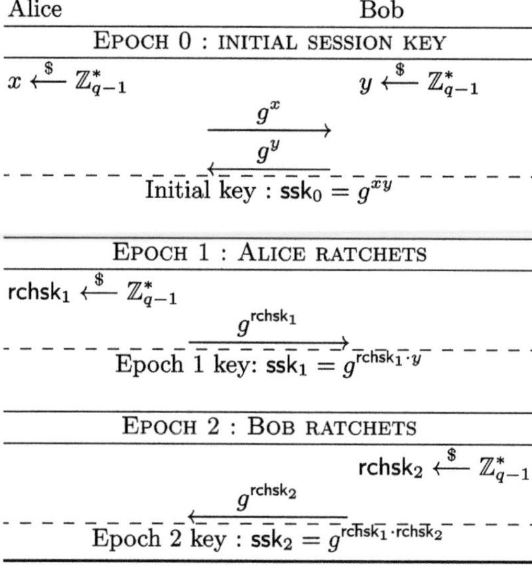

Fig. 1. Basic structure of the double ratchet.

3.1 The Double Ratchet

The Diffie-Hellman double-ratchet algorithm [18] was proposed by Marlinspike and Perrin and represents one of the main components of the Signal protocol. We depict its basic structure in Fig. 1. The double ratchet supposes the existence of an initial secret – which, in Fig. 1 we compute as the result of an interactive DH key-exchange (in epoch 0). Note that in Signal, this component is non-interactive.

Ratcheting begins in epoch 1, when Alice chooses a private ratchet key which we denote as rchsk_1. The corresponding public ratchet key $\mathsf{rchpk}_1 := g^{\mathsf{rchsk}_1}$ mod p is sent to Bob. The two parties update the session key, which becomes the DH product of Bob's prior contribution g^y and Alice's current ratchet public key rchpk_2.

In epoch 2, Bob initiates the ratchet in a similar way. At the end of this epoch, the resulting session key is the DH product of Alice's and Bob's public ratchet keys, rchpk_1 and rchpk_2.

Clearly, even an adversary that fully compromises Bob's initial state (learning y), cannot learn ssk_2, as its components are freshly and honestly generated. Thus, the protocol is PCS-secure. Similarly, even if an adversary corrupts the value rchsk_1, it cannot learn the past key ssk_0, thus achieving forward-secrecy (FS).

3.2 RHQC

The RHQC protocol depicted in Fig. 2 proposes the use of HQC with an optimization that consists to send only two polynomials instead of three. We recall,

Alice	Bob

Init Phase

INITIAL SESSION KEY

$(x_0^a, y_0^a) \xleftarrow{\$} \mathcal{R}_w^2$

$s_0 = x_0^a + h \cdot y_0^a$ $\xrightarrow{\;s_0\;}$

         $(x_0^b, y_0^b, e_0) \xleftarrow{\$} \mathcal{R}_w^2 \times \mathcal{R}_{w_e}$

         $\boldsymbol{m_0} \xleftarrow{\$} \mathbb{F}_2^k$

         $\mathsf{pk}_0 = x_0^b + h \cdot y_0^b$

         $v_0 = \boldsymbol{m_0}G + s_0 \cdot y_0^b + e_0$

         $\xleftarrow{(\mathsf{pk}_0, v_0)}$

$\boldsymbol{m_0} \leftarrow \mathsf{Dec}((x_0^a, y_0^a), (\mathsf{pk}_0, v_0))$

Session Key   Session Key

$\mathsf{ssk}_0 \leftarrow \boldsymbol{m_0}$ $\mathsf{ssk}_0 \leftarrow \boldsymbol{m_0}$

Ratcheting Phase

ALICE RATCHETS

$(x_1^a, y_1^a, e_1) \xleftarrow{\$} \mathcal{R}_w^2 \times \mathcal{R}_{w_e}$

$\boldsymbol{m_1} \xleftarrow{\$} \mathbb{F}_2^k$

$\mathsf{pk}_1 = x_1^a + h \cdot y_1^a$

$v_1 = \boldsymbol{m_1}G + \mathsf{pk}_0 \cdot y_1^a + e_1$

         $\xrightarrow{(\mathsf{pk}_1, v_1)}$

         $\boldsymbol{m_1} \leftarrow \mathsf{Dec}((x_0^b, y_0^b), (\mathsf{pk}_1, v_1))$

Session Key   Session Key

$\mathsf{ssk}_1 \leftarrow \boldsymbol{m_1}$ $\mathsf{ssk}_1 \leftarrow \boldsymbol{m_1}$

BOB RATCHETS

         $(x_2^b, y_2^b, e_2) \xleftarrow{\$} \mathcal{R}_w^2 \times \mathcal{R}_{w_e}$

         $\boldsymbol{m_2} \xleftarrow{\$} \mathbb{F}_2^k$

         $\mathsf{pk}_2 = x_2^b + h \cdot y_2^b$

         $v_2 = \boldsymbol{m_2}G + \mathsf{pk}_1 \cdot y_2^b + e_2$

         $\xleftarrow{(\mathsf{pk}_2, v_2)}$

$\boldsymbol{m_2} \leftarrow \mathsf{Dec}((x_1^a, y_1^a), (\mathsf{pk}_2, v_2))$

Session Key   Session Key

$\mathsf{ssk}_2 \leftarrow \boldsymbol{m_2}$ $\mathsf{ssk}_2 \leftarrow \boldsymbol{m_2}$

Fig. 2. RHQC: unwrapped protocol

in the case of a naïve ratchet Bob would send (pk, u, v) where pk and u are independent syndromes and u is a syndrome whose coordinates followed the $\mathcal{R}_{w_r}^2$ distribution while pk is $\mathcal{R}_w^2$ distributed. This optimization is possible due to the fact that the first coordinate of a HQC ciphertext is a syndrome of the same morphology as the public key HQC (for modified parameters, including the constraint that $w = w_r$ [16]). We notice that the parameters are changed compared to the standard HQC since we need to have the same Hamming weight in order to be able to do the rotation.

In [16] it is stated that HQC is similar to an ElGamal construction. As in classical ElGamal, the ciphertext (c_1, c_2) contains a NIKE public key c_1 and a ciphertext c_2 containing the message, which is symmetrically encrypted with the NIKE's key share. For HQC, we observe a strong analogy with the ElGamal construction. When Alice sends $s_0 = x_0^a + h y_0^a$ and Bob responds with $(u, v) = (x_0^b + h y_0^b, \; m_0 G + s_0 y_0^b + e_0)$, the values s_0 and u can be interpreted as public keys in a non-interactive key exchange (NIKE) setting.

More precisely, u plays a role analogous to the ElGamal component c_1, representing an ephemeral public key, while v corresponds to c_2, which embeds the message symmetrically encrypted under a shared key derived from the NIKE exchange.

The shared key is derived asymmetrically from the public values s_0 and u: Alice applies her secret y_0^a to Bob's public value u, computing $u \cdot y_0^a$, while Bob applies his secret y_0^b to Alice's public value s_0, computing $s_0 \cdot y_0^b$. The key distinction lies in the use of a symmetric encryption scheme that tolerates small discrepancies between these values, allowing correct decryption for keys that are *close* to $s_0 \cdot y_0^b$ (such as $u \cdot y_0^a$).

Overall, this interaction establishes a shared secret in a manner analogous to ElGamal, with the public values s_0 and u enabling secure key agreement.

3.3   Crucial Differences

The Diffie-Hellman ratchet is based on a NIKE. This ratchet is highly interesting in terms of efficiency and elegance and is secure due to NIKE's strong properties, which are:

1. The computed key is statistically indistinguishable from a random uniform distribution;
2. Corruption of one user's private key does not affect the security of shared keys between pairs of uncorrupted users;
3. Corruption of one shared symmetric key does not undermine the security of other shared uncorrupted keys.

Even though it is possible to build a KEM from a NIKE, the reverse does not hold. That being said, HQC is a KEM similar to an ElGamal construction, since the first part can be seen as a public key and the noise, as an equivalent of shared key in a Diffie-Hellman. Hence, RHQC treats HQC in a way similar to a NIKE, but without verifying if NIKE's properties hold. In particular, for this construction, item 2 outlined above does not hold for HQC.

4   Cryptanalysis of RHQC

We prove that RHQC protocol violates PCS. Unfortunately, the strong properties claimed for RHQC, and in particular, that scheme's PCS in the BRKE model [19], does not hold.

To make this proof possible we first suppose the existence of what we would call an extractor, aiming to extract the secret of the interlocutor's ratchet public key, then we show that this extractor exists. The supposition of the extractor is justified since as claimed earlier, it is used as a NIKE without checking the underlying properties.

4.1 Breaking PCS in RHQC

First, we propose to show the recursive construction and its consequences. For that we assume the existence of an extractor as defined in Definition 16 allowing us to break PCS by Theorem 1. We show later that this extractor exists, hence proving that RHQC is not PCS-secure.

In order to simplify the reading we explain briefly our notations: j stands for whether we are Alice or Bob, i stands for the epoch, (x_{i-1}^j, y_{i-1}^j) is my current sk, $c_i = (\mathsf{pk}_i, v_i)$ is public and (x_i^{1-j}, y_i^{1-j}) is the sk of the other party in the next epoch.

The extractor function f is such that $\mathsf{rchsk}_i = f(\mathsf{rchsk}_{i-1}, c_i)$ meaning the key update function is computable by an attacker having one ratched key.

Definition 16 (Extractor). *The property* Extractor *states that there exists a function taking as input, in the context of RHQC protocol, a* HQC *ciphertext* (pk_i, v_i) *and its private key* (x_{i-1}^j, y_{i-1}^j) *can recover the* $(x_i^{1-j}, y_i^{1-j}, e_i)$ *embedded in the* (pk_i, v_i), *or more formally, for a given transcript and* (w, w_e):

$$\text{Extractor} := \forall i \in \mathbb{N} \setminus \{0\}, \forall j \in \{0,1\}, \exists f : \mathcal{R}_w^2 \times \mathcal{R}^2 \longrightarrow \mathcal{R}_w^2 \times \mathcal{R}_{w_e},$$

$$(x_i^{1-j}, y_i^{1-j}, e_i) = f((x_{i-1}^j, y_{i-1}^j), (\mathsf{pk}_i, v_i))$$

Theorem 1 (Breaking PCS**).** *In the BRKE model proposed in [19], if we suppose the property* Extractor *true (meaning that a function exists) therefore we state that the RHQC protocol is not* PCS-*secure, or more formally:*

$$\text{BRKE} \models \text{Extractor} \implies \neg\text{PCS}(\text{RHQC})$$

Proof. Let's consider the following function:

$$r : \mathcal{R}_w^2 \times \mathcal{R}_{w_e} \longrightarrow \mathcal{R}_w^2$$
$$(x, y, e) \longmapsto (x, y)$$

Then we can build the following function, with f being the extractor:

$$r \circ f$$

We remark that the function $r \circ f$ is foldable.

Let's introduce $c \in \mathbb{N} \setminus \{0\}$ symbolizing the corruption/reveal's epoch, and set $j \in \{0,1\}$.

$$(x_{c+1}^{1-j}, y_{c+1}^{1-j}) = r \circ f[(x_c^j, y_c^j), (\mathsf{pk}_{c+1}, v_{c+1})]$$

$$(x_{c+2}^j, y_{c+2}^j) = r \circ f[r \circ f[(x_c^j, y_c^j), (\mathsf{pk}_{c+1}, v_{c+1})], (\mathsf{pk}_{c+2}, v_{c+2})]$$

$$(x_{c+3}^{1-j}, y_{c+3}^{1-j}) = r \circ f[r \circ f[r \circ f[(x_c^j, y_c^j), (\mathsf{pk}_{c+1}, v_{c+1})], (\mathsf{pk}_{c+2}, v_{c+2})], (\mathsf{pk}_{c+3}, v_{c+3})]$$

$$\vdots$$

We simplify the construction as follows, by using the foldable notation:

$$\forall i > c, (x_i^{\tilde{j}}, y_i^{\tilde{j}}) = \mathsf{foldl}[\ (r \circ f),\ (x_c^{j}, y_c^{j}),\ ((\mathsf{pk}_{c+1}, v_{c+1}), \cdots, (\mathsf{pk}_i, v_i))\ ]$$

Here $\tilde{j}$ is defined as $\tilde{j} := j + (i - c) \mod 2$, and foldl is a function of higher degree (taking function as arguments) as defined in Definition 15. Finally this shows trivially that the revelation of one secret key (a pair of (x, y)) implies the extraction for all $i > c$. We conclude the theorem holds.

Remark 2. Informally, suppose the existence of an extractor. Each time Bob sends a new public key, Alice can guess Bob's private key because of her knowing her own private key, and *vice-versa*. In other words, once an attacker obtains one of their private key, the adversary can disclose all the future session keys due to reccursion.

Remark 3. The main difference between Fig. 1 and Fig. 2 is that the secret used by one of the parties can not be known by the other party, due to the NIKE's properties. The existence of the extractor violates this rule.

Remark 4. RHQC can be seen as a protocol that embeds in its ciphertext the ciphertext of its secret key.

4.2 Extractor's Existence

We have seen, that if the extractor exists then PCS isn't achieved. The questions are: first if this extractor exists and secondly, if the extractor works for the RHQC's parameters.

HQC can be considered as a member of the same family as Ouroboros, BIKE, and so on. We focus on the fact that Ouroboros is a subpart of HQC. From Definition 8 and Definition 9 we remark the trivial relations, that we give as the followings Lemmas.

Lemma 1 (Ouroboros ciphertext to HQC ciphertext). *Every Ouroboros cipher can be written as a HQC cipher, or formally:*

$$\forall (u, v) \in \mathsf{Ouroboros}.\mathcal{C}, \forall m \in \mathsf{HQC}.\mathcal{M}, (u, v + \boldsymbol{m} \cdot \boldsymbol{G}) \in \mathsf{HQC}.\mathcal{C}$$

Lemma 2 (HQC ciphertext to Ouroboros ciphertext). *Every HQC cipher once decapsulated can be written as an Ouroboros cipher, or formally:*

$$\forall (u, v) \in \mathsf{HQC}.\mathcal{C}, (u, v - \mathsf{HQC}.\mathsf{Dec}(u, v) \cdot \boldsymbol{G}) \in \mathsf{Ouroboros}.\mathcal{C}$$

Remark 5. Informally Lemma 2 and Lemma 1 can be seen as follows:

$$v - uy = \boldsymbol{m}\boldsymbol{G} + \underbrace{xr_2 + yr_1 + e}_{\mathsf{Ouroboros}.\mathcal{C}}$$
$$\underbrace{\phantom{v - uy = \boldsymbol{m}\boldsymbol{G} + xr_2 + yr_1 + e}}_{\mathsf{HQC}.\mathcal{C}}$$

Input (x_{i-1}^j, y_{i-1}^j) and (pk_i, v_i)
Output $(x_i^{1-j}, y_i^{1-j}, e_i)$

$c_i := v_i - pk_i \cdot y_{i-1}^j$
// Notice that $c_i = m_i G + x_{i-1}^j y_i^{1-j} + x_i^{1-j} y_{i-1}^j + e_i$
$m_i \leftarrow \mathsf{HQC.Decode}(c_i)$
// Use of Lemma 2
$c_i' := c_i + m_i G$
$(x_i^{1-j}, y_i^{1-j}, e_i) \leftarrow \mathsf{Ouroboros.Decode}((x_{i-1}^j, y_{i-1}^j), c_i')$
if $\omega_H(x_i^{1-j}) \neq w \lor \omega_H(y_i^{1-j}) \neq w$
$\quad$ **return** $\perp$
return $(x_i^{1-j}, y_i^{1-j}, e_i)$

Fig. 3. Extractor

According to Lemma 2 we propose to explicit the extractor in Fig. 3. In few words, the attacker first open the ciphertext in order to obtain the message m_i. Now the attacker can convert from HQC ciphertext to Ouroboros ciphertext as stated in Lemma 2, by just adding $m_i G$ to the ciphertext. From now on, the attacker can decode and obtain the next ratchet secret key.

The decryption algorithm in Ouroboros allows us to extract x, y, and e. Ouroboros [12] presents a decoding algorithm of Gallager's code (or here Quasi-Cyclic (QC) code), named BitFlip described in Fig. 4. This algorithm takes as input the syndrome, the decoder, and a threshold. Since the proposed parameters for HQC in RHQC does not match those presented in Ouroboros, we need to estimate these threshold for each set of parameters. We found experimentally the threshold for the BitFlip's algorithm, in order to obtain an extractor with an overwhelming probability for its correctness. These values are given in Table 1. It confirms that RHQC is not PCS-secure.

Table 1. Guessing manually the BitFlip's threshold in order to decode for the proposed parameters of tested RHQC, with overwhelming probabilities

	n	w	w_r	w_e	threshold
rhqc-128-nistcompliant	19597	75	75	75	54
rhqc-128-32-optimized	13829	67	67	67	47

Input $s = xr_2 + yr_1 + e$, (x, y) and a threshold thr
Output (u, v, s) that is supposed to be equal to (r_2, r_1, e)

$u \leftarrow 0 \in \mathbb{F}_2^n, v \leftarrow 0 \in \mathbb{F}_2^n$
while iter $<$ iterMax $\wedge \, \omega_H(s) > w_e \wedge (\omega_H(u) \neq w_r \vee \omega_H(v) \neq w_r)$:
$\quad \sigma \leftarrow s \cdot_\mathbb{N} H$
$\quad$ **foreach** i such that $\sigma_i \geq$ thr :
$\quad\quad s \leftarrow s + H_i$
$\quad\quad$ **if** $i > n$:
$\quad\quad\quad v_{i-n} \leftarrow v_{i-n} + 1$
$\quad\quad$ **else**
$\quad\quad\quad u_i \leftarrow u_i + 1$
$\quad$ iter $\leftarrow$ iter $+ 1$
return (u, v, s)

Fig. 4. Algorithm Ouroboros' BitFlip [12].

5   On the Limits of Repairability of RHQC

In this section, we investigate whether the RHQC protocol can be repaired by an appropriate choice of parameters, or whether the attack presented in the previous section is inherent to the design. Our goal is to understand to what extent the trade-off between correctness and post-compromise security can be mitigated, and whether meaningful healing can be restored.

We begin by discussing the limitations of the initial extraction attack and explain why a more refined analysis is required. We then strengthen the attack by showing that recovering only partial secret information already suffices to compromise post-compromise security. To analyze this phenomenon, we introduce a new decoding algorithm, noisyBFmax.

We subsequently provide a probabilistic analysis of the decoding failure rate of noisyBFmax, which allows us to quantify the success probability of the extractor. Building on this analysis, we study how to maximize the extractor's success probability and derive concrete bounds on the healing behavior of RHQC. Finally, we apply these results to the rhqc-128 parameter set and discuss whether a viable repair strategy can be achieved in practice.

5.1   Necessary Conditions for the Repairability of RHQC

The repairability – consisting in the choice of parameters resistant to counter the attack – of RHQC is governed by two competing requirements. Correctness demands that the honest HQC decoder succeeds with sufficiently high probability, while post-compromise security (PCS) requires that the extraction process based on the Ouroboros decoder does not succeed too frequently. If extraction succeeds too often, secret information is recovered repeatedly, which directly compromises the PCS guarantees of the protocol.

For RHQC to be repairable, the extraction process, mainly the Ouroboros decoder, must fail with non-negligible probability. This condition is fundamental, as the security of RHQC relies on the fact that decoding in the honest execution dominates extraction in adversarial executions. Otherwise, an extractor exists that recovers secret material too frequently, undermining the intended security properties.

We consider the repairability of RHQC, if the DFR of HQC is lower than 2^{-1} and that the DFR of Ouroboros is higher than 2^{-1}, and that the parameters still guarantee 2-*DQCSD* and 3-*DQCSD-PT*.

Remark 6. For a given set of parameters (n, w), fixing w_e greater than the inflexion of the Ouroboros decoder, implies that the RHQC healing time is bounded linearly to the security parameter λ. Suppose the w_e is chosen, such that it leads to a Ouroboros' DFR's probability p.

This implies that at each round the extractor has a probability $1 - p$ to decode, hence breaking the protocol with $(1 - p)^k$ with k the number of rounds *i.e.* the probability that it is possible to decode successively. Fixing the w_e at the inflexion point, means that it can decode successively with a probability of 2^{-1} at each round, in other words the session heals after λ rounds. At the end the attacker has a probability of $2^{-\lambda}$ in order to break the PCS.

5.2   Limitations of the Initial Attack

In our setting, Ouroboros ciphertexts take the form $x \cdot r_2 + y \cdot r_1 + e$ where $\omega_H(e) > 0$. When the Hamming weight of e is nonzero, we refer to e as noise. To compute the DFR for Ouroboros ciphertexts, we propose a new decoding algorithm (which takes into account the noise), called `noisyBFmax`, which is based on the approach of [3]. This algorithm is described in Fig. 6 and is further detailed in Sect. 5.4. Notice since the analysis in [3], relies on a simplifying assumption, is more optimistic than that of [2]. Having an optimistic DFR provides a lower bound on the actual DFR; however, this is sufficient for the purpose of our attack analysis.

5.3   A Stronger Attack

We propose an enhanced attack Fig. 5 exploiting a key insight: recovering only one of the two secret polynomials, either r_1 or r_2, suffices to fully compromise the scheme and prevent post-compromise security (PCS) healing. Specifically, given the known values $\{h, x, y, r_1 + h \cdot r_2\}$, if `noisyBFmax` recovers r_2, it can compute $r_1 = (r_1 + h \cdot r_2) - h \cdot r_2$. Conversely, if it recovers r_1, then $(r_1 + h \cdot r_2) - r_1 = h \cdot r_2$; since the matrix representation $r_2 \cdot \text{rot}(h)$ is full-rank when the Hamming weight $\omega_H(h)$ is odd – a condition that holds with probability 2^{-1} due to the uniform random sampling of h in the ring $\mathcal{R}$ – inversion yields $\boldsymbol{r_2} = \boldsymbol{r_2} \cdot \text{rot}(\boldsymbol{h}) \cdot \text{rot}(\boldsymbol{h})^{-1}$. This partial recovery strengthens the attack, as its success probability is tied to the decoding failure rate (DFR) of getting at least one of the two polynomials, *i.e.* $\text{DFR}_\vee$, we later give more details in Sect. 5.6.

Table 2. Computed experimentally the inflexion points using `noisyBFmax` decoder (when extracting at least r_2 or r_1 or both), and analysis of RHQC's parameters for those points

	n	w	w_r	inflexion point w_e	Ouroboros's 1-DFR	HQC's DFR with w_e
rhqc-192	39733	114	114	$[\![11842, 11764]\!]$	$[0.492, 0.564333]$	$1 - 2^{-86}$
rhqc-128-128	16547	67	67	$[\![4714, 4683]\!]$	$[0.49, 0.55]$	$1 - 2^{-28}$
rhqc-128-64	15013	67	67	$[\![4020, 4047]\!]$	$[0.49, 0.56]$	$1 - 2^{-30}$
rhqc-128-32	13829	67	67	3458	0.5	$1 - 2^{-23}$

Input (x_{i-1}^j, y_{i-1}^j) and (pk_i, v_i)
Output $(x_i^{1-j}, y_i^{1-j}, e_i)$

$c_i := v_i - \mathsf{pk}_i \cdot y_{i-1}^j$
// Notice that $c_i = \boldsymbol{m_i G} + x_{i-1}^j y_i^{1-j} + x_i^{1-j} y_{i-1}^j + e_i$
$\boldsymbol{m_i} \leftarrow \mathsf{HQC.Decode}(c_i)$
// Use of Lemma 2
$c_i' := c_i + \boldsymbol{m_i G}$
$(\hat{x}_i^{1-j}, \hat{y}_i^{1-j}, \hat{e}_i) \leftarrow \mathtt{noisyBFmax}((x_{i-1}^j, y_{i-1}^j), c_i')$
// Extraction of all polynomials successful
if $c_i' = x_{i-1}^j \hat{y}_i^{1-j} + \hat{x}_i^{1-j} y_{i-1}^j + \hat{e}_i$
   | **return** $(\hat{x}_i^{1-j}, \hat{y}_i^{1-j}, \hat{e}_i)$
// Only extraction of $\hat{y}_i^{1-j}$ is successful
if $\omega_H(\hat{y}_i^{1-j}) = w \wedge \omega_H(\hat{x}_i^{1-j}) \neq w$
   | **return** $(h \cdot \hat{y}_i^{1-j} + \mathsf{pk}_i, \hat{y}_i^{1-j}, c_i' + \hat{y}_i^{1-j} \cdot x_{i-1}^j + y_{i-1}^j \cdot (h \cdot \hat{y}_i^{1-j} + \mathsf{pk}_i))$
// Only extraction of $\hat{x}_i^{1-j}$ is successful
if $2 \nmid \omega_H(h) \wedge \omega_H(\hat{x}_i^{1-j}) = w$
   | **return** $(\hat{x}_i^{1-j}, (\mathsf{pk}_i + \hat{x}_i^{1-j}) \cdot h^{-1}, \hat{x}_i^{1-j} y_{1-i}^j + (\mathsf{pk}_i + \hat{x}_i^{1-j}) \cdot h^{-1} x_{i-1}^j + c_i')$
// Fail otherwise
else
   | **return** $\perp$

Fig. 5. Extractor for a stronger attack

We computed in Table 2, according to the stronger attack (*cf.* Fig. 5), the different inflexion points for the proposed RHQC's parameters (*i.e.* for the fixed w and w_r) and investigate how the DFR of HQC's decoder behaves at those inflexion points. We notice, that the DFR of HQC's is higher than the Ouroboros's DFR. In other words, it is impossible to satisfy the requirements for the repairability with the proposed parameters in [16].

5.4   Introducing a New Decoder: `noisyBFmax`

Input $s = xr_2 + yr_1 + e$

Output (u, v, s) that is supposed to be equal to (r_2, r_1, e)

$u \leftarrow 0 \in \mathbb{F}_2^n, v \leftarrow 0 \in \mathbb{F}_2^n$

$\sigma \leftarrow s \cdot_{\mathbb{N}} H$

while iter $<$ iterMax $\wedge\ \omega_H(s) > w_e \wedge (\omega_H(u) \neq w_r \vee \omega_H(v) \neq w_r)$:

    $i \xleftarrow{\$} \operatorname{argmax} \sigma$

    if $i > n$:

        $v_{i-n} \leftarrow v_{i-n} + 1$

    else

        $u_i \leftarrow u_i + 1$

    foreach $j \in \operatorname{supp}(H_{i,\cdot})$:

        $s_j \leftarrow s_j + 1$

        if $s_j = 0$:

            $d \leftarrow -1$

        else

            $d \leftarrow 1$

        foreach $l \in \operatorname{supp}(H_{\cdot,j})$:

            $\sigma_l \leftarrow \sigma_l + d$

        iter $\leftarrow$ iter $+ 1$

return (u, v, s)

Fig. 6. Algorithm `noisyBFmax`[3]

As mentioned earlier, we propose a new algorithm dub `noisyBFmax` described in Fig. 6, based on `BFmax` [3]. The `noisyBFmax` algorithm extends `BFmax` except for its termination condition and its output (now we can output the e vector).

Notice that, as opposed to BitFlip, `noisyBFmax` only flips the bit corresponding to one of the coordinates of highest value in the matrix product over natural numbers $s \cdot_{\mathbb{N}} H$, where the BitFlip algorithm flips the bits corresponding to those that are greater than a threshold. This main improvement has two consequences[3]:

- The `noisyBFmax` is faster to compute than the original BitFlip. In the BitFlip algorithm we need each time that we modify s, to recompute $s \cdot_{\mathbb{N}} H$. This operation is costly. Since in `noisyBFmax` we only flip one bit, it is easier to predict the new weight in the new $s \cdot_{\mathbb{N}} H$, it is either $+1$ or -1 at some positions *cf.* Fig. 6.
- We are able to establish a theoretical DFR. As mentioned earlier, `noisyBFmax` flips one bit at each iteration, while BitFlip flips many bits at each iteration. Furthermore, in BitFlip the bits are flipped accordingly to whether the corresponding coordinates in $s \cdot_{\mathbb{N}} H$ are greater than a particular threshold. This

---

[3] Those observations also hold for `BFmax`.

strategy leads to some bits being mistakenly flipped, and it becomes hard to determine the probability of this event. Because at each iteration, the product $s \cdot_N H$ is recomputed, it becomes even harder to predict the new result, and how it affects the following iteration. On the other hand, `noisyBFmax` flips one bit at each iteration by choosing the maximum weight in the product $s \cdot_N H$. This strategy yields an easier probability model. In fact, we are less prone to mistakenly flip the wrong bit (here wrong and good means if the flipped bit is equal to the corresponding coordinates in r_1 or r_2 *i.e.* the vectors that we are reconstructing and corresponding to the word that is encoded). Furthermore, the algorithm does not need to recompute the product $s \cdot_N H$, but simply by readjusting with weight by $+1$ or -1, which is also more predictable.

5.5   Computing Theoretical `noisyBFmax`'s DFR

Since the `noisyBFmax` algorithm flips one bit at the time, it is easy to compute its DFR. To do so, we model the probability relying on Assumption 3. The main event that we encounter at each iteration for a syndrome $s = xr_2 + yr_1 + e$: "is one of the coordinates of highest value of the vector $s \cdot_N H$ corresponding to a position that once flipped is equal to the corresponding coordinate in the vector r_1 or r_2?".

Remark 7. This analysis is partly based on `BFmax`'s DFR analysis [3]. We recall that we add the capability to decode even with a noisy vector that we later dub e.

Assumption 3. *Each counter behaves as the sum of independent Bernoulli variables, all with the same parameter, which depends only on the value of the corresponding error bit (either 1 or 0).*

For a given syndrome $s = xr_2 + yr_1 + e$, we can rewrite in matrix from as follows: $s = rH^\top + e$, with $r = (r_2 \mid r_1) \in \mathbb{F}_2^{2n}$ and we recall that $H = (\mathrm{rot}(x) \mid \mathrm{rot}(y)) \in \mathbb{F}_2^{n \times 2n}$. We also recall the following Hamming weights:

- $\omega_H(r) = 2 \cdot w_r$
- Each row of $H^\top$ has a weight of $2 \cdot w$ and for each columns w
- $\omega_H(e) = w_e$

As stated before the algorithm starts by computing $s \cdot_N H$, to simplify our study we propose to denote this obtained vector as follows:

$$\sigma_i := \#\{j \in [\![0, r]\!] : H_{j,i} = 1 \wedge s_j = 1\}$$

Basically, σ_i represents the matrix product in $\mathbb{N}$ of s and the i-th column of H that we note $H_{\cdot,i}$.

With the aim of computing the decoding failure rate of `noisyBFmax` to extract the three vectors, we describe how we obtain the probability by explaining step

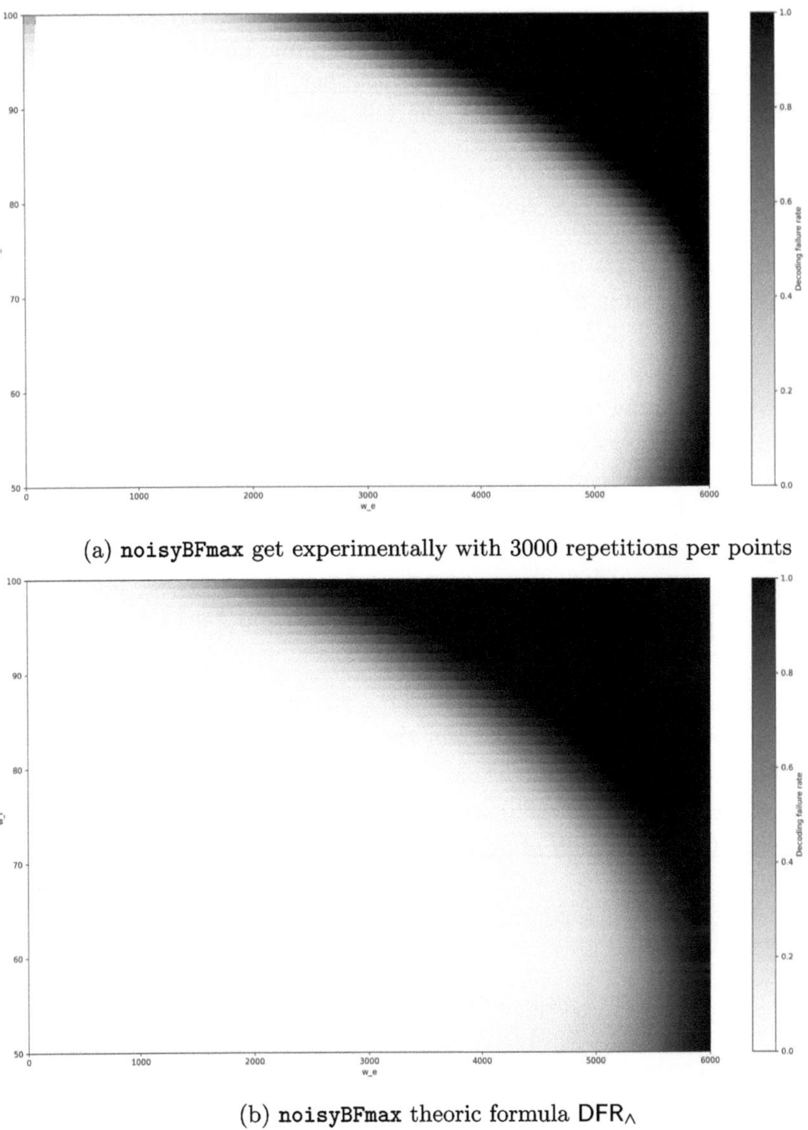

(a) **noisyBFmax** get experimentally with 3000 repetitions per points

(b) **noisyBFmax** theoric formula $\text{DFR}_\wedge$

Fig. 7. Comparison of the experimental and theoretical DFR for the extraction of the three vectors (r_2, r_1, e). Heatmaps for $n = 19597$. The white zone is where the decoding algorithm fails with a negligible probability, while the black zone the decoding algorithm fails with overwhelming probability, finally the gray zone is the zone where the algorithm fails with a probability of 0.5.

by step the link between the algorithm and the probabilistic model. As described before, the algorithm is successful if at each iteration the maximum weight in σ corresponds, once flipped, to the corresponding coordinate of r. We introduce the vector $\hat{\boldsymbol{r}}$ that is a temporary vector that is updated at each iteration, this vector correspond to $\hat{\boldsymbol{r}} \leftarrow \boldsymbol{s} \cdot_{\mathbb{N}} \boldsymbol{H}$. Since we flip one bit at a time the Hamming weight of $\hat{\boldsymbol{r}}$ varies by one, regardless of whether the correct bit has been found or not. Furthermore we introduce the following sets, with u corresponding to $\omega_H(\hat{\boldsymbol{r}})$:

$$J_0^{(u)} := \{i \in \mathbb{N} \mid \boldsymbol{r}_i = \hat{\boldsymbol{r}}_i\}, \ J_1^{(u)} := \{i \in \mathbb{N} \mid \boldsymbol{r}_i \neq \hat{\boldsymbol{r}}_i\}$$

We notice that at the first iteration (for $u = 2w_r$ since we iterate from $2w_r$ to 1) since the vector $\hat{\boldsymbol{r}}$ is initialized at $\boldsymbol{0} \in \mathbb{F}_2^{2n}$, we have $2w_r = \#J_1^{(2w_r)}$ and $n - 2w_r = \#J_0^{(2w_r)}$, at each correct guess the cardinal of $J_1^{(u)}$ is reducing and $J_0^{(u)}$ is growing and *vice versa* when guessed wrongly. We search the computation of successively guessing the right σ_i, meaning that at each iteration the set $J_1^{(u)}$ is growing by one. This succession of correct guesses gives us the following relation $u = \omega_H(\hat{\boldsymbol{r}}) = \#J_1^{(2w_r)}$, because each guesse reduce the Hamming weight of $\hat{\boldsymbol{r}}$.

The probability of success (the complementary of the DFR) that we are searching is the following:

$$\prod_{u=1}^{2w_r} \Pr\left[\max\{\sigma_j : j \in J_0^{(u)}\} < \max\{\sigma_j : j \in J_1^{(u)}\} \mid \hat{\boldsymbol{r}} \in \mathcal{S}_{2n,u}\right]$$

It means that at each iteration u (guessing $2w_r$ times correctly in a row), going from $2w_r$ to 1, the correct $\sigma_{j \in J_1^{(u)}}$ (for the bits not flipped yet and corresponding to a correct bit in the vector $\boldsymbol{r}$) has been chosen over the wrong $\sigma_{j \in J_0^{(u)}}$.

As mentioned earlier, the main component is to compute $\max_{i \in J}\{\sigma_i\}$. So we first define the probability of obtaining $\sigma_i = x$ for $x \in [\![0, w]\!]$, knowing the value $\hat{\boldsymbol{r}}_i$.

$$g_0^{(u)}(x) := \Pr[\sigma_i = x \mid \hat{\boldsymbol{r}}_i = 0] = \binom{w}{x} {\rho_0'}^x (1 - \rho_0')^{w-x}$$

$$g_1^{(u)}(x) := \Pr[\sigma_i = x \mid \hat{\boldsymbol{r}}_i = 1] = \binom{w}{x} {\rho_1'}^x (1 - \rho_1')^{w-x}$$

Before introducing ρ_1' and ρ_0' we first introduce ρ_0 and ρ_1, that correspond to the probabilities of obtaining a coordinate set to 1 in the matrix product $(\boldsymbol{s} - \boldsymbol{e}) \cdot_{\mathbb{N}} \boldsymbol{H}$ according to $\hat{\boldsymbol{r}}$.

$$\rho_1 := \Pr\left[(\boldsymbol{s} - \boldsymbol{e})_j = 1 \wedge \boldsymbol{H}_{j,i} = 1 \mid \hat{\boldsymbol{r}}_i = 1\right]$$

$$= \frac{1}{\binom{2n-1}{2w-1}} \sum_{\substack{l \in 2\mathbb{N}}}^{\min\{2w-1,u-1\}} \binom{u-1}{l} \binom{2n-u}{2w-1-l}$$

$$\rho_0 := \Pr\left[(\boldsymbol{s} - \boldsymbol{e})_j = 1 \wedge \boldsymbol{H}_{j,i} = 1 \mid \hat{\boldsymbol{r}}_i = 0\right]$$

$$= \frac{1}{\binom{2n-1}{2w-1}} \sum_{\substack{l \notin 2\mathbb{N}}}^{\min\{2w-1,u\}} \binom{u}{l} \binom{2n-1-u}{2w-1-l}$$

We now take into account the error $\boldsymbol{e}$. As a result, we now compute the probability corresponding to the matrix product of $\boldsymbol{s} \cdot_{\mathbb{N}} \boldsymbol{H}$ according to $\hat{\boldsymbol{r}}$. The matrix product can be interpreted as the chance of deciding which rows to add from the $\boldsymbol{H}$. In simpler words, this can be modeled as that there is $\frac{w_e}{n}$ of chance to pick an erroneous row, in other words, it was not supposed to yield a bit. We remodel our ρ into ρ' functions:

$$\rho_1' := \left(1 - \frac{w_e}{n}\right) \Pr\left[\boldsymbol{s}_j = 0\right] \Pr\left[(\boldsymbol{s} - \boldsymbol{e})_j = 1 \wedge \boldsymbol{H}_{j,i} = 1 \mid \boldsymbol{r}_i = 1\right]$$

$$+ \frac{w_e}{n} \Pr\left[\boldsymbol{s}_j = 1\right] \Pr\left[(\boldsymbol{s} - \boldsymbol{e})_j = 1 \wedge \boldsymbol{H}_{j,i} = 1 \mid \boldsymbol{r}_i = 0\right]$$

$$= \left(1 - \frac{w_e}{n}\right) \Pr\left[\boldsymbol{s}_j = 0\right] \rho_1 + \frac{w_e}{n} \Pr\left[\boldsymbol{s}_j = 1\right] \rho_0$$

$$\rho_0' := \left(1 - \frac{w_e}{n}\right) \Pr\left[\boldsymbol{s}_j = 1\right] \Pr\left[(\boldsymbol{s} - \boldsymbol{e})_j = 1 \wedge \boldsymbol{H}_{j,i} = 1 \mid \boldsymbol{r}_i = 0\right]$$

$$+ \frac{w_e}{n} \Pr\left[\boldsymbol{s}_j = 0\right] \Pr\left[(\boldsymbol{s} - \boldsymbol{e})_j = 1 \wedge \boldsymbol{H}_{j,i} = 1 \mid \boldsymbol{r}_i = 1\right]$$

$$= \left(1 - \frac{w_e}{n}\right) \Pr\left[\boldsymbol{s}_j = 1\right] \rho_0 + \frac{w_e}{n} \Pr\left[\boldsymbol{s}_j = 0\right] \rho_1$$

We notice that ρ_1' accounts for all the *incoherent choices*, while ρ_0' accounts for all the *coherent choices*. For example in ρ_1' we have $\left(1 - \frac{w_e}{n}\right)$ chance to have picked a wrong row, if the added error $\boldsymbol{e}_j$ is null or $\frac{w_e}{n}$ chances to pick a correct row, if the added error $\boldsymbol{e}_j$ is not null. We notice that ρ_0' is antonymous[4] to ρ_1'.

In order to compute $\Pr[\boldsymbol{s}_j = 0]$ or $\Pr[\boldsymbol{s}_j = 1]$, we build it using the following formulas (explained in more details in [17]). First we compute the chance to obtain a coefficient set to 1 in a polynomial which is the result of two polynomials of specific Hamming weight.

$$\tilde{p} := \Pr\left[\forall (a,b) \in \mathcal{R}_{w_r} \times \mathcal{R}_w, (ab)_i = 1\right] = \frac{1}{\binom{n}{w}\binom{n}{w_r}} \sum_{l \notin 2\mathbb{N}}^{\min\{w, w_r\}} \binom{n}{l}\binom{n-l}{w-l}\binom{n-w}{w_r-l}$$

Next from then we compute the probability to obtain 1 (resp. 0) for the codeword $xr_2 + yr_1$ (or, equivalently, also denoted by $\boldsymbol{r}\boldsymbol{H}^\top$), which is given by the following formula:

$$\Pr\left[\boldsymbol{r}\boldsymbol{H}_j^\top = 1\right] = 2\tilde{p}(1 - \tilde{p})$$

$$\Pr\left[\boldsymbol{r}\boldsymbol{H}_j^\top = 0\right] = (1 - \tilde{p})^2 \tilde{p}^2$$

Now there is missing only the error $\boldsymbol{e}$ that turns some coefficients to 0 if set to 1, otherwise to 1 if set to 0:

$$\Pr[\boldsymbol{s}_j = 1] = \Pr[(\boldsymbol{r}\boldsymbol{H}^\top + \boldsymbol{e})_j = 1] = \left(1 - \frac{w_e}{n}\right) \Pr\left[\boldsymbol{r}\boldsymbol{H}_j^\top = 1\right] + \frac{w_e}{n} \Pr\left[\boldsymbol{r}\boldsymbol{H}_j^\top = 0\right]$$

$$\Pr[\boldsymbol{s}_j = 0] = \Pr[(\boldsymbol{r}\boldsymbol{H}^\top + \boldsymbol{e})_j = 0] = \left(1 - \frac{w_e}{n}\right) \Pr\left[\boldsymbol{r}\boldsymbol{H}_j^\top = 0\right] + \frac{w_e}{n} \Pr\left[\boldsymbol{r}\boldsymbol{H}_j^\top = 1\right]$$

---

[4] We use this word and not negation since it's not a logical negation.

To compute `noisyBFmax`'s DFR, we notice that the algorithm succeeds if and only if, it has always flipped the good part each time. For the sake of brevity we define $\forall i \in \{0,1\}, \forall u \in [\![1, 2w_r]\!], \widetilde{\sigma}_{i,u} := \max\{\sigma_j : j \in J_i^{(u)}\}$. We can model it by the following, as explained before:

$$\mathsf{DFR}_\wedge(n, w, w_r, w_e) := 1 - \prod_{u=1}^{2w_r} \Pr\left[\widetilde{\sigma}_{0,u} < \widetilde{\sigma}_{1,u} \mid \hat{r} \in \mathcal{S}_{2n,u}\right]$$

$$= 1 - \prod_{u=1}^{2w_r} \sum_{x=0}^{w-1} \Pr\left[\widetilde{\sigma}_{0,u} = x \mid \hat{r} \in \mathcal{S}_{2n,u}\right] \Pr\left[\widetilde{\sigma}_{1,u} > x \mid \hat{r} \in \mathcal{S}_{2n,u}\right]$$

$$= 1 - \prod_{u=1}^{2w_r} \sum_{x=0}^{w-1} f_0^{(u)}(x) \cdot f_1^{(u)}(x)$$

We define functions f_0 and f_1, which cumulate the probabilities of the corresponding g functions in order to compute maximum of σ.

$$\forall x \in \mathbb{N}, f_1^{(u)}(x) := 1 - \left(\sum_{z=0}^{x} g_1^{(u)}(z)\right)^u$$

$$\forall x \in \mathbb{N}, f_0^{(u)}(x) := \begin{cases} \left(g_0^{(u)}(0)\right)^{2n-u} & \text{if } x = 0 \\ \left(\sum_{z=0}^{x} g_0^{(u)}(x)\right)^{2n-u} + \left(\sum_{z=0}^{x-1} g_0^{(u)}(x)\right)^{2n-u} & \text{otherwise} \end{cases}$$

Experimental and Theoretical Comparison. We compare the experimental and theoretical DFR in Fig. 7. We observe that the theoretical estimates closely match the experimental results on average. The only noticeable discrepancy occurs in the region around $(w, w_r, w_e) = (75, 75, 5400)$.

5.6   Maximizing `noisyBFmax`'s DFR for the Attack

We notice that the attacker does not need to retrieve all the three polynomials (r_2, r_1, e) for the attack to be successful. The attacker could find one of the three vectors and deduce the other two from the context *e.g.* the public key, and so on, as claimed in Sect. 5.3. If the algorithm has at least w_r successful guesses at each iteration then it can potentially retrieve either r_1 (or *resp.* r_2). The rest is composed of the sum of the error e, some wrong flipped bits, and of r_2 (or *resp.* r_1).

In order to compute $\mathsf{DFR}_\vee$ we assume the Markov chain described in Fig. 9. We give its transition matrix $A \in \mathbb{R}^{4w_r+1 \times 4w_r+1}$. We introduce the following notation $\pi^{(2w_r+1)} \in \mathbb{R}^{4w_r+1}$, which sets all the coordinates of $\pi^{(2w_r+1)}$ to 0 except the $(2w_r + 1)$-*th* coordinate which is set to 1. In order to compute the probabilities of each state after $2w_r$ iteration as the algorithm `noisyBFmax` states, we compute $\pi := N(\pi^{(2w_r+1)} A^{2w_r})$. We define N the function that normalize a vector, as $N(x) := \frac{1}{||x||_1} x$.

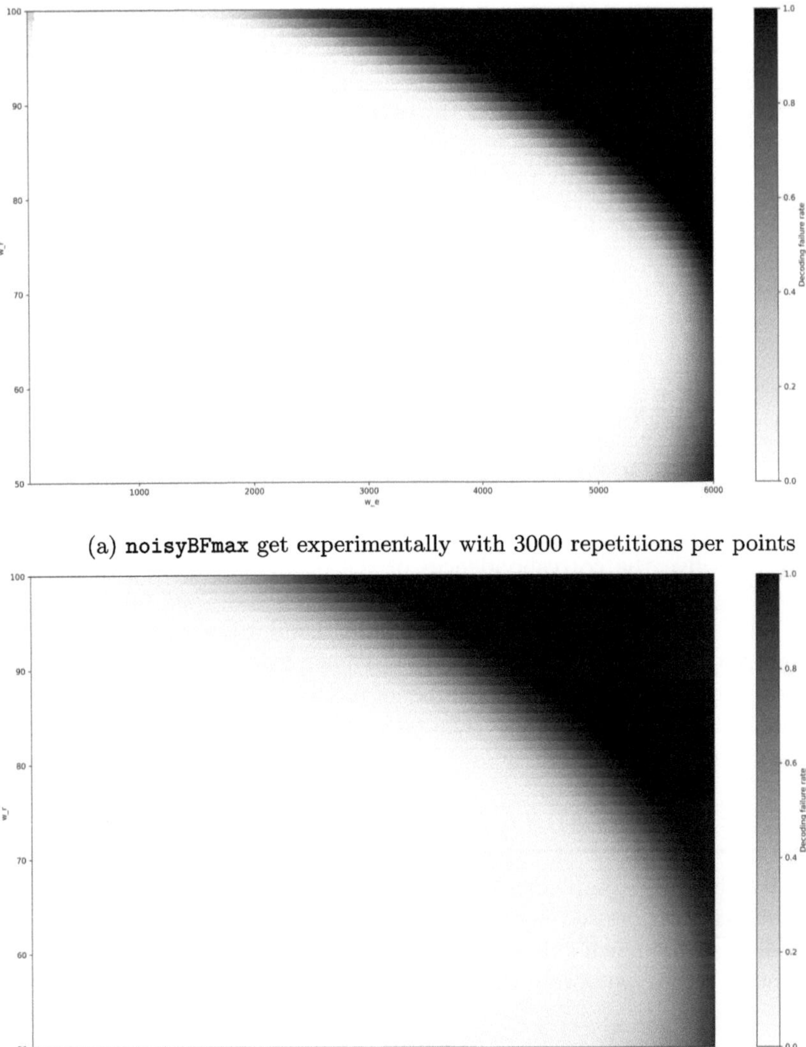

(a) **noisyBFmax** get experimentally with 3000 repetitions per points

(b) $\mathsf{DFR_V}$

Fig. 8. Comparison of the experimental and theoretical DFR for the extraction of one of the three vectors r_2 **,** r_1**,** e**.** Heatmaps for $n = 19597$. The white zone is where the decoding algorithm fails with a negligible probability, while the black zone the decoding algorithm fails with overwhelming probability, finally the gray zone is the zone where the algorithm fails with a probability of 0.5.

To obtain the decoding failure rate that extract at least one of the polynomials:

$$\mathsf{DFR_V}(n, w, w_r, w_e) := 1 - \sum_{k=1}^{w_r+1} \pi_k \cdot 2^{1-k}$$

Notice that we use the truncated cumulative negative exponential distribution to obtain $\mathrm{DFR}_\vee$. We justify this choice by stating that at the state 0 there is a probability of 1 to have successfully decoded, next at state 2 we have a probability of $\frac{1}{4}$ since a quarter of the outcome can fill entirely r_1 or r_2 and the rest does not fill one of them, and so on. Furthermore we take only odd indices since we analyze it for $2w_r \in 2\mathbb{N}$ and the indexation starts at 1.

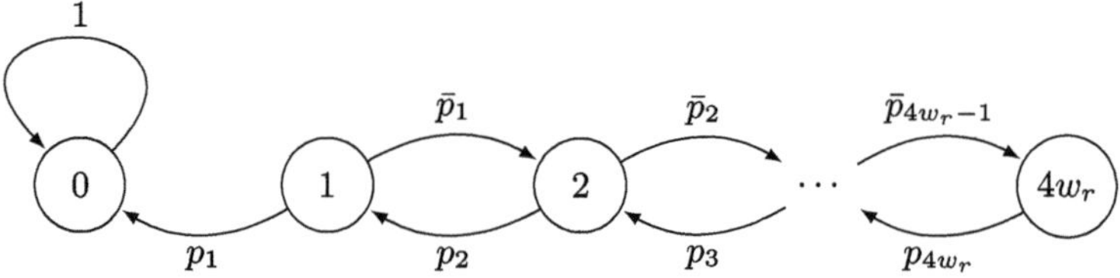

Fig. 9. Markov chain modeling the `noisyBFmax`'s DFR

We now give the correspondences of the probabilities used in the Markov chain in Fig. 9 above. First the algorithm starts at state $2w_r$ since both vectors u and v (*cf.* Fig. 6) have a Hamming weight of 0 and it is suppose to have $2w_r$. In other words, at this state there are $2w_r$ unknown values. Later, we either we flip a correct bit hence reducing the number of unknown values, or we flip the wrong bit and add an unknown value. The transition probabilities p_u corresponds to the prior probability:

$$p_u := \Pr\left[\max\{\sigma_j : j \in J_0^{(u)}\} < \max\{\sigma_j : j \in J_1^{(u)}\} \mid \hat{r} \in \mathcal{S}_{2n,u}\right]$$

We state that the complementary probability $\bar{p}_u$ symbolizes that the correct coordinate is not guessed correctly meaning that it adds an erroneous bit flip *i.e.* adding an unknown value.

In other words we obtain the following transition matrix:

$$A := \begin{pmatrix} 1 & 0 & 0 & 0 & \cdots & & 0 \\ p_1 & 0 & \bar{p}_1 & 0 & \cdots & & 0 \\ 0 & p_2 & 0 & \bar{p}_2 & \cdots & & 0 \\ \vdots & \ddots & \ddots & & \ddots & & \vdots \\ 0 & \cdots & 0 & p_{4w_r-1} & 0 & \bar{p}_{4w_r-1} \\ 0 & \cdots & 0 & 0 & p_{4w_r} & 0 \end{pmatrix}$$

Remark 8. We state that the computation of $\mathrm{DFR}_\wedge$ can be obtain by computing the product as mentioned earlier, or through the Markov by taking the coordinate of π corresponding to the state 0 *i.e.* $1 - \pi_1$.

Experimental and Theoretical Comparison. We compare the experimental and theoretical DFR in Fig. 8. We notice that the theoretical under estimates the experimental one. Plus we notice, that:

- there is a probability 0.6 of occurrences that are under 0.5 in the experimental one
- against a probability 0.77 in the theoretical one.

We can state that there is approximately, according to a sort of Monte-Carlo analysis in a reduced window, 0.17 in probability units of differences, that underestimate the code capacity to retrieve at least one of the two vectors r_1 or r_2. We suppose that this occured since we haven't take into account, in our probabilistic model, the case when the maximum of the wrong set is equal to the maximum of the good set, we refer the reader to the functions f_0 and f_1 described in Sect. 5.4.

5.7 Choice of Parameters to Counter the Attack

As seen previously for the fixed w and w_r proposed values we are not able to protect the RHQC. We propose varying the parameters w and w_r. We generate the heatmaps Fig. 10 for the Ouroboros and HQC decoder, in order to find a zone where HQC can decode while Ouroboros can't. We notice that there exists a spot where the repairability could be "considered". For $(n, w, wr, we) = (19597, 50, 50, 5600)$ gives a Ouroboros' DFR of 0.51 and for HQC's DFR 0.21. By the known attacks presented in HQC, the security parameters with those parameters is 2^{-132}, considering the best attack and the quantum acceleration. Since the HQC's DFR is too high, it is not a suitable candidate.

We notice that in order to recover the security Alice and Bob need to do 128 exchanges since the Ouroboros' DFR is 2^{-1}. In comparison with a naïve ratchet we are able to recover a security of 2^{-128} after the second exchange.

Since the actual DFR is higher than the predicted one, our analysis provides a lower bound on the DFR, which in turn yields a lower bound on the required parameters for RHQC when taking the attack into account.

Efficiency of RHQC over Naïve HQC Ratchet. We first recall that a naïve HQC-based ratchet achieves correctness in the sense that the HQC decoder fails with probability at most $2^{-\lambda}$, while providing a security level of λ bits.

To obtain an equivalent security and correctness criterion in the RHQC setting, we therefore seek a set of parameters for which the HQC decoding failure probability remains lower than $2^{-\lambda}$. At the same time, the decoding failure rate DFR_V of Ouroboros must be greater than $1 - 2^{-\lambda}$.

This separation ensures that HQC decoding succeeds with overwhelming probability, thereby guaranteeing correctness, while any extractor relying on Ouroboros decoding succeeds only with negligible probability, preserving the intended security properties of the protocol.

Thus, the n that we are searching for is between n_{RHQC} and $\frac{3}{2}n_{HQC}$. This is justified by the fact that in the naïve ratchet the interlocutor sends three

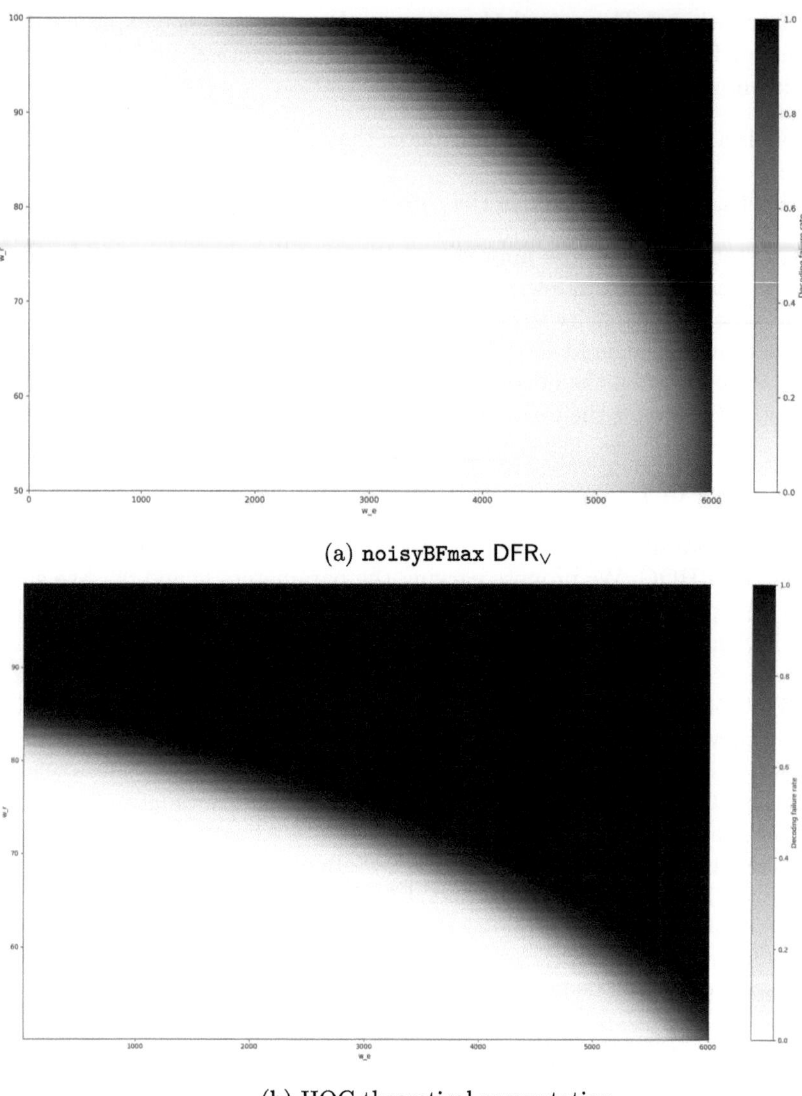

(b) HQC theoretical computation

Fig. 10. Comparison of noisyBFmax's DFR and HQC's DFR, in order to visually see overlapped zones. Heatmaps for $n = 19597$. The white zone is where the decoding algorithm fails with a negligible probability, while the black zone the decoding algorithm fails with overwhelming probability, finally the gray zone is the zone where the algorithm fails with a probability 0.5.

polynomials each of size n_{HQC} *i.e.* $3n_{\mathsf{HQC}}$ bits ; while in RHQC the interlocutor sends 2 polynomials of size n *i.e.* $2n$ bits. In otherwords while $2n < 3n_{\mathsf{HQC}}$ is satisfied then RHQC is more efficient than the naïve one. We recall that n needs to be primitive in order to have an appropriate ring $\mathcal{R}$.

More concretely, after the next sending operation the security is again at $2^{-\lambda}$, it has the same security guarantee and the same healing time than the naïve ratchet.

Unfortunately, we have exhaustively searched with an implementation[5] if this theorem is valid for RHQC-128 with $n \in [\![19597, \lceil \frac{3 \times 17669}{2} \rceil]\!]$. Unfortunately there is no valid n that satisfies what we have stated below. We conclude that RHQC-128 can not be as efficient and as secure as a naïve ratchet with HQC-128. We conjecture that it is also the case for the other parameters.

Notice that using another more accurate DFR would not change the conclusion that RHQC is in fact less efficient than naïve ratchet HQC for the same security parameter.

Conclusion for Alternative Parameters Resistant to the Attack. We have seen that the PCS and Correctness of RHQC is an equilibrium between the capacities of the external decoder (here HQC decoder) and the internal decoder (here Ouroboros decoder). Without changing RHQC, as demonstrated the protocol is not useable in practice compare to the naive ratchet. As an open question we may ask ourselves, would there exists any tuple of internal and external codes, that would not jeopardize the protocol?

6   Conclusion

We investigated the post-compromise security of the RHQC ratcheting protocol and showed that its design fundamentally fails to achieve healing after compromise. Our analysis reveals an inherent trade-off between correctness and post-compromise security when HQC is used in a NIKE-like fashion.

We proved that whenever parameters are chosen so that HQC decoding succeeds with overwhelming probability, the structure of RHQC enables the extraction of future ratchet secrets with non-negligible probability, thereby violating post-compromise security. Conversely, increasing the noise to prevent extraction inevitably breaks correctness. As a result, RHQC admits no parameter set that simultaneously achieves correctness, post-compromise security, and efficiency beyond that of a naïve post-quantum ratchet.

A central technical contribution of this work is the introduction of the `noisyBFmax` decoding algorithm. By enabling a precise probabilistic analysis of the decoding failure rate in the presence of noise, `noisyBFmax` proved crucial for rigorously characterizing the extractor's success probability. This analysis was instrumental in establishing the impossibility of repairing RHQC under its current design.

More broadly, our results highlight that post-quantum ratcheting protocols cannot rely on superficial analogies with Diffie–Hellman-based constructions. Instead, they require primitives with strong non-extractability properties.

Funding Information. This work was funded by X7PQC project.

---

[5] The implementation and its results are available at https://gitlab.xlim.fr/krejci/implem-pcs-rhqc.

A BRKE

<table>
<tr><td colspan="2" align="center">Oracle $\mathrm{Rcv}(u, ad, c)$</td></tr>
<tr><td>

Game $\mathsf{KIND}^{b}_{\mathrm{BR}}(\mathcal{A})$

For $u \in \{A, B\}:$
   $s_u \leftarrow 0;\ r_u \leftarrow 0$
   $e_u \leftarrow 0;\ EP_u[\cdot] \leftarrow \perp$
   $E_u^{\vdash} \leftarrow 0;\ E_u^{\dashv} \leftarrow 0$
   $adc_u[\cdot] \leftarrow \perp;\ is_u \leftarrow \mathsf{T}$
   $key_u[\cdot] \leftarrow \perp;\ XP_u \leftarrow \varnothing$
   $TR_u \leftarrow \varnothing;\ CH_u \leftarrow \varnothing$
   $oos_u \leftarrow \infty;\ forge_u \leftarrow \mathsf{F}$ G_1
   $VK_u[\cdot] \leftarrow \perp$ G_1

$(S_{A,S}, S_{A,R}) \xleftarrow{\$} init_{SR}$

$(S_{B,S}, S_{B,R}) \xleftarrow{\$} init_{SR}$
$S_A \leftarrow (S_{A,S}, S_{A,R})$
$S_B \leftarrow (S_{B,S}, S_{B,R})$

$b' \xleftarrow{\$} \mathcal{A}$
For $u \in \{A, B\}:$
   Require $TR_u \cap CH_u = \varnothing$
Stop with b'

</td><td>

Require $S_u \neq \ |$
If $is_u \wedge adc_{\bar{u}}[r_u] \neq (ad, c):$
   $is_u \leftarrow \mathsf{F}$
   $oos_u \leftarrow s_u$ G_1
   If $oos_u > r_u:\ forge_u \leftarrow \mathsf{T}$ G_1
If $r_u \in XP_{\bar{u}}:$
   $TR_u \xleftarrow{\cup} \{\mathsf{S}\} \times \mathbb{N} \times [s_u, \ldots]$
   $TR_u \xleftarrow{\cup} \{\mathsf{R}\} \times \mathbb{N} \times [r_u, \ldots]$
If $is_u:$
   $E_u^{\vdash} \leftarrow EP_{\bar{u}}[r_u]$
   $e_u \leftarrow e_u + 1$
$(S_1, S_2) \leftarrow S_u$
$vfk\|c_1\|c_2\|\sigma \leftarrow c;\ ad \leftarrow vfk$
Require $vfy_s(sgk, c_1\|c_2, \sigma)$
If $forge_u \wedge vfk \neq VK_{\bar{u}}[r_u]:$
         Abort G_1
$S_1 \leftarrow rcv_A(S_1, ad, c_2)$
Require $S_1 \neq \perp$
$(S_2, k.o) \leftarrow rcv_B(S_2, ad, c_1)$
Require $S_2 \neq \perp$
$S_u \leftarrow (S_1, S_2)$
If $S_u = \perp:$ Return $\perp$
If $is_u:\ k.o \leftarrow \diamond$
$key_u[R, E_u^{+}, r_u] \leftarrow k.o$
$r_u \leftarrow r_u + 1$
Return

</td></tr>
</table>

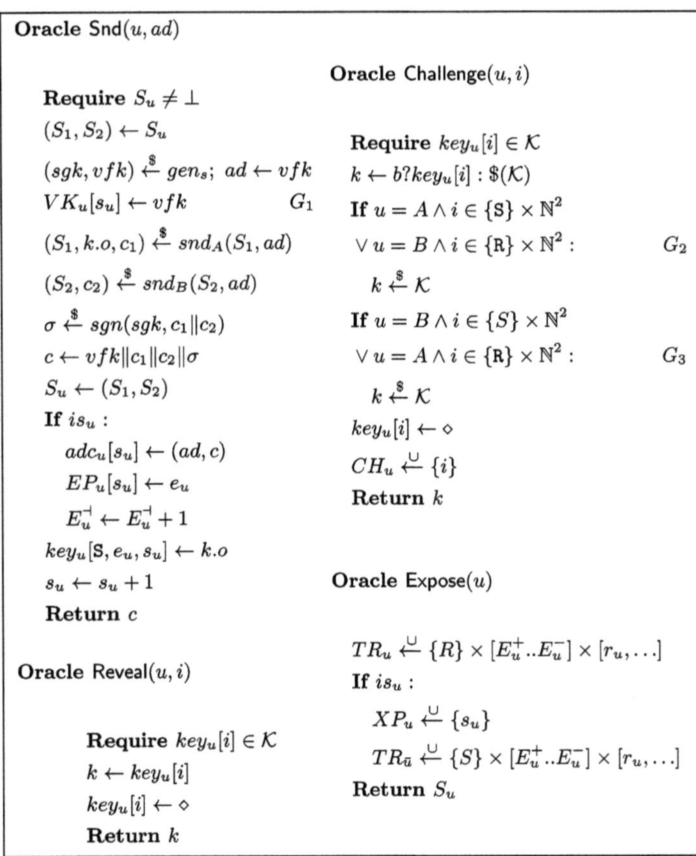

Fig. 11. Games $\mathsf{KIND}^b_{\mathrm{BR}}$, $b \in \{0,1\}$ for the BRKE scheme BR. Symbols S and R are labels that distinguish whether keys were established in a sending or a receiving operation [19].

References

1. Alwen, J., Coretti, S., Dodis, Y.: The double ratchet: Security notions, proofs, and modularization for the signal protocol. In: EUROCRYPT (2019). https://doi.org/10.1007/978-3-030-17653-2_5

2. Arpin, S., Lau, J.B., Mesnard, A., Perlner, R., Robinson, A., Tillich, J.P., Vasseur, V.: Error floor prediction with markov models for qc-mdpc codes. In: Annual International Cryptology Conference, pp. 221–252. Springer (2025). https://doi.org/10.1007/978-3-032-01855-7_8

3. Baldelli, A., Baldi, M., Chiaraluce, F., Santini, P.: Bf-max: an efficient bit flipping decoder with predictable decoding failure rate. In: Proceedings of the International Symposium on Information Theory (ISIT) (2025). https://doi.org/10.1109/isit63088.2025.11195380, https://arxiv.org/abs/2506.09689

4. Berlekamp, E., McEliece, R., Van Tilborg, H.: On the inherent intractability of certain coding problems (corresp.). IEEE Trans. Inform. theory **24**(3), 384–386 (2003). https://doi.org/10.1109/tit.1978.1055873

5. Blazy, O., Bossuat, A., Bultel, X., Fouque, P.A., Onete, C., Pagnin, E.: SAID: reshaping signal into an identity-based asynchronous messaging protocol with authenticated ratcheting. In: Proceedings of IEEE EuroS&P, pp. 294–309 (2019). https://doi.org/10.1109/EuroSP.2019.00030

6. Blazy, O., Boureanu, I., Lafourcade, P., Onete, C., Robert, L.: How fast do you heal? a taxonomy for post-compromise security in secure-channel establishment. In: Proceedings of USENIX (2023)

7. Boureanu, I., et al.: Post-compromise security with application-level key-controls – with a comprehensive study of the 5g akma protocol. In: Proceedings of AsiaCCS, pp. 231–247 (2025). https://doi.org/10.1145/3708821.3733910

8. Cohn-Gordon, K., Cremers, C., Dowling, B., Garratt, L., Stebila, D.: A formal security analysis of the signal messaging protocol. In: Proceedings of IEEE EuroS & P, pp. 451–466 (July 2017). https://doi.org/10.1109/eurosp.2017.27

9. Cohn-Gordon, K., Cremers, C.J.F., Garratt, L.: On post-compromise security. In: IEEE 29th Computer Security Foundations Symposium, CSF 2016, Lisbon, Portugal, 27 June 27 - 1 July 2016, pp. 164–178 (2016). https://doi.org/10.1109/CSF.2016.19

10. Cremers, C., Hale, B., Kohbrok, K.: The complexities of healing in secure group messaging: why Cross-Group effects matter. In: Proceedings of USENIX (2021)

11. Cremers, C., Medinger, N., Naska, A.: Impossibility results for post-compromise security in real-world communication systems. In: Proceedings of IEEE S& P, pp. 4391–4405 (2025). https://doi.org/10.1109/sp61157.2025.00229

12. Deneuville, J.C., Gaborit, P., Zémor, G.: Ouroboros: a simple, secure and efficient key exchange protocol based on coding theory. In: International Workshop on Post-Quantum Cryptography, pp. 18–34. Springer (2017). https://doi.org/10.1007/978-3-319-59879-6_2

13. Durak, F.B., Vaudenay, S.: Bidirectional asynchronous ratcheted key agreement with linear complexity. In: IWSEC (2019). https://doi.org/10.1007/978-3-030-26834-3_20

14. Jaeger, J., Stepanovs, I.: Optimal channel security against fine-grained state compromise: the safety of messaging. In: Shacham, H., Boldyreva, A. (eds.) CRYPTO 2018. LNCS, vol. 10991. Springer, Cham (2018). https://doi.org/10.1007/978-3-319-96884-1_2

15. Jost, D., Maurer, U., Mularczyk, M.: Efficient ratcheting: almost-optimal guarantees for secure messaging. In: Ishai, Y., Rijmen, V. (eds.) EUROCRYPT 2019. LNCS, vol. 11476. Springer, Cham (2019). https://doi.org/10.1007/978-3-030-17653-2_6

16. Juaneda, J., Dehez-Clementi, M., Deneuville, J.C., Lacan, J.: Rhqc: post-quantum ratcheted key exchange from coding assumptions. In: Proceedings of the International Symposium on Information Theory (ISIT) (2025). https://doi.org/10.1109/isit63088.2025.11195626, https://eprint.iacr.org/2025/481.pdf

17. Melchor, C.A., et al.: Hamming quasi-cyclic (hqc). NIST PQC Round **2**(4), 13 (2018). https://doi.org/10.1007/978-3-031-95963-9_33

18. Perrin, T., Marlinspike, M.: The double ratchet algorithm. GitHub wiki **112**(4) (2016)

19. Poettering, B., Rösler, P.: Towards bidirectional ratcheted key exchange. In: hacham, H., Boldyreva, A. (eds) CRYPTO 2018. CRYPTO 2018. LNCS, vol. 10991. Springer, Cham (2018). https://doi.org/10.1007/978-3-319-96884-1_1

On Breaking McEliece Keys Using Brute Force

Lorenz Panny[✉]

Technische Universität München, Munich, Germany
`lorenz@yx7.cc`

Abstract. In the McEliece public-key encryption scheme, a private key is almost always not determined uniquely by its associated public key. We highlight a structural characterization of equivalent private keys that reduces the cost estimate for a simple private-key search using the support-splitting algorithm (SSA) by a polynomial but practically very substantial factor. In addition, we show how to apply the attack to extended codes in order to further improve the performance of the attack. (All of these techniques appear to be known to experts, but not all details have previously been laid out in the literature.)

In addition to spelling out the—thus far—missing details underlying these attack strategies, we provide an optimized software implementation of the SSA for this kind of key search and demonstrate its capabilities in practice by solving a key-recovery challenge with a naïve a-priori cost estimate of 2^{91} bit operations in just ≈ 1470 core days, testing ≈ 7700 private-key candidates per core and second in the process. We stress that the speedup from those equivalences on private keys and from our implementation techniques is merely polynomial and does not indicate any weakness in realistic instantiations of the McEliece cryptosystem, whose parameter choices are primarily constrained by decoding attacks rather than ludicrously more expensive key-recovery attacks.

Keywords: Code-based cryptography · concrete cryptanalysis · Goppa codes

1 Introduction

Code-based cryptography, and McEliece's public-key encryption scheme [10] in particular, are one of the primary candidates for post-quantum cryptography. The idea is simple: Decoding is computationally hard for *random* linear codes, whereas there exist efficient decoders for some more structured families of codes. Users can thus generate an efficiently decodable code in private and "scramble" it into an equivalent code which "appears" random and can be published. (Concretely, for the secret code, the standard choice is a Goppa code over the binary

Date of this document: 2026-01-29.

M. Bardet and R. Niederhagen (Eds.): PQCrypto 2026, LNCS 16492, pp. 275–308, 2026.
https://doi.org/10.1007/978-3-032-22698-3_9

finite field $\mathbb{F}_2$, which can be decoded efficiently using algorithms due to Patterson [13] or Bernstein [4].) The secret transformation from the structured private code to the public random-looking code thus forms a trapdoor that allows the private-key holder to decode efficiently, while (presumably) nobody else will be able to do so. As a consequence, as pointed out in McEliece's original paper:

> It appears that an eavesdropper has two basic attacks to try; first, to try to recover G from G' and so to be able to use Patterson's algorithm. Second, he might attempt to recover $\mathbf{u}$ from $\mathbf{x}$ without learning G.   [10]

These two approaches are nowadays known as the "key-recovery attack" and the "decoding attack" against McEliece, respectively. For decoding, the state of the art is *information-set decoding (ISD)*, of which there exist a large number of variants: See [2, § 1] for a long list of references. In comparison, the key-recovery problem has been receiving relatively slim consideration in the literature. The reason for this seems to be that parameter choices for McEliece have always been constrained primarily by the decoding attack, which has a much lower complexity than all known key-recovery attacks. Indeed, as pointed out by McEliece:

> The first attack seems hopeless if n and t are large enough because there are so many possibilities for G, not to mention the possibilities for S and P.   [10]

However, for independent applications that might rely on the hardness of the McEliece key-recovery problem only, and in the interest of gaining sufficient clarity about the situation in general, there still seems to be value in determining the exact difficulty of this problem.

In this paper, we theoretically investigate and practically optimize a well-known approach for the key-recovery problem, which falls into the category of "smart brute force": Enumerate part of the private-key components (the Goppa polynomial g and *set* of evaluation points $\{\alpha_1, ..., \alpha_n\}$) and check in an efficient manner, using Sendrier's *support-splitting algorithm* [15], whether there exists a valid assignment for the remaining component (the permutation of evaluation points) that leads the key-generation routine to produce the targeted public key.

The historical lack of concrete cost estimates for the McEliece key-recovery problem prompted the *Technology Innovation Institute (TII)* in Abu Dhabi to issue a set of challenge instances for this problem, covering estimated difficulties between 22 and 255 bits. The largest challenge instance that was solved during the admissible time span (May 2023 to May 2024) was a McEliece public key with parameters $(m, t, n) = (8, 5, 253)$ and an a-priori difficulty estimate of 83 bits. This estimate matches the result of multiplying the number of private keys up to permutation ($\approx 2^{tm}/t \cdot \binom{2^m}{n}$) by a rough cost estimate for Gauß elimination (n^3), corresponding to a straightforward black-box application of the support-splitting algorithm to the key-recovery problem while setting constant factors in the cost of linear algebra to one. We demonstrate that this naïve estimate for the complexity of a brute-force key search overshoots the actual cost in two orthogonal ways: First, the *number* of guesses required is smaller (by a logarithmic factor) than the number of private keys, since a polynomially large set of private keys corresponds to any given public key. Second, the cost of testing each candidate private key can be *amortized* across multiple guesses, resulting in a lower cost per guess compared to testing each guess completely separately and independently. We further describe and demonstrate some useful implementation techniques which drastically speed up the key search in practice.

After the conclusion of the challenge, our implementation was further improved by incorporating the option to run the attack using extended Goppa codes, which introduces additional equivalences on private-key data, thereby accelerating the attack by another factor of $\approx n$. This renders it feasible to solve the McEliece key-recovery problem for even larger parameter sets: The biggest example we have conquered to date is TII's challenge instance with an a-priori difficulty estimate of 91 bits, which took less than a (wall-clock) day on a potent server.

2   Preliminaries

2.1   Definitions and Notation

The following definitions are all standard in coding theory: A *(linear) code* in $\mathbb{F}_q^n$ is a subspace $C \subseteq \mathbb{F}_q^n$. The *(Hamming) weight* of a vector $c \in \mathbb{F}_q^n$ is the number of nonzero coordinates in c. The *enumerator* $\mathcal{W}(C)$ of a linear code $C \subseteq \mathbb{F}_q^n$ is the vector $(w_0, w_1, ..., w_n) \in \mathbb{Z}_{\geq 0}^{n+1}$ where $w_i = \left|\{c \in C \mid \mathrm{wt}(c) = i\}\right|$. The *dual* of a code C is the code $C^{\perp} = \left\{w \in \mathbb{F}_p^n \mid \forall v \in C.\ \langle v, w \rangle = 0\right\}$. The *hull* of C is the code $C \cap C^{\perp}$. Two codes are *permutation-equivalent* if one can be obtained from the other by permuting the coordinates of the ambient space $\mathbb{F}_q^n$.

Throughout, let $\mathsf{Irr}_t(q)$ denote the number of monic irreducible polynomials over $\mathbb{F}_q$ of degree t. Note $q^t - \log_2(t) \cdot q^{t/2} \leq t \cdot \mathsf{Irr}_t(q) \leq q^t$, hence $\mathsf{Irr}_t(q) \approx q^t/t$.

We write $\mathbb{F}_q[x]_{\leq t}$ for the set of polynomials in $\mathbb{F}_q[x]$ of degree $\leq t$; similarly for "$<$" in place of "$\leq$".

2.2   Goppa Codes

Fix a prime power $q = p^m$ and let t, n be positive integers such that $tm \leq n \leq q$.

For a monic squarefree polynomial $g \in \mathbb{F}_q[x]$ of degree t and a length-n sequence $L = (\alpha_1, ..., \alpha_n)$ of distinct elements $\alpha_i \in \mathbb{F}_q$ satisfying $g(\alpha_i) \neq 0$, the *Goppa code* defined by g and L is the $\mathbb{F}_p$-vector space

$$\Gamma(g, L) \;=\; \left\{ c \in \mathbb{F}_p^n \;\middle|\; \forall f \in \mathbb{F}_q[x]_{<t}.\ \sum_{i=1}^{n} c_i (f/g)(\alpha_i) = 0 \right\}.$$

Identifying elements of $\mathbb{F}_{p^m}$ with vectors in $\mathbb{F}_p^m$ using an arbitrary $\mathbb{F}_p$-vector space isomorphism, a parity-check matrix of $\Gamma(g, L)$ is given by [9, Ch. 12, § 3]

$$\begin{bmatrix} \alpha_1^0/g(\alpha_1) & \cdots & \alpha_n^0/g(\alpha_n) \\ \hline \alpha_1^1/g(\alpha_1) & \cdots & \alpha_n^1/g(\alpha_n) \\ \hline \vdots & \ddots & \vdots \\ \hline \alpha_1^{t-1}/g(\alpha_1) & \cdots & \alpha_n^{t-1}/g(\alpha_n) \end{bmatrix} \in \mathbb{F}_p^{tm \times n}.$$

Notice that permuting L evidently produces equivalent Goppa codes. We shall write $\mathsf{set}(L)$ for the *set* $\{\alpha_1, ..., \alpha_n\}$ containing all the elements in L.

Extended Goppa Codes. We now additionally allow for the list of evaluation points to contain a new element ∞, so that the list $\widehat{L}$ will consist of $n+1$ distinct elements of $\mathbb{P}^1\mathbb{F}_q = \mathbb{F}_q \sqcup \{\infty\}$. Note that we do not require $\infty \in \widehat{L}$; thus, the definition here is more general than the definition from [9, Ch. 12, §4]. By convention, for a nonzero rational expression $f(x) = f_1(x)/f_2(x)$ with $f_1, f_2 \in \mathbb{F}_q[x]$, we set $f(\infty) = 0$ when $\deg(f_1) < \deg(f_2)$, $f(\infty) = \mathrm{lc}(f_1)/\mathrm{lc}(f_2)$ when $\deg(f_1) = \deg(f_2)$ and $f(\infty) = \infty$ when $\deg(f_1) > \deg(f_2)$.

With this, the *extended Goppa code* defined by g and $\widehat{L}$ is the $\mathbb{F}_p$-vector space

$$\widehat{\Gamma}(g, \widehat{L}) = \left\{ c \in \mathbb{F}_p^{n+1} \,\middle|\, \forall f \in \mathbb{F}_q[x]_{\leq t}. \sum_{i=1}^{n+1} c_i (f/g)(\alpha_i) = 0 \right\}.$$

The following lemma shows that this definition is indeed a generalization of [9, Ch. 12, §4], where extended Goppa codes are constructed by "adding an overall parity check":

Lemma 1. *If $\widehat{L}$ is obtained by extending a list $L = (\alpha_1, ..., \alpha_n) \in \mathbb{F}_q^n$ with $\alpha_{n+1} = \infty$, i.e., $\widehat{L} = L \,\|\, (\infty)$, then $\widehat{\Gamma}(g, \widehat{L}) = \{ c \,\|\, (-c_1 - \cdots - c_n) \,|\, c \in \Gamma(g, L) \}$.*

Proof. See Appendix A.1.

Thus, for $\widehat{L} = L \,\|\, (\infty)$ in particular, a parity-check matrix of $\widehat{\Gamma}(g, \widehat{L})$ is given by

$$\left[\begin{array}{ccc|c} \alpha_1^0/g(\alpha_1) & \cdots & \alpha_{n+1}^0/g(\alpha_{n+1}) & 0 \\ \hline \alpha_1^1/g(\alpha_1) & \cdots & \alpha_{n+1}^1/g(\alpha_{n+1}) & 0 \\ \hline \vdots & \ddots & \vdots & \vdots \\ \hline \alpha_1^{t-1}/g(\alpha_1) & \cdots & \alpha_{n+1}^{t-1}/g(\alpha_{n+1}) & 0 \\ 1 & \cdots & 1 & 1 \end{array} \right] \in \mathbb{F}_p^{(tm+1)\times(n+1)}.$$

In general, the column $(0, 0, ..., 0, 1)$ is associated to the element ∞ in the list $\widehat{L}$; if $\mathsf{set}(\widehat{L}) \not\ni \infty$, no such column appears. It should therefore not come as a surprise that a Goppa code can be recovered from its associated extended Goppa code:

Corollary 2. *Let $g^{(1)}, g^{(2)} \in \mathbb{F}_q[x]$ be polynomials as in the definition of an (extended) Goppa code and let $L^{(1)}, L^{(2)}$ be lists of n distinct elements of $\mathbb{F}_q$ each. If $\widehat{\Gamma}(g^{(1)}, L^{(1)} \,\|\, (\infty)) = \widehat{\Gamma}(g^{(2)}, L^{(2)} \,\|\, (\infty))$, then $\Gamma(g^{(1)}, L^{(1)}) = \Gamma(g^{(2)}, L^{(2)})$.*

Proof. By Lemma 1, the last coordinate of each code word that is "lost" when transitioning from $L^{(i)} \| (\infty)$ to $L^{(i)}$ contains entirely redundant information. $\square$

As a consequence of Lemma 1, the extended Goppa code $\widehat{C} = \widehat{\Gamma}(g, L \| (\infty))$ associated to a Goppa code $C = \Gamma(g, L)$ can be constructed efficiently from C without knowledge of g or L, by adding an overall parity-check symbol to C. Together with Corollary 2, this reduces solving permutation equivalence for two Goppa codes $C^{(1)}$ and $C^{(2)}$ to solving permutation equivalence for the associated *extended* Goppa codes $\widehat{C}^{(i)}$, provided that the permutation $\pi \in \mathcal{S}_n$ realizing the equivalence between $\widehat{C}^{(1)}$ and $\widehat{C}^{(2)}$ can be forced to map the positions of ∞ in the lists $\widehat{L}^{(i)}$ defining the two extended codes to one another. (We will see in Sect. 3.1 that this is indeed possible.)

2.3 Key Search

The most obvious approach to recovering a McEliece private key is to simply guess the pair (g, L), compute the associated public key, and check for equality. Since there are $q!/(q-n)!$ choices for L, it is easily seen that $\mathsf{Irr}_t(q) \cdot q!/(q-n)!$ attempts suffice on average. (This is under the assumption that g is irreducible.)

One may gain a reduction factor of $n!$ in the number of attempts by guessing $\mathsf{set}(L)$ instead of L, and consequently checking for permutation equivalence of the resulting codes rather than equality. This test can be performed efficiently in practice using the *support-splitting algorithm* [15]. Using this approach, the expected number of required guesses appears to be $\mathsf{Irr}_t(q) \cdot \binom{q}{n}$, although testing each guess now requires slightly more computation than before.

However, as it turns out, the actual complexity of a brute-force key search is even lower than this: The reason is that every public key has a relatively large number of equivalent private keys associated to it, and recovering any equivalent key suffices; indeed, finding *the* private key is impossible since it is information-theoretically indistinguishable from its equivalent keys. We will analyze these additional equivalences in the upcoming Sect. 3.

Using Extended Goppa Codes. Furthermore, it has previously been pointed out that *extending* the Goppa code under attack yields a speedup for the attack: This observation is briefly mentioned, albeit without any details, in [8, § 2.2.1] and [12, p. 126]. We will elaborate on this approach in Sect. 3.1.

3 Equivalent Keys

In this section, we study an important algebraic relationship on the data defining a Goppa code which induces equivalences on the resulting codes. The protagonist is the following group of transformations:

Definition 3. *The* affine semilinear group *of a finite field* $\mathbb{F}_q$ *is the subgroup*

$$\mathrm{A\Gamma L}(q) := \left\{ (x \mapsto Ax^\varphi + B) \ \middle| \ A \in \mathbb{F}_q^\times, \ B \in \mathbb{F}_q, \ \varphi \in \mathrm{Aut}(\mathbb{F}_q) \right\}$$

of $\mathrm{Sym}(\mathbb{F}_q)$. *Its elements are called* affine semilinear transformations.

One subtle detail in Definition 3 is that elements of $\mathrm{A\Gamma L}(q)$ might be viewed either as a triple (A, B, φ) or as a permutation in $\mathrm{Sym}(\mathbb{F}_q)$. It is easy to see that these two viewpoints are indeed equivalent:

Lemma 4. *Consider the triples* (A, B, φ) *and* (A', B', φ') *with* $A, A' \in \mathbb{F}_q^\times$, $B, B' \in \mathbb{F}_q$, *and* $\varphi, \varphi' \in \mathrm{Aut}(\mathbb{F}_q)$.
If $Ax^\varphi + B = A'x^{\varphi'} + B'$ *holds for all* $x \in \mathbb{F}_q$, *then* $(A, B, \varphi) = (A', B', \varphi')$.

Proof. See Appendix A.2.

Corollary 5. *The cardinality of* $\mathrm{A\Gamma L}(q)$ *equals* $(q-1)qm$ *where* $m = \log_p(q)$.

Remark 6. Explictly, in the "triples" viewpoint, formulas for computing in $\mathrm{A\Gamma L}(q)$ are given as follows:

$$(A, B, \varphi)^{-1} = \left((1/A)^{\varphi^{-1}}, (-B/A)^{\varphi^{-1}}, \varphi^{-1}\right);$$
$$(A', B', \varphi') \circ (A, B, \varphi) = \left(A'A^{\varphi'}, A'B^{\varphi'} + B', \varphi' \circ \varphi\right).$$

The group $\mathrm{A\Gamma L}(q)$ evidently acts on $\mathbb{F}_q$. We extend this action to subsets of $\mathbb{F}_q$ by element-wise application and to vectors in $\mathbb{F}_q^n$ by coordinate-wise application. Furthermore, we define an action on polynomials in $\mathbb{F}_q[x]$ by acting on the roots:

Definition 7. *Let* $h \in \mathbb{F}_q[x]$ *denote a polynomial of degree* d *and* $\varrho_1, ..., \varrho_d$ *its (not necessarily distinct) roots in* $\overline{\mathbb{F}_q}$. *For* $\tau = (x \mapsto Ax^\varphi + B) \in \mathrm{A\Gamma L}(q)$, *lift* φ *to an arbitrary automorphism* $\Phi \in \mathrm{Aut}(\overline{\mathbb{F}_q})$ *which restricts to* φ *in* $\mathrm{Aut}(\mathbb{F}_q)$,[1] *and define* $\tau * h$ *as the polynomial* $\mathrm{lc}(h) \cdot \prod_{j=1}^d (x - A\varrho_j^\Phi - B) \in \mathbb{F}_q[x]$.

Lemma 8. *The group action from Definition 7 is well-defined.*

Proof. See Appendix A.3.

The following main theorem is a generalization of a result originally due to Moreno [11], which was restricted to the important special case of irreducible g and $\mathsf{set}(L) = \mathbb{F}_q$, in characteristic 2 only. The cryptographic literature usually attributes Moreno's result to Gibson [7], who appears to have rediscovered it later and introduced it to the cryptanalytic context. The generalization given here is essentially due to [3], who declares it to be "well known":

Theorem 9. *Let* g *and* L *be as in Sect. 2.2 and let* $\tau \in \mathrm{A\Gamma L}(q)$. *Then*

$$\Gamma(\tau * g, \tau * L) = \Gamma(g, L).$$

Proof. This is proved in [3, Proposition 3].

---

[1] The obvious way to do this is to lift $\varphi \colon \mathbb{F}_q \to \mathbb{F}_q$, $x \mapsto x^{p^k}$ to $\Phi \colon \overline{\mathbb{F}_q} \to \overline{\mathbb{F}_q}$, $x \mapsto x^{p^k}$.

Regrettably, however, the group action by $A\Gamma L(q)$ on the set of McEliece private keys does not immediately lead to either lower *or* upper bounds on the number of equivalent private keys per public key. This is due to two separate, counteracting effects:

- It can occasionally happen that some of the equivalences induced by $A\Gamma L(q)$ as in the theorem are *already* explained by permutation equivalence: This is the case whenever $A\Gamma L(q)$ stabilizes the polynomial g and acts as a permutation on the list L, i.e., stabilizes $\mathsf{set}(L)$. As a consequence, simply multiplying the number of equivalences coming from $A\Gamma L(q)$ by the cardinality $n!$ of $\mathcal{S}_n$ leads to overcounting the number of equivalent private keys in general.
- Not all equivalences on public keys are explained by the action of $A\Gamma L(q)$: We refer to this phenomenon as "spurious equivalences". They, too, are rare, but they may in general lead to undercounting the number of equivalent private keys when estimating it via $A\Gamma L(q)$.

It seems difficult to strictly prove anything about the prevalence and impact of those effects for a given choice of parameters.

From a practical standpoint, however, since both of these exceptional cases occur only exceedingly rarely when concerned with reasonably large parameter sets, we may for our cryptanalytic purposes assume that we are in the average situation, in which the equivalent keys are indeed in bijection with $A\Gamma L(q)$ and the count resulting from Heuristic 10 is therefore essentially (or exactly) correct.

Heuristic 10. *Generically, the number of irreducible Goppa codes with parameters $p, m, q = p^m, t, n$ modulo permutation equivalence can be estimated as*

$$\mathsf{Irr}_q(t) \cdot \binom{q}{n} / ((q-1)qm) \, .$$

Also note that public keys having more equivalent private keys are more likely to be sampled during key generation, hence the distribution of public keys is biased towards the "weaker" ones with respect to a brute-force key-search attack.

3.1   Equivalences Between Extended Goppa Codes

The following results are known to experts and have appeared before in [3], but do not appear to have experienced widespread recognition in the cryptography community.

Definition 11. *The* projective semilinear group *of $\mathbb{F}_q$ is the subgroup*

$$P\Gamma L(q) := \left\{ \left(x \mapsto \frac{Ax^\varphi + B}{Cx^\varphi + D}\right) \;\middle|\; A, B, C, D \in \mathbb{F}_q, \det\left(\begin{smallmatrix} A & B \\ C & D \end{smallmatrix}\right) \neq 0, \varphi \in \mathrm{Aut}(\mathbb{F}_q) \right\}$$

of $\mathrm{Sym}(\mathbb{P}^1\mathbb{F}_q)$, where by convention $1/0 = \infty$ and $\infty \mapsto A/C$. Its elements are called projective semilinear transformations.

Lemma 12. *The cardinality of* $\mathrm{P\Gamma L}(q)$ *equals* $(q^2 - 1)qm$ *where* $m = \log_p(q)$.

Proof. See Appendix A.4.

As before, we extend the action of $\mathrm{P\Gamma L}(q)$ on $\mathbb{P}^1\mathbb{F}_q$ to subsets of $\mathbb{P}^1\mathbb{F}_q$ by element-wise application, to vectors in $(\mathbb{P}^1\mathbb{F}_q)^{n+1}$ by coordinate-wise application, and to polynomials $g \in \mathbb{F}_q[x]$ with no roots in $\mathbb{F}_q$ by acting on the roots (analogously to Definition 7 and Lemma 8).

Theorem 13. *Let* g *and* $\widehat{L}$ *be as in Sect. 2.2, with the additional restriction that* g *have no roots in* $\mathbb{F}_q$, *and let* $\tau \in \mathrm{P\Gamma L}(q)$. *Then*

$$\widehat{\Gamma}(\tau * g,\ \tau * \widehat{L}) = \widehat{\Gamma}(g, \widehat{L}).$$

Proof. This is proved in [3, Theorem 1]. $\qquad\qquad\qquad\qquad\qquad\qquad\square$

Just like for the action of $\mathrm{A\Gamma L}(q)$, this yields an estimate for the number of equivalence classes of extended Goppa codes:

Heuristic 14. *Generically, the number of extended irreducible Goppa codes with parameters* $p, m, q = p^m, t, n$ *modulo permutation equivalence can be estimated as*

$$\mathsf{Irr}_q(t) \cdot \binom{q+1}{n+1} \Big/ \big((q^2 - 1)qm\big).$$

The ratio between the quantities from Heuristic 14 and Heuristic 10 equals $\binom{q+1}{n+1} / (q+1) / \binom{q}{n} = 1/(n+1)$, which translates to a speedup factor of about $n+1$ in the attack when using extended codes. (In TII's McEliece Challenges, $n \approx q$.)

Restricting Equivalences Between Extended Goppa Codes. The main application of the action by $\mathrm{P\Gamma L}(q)$ on extended codes is that there are more equivalences between Goppa codes after extending than there are between the original Goppa codes, hence the probability of finding parameters (g, L) such that the resulting extended Goppa code is equivalent to a given extended Goppa code increases by a factor of approximately $n+1$ compared to when not extending the codes (according to Heuristics 10 and 14).

The strategy is as follows: Given a Goppa code $C = \Gamma(g, L)$ with unknown parameters g, L, we extend C by adding an overall parity check, yielding the extended Goppa code $\widehat{C} = \widehat{\Gamma}(g, L \,\|\, (\infty))$. Using a brute-force search over $(g', \widehat{L}')$ and a solver for permutation equivalence, we obtain an extended Goppa code $\widehat{C}' = \widehat{\Gamma}(g', \widehat{L}')$ which is permutation-equivalent to $\widehat{C}$. For ease of notation, we view such an equivalence as a bijection $\widehat{\pi} \colon \mathsf{set}(L \,\|\, (\infty)) \to \mathsf{set}(\widehat{L}')$.

The "lucky" case is $\infty \in \widehat{L}'$ and $\widehat{\pi}(\infty) = \infty$, since in this case we can immediately invoke Corollary 2 to conclude that $C' = \Gamma(g', L')$, where L' is $\widehat{L}'$ with ∞ removed, defines a code equivalent to $\Gamma(g, L) = C$, so (g', L') is a valid solution to our key-recovery problem.

Otherwise, we may again exploit the action of $\mathrm{P\Gamma L}(q)$ on the pair $(g', \widehat{L}')$ to position ourselves in the "lucky" case: In essence, one looks for some $\tau \in \mathrm{P\Gamma L}(q)$ that maps the given element $\widehat{\pi}(\infty) \in \mathbb{F}_q$ to ∞. Then, using Theorem 13, the pair $g'' := \tau * g'$ and $\widehat{L}'' := \tau * \widehat{L}'$ still satisfies $\widehat{\Gamma}(g'', \widehat{L}'') = \widehat{C}'$, which is still permutation-equivalent to $\widehat{C}$, but now with a permutation $\mathsf{set}(L \,\|\, (\infty)) \to \mathsf{set}(L'')$ that fixes ∞, thus leaving us in the "lucky" case.

Finding a $\tau \in \mathrm{P\Gamma L}(q)$ that takes a given $\alpha \in \mathbb{F}_q$ to ∞ is of course easy enough: One such example is $\tau = \left(x \mapsto \frac{1}{x-\alpha}\right)$.

4   The Support-Splitting Algorithm

In the year 2000, Sendrier introduced a practically efficient algorithm for testing whether two linear codes are permutation-equivalent, and if so, to recover the permutation [15]. The approach crucially relies on *permutation invariants* of linear codes: Required are efficiently computable values associated to a linear code which are (1) invariant under permutations, and (2) discriminant, i.e., they tend to take on different values for codes which aren't permutation-equivalent.

We remark that not much has been proven about either the correctness or the complexity of this algorithm. Empirically, however, it appears to work very well for random codes as well as for the family of Goppa codes used in McEliece.

Splitting the Support. Provided a sufficiently discriminant invariant $\mathcal{V}$, given two codes $C, C' \subseteq \mathbb{F}_q^n$, it is conceptually easy to recover a permutation $\pi \in \mathcal{S}_n$ connecting the two codes, assuming one exists: The core subroutine takes as input two partitions $\{1, ..., n\} = S_1 \,\dot\cup\, \cdots \,\dot\cup\, S_\ell = T_1 \,\dot\cup\, \cdots \,\dot\cup\, T_\ell$ such that $\pi(S_i) = T_i$ for all $i \in \{1, ..., \ell\}$, and outputs another, finer pair of partitions with the same property. Repeating this process will eventually yield a partition with all $|S_i| = |T_i| = 1$, which allows us to read off π. (If the codes are in fact not permutation-equivalent, the subroutine should either detect this and fail, or output an arbitrary finer partition: One may simply check at the end that π is a valid solution.)

We say that the partitions $S_1 \,\dot\cup\, \cdots \,\dot\cup\, S_\ell$ and $T_1 \,\dot\cup\, \cdots \,\dot\cup\, T_\ell$ are *"compatible"* if $|S_i| = |T_i|$ holds for all $i \in \{1, ..., \ell\}$, i.e., if the cardinalities of each pair of sets in the partitions with the same index match up.

Initial Partition. The refining step below assumes that a relatively fine partition of the set of positions of C and C' has already been computed. Obtaining such an initial partition can be done easily by puncturing both codes C and C' at each position $i \in \{1, ..., n\}$ and computing the invariants $\mathcal{V}$ associated to each punctured code C_i resp. C_i': The partition is then given by grouping all i with the same $\mathcal{V}(C_i)$ together into one S_k, and similarly for $\mathcal{V}(C_i')$ into T_k.

If $\mathcal{V}(C) \neq \mathcal{V}(C')$, or if the partitions for C and C' resulting from the initial puncturings are not compatible, the codes cannot be permutation-equivalent.

Refining Step. The refining procedure works as follows: Iterate over nonempty subsets $I \subseteq \{1, ..., \ell\}$, for instance in order of increasing cardinality up to some predetermined constant bound. For each such I, puncture C at the positions in $J := \bigcup_{i \in I} S_i$ to obtain a code C_J. Then compute the associated invariant $\mathcal{V}$ for all further puncturings $C_{J \cup \{j\}}$ at each position j. Now, hopefully, $\mathcal{V}$ is nonconstant on $\{C_{J \cup \{j\}} \mid j \in S_k\}$ for some S_k with $k \notin I$, so that we may refine the partition by splitting such a S_k into multiple sets $S_{k,1} \dot\cup \cdots \dot\cup S_{k,r} = S_k$. Applying the same procedure to C' with the T_k leads to a partition $T_{k,1} \dot\cup \cdots \dot\cup T_{k,r} = T_k$ for which $\pi(S_{k,i}) = T_{k,i}$. In this case, we have thus successfully refined the partition. The refining step can fail in two ways:

- First, it could happen that there are no more subsets $I \subseteq \{1, ..., \ell\}$ among those considered for which $\mathcal{V}$ refines the partition after puncturing at the positions indicated by I. In that case, one may resort to brute-forcing parts of the permutation π in order to refine the partition anyway—in a possibly incorrect way, but of course a valid guess must exist if the codes are actually permutation-equivalent, so a backtracking search will eventually succeed.
- Second, if the newly refined partitions are not compatible, then the codes cannot be permutation-equivalent.

Remark 15. The original description of the support-splitting algorithm [15] also applies *shortenings* in addition to puncturings to the input codes. We found that this adds only little discriminatory power while significantly complicating the algorithms, hence we decided not to use shortenings in our implementation.

Hull Enumerators. The key insight in [15] was that the *enumerator* of the *hull* of a code forms a permutation invariant which is almost always efficiently computable and sufficiently discriminant, at least in practice, to enable the support-splitting algorithm to work well.

On average, hulls are random-looking subspaces of relatively small dimension: It was proven in [14, Theorem 4] that the dimension of the hull for a random code roughly obeys a discrete half-normal distribution;[2] hence, the probability of it exceeding a certain $\ell_0 \in \mathbb{Z}_{\geq 0}$ is bounded above by $q^{-\Omega(\ell_0^2)}$, which shrinks at a superexponential rate as ℓ_0 grows.

As a consequence, computing the hull enumerator of a sufficiently random code can almost always be done very quickly: Since the dimension of the hull is overwhelmingly likely to be tiny, one may simply iterate over all hull vectors and tally their weights. Indeed, the core observation in [15] was that the hull enumerator is (empirically) an efficiently computable and sufficiently discriminant invariant $\mathcal{V}$ to render the support-splitting approach highly effective in practice.

---

[2] Asymptotically, the proportion of n-dimensional codes over $\mathbb{F}_q$ with hull dimension ℓ approaches $R_\ell := C / \prod_{i=1}^{\ell} (q^i - 1) \approx C / q^{\ell(\ell+1)/2}$, where C is a constant (dependent on q) which satisfies $0.419 < C < 1$. Note that $\sum_{\ell=\ell_0}^{\infty} R_\ell \in \Theta(R_{\ell_0})$.

Optimizations. Implementing the support-splitting algorithm in a straightforward manner, using standard linear-algebra routines and hash tables for keeping track of the partitions S_k and T_k, leads to significant overheads from dynamic memory allocations and unpredictable memory-access patterns: See Sect. 5.

We foreshadow that there are two very useful optimizations for the support-splitting algorithm when applied to brute-force key search:

- First, noticing that almost all candidate codes are actually *not* equivalent to the target code, instead of implementing and running the full support-splitting algorithm inside the brute-force search, it is enough to build a simple and fast *filter* which will reject most inequivalent codes swiftly, but need not be perfectly correct, nor recover the permutation in full. See Sect. 5.5.
- Second, since one of the input codes remains fixed, one may precompute good puncturing locations by essentially running only one side of the support-splitting algorithm for the target code and noting which puncturings worked well to refine the partition, then performing only those puncturings for the candidate equivalent code at runtime while skipping the rest. See Sect. 5.6.

5 Efficient Key Search

In the context of a brute-force key search, in which checking for (permutation) equivalence contributes a multiplicative factor to the overall complexity, it is clearly desirable to minimize the cost per equivalence test.

To set a baseline, let us first discuss the main limitations of a straightforward implementation: Processing a single guess at a time (per thread), representing codes as generator matrices or parity-check matrices, and using generic linear-algebra libraries for the hull and punctured-hull computations. This approach is prone to suffering from several effects causing slowdown:

- Plenty of conditional branches, which may cause mispredictions and therefore expensive rollbacks and cache invalidations. This includes many conditions whose values are essentially (difficult-to-predict) coinflips, such as during the computation of a reduced row echelon form using Gauß elimination.
- Relatively complex, a priori variably-sized data structures. Depending on implementation specifics, these data structures may incur slowdowns in thread-safe memory management on many-core machines. In addition, for large data structures, another issue is that unpredictable memory-access patterns may cause the processor to stall while waiting for data to be fetched from main memory to a fast cache located closer to the processing core.

By contrast, in the following, we describe a collection of techniques designed to work around these issues on typical contemporary many-core CPUs. The key strategy employed in this work is to rephrase the entire equivalence test as a **binary circuit**, which is much more amenable to fast parallel evaluation, on simpler hardware, than the original high-level algorithm. As a byproduct, the same circuit can easily be ported to other platforms, such as GPUs, FPGAs, or even ASICs, to obtain efficient implementations of the key search.

Remark 16. It seems very much conceivable that generic circuit-optimization techniques could help reduce the number of logical operations in the circuits constructed via our approach, leading to a faster key-recovery attack on any of the aforementioned hardware platforms. We have not explored this possibility.

Remark 17. The main case of interest going forward will be binary codes ($q = 2$). However, whenever the algorithms given in the following are easily expressed for general q, we have refrained from needlessly specializing to $q = 2$. Throughout, we will identify the values $0, 1 \in \mathbb{F}_2$ with the booleans false and true respectively.

Moreover, note that some of the algorithms are formulated using (fixed-length) loops and branching for clarity: These abstractions are not admissible in a circuit to evaluate the algorithm and will have to be unrolled into copies of the loop body and conditional assignments using bitmasks, respectively. See the difference between Algorithm 1 and Algorithm 2 for the latter conversion.

The algorithmic building blocks given in Sects. 5.2 and 5.3 are essentially from [15, § 6.1]. We reiterate them here for clarity and completeness, and because some of our optimizations (Sect. 6.1) interact with those details.

5.1 Preliminaries

Throughout the rest of the paper, we adhere to the following definitions and notational conventions.

- A *q-ary code* of dimension m and length n is an m-dimensional subspace of $\mathbb{F}_q^n$. Codes are represented using a *basis matrix* in $\mathbb{F}_q^{m \times n}$, whose rows form an $\mathbb{F}_q$-basis of the code. Occasionally, basis matrices may be padded (or interleaved) with zero rows.
- The *dual* code $C^\perp$ associated to a code C is its orthogonal complement with respect to the standard inner product. It equals the right kernel of a basis matrix. The *hull* of a code C is the intersection $C \cap C^\perp$.
- *Puncturing* a code $C \subseteq \mathbb{F}_q^n$ at position $i \in \{1, ..., n\}$ means projecting it to the subspace $\mathbb{F}_q^{i-1} \times \{0\} \times \mathbb{F}_q^{n-i}$. On a basis matrix, this can be realized by filling the ith column with zeroes.
- The *weight* $\mathrm{wt}(c) \in \{0, ..., n\}$ of a code word $c \in \mathbb{F}_q^n$ is the number of nonzero coordinates in c. The *(weight) enumerator* $\mathcal{W}(C)$ of a code $C \subseteq \mathbb{F}_q^n$ is the integer vector $(w_0, ..., w_n) \in \mathbb{Z}_{\geq 0}^{n+1}$, where $w_i = \big|\{c \in C \mid \mathrm{wt}(c) = i\}\big|$.

5.2 Keeping Pivots on the Diagonal

A useful trick to increase the amount of deterministic code paths in the linear-algebra routines is to ensure all pivots are kept on the main diagonal inside the row echelon form computation, by inserting zero rows between non-zero rows in the matrix as appropriate. (This is a non-standard choice: Most descriptions of Gauß elimination keep "empty" rows at the end.) See Fig. 1 for an example.

$$\begin{bmatrix}1&0&0&1&0&0&1&1&0&0\\0&1&0&0&0&0&0&1&0&0\\0&0&1&1&0&0&1&0&0&0\\0&0&0&0&1&0&1&0&0&0\\0&0&0&0&0&1&0&1&0&0\\0&0&0&0&0&0&0&0&1&0\\0&0&0&0&0&0&0&0&0&1\\0&0&0&0&0&0&0&0&0&0\\0&0&0&0&0&0&0&0&0&0\\0&0&0&0&0&0&0&0&0&0\end{bmatrix} \qquad \begin{bmatrix}1&0&0&1&0&0&1&1&0&0\\0&1&0&0&0&0&0&1&0&0\\0&0&1&1&0&0&1&0&0&0\\0&0&0&0&0&0&0&0&0&0\\0&0&0&0&1&0&1&0&0&0\\0&0&0&0&0&1&0&1&0&0\\0&0&0&0&0&0&0&0&0&0\\0&0&0&0&0&0&0&0&0&0\\0&0&0&0&0&0&0&0&1&0\\0&0&0&0&0&0&0&0&0&1\end{bmatrix}$$

Fig. 1. Generating matrices of the same 7-dimensional subspace of $\mathbb{F}_2^{10}$ given in standard reduced row echelon form (left) and in the "diagonal standard form" (right) that is employed in [15] and in this work.

Definition 18. *A square matrix M is in* diagonal standard form *if its nonzero rows are in reduced row echelon form and all pivots lie on the main diagonal.*

This form of a matrix is very convenient for the linear-algebraic types of computational tasks that appear in coding theory: In particular, having a generator matrix of some code in this form allows us to directly read off a basis of the right kernel of the matrix, i.e., a generator matrix of the dual code. The following result was used without proof in [15, § 6.1.1]:

Lemma 19. *A matrix M in diagonal standard form is idempotent, i.e., $M^2 = M$. In particular, the nonzero columns of $\mathbb{1} - M$ form a basis of the right kernel of M.*

Proof. See Appendix A.5.

Using the diagonal standard form was already suggested in the original description of the support-splitting algorithm; however, the motivation there seems to have been to enable Algorithm 4 for punctured hulls given in the following Sect. 5.3, rather than to optimize the circuit associated to the linear-algebra computation. Indeed, the diagonal standard form (and a transformation matrix) can be computed using a variant of Gauß elimination that involves fewer case distinctions based on the locations of the pivots; see Algorithms 1 and 2.

Lemma 20. *Algorithm 2 is correct and requires $6n^3 + O(n^2)$ logical operations. If the output L is not needed, omitting its computation reduces this to $2n^3 + O(n^2)$.*

Proof. Several routine verifications. (See also the comments in Algorithm 2.) □

From the given formulation of Algorithm 2, it is straightforward to construct a binary circuit that is equivalent to evaluating the entire algorithm: See Fig. 3 in Appendix B for a tiny example. Note that this is just for illustration: We do not actually ever compute or export a graph representation of the circuit for the fast SSA filter at any point; rather, we write software (very similar to Algorithm 2) to evaluate the circuit straight away. See also Sect. 6.1.

Algorithm 1: Transforming a matrix to diagonal standard form.
— Restartable: If the kth column is replaced, continue the main loop from that k.

Input: $A, B \in \mathbb{F}_q^{n \times n}$.
Output: $L, R \in \mathbb{F}_q^{n \times n}$ such that R is in diagonal standard form, and such that there exists $T \in \mathrm{GL}_n(\mathbb{F}_q)$ with $L = TA$ and $R = TB$.

```
// Initialize output variables.
(L, R) ← (A, B)
// Outer loop. Iterate over columns from left to right.
for k from 1 to n do
    if R_kk = 0 then
        // We don't have a pivot. Try to find one.
        for i from 1 to n do
            if i = k then
                continue
            // Does column k not yet have a pivot in row k, but in row i?
            if R_kk = 0 and (i ≥ k or R_ii = 0) and R_ik ≠ 0 then
                L_k ← L_k + L_i
                R_k ← R_k + R_i
                break
        if R_kk = 0 then
            continue
    // Rescale row k row so that the pivot equals 1.
    L_k ← R_kk^{-1} · L_k
    R_k ← R_kk^{-1} · R_k
    // Inner loop: Zero out the rest of column k.
    for i from 1 to n do
        if i = k then
            continue
        if R_ik = 0 then
            continue
        L_i ← L_i − R_ik · L_k
        R_i ← R_i − R_ik · R_k
return (L, R)
```

Another important property of Algorithms 1 and 2 is that they are *restartable*: When some of the columns of the input matrix are substituted, the execution of the algorithm can continue from the new columns and thereby reuse all the work done up until the first modified column, resulting in a much lower amortized cost. This is very useful in the context of McEliece key recovery, which involves a brute-force search over subsets of possible column vectors. See Sect. 6.2 and also [5, § 4], where a very similar approach was used for the decoding attack.

Remark 21. When applied in the context of Algorithm 3, the input matrix B to Algorithm 2 is symmetric. This causes the transformation matrix T to become

---

Algorithm 2: Transforming a matrix over $\mathbb{F}_2$ to diagonal standard form.
- Constant-time: There are no input-dependent branches or memory accesses.
- Restartable: If the kth column is replaced, continue the main loop from that k.
- Note: The output usually differs from the one produced by Algorithm 1.

Input: $A, B \in \mathbb{F}_2^{n \times n}$.
Output: $L, R \in \mathbb{F}_2^{n \times n}$ such that R is in diagonal standard form, and such that
   there exists $T \in \mathrm{GL}_n(\mathbb{F}_2)$ with $L = TA$ and $R = TB$.

```
// Initialize output variables.
(L, R) ← (A, B)
// Outer loop: Iterate over columns from left to right.
for k from 1 to n do
    // Inner loop: Try to find a row with a pivot and add it to the correct row.
    for i from 1 to n do
        if i = k then
            continue
        // Does column k not yet have a pivot in row k, but in row i?
        m ← R_kk
        if i < k then
            m ← m ∨ R_ii
        m ← ¬m
        m ← m ∧ R_ik
        // If so, add row i to row k.
        for j from 1 to n do
            L_kj ← L_kj ⊕ (m ∧ L_ij)
        for j from k to n do
            R_kj ← R_kj ⊕ (m ∧ R_ij)
    // Inner loop: Try to zero out the rest of column k assuming we have a pivot.
    for i from 1 to n do
        if i = k then
            continue
        // Does column k contain a one in row i?
        m ← R_ik
        // If so, add row k to row i.
        for j from 1 to n do
            L_ij ← L_ij ⊕ (m ∧ L_kj)
        for j from k to n do
            R_ij ← R_ij ⊕ (m ∧ R_kj)

return (L, R)
```

---

symmetric as well (it equals $(B + D)^{-1}$ where D is the diagonal part of $\mathbb{1} - R$),
but unfortunately, we have not succeeded in exploiting this fact to eliminate
redundancy and accelerate the algorithm.

Remark 22. Some common optimizations for linear algebra over small finite
fields, such as the "Four Russians" method [6], unfortunately do not apply in our

---

Algorithm 3: Computing the hull of a code in diagonal standard form.

Input: $M \in \mathbb{F}_q^{n \times n}$ in diagonal standard form, defining a code $C \subseteq \mathbb{F}_q^n$.
Output: $H \in \mathbb{F}_q^{\ell \times n}$ a basis matrix of the hull $C \cap C^\perp$.

$A \leftarrow \mathbb{0} \in \mathbb{F}_q^{n \times n}$
$B \leftarrow M$
// Iterate over all rows.
for k **from** 1 **to** n **do**
   // If this row is zero, copy in the corresponding row of $(\mathbb{1} - M)^\mathsf{T}$.
   if $M_{kk} = 0$ **then**
     $A_{kk}, B_{kk} \leftarrow 1$
     for j **from** 1 **to** $k-1$ **do**
       $A_{kj}, B_{kj} \leftarrow -M_{jk}$

// Compute the diagonal standard form of B.
Apply Algorithm 1 to the input (A, B), obtaining matrices $L, R \in \mathbb{F}_q^{n \times n}$.
// Read off a basis of the hull from the nonzero columns of $(\mathbb{1} - R)^\mathsf{T}$.
Initialize $\ell \leftarrow 0$ and $H \in \mathbb{F}_q^{0 \times n}$.
for k **from** 1 **to** n **do**
   if $R_{kk} = 0$ **then**
     Append a zero row to H.
     $\ell \leftarrow \ell + 1$
     $H_{\ell k} \leftarrow 1$
     for i **from** 1 **to** $k-1$ **do**
       $H_{\ell i} \leftarrow -R_{ik}$

return H

Algorithm 4: Computing the hull of a singly-punctured code (over $\mathbb{F}_2$).

Input: $H \in \mathbb{F}_2^{\ell \times n}$ a basis matrix of the hull of a code $C \subseteq \mathbb{F}_2^n$,
     the matrix $L \in \mathbb{F}_2^{n \times n}$ as computed by Algorithm 3 for C,
     an index $r \in \{1, ..., n\}$.
Output: $H' \in \mathbb{F}_2^{\ell' \times n}$ a basis matrix of the hull of the code C punctured at r.

$H' \leftarrow H$
// If r is in the support, shorten the code at r.
for k **from** ℓ **down to** 1 **do**
   if H_{kr} **then**
     for i **from** 1 **to** $k-1$ **do**
       if H_{ir} **then**
         $H'_i \leftarrow H_i \oplus H_k$
     Delete the kth row from H'.
     return H'

// Otherwise, the hull is either augmented by a suitable vector, or unchanged.
if $L_{r,r} = 0$ **then**
   Append the row L_r of L to H'.
return H'

---

setting: This is because it relies on fast random access to precomputed tables, which becomes expensive in the circuit abstraction.

5.3   Computing Everywhere Punctured Hulls, All at once

All of the following is essentially explained in [15, §6.1.2]. In this section, we give a simplified and streamlined account for our particular application.

Lemma 23. *Let C be a code given by a square matrix $M \in \mathbb{F}_q^{n \times n}$ in diagonal standard form. Then the hull $C \cap C^\perp$ equals the (right) kernel of $\mathbb{1} + M - M^\mathsf{T}$.*

Proof. This follows from the general fact that $(C_1 \cap C_2)^\perp = C_1^\perp + C_2^\perp$ holds for any two codes C_1, C_2, combined with Lemma 19.   □

What this entails is that computing the hull of a linear code can be done entirely *in place*: The nonzero rows of $\mathbb{1} - M$ correspond exactly to the zero rows of M, hence computing the hull via Lemma 23 involves flipping all coefficients lying above the diagonal across the diagonal, negating them, and filling the diagonal with ones, then computing the diagonal standard form again and reading off the kernel. See Algorithm 3.

In addition, Lemma 23 also allows for computing the hulls of *punctured* codes very easily after the hull has been computed: This was detailed for the case $q = 2$ in [15, §5.3.1]. See Algorithm 4.

Remark 24. The algorithms in this paper only require singly-punctured hull enumerators. However, if further puncturings are required, this could easily be achieved using the same methods by keeping track of the matrices L, R computed by Algorithm 1 over the course of multiple sequential applications of Algorithm 4.

5.4   Computing Weight Enumerators

Computing the weight enumerator of a low-dimensional code over a small finite base field is generally straightforward: Simply enumerate all linear combinations of a basis of the code and record the weight of each code word encountered this way. An optimized method of performing this enumeration (for $q = 2$) consists in iterating over the vectors determining linear combinations of a basis according to a *Gray code*, i.e., a way of arranging all bit vectors of a given length in such a way that every pair of two adjacent vectors has Hamming distance one. The details are elaborated in Algorithm 5.

Each individual count inside a weight-enumerator data structure is represented in our binary circuit as a standard ripple-carry incrementer of some suitable (a priori fixed) bit length w. Every such counter also features an overflow bit o to prevent further processing of wrong results after an integer wraparound occured. See Algorithm 6. We note that the counts could alternatively be stored in unary representation, but this scales much worse: Incrementing a w-bit binary number takes $2w + O(1)$ bit operations, while incrementing a unary number capable of storing w-bit integers takes $2^w + O(1)$ bit operations.

Algorithm 5: Weight enumerator of a low-dimensional code (over $\mathbb{F}_2$).

Input: $H \in \mathbb{F}_2^{\ell \times n}$ a basis matrix of some code in $\mathbb{F}_2^n$.
Output: Weight enumerator $(w_0, ..., w_n) \in \mathbb{Z}_{\geq 0}^{n+1}$ of the code generated by H.

Initialize counters $w_0, ..., w_n$ to zero.
Initialize $c \leftarrow 0 \in \mathbb{F}_2^n$.
Increment w_0.
for s **from** 1 **to** $2^\ell - 1$ **do**
    $i \leftarrow \nu_2(s)$ // The number of trailing zero bits.
    $c \leftarrow c \oplus H_{i+1}$
    // Compute the weight of c.
    Initialize a counter k to zero.
    for j **from** 1 **to** n **do**
        if c_j **then**
            Increment k.
    // Increment the associated counter.
    for j **from** 1 **to** n **do**
        if $k = j$ **then**
            Increment w_j.

return $(w_0, ..., w_n)$

5.5 Fast Filtering Using Hull Enumerators

In the context of a key-recovery attack against McEliece, the main contributing factor of the attack complexity is the cost of repeated permutation-equivalence tests with one of the two inputs (the target public key) remaining fixed. As such, our main goal is to optimize those equivalence tests as much as possible, yielding a "fast filter". Crucially, the construction of the fast filter itself may utilize liberal amounts of precomputation involving the target public-key code.

The key observation is that (1) for codes to possibly be equivalent, the hull enumerators and the multisets of singly-punctured hull enumerators of the two codes must be identical, and (2) it is acceptable for this equivalence test to be imperfect, opening up the potential to achieve much faster execution times by admitting a small chance of false positives.

In the context of our attack, we successfully exploit these two observations to obtain a fast (but imperfect) equivalence check as follows:

- **Puncturings only.** While the original description of the support-splitting code applies both puncturings and shortenings to the input codes, we refrain from using shortenings for simplicity. (See Remark 15.)
- **Single puncturings only.** The full support-splitting algorithm involves a recursive procedure to further discriminate the positions of the two input codes corresponding to each other until the exact permutation inducing the equivalence has been determined. To trade speed for correctness, we instead

---

Algorithm 6: Incrementing a w-bit integer using bit operations.

Input: Bit array $[b_0, ..., b_{w-1}; o]$ representing $n = b_0 + 2b_1 + \cdots + 2^{w-1}b_{w-1}$
    if $o = \mathsf{false}$, else $n = \infty$, and a bit c.
Output: Bit array $[b'_0, ..., b'_{w-1}; o']$ representing $n' = n + c$ if $n + c < 2^w$,
    else $n' = \infty$.

for i **from** 0 **to** $w - 1$ **do**
    $b'_i \leftarrow b_i \oplus c$
    $c \leftarrow b_i \wedge c$
$o' \leftarrow o \vee c$
return $[b'_0, ..., b'_{w-1}; o']$

---

stop after the first refining step and post-process the resulting stream of candidate equivalent codes using a slower but perfectly correct implementation of the full support-splitting algorithm only afterwards. (See Sect. 5.7.)

- **Sets instead of multisets.** In theory, we would like to compare the multisets of singly-punctured hull enumerators of an input code to the (precomputed) multiset corresponding to the target public-key code. In reality, this multiset comparison can be approximated by instead simply checking for the presence or absence of certain elements of one multiset in the other multiset: As soon as an expected hull enumerator cannot be found, or an unexpected hull enumerator is encountered, the respective code can immediately be discarded.

The resulting fast filtering method is detailed in Algorithm 7. It relies on the following data structure as input:

Definition 25. *For a code $C \subseteq \mathbb{F}_q^n$, a* fast filter *is the following data structure:*

- *The first component is the hull enumerator of C.*
- *The second component is a list of tuples $(b, v) \in \{\mathsf{true}, \mathsf{false}\} \times \mathbb{Z}_{\geq 0}^{n+1}$ with the property that $b = \mathsf{true}$ if and only if the vector v occurs as one (or multiple) of the singly-punctured hull enumerators of C.*

In a nutshell, this data structure contains information about singly-punctured hull enumerators whose presence or absence quickly establishes (with certainty) the non-equivalence of "most" random codes to the target code: Check for the presence of enumerators which appear for the target code C but are unlikely to appear in a random code, and check for the absence of enumerators which are likely to appear for a random code but do not appear for C.

The way a "fast filter" is constructed for a given target code C is simple: We sample many random Goppa codes, compute all their singly-punctured hull enumerators, and use a greedy approach to select those enumerators into the filter first whose presence or absence leads to the strongest filtering. See Algorithm 8.

Remark 26. The "fast filtering" approach inherently offers a tradeoff between the complexity (hence the computational effort) of the employed strategy and the quality of the filtering (hence the rate of false positives).

Algorithm 7: Evaluating a fast filter for permutation equivalence.

Input: Fast filter $\mathcal{F} = \big(u, [(b_1, v_1), ..., (b_\ell, v_\ell)]\big)$, some code $C' \subseteq \mathbb{F}_q^n$.
Output: Boolean indicating whether C' passed the filter $\mathcal{F}$ or not.

// First make sure the hull enumerators match.
Compute the hull enumerator u' of C'.   // Algorithms 3 and 5
if $u' \neq u$ **then**
  | **return** false

// Verify that all forbidden singly-punctured hull enumerators are absent.
for k **from** 1 **to** n **do**
  | Compute the hull enumerator v'_k of C' punctured at k.   // Algorithms 4 and 5
  | **for** i **from** 1 **to** ℓ **do**
  | | **if** $b_i =$ false **and** $v'_k = v_i$ **then**
  | | | **return** false

// Verify that all required singly-punctured hull enumerators are present.
for i **from** 1 **to** ℓ **do**
  | **if** $b_i =$ true **then**
  | | $r \leftarrow$ false
  | | **for** k **from** 1 **to** n **do**
  | | | **if** $v'_k = v_i$ **then**
  | | | | $r \leftarrow$ true
  | | | | **break**
  | | **if** $r =$ false **then**
  | | | **return** false

// All checks passed!
return true

In particular, with the greedy approach used in Algorithm 8, a fast filter can simply be truncated at the end in order to increase the filter's throughput at the expense of some of its distinguishing strength.

Remark 27. One side effect of the particular "fast filtering" technique employed in this work is that the key search proceeds at a much higher rate for some target codes than others: For example, in the most extreme case, the hull enumerator of the public-key code itself would be overwhelmingly unlikely to appear for random Goppa codes, hence a fast filter could consist of simply checking the hull enumerator (without applying any puncturings at all). This effect is visible in Tables 1 and 2 , where smaller "$\# \mathcal{F}$" correlates with higher throughput overall.

The fact that one of the input codes remains fixed implies that bounds on the integers that can appear in weight enumerators, as needed for the algorithms in Sect. 5.4, are readily available: They can simply be chosen according to the weight enumerators observed for the target public key. While the enumerators computed for a candidate equivalent code may in fact have larger entries, this

---

Algorithm 8: Constructing a fast filter for permutation equivalence.

Input: Goppa code $C \subseteq \mathbb{F}_p^n$ with $q = p^m$ and $t = \deg(g)$; sample count $K \in \mathbb{Z}_{\geq 1}$.
Output: Fast filter $\mathcal{F}$ which C passes, whereas a random Goppa code with the same parameters is "unlikely" to pass (depending on K).

Compute the hull enumerator $u \in \mathbb{Z}_{\geq 0}^{n+1}$ of C.
Compute the set of all singly-punctured hull enumerators $V_{yes} \subseteq \mathbb{Z}_{\geq 0}^{n+1}$ of C.
for k **from** 1 **to** K **do**
> Sample a random Goppa code C'_k of parameters (p, m, t, n).
> Compute the set of all singly-punctured hull enumerators $V'_k \subseteq \mathbb{Z}_{\geq 0}^{n+1}$ of C'_k.

$\mathcal{V} \leftarrow V_{yes} \cup \bigcup_{k=1}^{K} V'_k$
$\mathcal{C} \leftarrow \{C'_1, ..., C'_K\}$
$\mathcal{F} \leftarrow (u, [\,])$
while $\mathcal{V} \neq \emptyset$ **do**
> Filter $\mathcal{C}$ through $\mathcal{F}$ and only keep the codes that pass.
> // At this point one could optionally **break** early once the empirical rate $|\mathcal{C}|/K$ of false positives has fallen below a given target false-positive rate.
> **if** $\mathcal{C} = \emptyset$ **then**
>> **break**
>
> **for each** $v \in \mathcal{V}$ **do**
>> $b_v \leftarrow (v \in V_{yes})$
>> Compute the proportion ε_v of codes in $\mathcal{C}$ passing the filter $(u, [(b_v, v)])$.
>
> Find a $v \in \mathcal{V}$ with ε_v minimal among all v and remove v from $\mathcal{V}$.
> Append (b_v, v) to the second component of $\mathcal{F}$.

return $\mathcal{F}$

---

cannot possibly occur for a valid solution, hence this scenario can be detected (and the offending codes discarded) by simply inspecting the overflow bit.

5.6   Precomputation for the Full SSA

For general inputs, the simple filter obtained in the previous Sect. 5.5, which checks for the presence or absence of certain enumerators within the set of singly-punctured hull enumerators, may not be selective enough. In that case, one could proceed with precomputing the full SSA as described in Sect. 4: Instead of relying only on singly-punctured hulls, continue down the recursion and puncture out more positions of the code as identified by their punctured hull enumerators.

An important detail is that this can be done as a one-time precomputation for one side of the equivalence test, leaving only the candidate equivalent key to be processed at runtime (following a predictable pattern determined beforehand), which is beneficial in the context of a key-recovery attack: It again enables the whole equivalence test to be phrased as a binary circuit that does not involve any unpredictable control flow or complicated data structures.

We also note that there is a tradeoff between the one-time precomputation cost and the online phase of the attack: Trying (in the notation of Sect. 4) a larger variety of puncturing sets I at each refining step yields possibly much shorter and therefore more efficient strategies for the resulting equivalence test.

In our implementation of the key-recovery attack (see Sect. 6), we initially tested a proof-of-concept implementation of this more general approach for the first fast filtering stage, but it quickly became evident that singly-punctured hulls almost always provide strong enough filtering in practice, hence the full "precomputed SSA" approach was abandoned for that purpose and we settled for the simpler strategy described in Sect. 5.5. We do however use the more general method outlined here when post-processing the codes that passed the fast filter, as described in the following Sect. 5.7.

5.7 Post-processing Codes Passing the Filter

The fast filter from Sect. 5.5 is not perfect: It does allow for false positives, i.e., actually inequivalent codes which nevertheless exhibit the correct set of singly-punctured hull enumerators, to be incorrectly identified as candidate equivalent codes—albeit at a very slow rate, assuming the conditions tested by the fast filter are strong enough, meaning they are satisfied only for a miniscule proportion of random Goppa codes.

Since those false positives are very rare in practice, a second, strictly correct (but more expensive) filtering stage can eliminate them at almost no additional cost per guess: We simply re-run the standard support-splitting algorithm (with a precomputed strategy—see Sect. 5.6) in order to distinguish the true solution from the false positives that are erroneously passing through the filter. As a byproduct of establishing equivalence to the target code, the SSA at the same time also recovers a permutation that realizes the equivalence between the public-key code and the solution to the key-recovery problem.

6 Implementation

Our parallelized C++ implementation of the McEliece key-recovery attack using the support-splitting algorithm is available for download at the following link:

$$\text{https://yx7.cc/code/goppify/goppify-latest.tar.xz}$$

In this section, we specialize to $p = 2$ and $q = 2^m$; this is the only case that is currently supported by the implementation. Let w denote the number of bits in a register of the target architecture. (The implementation hardcodes $w = 64$.)

6.1 Bitslicing the Fast SSA Filter

The most effective optimization employed in our brute-force software to recover McEliece keys is *bitslicing*. Generically, this technique refers to rewriting a given computation as a binary circuit, then evaluating the circuit on w independent inputs *in parallel* using the processor's bitwise logic instructions on registers

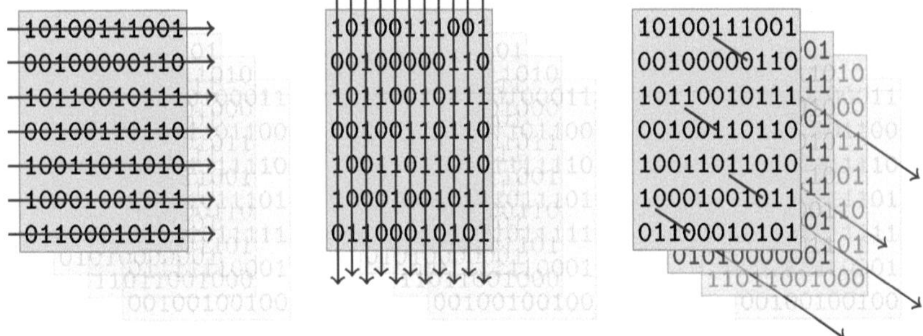

Fig. 2. Illustration of the ways a list of matrices over $\mathbb{F}_2$ can be stored in, in (from left to right) row-major, column-major, and bitsliced order. Each arrow indicates the set of bits stored inside a single bit vector (i.e., CPU register) within the target machine.

holding w bits each. This is fundamentally the same concept as batching multiple instances of the same computation using vector instructions, but here it is applied at the level of single bits held in general-purpose CPU registers. See Fig. 2.

In the context of linear algebra over $\mathbb{F}_2$, which the support-splitting algorithm heavily relies on, this yields to several important optimizations over the straightforward approach working on one matrix in row-major form at a time:

- **Predictable execution flow:** Avoiding conditional branches and variable-length loops assists the processor in effectively pipelining the execution of the program and helps prevent expensive mispredictions (and the resulting rollbacks) on architectures that rely on speculative execution.
- **Predictable memory-access pattern:** Avoiding random accesses to large memory regions is a crucial consideration in optimizing computations for modern CPUs since fetching data from main memory incurs a potentially very large time penalty. Using data-independent memory-access patterns enables the memory controller on superscalar architectures to prefetch the required information into a lower (faster) level of the cache hierarchy while previous steps of the program are in the process of being executed, resulting in much smaller memory-access latencies and, therefore, higher throughput.

On the opposite side, the primary drawbacks of bitslicing computations are:

- **Random accesses are expensive:** While loading or storing data from or to an array with variable index is expressible in the circuit abstraction (for an example, see Remark 28 and the pivoting step in Algorithm 2), it comes at a linear time cost in the size of the array that is being accessed. In comparison, the RAM model of computation stipulates that a memory access can be performed in constant time, independently of the size of the memory, while more realistic models of computation assign a nonconstant but still sublinear time cost.
- **Integer arithmetic is expensive:** Modern processors typically perform a very large number of bit operations per assembly instruction or clock cycle.

Logical bit operations, as employed for bitslicing, offer among the worst throughput in terms of bit operations per unit of time. By comparison, integer arithmetic in non-bitsliced representation benefits from specialized silicon inside the CPU, enabling it to perform integer operations with throughput often significantly greater than one instruction per cycle, despite the fact that those operations actually consist of a possibly very large number of bit operations. Therefore, emulating nontrivial computations using relatively primitive operations which could—in non-bitsliced representation—be run through specialized hardware is inherently much slower than simply using the built-in instructions. Nevertheless, when only a small number of simple (say) integer operations is required as part of a larger circuit that can more favorably be expressed in terms of bit operations, it may be beneficial to perform them in the bitsliced representation anyway.

Luckily, neither of those disadvantages has a big impact in our context: The vast majority of the time is spent on linear algebra over $\mathbb{F}_2$, where packing multiple instances into a set of registers in order to exploit the parallelism inherently provided by register-sized bitwise operators offers a clear advantage over using those same hardware units to execute only a single instance at a time.

Remark 28. Algorithm 1, 6 and 9 are all given in non-bitsliced form for ease of notation. In all cases, converting them into a bitslicable circuit is straightforward: The most important translation step is to replace all conditional expressions by equivalent sequences of bit operations, similar to constant-time cryptographic code: In essence, the conditional assignment "**if** C **then** $R \leftarrow A$ **else** $R \leftarrow B$" turns into the computation of *both* branches $R_{\text{true}} \leftarrow A$ and $R_{\text{false}} \leftarrow B$, followed by the combination of the two possible results using a bitmask, i.e., computing $R \leftarrow (C \wedge R_{\text{true}}) \vee (\neg C \wedge R_{\text{false}})$. Similarly, random accesses to memory can be emulated by iterating over all memory cells that could possibly be accessed and conditionally reading or writing the cell using a bitmask each time.

Shortcuts. Recall that our implementation processes multiple instances of the hull and punctured-hull computations in parallel via bitslicing. For example, when *all* bits in the register holding the value m in Algorithm 2 are unset, the following loops have no effect and can thus be skipped altogether in bitsliced or vectorized software, resulting in noticeable speedups when only a small proportion of the input instances really do require the evaluation of that code path. We refer to this as a *shortcut*. Note that this breaks the circuit abstraction.

6.2   Orchestrating the Key Recovery

On top of the "fast filter" core for rapid batch testing of code equivalences using the bitsliced representation, our key-recovery attack tool consists of several more higher-level procedures that will be detailed below.

Our implementation of the algorithms described in this paper is written in C++23, making extensive use of its efficient and convenient multithreading functionality. We employ the NTL library for computing in $\mathbb{F}_{2^m}$ and $\mathbb{F}_{2^m}[x]$ outside of the bitsliced representation (i.e., for the computations involving $\mathbb{F}_{2^m}$ in Algorithm 10). Note that we exclusively work with parity-check matrices for manipulating Goppa codes, which are slightly easier (or at least more convenient) to construct than generator matrices.

The Extended-Codes Version. For simplicity, in the following, we describe the version of the main algorithm that does not use extended Goppa codes. The only changes necessary to run the extended-code version are:

- Run the precomputation for the fast filter (Algorithm 8) for the extended version of the target public-key code instead of the target code itself.
- Instead of brute-forcing combinations of Goppa parity-check columns as below, brute-force combinations of *extended*-Goppa parity-check columns, which may or may not include a column $(0, ..., 0, 1)$ associated to $\infty \in \mathsf{set}(\widehat{L})$.
- Add a post-processing step to obtain a solution for the McEliece key-recovery problem given a solution for the key-recovery problem on extended codes: See Sect. 3.1.

The Main Loop. Until a solution is found, each processing core repeatedly samples w random (irreducible) polynomials $g_1, ..., g_w \in \mathbb{F}_{2^m}[x]$ of degree t. For each $\alpha \in \mathbb{F}_{2^m}$, it computes the associated columns

$$v_\alpha^{(k)} := \begin{bmatrix} \alpha^0/g_k(\alpha) \\ \hline \alpha^1/g_k(\alpha) \\ \hline \vdots \\ \hline \alpha^{t-1}/g_k(\alpha) \end{bmatrix} \in \mathbb{F}_2^{tm} \tag{$*$}$$

of a Goppa parity-check matrix (see Sect. 2.2). The collection of $2^m \cdot w$ columns $\{v_\alpha^{(k)} \mid k \in \{1, ..., w\}, \alpha \in \mathbb{F}_{2^m}\}$ is then bitsliced into $2^m \cdot tm$ width-w registers $\{r_i(\alpha) \mid i \in \{1, ..., tm\}, \alpha \in \mathbb{F}_{2^m}\}$, with $r_i(\alpha)$ containing the ith coefficient in each of the columns $v_\alpha^{(1)}, ..., v_\alpha^{(w)} \in \mathbb{F}_2^{tm}$.

Finally, the algorithm picks a random ordering for the 2^m elements of $\mathbb{F}_{2^m}$ and thus for the bitsliced columns $(r_1(\alpha), ..., r_{tm}(\alpha))$ that will be combined into candidate parity-check matrices. See Algorithm 10 for details.

Iterating over Length-n Subsets of $\mathbb{F}_q$. For each choice of the columns $r_i(\alpha)$, the algorithm now enumerates a certain (configurable) number of length-n subsets of those columns, which corresponds to guessing the set of Goppa evaluation points $\mathsf{set}(L)$. These subsets are enumerated in a *depth-first* fashion, systematically constructing all possible combinations of column sets in the candidate Goppa parity-check matrix by filling in the columns from left to right, recursing further to the right whenever possible, and only continuing with the next choice for the "current" column after the algorithm has run out of options for all columns to the right. This enumeration procedure can be implemented using a *stack* data structure; see Algorithm 9 for details.

One major benefit of enumerating subsets of $\mathbb{F}_{2^m}$ in this particular order is that almost all of the time, modifications occur exclusively near the end of the candidate parity-check matrix, which means most of the work involved in the linear-algebra routines can be reused and therefore amortized across multiple guesses for $\mathsf{set}(L)$. This important optimization owes crucially to the fact that the particular variant of Gauß elimination used in Algorithm 2 finalizes the columns of the reduced matrix in diagonal standard form sequentially from left to right, which renders it possible to restart the elimination process midway and continue from whichever column has been swapped out. This is similar to the techniques described in [5, § 4].

Algorithm 9: Searching for a valid subset of column vectors.

Input: Sequence $v_1, .., v_\ell$ of column vectors in $\mathbb{F}_q^d$, dimension $n \in \{1, ..., \ell\}$, and a function $\mathsf{check} \colon \mathbb{F}_q^{d \times n} \to \{\mathsf{false}, \mathsf{true}\}$.

Output: Iterator over subsets $\{i_1, ..., i_n\} \subseteq \{1, ..., \ell\}$ satisfying $\mathsf{check}(R) = 1$, where R is the diagonal standard form of the matrix $\left(v_{i_1} \mid \cdots \mid v_{i_n} \right)$.

Initialize an empty stack $\mathcal{S}$ holding values in $\{1, ..., \ell\}^* \times \mathbb{F}_q^{d \times d} \times \mathbb{F}_q^{d \times n}$.

Push $\left((\,), \mathbb{1}, \mathbb{0} \right)$ onto $\mathcal{S}$.

while $\mathcal{S}$ is not empty **do**

> Pop the top value $\left((i_1, ..., i_k), L, R \right)$ from $\mathcal{S}$.
>
> **if** $k = n$ **then**
>
>> /* At this point, rather than enumerating all $\binom{\ell}{n}$ subsets, one could increment a counter and return early once some limit was reached.   */
>>
>> **if** $\mathsf{check}(R)$ **then**
>>
>>> **yield** $\{i_1, ..., i_k\}$
>
> $j \leftarrow i_k + 1$ // convention: $i_0 = 0$
>
> **if** $j \leq \ell$ **then**
>
>> **if** $0 < k \leq n$ **then**
>>
>>> // Note on the stack where to continue after the recursive step.
>>>
>>> $(L', R') \leftarrow (L, R)$
>>>
>>> Replace the kth column of R' by the vector $L \cdot v_j$.
>>>
>>> Apply the kth iteration of Algorithm 1 or 2 to the pair (L', R').
>>>
>>> Push $\left((i_1, ..., i_{k-1}, j), L', R' \right)$ onto $\mathcal{S}$.
>>
>> **if** $0 \leq k < n$ **then**
>>
>>> // Set up the stack for entering a recursive depth-first step next.
>>>
>>> Replace the $(k+1)^{\mathrm{th}}$ column of R by the vector $L \cdot v_j$.
>>>
>>> Apply the $(k+1)^{\mathrm{th}}$ iteration of Algorithm 1 or 2 to the pair (L, R).
>>>
>>> Push $\left((i_1, ..., i_k, j), L, R \right)$ onto $\mathcal{S}$.

Running the Filter. Once the bitsliced candidate parity-check matrices have been set up in the way outlined above, all that is left to do is to run the fast filter developed in Sect. 5.5 on the bitsliced inputs in parallel. This yields a single register containing one bit per candidate parity-check matrix, indicating whether the respective instance has passed the filter. For each parity-check matrix that passed the filter, we reconstruct the matrix in non-bitsliced representation and run a slower non-bitsliced implementation of the full SSA (see Sect. 5.7) to discover whether the code is truly permutation-equivalent to the target public-key code or a false positive has passed the fast filter.

Algorithm 10: The main key-recovery algorithm.

Input: Fast filter $\mathcal{F}$ for a Goppa code $C \subseteq \mathbb{F}_2^n$ with $q = 2^m$ and $t = \deg(g)$.

Output: Goppa polynomial g and list L of evaluation points defining C.

while true **do**

    Sample w irreducible polynomials $g_1, ..., g_w \in \mathbb{F}_{2^m}[x]$ of degree t.

    Compute the associated columns $v_\alpha^{(1)}, ..., v_\alpha^{(w)}$ according to Equation $(*)$.

    For each $\alpha \in \mathbb{F}_{2^m}$, bitslice the list $\left[v_\alpha^{(1)}, ..., v_\alpha^{(w)}\right] \in (\mathbb{F}_2^{tm})^w$ of w independent columns into a list of length-w registers $r(\alpha) = \left[r_1(\alpha), ..., r_{tm}(\alpha)\right] \in (\mathbb{F}_2^w)^{tm}$.

    Sample a random bijection $\iota \colon \{1, ..., 2^m\} \to \mathbb{F}_{2^m}$ and let

    $S \leftarrow \left[r(\iota(1)), ..., r(\iota(2^m))\right] \in \left((\mathbb{F}_2^w)^{tm}\right)^{2^m}$.

    Execute the bitsliced version of Algorithm 9 with inputs S and n, using the bitsliced version of Algorithm 7 with input $\mathcal{F}$ for the check function.

    for each *index set* $\{i_1, ..., i_n\} \subseteq \{1, ..., 2^m\}$ *returned by Algorithm 9 for the kth bit of the bitsliced computation* **do**

        Rebuild the corresponding Goppa code $C' := \Gamma(g_k, [\iota(i_1), ..., \iota(i_n)])$.

        Run the standard SSA on input (C, C'), yielding a result $\pi \in \mathcal{S}_n \cup \{\bot\}$.

        if $\pi \neq \bot$ **then**

            $L \leftarrow \left[\iota(i_{\pi(1)}), ..., \iota(i_{\pi(n)})\right]$

            return (g, L)

Remark 29. Algorithm 10 can easily be adjusted—following essentially the same structure—to work with any other efficient implementation of the fast filter, such as CPU implementations using dedicated vector registers and instructions, GPU implementations, or hardware implementations on FPGAs or ASICs.

6.3 Estimates

An overview of the estimated cost of breaking various (smaller) challenge instances of the McEliece key-recovery problem using our implementation of the attack is displayed in Tables 2 and 1 (including, resp. without, the use of extended codes).

Baseline: Linear Algebra Using M4RI. The M4RI library [1] is a highly optimized implementation of the "Four Russians" [6] approach to linear algebra over $\mathbb{F}_2$. Comparing the performance of our bitsliced implementation of Gauß elimination (Algorithm 2) to M4RI reveals that our implementation achieves roughly twice the throughput of MARI when computing reduced echelon forms of random square matrices over $\mathbb{F}_2$ of dimensions $n = 253$. This suggests that the vectorized circuit-based approach employed in this paper is presumably superior when many instances of the same linear-algebra task can be batched, even when the relatively complicated hardware required to run M4RI is available.

6.4   Breaking the "83-Bit" Instance

In this section we report on details of the successful private-key recovery for the largest solved instance (estimated 83 bits of security) of TII's McEliece Challenges. The target public-key file `pk_McEliece_83.txt`, along with the public-key files for all other difficulty levels, are available at https://github.com/ElenaKirshanova/tii_decoding_challenge/blob/main/public_keyRec/.

Solving the challenge was done by simply invoking the script `./solve.sh 83` from (a previous version of) the code package without any further modifications. This script first runs the precomputation stage for the target code as described in Sects. 5.5 and 5.6, followed by the main key-recovery program (Algorithm 10).

In a stroke of luck, for the particular target public-key code from the challenge, the hull enumerator alone is already quite rare: It only occurs for one in about 3350 random codes. Adding just one additional check for the presence of a certain singly-punctured hull enumerator lowers this proportion below one in a million, resulting in a high rate of filtering for this target key, as indicated in Table 1.

In another stroke of luck, the private key was encountered significantly faster than expected: While Table 1 suggests an estimated $2^{40.08}$ guesses, our software recovered a valid private key for the challenge instance after only $2^{39.04}$ guesses using about 1735 core days over the course of about 3.4 wall-clock days.

The hardware platform used to solve the challenge was a server with two AMD EPYC 9754 processors (containing a total of 256 cores implementing the Zen 4c microarchitecture) with dynamic frequency scaling (base clock 2.25 GHz, boost clock up to 3.1 GHz) and hyperthreading (for a total of 512 threads) enabled. Note that these timings are not exactly comparable to the estimates given in Table 1 since dynamic frequency scaling and hyperthreading were enabled at the time of the record run while they are disabled in Table 1.

6.5   Breaking the "91-Bit" Instance

After the conclusion of TII's McEliece Challenges, our attack implementation was strenghtened by adding the extended-codes optimization laid out in this paper. The outcome is a speedup factor on the order of n, which not only reduces the cost for solving the 83-bit challenge instance from about 1400 core days to about 6.3 core days, but also puts even larger challenge instances easily within reach: In an example run, we've successfully solved the TII McEliece Challenge instance with an a-priori difficulty estimate of 91 bits using only 161 core days on the same hardware configuration that was used to generate Tables 2 and 1.

Acknowledgements. This work was provoked by the *TII McEliece Challenges*. (https://crowdchallenge.tii.ae/mceliece-challenges/) Thanks to Andre Esser for encouraging me to delve into this topic, to Violetta Weger for educating me about some aspects of coding theory, and to Marius Stelzner for pointing out an assortment of small mistakes in a previous version. I also wish to thank my previous employer, Academia Sinica, whose equipment was used during part of this research.

Table 1. Overview of the smaller parameter sets from the *TII McEliece Challenges* together with attack complexity estimates using our optimized key-search software *without* the use of extended Goppa codes. The empirical throughput (private-key guesses per core and second) was measured on an AMD EPYC 9754 processor (Zen 4c microarchitecture) running at $2.25\,\mathrm{GHz}$ with hyperthreading disabled. The required number of guesses was estimated based on Heuristic 10. The columns "$\#\,\mathcal{F}$" and "$\approx \Pr[\mathcal{F}\mapsto\text{true}]$" refer to the length of the used fast filter $\mathcal{F}$, not including the unpunctured hull enumerator itself, and the empirical probability for a random code to pass the filter $\mathcal{F}$, respectively. All filters were constructed by running Algorithm 8 with $K = 100{,}000$. Note that no attempt was made to optimize the estimated total duration of the attack by adjusting the length of the filter.

instance	m	t	n	$\approx \#$ guesses	$\#\,\mathcal{F}$	$\approx \Pr[\mathcal{F}\mapsto\text{true}]$	guesses/(core·s)	$\approx$ core time
41	5	2	27	$2^{14.30}$	5	$2^{-6.31}$	$2^{16.77}$	$\approx 0.2\,\mathrm{s}$
43	5	2	26	$2^{16.47}$	6	$2^{-4.25}$	$2^{14.92}$	$2^{1.54}\,\mathrm{s} \approx 2.9\,\mathrm{s}$
44	6	2	61	$2^{11.76}$	10	$2^{-10.76}$	$2^{16.84}$	$\approx 0.0\,\mathrm{s}$
45	6	3	62	$2^{12.83}$	9	$2^{-5.53}$	$2^{13.77}$	$\approx 0.5\,\mathrm{s}$
46	6	4	63	$2^{13.44}$	4	$2^{-13.43}$	$2^{17.49}$	$\approx 0.1\,\mathrm{s}$
47	5	2	23	$2^{21.42}$	7	$2^{-6.48}$	$2^{17.43}$	$2^{3.99}\,\mathrm{s} \approx 15.9\,\mathrm{s}$
48	6	2	60	$2^{15.69}$	4	$2^{-15.69}$	$2^{18.68}$	$\approx 0.1\,\mathrm{s}$
49	5	2	21	$2^{23.62}$	8	$2^{-10.48}$	$2^{20.18}$	$2^{3.44}\,\mathrm{s} \approx 10.9\,\mathrm{s}$
50	6	3	61	$2^{17.20}$	14	$2^{-5.41}$	$2^{13.76}$	$2^{3.44}\,\mathrm{s} \approx 10.9\,\mathrm{s}$
51	6	4	62	$2^{18.41}$	2	$2^{-18.43}$	$2^{18.64}$	$\approx 0.9\,\mathrm{s}$
52	6	5	63	$2^{19.12}$	17	$2^{-7.26}$	$2^{15.22}$	$2^{3.89}\,\mathrm{s} \approx 14.9\,\mathrm{s}$
53	6	3	60	$2^{21.13}$	3	$2^{-20.12}$	$2^{18.49}$	$2^{2.64}\,\mathrm{s} \approx 6.2\,\mathrm{s}$
55	6	4	61	$2^{22.78}$	16	$2^{-17.58}$	$2^{18.46}$	$2^{4.32}\,\mathrm{s} \approx 20.0\,\mathrm{s}$
57	6	3	59	$2^{24.71}$	8	$2^{-17.37}$	$2^{18.40}$	$2^{6.31}\,\mathrm{s} \approx 1.3\,\mathrm{min}$
58	6	2	57	$2^{25.63}$	20	$2^{-15.15}$	$2^{18.82}$	$2^{6.81}\,\mathrm{s} \approx 1.9\,\mathrm{min}$
59	6	4	60	$2^{26.71}$	15	$2^{-17.93}$	$2^{18.47}$	$2^{8.24}\,\mathrm{s} \approx 5.1\,\mathrm{min}$
60	6	3	58	$2^{28.01}$	10	$2^{-19.41}$	$2^{18.78}$	$2^{9.24}\,\mathrm{s} \approx 10.0\,\mathrm{min}$
63	6	2	55	$2^{31.10}$	4	$2^{-19.78}$	$2^{19.09}$	$2^{12.01}\,\mathrm{s} \approx 1.1\,\mathrm{h}$
65	6	2	54	$2^{33.56}$	14	$2^{-17.80}$	$2^{18.66}$	$2^{14.90}\,\mathrm{s} \approx 8.5\,\mathrm{h}$
66	6	3	56	$2^{33.90}$	15	$2^{-7.06}$	$2^{15.10}$	$2^{18.80}\,\mathrm{s} \approx 5.3\,\mathrm{d}$
68	6	2	53	$2^{35.85}$	2	$2^{-19.74}$	$2^{19.45}$	$2^{16.40}\,\mathrm{s} \approx 1.0\,\mathrm{d}$
69	6	4	57	$2^{36.65}$	16	$2^{-17.56}$	$2^{18.82}$	$2^{17.83}\,\mathrm{s} \approx 2.7\,\mathrm{d}$
70	8	5	255	$2^{26.68}$	28	$2^{-9.28}$	$2^{11.82}$	$2^{14.86}\,\mathrm{s} \approx 8.3\,\mathrm{h}$
71	6	6	60	$2^{38.13}$	9	$2^{-17.23}$	$2^{18.79}$	$2^{19.34}\,\mathrm{s} \approx 7.7\,\mathrm{d}$
72	7	5	125	$2^{34.26}$	2	$2^{-23.77}$	$2^{16.22}$	$2^{18.04}\,\mathrm{s} \approx 3.1\,\mathrm{d}$
73	7	6	126	$2^{35.61}$	1	$2^{-23.92}$	$2^{16.09}$	$2^{19.52}\,\mathrm{s} \approx 8.7\,\mathrm{d}$
74	7	8	128	$2^{36.20}$	26	$2^{-6.95}$	$2^{10.79}$	$2^{25.41}\,\mathrm{s} \approx 1.41\,\mathrm{yr}$
76	6	7	60	$2^{43.91}$	3	$2^{-18.87}$	$2^{19.05}$	$2^{24.85}\,\mathrm{s} \approx 0.96\,\mathrm{yr}$
77	7	5	124	$2^{39.23}$	6	$2^{-19.15}$	$2^{15.90}$	$2^{23.33}\,\mathrm{s} \approx 4.0\,\mathrm{mo}$
78	6	8	61	$2^{45.78}$	5	$2^{-18.29}$	$2^{18.48}$	$2^{27.31}\,\mathrm{s} \approx 5.26\,\mathrm{yr}$
79	7	6	125	$2^{41.00}$	5	$2^{-19.46}$	$2^{15.92}$	$2^{25.08}\,\mathrm{s} \approx 1.12\,\mathrm{yr}$
80	7	7	126	$2^{42.39}$	2	$2^{-21.02}$	$2^{16.02}$	$2^{26.36}\,\mathrm{s} \approx 2.74\,\mathrm{yr}$
81	7	8	127	$2^{43.20}$	5	$2^{-18.43}$	$2^{15.38}$	$2^{27.82}\,\mathrm{s} \approx 7.52\,\mathrm{yr}$
82	6	8	60	$2^{49.72}$	6	$2^{-18.92}$	$2^{18.59}$	$2^{31.13}\,\mathrm{s} \approx 74.34\,\mathrm{yr}$
83	8	5	253	$2^{40.08}$	1	$2^{-19.94}$	$2^{13.22}$	$2^{26.86}\,\mathrm{s} \approx 3.86\,\mathrm{yr}$
84	8	6	254	$2^{41.42}$	28	$2^{-10.64}$	$2^{12.61}$	$2^{28.80}\,\mathrm{s} \approx 14.86\,\mathrm{yr}$
85	8	8	256	$2^{42.01}$	25	$2^{-10.31}$	$2^{9.98}$	$2^{32.03}\,\mathrm{s} \approx 138.8\,\mathrm{yr}$
86	7	5	122	$2^{48.22}$	1	$2^{-19.23}$	$2^{16.44}$	$2^{31.78}\,\mathrm{s} \approx 117.0\,\mathrm{yr}$
87	7	8	126	$2^{49.19}$	4	$2^{-18.28}$	$2^{15.79}$	$2^{33.40}\,\mathrm{s} \approx 359.4\,\mathrm{yr}$
88	7	9	127	$2^{50.03}$	26	$2^{-6.78}$	$2^{12.13}$	$2^{37.90}\,\mathrm{s} \approx 8{,}155\,\mathrm{yr}$
89	8	5	252	$2^{46.06}$	1	$2^{-21.19}$	$2^{13.23}$	$2^{32.83}\,\mathrm{s} \approx 242.2\,\mathrm{yr}$
90	7	5	121	$2^{52.34}$	4	$2^{-17.60}$	$2^{16.20}$	$2^{36.14}\,\mathrm{s} \approx 2{,}399\,\mathrm{yr}$
91	8	6	253	$2^{47.82}$	18	$2^{-13.32}$	$2^{13.02}$	$2^{34.79}\,\mathrm{s} \approx 944.4\,\mathrm{yr}$
92	8	7	254	$2^{49.19}$	4	$2^{-19.14}$	$2^{13.10}$	$2^{36.10}\,\mathrm{s} \approx 2{,}329\,\mathrm{yr}$
93	8	8	255	$2^{50.01}$	29	$2^{-9.06}$	$2^{11.71}$	$2^{38.30}\,\mathrm{s} \approx 10{,}696\,\mathrm{yr}$
94	7	5	120	$2^{56.26}$	7	$2^{-18.34}$	$2^{16.23}$	$2^{40.03}\,\mathrm{s} \approx 35{,}557\,\mathrm{yr}$
95	7	7	123	$2^{57.38}$	2	$2^{-23.08}$	$2^{16.39}$	$2^{40.99}\,\mathrm{s} \approx 69{,}152\,\mathrm{yr}$
96	9	8	512	$2^{47.83}$	4	$2^{-20.24}$	$2^{8.35}$	$2^{39.48}\,\mathrm{s} \approx 24{,}359\,\mathrm{yr}$
97	7	8	124	$2^{59.55}$	12	$2^{-15.02}$	$2^{16.19}$	$2^{43.36}\,\mathrm{s} \approx 358{,}402\,\mathrm{yr}$
99	7	9	125	$2^{61.42}$	5	$2^{-19.82}$	$2^{16.09}$	$2^{45.32}\,\mathrm{s} \approx 1{,}395{,}262\,\mathrm{yr}$

Table 2. Overview of the smaller parameter sets from the *TII McEliece Challenges* together with attack complexity estimates using our optimized key-search software *including* the use of extended Goppa codes. The empirical throughput (private-key guesses per core and second) was measured on an AMD EPYC 9754 processor (Zen 4c microarchitecture) running at 2.25 GHz with hyperthreading disabled. The required number of guesses was estimated based on Heuristic 14. The columns "$\#\,\mathcal{F}$" and "$\approx \Pr[\mathcal{F} \mapsto \text{true}]$" refer to the length of the used fast filter $\mathcal{F}$, not including the unpunctured hull enumerator itself, and the empirical probability for a random code to pass the filter $\mathcal{F}$, respectively. All filters were constructed by running Algorithm 8 with $K = 100{,}000$. Note that no attempt was made to optimize the estimated total duration of the attack by adjusting the length of the filter.

instance	m	t	n	$\approx \#$ guesses	$\#\,\mathcal{F}$	$\approx \Pr[\mathcal{F} \mapsto \text{true}]$	guesses/(core·s)	$\approx$ core time
41	5	2	27	$2^{9.49}$	3	$2^{-8.49}$	$2^{17.73}$	$\approx 0.0\,$s
43	5	2	26	$2^{11.71}$	5	$2^{-4.34}$	$2^{14.83}$	$\approx 0.1\,$s
44	6	2	61	$2^{5.81}$	2	$2^{-5.81}$	$2^{11.93}$	$\approx 0.0\,$s
45	6	3	62	$2^{6.85}$	5	$2^{-3.53}$	$2^{11.42}$	$\approx 0.0\,$s
46	6	4	63	$2^{7.44}$	1	$2^{-7.44}$	$2^{13.70}$	$\approx 0.0\,$s
47	5	2	23	$2^{16.83}$	11	$2^{-8.20}$	$2^{18.75}$	$\approx 0.3\,$s
48	6	2	60	$2^{9.76}$	1	$2^{-9.76}$	$2^{15.73}$	$\approx 0.0\,$s
49	5	2	21	$2^{19.16}$	10	$2^{-5.53}$	$2^{16.51}$	$2^{2.65}\,$s $\approx 6.3\,$s
50	6	3	61	$2^{11.24}$	4	$2^{-11.25}$	$2^{16.75}$	$\approx 0.0\,$s
51	6	4	62	$2^{12.44}$	1	$2^{-12.43}$	$2^{17.28}$	$\approx 0.0\,$s
52	6	5	63	$2^{13.12}$	4	$2^{-13.12}$	$2^{17.05}$	$\approx 0.1\,$s
53	6	3	60	$2^{15.20}$	3	$2^{-15.19}$	$2^{17.81}$	$\approx 0.2\,$s
55	6	4	61	$2^{16.83}$	7	$2^{-16.84}$	$2^{18.38}$	$\approx 0.3\,$s
57	6	3	59	$2^{18.81}$	12	$2^{-18.83}$	$2^{18.43}$	$2^{0.37}\,$s $\approx 1.3\,$s
58	6	2	57	$2^{19.77}$	19	$2^{-14.07}$	$2^{18.50}$	$2^{1.27}\,$s $\approx 2.4\,$s
59	6	4	60	$2^{20.78}$	2	$2^{-20.78}$	$2^{17.99}$	$2^{2.79}\,$s $\approx 6.9\,$s
60	6	3	58	$2^{22.13}$	3	$2^{-19.80}$	$2^{18.81}$	$2^{3.32}\,$s $\approx 10.0\,$s
63	6	2	55	$2^{25.29}$	1	$2^{-19.18}$	$2^{19.31}$	$2^{5.98}\,$s $\approx 1.1\,$min
65	6	2	54	$2^{27.77}$	3	$2^{-19.66}$	$2^{18.92}$	$2^{8.85}\,$s $\approx 7.7\,$min
66	6	3	56	$2^{28.06}$	15	$2^{-5.70}$	$2^{14.23}$	$2^{13.84}\,$s $\approx 4.1\,$h
68	6	2	53	$2^{30.10}$	2	$2^{-21.57}$	$2^{19.12}$	$2^{10.97}\,$s $\approx 33.5\,$min
69	6	4	57	$2^{30.79}$	11	$2^{-18.77}$	$2^{18.56}$	$2^{12.23}\,$s $\approx 1.3\,$h
70	8	5	255	$2^{18.68}$	4	$2^{-17.74}$	$2^{12.54}$	$2^{6.14}\,$s $\approx 1.2\,$min
71	6	6	60	$2^{32.20}$	4	$2^{-20.23}$	$2^{18.58}$	$2^{13.61}\,$s $\approx 3.5\,$h
72	7	5	125	$2^{27.29}$	2	$2^{-18.00}$	$2^{16.14}$	$2^{11.15}\,$s $\approx 37.8\,$min
73	7	6	126	$2^{28.62}$	0	$2^{-21.82}$	$2^{15.97}$	$2^{12.65}\,$s $\approx 1.8\,$h
74	7	8	128	$2^{29.19}$	19	$2^{-8.48}$	$2^{11.10}$	$2^{18.09}\,$s $\approx 3.2\,$d
76	6	7	60	$2^{37.98}$	4	$2^{-19.72}$	$2^{18.24}$	$2^{19.73}\,$s $\approx 10.1\,$d
77	7	5	124	$2^{32.26}$	6	$2^{-18.96}$	$2^{15.84}$	$2^{16.43}\,$s $\approx 1.0\,$d
78	6	8	61	$2^{39.83}$	7	$2^{-20.08}$	$2^{18.49}$	$2^{21.34}\,$s $\approx 1.0\,$mo
79	7	6	125	$2^{34.02}$	5	$2^{-19.19}$	$2^{15.74}$	$2^{18.28}\,$s $\approx 3.7\,$d
80	7	7	126	$2^{35.40}$	1	$2^{-20.74}$	$2^{16.01}$	$2^{19.39}\,$s $\approx 7.9\,$d
81	7	8	127	$2^{36.20}$	6	$2^{-19.75}$	$2^{15.34}$	$2^{20.86}\,$s $\approx 22.1\,$d
82	6	8	60	$2^{43.78}$	3	$2^{-22.40}$	$2^{18.31}$	$2^{25.48}\,$s $\approx 1.48\,$yr
83	8	5	253	$2^{32.09}$	1	$2^{-25.90}$	$2^{13.03}$	$2^{19.06}\,$s $\approx 6.3\,$d
84	8	6	254	$2^{33.42}$	25	$2^{-9.19}$	$2^{11.92}$	$2^{21.50}\,$s $\approx 1.1\,$mo
85	8	8	256	$2^{34.00}$	9	$2^{-17.69}$	$2^{10.03}$	$2^{23.97}\,$s $\approx 6.2\,$mo
86	7	5	122	$2^{41.28}$	1	$2^{-20.37}$	$2^{16.34}$	$2^{24.94}\,$s $\approx 1.02\,$yr
87	7	8	126	$2^{42.20}$	2	$2^{-21.41}$	$2^{15.64}$	$2^{26.56}\,$s $\approx 3.14\,$yr
88	7	9	127	$2^{43.03}$	19	$2^{-8.56}$	$2^{13.75}$	$2^{29.28}\,$s $\approx 20.69\,$yr
89	8	5	252	$2^{38.08}$	2	$2^{-22.05}$	$2^{13.14}$	$2^{24.94}\,$s $\approx 1.02\,$yr
90	7	5	121	$2^{45.41}$	2	$2^{-20.77}$	$2^{16.17}$	$2^{29.24}\,$s $\approx 20.12\,$yr
91	8	6	253	$2^{39.83}$	4	$2^{-19.07}$	$2^{12.91}$	$2^{26.92}\,$s $\approx 4.03\,$yr
92	8	7	254	$2^{41.20}$	1	$2^{-20.46}$	$2^{13.07}$	$2^{28.12}\,$s $\approx 9.27\,$yr
93	8	8	255	$2^{42.01}$	3	$2^{-18.10}$	$2^{12.68}$	$2^{29.32}\,$s $\approx 21.27\,$yr
94	7	5	120	$2^{49.34}$	10	$2^{-18.05}$	$2^{15.97}$	$2^{33.37}\,$s $\approx 352.6\,$yr
95	7	7	123	$2^{50.42}$	2	$2^{-19.79}$	$2^{16.17}$	$2^{34.26}\,$s $\approx 650.0\,$yr
96	9	8	512	$2^{38.83}$	1	$2^{-19.91}$	$2^{8.34}$	$2^{30.49}\,$s $\approx 47.93\,$yr
97	7	8	124	$2^{52.58}$	17	$2^{-10.17}$	$2^{15.03}$	$2^{37.55}\,$s $\approx 6{,}385\,$yr
99	7	9	125	$2^{54.44}$	2	$2^{-24.81}$	$2^{16.06}$	$2^{38.38}\,$s $\approx 11{,}305\,$yr

A   Proofs

A.1   Proof of Lemma 1

Proof. First, note that $\alpha_{n+1} = \infty$, which implies that $(f/g)(\alpha_{n+1}) = 0$ whenever $\deg(f) < \deg(g) = t$. Call this property "$\dagger$".

Inclusion "$\subseteq$": Let $\widehat{c} = (c_1, ..., c_{n+1}) \in \widehat{\Gamma}(g, \widehat{L})$ and write $c = (c_1, ..., c_n) \in \mathbb{F}_q^n$. By assumption, we have $\ddagger$: $\forall f \in \mathbb{F}_q[x]_{\leq t}$. $\sum_{i=1}^{n+1} c_i(f/g)(\alpha_i) = 0$, which implies $\forall f \in \mathbb{F}_q[x]_{<t}$. $\sum_{i=1}^{n} c_i(f/g)(\alpha_i) = 0$ thanks to $\dagger$, hence $c = (c_1, ..., c_n) \in \Gamma(g, L)$. It remains to show that $c_{n+1} = -c_1 - \cdots - c_n$: This is immediate by instantiating $\ddagger$ with $f = g$.

Inclusion "$\supseteq$": Let $c = (c_1, ..., c_n) \in \Gamma(g, L)$ and set $\widehat{c} = (c_1, ..., c_n, c_{n+1}) \in \mathbb{F}_q^{n+1}$ where $c_{n+1} = -c_1 - \cdots - c_n$. Suppose given some $f \in \mathbb{F}_q[x]_{\leq t}$. If $\deg(f) < t$, then $\sum_{i=1}^{n} c_i(f/g)(\alpha_i) = 0$ by assumption, which (thanks to $\dagger$) is equivalent to the desired statement $\sum_{i=1}^{n+1} c_i(f/g)(\alpha_i) = 0$. Now suppose $\deg(f) = t$: Setting $h = \mathrm{lc}(f)$, we get $f = gh + r$ for some $r \in \mathbb{F}_q[x]$ with $\deg(r) < t$. From the implication we just proved (now applied to r instead of f), we get $\sum_{i=1}^{n+1} c_i(r/g)(\alpha_i) = 0$. Hence

$$\sum_{i=1}^{n+1} c_i(f/g)(\alpha_i) = \sum_{i=1}^{n+1} c_i(h+r/g)(\alpha_i) = h \underbrace{\sum_{i=1}^{n+1} c_i}_{=0} + \underbrace{\sum_{i=1}^{n+1} c_i(r/g)(\alpha_i)}_{=0} = 0,$$

which was to be demonstrated. $\qquad\square$

A.2   Proof of Lemma 4

Proof. Since φ, φ' are field automorphisms, they leave $0, 1 \in \mathbb{F}_q$ invariant. Hence, substituting $x = 0$ into $Ax^\varphi + B = A'x^{\varphi'} + B'$ yields $B = B'$, and substituting $x = 1$ then shows $A+B = A'+B$, hence $A = A'$. Finally, if $Ax^\varphi + B = A + x^{\varphi'} + B$ for all $x \in \mathbb{F}_q$, then $x^\varphi = x^{\varphi'}$ for all $x \in \mathbb{F}_q$, therefore $\varphi - \varphi'$ as maps. $\qquad\square$

A.3   Proof of Lemma 8

Proof. Let $\sigma \in \mathrm{Gal}(\overline{\mathbb{F}_q}/\mathbb{F}_q)$. Since h is defined over $\mathbb{F}_q$, there is a permutation π of the set $\{1, ..., d\}$ such that $\varrho_j^\sigma = \varrho_{\pi(j)}$ for all j. Utilizing the fact that $\mathrm{Aut}(\overline{\mathbb{F}_q})$ is abelian and hence $\Phi\sigma = \sigma\Phi$, we therefore get

$$(A\varrho_j^\Phi + B)^\sigma = A\varrho_j^{\Phi\sigma} + B = A\varrho_{\pi(j)}^\Phi + B.$$

This shows that σ acts as a permutation on the elements $A\varrho_j^\Phi + B$, which by definition make up the roots of $\tau * h$, and therefore $\tau * h$ must be defined over $\mathbb{F}_q$.

It remains to show that the choice of lift Φ does not matter: This is because for all $\Phi, \Phi' \in \mathrm{Aut}(\overline{\mathbb{F}_q})$ which restrict to φ in $\mathrm{Aut}(\mathbb{F}_q)$, we have $\Phi^{-1}\Phi' \in \mathrm{Gal}(\overline{\mathbb{F}_q}/\mathbb{F}_q)$. Let π again denote a permutation such that $\varrho_j^{\Phi^{-1}\Phi'} = \varrho_{\pi(j)}$ for all j. Then

$$\varrho_j^{\Phi'} = \varrho_j^{\Phi'\Phi\Phi^{-1}} = \varrho_{\pi(j)}^\Phi,$$

thus replacing Φ by Φ' merely induces a permutation on the elements $A\varrho_j^\Phi + B$, which leaves the polynomial $\tau * h$ invariant. $\qquad\square$

A.4   Proof of Lemma 12

Proof. (Sketch.) For brevity, we give a proof sketch for the following (stronger) claim, morally similar to Lemma 4: The group $\mathrm{P\Gamma L}(q)$ is in bijection with the set

$$S = \left\{(A, B, C, D, \varphi) \in \mathbb{F}_q^4 \times \mathrm{Aut}(\mathbb{F}_q) \;\middle|\; \det\!\left(\begin{smallmatrix} A & B \\ C & D \end{smallmatrix}\right) \neq 0\right\}$$

modulo the equivalence relation

$$(A,B,C,D,\varphi) \sim (A',B',C',D',\varphi') \iff \varphi = \varphi' \text{ and } \exists \lambda \in \mathbb{F}_q^\times .\ \left(\begin{smallmatrix} A' & B' \\ C' & D' \end{smallmatrix}\right) = \lambda\left(\begin{smallmatrix} A & B \\ C & D \end{smallmatrix}\right),$$

by identifying the class of (A, B, C, D, φ) with the map $x \mapsto \frac{Ax^\varphi + B}{Cx^\varphi + D}$ in $\mathrm{Sym}(\mathbb{P}^1\mathbb{F}_q)$.

This mapping from $S/\!\sim$ to $\mathrm{P\Gamma L}(q)$ is obviously well-defined and surjective. Moreover, after defining a group structure on $S/\!\sim$ using the *symbolic* composition of the associated functions in $\mathrm{P\Gamma L}(q)$, this map becomes a group homomorphism. To prove injectivity, let $(A, B, C, D, \varphi) \in S$ such that $\tau\colon x \mapsto \frac{Ax^\varphi + B}{Cx^\varphi + D} \in \mathrm{P\Gamma L}(q)$ is the identity map on $\mathbb{P}^1\mathbb{F}_q$. Then, substituting the points $0, 1, \infty$ into $\tau(x) = x$:

$$\infty = \tau(\infty) = A/C\,;$$
$$0 = \tau(0) = B/D\,;$$
$$1 = \tau(1) = (A + B)/(C + D)\,.$$

Together, these imply $B = C = 0$ and $A = D$, hence $\tau\colon x \mapsto x^\varphi$. Finally, $x^\varphi = x$ for all $x \in \mathbb{F}_q$ implies $\varphi = \mathrm{id} \in \mathrm{Aut}(\mathbb{F}_q)$. In summary, $(A, B, C, D, \varphi) = (\lambda, 0, 0, \lambda, \mathrm{id})$ for some $\lambda \in \mathbb{F}_q^\times$. $\qquad\square$

A.5   Proof of Lemma 19

Proof. Let M_{ij} denote the coefficient of M in the ith row and j^{th} column. The entry in the ith row and j^{th} column of M^2 thus equals $c = \sum_{k=1}^n M_{ik}M_{kj}$. Since all entries of M below the diagonal are zero, this sum shortens to $c = \sum_{k=i}^j M_{ik}M_{kj}$. For each k, if $M_{kk} = 1$, then all M_{ik} with $i < k$ lie above a pivot and therefore must be zero, and if $M_{kk} = 0$, then the entire k^{th} row, thus all M_{kj}, must be zero. Since in both cases, it follows that $M_{ik}M_{kj} = 0$ unless $k = i$, we are left with $c = M_{ii}M_{ij}$. Now, if $M_{ii} = 1$, then $c = M_{ij}$ as claimed. If on the other hand $M_{ii} = 0$, then the entire i^{th} row is zero and it follows that $c = M_{ij} = 0$.

From $M^2 = M$ we get $M \cdot (\mathbb{1} - M) = 0$, hence the columns of $\mathbb{1} - M$ are indeed contained in the right kernel of M. The matrix $\mathbb{1} - M$ is upper triangular with every nonzero column having a 1 on the diagonal, hence the nonzero columns are linearly independent. Finally, from the rank–nullity theorem, the nonzero columns of $\mathbb{1} - M$ must form a basis of the right kernel since they correspond precisely to the zero rows of M. $\qquad\square$

B   Example: Boolean Circuit for Linear Algebra

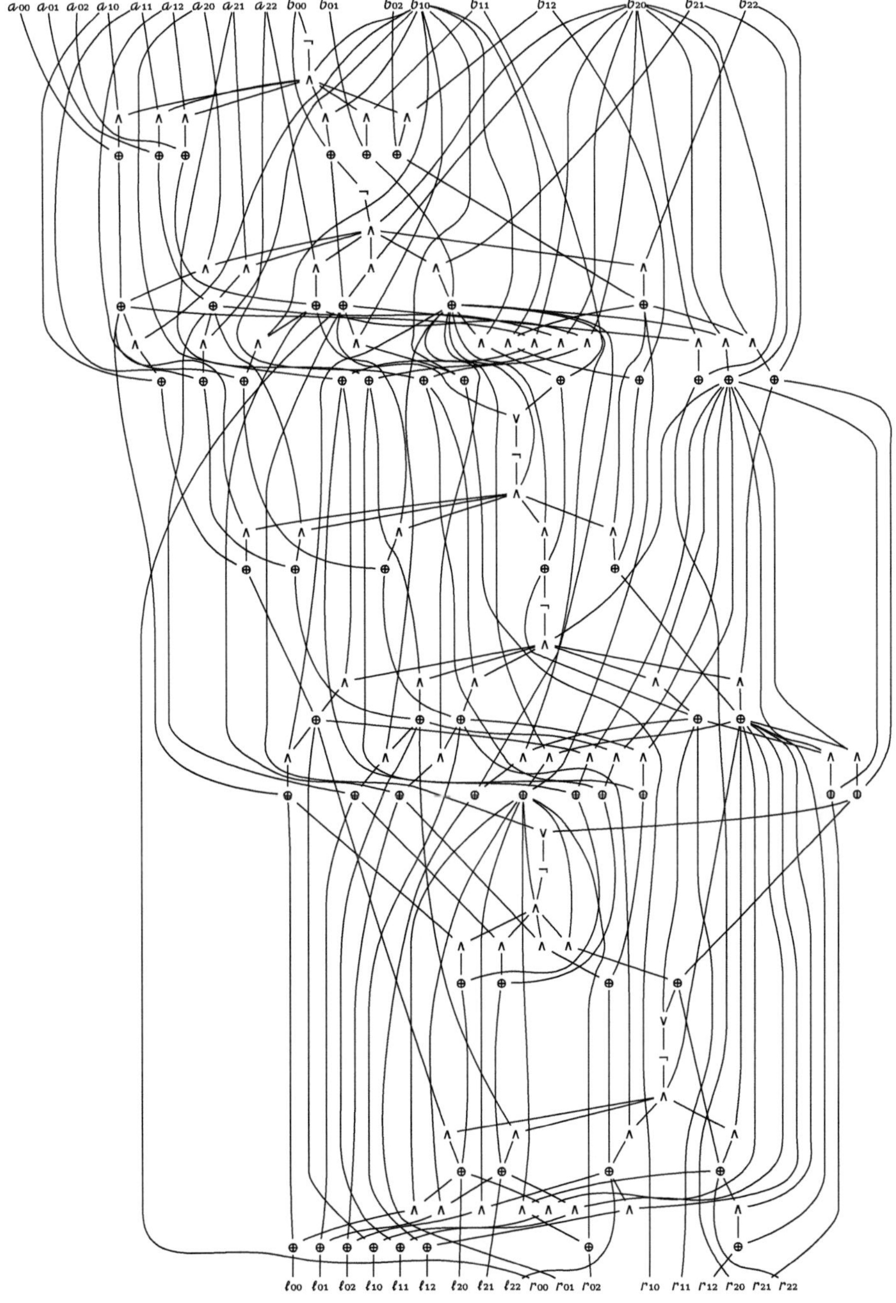

Fig. 3. Logic circuit constructed by Algorithm 2 for $n = 3$.

References

1. Albrecht, M., Bard, G.: The M4RI Library. The M4RI Team (2025). https://bitbucket.org/malb/m4ri
2. Albrecht, M.R., et al.: Classic McEliece: conservative code-based cryptography. Tech. rep. (2022). https://classic.mceliece.org/mceliece-rationale-20221023.pdf
3. Berger, T.P.: On the cyclicity of Goppa codes, parity-check subcodes of Goppa codes, and extended Goppa codes. Finite Fields Appl. **6**(3), 255–281 (2000). https://doi.org/10.1006/ffta.2000.0277
4. Bernstein, D.J.: Understanding binary-Goppa decoding. IACR Commun. Cryptol. **1**(1) (2024). https://doi.org/10.62056/angy4fe-3
5. Bernstein, D.J., Lange, T., Peters, C.: Attacking and defending the McEliece cryptosystem. In: PQCrypto 2008. LNCS, vol. 5299, pp. 31–46. Springer (2008). https://ia.cr/2018/318
6. Арлазаров, ВЛ, Диниц, ЕА, Кронрод, МА, Фараджев, ИА: Об экономном построении транзитивного замыкания ориентированного графа. Доклады Академии Наук СССР **194**, 487–488 (1970)
7. Gibson, J.K.: Equivalent Goppa codes and trapdoors to McEliece's public key cryptosystem. In: EUROCRYPT 1991. LNCS, vol. 547, pp. 517–521. Springer (1991). https://doi.org/10.1007/3-540-46416-6_46
8. Loidreau, P., Sendrier, N.: Weak keys in the McEliece public-key cryptosystem. IEEE Trans. Inf. Theory **47**(3), 1207–1211 (2001)
9. MacWilliams, F.J., Sloane, N.J.A.: The Theory of Error-Correcting Codes. North-Holland Publishing Company, 3 edn. (1981)
10. McEliece, R.J.: A public-key cryptosystem based on algebraic coding theory. The Deep Space Network Progress Report 42-44 (1978). https://ipnpr.jpl.nasa.gov/progress_report/42-44/44N.PDF
11. Moreno, O.: Symmetries of binary Goppa codes (corresp.). IEEE Trans. Inf. Theory **25**(5), 609–612 (1979). https://doi.org/10.1109/tit.1979.1056089
12. Overbeck, R., Sendrier, N.: Code-based cryptography. In: Bernstein, D.J., Buchmann, J., Dahmen, E. (eds.) Post-Quantum Cryptography, pp. 95–145. Springer (2009)
13. Patterson, N.J.: The algebraic decoding of Goppa codes. IEEE Trans. Inf. Theory **21**(2), 203–207 (1975). https://doi.org/10.1109/TIT.1975.1055350
14. Sendrier, N.: On the dimension of the hull. SIAM J. Discrete Math. **10**(2), 282–293 (1997). https://inria.hal.science/inria-00074009/document
15. Sendrier, N.: Finding the permutation between equivalent linear codes: The support splitting algorithm. IEEE Trans. Inf. Theory **46**(4), 1193–1203 (2000). https://inria.hal.science/inria-00073037/document

Cryptanalysis and Fault Attacks

Handling Noisy Plaintext Checking Oracles with SPiRiT

Application to Kyber

Paco Poilbout[1]([✉]), Thomas Roche[2], and Laurent Imbert[3]

[1] Mons, Belgium
`pacopoilbout@gmail.com`
[2] NinjaLab, Montpellier, France
`thomas.roche@ninjalab.io`
[3] CNRS, Université de Montpellier, LIRMM, Montpellier, France
`laurent.imbert@lirmm.fr`

Abstract. Post-Quantum key encapsulation mechanisms based on the re-encryption framework of Fujisaki and Okamoto have proved very sensitive to Plaintext Checking Oracle (PCO) attacks. The first theoretic works on PCO attacks were rapidly followed by practical attacks on real implementations, notably on NIST standardized ML-KEM. The actual realization of a PCO relies on side-channel leakages that are inherently noisy; even more so if the implementation embeds side-channel countermeasures.

In this paper we tackle the often overlooked complications caused by highly noisy PCOs. We demonstrate that the impact of wrong oracle answers can be very efficiently reduced with the use of the so-called *Sequential Probability Ratio Test* (SPRT). This test can be seen as an elegant and natural early abort strategy on top of the commonly used approaches based on majority-voting or the likelihood ratio test. As far as we know, this is the first use of SPRT in the context of side-channel attacks. We show that it allows to divide by a factor up to 3 the attack complexity compared to the traditional approaches. By establishing new comparisons with recently published noisy PCO attacks we emphasize that SPRT should be considered as the novel baseline for all future works in this line of research.

Keywords: ML-KEM · Side-channel attacks · Plaintext checking oracle · Majority voting · SPRT

1 Introduction

After a thorough evaluation process, NIST standardized five algorithms for digital signature and encryption that are believed to remain secure even in the

---

P. Poilbout—Independent Researcher.
This work was done during Paco Poilbout Master Research Internship at NinjaLab and LIRMM.

M. Bardet and R. Niederhagen (Eds.): PQCrypto 2026, LNCS 16492, pp. 311–341, 2026.
https://doi.org/10.1007/978-3-032-22698-3_10

presence of a quantum adversary. In particular, NIST endorsed ML-KEM [10], a Module-Lattice-Based Key-Encapsulation Mechanism (KEM for short) based on CRYSTALS-Kyber [17].

Building solid protection against side-channel attacks for these novel class of algorithms remains a challenge of utmost importance. In particular, numerous side-channel attacks against several implementations of Kyber have already been proposed. In this paper, we are interested in a family of attacks that take advantage of the re-encryption process present in most PQC KEMs through the FO-transform, by creating a so-called *Plaintext-Checking Oracle* (PCO for short) [7,13,16]. The practical realization of such an oracle exploits side-channel leakages in a way that has proven to be extremely advantageous for the attacker compared to traditional side-channel attacks [1].

Over the past years, several improvements have been suggested to drastically reduce the complexity of PCO attacks (in terms of number of oracle queries, i.e. number of side-channel traces); notably the formalization of efficient binary search trees due to Qin *et al.* [14], and the multi-plaintext (or multi-valued) oracle paradigm [15,19,22].

In this paper, we study a largely overlooked issue of side-channel based PCO attacks: depending on the side-channel leakage strength, the practical realization of a PCO might provide a wrong answer with non-negligible probability. While most of the literature assumes (or practically builds) PCOs with negligible probability of error, it seems reasonable to ask what happens when the attacker is unable to do so. For instance, due to the use of dedicated side-channel countermeasures which reduce the amount of information that an attacker is able to capture through side-channel (see *e.g.* a formal study of masking in this context [1]).

The ultimate goal of a PCO attack is to recover all the digits of the private key. For each digit, the attacker queries an oracle whose response allows to walk down one step in a decision tree until the corresponding digit is fully recovered. The same process is repeated for each digit. Since the side-channel realization of this oracle might provide a wrong answer, a natural and widely used solution is to rely on majority-voting (see, *e.g.* [16]), i.e. each step in descending the decision tree is taken based on the most frequent response obtained after repeated independent queries addressed to the oracle.

Over the past years, majority-voting (or its generalization to the likelihood ratio test) has thus become the method of choice for addressing the issue of noisy PCOs, and also the baseline for comparing advanced techniques for handling noisy PCOs [5,9,18]. Surprisingly, in all these works, majority voting (or likelihood ratio test) is always exploited in its most naive version. In particular, although natural, early abort strategies are never considered.

In this work, we propose to set a new baseline provided by the so-called *Sequential Probability Ratio Test* (SPRT for short). In its simplest expression, SPRT can be seen as an elegant early-abort strategy on top of majority-voting[1],

---

[1] More generally, SPRT can be seen as an elegant early-abort strategy on top of likelihood updating.

de facto reducing the number of oracle queries for free. To our knowledge, this is the first time that SPRT is proposed in the side channel context. This could be explained by the *online* nature of the early-abort strategy (the attacker must analyze a side-channel trace before the next side-channel acquisition), which could be an issue in some contexts. However, PCO attacks are inherently online side-channel attacks (at least for Kyber) and therefore the use of SPRT does not add new constraints for the attacker.

As with the literature on this subject, while all our contributions are presented in the context of Kyber, they are completely generic and would also apply to any KEM based on the re-encryption framework.

Related Works:

In [20], the authors tackled a Kyber implementation involving side-channel countermeasures with a deep-learning trained PCO which revealed a relatively high probability of error. In order to reduce this probability of error, their solution refined the majority-voting test into a more general likelihood ratio test by exploiting all the deep-learning network output information.

To our knowledge, only four recent papers propose sophisticated solutions to the issue of noisy oracles, namely Guo *et al.* [5] and Shen *et al.* [18] in 2023, Li *et al.* [9] in 2025, and a very recent preprint[2] from Hermelink, Mårtensson and Tran [6] of particular interest.

We first observe that the SCA-LDPC attack *on Kyber* from [5] exploits the Full Domain (FD) oracle model (this is also the case for the more recent [3]). However, such an oracle model represents a much more powerful attacker than the PCO model and therefore goes beyond the scope of this paper. Although the use of SPRT in this model may also have some impact, we leave this investigation for future work.

We present and analyze [18] and [9] in details in Sects. 6 and 7 respectively. We show that the usage of SPRT as the proper baseline reduces their complexity gains to almost nothing at best, and even incur significant negative returns in the worst cases.

The results presented in [6] by Hermelink *et al.* are based on joint-probabilities and soft-analytic techniques that are particularly relevant in the multi-plaintext setting. Yet, their approach also applies in the single PCO case. We present comparisons with our new baseline in both cases in Sect. 8.

Contributions and Paper Organization:

In Sect. 2 we present the notations used throughout this paper, and all necessary information about our target key encapsulation scheme ML-KEM. We recall the principles of plaintext checking (and multi-plaintext checking) oracle attacks in Sect. 3. In Sect. 4, we then explain how these idealized oracles are implemented

---

[2] We thank the anonymous reviewer for bringing this important article to our attention, which we had missed during the initial submission.

in real life using side-channel analysis and we introduce the concept of *noisy* plaintext checking oracles. Our contributions follow:

- In Sect. 4.4 we show that side-channel based noisy oracles should not be handled with the traditional likelihood ratio test but with the SPRT, an elegant early-abort strategy built on top of the likelihood ratio test. Our simulations demonstrate that the use of SPRT results in dividing the number of oracle queries by a factor ranging from 2 to 3, at no extra cost.
- In Sect. 5, we propose a simple, yet effective way to improve the multi-plaintext checking oracle attack from Tanaka *et al.* [19]. We show that their approach can be combined with SPRT when the oracle is noisy.
- In Sect. 6, we study the recent attack from [9]. This algorithm is well adapted to muti-plaintext checking oracles and has been specifically developed to handle noisy oracles. We demonstrate that the use of SPRT as the baseline instead of majority voting significantly reduces or voids the complexity gains claimed in [9]: from the claimed -43.9% gain we end up with a modest -12% gain in the best case (very low level of noise). In the worst case (*i.e.* higher level of noise) [9] solution incurs a drastic penalty of $+63.4\%$ compared to the new baseline (see Tables 4 and 5).
- In Sect. 7, we study another recent algorithm [18] proposed to handle noisy oracles, in the specific case of a single plaintext checking oracle. We show that the use of SPRT as the baseline considerably reduces the complexity gain claimed in [18]: from -63.7% down to -18.8% gain in the best case (very low level of noise) to a $+18.8\%$ penalty in the worst cases (higher level of noise) (see Tables 8 and 9). Yet, we show that combining SPRT together with the approach from [18] is advantageous: the resulting algorithm is much simpler and results in the best attack complexity.
- Finally, in Sect. 8, we compare the SPRT approach with the techniques proposed in [6]. In the multi-plaintext setting, the BP approach from Harmelink*et al.* allows to reduce the number of oracle queries by a factor close to two at the cost of a significant increase in complexity. In the single PCO model, SPRT has to be favoured since it requires slightly fewer traces while remaining less expensive.

2   Notations and ML-KEM

In this section, we introduce the notations used in this paper. We recall the set of algorithms from the CRYSTAL-Kyber suite, in particular the CPA Public Key Encryption scheme and CCA Key Encapsulation Mechanism. We also give the NIST standardized (under ML-KEM) security parameters. For more details about these algorithms, we refer to their specifications [10].

2.1   Notations

Let $R = \mathbb{Z}[X]/(X^n + 1)$, $R_q = \mathbb{Z}_q[X]/(X^n + 1)$ with $q = 3329$ a prime number and $n = 2^8$. For a distribution ψ, $x \xleftarrow{\$} \psi$ denotes a random sample from ψ,

$x \xleftarrow{\$} \psi^n$ denotes n random, independent samples from ψ and $x \xleftarrow{\sigma} \psi$ denotes the deterministic sample of the coin σ from ψ. The same notations hold when is ψ a set, in this case the random samples are drawn uniformly from the set ψ.

Moreover, $U(q)$ designates the uniform distribution over the set $\mathbb{Z}_q$ and β_η the centered binomial distribution implemented as $\sum_{i=1}^{\eta}(a_i - b_i)$, with $a_i, b_i \xleftarrow{\$} \{0,1\}$ for all $i = 1, \ldots, \eta$.

A vector of n bits or a polynomial in R_q will be both denoted with small caps, $e.g.$ x. And the ith coefficient of x is $x[i-1]$ ($i.e.$ the indexes start at 0). A vector or set of polynomials will be denoted with bold font ($e.g.$ $\mathbf{x}$), whereas a matrix of polynomials with bold capital font ($e.g.$ $\mathbf{A}$).

Finally, $\lceil s \rfloor$ denotes the closest integer from the value s (and when s is at equal distance between two integers, the greater of the two is chosen), $|s|$ the absolute value of s and $\Pr(A)$ the probability of event A.

2.2 CRYSTAL-Kyber PKE Scheme

With the above notations, we recall hereafter the CRYSTAL-Kyber PKE scheme, with its three algorithms: key generation, encryption and decryption. Security parameters are recalled in Table 1.

Algorithm 1. Kyber.CPAPKE.KeyGen():

Output: $(\mathbf{pk}, \mathbf{sk})$ with $\mathbf{pk} \in R_q^{k \times k} \times R_q^k$ and $\mathbf{sk} \in R_q^k$

1: $(\rho, \sigma) \xleftarrow{\$} \{0,1\}^{256} \times \{0,1\}^{256}$
2: $\mathbf{A} \xleftarrow{\rho} U(q)^{k \times k}$
3: $(\mathbf{s}, \mathbf{e}) \xleftarrow{\sigma} \beta_{\eta_1}^k \times \beta_{\eta_1}^k$
4: $\mathbf{t} \leftarrow \mathbf{As} + \mathbf{e}$
5: $\mathbf{pk} \leftarrow (\mathbf{A}, \mathbf{t})$
6: $\mathbf{sk} \leftarrow \mathbf{s}$
7: **return** $(\mathbf{pk}, \mathbf{sk})$

Algorithm 2. Kyber.CPAPKE.Dec($\mathbf{sk}, \mathbf{c}$):

Input: Secret key $\mathbf{sk} \in R_q^k$ and Ciphertext $\mathbf{c} := (\mathbf{c_1}, c_2)$
Output: Message m
1: $\mathbf{u'} := \mathsf{Decompress}_q(\mathbf{c_1}, d_u)$
2: $v' := \mathsf{Decompress}_q(c_2, d_v)$
3: $m' \leftarrow v' - \mathbf{sk}^T \mathbf{u'}$
4: $m := \mathsf{Compress}_q(m', 1)$
5: **return** m

Algorithm 3. Kyber.CPAPKE.Enc($\mathbf{pk}, m, r$):

Input: Public key $\mathbf{pk} := (\mathbf{A}, \mathbf{t})$ with $A \in R_q^{k \times k}$ and $t \in R_q^k$
Input: Message $m \in \{0,1\}^{256}$
Input: Random coin $r \in \{0,1\}^{256}$
Output: Ciphertext $\mathbf{c} := (\mathbf{u}, v)$
  1: $(\mathbf{r}, \mathbf{e}_1, e_2) \xleftarrow{r} \beta_{\eta_1}^k \times \beta_{\eta_2}^k \times \beta_{\eta_2}$
  2: $\mathbf{u}' \leftarrow \mathbf{A}^T \mathbf{r} + \mathbf{e}_1$
  3: $v' \leftarrow \mathbf{t}^T \mathbf{r} + e_2 + \left\lceil \frac{q}{2} \right\rfloor m$
  4: $\mathbf{u} := \mathsf{Compress}_q(\mathbf{u}', d_u)$
  5: $v := \mathsf{Compress}_q(v', d_v)$
  6: **return** $(\mathbf{u}, v)$

The $\mathsf{Compress}_q$ and $\mathsf{Decompress}_q$ functions are defined as:

$$\mathsf{Compress}_q(x, d) = \left\lceil (2^d/q) \cdot x \right\rfloor \bmod 2^d$$

$$\mathsf{Decompress}_q(x, d) = \left\lceil (q/2^d) \cdot x \right\rfloor$$

2.3 ML-KEM

From the PKE scheme of Kyber, a key encapsulation mechanism is constructed (standardized under the name ML-KEM [10]. It is based on a variant of the FO (Fujisaki-Okamoto) transform [4] to ensure IND-CCA2 security.

The Kyber.CCAKEM.Decaps($\mathbf{sk}', \mathbf{c}$) algorithm is the target of the plaintext-checking oracle attacks (that can be seen as a subclass of the *key-mismatch* attacks) studied in this paper. In order to avoid chosen ciphertexts attacks, the FO-transform ensures that the Kyber.CCAKEM.Decaps input $\mathbf{c}$ is correct, otherwise the decapsulated session key K is not output by the algorithm. To this end, after the decryption of the ciphertext $\mathbf{c}$ into the message $\hat{m}$, the message is re-encrypted into $\hat{\mathbf{c}}$ and the equality of $\mathbf{c}$ and $\hat{\mathbf{c}}$ is verified.

Algorithm 4. Kyber.CCAKEM.KeyGen():

Output: Public key $\mathbf{pk}$ and Secret key $\mathbf{sk}'$
  1: $z \xleftarrow{\$} \{0,1\}^{256}$
  2: $(\mathbf{pk}, \mathbf{sk}) \leftarrow$ Kyber.CPAKEM.Keygen()
  3: $\mathbf{sk}' := (\mathbf{sk}\|\mathbf{pk}\|\mathbf{H}(\mathbf{pk})\|z)$
  4: **return** $(\mathbf{pk}, \mathbf{sk}')$

In the above algorithms, J, G and H are hash functions based on the Keccak permutation.

Algorithm 5. Kyber.CCAKEM.Encaps(**pk**):

Input: Public key $\mathbf{pk} := (\mathbf{A}, \mathbf{t})$

1: $m' \xleftarrow{\$} \{0,1\}^{256}$
2: $(K, r) \leftarrow \mathbf{G}(m\|\mathbf{H}(\mathbf{pk}))$
3: $\mathbf{c} \leftarrow$ Kyber.CPAKEM.Enc($\mathbf{pk}, m, r$)
4: **return** $(\mathbf{c}, K)$

Algorithm 6. Kyber.CCAKEM.Decaps($\mathbf{sk'}, \mathbf{c}$):

Input: Ciphertext $\mathbf{c} := (\mathbf{c}_1, c_2)$, secret key $\mathbf{sk'} := (\mathbf{sk}\|\mathbf{pk}\|\mathbf{H}(\mathbf{pk})\|z)$
Output: Shared key K

1: $\hat{m} \leftarrow$ Kyber.CPAPKE.Dec($\mathbf{sk}, \mathbf{c}$)
2: $(K, r') \leftarrow \mathbf{G}(\hat{m}\|\mathbf{H}(\mathbf{pk}))$
3: $\hat{\mathbf{c}} \leftarrow$ Kyber.CPAKEM.Enc($\mathbf{pk}, \hat{m}, r'$)
4: **if** $\mathbf{c} \neq \hat{\mathbf{c}}$ **then**
5:      $K := \mathbf{J}(z\|\mathbf{c}))$
6: **return** K

2.4   Parameters

Table 1. Parameter sets of ML-KEM

parameter sets	n	k	q	η_1	η_2	d_U	d_V
Kyber512	256	2	3329	3	2	10	4
Kyber768	256	3	3329	2	2	10	4
Kyber1024	256	4	3329	2	2	11	5

3   Attack on Kyber Using Plaintext Checking Oracles

3.1   Plaintext Checking Oracles

Following the seminal work of Huguenin-Dumittan and Vaudenay [7], one can define a *single* PCO as follows. Let $\bar{m}$ be an arbitrarily chosen reference plaintext, and Dec(sk, c) a generic decryption procedure. Then, a PCO can be defined as:

$$\mathcal{O}(c, \bar{m}) = \begin{cases} 1 & \text{if Dec}(sk, c) = \bar{m} \\ 0 & \text{otherwise.} \end{cases} \tag{1}$$

In [19], the authors extend the single PCO to multiple reference plaintexts $\{\bar{m}_i\}_{0 \leq i < n}$. The so-called *multi-plaintext checking oracle* (M-PCO) is defined as:

$$\mathcal{O}(c, \{\bar{m}_i\}_{0 \leq i < n}) = i \ \text{ iff } \ \text{Dec}(sk, c) = \bar{m}_i \tag{2}$$

It is worth noticing that the above oracle is well defined since the forged cyphertext c can only decrypt to one of the $\bar{m}_i$ by construction (see Sect. 3.3).

In all the previous works (starting with [7]), the authors assume that $\bar{m} = 0$ in the case of a single PCO and, that $\bar{m}_i$ is the null vector except for the first $\lceil \log_2(n) \rceil$ coefficients that encode the binary representation of i for $0 \leq i < n$ in the case of a M-PCO. Moreover n is chosen to be a power of 2. We shall use the same assumptions in the sequel.

In the rest of this section we will detail the key-recovery PCO and M-PCO attacks on Kyber. In Sect. 4, we shall define *noisy* versions of these oracles that can be constructed in practice through side-channel analysis.

3.2   Plaintext Checking Oracle Attack

The attack will recover, one by one, each of the 256 coefficients of the k polynomials in R_q that form Kyber secret key $\mathbf{sk}$. To this end, the attacker creates specific ciphertexts $\mathbf{c} = (\mathbf{c_1}, c_2)$ and send them through Kyber.CCAKEM.Decaps (Algorithm 6). From the description of Kyber.CPAPKE.Dec (Algorithm 2), we have the following computation of the decompressed message m':

$$m' = v' - \mathbf{sk}^T \mathbf{u'},$$

where $\mathbf{u'} = \mathsf{Decompress}_q(\mathbf{c_1}, d_u)$ and $v' = \mathsf{Decompress}_q(c_2, d_v)$. By choosing $\mathbf{c_1}$ such that all its polynomials are null except for a single one, it can be easily checked that $\mathbf{u'}$ has the same structure and the above equation rewrites:

$$m' = v' - sk \times u', \tag{3}$$

where u' (*resp.* c_1) denotes the non-null polynomial of $\mathbf{u'}$ (*resp.* $\mathbf{c_1}$) and sk the corresponding polynomial of $\mathbf{sk}$. In all the following we will then, *w.l.o.g.*, consider a unique polynomial.

Now recall that the decrypted message m is the 256 long binary vector $m = \mathsf{Compress}_q(m', 1)$. The attacker will construct ciphertexts (c_1, c_2) such that m is the null vector except for its first element and $m[0]$ depends on the value of a single coefficient of sk, say $sk[i]$ for some $0 \leq i < 256,$.

In order to recover $sk[i]$, one first needs to shift its position to the first one. This is possible thanks to u': by taking $u' = -\alpha X^{256-i}$, for some non-null value α, it is easy to see that the first coefficient of m' will be

$$m'[0] = v'[0] + \alpha sk[i]$$

If we take α such that, $\forall s \in \{-\eta_1, -\eta_1 + 1, \cdots, \eta_1\}, \mathsf{Compress}_q(\alpha s, 1) = 0$, then by setting v' a constant polynomial (*i.e.* $v'[i] = 0$ for $i = 1, \ldots, 255$), the message $m = \mathsf{Compress}_q(v' - sk \times u', 1)$ has all its coefficients equel to zero except the first one, whose value is:

$$m[0] = \mathsf{Compress}_q(v'[0] + \alpha sk[i], 1) = \begin{cases} 0 & \text{if } |(v'[0] + \alpha sk[i]) \bmod q - \frac{q}{2}| > \lceil \frac{q}{4} \rceil \\ 1 & \text{otherwise} \end{cases}$$

Since $sk[i] \in \{-\eta_1, \cdots, \eta_1\}$, for well chosen values of $v'[0]$ and α, one can divide the search space by 2. For instance:

$$m[0] = \mathsf{Compress}_q(v'[0] + \alpha sk[i], 1) = \begin{cases} 0 & \text{if } sk[i] \leq 0 \\ 1 & \text{otherwise} \end{cases}$$

The attack will then adaptively choose successive values of $v'[0]$ and follow a binary search (as illustrated in Fig. 1). Since the search space is of size $2\eta_1 + 1$, the attacker can expect to recover the value of a coefficient in about $\lceil \log_2(2\eta_1 + 1) \rceil$ oracle queries, assuming that the tree is balanced.

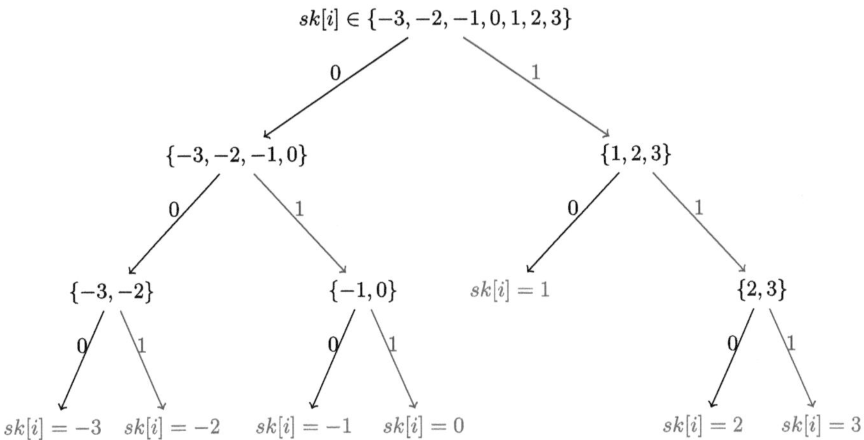

Fig. 1. A *balanced* binary research tree for Kyber512.

Taking into account the fact that the coefficients of sk are randomly drawn from the centered binomial distribution β_{η_1}, Qin *et al.* [14] were able to exhibit, in the case of Kyber 512 (*resp.* 768, 1024), a lower bound on the average calls to the oracle: 2.375 (*resp.* 2.125, 2.125). Moreover, they propose the most efficient binary tree for the search: for Kyber 512 (*resp.* 768, 1024), this tree results in 2.56 (*resp.* 2.31, 2.31) calls on average to the oracle.

Notwithstanding the fact that our contributions are completely independent from the choice of the selected binary tree, our costs estimations for the PCO attacks will be conducted with [14] so-called *optimal tree*.

Assuming that the binary search has an average number of calls to the oracle of o to retrieve a key coefficient, the overall attack will require $k \times 256 \times o$ calls in average. It can be observed that if the oracle answers incorrectly once during this whole attack process, it will affect a unique coefficient. It is usually observed in the literature (when considering oracles that can be sometimes wrong) that a single coefficient error in the final key (at an unknown position) can be brute-forced (this is true for all versions of Kyber). Therefore, an oracle that would answer incorrectly with probability $p_e = \frac{1}{k \times 256 \times o}$ would be *correct enough* to apply the above attack. For Kyber-1024, with the optimal tree, this corresponds to $p_e \approx 5 \cdot 10^{-4}$. Hence, we often find in the literature the threshold $p_e = 10^{-4}$, and equivalently the success rate's lower bound $\sigma = 1 - 10^{-4}$ for a *correct enough* oracle.

3.3 Multi-plaintext Checking Oracle Attack

Tanaka *et al.* [19] show that the access to a M-PCO (as defined in Sect. 3.1) allows to reduce the number of oracle queries. Moreover, they demonstrate that such an oracle can be built in practice from side-channel leakages.

Following [19], the number of references messages will be set to 2^N. Moreover, $\forall i \in \{0, \cdots, 2^N - 1\}$ and $\forall j \in \{0, \cdots, 255\}, \bar{m}_i[j] = \lfloor \frac{i}{2^j} \rfloor \bmod 2$. In practice, N cannot be very large because the number of reference messages (and then the cost of the oracle's training) grows exponentially with N, *w.l.o.g.* we will take $N = 8$ in our cost estimations.

From the above description, the extension from single plaintext to multi-plaintext is quite straightforward: for some block index $a \in \{0, \cdots, 255 - N\}$, we now define

$$u' = -\alpha \cdot X^{256-a} \text{ and } v' = \sum_{i=0}^{N-1} \beta_i X^i$$

with α as before and for some chosen coefficient values β_i. We then have $m = \mathsf{Compress}_q(v' - sk \times u', 1)$ with all its coefficients null but the N firsts, whose values are, for $0 \leq i < N$,

$$m[i] = \mathsf{Compress}_q(\beta_i + \alpha sk[a + i], 1)$$

$$= \begin{cases} 0 & \text{if } |(\beta_i + \alpha sk[a+i]) \bmod q - \frac{q}{2}| > \lceil \frac{q}{4} \rfloor \\ 1 & \text{otherwise} \end{cases}$$

Hence, m takes the value of one of the reference plaintexts, depending on the values $(\beta_i, \alpha, sk[a + i])$, and the oracle will tell which one. This allows to work simultaneously (and without dependence since the β_i can be chosen independently from each others) on N consecutive key coefficients. When the binary search is finished for all of them, the next block is processed. This is extremely powerful and results in a gain up to 87% oracle calls (see [19]) compared to the single plaintext oracle approach.

Let us remark that the authors of [19] also show that, for Kyber 512[3], the *optimal tree* [14] is too unbalanced (its longest path leads to 4 oracle calls) and should be replaced by a more balanced binary tree (that has a maximum of 3 oracle calls). This comes from the fact that in the M-PCO attack, all coefficient of a block must be retrieved before starting to work on the next block. In Sect. 5, we will show how to slightly relax this constraint and improve the overall cost of M-PCO attacks.

---

[3] For Kyber 768 and 1024, there is no difference.

4   Noisy Plaintext Checking Oracles

We have seen that the (M-)PCOs defined in Sect. 3 lead to efficient key-recovery attacks on Kyber. In practice, such oracles are usually built from side-channel leakages, see *e.g.* [9,18–20]. In this context, and very often in practice, the oracle may answer incorrectly with some non-null probability, we will refer to a *noisy oracle* (and denote it $\tilde{\mathcal{O}}$). In the literature, the considered noisy oracles have often a very small probability of error, and few papers actually tackle the issue of non-negligible error probabilities. This is however typically what one would expect from a Kyber implementation embedding side-channel countermeasures (*e.g.* masking). For instance, [20] considers masked implementations and indeed, in this case, the oracle error probability is important.

A naive, yet effective, way to handle this noise is to make repeated calls to the oracle and choose the most frequent answer: this is the *majority-voting* approach. As we will see, side-channel based PCOs provide richer information than just a binary value. This extra information can be used to reduce the number of repeated calls thanks to a probability ratio test (as it is done in [20] and traditionally in profiled side-channel analysis literature). In this section, we will first properly define a noisy oracle based on side-channel leakages, recall the classical approach of Probability Ratio Testing (PRT for short) and then introduce the Wald's test [21] (or Sequential Probability Ratio Test, SPRT for short). We will show that using the latter allow to divide the number of repeated oracle calls by a factor between 2 and 3. We will see that SPRT is just PRT with early-arbort and has then a unique drawback: making the attack *online* (the attacker cannot harvest the side-channel traces in advance). This drawback does not apply for PCO attacks since they are already online attacks due to the decision tree procedure presented in the previous section.

To our knowledge – in the context of PCO attack on Kyber – there are only two papers that specifically focus on strongly noisy oracles, namely [9, 18], which propose high-level attack procedures to cope with the noise. These two approaches will be presented and compared to in the next Sects. 7 and 6 respectively.

4.1   Practical Considerations

Many recent publications (see, *e.g.*, [9,12,18–20,23]) demonstrate that the message value can be reliably recovered using profiled side-channel analysis. These publications focus on different implementations of Kyber (and other FO-transform based KEM schemes), on different Hardware technology and using different side-channel acquisition chains. We identify two main reasons to explain the success of these attacks in practice:

– As recalled in [1], the side-channel attacker is in a very advantageous position compared to classical (profiled) side-channel analysis contexts. The manipulation of $\hat{m}$ (see line 2 and 3 of Algorithm 6) results in *"[...] hundreds,*

thousands or even millions of intermediate bytes/words" that are deterministically determined by the value $\hat{m}$. Moreover, in its simple form, the oracle
only needs to distinguish two different messages (which, thanks to the hash
function $\mathbf{G}$, have nothing in common very quickly during the computation).
- As recalled in many of the cited publications, the side-channel profiling step
  can be executed directly on the target device. Indeed, for any chosen message
  $\hat{m}$ it is easy to build a ciphertext $\mathbf{c} = (\mathbf{c_1}, \mathbf{c_2})$ which will be decrypted (for all
  secret key $\mathbf{sk}$) into $\hat{m}$.

To our knowledge, this situation is unique in the field of side-channel and gives
to the attacker a huge advantage that results in very efficient attacks, even when
the implementation involves side-channel countermeasures.

The purpose of this paper is not to provide another proof that this threat is
real, but to show that, even in the case where the oracle is not perfect (and then
answers with some relatively high probability of error), these kind of attacks are
more efficient than expected from the state-of-the-art.

Concretely, there are two different approaches in the literature to construct
an oracle in practice: using template profiling or deep-learning (DL for short)
training. In both cases, the attacker must run the Kyber.CCAKEM.Decaps algorithm over chosen ciphertexts that decrypt into the reference message $\bar{m}$ (or, in
case of multi-plaintext, one of the messages $\bar{m}_i$) and train the DL network (or
equivalently infer the multivariate Gaussian distribution for the templates) with
the captured side-channel execution traces. In the following section, we formally
define the *noisy* PCOs that result from this training.

4.2   Noisy Plaintext Checking Oracles Definition

Let us consider a side-channel attacker able to capture a side-channel execution
trace l during the execution of Kyber.Decaps(c, sk) for a chosen value of c and
an unknown key sk. We define a generic noisy PCO as follows (given a reference
message $\bar{m}$):

$$\tilde{\mathcal{O}}(c, \bar{m}, l) = \Pr(\mathrm{Dec}(sk, c) = \bar{m}|l)$$

and a noisy M-PCO (given multiple reference plaintexts $\{\bar{m}_i\}_{0 \leq i < n}$):

$$\tilde{\mathcal{O}}(c, \{\bar{m}_i\}_{0 \leq i < n}, l) = \{\Pr(\mathrm{Dec}(sk, c) = \bar{m}_i|l)\}_{0 \leq i < n}$$

Note that these definitions are slightly more general than what is usually
found in the literature, and provide more granularity. From a noisy oracle, we
can define its *Bernoulli* version, denoted $\tilde{\mathcal{O}}_{\mathcal{B}}$, which is more common in the
literature:

$$\tilde{\mathcal{O}}_{\mathcal{B}}(c, \bar{m}, l) = \begin{cases} 1 & \text{if } \tilde{\mathcal{O}}(c, \bar{m}, l) > 0.5 \\ 0 & \text{otherwise.} \end{cases}$$

Equivalently, for the noisy M-PCO, its (categorical) Bernoulli version is:

$$\tilde{\mathcal{O}}_{\mathcal{B}}(c, \{\bar{m}_i\}_{0 \leq i < n}, l) = \mathrm{argmax}_i(\tilde{\mathcal{O}}(c, \{\bar{m}_i\}_{0 \leq i < n}, l))$$

For the Bernoulli versions of the oracles, one can define a probability p_e of giving an erroneous answer (it can be computed analytically if the probability mass function of the corresponding noisy oracle is known, or estimated – by submitting traces with known labels[4]). The popularity of the Bernoulli oracle in the literature certainly comes from their simplicity and notably the fact that one can compare attack algorithms costs with respect to the unique parameter p_e. Hence, when comparing our results with the literature, we will need to use these Bernoulli versions.

However, they are truncated version of the original noisy oracles, since part of the information is lost. And in fact, as observed in [20], the side-channel based oracles (built from template profiling or DL training) coincide with our original definition.

From a Noisy M-PCO to N Noisy PCOs. The M-PCO attack principle is recalled in Sect. 3.3, when the oracle is not noisy. In this case, with a single call to the oracle, the attacker retrieves information about n key coefficients and will treat these n information independently (n independent decision trees are followed) as if, these information were coming from n distinct calls to a PCO. To this end, the reference messages set cannot be arbitrarily selected, in fact they are chosen such that $\bar{m}_i$ (which is a vector of 256 binary coefficients) $N = \lceil \log_2(n) \rceil$ first coefficients coincide with the binary representation of i and the rest is set to 0. In this specific context, the above definition of a noisy M-PCO is not adapted, and, *w.l.o.g.*, one can transform such an oracle as follows:

$$\widetilde{\mathcal{MO}}(c, \{\bar{m}_i\}_{0 \leq i < N}, l) = \{\mathrm{Pr}(\mathrm{Dec}(sk, c)[i] = 0 | l)\}_{0 \leq i < N},$$

where $\mathrm{Dec}(sk, c)[i]$ is the ith coefficient of $\mathrm{Dec}(sk, c)$.

And we have, for $0 \leq i < N$:

$$\mathrm{Pr}(\mathrm{Dec}(sk, c)[i] = 0 | l) = \sum_{m_j \ s.t. \ m_j[i]=0} \mathrm{Pr}(\mathrm{Dec}(sk, c) = \bar{m}_j | l)$$

One can remark that, for $0 \leq j < n$:

$$\mathrm{Pr}(\mathrm{Dec}(sk, c) = \bar{m}_j | l) = \prod_{i=0}^{N-1} \mathrm{Pr}(\mathrm{Dec}(sk, c)[i] = \bar{m}_j[i] | l)$$

Therefore $\widetilde{\mathcal{MO}}(c, \{\bar{m}_i\}_{0 \leq i < N}, l)$ and $\tilde{\mathcal{O}}(c, \{\bar{m}_i\}_{0 \leq i < s}, l)$ are completely equivalent, since it is possible to construct one from the other and vice versa.

We then end up with N *virtual* (because they come from a single oracle call) noisy single PCO. Following the attack strategy, we choose to handle them independently. We hence only have to focus on noisy single PCOs in the rest of this section.

---

[4] For instance, the traces from the validation set that was used for the oracle training.

First let us present the natural *Probability Ratio Testing* (*PRT* for short) which is systematically used in the literature. Then we will introduce Wald's test [21] (or *Sequential Probability Ratio Testing, SPRT* for short) in this context.

4.3　PRT Applied to a Noisy Plaintext-Checking Oracle

Given a side-channel sample l, the probability mass function of the associated message m being equal to the reference message $\bar{m}$ (or not) is directly given by the noisy PCO call:

$$\tilde{\mathcal{O}}(c, \bar{m}, l) = \Pr(\mathrm{Dec}(sk, c) = \bar{m}|l) = 1 - \Pr(\mathrm{Dec}(sk, c) \neq \bar{m}|l)$$

In a more general setting, this oracle can be seen as two probability mass functions:

$$f(l, \theta_0) = \Pr(\mathrm{Dec}(sk, c) = \bar{m}|l)$$
$$f(l, \theta_1) = \Pr(\mathrm{Dec}(sk, c) \neq \bar{m}|l)$$

where θ_0 (*resp.* θ_1) is the distribution parameter of the side-channel data when Kyber.CCAKEM.Decaps manipulates a decrypted message $m = \bar{m}$ (*resp.* $m \neq \bar{m}$).

As previously stated, in a noisy oracle context (*i.e.* $f(l, \theta_i)$ takes other values than just 0 or 1), the attacker will repeatedly request the oracle with side-channel data $\{l_i\}_{0 \leq i < T}$ generated from T executions of Kyber.CCAKEM.Decaps over a single crafted ciphertext c. From this data, the attacker wants to choose (with a very small error probability) between one of these two hypotheses:

$$\mathbf{H}_0 : m = \bar{m}$$
$$\mathbf{H}_1 : m \neq \bar{m}$$

where m is the decrypted message from the ciphertext c. In the setting of a side-channel attack, the hypotheses are fully symmetric: accepting $\mathbf{H}_0$ is rejecting $\mathbf{H}_1$ and vice versa.

Let

$$\Lambda_T = \prod_{i=0}^{T-1} \frac{f(l_i, \theta_0)}{f(l_i, \theta_1)}$$

be the *likelihood ratio* between these two distributions. Assuming that the oracle is properly estimated (*i.e.* the profiling step has converged), the NeymanPearson lemma [11] tells us that Λ_T is the strongest metric to accept or reject hypothesis $\mathbf{H}_0$. This test relies on reasonable assumptions about the distributions regularity conditions, which we assume to hold throughout the sequel. Interested readers shall refer to, *e.g.*, [8, Theorem 12.4.2] for a proper definition of these assumptions. In our simple symmetric case, the test can be re-stated as:

$$\text{accept } \mathbf{H}_0 \; \textit{if } \Lambda_T \geq 1$$
$$\text{accept } \mathbf{H}_1 \; \textit{if } \Lambda_T < 1$$

This probability ratio test of hypothesis (so-called *likelihood test*) is typically followed in all the literature of (profiled) side-channel analysis (since the seminal work of Chari *et al.* [2]), often without mentioning it. For instance, the authors of [20] strictly apply this test over the a trained DL network and compare the message complexity of their attack to the majority-voting approach. It can be observed that the majority-voting approach is equivalent to conducting the likelihood test over an oracle that involves Bernoulli distributions (*i.e.* the so-called Bernoulli oracle in the previous section) with the probability of error p_e as parameter.

In the classical Gaussian template setting, the probability mass functions follows a multivariate Gaussian distribution where the mean and covariance matrix have been estimated during the profiling phase. For DL-based approaches, as experimented in [20] on two very classical network architectures (namely a CNN and a MLP), one can also extract from the trained network the probability score for an oracle query. The neural network then directly acts as an oracle to the distribution probability mass function.

It is hard to tell, a priori, what will be the best tool to build the oracle (DL or template), it will depend on the target processor and the means of capturing the sensitive leakages. We can remark however that, while it is always possible to turn a noisy oracle into a Bernoulli oracle (as seen in the previous section), this is not a good idea as it usually means loosing information (as observed in [20]). Except in specific contexts where oracles are trained on insufficient traces, or for certain DL architectures that do not provide reliable probability scores.

Be that as it may, most of the literature on PCO attacks illustrate their work on a Bernoulli oracle, for its simplicity but also maybe to avoid over-tuning a method for a specific profiling technique or leakage function.

4.4   SPRT Applied to a Noisy Plaintext-Checking Oracle

In this section, we present the *Sequential Probability Ratio Testing* (*SPRT* for short), also referred to as Wald's test [21] in the literature. The seminal work of Wald in the early 1940's has had a profound impact in extremely diverse scientific domains, from medical studies to econometrics. Extensions and improvements of the Wald's test have been proposed in many different cases, depending on the a priori knowledge of the experimenter: the number of distributions, theirs forms, etc. Surprisingly, as far as we know, it was never considered in the field of side-channel analysis.

However, (supervised) side-channel analysis perfectly fits the basic setup of Wald's test, and we will see that it is particularly interesting in the case of PCO attacks.

Algorithm 7. Sequential Probability Ratio Test (SPRT)

Input: Hypotheses $\mathbf{H}_0, \mathbf{H}_1$ with densities $f(\cdot, \theta_0)$ and $f(\cdot, \theta_1)$
Input: Error probabilities α, β
Output: Decision: accept $\mathbf{H}_0$ or $\mathbf{H}_1$

  1: $t \leftarrow 0$
  2: $\Lambda_0^{\log} \leftarrow 0$
  3: $A \leftarrow \log\left(\dfrac{\alpha}{1-\beta}\right)$
  4: $B \leftarrow \log\left(\dfrac{1-\alpha}{\beta}\right)$
  5: **while** true **do**
  6:     Obtain a new observation l_t from the oracle
  7:     $\Lambda_{t+1}^{\log} \leftarrow \Lambda_t^{\log} + \log f(l_t, \theta_0) - \log f(l_t, \theta_1)$
  8:     $t \leftarrow t + 1$
  9:     **if** $\Lambda_t^{\log} \leq A$ **then**
10:        **return Accept $\mathbf{H}_0$**   ▷ Type I error: α
11:     **else if** $\Lambda_t^{\log} \geq B$ **then**
12:        **return Accept $\mathbf{H}_1$**   ▷ Type II error: β

Applying Wald's test in our context is straightforward as it is directly based on the likelihood test. It can be seen as an *early abort* strategy in the likelihood test (which is inherently a fixed sample-size test). In our context, this early abort strategy will have a huge impact on the message complexity of the attack. And it is pretty easy to see it: the value of T (the number of repeated calls to the noisy oracle) must be high enough such that wrongly accepting $\mathbf{H}_0$ happens with very low error probability (a typical chosen value for this error probability is 10^{-4}, see Sect. 3.2). It can be observed that the likelihood ratio value Λ_T actually provides a direct information on the probability of error of accepting or rejecting $\mathbf{H}_0$ (the closer Λ_T is to 1, the higher is the probability of error). Hence, in many cases, one can safely stop the oracle calls before reaching T.

In the SPRT process, the number of oracle requests is not a priori bounded and, at each new oracle output, the likelihood ratio is updated. At step t,

$$\Lambda_t = \prod_{i=0}^{t-1} \frac{f(l_i, \theta_0)}{f(l_i, \theta_1)},$$

and the test checks the value of Λ_t with respect to pre-defined thresholds A and B.

Algorithm 7 describes the complete SPRT procedure, with $\log(\Lambda_t)$ denoted as $\Lambda_t^{\log 5}$ and α and β the probability of Type 1 and Type 2 errors. In our symmetric context, one usually wants $\alpha = \beta = 10^{-4}$. Moreover, we denote by σ the expected probability of success, *i.e.* $\sigma = 1 - \alpha$.

---

[5] We use here the log likelihood notations as it is usually done in practice.

4.5   Oracle Cost Estimations and Comparisons

In order to estimate the impact of the use of SPRT in the PCO attacks, we conducted several simulations based on simple models: the Bernoulli oracle (as it is the most common in the literature) and the Gaussian template oracle.

For the former, we simply choose a probability of error p_e to define the Bernoulli distributions, p_e will take various values from (close to) 0 to 0.44. For the latter, we use a simple leakage model: pooled univariate Gaussian distribution. Hence, the message $m = 0$ (*resp.* $m = 1$) will produce a synthetic side-channel trace randomly drawn from a Gaussian distribution with mean μ_0 (*resp.* μ_1) and standard deviation s (common to 0 and 1). μ_0 (*resp.* μ_1) is arbitrarily set to 0 (*resp.* 1) while s will takes various values from 0 to 3.34. From $\mu_1 - \mu_0$ and s, we computed the error probability p_e of the Bernoulli version of this noisy oracle (s is then chosen such that the error probability spectrum is the same for both noisy oracles). This allows to draw the Bernoulli and Gaussian experiments on the same figure, for each error probability p_e tested.

Then, for each case, we systematically estimate, through simulations (over 10^6 tests), the average number of oracles calls in order to reach a decision ($m = 0$ or $m = 1$) with success probability $\sigma = 1 - 10^{-4}$. The experiments are conducted both for the likelihood test and Wald's test, the results are depicted in Fig. 2. On the right sub-figure, the ratio gain of using SPRT over likelihood is shown. Interestingly, for both types of distributions, the gain is very similar, it reaches 2 as soon as the oracle is noisy (*i.e.* when repeated calls are actually needed). It even gets close to 3 for highly noisy oracles ($p_e \geq .25$).

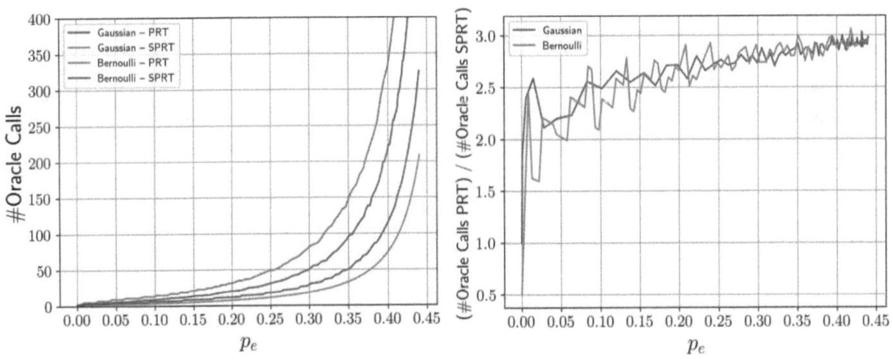

Fig. 2. Number of Oracle Calls Comparison for PRT vs. SPRT.

5   Impact on Noisy Multi-plaintext Checking Oracle Attacks

As explained in Sect. 3.3, the attack using a multi-plaintext checking oracle (M-PCO) does not use the optimal tree from [14] but the more balanced one instead.

Tanaka *et al.* [19] explain why: for each block, the total number of oracle calls for the full recovery of the block will be the highest number of calls among all coefficients of the block.

Let us consider the following example on Kyber-512. For the block $(sk[0], sk[1], sk[2], sk[3]) = (0, 2, -1, -3)$, if we are using the optimal tree, -3 is recovered in 4 oracle queries whereas 0 requires only 2 queries. Since the coefficients of a block are all retrieved together, one must make 4 queries in order to retrieve -3 even if 0 is already found.

Ideally, we would like to replace the finished coefficients by new ones as soon as possible, in order to remove the useless queries. However, if we want to treat blocks of coefficients that are not following each other, this would require the crafted Kyber ciphertext $c = (c_1, c_2)$ to be such that the polynomial c_1 has more than one non-null monomial. In turn, this would make a message coefficients dependent from two or more key coefficients (this comes from the polynomial multiplication in Eq. (3)). And, as far as we known, this situation does not allow to mount an attack.

All in all, the only degree of liberty the attacker has, is to choose a position a, a block length N and shift the block of N consecutive coefficients of sk into the N first positions. A simple, yet modest, improvement of the multi-plaintext checking oracle attack described in [19] is then, whenever the leading coefficient of a block has been found, to shift the selected block by one[6] coefficient instead of waiting for all the N coefficients of sk to be found before shifting by N as it was originally proposed.

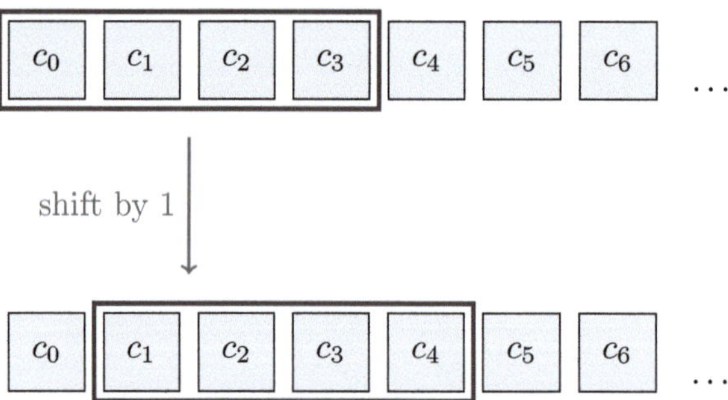

This transformation is at least as good as the classical method because we introduce flexibility in the positions of the blocks and then takes less oracle calls in average. We will still use the balanced tree as it gives better results, even with this shifting mechanism.

Table 2 gives the average number of calls to recover the full secrete key with a block size of $N = 8$ for a perfect (non-noisy) oracle (these averages have been estimated over 10^4 different secret keys, as it will be the case for all results shown in this section and the following). The discrepancy of results between Kyber 512

---

[6] In practice, if multiple leading coefficients are already known, the next block of computation will begin with the next unknown coefficient.

and the two others comes from the difference in the attack decision binary trees (see Sect. 3.2).

Table 3 shows the results for a noisy Bernoulli multi-plaintext oracle (for comparison purpose with the literature), depending on the use of majority-voting[7] (*i.e.* PRT) or SPRT and the use of shifting or not. As expected, the use of SPRT provides a huge benefit without any disadvantage. Moreover, it can be checked that the shifting method gives even better results when combined with SPRT. This comes from the fact that the standard deviation of the number of calls

Table 2. Comparison of calls between estimation of classical multi-plaintext attack from [19] and simulation of shifting multi-plaintext attacks for different versions of Kyber with $N = 8$, under the assumption of a perfect oracle.

Accuracy	Method	#TotalCalls
Kyber 512	Classical	192 *(ref)*
	Shifting	189.81 (1.1%)
Kyber 768	Classical	283.21 *(ref)*
	Shifting	253.82 (10.4%)
Kyber 1024	Classical	377.61 *(ref)*
	Shifting	338.18 (10.4%)

Table 3. Comparison of number of oracle calls and number of errors per key between majority voting and SPRT methods, with and without shifting, for all versions of Kyber. Block size $N = 8$ and noisy oracle with $p_e = 0.1$.

Accuracy	Method	#TotalCalls	#Error/#Coeff
Kyber 512	Classical MV (t=11)	2111.99 *(ref)*	0.007/512
	Shifting MV (t=11)	2087.95 (1.1%)	0.008/512
	Classical SPRT	1158.65 (45.1%)	0.001/512
	Shifting SPRT	1084.41 (48.7%)	0.000/512
Kyber 768	Classical MV (t=11)	3115.53 *(ref)*	0.012/768
	Shifting MV (t=11)	2792.34 (10.4%)	0.010/768
	Classical SPRT	1323.37 (57.5%)	0.015/768
	Shifting SPRT	1159.88 (62.8%)	0.013/768
Kyber 1024	Classical MV (t=11)	4153.44 *(ref)*	0.015/1024
	Shifting MV (t=11)	3721.96 (10.4%)	0.013/1024
	Classical SPRT	1763.45 (57.6%)	0.019/1024
	Shifting SPRT	1545.98 (62.8%)	0.020/1024

---

[7] They are denoted "MV ($t = 11$)" in the table, as the number of repetition is 11.

is quite high for SPRT (compared to PRT) and then benefits from the greater granularity of the new shifting method.

6   Grafting Tree

In [9] the authors propose an original method to correct key coefficients errors after a M-PCO attack with a noisy oracle. Their results (reproduced in Table 4) show significant gains (ranging from about -22% to -44% depending on the oracle's p_e). We will however advocate that the extent of these gains can be largely explained by their comparison to the naive majority voting approach, i.e. without using any early abort strategy. The core idea of [9] correction follows three steps:

1. Recover a *rough* coefficient $\hat{sk}[i]$ by performing the M-PCO attack
2. Build an optimal decision tree assuming that the value $\hat{sk}[i]$ is correct and perform the coefficient recovery using this tree. Compare the new value $\hat{sk}'[i]$ with $\hat{sk}[i]$. If they are the same, stop at this step and return $\hat{sk}[i]$.
3. Perform another coefficient recovery with the original tree and compare the new value $\hat{sk}''[i]$ to the others. If $\hat{sk}''[i] = \hat{sk}'[i]$, then return $\hat{sk}'[i]$, otherwise return $\hat{sk}[i]$.

The algorithm is well-suited to oracles that are moderately noisy. Indeed, as the number of errors in the first or second stage are relatively low, stage 3 is rarely required. Also, since the second tree is built assuming that $\hat{sk}[i]$ is correct, it only needs two calls to the oracle if $\hat{sk}[i]$ is confirmed. For noisier oracles, the authors use majority-voting to artificially raise the quality of the oracle to a more practical threshold. It is thus very easy and natural to replace the majority-voting with SPRT in their method.

For Kyber-1024[8] the authors of [9] propose different strategies depending on the oracle's probability of error (p_e):

- If $p_e \in [0.001; 0.017]$, the Grafting Tree method does not produce more than one incorrect coefficient per key (on average), so it can be used without majority-voting.
- If $p_e \in]0.017; 0.050]$, the authors propose to improve the quality of the oracle with majority-voting for the second and third steps only.
- If $pe > 0.050$, the authors propose to improve the quality of the oracle using majority-voting for all steps.

As a result, their approach uses majority-voting to reach a probability of error within the *healthy zone* $[0; 0.017]$.

Table 4, which is directly extracted from [9], shows the comparison between the classical majority voting method and the method from [9]. The attack simulation is on Kyber-1024 using a noisy Bernoulli M-PCO of block size $N = 8$.

---

[8] Kyber-1024 is the only context where the authors of [9] consider really noisy oracles, *i.e.* for $p_e > 0.017$.

In Table 4, MV stands for majority voting and the value t is the number of experiments.

Table 5 shows the attack's cost for Kyber-1024 with a noisy Bernoulli M-PCO of block size $N = 8$. For fair comparison, the [9] results of Table 5 have been recomputed using the shifting mechanism presented in the previous section and the appropriate algorithm depending on the probability of error: for $p_e \in \{0.001, 0.017\}$ we did not use any correction on the oracle, for $p_e = 0.050$ we used majority voting ($t = 3$) in the second and third steps and for $p_e = 0.100$ we used majority voting ($t = 3$) for every steps.

The goal of Table 5 is to show that the gain evaluation of the attack from [9] is overestimated as it was originally compared to under-performing statistical method.

The results indicate that for $p_e \leq 0.017$, the average gain of the method proposed in [9] over the SPRT is relatively modest, approximately -12%. This contrasts with the original paper, where the reported improvement over previous methods was about -44%. For noisier oracles, the advantage even disappears. In fact, under such conditions, the method of [9] requires more calls on average than the SPRT, with overheads of approximately 17.8% for $p_e = 0.050$ and 63.4% for $p_e = 0.1$.

The differences between the number of errors (see the **#Error/#Coeff** column) in Table 5 are explained by the discret aspect of the different approaches which makes some accuracy values unreachable. While our goal is to have fewer than 1 erroneous coefficient per full key recovery (as explained in Sect. 3.2), reaching exactly this goal is often not possible. It is then important to take into consideration the combination of the average number of traces and the average number of errors to have a more accurate interpretation of the results.

Taking this into account, the advantage of using [9] compared to SPRT alone is close to nothing for $p_e \leq 0.017$ and even negative after that point.

Table 4. Comparison between majority-voting and [9] for Kyber 1024 with $N = 8$ under a noisy oracle with $p_e \in \{0.001, 0.050, 0.100\}$.

Accuracy	Method	#TotalCalls	#Error/#Coeff
$p_e = 0.001$	MV (t = 3)	1152 *(ref)*	0.000/1024
	[9]	635.5 (43.9%)	0.003/1024
$p_e = 0.050$	MV (t = 5)	1888 *(ref)*	0.372/1024
	[9]	1332 (29.4%)	0.351/1024
$p_e = 0.100$	MV (t=7)	2643 *(ref)*	0.477/1024
	[9]	2041 (22.8%)	0.641/1024

Table 5. Comparison of calls and number of error per key between our SPRT method and the method from [9] with shifting for Kyber 1024 with $N = 8$ under a noisy oracle with $p_e \in \{0.001, 0.017, 0.050, 0.100\}$.

Accuracy	Method	#TotalCalls	#Error/#Coeff
$p_e = 0.001$	Shifting SPRT	677.66 *(ref)*	0.000/1024
	Shifting [9]	596.34 (-12.0%)	0.003/1024
$p_e = 0.017$	Shifting SPRT	692.85 *(ref)*	0.172/1024
	Shifting [9]	626.44 (-9.6%)	0.924/1024
$p_e = 0.050$	Shifting SPRT	1086.54 *(ref)*	0.041/1024
	Shifting [9]	1279.7 (+17.8%)	0.518/1024
$p_e = 0.100$	Shifting SPRT	1165.65 *(ref)*	0.341/1024
	Shifting [9]	1905.10 (+63.4%)	0.707/1024

7   Checking by Block

In this section, we assume that the attacker does not have access to a M-PCO[9], and therefore consider a single PCO. In [18], Shen *et al.* propose a checking method to quickly (in terms of number of oracle calls) detect if a block of $N \in \{2, 4\}$ consecutive key coefficients were correctly guessed. In fact, the *Grafted Tree* method [9] from the same group of authors, can be seen as an extension of the checking-by-block method to a M-PCO.

Similarly to [9], the authors of [18] exhibit impressive gains (results are reproduced in Table 8[10]), ranging from -45% to about -63% depending on the oracle's p_e. Here again, we will show that shifting from naive majority voting to SPRT as a baseline mecanism removes a large part of these gains. This is particularly interesting in the case of the checking-by-block method as it is actually built upon a complicated, ad-hoc early abort strategy (in the case of a *low accuracy oracle*, *i.e.* noisy oracle with $p_e \geq 0.010$, as per [18]). In fact, we will show next that using SPRT for the oracle calls allows to completely remove their ad-hoc early abort strategy and solely keep the core of checking-by-block strategy, greatly simplifying the approach and making it the exact equivalent of the *Grafted Tree* method for single PCOs.

---

[9] Several reasons could force an attacker to use a single PCO. For instance because the oracle training becomes too expensive for multi-plaintext, or leads to higher probabilities of error. Another practical reason could be that the attacker uses a pre-trained oracle in order to reduce the overall attack complexity.

[10] All results in this section are given for Kyber-512, to follow the choice of [18].

7.1   Method Description

The main idea is to use well-constructed ciphertexts to check coefficient blocks of size N with only 2 queries to the oracle. The authors of [18] demonstrate that such ciphertexts exist and can be iteratively computed for each particular block (for $N \leq 4$).

The attack procedure starts by building a *rough* key $\hat{sk}$ using a noisy PCO. Since some coefficients of $\hat{sk}$ might be erroneous, the attacker can check the correctness of a block of N coefficients with only two calls to the oracle. To do so, the attacker uses pairs of expressly crafted ciphertexts (ct_1, ct_2) allowing them to decide whether ot not a block is correct.

Example: Let us consider the first block of size 2 from $\hat{sk}$, *i.e.* $(\hat{sk}[0], \hat{sk}[1])$. [18] shows that there exists a pair of ciphertexts (ct_1, ct_2) such that $(\mathcal{O}(ct_1, \hat{m}), \mathcal{O}(ct_2, \hat{m})) = (0, 1)$ if and only if $(sk[0], sk[1]) = (\hat{sk}[0], \hat{sk}[1])$, and $(\mathcal{O}(ct_1, \hat{m}), \mathcal{O}(ct_2, \hat{m})) \neq (0, 1)$ otherwise. In all the following we shall assume, *w.l.o.g.*, that $\hat{m}$ is the message with all 0 coefficients.

For instance (for Kyber-512), for $(\hat{sk}[0], \hat{sk}[1]) = (0, 2)$, the ciphertexts $ct_1 = (32 - 48 \cdot X^{255}, 5)$ and $ct_2 = (22 - 43 \cdot X^{255}, 5)$ produce the following oracle outputs (Table 6):

Table 6. $\mathcal{O}(ct_1)\|\mathcal{O}(ct_2)$ for $[-3, 3] \times [-3, 3]$ from [18]

$sk[0]\backslash sk[1]$	-3	-2	-1	0	1	2	3
-3	"11"	"11"	"11"	"11"	"11"	"11"	"11"
-2	"11"	"11"	"11"	"11"	"11"	"11"	"11"
-1	"11"	"11"	"11"	"11"	"11"	"11"	"11"
0	"11"	"11"	"11"	"11"	"11"	"01"	"00"
1	"11"	"11"	"11"	"11"	"00"	"00"	"00"
2	"11"	"11"	"00"	"00"	"00"	"00"	"00"
3	"11"	"00"	"00"	"00"	"00"	"00"	"00"

Because $\mathcal{O}(ct) = \mathsf{Compress}_q(v' - sk[0]u'[0] - sk[1]u'[255], 1)$, such ciphertexts pair exist for each different blocks of size 2, with $sk[i] \in \{-3, \ldots, 3\}$, which represents 49 different pairs. But for larger blocks, the existence of these cipher pairs is not guaranteed, and when they do not exist, the blocks are divided in half to test smaller blocks. The ciphertexts pairs are constructed by exhaustive search through the whole space of coefficients and ciphertexts. To reduce computation time, the construction of these pairs is limited to blocks of size 4.

Correction and recovery are then carried out according to two different algorithms, one for high-accuracy oracles with reliable responses, and the other for low-accuracy oracles requiring additional corrections. In [18], the accuracy threshold (between high and low) is around 0.99 (or equivalently $p_e = 0.01$). These two processes are described hereafter:

For High-Accuracy:

1. Recover a rough key $\hat{sk}$ by executing the classical attack method with the optimal tree
2. Check all blocks using the method explained above and mark any suspicious blocks
3. For each suspect block, perform another retrieval for each coefficient in the blocks and replace the suspect coefficients with these coefficients. Finally return the key.

For Low-Accuracy:

1. Define constants cc_1, cc_2 and the list cc_t depending on the oracle's probability of error p_e (see Table 7). A round counter r is initialized to 1.
2. Recover a rough key $\hat{sk}$ by executing the classical attack method with the optimal tree.
3. Check all blocks using the method explained above and mark any suspicious blocks.
4. For each block, perform coefficient recovery. If the block has been marked as non-suspicious, add cc_1 to the *confidence level* of the value found. If the block was marked as suspicious, add cc_2.
5. For each coefficient, replace the value of $sk[i]$ by the value with the highest confidence level. If this confidence level is greater than the threshold $cc_t[r]$ for round r, mark the coefficient as "Finished".
6. If all coefficients are marked as "Finished", return the key, otherwise increment the round counter r by one and go back to step (2).

Table 7. The precomputed parameters from [18]

p_e	cc_1	cc_2	$cc_t[r]$, for $r = 1, 2, \ldots$
0.04	4	3	$\{5, 9, 11, 14, 14, 18, 18, 18, 18, 22, 22, \ldots\}$
0.05	4	3	$\{5, 9, 12, 13, 13, 16, 17, 17, 21, 21, 21, \ldots\}$
0.10	3	4	$\{5, 9, 13, 16, 20, 20, 20, 22, 24, 25, 26, \ldots\}$

The figures from Table 7 have been found experimentally by testing and selecting the best couple (cc_1, cc_2) and the list cc_t for a given probability of error p_e.

For reference, the results of [18] approach are recalled in Table 8. As before, the gains are relative to the naive majority voting. As in the previous section, we will show that these impressive gains are, for a large part, artificial and are lost when using SPRT as the baseline.

Table 8. Comparison between majority-voting and [18, LA].

Accuracy	Method	#TotalCalls	#Error/#Coeff
$p_e = 0.04$	MV (t = 7)	9185.0 *(ref)*	0.11/512
	[18, LA]	3424.91 (62.7%)	0.05/512
$p_e = 0.05$	MV (t = 7)	9185.0 *(ref)*	0.11/512
	[18, LA]	3874.5 (57.8%)	0.15/512
$p_e = 0.10$	MV (t = 11)	14433.3 *(ref)*	0.39/512
	[18, LA]	7773.9 (46.1%)	0.25/512

7.2   Comparison with SPRT

Similarly to the previous Sect. 5, we study here the addition of SPRT to the checking-by-block method. The intuition is that the ad-hoc early-abort strategy of [18] in the case of low accuracy oracles can be removed by the use of SPRT (which is, inherently, an early-abort strategy).

To compare with the algorithm cost (in terms of number of call to the noisy oracle) of [18]'s approach for the low-accuracy ([18, LA] for short) cases, we tested two approaches:

- SPRT alone;
- SPRT to reach the oracle accuracy of $p_e = 0.01$ and then, with this less-noisy (but more costly) oracle, apply [18]'s approach for the high-accuracy ([18, HA] for short) cases.

To compare with [18, LA]'s results, we focus on their considered cases: $p_e = 0.04, 0.05$ and 0.1, the results are given in Table 9.

Firstly, the results of the Tables 8 and 9 show that the gain is considerably reduced if the SPRT method is used as the reference method instead of majority voting. The gain drops from -63% to -19% in the best case and, for the noisier oracles with $p_e = 0.10$, the [18, LA] method is even less efficient than the reference SPRT method. These results highlights the importance of choosing the SPRT method as the reference.

The results also show that the SPRT + [18, HA] is always the best, demonstrating that the use of SPRT completely voids the [18, LA] ad-hoc early-abort strategy.

8   Belief Propagation and Joint Probabilities

In a recent preprint [6][11], Hermelink, Mårtensson and Tran propose a powerful approach to handle noisy PCO. Although their solution is particularly relevant

---

[11] Posted concurrently to the writing of the present paper.

Table 9. Comparison between SPRT alone, [18, LA] and SPRT + [18, HA]

Accuracy	Method	#TotalCalls	#Error/#Coeff
$p_e = 0.04$	SPRT	4217.71 *(ref)*	0.10/512
	[18, LA]	3424.91 (18.8%)	0.05/512
	SPRT + [18, HA]	3457.1 (18.0%)	0.08/512
$p_e = 0.05$	SPRT	4371.74 *(ref)*	0.20/512
	[18, LA]	3874.5 (11.4%)	0.15/512
	SPRT + [18, HA]	3561.8 (18.5%)	0.18/512
$p_e = 0.10$	SPRT	6557.8 *(ref)*	0.21/512
	[18, LA]	7773.9 (+18.5%)	0.25/512
	SPRT + [18, HA]	5946.3 (-9.3%)	0.06/512

for multi-plaintext oracles, the authors also provide results for the single PCO case.

Fortunately, the comparison is quite easy to do as the new proposal [6] models noisy oracles in a very similar way to that in Sect. 4.2. They tackle exactly the same issue and compare their results to the same papers [9, 18]. Roughly speaking, [6] original approach uses joint probabilities (or belief-propagation (BP) for a more efficient, albeit less precise, solution) in order to exploit the correlation between the secret key's coefficients (involved in a multi-PCO) during the likelihood updating. They use an early abort criterion based on the entropy of the subkey being less than some arbitrary values, which seems less robust than the SPRT thresholds.

In Table 10, we show that [6] compares favorably to the simple use of SPRT in the case of multi-plaintext oracles. However, our cost comparisons reveal that their approach has a higher complexity. In the single PCO case however, the SPRT approach requires slightly fewer traces (see Table 11) while remaining less costly.

We note that the approach from [6] does not allow to break down blocks of N key coefficients. The average number of queries for this attack is then computed over the *successful* attacks only (*i.e.* for the attacks that have 0 erroneous blocks). Our attacks, as in the rest of the literature, are considered successful when the average number of erroneous coefficients is less than 1 for the whole secret key.

8.1   Multi-plaintext Oracle

We aligned our comparisons with the values reported in [6]. Table 10 gives the average number of queries for both approaches for Kyber 1024 and a multi-plaintext oracle of size $N = 8$ coefficients. For $N > 5$, the cost of the optimal attack from [6] makes it intractable. So the results are only given for the BP strategy.

The BP approach, considering the $N = 8$ key coefficients of a block together instead of independently, requires slightly less than half as many queries. This is a significant improvement compared to our solution. This improvement, however, comes at a cost.

Table 10. Number of oracle queries between our shifting SPRT and the BP method from [6] for Kyber 1024 with $N = 8$ under a noisy oracle with $p_e \in \{0.05, 0.10, 0.20\}$.

Accuracy	Method	#TotalCalls
$p_e = 0.05$	Shifting SPRT	1086.54 *(ref)*
	BP [6]	623.36 (-42.6%)
$p_e = 0.10$	Shifting SPRT	1165.65 *(ref)*
	BP [6]	706.56 (-39.4%)
$p_e = 0.20$	Shifting SPRT	1786.1 *(ref)*
	BP [6]	817.92 (-54.2%)

Cost Comparison: Let us denote by K_N^{SPRT} the average number of queries needed to recover one block of N coefficients in the SPRT multi-plaintext attack. Similarly, let K_N^{BP} denote the average number of queries needed to recover one block of N coefficients using the BP algorithm from [6]. Given the values from Table 10 for $N = 8$, we made the reasonable assumption that $K_8^{BP} \approx K_8^{SPRT}/2$.

In the multi-plaintext context, the SPRT attack requires 4 floating point operations (including 2 inequality checks and 2 multiplications[12]), for each coefficient of the block, per query. The overall complexity of the attack (for one block of N coefficients) is then:

$$C_N^{SPRT} = 4N \cdot K_N^{SPRT} \tag{4}$$

In [6] the cost of the BP attack is (aggregating all floating point operations together):

$$C_N^{BP} = K_N^{BP} \cdot \left((2^N + 7) \cdot N \cdot (2\eta + 1) + N \right) \tag{5}$$

While these costs are difficult to compare since the number of queries K_N^{SPRT} and K_N^{BP} are not known a priori, it appears clearly that the BP attack from [6] has a much higher complexity than the SPRT approach for the classical setting of $N = 8$ (using our estimation $K_8^{BP} \approx \frac{K_8^{SPRT}}{2}$).

---

[12] For a fair comparison we assume, as in [6], that the probabilities are multiplied instead of adding their log.

8.2   Single Plaintext Checking Oracle

For the single PCO case, Table 11 shows that our method is slightly better or at least as efficient (in terms of the average number of queries) as the optimal attack from [6]. This is not surprising since their attack is designed for the multi-plaintext oracle setting. Also, while the algorithmic costs of the two approaches are greatly reduced, the SPRT remains cheaper than [6].

Table 11. Comparison between SPRT and the optimal attack from [6] for a single PCO under a noisy oracle with $p_e \in \{0.10, 0.45, 0.49\}$.

Accuracy	Method	#TotalCalls
$p_e = 0.10$	SPRT	8777.8 *(ref)*
	Optimal [6]	10368.0 (+18.1%)
$p_e = 0.45$	SPRT	674 946.5 *(ref)*
	Optimal [6]	722 380.8 (+7.0%)
$p_e = 0.49$	SPRT	18 907 728.26 *(ref)*
	Optimal [6]	19 319 142.91 (+2.1%)

Cost Comparison: Denoting by K_1^{OPT} the average number of queries needed to recover one coefficient in the optimal attack from [6], the attack complexity (again in terms of number of floating point operations) for one coefficient becomes:

$$\mathcal{C}_1^{OPT} = K_1^{OPT} \cdot (4\eta + 2) \tag{6}$$

For the SPRT attack, the cost is:

$$\mathcal{C}_1^{SPRT} = 4K_1^{SPRT} \tag{7}$$

Since our experiments show that $K_1^{OPT} \approx K_1^{SPRT}$ (as per Table 11), we have

$$\mathcal{C}_1^{OPT} \approx \mathcal{C}_1^{SPRT} \times \frac{2\eta + 1}{2}. \tag{8}$$

Since $\eta \in \{2, 3\}$, this makes the [6] approach for $N = 1$ slightly more expensive than the SPRT solution for no benefit.

9   Conclusion

In this paper we consider *plaintext-checking oracle* attacks on Kyber when oracles are *noisy* (*i.e.* oracles that can be erroneous). We show that, in this context of online (*i.e.* adaptive) attacks, the use of Sequential Probability Ratio Test (SPRT) can efficiently replace the classical majority-voting or likelihood ratio test strategies.

To evaluate the proposed method, we conducted several simulations using oracles with varying noise levels and compared the outcomes with previous results obtained under similar models and attack strategies.

Our results demonstrate that using SPRT – in comparison to other classical baselines – achieves a significant reduction in the number of oracle calls while maintaining the same level of flexibility in online attack scenarios. Furthermore, we showed that recent improvement techniques proposed in [9] and [18] are substantially affected by this change – sometimes performing worse, but also potentially serving as complementary methods. Overall, the proposed SPRT-based strategy establishes a new baseline in this particular case, combining strong efficiency with high adaptability compared to existing approaches.

In the last revision of this paper, we added a comparison to the recent preprint [6] from Hermelink *et al.*. We show that [6]'s approach improves significantly (in terms of number of oracle queries) the simple use of SPRT in the multi-plaintext setting, at the cost of a higher algorithmic complexity. In the binary case, we show that [6]'s approach does not perform better than ours, while still being more costly.

Future work could extend this approach to other attack scenarios (*e.g.* the *Full Domain* oracle model) and other post-quantum KEMs. Evaluating the SPRT-based strategy across different schemes would help assess its generality and potential as a versatile tool for efficient online attacks.

Acknowledgements. We would like to thank the anonymous reviewers for their careful reading and very constructive comments. And particularly, for pointing out the highly relevant preprint [6] which we had missed.

References

1. Azouaoui, M., Bronchain, O., Hoffmann, C., Kuzovkova, Y., Schneider, T., Standaert, F.X.: Systematic study of decryption and re-encryption leakage: the case of Kyber. In: Balasch, J., O'Flynn, C. (eds.) COSADE 2022. LNCS, vol. 13211, pp. 236–256. Springer, Cham (2022). https://doi.org/10.1007/978-3-030-99766-3_11
2. Chari, S., Rao, J.R., Rohatgi, P.: Template attacks. In: Kaliski, Jr., B.S., Koç, Çetin Kaya., Paar, C. (eds.) CHES 2002. LNCS, vol. 2523, pp. 13–28. Springer, Heidelberg (2003). https://doi.org/10.1007/3-540-36400-5_3
3. Dong, H., Guo, Q.: Multi-value plaintext-checking and full-decryption oracle-based attacks on HQC from offline templates. IACR Trans. Cryptogr. Hardw. Embed. Syst. **2025**(4), 254––289 (2025). https://doi.org/10.46586/tches.v2025.i4.254-289. https://tches.iacr.org/index.php/TCHES/article/view/12410
4. Fujisaki, E., Okamoto, T.: Secure integration of asymmetric and symmetric encryption schemes. In: Wiener, M.J. (ed.) CRYPTO'99. LNCS, vol. 1666, pp. 537–554. Springer, Heidelberg (1999). https://doi.org/10.1007/3-540-48405-1_34

5. Guo, Q., Nabokov, D., Nilsson, A., Johansson, T.: SCA-LDPC: a code-based framework for key-recovery side-channel attacks on post-quantum encryption schemes. In: Guo, J., Steinfeld, R. (eds.) ASIACRYPT 2023, Part IV. LNCS, vol. 14441, pp. 203–236. Springer, Singapore (2023). https://doi.org/10.1007/978-981-99-8730-6_7

6. Hermelink, J., Mårtensson, E., Tran, M.: Noise-tolerant plaintext-checking oracle attacks – a soft-analytic approach applied to ML-KEM. Cryptology ePrint Archive, Report 2025/1496 (2025). https://eprint.iacr.org/2025/1496

7. Huguenin-Dumittan, L., Vaudenay, S.: Classical misuse attacks on NIST round 2 PQC - the power of rank-based schemes. In: Conti, M., Zhou, J., Casalicchio, E., Spognardi, A. (eds.) ACNS 2020, Part I. LNCS, vol. 12146, pp. 208–227. Springer, Cham (2020). https://doi.org/10.1007/978-3-030-57808-4_11

8. Lehmann, E.L., Romano, J.P.: Testing statistical hypotheses. Springer Texts in Statistics, 3rd edn. Springer, New York (2005)

9. Li, J., et al.: Grafted trees bear better fruit: an improved multiple-valued plaintext-checking side-channel attack against kyber. In: 2025 Design, Automation & Test in Europe Conference (DATE), pp. 1–7 (2025). https://doi.org/10.23919/DATE64628.2025.10992764

10. Module-Lattice-Based Key-Encapsulation Mechanism Standard: National Institute of Standards and Technology, NIST FIPS PUB 203. U.S. Department of Commerce (2024)

11. Neyman, J., Pearson, E.S.: On the problem of the most efficient tests of statistical hypotheses. Philos. Trans. Roy. Soc. London Series A Containing Papers of a Mathematical or Physical Character **231**, 289–337 (1933). http://www.jstor.org/stable/91247

12. Ngo, K., Dubrova, E., Guo, Q., Johansson, T.: A side-channel attack on a masked IND-CCA secure Saber KEM implementation. IACR TCHES **2021**(4), 676–707 (2021). https://doi.org/10.46586/tches.v2021.i4.676-707. https://tches.iacr.org/index.php/TCHES/article/view/9079

13. Qin, Y., Cheng, C., Ding, J.: An efficient key mismatch attack on the NIST second round candidate Kyber. Cryptology ePrint Archive, Report 2019/1343 (2019). https://eprint.iacr.org/2019/1343

14. Qin, Y., Cheng, C., Zhang, X., Pan, Y., Hu, L., Ding, J.: A systematic approach and analysis of key mismatch attacks on lattice-based NIST candidate KEMs. In: Tibouchi, M., Wang, H. (eds.) ASIACRYPT 2021, Part IV. LNCS, vol. 13093, pp. 92–121. Springer, Cham (2021). https://doi.org/10.1007/978-3-030-92068-5_4

15. Rajendran, G., Ravi, P., D'Anvers, J.P., Bhasin, S., Chattopadhyay, A.: Pushing the limits of generic side-channel attacks on LWE-based KEMs - parallel PC oracle attacks on Kyber KEM and beyond. IACR TCHES **2023**(2), 418–446 (2023). https://doi.org/10.46586/tches.v2023.i2.418-446

16. Ravi, P., Roy, S.S., Chattopadhyay, A., Bhasin, S.: Generic side-channel attacks on CCA-secure lattice-based PKE and KEMs. IACR TCHES **2020**(3), 307–335 (2020). https://doi.org/10.13154/tches.v2020.i3.307-335. https://tches.iacr.org/index.php/TCHES/article/view/8592

17. Schwabe, P., et al.: CRYSTALS-KYBER. Technical report, National Institute of Standards and Technology (2022). https://csrc.nist.gov/Projects/post-quantum-cryptography/selected-algorithms-2022

18. Shen, M., Cheng, C., Zhang, X., Guo, Q., Jiang, T.: Find the bad apples: an efficient method for perfect key recovery under imperfect SCA oracles - a case study of Kyber. IACR TCHES **2023**(1), 89–112 (2023). https://doi.org/10.46586/tches.v2023.i1.89-112

19. Tanaka, Y., Ueno, R., Xagawa, K., Ito, A., Takahashi, J., Homma, N.: Multiple-valued plaintext-checking side-channel attacks on post-quantum KEMs. IACR TCHES **2023**(3), 473–503 (2023). https://doi.org/10.46586/tches.v2023.i3.473-503
20. Ueno, R., Xagawa, K., Tanaka, Y., Ito, A., Takahashi, J., Homma, N.: Curse of re-encryption: a generic power/EM analysis on post-quantum KEMs. IACR TCHES **2022**(1), 296–322 (2022). https://doi.org/10.46586/tches.v2022.i1.296-322
21. Wald, A.: Sequential tests of statistical hypotheses. Ann. Math. Statist. **16**(4), 117–186 (1945). http://dml.mathdoc.fr/item/1177731118
22. Xagawa, K., Ito, A., Ueno, R., Takahashi, J., Homma, N.: Fault-injection attacks against NIST's post-quantum cryptography round 3 KEM candidates. In: Tibouchi, M., Wang, H. (eds.) ASIACRYPT 2021, Part II. LNCS, vol. 13091, pp. 33–61. Springer, Cham (2021). https://doi.org/10.1007/978-3-030-92075-3_2
23. Xu, Z., Pemberton, O., Roy, S., Oswald, D., Yao, W., Zheng, Z.: Magnifying side-channel leakage of lattice-based cryptosystems with chosen ciphertexts: the case study of kyber. IEEE Trans. Comput. **71**, 1 (2021). https://doi.org/10.1109/TC.2021.3122997

Refined Modelling of the Primal Attack, and Variants Against Module-LWE

Paola de Perthuis[1][(✉)] and Filip Trenkić[2]

[1] Centrum Wiskunde and Informatica (CWI), Amsterdam, The Netherlands
`Paola.de.Perthuis@cwi.nl`
[2] King's College London, London, UK

Abstract. The primal attack reduces Learning with Errors (LWE) to the unique Shortest Vector Problem (uSVP), and then applies lattice reduction such as BKZ to solve the latter. Estimating the cost of the attack is required to evaluate the security of constructions based on LWE.

Existing fine-grained estimators for the cost of the primal attack, due to Dachman-Soled–Ducas–Gong–Rossi (CRYPTO 2020) and Postlethwaite–Virdia (PKC 2021), differ from experimental data as they implicitly assume the unique shortest vector is resampled several times during the attack, changing its length. Furthermore, these estimators consider only the first two moments of the LWE secret and error, and therefore do not differentiate between distinct centred distributions with equal variances. We remedy both issues by initially fixing the short vector's length, and later integrating over its distribution. We provide extensive experimental evidence that our estimators are more accurate and faithfully capture the behaviour of different LWE distributions.

In the case of Module-LWE, lattice reduction utilising the module structure could lead to cheaper attacks. We build upon the analysis of module lattice reduction by Ducas–Engelberts–Perthuis (Asiacrypt 2025), providing a simulator for Module-BKZ generalising the BKZ simulator of Chen–Nguyen (Asiacrypt 2011). We design estimators for a module variant of the primal attack, supporting our analysis with experimental evidence. Asymptotically, we show the module primal attack over a degree d number field K has a reduced cost, resulting in a subexponential gain, whenever the discriminant Δ_K satisfies $|\Delta_K| < d^d$, one such case being non-power-two cyclotomics.

Keywords: Cryptanalysis · Module Lattices · Learning With Errors

1 Introduction

The Learning with Errors (LWE) and NTRU problems serve as central hardness assumptions in lattice-based cryptography, underpinning many primitives and advanced constructions. Module-LWE (MLWE), the algebraically structured variant of LWE, is used extensively in post-quantum standards including

M. Bardet and R. Niederhagen (Eds.): PQCrypto 2026, LNCS 16492, pp. 342–376, 2026.
https://doi.org/10.1007/978-3-032-22698-3_11

CRYSTALS-Kyber [13] and SMAUG-T [18], while NTRU+ [30] relies on the hardness of NTRU.

The *primal attack* refers to a family of attacks which reduce LWE and NTRU to the unique Shortest Vector Problem (uSVP), then apply lattice reduction algorithms, the most common of which is BKZ [44,46]. The BKZ algorithm is parameterised by a blocksize β, which corresponds to the quality of lattice reduction, and implemented variants have complexity $2^{\Theta(\beta)}$ [34]. Evaluating the cost of the primal attack is thus directly dependent on estimating the minimal blocksize β such that BKZ-β recovers the unique shortest vector [2,5,6].

Initial estimates gave a single blocksize β which was likely to succeed in solving the instance [6], but later works reported that smaller blocksizes often have a non-negligible probability of success [4,9]. More recent works [19,42] aimed to capture these low-probability events by instead estimating, for each blocksize β, the probability that BKZ-β would recover the unique shortest vector. These models rely on a BKZ simulator [10,17], which predicts the evolution of the profile – the lengths of vectors in the lattice basis – during the execution of BKZ. We note that these estimators are designed for LWE instances where the secret and error are sampled coordinatewise from a discrete Gaussian distribution, but in practice a variety of other distributions are used. One unsatisfying solution provided in [42] is to model an arbitrary distribution by a discrete Gaussian of the same variance.

Many real-world schemes use structured lattice assumptions, such as NTRU and MLWE, where the lattices arise as modules over the ring of integers in a number field [26,31,36]. The use of module lattices can be crucial for efficiency and small key sizes, but the algebraic structure opens potential avenues for attack. In [32,39], module variants of the standard reduction algorithms were first proposed, with a study of their behavior on worst-case instances. Analysis of experimental behavior was not immediate, because of the challenges posed by the implementation of module-lattice reduction. Then, [29] gave a predictive analysis of the reduction for NTRU instances, with a negative result. Most recently, [21] provided an average-case study of the Module-BKZ (mBKZ) algorithm, predicting the quality of mBKZ-reduced lattice bases, depending on the blocksize and the underlying number field.

Crucially, it was shown that for lattices over non-power-two cyclotomic number fields, the Module-BKZ algorithm achieves the same basis quality as BKZ-β while using a sublinearly smaller blocksize, in particular providing a gain in $\Theta(\beta/\ln\beta)$.

Contributions. Broadly, this article seeks the comprehension of dependencies in the primal attack. While a unique short vector may be initially drawn from a random distribution, it does not change during the attack itself; and when considering attacks against module lattices, there are multiple short vectors resulting from the action of roots of unity, which do not behave independently. Our goal is to introduce statistical models which account for and quantify these phenomena.

Our first contribution is to refine existing estimators [19,42] for the success probability of the primal attack. For small blocksizes where experiments are feasible, these lack accuracy, and we explain this is due to a heuristic that implicitly assumes the short vector is resampled several times during the attack (Sect. 3.1). We provide new estimators to remedy this. Our technique is to model the success probability assuming the length λ_1 of the shortest vector is known, and then integrate over the randomness of λ_1 (Sect. 3.2). A similar technique was used in [23] to improve analysis of the dual attack. Concretely, we use that the projection of the short vector into a random subspace follows a beta distribution, whereas previous works use a chi-squared distribution – this discrepancy was noted in [11]. We provide extensive experimental evidence, concluding that our estimators are more accurate (Fig. 3) and moreover able to differentiate between LWE distributions with the same mean and variance (Fig. 5).

Our second contribution is to build upon the analysis of Module-BKZ in [21], in particular addressing Open Questions 1, 2 and 4. First, we propose a simulator analogous to the BKZ simulator of [17] for the evolution of a basis profile during Module-BKZ (Sect. 4). Using this, we adapt our estimators to predict the success probability of a module analogue of the primal attack, which can outperform the standard primal attack. We support our analysis with experiments (Sect. 5.4), though because of the limitations of current implementations, they were conducted for cyclotomic number fields of low degree. We hence complement them with an asymptotic analysis (Sect. 5.2). In particular, we show that if β is the $\mathbb{Q}$-blocksize required by Module-BKZ to solve Module-LWE, then BKZ requires a blocksize of

$$\beta_{\mathrm{eq}} = \beta + \frac{1}{d} \ln \frac{d^d}{|\Delta_K|} \ln \left(\frac{q^u |\Delta_K|^{1/d}}{\sigma^2 2\pi e} \right) \frac{\beta}{(\ln \beta)^2} + o\left(\frac{\beta}{(\ln \beta)^2} \right).$$

where K is the underlying degree-d number field with discriminant Δ_K, q and σ are the MLWE modulus and noise width, and $u \in (0, 2)$ pertains to the number of samples. Hence, the sublinear gain provided by Module-BKZ for non-power-two cyclotomics translates to a sublinear gain on the blocksize for which the module primal attack succeeds.

Finally, for this comparison to be exhaustive, we analyse variants of the standard primal attack against MLWE (Sect. 6). Rather than reducing to unique-SVP, one can embed several short vectors in the module lattice, obtained from the action of the roots of unity in the number field: then, finding any one of them recovers the secret. Such attacks were proposed in [40,49], with experimental evidence to suggest embedding more short vectors can be beneficial, which we confirm by proposing an extension of our estimators to this scenario, and comparing to experiments.

Our code is open source and available at https://github.com/FTcode/beta-is-better (Sect. 3) and https://github.com/FTcode/mPrimal (Sect. 4, Sect. 5, Sect. 6).

2   Preliminaries

We write $\mathbb{N}, \mathbb{Z}, \mathbb{Q}, \mathbb{R}$ and $\mathbb{C}$ for the naturals, integers, rationals, reals, and complex numbers respectively, and $\mathbb{Z}_q$ for the integers modulo q. We write $\ln$ for the natural logarithm, ϕ for Euler's totient function, Γ for the Gamma function, and ψ for the digamma function. In Euclidean space $\mathbb{R}^n$ we write $B_n(r)$ for the n-ball of radius r, and $S_{n-1}(r)$ for the corresponding $(n-1)$-sphere. If r is omitted, it is understood to be 1.

2.1   Probability

We use $\mathbb{P}, \mathbb{V}$, and $\mathbb{E}$ to denote probability, variance, and expectation. For a distribution $\mathcal{X}$ on a set S, we use $\mathcal{X}^n$ to denote the distribution on S^n with components identically independently distributed (iid) according to $\mathcal{X}$. We write $\mathcal{N}(\mu, \sigma^2)$ for the normal (continuous Gaussian) distribution with mean μ and variance σ^2, $\mathrm{Bin}(n, p)$ for the binomial distribution with n trials and success probability p, $\mathcal{U}(S)$ for the uniform distribution on a finite nonempty set S, and $\mathrm{Beta}(a, b)$ for the beta distribution with shape parameters a and b. The sum of the squares of n independent $\mathcal{N}(0, \sigma^2)$ variables is the scaled chi-squared distribution $\sigma^2 \chi_n^2$.

The discrete Gaussian on $\mathbb{Z}$ with mean 0 and parameter σ is defined by the probability mass function

$$D_{\mathbb{Z},\sigma}(x) = \frac{e^{-x^2/2\sigma^2}}{\sum_{y \in \mathbb{Z}} e^{-y^2/2\sigma^2}} \cdot$$

Note that σ^2 does not correspond exactly to the variance of the distribution. However, for sufficiently large σ, many properties of the discrete Gaussian (including the variance) approach those of the continuous Gaussian, a phenomenon known as *smoothing* [38].

Definition 1 (Random Subspace). *A (uniformly) random β-dimensional subspace of $\mathbb{R}^N$ is sampled by choosing an arbitrary β-dimensional subspace $S \subset \mathbb{R}^N$ and applying a uniformly random orthogonal transformation $T \in O(N)$.*[1]

2.2   Lattices

Definition 2 (Lattice). *A rank n lattice is the integer span of n linearly independent vectors $\mathbf{b}_1, \ldots, \mathbf{b}_n \in \mathbb{R}^d$, called a basis. We write these as columns of a matrix $\mathbf{B}$. The lattice generated by $\mathbf{B}$ is $\Lambda(\mathbf{B}) = \{x_1 \mathbf{b}_1 + \cdots + x_n \mathbf{b}_n \mid x_i \in \mathbb{Z}\}$.*

---

[1] Formally, the set of all β-dimensional subspaces of $\mathbb{R}^N$ is called the *Grassmannian manifold* and denoted $\mathrm{Gr}_\beta(\mathbb{R}^N)$. The orthogonal group $O(N)$, which acts transitively on $\mathrm{Gr}_\beta(\mathbb{R}^N)$, is compact and thus admits a unique finite *Haar measure*, which is a natural uniform measure on the group. The distribution we have defined on $\mathrm{Gr}_\beta(\mathbb{R}^N)$ is simply the *push-forward* of this Haar measure under the action of $O(N)$.

Definition 3 (Gram–Schmidt Orthogonalisation, GSO). *For any lattice basis* $\mathbf{b}_1, \ldots, \mathbf{b}_n$*, the Gram–Schmidt orthogonalisation is the set of orthogonal vectors denoted* $\mathbf{b}_1^*, \ldots, \mathbf{b}_n^*$ *and defined by*

$$\mathbf{b}_i^* = \mathbf{b}_i - \sum_{j<i} \mu_{i,j} \cdot \mathbf{b}_j^* \ \ where \ \mu_{i,j} = \frac{\langle \mathbf{b}_i, \mathbf{b}_j^* \rangle}{\langle \mathbf{b}_j^*, \mathbf{b}_j^* \rangle}.$$

Definition 4 (Lattice Volume). *Given any basis* $\mathbf{B}$ *for a lattice* Λ*, its volume is defined as the volume of the parallelepiped* $\mathcal{P}(\mathbf{B}) = \{\mathbf{B}\mathbf{x} \mid \mathbf{x} \in [0,1)^n\}$,

$$\mathrm{vol}(\Lambda) = \sqrt{\det\left(\mathbf{B}^T\mathbf{B}\right)} = \prod_{i=1}^{n} ||\mathbf{b}_i^*||.$$

Definition 5 (Lattice Minima). *For a rank n lattice Λ we define, for each* $i \in \{1, \ldots, n\}$*, the ith minimum*

$$\lambda_i(\Lambda) = \underset{r \in \mathbb{R}^+}{arg\ min}\{\mathrm{rank}(\mathrm{span}_{\mathbb{R}}(\Lambda \cap B_n(r))) = i\}.$$

Definition 6 (Gaussian Heuristic). *For a rank n lattice of unit volume, the Gaussian heuristic for the shortest vector approximates the first minimum as*

$$\mathrm{gh}_{\mathbb{Q}}(n) = \frac{2^{\frac{1}{n}}\Gamma\left(1 + \frac{1}{n}\right)}{\mathrm{vol}(B_n)^{\frac{1}{n}}} \approx \sqrt{\frac{n}{2\pi e}}.$$

By appropriate scaling, we define the Gaussian heuristic for a lattice of arbitrary volume, $\mathrm{gh}_{\mathbb{Q}}(\Lambda) = \mathrm{gh}_{\mathbb{Q}}(n) \cdot \mathrm{vol}(\Lambda)^{1/n}$. We write $\mathrm{lgh}_{\mathbb{Q}}(\cdot) = \ln \mathrm{gh}_{\mathbb{Q}}(\cdot)$, and may omit the subscript.

Definition 7 (Projected Sublattices). *Let* $\mathbf{B} = (\mathbf{b}_1, \ldots, \mathbf{b}_n)$ *be a basis for a lattice Λ. We define the linear map π_i as the projection orthogonal to the span of* $\{\mathbf{b}_1, \ldots, \mathbf{b}_{i-1}\}$*. For indices $1 \le i < j \le n$ we define the projected subbasis*

$$\mathbf{B}_{[i:j]} = (\pi_i(\mathbf{b}_i), \ldots, \pi_i(\mathbf{b}_j))$$

and the corresponding projected sublattice $\Lambda_{[i:j]} = \Lambda(\mathbf{B}_{[i:j]})$.

If the index j is omitted, we understand it to mean $j = n$. We may also write $\Lambda_{[i:j]}^{(1)}$ to denote the normalised projected sublattice, scaled to have volume 1.

2.3   Lattice Problems

Lattices are a rich source of computational problems. A simple problem is to find a shortest (nonzero) vector in a lattice; we further consider promise problem variants, where we are guaranteed that the lattice satisfies some additional property.

Definition 8 (Shortest Vector Problem, SVP). *Given a lattice Λ, find a vector* $\mathbf{v} \in \Lambda$ *of length* $\lambda_1(\Lambda)$.

Definition 9 (Unique Shortest Vector Problem, uSVP$_\gamma$). *Given a lattice Λ and $\gamma \geq 1$ with the promise that $\lambda_2(\Lambda) > \gamma\lambda_1(\Lambda)$, find the vector $\mathbf{v} \in \Lambda$ (unique up to sign) of length $\lambda_1(\Lambda)$. If omitted, $\gamma = 1$.*

While previously it was thought that the factor $\gamma = \lambda_2(\Lambda)/\lambda_1(\Lambda)$ determines the difficulty of solving SVP on a lattice, it is now understood that the hardness is mainly driven by the ratio $f = \mathrm{gh}(\Lambda)/\lambda_1(\Lambda)$ [1,4,9].

Definition 10 (f-unusual-SVP [24]). *Given a lattice Λ and $f \geq 1$ with the promise that $\lambda_1(\Lambda) \leq \mathrm{gh}(\Lambda)/f$, find a vector $\mathbf{v} \in \Lambda$ of length $\lambda_1(\Lambda)$.*

A commonly used problem in cryptography is *Learning with Errors* or LWE [43], the presumed hardness of which is the underlying security assumption in many lattice-based schemes.

Definition 11 (LWE$_{n,m,q,\chi}$). *Let n, m, q be positive integers and χ a probability distribution on $\mathbb{Z}_q$. We call m the number of samples and q the modulus. Sample $\mathbf{A} \leftarrow \mathcal{U}(\mathbb{Z}_q^{n \times m})$, a secret vector $\mathbf{s} \leftarrow \chi^n$, an error vector $\mathbf{e} \leftarrow \chi^m$, and compute*

$$\mathbf{b} = \mathbf{A}^T\mathbf{s} + \mathbf{e} \pmod{q}$$

An instance of LWE$_{n,m,q,\chi}$ *is the pair $(\mathbf{A}, \mathbf{b})$ and the goal is to recover the secret vector $\mathbf{s}$.*

For cryptographic functionalities, the distribution χ should satisfy some notion of 'smallness', when considered as a distribution on $\mathbb{Z}$ using the balanced coset representatives $\{-\lceil q/2 \rceil + 1, \ldots, \lfloor q/2 \rfloor\}$. Often notation is abused to write χ as a probability distribution on $\mathbb{Z}$, with the understanding that we mean its reduction modulo q. Note that the given formulation, where $\mathbf{s}$ is sampled coordinatewise from χ, is known as *normal form* LWE. The original formulation samples $\mathbf{s} \leftarrow \mathcal{U}(\mathbb{Z}_q^n)$, but a standard reduction [7] maps LWE with uniform $\mathbf{s}$ and m samples to normal form LWE with $m - n$ samples.

2.4   Lattice Reduction

A lattice reduction algorithm takes as input a basis for a lattice, and outputs a basis of better quality, called a reduced basis. The celebrated LLL algorithm [33] runs in polynomial time but provides relatively weak lattice reduction: a stronger notion of reduction is achieved by the BKZ algorithm [44,46].

Definition 12 (BKZ-reduced). *Let $2 \leq \beta \leq n$. A basis $\mathbf{B}$ of a rank n lattice Λ is BKZ-β reduced if it is LLL-reduced and for all $i \in \{1, \ldots, n-1\}$,*

$$||\mathbf{b}_i^*|| = \lambda_1(\Lambda_{[i:\min(i+\beta-1,n)]})$$

The quantity β is called the blocksize. We say a basis is *HKZ-reduced* if it is BKZ-reduced with $\beta = n$. The BKZ algorithm requires access to an oracle O_{SVP} which solves SVP in lattices of rank at most β. This oracle is repeatedly called on projected sublattices $\Lambda_{[i:\min(i+\beta-1,n)]}$, known as *blocks*, and if the output vector $\mathbf{v}$ is shorter than the current first vector in the block, it is inserted into the basis at the beginning of the block. A high-level description is given in, for example, [42, Alg. 1].

BKZ in Practice. In its original form, BKZ terminates only once no insertions were made during the previous tour, guaranteeing a BKZ-β reduced basis. In practice we do not run the algorithm to termination, but instead provide a fixed maximum number of tours τ. We also consider Progressive-BKZ, where we run a fixed number of tours τ at each blocksize $\beta = 3, 4, \ldots, n$ sequentially, or until some termination condition is met.[2]

2.5 Predicting Lattice Reduction

Definition 13 (Basis Profile). *For a basis* $\mathbf{B}$ *of a rank n lattice Λ with GSO* $\mathbf{b}_1^*, \ldots, \mathbf{b}_n^*$, *the basis profile is the sequence* $(\ell_i)_{i=1}^n$ *where* $\ell_i = \ln \|\mathbf{b}_i^*\|$.

A common heuristic, based on observed behaviour, is that after lattice reduction the profile ℓ_i decreases linearly.

Definition 14 (Geometric Series Assumption, GSA [45]). *For β sufficiently large, there is a constant $\alpha > 1$ (depending only on β) such that the profile after BKZ-β reduction of a random full-rank n lattice basis satisfies*

$$\mathbb{E}[\ell_i] = \mathbb{E}[\ell_1] - (i - 1)\ln\alpha.$$

Equivalently, for all $1 \le i \le n$,

$$\mathbb{E}[\ell_i] = \frac{n + 1 - 2i}{2}\ln\alpha + \frac{1}{n}\ln\mathrm{vol}(\Lambda)$$

where

$$\ln\alpha = \frac{2}{\beta - 1}\mathbb{E}_{\mathbf{s}}[\ln\|\mathbf{s}\|]$$

and $\mathbf{s}$ is a shortest vector in one of the random normalised projected sublattices $\Lambda_{[j:j+\beta-1]}^{(1)}$ for $1 \le j \le n - \beta + 1$.

In the analysis of BKZ algorithms, it is standard to assume that for sufficiently large β the normalised projected sublattices behave as random unit volume lattices, and we hence apply the Gaussian heuristic.

Definition 15. *For $\beta \ge 45$, define α_β by*

$$\ln\alpha_\beta = \frac{2}{\beta - 1}\cdot\mathrm{lgh}(\beta)$$

BKZ Simulation. The GSA only predicts the profile once sufficiently many tours have been run, and furthermore does not capture the true shape of the profile [1]. For refined predictions we may use *BKZ simulators*, which accept as input a basis profile $(\ell_i)_{i=1}^n$, a blocksize β, and number of tours τ, and the output is a prediction for the resulting profile. In this work we consider the deterministic simulator[3] introduced in [17], which we write as BKZSim.

---

[2] In the context of the primal attack, when the embedded vector has been found.

[3] While there also exist probabilistic simulators [10], we do not consider them in this work.

2.6   Primal Attack and Blocksize Estimation

The *primal attack* refers to a family of algorithms for solving LWE which transform LWE instances into uSVP instances, and apply lattice reduction algorithms.

Definition 16 (Bai–Galbraith Embedding [8]). *Given an instance of* $\mathrm{LWE}_{n,m,q,\chi}$, *define the Bai–Galbraith embedding*[4] *as the block matrix*

$$\mathbf{B} = \begin{pmatrix} q\mathbf{I}_m & -\mathbf{A}^T & \mathbf{b} \\ & \mathbf{I}_n & \\ & & t \end{pmatrix}$$

where $t \in \mathbb{R}$ *is the* embedding coefficient. *This gives a rank* $N = (n + m + 1)$ *lattice* $\Lambda = \Lambda(\mathbf{B})$ *containing the vector* $\mathbf{v} = (\mathbf{e}, \mathbf{s}, t)$.

This is a specialisation of a more general method of Kannan [28]. The vector $\mathbf{v}$ is called the *embedded vector*. Since $\mathbf{e}$ and $\mathbf{s}$ are sampled from a short distribution χ, the embedded vector is short, and under appropriate conditions is the unique shortest vector [35]. The embedding coefficient is often chosen in practice as $t = 1$, though formally one should choose $t = \sigma$ [35]. Indeed, if we view Λ as an instance of f-unusual-SVP, then σ is the choice maximising the expected value of the ratio $f = \mathrm{gh}(\Lambda)/\lambda_1(\Lambda)$.

Solving the uSVP Instance. After forming the lattice $\Lambda = \Lambda(\mathbf{B})$ the primal attack aims to recover $\mathbf{v}$ by applying the BKZ algorithm. The mechanism by which BKZ recovers the short vector was suggested in [6] and studied further in [4,9]. In brief, when the O_{SVP} oracle is called at position $i = N - \beta + 1$ (on the 'terminal block') the projection $\pi_{N-\beta+1}(\mathbf{v})$ of the embedded vector will be inserted if it is a shortest vector in the projected sublattice, leading to the success condition:

$$\|\pi_{N-\beta+1}(\mathbf{v})\| \leq \|\mathbf{b}^*_{N-\beta+1}\|. \tag{1}$$

If this occurs then, by a similar argument, in the following tour a projection of $\mathbf{v}$ will likely be inserted at position $i = N - 2\beta + 2$. Subsequent tours will continue to insert projections of $\mathbf{v}$ at earlier positions in the basis, until eventually the applications of LLL within BKZ are sufficient to recover $\mathbf{v}$ [4, §4.1].

Prediction via the GSA. An estimate for the smallest blocksize for which BKZ will recover the embedded vector, assuming the GSA, was given in [6] and is sometimes referred to as the '2016 estimate'. If $\sigma^2 = \mathbb{V}(\chi)$, then $\mathbb{E}[\|\mathbf{v}\|^2] = N\sigma^2$, and the projection into the heuristically random β-dimensional subspace spanned by $\Lambda_{[N-\beta+1]}$ has expected square norm $\mathbb{E}[\|\pi_{N-\beta+1}(\mathbf{v})\|^2] = \beta\sigma^2$.

---

[4] We note that variants exist for LWE instances where $\mathbf{e}$ and $\mathbf{s}$ are sampled from different distributions, or when these distributions are not centred at zero [4,42], but we will not consider those scenarios.

On the other hand, after several tours of BKZ-β the profile converges towards the GSA, with the slope predicted by α_β. Thus, Eq. (1) becomes

$$\sigma\sqrt{\beta} \leq \alpha_\beta^{(2\beta-N-1)/2}\mathrm{vol}(\Lambda)^{1/N} \tag{2}$$

and the first successful blocksize is estimated as the smallest β satisfying this inequality. If the attacker is free to choose the number of LWE samples m, then β and m may be optimised simultaneously.

Prediction via Simulation. The 2016 estimate has several shortcomings. Firstly, it assumes the GSA, which does not capture the true shape of the profile, and only applies when sufficiently many tours are run. Secondly, it only provides a single blocksize which is likely to be successful, but smaller blocksizes may still solve the instance.

A more fine-grained estimation technique, introduced in [19], models an attacker running Progressive-BKZ and estimates the probability mass function for the blocksize β^* at which the shortest vector will be recovered. The analogous model predicting the success probability of (fixed blocksize) BKZ-β, when running a maximum number of tours τ, was introduced in [42]. The idea is to simulate the tour-by-tour evolution of the basis profile $(\ell_i)_{i=1}^N$ using BKZSim. After each tour it is assumed that the projection of the embedded vector into the terminal block has square norm following a chi-squared distribution,

$$||\pi_{N-\beta+1}(\mathbf{v})||^2 \sim \sigma^2\chi_\beta^2 \tag{3}$$

and is inserted into the basis if shorter than $\mathbf{b}_{N-\beta+1}^*$, which occurs with probability $\mathbb{P}(\sigma^2\chi_\beta^2 \leq \exp(2 \cdot \ell_{N-\beta+1}))$. Note that this approach requires a prediction of the initial profile, when the Bai–Galbraith embedding $\mathbf{B}$ is only LLL-reduced. This exhibits a characteristic *Z-shape* [27], which is well-understood. We write $\mathsf{LLLSim}(n, m, q, \chi)$ for the algorithm described in [42, App. B] which outputs the predicted Z-shape resulting from an instance of $\mathrm{LWE}_{n,m,q,\chi}$.

2.7   Number Fields

Let $K \cong \mathbb{Q}[X]/P(X)$ be a number field of degree $d = [K : \mathbb{Q}] = \deg P$. We write $\mathcal{O}_K$ for the ring of integers, Δ_K for the discriminant, and μ_K for the set of roots of unity. K admits d distinct embeddings (injective field homomorphisms) into $\mathbb{C}$, each one corresponding to evaluating polynomials in K at one of the roots of P in $\mathbb{C}$. We define the *canonical embedding* $\sigma : K \to \mathbb{C}^d, x \mapsto (\sigma_i(x))_{i=1}^d$. We have $d = d_\mathbb{R} + 2d_\mathbb{C}$, where $d_\mathbb{R}$ denotes the number of real embeddings, and $d_\mathbb{C}$ the number of complex embeddings up to conjugation. We define the ring $K_\mathbb{R} = K\otimes_\mathbb{Q}\mathbb{R} \cong \mathbb{R}^{d_\mathbb{R}} \times \mathbb{C}^{d_\mathbb{C}}$, and for any $z \in K_\mathbb{R}$ define the complex conjugate $\bar{z} = \sigma^{-1}(\overline{\sigma(z)})$, and square root $z^{1/2} = \sigma^{-1}(\sigma(z)^{1/2})$, where σ has been extended to $K_\mathbb{R}$ and the conjugation and square root are applied componentwise.

The field trace $\mathrm{Tr} : K_\mathbb{R} \to \mathbb{R}, x \mapsto \sum_{j=1}^d \sigma_j(x)$ induces an inner product $\langle x, y\rangle_{\mathrm{Tr}} = \mathrm{Tr}(x\bar{y})$, which corresponds to $\langle\sigma(x), \sigma(y)\rangle_\mathbb{C}$. This extends to $K_\mathbb{R}^m$

by $\langle \mathbf{x}, \mathbf{y} \rangle_{\mathrm{Tr}} = \sum_{i=1}^{m} \langle x_i, y_i \rangle_{\mathrm{Tr}}$. On the other hand, we also define $\langle \mathbf{x}, \mathbf{y} \rangle_K = \sum_{i=1}^{m} x_i \bar{y}_i$. We write $\|\mathbf{x}\| = \langle \mathbf{x}, \mathbf{x} \rangle_{\mathrm{Tr}}^{1/2}$ and $\|\mathbf{x}\|_K = \langle \mathbf{x}, \mathbf{x} \rangle_K^{1/2}$. The algebraic norm is $\mathrm{N}(x) = \prod_{i=1}^{d} \sigma_i(x)$ and satisfies, by the arithmetic-geometric inequality, $\sqrt{d}\,\mathrm{N}(x)^{1/d} \leq \|x\|$. For $\mathbf{x} \in K_{\mathbb{R}}^m$ we use the shorthand $\mathrm{N}(\mathbf{x}) = \mathrm{N}(\langle \mathbf{x}, \mathbf{x} \rangle_K^{1/2})$.

Cyclotomic Fields. Let $c \in \mathbb{N}$ be odd or a multiple of 4. The cyclotomic number field with *conductor* c is $K = \mathbb{Q}(\omega_c) \cong \mathbb{Q}[X]/\Phi_c(X)$, where ω_c is a primitive c-th root of unity, and Φ_c is the c-th cyclotomic polynomial. The degree is $[K : \mathbb{Q}] = \deg \Phi_c = \phi(c)$. We have $|\mu_K| = c$ when c is even, and $|\mu_K| = 2c$ when c is odd.

The Cyclic Embedding. For $K = \mathbb{Q}(\omega_c)$ a cyclotomic field, consider the *cyclic ring* $\mathcal{C} = \mathbb{R}[X]/(X^c - 1)$. We view $\mathcal{C}$ as a Euclidean vector space equipped with the *coefficient inner product* $\langle \sum_{i=0}^{c-1} a_i X^i, \sum_{i=0}^{c-1} b_i X^i \rangle_{\mathrm{coeff}} := \sum_{i=0}^{c-1} a_i b_i$. The appropriately scaled discrete Fourier transform

$$\mathcal{F} : \mathcal{C} \to \mathbb{C}^c, \quad f(X) \mapsto \frac{1}{\sqrt{c}} \left(f(\omega_c^j) \right)_{j=0}^{c-1}$$

provides an isometry with $\mathbb{C}^c$ (equipped with the standard inner product).

On the other hand, the canonical embedding $\sigma : K \to \mathbb{C}^{\phi(c)}$ is an isometry (using the trace inner product on K), and there is a trivial isometry $\mathsf{pad} : \mathbb{C}^{\phi(c)} \to \mathbb{C}^c$ by null padding at positions corresponding to non-primitive c-th roots of unity.

Definition 17 (Cyclic Embedding). *In the notation above, the cyclic embedding* $\theta : K \to \mathcal{C}$ *is defined as the isometry completing the commutative diagram*

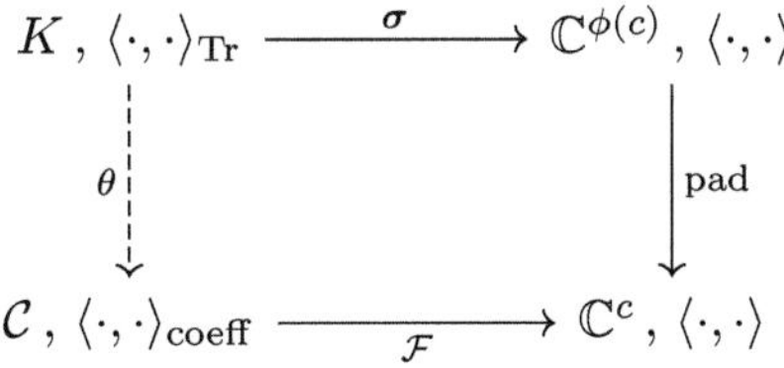

The cyclic embedding has been used, implicitly or explicitly, in several existing works [12, 20–22]. The utility of the cyclic embedding in this paper is twofold. Firstly, the ring of integers $\mathcal{O}_K = \mathbb{Z}[\omega_c]$ is mapped under θ to elements of $\frac{1}{\sqrt{c}}\mathbb{Z}[X]/(X^c - 1)$;[5] hence, multiplying elements of K by a factor $\sqrt{c}$ results in a scaled isometric embedding of $\mathcal{O}_K$ in $\mathbb{Z}^c$. This representation allows us, in

---

[5] Let $a \in \mathcal{O}_K$. By definition, denoting $\theta(a) = \sum_{k=0}^{c-1} b_k X^k$, $b_k = \frac{1}{c} \sum_{i=1}^{d} \sqrt{c} \cdot \sigma_i(a) \cdot \sigma_i(\omega_c^{-k}) = \frac{1}{\sqrt{c}} \sum_{i=1}^{d} \sigma_i(a\omega_c^{-k}) = \frac{1}{\sqrt{c}}\mathrm{Tr}(a\omega_c^{-k})$. As both a and ω_c are in the ring $\mathcal{O}_K$, $a\omega_c^{-k}$ also is, and its trace is in $\mathbb{Z}$.

implementations, to view module lattices as integer lattices using the standard inner product – whereas using the canonical embedding would lead to irrational values, and using the coefficient embedding would require a different inner product.

Secondly, the cyclic embedding allows us to efficiently sample from distributions on $\mathcal{O}_K$ which are close to spherical with respect to the geometry defined by the trace inner product. This technique was introduced in [20], which concerns the primal formulation of Ring-LWE, and we will utilise it when generating instances of Module-LWE for experiments.

In particular, viewing $K = \mathbb{Q}[X]/\Phi_c(X)$, there is a canonical projection $\pi : \mathcal{C} \to K$ by reducing modulo Φ_c (note that for any x in K, $\theta(x) \bmod \Phi_c = x$). This induces a $\mathbb{R}$-linear map $\pi_{\mathbb{R}} : \mathcal{C} \to K_{\mathbb{R}}$. Furthermore, we define the rounding map $\lfloor \cdot \rceil : K_{\mathbb{R}} \to \mathcal{O}_K$ by rounding each coefficient, $\sum_{i=0}^{d-1} a_i X^i \to \sum_{i=0}^{d-1} \lfloor a_i \rceil X^i$.

Definition 18. *With the notation above, we write χ_σ to mean the distribution on $\mathcal{O}_K$ sampled as follows.*

1. *Sample $g = \sum_{i=0}^{c-1} g_i X^i \in \mathcal{C}$ with each $g_i \leftarrow \mathcal{N}(0, \sigma^2/c)$*
2. *Return the rounded reduction $\lfloor \pi_{\mathbb{R}}(g) \rceil \in \mathcal{O}_K$.*

We note that $\pi_{\mathbb{R}}(g)$ is distributed as a continuous, spherical Gaussian with variance $d\sigma^2$ on $K_{\mathbb{R}}$ [20, Theorem 5]. However this is no longer true after the rounding step, with the distortion more pronounced for smaller σ. Nevertheless, for $a \leftarrow \chi_\sigma$ we have $\mathbb{E}[||a||^2] \approx d\sigma^2$, and similar to the integer discrete Gaussian $D_{\mathbb{Z},\sigma}$, this approximation improves for larger σ.

2.8 Module Lattices

A *fractional ideal* of $\mathcal{O}_K$ is an $\mathcal{O}_K$-submodule $\mathfrak{J} \subseteq K$ for which there exists $x \in K \setminus \{0\}$ such that $x\mathfrak{J} \subseteq \mathcal{O}_K$. The algebraic norm is $N(\mathfrak{J}) = [\mathcal{O}_K : x\mathfrak{J}]/|N(x)|$ for any such x. A rank r $\mathcal{O}_K$-module is a set of the form $\mathcal{M} = \sum_{i=1}^{r} \mathbf{b}_i \mathfrak{J}_i$ for nonzero fractional ideals $\mathfrak{J}_1, \ldots, \mathfrak{J}_r$ and $K_{\mathbb{R}}$-linearly independent vectors $\mathbf{b}_1, \ldots, \mathbf{b}_r \in K_{\mathbb{R}}^m$. $\mathcal{M}$ is said to be a *free* module if $\mathfrak{J}_1 = \cdots = \mathfrak{J}_r = \mathcal{O}_K$. The set $\mathfrak{B} = (\mathbf{b}_i, \mathfrak{J}_i)_{i=1}^r$ is a *pseudobasis* for $\mathcal{M}$, and called *unital* if $\mathcal{O}_K \subseteq \mathfrak{J}_i$ for all i. We write $\mathbf{B}$ for the matrix with columns $\mathbf{b}_1, \ldots, \mathbf{b}_r$. The module has $K_{\mathbb{R}}$-determinant $\det_{K_{\mathbb{R}}}(\mathcal{M}) = \det(\overline{\mathbf{B}}^T \mathbf{B}) \prod_{i=1}^r \mathfrak{J}_i$.

If we extend the canonical embedding $\boldsymbol{\sigma} : K \to \mathbb{C}^d$ componentwise to elements of $\mathcal{M}$, then $\boldsymbol{\sigma}(\mathcal{M})$ is an rd-dimensional lattice in $\mathbb{C}^{rd} \cong \mathbb{R}^{2rd}$, called a *module lattice*. We will abuse notation and write $\mathcal{M}$ to mean both the $\mathcal{O}_K$-module and the module lattice. The $\mathbb{Q}$-determinant is the volume of the module lattice, $\det_{\mathbb{Q}}(\mathcal{M}) = |\Delta_K|^{r/2} N(\det_{K_{\mathbb{R}}}(\mathcal{M}))$.

It has been shown, under certain conditions on K and r, that the first minimum of a random (formally defined using the Haar measure) unit volume rank r module lattice over a number field K is asymptotically concentrated around $(|\mu_K| \cdot \mathrm{vol}(B_{rd}))^{-rd}$ [25]. For cyclotomic K, this was adapted to give the *module Gaussian heuristic*, and justified experimentally, in [21].

Definition 19 (Module Gaussian Heuristic). *Let $\mathcal{M}$ be a rank r module lattice of unit volume over $K = \mathbb{Q}(\omega_c)$. The Gaussian heuristic for $\mathcal{M}$ approximates the first minimum as*

$$\mathrm{gh}_K(r) = \mathrm{gh}_{\mathbb{Q}}(rd) \cdot \left(\frac{|\mu_K|}{2}\right)^{1/rd}.$$

We write $\mathrm{lgh}_K(\cdot) = \ln \mathrm{gh}_K(\cdot)$. Again, by appropriate scaling, we define the module Gaussian heuristic for arbitrary $\mathcal{M}$ as $\mathrm{gh}_K(\mathcal{M}) = \mathrm{gh}_K(r) \cdot \det_{\mathbb{Q}}(\mathcal{M})^{1/rd}$.

Module-LWE provides another hardness assumption for cryptography [16, 31], and the algebraic structure can be utilised for better efficiency and smaller public key sizes, compared to unstructured LWE.

Definition 20 (MLWE$_{K,r,m,q,\chi}$). *Let r, m, q be positive integers and χ a probability distribution on $R_q = \mathcal{O}_K/q\mathcal{O}_K$. Sample $\mathbf{A} \leftarrow \mathcal{U}(R_q^{r \times m})$, a secret vector $\mathbf{s} \leftarrow \chi^r$, and error vector $\mathbf{e} \leftarrow \chi^m$, and compute*

$$\mathbf{b} = \mathbf{A}^T\mathbf{s} + \mathbf{e} \quad (\mathrm{mod}\ q\mathcal{O}_K)$$

An instance of MLWE$_{K,r,m,q,\chi}$ is the pair $(\mathbf{A}, \mathbf{b})$ and the goal is to recover the secret vector $\mathbf{s}$.

Again, we may abuse notation and give χ as a distribution on $\mathcal{O}_K$, with the understanding that we mean its reduction modulo $q\mathcal{O}_K$.

Note that formally the problem should be defined using the *dual ring* $R_q^\vee$ [37], but we have chosen to use the *primal* formulation, as is commonly done for practical purposes [14, 20]. As with LWE we consider *normal form* MLWE, noting that recent works [15] extend the standard reduction [7] to the module setting.

2.9   Module Lattice Reduction

Definition 21 (GSO over $K_{\mathbb{R}}$). *Given $\mathbf{B} = (\mathbf{b}_1, \dots, \mathbf{b}_r)$ which are $K_{\mathbb{R}}$-linearly independent, the GSO is*

$$\mathbf{b}_i^* = \mathbf{b}_i - \sum_{j<i} \mu_{i,j}\mathbf{b}_j^* \text{ where } \mu_{i,j} = \frac{\langle \mathbf{b}_i, \mathbf{b}_j^* \rangle_K}{\langle \mathbf{b}_j^*, \mathbf{b}_j^* \rangle_K}$$

As in the unstructured case, for a pseudobasis $\mathfrak{B} = (\mathbf{b}_i, \mathfrak{I}_i)_{i=1}^r$ of a module lattice $\mathcal{M}$ we define π_i as the $K_{\mathbb{R}}$-linear projection away from the span of $\{\mathbf{b}_1, \dots, \mathbf{b}_{i-1}\}$.

For $1 \leq i < j \leq r$ we define the *projected subbasis* $\mathfrak{B}_{[i:j]} = (\pi_i(\mathbf{b}_k), \mathfrak{I}_k)_{k=i}^j$ and the corresponding *projected submodule* $\mathcal{M}_{[i:j]} = \pi_i(\mathbf{b}_i)\mathfrak{I}_i + \dots + \pi_i(\mathbf{b}_j)\mathfrak{I}_j$.

Definition 22 (K-profile). *The pseudobasis $\mathfrak{B} = (\mathbf{b}_i, \mathfrak{I}_i)_{i=1}^r$ has K-profile $(\ell_i^K)_{i=1}^r$ where $\ell_i^K = \ln \det_{\mathbb{Q}}(\mathbf{b}_i^* \cdot \mathfrak{I}_i)$.*

Definition 23 (mBKZ$_K^{\beta_K}$**-reduced**). *Let* $2 \le \beta_K \le r$. *A pseudobasis* $\mathfrak{B}$ *of a rank* r *module* $\mathcal{M}$ *is* mBKZ$_K^{\beta_K}$*-reduced if for all* $i \in \{1, \ldots, r-1\}$,

$$||\mathbf{b}_i^*|| = \lambda_1(\mathcal{M}_{[i:\min(i+\beta_K-1,r)]}) \, .$$

To achieve this, we apply the Module-BKZ algorithm, an overview of which is given in [21, Alg. 1]. In practice we will consider running mBKZ$_K^{\beta_K}$ for a fixed number of tours τ, and also consider Progressive-mBKZ$_K$ which runs τ tours at each blocksize $\beta_K = 3, 4, \ldots$ sequentially.

Note that mBKZ using the K-blocksize β_K calls the SVP oracle on lattices of $\mathbb{Q}$-dimension at most $\beta = d\beta_K$, which we call the $\mathbb{Q}$-blocksize.

Definition 24 (Module-GSA, mGSA [21]). *Let* K *be a number field of degree* d. *Let* $\mathcal{M}$ *be a random rank* r *module over* K, *and let* $\mathfrak{B}$ *be an* mBKZ$_K^{\beta_K}$*-reduced pseudobasis of* $\mathcal{M}$ *for some sufficiently large* $\beta_K \ll r$. *Then there is a constant* $\alpha_K > 1$ *(depending on* β_K*) such that* $\mathbb{E}[\ell_i^K] = \mathbb{E}[\ell_1^K] - (i-1)\ln\alpha_K$.

Equivalently, $\mathbb{E}[\ell_i^K] = \frac{r+1-2i}{2}\ln\alpha_K + \frac{1}{r}\ln\det_{\mathbb{Q}}(\mathcal{M})$ for all $1 \le i \le r$, with

$$\ln\alpha_K = \frac{2d}{\beta_K - 1}\left(\mathbb{E}_\mathbf{s}[\ln||\mathbf{s}||] + \frac{1}{2d}\ln\frac{|\Delta_K|}{d^d} + \mathbb{E}_\mathbf{s}\left[\ln\frac{\sqrt{d}\mathrm{N}(\mathbf{s})^{1/d}}{||\mathbf{s}||}\right] + \frac{\mathbb{E}_{\mathfrak{J}}[\ln\mathrm{N}(\mathfrak{J})]}{d}\right)$$

where $\mathbf{s}$ is a shortest vector in one of the random normalised projected module lattices $\mathcal{M}_{[j:j+\beta_K-1]}^{(1)}$ for $1 \le j \le r-\beta_K+1$, and $\mathfrak{J}$ is the corresponding fractional ideal in the random unital pseudobasis $\mathfrak{B}$.[6] We write $\mathrm{slope}_K(\beta_K) = -\ln\alpha_K$. The four terms in the expression for $\ln\alpha_K$ are examined in [21, §4], under the further heuristic assumption that the projected sublattices behave as random unit volume lattices. The first may be estimated by the module-lattice Gaussian heuristic as $\mathrm{lgh}_K(\beta_K)$. The second depends only on K and is called the *discriminant gap*. The third is the *skewness gap* and modelled as $\mathrm{skew}_K(\beta_K)$ where

$$\mathrm{skew}_K(r) = \frac{\ln d}{2} + \frac{d_{\mathbb{R}}\psi(r/2) + 2d_{\mathbb{C}}(\psi(r) - \ln 2)}{2d} - \frac{\psi(rd)}{2}$$

Finally, the fourth term is the *index gap*. Under suitable heuristics this was shown to be exponentially small, and in practice is almost always zero for the lattices and blocksizes we consider [21, §4.5]. Moreover, embeddings of MLWE lattices are free, hence falling in the principal ideal class, and our experiments take as input bases with all fractional ideals $\mathfrak{J}_1, \ldots, \mathfrak{J}_r$ equal to $\mathcal{O}_K$ instead of more general pseudobases.

3 The Success Probability of Solving SVP via BKZ

In this section, we propose a new model for the success probability of solving SVP via BKZ. We apply our model to LWE, comparing to extensive experimental data, and demonstrate that it is not only more accurate than the existing

---

[6] As $\mathbf{s}$ is a shortest vector in the module, $\mathcal{O}_K \subseteq \mathfrak{J}$. The rest of the pseudobasis is made unital by applying [32, Alg. 3.2] in the mBKZ reduction.

estimators in [42], but also capable of capturing the difference in security between different distributions χ.

3.1   The Beta Distribution Model

We have seen that existing models for estimating the success probability apply the heuristic assumption that, after each tour, the projection of the embedded vector in the terminal block has square norm following a chi-squared distribution. Indeed, modelling $S = \mathrm{span}_{\mathbb{R}}(\Lambda_{[N-\beta+1]}) \subset \mathbb{R}^N$ as a random[7] β-dimensional subspace, and modelling $\mathbf{v}$ as sampled coordinatewise from a continuous Gaussian with variance σ^2, it follows that $||\pi_{N-\beta+1}(\mathbf{v})||^2 \sim \sigma^2 \chi_\beta^2$.

However, this reasoning implicitly assumes that $\mathbf{v}$ is rerandomised each tour. In reality, when attempting to solve a single instance, $\mathbf{v}$ is fixed – it is only the subspace S which is rerandomised each tour.

Lemma 1. *Let $\mathbf{v} \in \mathbb{R}^N$ be arbitrary, and let $S \subset \mathbb{R}^N$ be a uniformly random β-dimensional subspace. The projection of $\mathbf{v}$ onto S, denoted $\pi_S(\mathbf{v})$, has square norm following a beta distribution:*

$$||\pi_S(\mathbf{v})||^2 \sim ||\mathbf{v}||^2 \cdot Beta\left(\frac{\beta}{2}, \frac{N-\beta}{2}\right).$$

Proof. See [41, App. A].

As a consequence of Lemma 1 and the preceding discussion, we propose new estimators for the success probability of solving SVP via BKZ, essentially replacing the chi-squared distributions in [42] with the appropriate beta distributions. We have also decided to phrase our algorithms for a general lattice Λ, rather than one arising via the primal attack applied to an LWE instance. We require as input two properties of the lattice: an initial basis profile, and the first minimum λ_1. While in general computing λ_1 is a hard problem, for LWE lattices λ_1 is a random variable following a known distribution, and we will later integrate over this distribution (Sect. 3.2). The new estimators BKZSuccess and ProgBKZSuccess are described in Algorithms 1 and 2.

3.2   Application to LWE

To apply these estimators to the case of $\mathrm{LWE}_{n,m,q,\chi}$, where we reduce the Bai-Galbraith lattice Λ with embedded vector $\mathbf{v}$, we use for the initial profile the predicted Z-shape $(\ell_i)_{i=1}^N = \mathsf{LLLSim}(n, m, q, \chi)$. However, the first minimum $\lambda_1(\Lambda)$, which is the norm of the embedded vector $\mathbf{v}$, is not deterministic: it is a random variable depending on the LWE instance. We capture this as follows (choosing BKZSuccess for illustration). Assuming the probability density function f_V of the random variable $V = ||\mathbf{v}||^2$ is known, we estimate the success probability against a random $\mathrm{LWE}_{n,m,q,\chi}$ instance by computing the integral

---

[7] As per Definition 1.

```
1  BKZSuccess((ℓᵢ)ᴺ_{i=1}, λ₁, β, τ)
```

2 $p_{\text{tot}} \leftarrow 0$
3 **for** tour $\leftarrow 1$ **to** τ **do**
4    $\quad (\ell_i)_{i=1}^N \leftarrow \mathsf{BKZSim}((\ell_i)_{i=1}^N, \beta, 1)$
5    $\quad p_{\text{new}} \leftarrow \mathbb{P}\big(\lambda_1^2 \cdot \mathrm{Beta}\big(\frac{\beta}{2}, \frac{N-\beta}{2}\big) \leq \exp(2 \cdot \ell_{N-\beta+1})\big)$
6    $\quad p_{\text{tot}} \leftarrow p_{\text{tot}} + (1 - p_{\text{tot}}) \cdot p_{\text{new}}$
7 **end**
8 **return** p_{tot}

Algorithm 1: Proposed estimator for the success probability of solving SVP via τ tours of BKZ-β.

```
1  ProgBKZSuccess((ℓᵢ)ᴺ_{i=1}, λ₁, τ)
```

2 $p_{\text{tot}} \leftarrow 0,\ P \leftarrow \{\},\ \beta \leftarrow 3$
3 **while** $\beta < 40$ **do**
4    $\quad (\ell_i)_{i=1}^N \leftarrow \mathsf{BKZSim}((\ell_i)_{i=1}^N, \beta, \tau)$
5    $\quad \beta \leftarrow \beta + 1$
6 **end**
7 **while** $\beta \leq N$ **do**
8    $\quad$ **for** tour $\leftarrow 1$ **to** τ **do**
9      $\quad\quad (\ell_i)_{i=1}^N \leftarrow \mathsf{BKZSim}((\ell_i)_{i=1}^N, \beta, 1)$
10     $\quad\quad p_{\text{new}} \leftarrow \mathbb{P}\big(\lambda_1^2 \cdot \mathrm{Beta}\big(\frac{\beta}{2}, \frac{N-\beta}{2}\big) \leq \exp(2 \cdot \ell_{N-\beta+1})\big)$
11     $\quad\quad p_{\text{tot}} \leftarrow p_{\text{tot}} + (1 - p_{\text{tot}}) \cdot p_{\text{new}}$
12   $\quad$ **end**
13   $\quad P[\beta] \leftarrow p_{\text{tot}}$
14   $\quad$ **if** $p_{tot} \geq 0.999$ **then**
15     $\quad\quad$ **break**
16   $\quad$ **end**
17   $\quad \beta \leftarrow \beta + 1$
18 **end**
19 **return** P

Algorithm 2: Proposed estimator for the success probability of solving uSVP via Progressive-BKZ, with τ tours at each blocksize. Returns the cumulative mass function $P[\beta]$ of solving the instance in the round using block size β.

$$p = \int_{\mathrm{Supp}(V)} \mathsf{BKZSuccess}((\ell_i)_{i=1}^N, \sqrt{v}, \beta, \tau) \cdot f_V(v)\, \mathrm{d}v\,.$$

In practice, χ is typically a discrete probability distribution, thus $\mathrm{Supp}(V)$ is a discrete set, and the integral becomes a sum:

$$p = \sum_{v \in \mathrm{Supp}(V)} \mathsf{BKZSuccess}((\ell_i)_{i=1}^N, \sqrt{v}, \beta, \tau) \cdot \mathbb{P}(||\mathbf{v}||^2 = v).$$

We compute p by computing each term numerically.[8] The first factor is given by the output of Algorithm 1.[9] Recalling that the embedded vector is given by $\mathbf{v} = (\mathbf{e}, \mathbf{s}, t)$, where $\mathbf{e} \leftarrow \chi^m$, $\mathbf{s} \leftarrow \chi^n$ and t is the embedding coefficient, we compute the second factor exactly for certain distributions χ, and approximate it for others.

- *Centred Binary:* If $\chi = \mathcal{U}(\{-1, 1\})$ then $||\mathbf{v}||^2 = n + m + t^2$ is constant, and so the sum contains only one term.
- *Ternary:* If $\chi = \mathcal{U}(\{-1, 0, 1\})$ then $||\mathbf{v}||^2 \sim t^2 + \mathrm{Bin}(n + m, 2/3)$.
- *Discrete Gaussian:* If $\chi = D_{\mathbb{Z}, \sigma}$ then it is difficult to capture the distribution of $||\mathbf{v}||^2$ exactly. However, note that if χ were a *continuous* Gaussian $\chi = \mathcal{N}(0, \sigma^2)$ we would have $||\mathbf{v}||^2 \sim \sigma^2 \chi^2_{n+m} + t^2$. Thus we make the following approximation,

$$\mathbb{P}(||\mathbf{v}||^2 = v) \approx \mathbb{P}\left(v - \frac{1}{2} \leq \sigma^2 \chi^2_{n+m} + t^2 < v + \frac{1}{2}\right).$$

Furthermore, we note that we need not restrict ourselves, as we have done so far, to the regime where the LWE secret and error are sampled coordinatewise from some distribution χ. The model is far more general and can easily be adapted to, for example, sparse binary or ternary secrets.

3.3   Comparison to Experiments

To assess the accuracy of our new estimators, we compare to extensive experimental data.

Table 1. LWE parameter sets used for testing the primal attack and success probability simulators, also used in [42].

n	q	m	σ	β_{GSA}
93	257	105	1	61
100	257	104	$\sqrt{2/3}$	60

LWE Parameters. We consider LWE with two parameter sets, listed in Table 1. Each parameter set consists of n, q, m and σ^2, as well as the blocksize prediction β_{GSA} given by the 2016 estimate. For both parameter sets, we consider the discrete Gaussian distribution $\chi = D_{\mathbb{Z}, \sigma}$. For the $n = 93$ parameter set, where $\sigma = 1$, we may also consider the centred binary distribution

---

[8] If $\mathrm{Supp}(V)$ is infinite, we reduce to only finitely many terms by considering appropriate tail bounds on the distribution.

[9] We note that the calls to BKZSim within Algorithm 1 are independent of the input $\lambda_1 = v$, hence the profile simulation can be amortised.

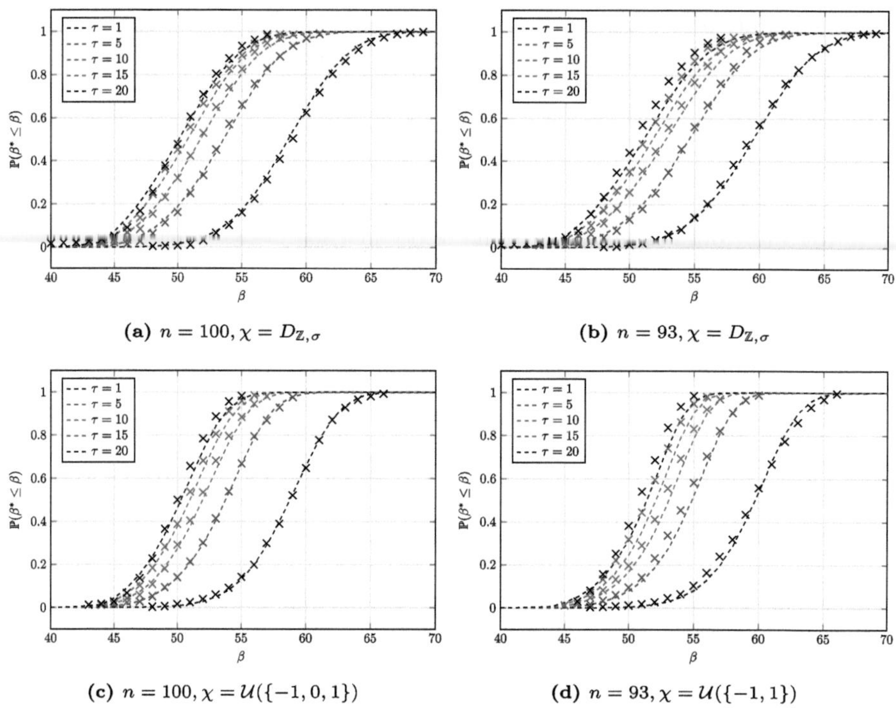

Fig. 1. Comparison of estimated and experimental success probabilities for Progressive-BKZ. Dashed lines are estimations, crosses are experimental data. For each subfigure, 1000 experiments were run. See Table 1 for full parameter sets.

$\chi = \mathcal{U}(\{-1, 1\})$. For the $n = 100$ parameter set, where $\sigma = \sqrt{2/3}$, we may consider for comparison the ternary distribution $\chi = \mathcal{U}(\{-1, 0, 1\})$.[10]

Implementation Details. We provide implementations in Python of Algorithms 1 and 2, and their applications to LWE as detailed in Sect. 3.2. We implement the primal attacks using BKZ 2.0 as provided in `fpylll` [47].

We note that the runtime of our new estimators is not noticeably different to the original estimators. Indeed, the runtime is dominated by the BKZ simulator, which remains unchanged.

We also note that the success probabilities (both experimental and estimated) are higher than those reported in the published version of [42], due to a slightly different Bai–Galbraith embedding; it is now standard practice to place the q-vectors at the *start* of the basis, as opposed to the middle, which gives a more extreme Z-shape. Their estimators have been updated to account for this improvement, allowing for fair comparison to our estimators.

---

[10] While the variance of $D_{\mathbb{Z},\sigma}$ may differ from σ^2, since we are not ensuring any conditions relating to smoothing, these examples were chosen in [42] to give different distributions in the same 'ballpark'.

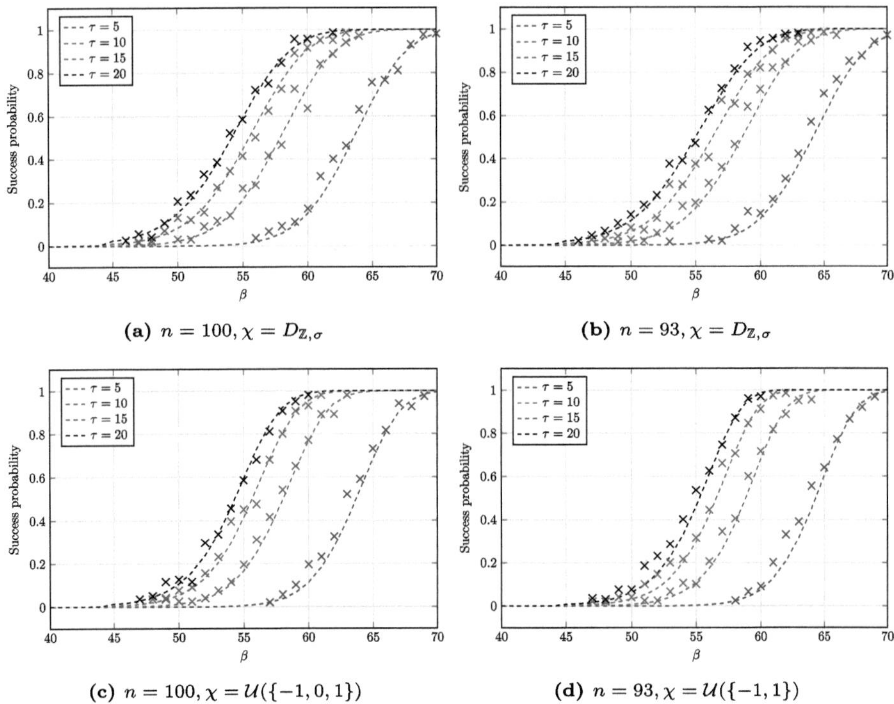

Fig. 2. Comparison of estimated and experimental success probabilities for BKZ-β. Dashed lines are estimations, crosses are experimental data. For each blocksize in each subfigure, 200 experiments were run. See Table 1 for full parameter sets.

Measuring Accuracy. To evaluate our estimators against those from [42], we compute the total squared error between estimated and experimental probabilities.

For Progressive-BKZ, the estimators give a prediction for the cumulative mass function $\mathbb{P}(\beta^* \leq \beta)$, where β^* is the blocksize at which the short vector is recovered. From this we may extract a probability mass function $f_{\text{est}}(\beta)$. On the other hand, by counting how many experiments succeed at each blocksize, we obtain an experimental probability mass function $f_{\text{exp}}(\beta)$. The total square error is then $\sum_{\beta}(f_{\text{est}}(\beta) - f_{\text{exp}}(\beta))^2$.

For BKZ-β, we obtain for each β an estimate $f_{\text{est}}(\beta)$ of the success probability when using β, and an experimental probability $f_{\text{exp}}(\beta)$. The total square error is again $\sum_{\beta}(f_{\text{est}}(\beta) - f_{\text{exp}}(\beta))^2$.

In each case we also provide a statistical baseline, to understand when the distances become significant. In particular, we compute the expected total square error if the same number of samples were drawn again from the experimentally obtained distribution and used to estimate it, as explained in [41, App. B].

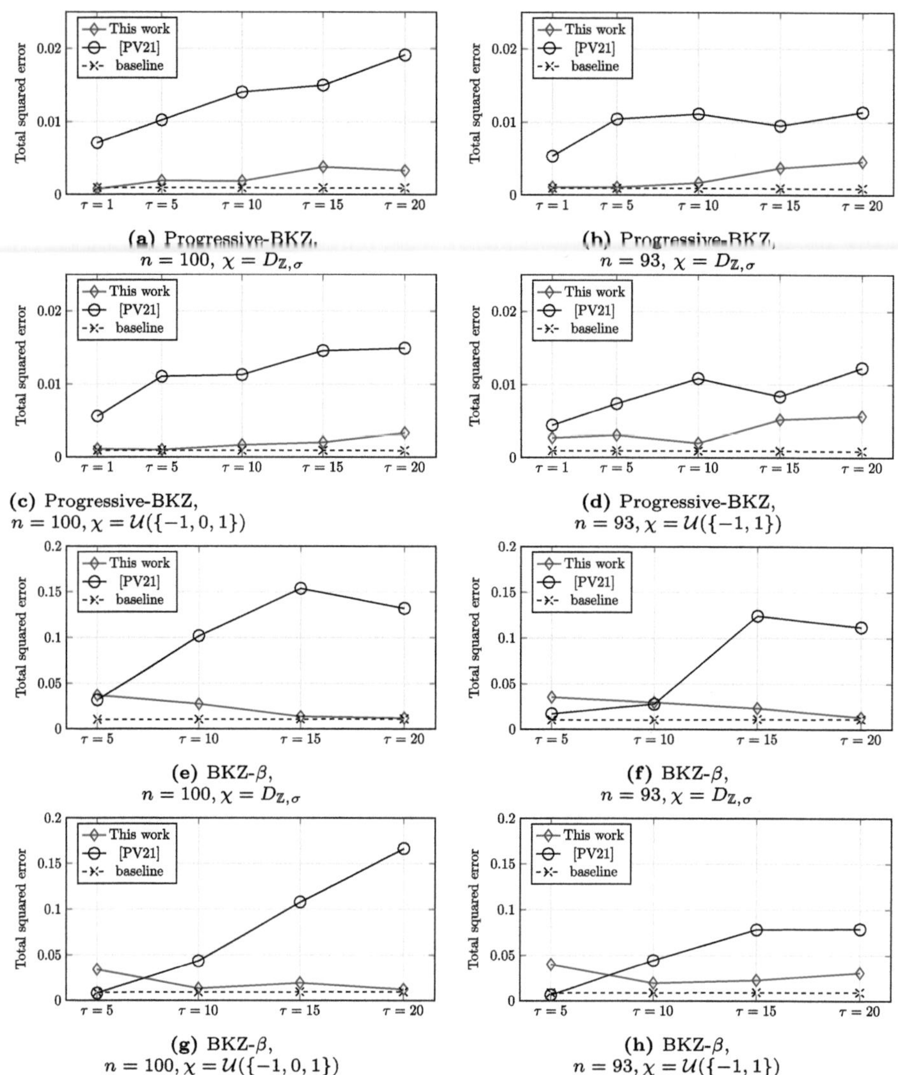

Fig. 3. Total squared error between estimated and experimental success probabilities, compared to a baseline of the expected total squared error if drawing the same number of samples again from the experimental distribution (see [41, App. B] for details).

Results and Observations. In Figs. 2 and 1 we show the output of our new estimators alongside experimental success probabilities. In Fig. 3 we show, for both our new estimators and the old [42] estimators, the total squared error to the experiments. To illustrate the qualitative difference between the old and new estimators, we compare their outputs in Fig. 4. Finally, in Fig. 5, we illustrate the difference in success probability for the various error and secret distributions (centred binary, ternary, and discrete Gaussian).

From Fig. 3 we see that our new model provides a consistent improvement in accuracy for Progressive-BKZ. In the case of BKZ-β, our model is marginally worse for $\tau = 5$ tours, but superior in all other cases.

In particular, when a larger number of tours are run, the [42] estimators vastly overestimate the success probability (see Fig. 4). This is due to implicitly assuming the embedded vector is sampled freshly each tour, and hence it always has a chance to be unusually small. These probabilities accumulate each tour, making the effect more pronounced when more tours are run. Our new model eliminates this flaw by design.

Furthermore, our new model is able to faithfully capture the difference in security between the different secret and error distributions (Fig. 5), whereas the old estimators are blind to the difference.

However, our new estimators often slightly *underestimate* the success probability. The cause of this is unclear; it is possibly due to the BKZ 2.0 algorithm in practice applying certain improvements to the basis quality (local block rerandomisation and preprocessing) which are not captured by the model.

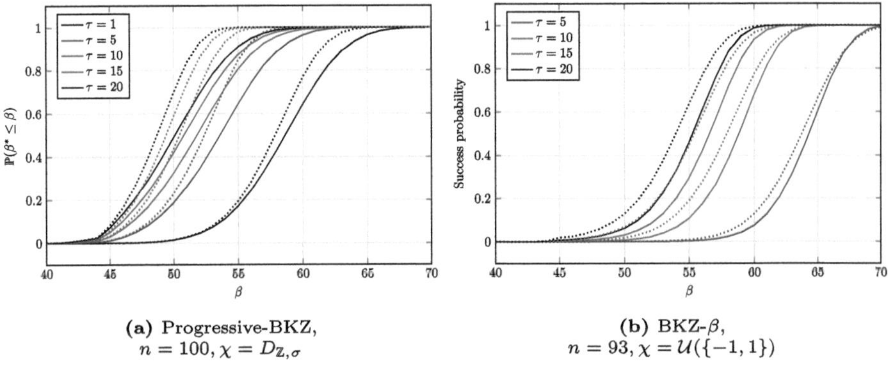

(a) Progressive-BKZ,
$n = 100, \chi = D_{\mathbb{Z},\sigma}$

(b) BKZ-β,
$n = 93, \chi = \mathcal{U}(\{-1, 1\})$

Fig. 4. Comparison between our estimators (solid) and those in [42] (dotted).

4 Module-BKZ Profile Simulation

In this section, we propose an algorithm to simulate the evolution of the K-profile of a pseudobasis when running Module-BKZ, and we verify its accuracy experimentally.

4.1 Algorithm Description

Suppose we have a pseudobasis $\mathfrak{B}$ with K-profile $(\ell_i)_{i=1}^{\rho}$. During a tour of $\mathrm{mBKZ}_K^{\beta_K}$, when the SVP oracle is called at position i, it will find the shortest

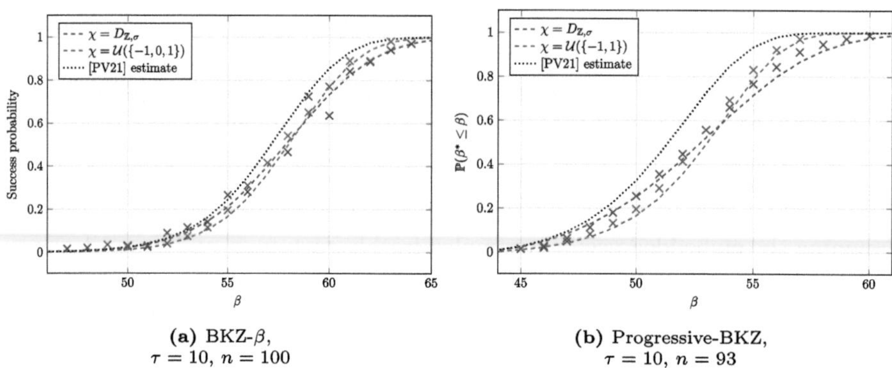

(a) BKZ-β,
$\tau = 10$, $n = 100$

(b) Progressive-BKZ,
$\tau = 10$, $n = 93$

Fig. 5. Comparison between the various secret and error distributions. Crosses are experiments, dashes are our estimators, dots are [42] estimators.

vector $\mathbf{w}$ in the projected module lattice $\mathcal{M}_{[i:\ i+b-1]}$ where $b = \min(\beta_K, \rho - i + 1)$ is the K-rank of the local block. Then, the corresponding ideal $\mathfrak{J}$ is computed, and $(\mathbf{w}, \mathfrak{J})$ is inserted into the pseudobasis $\mathfrak{B}$ at position i.

Following this insertion operation, the updated value of the K-profile at position i, which we denote by ℓ'_i, is thus given by:

$$\ell'_i = \ln \det_{\mathbb{Q}}(\mathbf{w}\mathfrak{J}) = \frac{1}{2} \ln |\Delta_K| + \ln \mathrm{N}(\mathbf{w}) + \ln \mathrm{N}(\mathfrak{J})$$

$$= d \ln(\|\mathbf{w}\|) + \frac{1}{2} \ln \frac{|\Delta_K|}{d^d} + d \ln \frac{\sqrt{d}\mathrm{N}(\mathbf{w})^{1/d}}{\|\mathbf{w}\|} + \ln \mathrm{N}(\mathfrak{J})$$

To obtain a formula for the average-case behaviour, we take expectations and follow the heuristic analysis in [21]. For large enough ranks $b \geq \lfloor 45/d \rfloor$,

$$\mathbb{E}[\ell'_i] \approx d \lgh_K(b) + \frac{1}{2} \ln \frac{|\Delta_K|}{d^d} + d \operatorname{skew}_K(b) + 0$$

For smaller ranks $b \leq \lfloor 45/d \rfloor$, the heuristic analysis is inaccurate, and we instead use experimental data for the average profile of a mHKZ_K-reduced rank $\lfloor 45/d \rfloor$ module lattice.

We iteratively apply this reasoning at each position in the basis, to obtain the simulator $\mathrm{mBKZSim}_K$ presented in Algorithm 3. We note that setting $K = \mathbb{Q}$ recovers the original simulator BKZSim.

4.2   Implementation

We provide a Python implementation of the simulator, which we use in Fig. 6 to compare experimental and simulated K-profiles. We see in particular the tails of the simulated profiles reflect those of the experimental profiles more accurately than the simple Module-GSA.

1 $\mathsf{mBKZSim}_K((\ell_i)_{i=1}^{\rho}, \beta_K, \tau)$

2 /* Pre-processing */

3 $(h_i) \leftarrow$ average profile of mHKZ_K-reduced unit-volume rank $\lfloor 45/d \rfloor$ module lattice

4 **for** $b \leftarrow 1$ **to** $\lfloor 45/d \rfloor$ **do**

5 $\quad$ $c_b \leftarrow h_{\lfloor 45/d \rfloor - b + 1} - \dfrac{1}{b} \displaystyle\sum_{i=\lfloor 45/d \rfloor - b + 1}^{\lfloor 45/d \rfloor} h_i$

6 **end**

7 **for** $b \leftarrow \lfloor 45/d \rfloor + 1$ **to** β_K **do**

8 $\quad$ $c_b \leftarrow d \lg h_K(b) + \dfrac{1}{2} \ln \dfrac{|\Delta_K|}{d^d} + d \operatorname{skew}_K(b)$

9 **end**

10 /* Profile simulation */

11 **for** tour $\leftarrow 1$ **to** τ **do**

12 $\quad$ $\phi \leftarrow$ true

13 $\quad$ $t \leftarrow \min(\lfloor 45/d \rfloor, \beta_K)$

14 $\quad$ **for** $i \leftarrow 1$ **to** $\rho - t + 1$ **do**

15 $\quad\quad$ $b \leftarrow \min(\beta_K, \rho - i)$ $\qquad\qquad$ // Dimension of local block

16 $\quad\quad$ $f \leftarrow \min(i + \beta_K, \rho)$ $\qquad\qquad$ // End index of local block

17 $\quad\quad$ $\ln V \leftarrow \sum_{j=1}^{f} \ell_j - \sum_{j=1}^{i-1} \ell'_j$

18 $\quad\quad$ **if** $\phi =$ true **then**

19 $\quad\quad\quad$ **if** $\ln V / b + c_b < \ell_i$ **then**

20 $\quad\quad\quad\quad$ $\ell'_i \leftarrow \ln V / b + c_b$

21 $\quad\quad\quad\quad$ $\phi \leftarrow$ false

22 $\quad\quad\quad$ **end**

23 $\quad\quad$ **end**

24 $\quad\quad$ **else**

25 $\quad\quad\quad$ $\ell'_i \leftarrow \ln V / b + c_b$

26 $\quad\quad$ **end**

27 $\quad$ **end**

$\quad$ // Insert tail

28 $\quad$ $\ln V \leftarrow \sum_{i=1}^{\rho} \ell_i - \sum_{i=1}^{\rho - t} \ell'_i$

29 $\quad$ **for** $i \leftarrow \rho - t + 2$ **to** ρ **do**

30 $\quad\quad$ $\ell'_i \leftarrow \ln V / t + h_{i + \lfloor 45/d \rfloor - \rho}$

31 $\quad$ **end**

$\quad$ // Overwrite old profile with new profile

32 $\quad$ $(\ell_i)_{i=1}^{\rho} \leftarrow (\ell'_i)_{i=1}^{\rho}$

33 **end**

34 **return** $(\ell_i)_{i=1}^{\rho}$

Algorithm 3: Proposed algorithm for simulating τ tours of $\mathrm{mBKZ}_K^{\beta_K}$ on a given K-profile $(\ell_i)_{i=1}^{\rho}$.

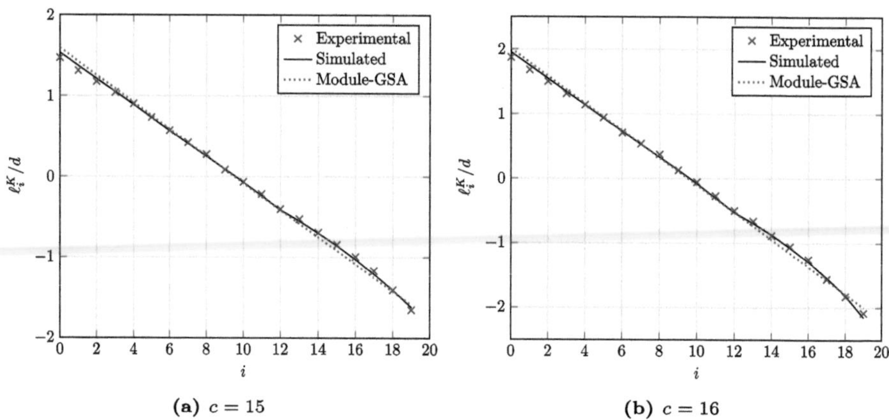

(a) $c = 15$ **(b)** $c = 16$

Fig. 6. Comparison between the Module-GSA, the simulated profiles using Algorithm 3, and the experimental profiles taken from [21]. Each experimental profile is the average over 5 lattices. Random module lattices of $\mathbb{Q}$-rank 160 were reduced with blocksize $\beta_K = 64/d$ for 30 tours.

5   The Module Primal Attack

The standard primal attack can be applied to Module-LWE instances, but does not utilise the algebraic structure. On the other hand, Module-BKZ allows for a module analogue of the primal attack. We generalise our improved model for the primal attack to the module setting, and compare the two attacks.

Definition 25 (Module-Bai–Galbraith Embedding). *Given an instance of normal form Module-LWE,* $(\mathbf{A}, \mathbf{b}) \leftarrow \mathrm{MLWE}_{K,r_K,m_K,q,\chi}$, *let* $\rho_K = r_K + m_K + 1$. *We define the Module-Bai–Galbraith lattice as the the rank* ρ_K *free module* $\mathcal{M}$ *over* $\mathcal{O}_K$ *with* K*-basis given by the columns of*

$$\mathbf{M} = \begin{pmatrix} q\mathbf{I}_{m_K} & -\mathbf{A}^T & \mathbf{b} \\ & \mathbf{I}_{r_K} & \\ & & t \end{pmatrix} \in K^{\rho_K \times \rho_K}$$

where $t \in K$ *is the embedding coefficient.*

The module lattice $\mathcal{M}$ contains a rank 1 module sublattice $\mathcal{V} = \mathbf{v}\mathcal{O}_K$, where $\mathbf{v} = (\mathbf{e}, \mathbf{s}, t)^T$ contains the error $\mathbf{e}$ and secret $\mathbf{s}$. From the K-basis we may compute the volume $\det_{\mathbb{Q}}(\mathcal{M}) = |\Delta_K|^{\rho_K/2} q^{m_K d} \mathrm{N}(\|t\|_K)$. The *module primal attack* against MLWE consists of forming this lattice, and applying mBKZ with the goal of recovering $\mathcal{V}$.

The Shortest Vector. Unlike in the standard primal attack where the embedding gives a uSVP instance, we have instead embedded a dense sublattice $\mathcal{V} \subset \mathcal{M}$

which contains many short vectors $\{\zeta\mathbf{v}\}_{\zeta\in\mu_K}$. While $\mathbf{v}\in\mathcal{V}$ minimises the *algebraic norm*, it is possible that there is some element in $\mathbf{w}\in\mathcal{V}$ with shorter Euclidean norm. However, we can justify that this is unlikely when ρ_K is sufficiently large. For any $\mathbf{w}\in\mathcal{V}$ we have

$$||\mathbf{w}|| \geq \sqrt{d}\mathrm{N}(\mathbf{w})^{1/d} \geq \sqrt{d}\mathrm{N}(\mathbf{v})^{1/d}$$

and, as ρ_K increases, we expect this lower bound to rapidly tend to $||\mathbf{v}||$. Indeed, modelling $\mathbf{v}$ as spherically sampled,[11] we may apply the skewness model $\mathrm{skew}_K(\rho_K)$ (see Sect. 2.9) as a heuristic lower bound,

$$0 \geq \mathbb{E}_\mathbf{v}\left[\ln\frac{\sqrt{d}\mathrm{N}(\mathbf{v})^{1/d}}{||\mathbf{v}||}\right] \geq \mathrm{skew}_K(\rho_K) = \frac{1 - d_\mathbb{R} - d_\mathbb{C}}{2d\rho_K} + o\left(\frac{1}{\rho_K}\right).$$

In particular, even if there *is* a shorter vector, it is not much shorter than $\mathbf{v}$. We henceforth always make the assumption that $\mathbf{v}$ is a shortest vector, and moreover that $\mu_K\,\mathbf{v} = \{\zeta\mathbf{v}\}_{\zeta\in\mu_K}$ is the set of shortest vectors. We note that a shorter vector $\mathbf{w}\in\mathcal{V}$ would increase the chance of mBKZ recovering $\mathcal{V}$ and hence $\mathbf{v}$, so this assumption is pessimistic for an attacker.

Choice of Embedding Coefficient. The notion of f-unusual-SVP does not demand uniqueness of the shortest vector, and we may still heuristically assume that the hardness of recovering any one of the shortest vectors is driven by the ratio $f = \mathrm{gh}_K(\mathcal{M})/\lambda_1(\mathcal{M})$. To maximise f, note the factor dependent on t is

$$\frac{\mathrm{N}(||t||_K)^{1/d(r_K+m_K+1)}}{\sqrt{d(r_K + m_K)\sigma^2 + ||t||^2}}$$

and we recall the inequality $\mathrm{N}(||t||_K)^{1/d} \leq ||t||/\sqrt{d}$, with equality when $t \in \mathbb{Q}\cdot\mu_K$. Thus we choose t rational; the above then simplifies, and is maximised at $t = \sigma$.[12]

5.1   Blocksize Prediction Using the Module-GSA

We now adapt the [6] blocksize analysis to the module setting, estimating the blocksize β_K required for the module primal attack to succeed, assuming the mGSA. Let $(\mathbf{A}, \mathbf{b}) \leftarrow \mathrm{MLWE}_{K,r_K,m_K,q,\chi}$, and let $\mathcal{M}$ be the corresponding Module-Bai–Galbraith lattice with embedded vector $\mathbf{v}$. When a tour of $\mathrm{mBKZ}_K^{\beta_K}$ reaches the terminal block, a projection of an embedded vector $\mathbf{w}\in\mu_K\mathbf{v}$ is inserted if it is a shortest vector. Under any K-linear projection π, the projections of the embedded vectors will all have the same length,

$$||\pi(\zeta\mathbf{v})|| = ||\zeta\pi(\mathbf{v})|| = ||\pi(\mathbf{v})||\quad \forall\zeta\in\mu_K$$

---

[11] Such a distribution is obtained through a spherical sampling on the cyclic embedding.

[12] If σ is irrational, we may choose an arbitrarily good rational approximation.

hence we need only consider one shortest vector $\mathbf{v}$, leading to the success condition

$$||\pi_{\rho_K - \beta_K + 1}(\mathbf{v})|| \leq \lambda_1(\mathcal{M}_{[\rho_K - \beta_K + 1]}). \tag{4}$$

Using the beta distribution model from Sect. 3.1 for the squared norm of the projection of $\mathbf{v}$, we compute the expected logarithm of the norm as

$$\mathbb{E}\left[\ln ||\pi_{\rho_K - \beta_K + 1}(\mathbf{v})||\right] = \mathbb{E}\left[\ln ||\mathbf{v}||\right] + \frac{1}{2}\,\mathbb{E}\left[\ln X\right]$$

where $X \sim \mathrm{Beta}\left(\frac{d\beta_K}{2}, \frac{d(\rho_K - \beta_K)}{2}\right)$. Following the [6] paradigm we consider the case where $\mathbf{v}$ is a spherical Gaussian, yielding

$$\mathbb{E}\left[\ln ||\pi_{\rho_K - \beta_K + 1}(\mathbf{v})||\right] = \ln(\sigma\sqrt{2}) + \frac{1}{2}\,\psi\left(\frac{d\beta_K}{2}\right) = \ln\left(\sigma\sqrt{d\beta_K}\right) - \frac{1}{2d\beta_K} + o\left(\frac{1}{\beta_K}\right).$$

On the other hand, after running $\mathrm{mBKZ}_K^{\beta_K}$, we assume the shortest vector in the terminal block behaves according to the module Gaussian heuristic,

$$\lambda_1(\mathcal{M}_{[\rho_K - \beta_K + 1]}) = \mathrm{gh}_K(\beta_K) \cdot \det_{\mathbb{Q}}(\mathcal{M}_{[\rho_K - \beta_K + 1]})^{\frac{1}{d\beta_K}}$$

From the definition of the K-profile and the mGSA we derive

$$\mathbb{E}\left[\ln \det_{\mathbb{Q}}(\mathcal{M}_{[\rho_K - \beta_K + 1]})\right] = \beta_K\left(\frac{1}{\rho_K}\ln\det_{\mathbb{Q}}(\mathcal{M}) + \frac{\rho_K - \beta_K}{2}\mathrm{slope}_K(\beta_K)\right)$$

Note that $\mathrm{slope}_K(\beta_K) = -\ln\alpha_K < 0$ from Definition 24. Taking logs and expectations in Eq. (4), substituting the above and simplifying, we attain the mGSA success condition:

$$\ln(\sigma\sqrt{2}) + \frac{1}{2}\psi\left(\frac{d\beta_K}{2}\right) \leq \mathrm{lgh}_K(\beta_K) + \frac{\ln\det_{\mathbb{Q}}(\mathcal{M})}{d\rho_K} + \frac{\rho_K - \beta_K}{2d}\mathrm{slope}_K(\beta_K) \tag{5}$$

5.2 Asymptotic Comparison to the Standard Primal Attack

The standard primal attack can also be applied to MLWE instances, by ignoring the module structure and embedding only one vector (in the language of Definition 26 later, using the ℓ-embedding with $\ell = 1$). The resulting lattice Λ has rank $d(r_K + m_K) + 1$, volume $|\Delta_K|^{d(r_K + m_K)/2} q^{m_K d}\sigma$, and follows the GSA success condition

$$\ln(\sigma\sqrt{2}) + \frac{1}{2}\psi\left(\frac{\beta}{2}\right) < \mathrm{lgh}_{\mathbb{Q}}(\beta) - \frac{d(r_K + m_K) + 1 - \beta}{\beta - 1} + \frac{\mathrm{vol}(\Lambda)}{d(r_K + m_K) + 1} \tag{6}$$

We may thus asymptotically compare the blocksizes required by the standard and module primal attacks.

Theorem 1 (Asymptotic Relation Between BKZ and Module-BKZ Blocksizes). *Let $\beta = d\beta_K$ where β_K is the minimal blocksize satisfying the Module-GSA success condition Eq. (5). Let β_{eq} be the minimal blocksize satisfying the corresponding GSA success condition, Eq. (6).*

If σ and q are fixed and $m_K = \alpha r_K + o(r_K)$, then

$$\beta_{\mathrm{eq}} = \beta + \frac{1}{d}\ln\frac{d^d}{|\Delta_K|}\ln\left(\frac{q^{2\alpha/(1+\alpha)}|\Delta_K|^{1/d}}{\sigma^2 2\pi e}\right)\frac{\beta}{(\ln\beta)^2} + o\left(\frac{\beta}{(\ln\beta)^2}\right).$$

We provide a proof in the full version [41]. In the process we additionally prove the following lemma relating $r_K + m_K$ to β asymptotically, which is itself insightful.

Lemma 2 (Asymptotic Relation Between Dimension and Blocksize in the Module Primal Attack). *Let $r = dr_K$, $m = dm_K$, and let $\beta = d\beta_K$ where β_K is the minimal blocksize satisfying the Module-GSA success condition Eq. (5). If σ and q are fixed and $m_K = \alpha r_K + o(r_K)$, then*

$$r + m = \beta + C_f \cdot \frac{\beta}{\ln\beta} + C_K C_f \cdot \frac{\beta}{(\ln\beta)^2} + o\left(\frac{\beta}{(\ln\beta)^2}\right),$$

where $C_f = \ln\left(\dfrac{q^{2\alpha/(1+\alpha)}|\Delta_K|^{1/d}}{\sigma^2 2\pi e}\right)$ and $C_K = \dfrac{1}{d}\ln\dfrac{d^d}{|\Delta_K|} + \ln(2\pi e)$.

When K is a cyclotomic number field with conductor a power of two, then $|\Delta_K| = d^d$ and thus Theorem 1 simply implies that $\beta_{\mathrm{eq}} - \beta = o(\beta/(\ln\beta)^2)$. On the other hand, for all other cyclotomic fields, $|\Delta_K| < d^d$ and so the module primal attack succeeds with smaller blocksizes, with the gap driven by the factor $\ln(d^d/|\Delta_K|)/d$. This factor, corresponding to the 'discriminant gap' term in [21], depends only on the radical (product of distinct prime factors) of the conductor, growing with the number of small odd primes in its decomposition [21, §4.3].

The other factor C_f increasing the gap is directly impacted by the $\mathbb{Q}$-determinant of the module lattice and the length of its shortest vector – though related to usual measures of hardness of a short vector recovery, the importance of the discriminant in its value should be noted.

5.3   Prediction via Simulation

For more fine-grained predictions, we adapt our SVP estimators (Algorithms 1 and 2) to obtain mBKZSuccess and mProgBKZSuccess. The first is presented in Algorithm 4, and the second follows analogously.

To apply these to Module-LWE we additionally (as in Sect. 3.2) require an initial profile for the Module-Bai–Galbraith lattice, and the probability distribution of $||\mathbf{v}||^2$. For the initial profile, we use a simple adaptation of LLLSim returning instead a K-profile, which we call mLLLSim. In our experiments, we use $\mathbf{v} \sim \chi_\sigma^{\rho_K}$, and thus model $||\mathbf{v}||^2 \sim \sigma^2 \chi_{d\rho_K}^2$.

---

1 $\mathsf{mBKZSuccess}_K((\ell_i^K)_{i=1}^{\rho}, \lambda_1, \beta_K, \tau)$

---

2 $p_{\text{tot}} \leftarrow 0$

3 **for** tour $\leftarrow 1$ **to** τ **do**

4     $(\ell_i)_{i=1}^{\rho} \leftarrow \mathsf{mBKZSim}((\ell_i^K)_{i=1}^{\rho}, \beta_K, 1)$

5     $\ln V \leftarrow \sum_{i=\rho-\beta_K+1}^{\rho} \ell_i^K$ // Volume of terminal block

6     $\lambda_1' \leftarrow \exp(\lg h_K(\beta_K) + \ln V / d\beta_K)$ // mGH for terminal block

7     $p_{\text{new}} \leftarrow \mathbb{P}\left(\lambda_1^2 \cdot \mathrm{Beta}\left(\frac{d \cdot \beta_K}{2}, \frac{d \cdot \rho - d \cdot \beta_K}{2}\right) \leq (\lambda_1')^2\right)$

8     $p_{\text{tot}} \leftarrow p_{\text{tot}} + (1 - p_{\text{tot}}) \cdot p_{\text{new}}$

9 **end**

10 **return** p_{tot}

Algorithm 4: Proposed estimator for the success probability of solving SVP via τ tours of $\mathrm{mBKZ}_K^{\beta_K}$.

5.4 Experiments

MLWE Parameters. We consider Module-LWE with four parameter sets, listed in Table 2. Each parameter set consist of the conductor c for the underlying number field $K = \mathbb{Q}(\omega_c)$, as well as the MLWE parameters r_K, m_K, q, and a parameter σ for the width of $\chi = \chi_\sigma$ as per Definition 18. We also provide the GSA and mGSA predictions for the standard and module primal attacks, given as $\mathbb{Q}$-blocksizes β_{mGSA} and β_{GSA} respectively. The parameter sets are chosen to keep β_{mGSA} roughly constant while comparing different number fields.[13]

Table 2. MLWE parameter sets used for testing the primal attacks. We choose a fixed number of samples m_K slightly larger than r_K, as is typically optimal, see [6, Table 1].

c	r_K	m_K	q	σ	β_{mGSA}	β_{GSA}
3	59	60	48000	11	60	66
5	29	30	30000	12	60	62
7	18	21	10000	10	60	56
8	29	30	20000	8	60	49

Implementation Details. We provide an implementation of the structured primal attack in Python, building upon the implementation of Module-BKZ provided in [21]. Module lattices are represented using the cyclic embedding. The SVP oracle is implemented using sieving, as provided by (the Python wrapper for) the **g6k** library [3].

---

[13] Interestingly, for $c = 7$ we have $\beta_{\mathrm{mGSA}} > \beta_{\mathrm{GSA}}$ despite mBKZ providing an improved slope; this is due to the differences in the rank, volume, and shortest vector length in the embedding lattices.

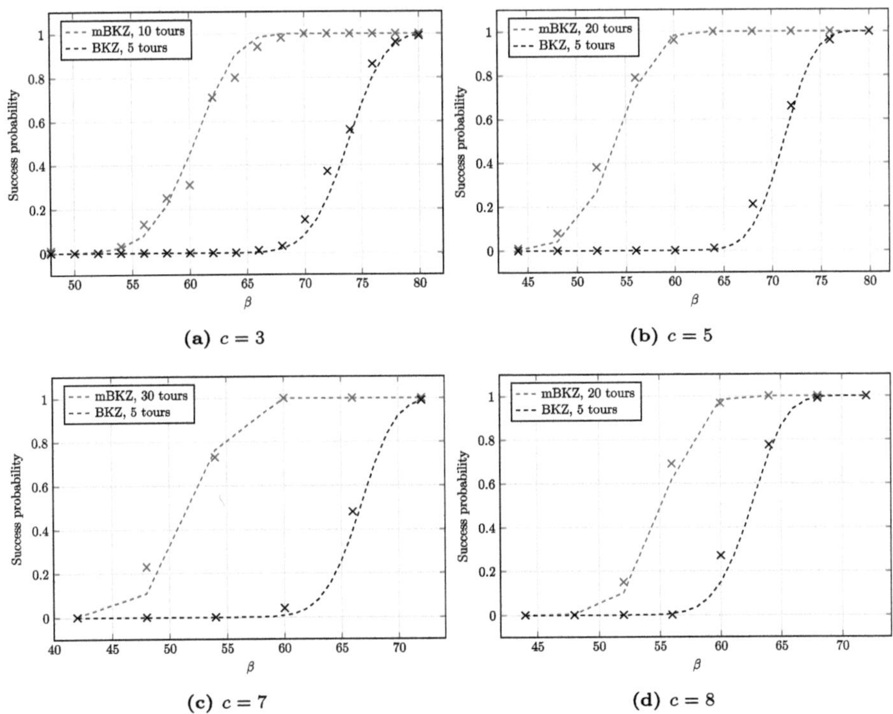

Fig. 7. Success probabilities for both the module primal attack using $\mathrm{mBKZ}_K^{\beta/d}$, and the standard primal attack using BKZ-β. Dashed lines are estimations, crosses are experimental data. For each blocksize in each subfigure, 200 experiments were run. See Table 2 for full parameter sets.

Methodology for Comparison. In our experiments, we allow fair comparison between BKZ and Module-BKZ as follows.

For primal attacks using a fixed blocksize, we compare BKZ-β to $\mathrm{mBKZ}_K^{\beta_K}$, where $\beta = d \cdot \beta_K$ is the $\mathbb{Q}$-blocksize of $\mathrm{mBKZ}_K^{\beta_K}$, ensuring the SVP oracles in each algorithm operate on lattices of the same dimension. Furthermore, a single tour of BKZ applies the oracle at each consecutive index i, whereas in mBKZ it is only applied at indices which are a multiple of d. Thus to balance the number of oracle calls, we compare τ tours of BKZ to $d \cdot \tau$ tours of mBKZ.

For primal attacks using a progressive strategy, the situation is more complicated. Progressive-BKZ uses each blocksize $\beta \geq 2$, whereas Progressive-mBKZ can only utilise $\mathbb{Q}$-blocksizes $\beta \geq 2d$ that are multiples of d. Nevertheless, we will compare Progressive-BKZ with τ tours at each blocksize to Progressive-mBKZ with $d \cdot \tau$ tours at each blocksize, which ensures close runtimes while keeping the cost for Progressive-mBKZ slightly lower – a more detailed cost comparison may be found in [41, App. D].

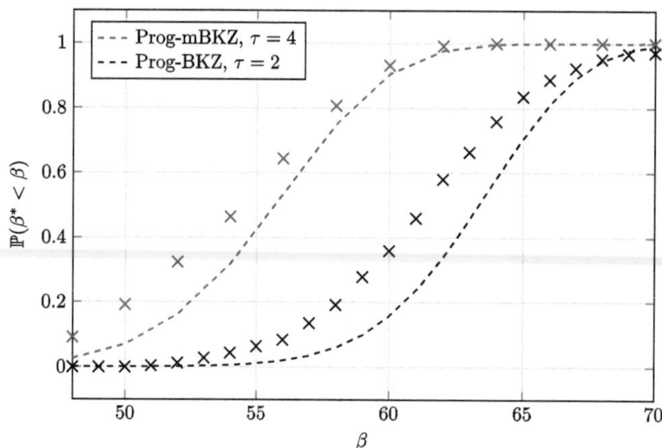

Fig. 8. Success probabilities for both the module primal attack using Progressive-mBKZ$_K$ and the standard primal attack using Progressive-BKZ, applied to Module-LWE instances with the $c = 3$ parameter set (Table 2). Dashed lines are estimations, crosses are experimental data. For each attack, 250 experiments were run.

Results and Observations In Figs. 7 and 8 we compare the estimators to experiments. We observe that our estimators are relatively accurate, although tend to underestimate the success probability, especially in Fig. 8. We suspect this is a consequence of optimisations in **g6k**, especially on-the-fly lifting, which are not captured in the model.

Regardless, the experiments and predictions show that the module primal attack appears superior in all cases, even when $\beta_{\mathrm{mGSA}} > \beta_{\mathrm{GSA}}$. To explain this, note that the GSA and mGSA success conditions assume sufficiently many tours have been run for convergence, and thus the relative convergence speeds of the algorithms are unaccounted for. For example in the $c = 8$ parameter set, writing τ and $\tau_K = \mathrm{d} \cdot \tau$ for the number of tours in each case, the estimators predict that the standard attack is eventually superior when $\tau \geq 11$.

Furthermore, note that when balancing total oracle calls as we have done, that Module-BKZ makes a factor d *more* oracle calls on the terminal block ($d\tau$ as opposed to τ), and thus has more 'chances' to find a projection of the embedded vector, which is not captured in the GSA/mGSA.

6   Modelling Attacks with Multiple Embedded Vectors

Thus far, we have considered two attacks against Module-LWE: the standard primal attack, which embeds one short vector to give a uSVP instance; and the module primal attack, which embeds d short vectors generating a dense sublattice. To use Module-BKZ, it is necessary to embed the entire dense sublattice. However if we only consider BKZ, we are free to embed only part of it, generated by $1 \leq \ell \leq d$ short vectors.

It is possible that choosing $\ell > 1$ may be advantageous compared to the usual primal attack using $\ell = 1$. Intuitively, embedding more vectors should increase the probability at least one projection is short.[14]. Embeddings of this form have previously been considered in [40,49], where it was observed experimentally for certain parameter sets that $\ell \approx 2, 3$ was optimal. In this section we investigate such embeddings, proposing a model for the success probability which takes into account the presence of multiple embedded vectors.

6.1   Extended Bai–Galbraith Embeddings

Let K be a cyclotomic field with $\theta : K \to \mathcal{C} \cong \mathbb{R}^c$ the cyclic embedding.

Definition 26 (ℓ-embedding). *For $(\mathbf{A}, \mathbf{b}) \leftarrow \mathrm{MLWE}_{K,r,m,q,\chi}$ and an integer $1 \leq \ell \leq d$, we define the ℓ-embedding as the matrix where $\mathbf{B} \in \mathbb{R}^{c(m+r) \times d(m+r)}$ is a $\mathbb{Z}$-basis, under the cyclic embedding θ, for the module lattice with K-basis*

$$\begin{bmatrix} q\mathbf{I}_m & -\mathbf{A}^T \\ & \mathbf{I}_r \end{bmatrix},$$

the vectors $\mathbf{b}_i = \theta(\omega_c^i \mathbf{b}) \in \mathbb{R}^{c(m+r)}$ are rotations of $\mathbf{b}$ in the cyclic embedding, and $\mathbf{T}_\ell \in \mathbb{R}^{\ell \times \ell}$ is the 'embedding submatrix' with columns $\mathbf{t}_i$.

This yields a (non full rank) lattice $\Lambda = \Lambda(\mathbf{M}_\ell) \subset \mathbb{R}^{cm+cr+\ell}$ of rank $N = dm + dr + \ell$, which contains the short vectors $\mathbf{v}_i = \big(\theta(\omega_c^i \mathbf{e}), \theta(\omega_c^i \mathbf{s}), \mathbf{t}_i\big)$ for $i = 0, \ldots, \ell - 1$. Furthermore, suppose there is another root of unity in the $\mathbb{Z}$-span of the first ℓ, say $\omega_c^k = \sum_{i=0}^{\ell-1} z_i \omega_c^i$. Then for each such ω_c^k (up to sign), Λ additionally contains a short vector $\mathbf{v}_k = \big(\theta(\omega_c^k \mathbf{e}), \theta(\omega_c^k \mathbf{s}), \sum_{i=0}^{\ell-1} z_i \mathbf{t}_i\big)$.

6.2   Success Probability Model

To model the success probability of recovering an embedded vector with BKZ, we adapt our existing estimators (Algorithms 1 and 2) as follows.

First, we compute the set R of all roots of unity in $\mathrm{span}_{\mathbb{Z}}\{1, \omega_c, \ldots \omega_c^{\ell-1}\}$, up to sign, represented as coefficients $\mathbf{z} = (z_0, \ldots, z_{\ell-1})$ of the linear combination.[15]

Then, given $V = ||(\mathbf{e}, \mathbf{s})||$, the corresponding vectors in Λ have square norms $V^2 + ||\sum_i z_i \mathbf{t}_i||^2$. We make the assumption that their projections into the terminal block are independent. This heuristic has previously been considered, for example in [11, Heuristic 1]. Thus the shortest projection has square norm distributed as the minimum M of $|R|$ beta distributions,

$$M \sim \min_{\mathbf{z} \in R} \left(\left(V^2 + ||*||\sum_i z_i \mathbf{t}_i \Big.^2 \right) \cdot \mathrm{Beta}\left(\frac{\beta}{2}, \frac{N-\beta}{2} \right) \right).$$

---

[14] Recall that Module-BKZ uses K-linear projections, and thus all embedded vectors had the same length after projection into the terminal block. On the contrary, BKZ uses only $\mathbb{Q}$-linear projections, allowing the projected lengths to differ.

[15] This depends only on the conductor, and can be precomputed with some basic number theory.

So after each oracle call in the terminal block, the smallest projection is inserted with probability $\mathbb{P}(M \leq \exp(2 \cdot \ell_{N-\beta+1}))$. By simulating the profile with BKZSim, we attain a success probability prediction for each V. To apply this to LWE, we integrate over the distribution of V (see Sect. 3.2).[16]

6.3 Experiments and Observations

We provide implementations of the ℓ-embedding attacks, and corresponding estimators, in our codebase. For the embedding submatrix we choose $\mathbf{T}_\ell = (\sigma\sqrt{\ell})\mathbf{I}_\ell$, which we justify in [41, App. E]. In Fig. 9 we compare our estimations and experiments for a fixed blocksize, number of tours, and Module-LWE parametersiation, with ℓ varying. Additionally, we show the 'naive prediction' when the presence of multiple embedded vectors is not accounted for.

We observe that our model improves upon the naive prediction, but still underestimates success probabilities; a more thorough analysis of these ℓ-embeddings, and in particular of the angle dependency between the shortest vectors (and their projections) should be considered for future work.

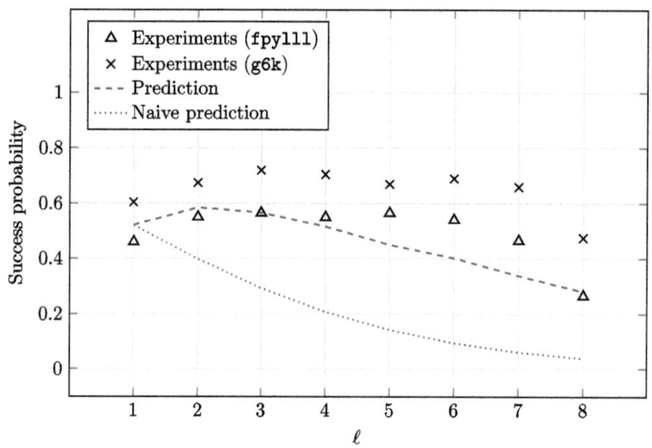

Fig. 9. Comparison of predicted and experimental success probabilities for the ℓ-embedding primal attacks. We use the Module-LWE parameters $c = 15$, $r = 14$, $m = 15$, $q = 2100$, $\sigma = 4$ and run BKZ-58 for 10 tours. For each ℓ, 200 experiments were run, using both `fpylll` (enumeration) and `g6k` (sieving).

Acknowledgements. We thank Léo Ducas and Eamonn Postlethwaite for helpful discussions and comments. We also thank King's College London e-Research [48] for providing the computational resources used to run our experiments.

---

[16] For our initial profile, we use a Z-shape prediction, adapted for ℓ-embeddings.

References

1. Albrecht, M., Ducas, L.: Lattice attacks on NTRU and LWE: a history of refinements. Cryptology ePrint Archive, Report 2021/799 (2021). https://eprint.iacr.org/2021/799
2. Albrecht, M.R., et al.: Estimate all the LWE, NTRU schemes! In: Catalano, D., De Prisco, R. (eds.) SCN 2018. LNCS, vol. 11035, pp. 351–367. Springer, Cham (2018). https://doi.org/10.1007/978-3-319-98113-0_19
3. Albrecht, M.R., Ducas, L., Herold, G., Kirshanova, E., Postlethwaite, E.W., Stevens, M.: The general sieve kernel and new records in lattice reduction. In: Ishai, Y., Rijmen, V. (eds.) EUROCRYPT 2019, Part II. LNCS, vol. 11477, pp. 717–746. Springer, Cham (2019). https://doi.org/10.1007/978-3-030-17656-3_25
4. Albrecht, M.R., Göpfert, F., Virdia, F., Wunderer, T.: Revisiting the expected cost of solving uSVP and applications to LWE. In: Takagi, T., Peyrin, T. (eds.) ASIACRYPT 2017, Part I. LNCS, vol. 10624, pp. 297–322. Springer, Cham (2017). https://doi.org/10.1007/978-3-319-70694-8_11
5. Albrecht, M.R., Player, R., Scott, S.: On the concrete hardness of learning with errors. J. Math. Cryptol. **9**(3), 169–203 (2015). http://www.degruyter.com/view/j/jmc.2015.9.issue-3/jmc-2015-0016/jmc-2015-0016.xml
6. Alkim, E., Ducas, L., Pöppelmann, T., Schwabe, P.: Post-quantum key exchange - a new hope. In: Holz, T., Savage, S. (eds.) USENIX Security 2016, pp. 327–343. USENIX Association (2016). https://www.usenix.org/conference/usenixsecurity16/technical-sessions/presentation/alkim
7. Applebaum, B., Cash, D., Peikert, C., Sahai, A.: Fast cryptographic primitives and circular-secure encryption based on hard learning problems. In: Halevi, S. (ed.) CRYPTO 2009. LNCS, vol. 5677, pp. 595–618. Springer, Heidelberg (2009). https://doi.org/10.1007/978-3-642-03356-8_35
8. Bai, S., Galbraith, S.D.: Lattice decoding attacks on binary LWE. In: Susilo, W., Mu, Y. (eds.) ACISP 2014. LNCS, vol. 8544, pp. 322–337. Springer, Cham (2014). https://doi.org/10.1007/978-3-319-08344-5_21
9. Bai, S., Miller, S., Wen, W.: A refined analysis of the cost for solving LWE via uSVP. In: Buchmann, J., Nitaj, A., Rachidi, T. (eds.) AFRICACRYPT 2019. LNCS, vol. 11627, pp. 181–205. Springer, Cham (2019). https://doi.org/10.1007/978-3-030-23696-0_10
10. Bai, S., Stehlé, D., Wen, W.: Measuring, simulating and exploiting the head concavity phenomenon in BKZ. In: Peyrin, T., Galbraith, S. (eds.) ASIACRYPT 2018, Part I. LNCS, vol. 11272, pp. 369–404. Springer, Cham (2018). https://doi.org/10.1007/978-3-030-03326-2_13
11. Bambury, H., Nguyen, P.Q.: Improved provable reduction of NTRU and hypercubic lattices. In: Saarinen, M.J., Smith-Tone, D. (eds.) Post-Quantum Cryptography - 15th International Workshop, PQCrypto 2024, Part I, pp. 343–370. Springer, Cham (2024). https://doi.org/10.1007/978-3-031-62743-9_12
12. Bonnoron, G., Ducas, L., Fillinger, M.: Large FHE gates from tensored homomorphic accumulator. In: Joux, A., Nitaj, A., Rachidi, T. (eds.) AFRICACRYPT 2018. LNCS, vol. 10831, pp. 217–251. Springer, Cham (2018). https://doi.org/10.1007/978-3-319-89339-6_13
13. Bos, J.W., et al.: CRYSTALS - kyber: a CCA-secure module-lattice-based KEM. In: 2018 IEEE European Symposium on Security and Privacy, pp. 353–367. IEEE Computer Society Press (2018). https://doi.org/10.1109/EuroSP.2018.00032

14. Boudgoust, K., Jeudy, C., Roux-Langlois, A., Wen, W.: On the hardness of module learning with errors with short distributions. J. Cryptol. **36**(1), 1 (2023). https://doi.org/10.1007/s00145-022-09441-3
15. Boudgoust, K., Jeudy, C., Tairi, E., Wen, W.: Hardness of m-LWE with general distributions and applications to leaky variants. Cryptology ePrint Archive, Paper 2025/1472 (2025). https://eprint.iacr.org/2025/1472
16. Brakerski, Z., Gentry, C., Vaikuntanathan, V.: (leveled) fully homomorphic encryption without bootstrapping. In: Proceedings of the 3rd Innovations in Theoretical Computer Science Conference, ITCS 2012, pp. 309–325. Association for Computing Machinery, New York, NY, USA (2012). https://doi.org/10.1145/2090236.2090262
17. Chen, Y., Nguyen, P.Q.: BKZ 2.0: better lattice security estimates. In: Lee, D.H., Wang, X. (eds.) ASIACRYPT 2011. LNCS, vol. 7073, pp. 1–20. Springer, Heidelberg (2011). https://doi.org/10.1007/978-3-642-25385-0_1
18. Cheon, J.H., Choe, H., Hong, D., Yi, M.: SMAUG: pushing lattice-based key encapsulation mechanisms to the limits. In: Carlet, C., Mandal, K., Rijmen, V. (eds.) SAC 2023. LNCS, vol. 14201, pp. 127–146. Springer, Cham (2024). https://doi.org/10.1007/978-3-031-53368-6_7
19. Dachman-Soled, D., Ducas, L., Gong, H., Rossi, M.: LWE with side information: attacks and concrete security estimation. In: Micciancio, D., Ristenpart, T. (eds.) CRYPTO 2020, Part II. LNCS, vol. 12171, pp. 329–358. Springer, Cham (2020). https://doi.org/10.1007/978-3-030-56880-1_12
20. Ducas, L., Durmus, A.: Ring-LWE in polynomial rings. In: Fischlin, M., Buchmann, J., Manulis, M. (eds.) PKC 2012. LNCS, vol. 7293, pp. 34–51. Springer, Heidelberg (2012). https://doi.org/10.1007/978-3-642-30057-8_3
21. Ducas, L., Engelberts, L., de Perthuis, P.: Predicting module lattice reduction. In: ASIACRYPT (2025). https://eprint.iacr.org/2025/1904
22. Ducas, L., Prest, T.: Fast Fourier orthogonalization, pp. 191–198 (2016). https://doi.org/10.1145/2930889.2930923
23. Ducas, L., Pulles, L.N.: Accurate score prediction for dual-sieve attacks. J. Cryptol. **39**(1), 8 (2026). https://doi.org/10.1007/S00145-025-09560-7
24. Ducas, L., van Woerden, W.P.J.: On the lattice isomorphism problem, quadratic forms, remarkable lattices, and cryptography. In: Dunkelman, O., Dziembowski, S. (eds.) EUROCRYPT 2022, Part III. LNCS, vol. 13277, pp. 643–673. Springer, Cham (2022). https://doi.org/10.1007/978-3-031-07082-2_23
25. Gargava, N., Serban, V., Viazovska, M., Viglino, I.: Effective module lattices and their shortest vectors (2024). https://arxiv.org/abs/2402.10305
26. Hoffstein, J., Pipher, J., Silverman, J.H.: NTRU: a ring-based public key cryptosystem. In: Third Algorithmic Number Theory Symposium (ANTS). LNCS, vol. 1423, pp. 267–288. Springer, Cham (1998)
27. Howgrave-Graham, N.: A hybrid lattice-reduction and meet-in-the-middle attack against NTRU. In: Menezes, A. (ed.) CRYPTO 2007. LNCS, vol. 4622, pp. 150–169. Springer, Heidelberg (2007). https://doi.org/10.1007/978-3-540-74143-5_9
28. Kannan, R.: Minkowski's convex body theorem and integer programming. Math. Oper. Res. **12**(3), 415–440 (1987). http://www.jstor.org/stable/3689974
29. Karenin, A., Kirshanova, E.: Finding dense submodules with algebraic lattice reduction. In: Vaudenay, S., Petit, C. (eds.) AFRICACRYPT 2024. LNCS, vol. 14861, pp. 403–427. Springer, Cham (2024). https://doi.org/10.1007/978-3-031-64381-1_18
30. Kim, J., Park, J.H.: NTRU+: compact construction of NTRU using simple encoding method. Cryptology ePrint Archive, Report 2022/1664 (2022). https://eprint.iacr.org/2022/1664

31. Langlois, A., Stehlé, D.: Worst-case to average-case reductions for module lattices. DCC **75**(3), 565–599 (2015). https://doi.org/10.1007/s10623-014-9938-4

32. Lee, C., Pellet-Mary, A., Stehlé, D., Wallet, A.: An LLL algorithm for module lattices. In: Galbraith, S.D., Moriai, S. (eds.) ASIACRYPT 2019, Part II. LNCS, vol. 11922, pp. 59–90. Springer, Cham (2019). https://doi.org/10.1007/978-3-030-34621-8_3

33. Lenstra, A.K., Lenstra, H. W., J., Lovász, L.: Factoring polynomials with rational coefficients. Mathematische Annalen **261**(4), 515–534 (1982). https://doi.org/10.1007/BF01457454

34. Li, J., Nguyen, P.Q.: A complete analysis of the BKZ lattice reduction algorithm. Cryptology ePrint Archive, Report 2020/1237 (2020). https://eprint.iacr.org/2020/1237

35. Lyubashevsky, V., Micciancio, D.: On bounded distance decoding, unique shortest vectors, and the minimum distance problem. In: Halevi, S. (ed.) CRYPTO 2009. LNCS, vol. 5677, pp. 577–594. Springer, Heidelberg (2009). https://doi.org/10.1007/978-3-642-03356-8_34

36. Lyubashevsky, V., Peikert, C., Regev, O.: On ideal lattices and learning with errors over rings. In: Gilbert, H. (ed.) EUROCRYPT 2010. LNCS, vol. 6110, pp. 1–23. Springer, Heidelberg (2010). https://doi.org/10.1007/978-3-642-13190-5_1

37. Lyubashevsky, V., Peikert, C., Regev, O.: A toolkit for ring-LWE cryptography. In: Johansson, T., Nguyen, P.Q. (eds.) EUROCRYPT 2013. LNCS, vol. 7881, pp. 35–54. Springer, Heidelberg (2013). https://doi.org/10.1007/978-3-642-38348-9_3

38. Micciancio, D., Regev, O.: Worst-case to average-case reductions based on Gaussian measures. SIAM J. Comput. **37**(1), 267–302 (2007). https://doi.org/10.1137/S0097539705447360

39. Mukherjee, T., Stephens-Davidowitz, N.: Lattice reduction for modules, or how to reduce ModuleSVP to ModuleSVP. In: Micciancio, D., Ristenpart, T. (eds.) CRYPTO 2020, Part II. LNCS, vol. 12171, pp. 213–242. Springer, Cham (2020). https://doi.org/10.1007/978-3-030-56880-1_8

40. Nakamura, S., Yasuda, M.: An extension of Kannan's embedding for solving ring-based LWE problems. In: Paterson, M.B. (ed.) 18th IMA International Conference on Cryptography and Coding. LNCS, vol. 13129, pp. 201–219. Springer, Cham (2021). https://doi.org/10.1007/978-3-030-92641-0_10

41. de Perthuis, P., Trenkić, F.: Refined modelling of the primal attack, and variants against module-learning with errors. Cryptology ePrint Archive, Paper 2025/2195 (2025). https://eprint.iacr.org/2025/2195

42. Postlethwaite, E.W., Virdia, F.: On the success probability of solving unique SVP via BKZ. In: Garay, J. (ed.) PKC 2021, Part I. LNCS, vol. 12710, pp. 68–98. Springer, Cham (2021). https://doi.org/10.1007/978-3-030-75245-3_4

43. Regev, O.: On lattices, learning with errors, random linear codes, and cryptography. J. ACM **56**(6) (2009). https://doi.org/10.1145/1568318.1568324

44. Schnorr, C., Euchner, M.: Lattice basis reduction: improved practical algorithms and solving subset sum problems. Math. Program. **66**, 181–199 (1994). https://doi.org/10.1007/BF01581144

45. Schnorr, C.P.: Lattice reduction by random sampling and birthday methods. In: Alt, H., Habib, M. (eds.) STACS 2003, pp. 145–156. Springer, Heidelberg (2003)

46. Schnorr, C.: A hierarchy of polynomial time lattice basis reduction algorithms. Theoret. Comput. Sci. **53**(2), 201–224 (1987). https://doi.org/10.1016/0304-3975(87)90064-8. https://www.sciencedirect.com/science/article/pii/0304397587900648

47. Development team, T.F.: fpylll, a Python wrapper for the fplll lattice reduction library, Version: 0.6.4 (2025). https://github.com/fplll/fpylll
48. Development team, T.K.: King's Computational Research, Engineering and Technology Environment (CREATE) (2025)
49. Uesugi, S., Okumura, S., Miyaji, A.: Revisiting an extension of Kannan's embedding for ring-LWE. In: You, I., Choraś, M., Shin, S., Kim, H., Astillo, P.V. (eds.) Mobile Internet Security, pp. 167–180. Springer, Singapore (2024)

A Collision Attack on the LTZ Hash Function Based on a Conjecture on Supersingular Non-superspecial Isogeny Graphs of Dimension 2

Ryo Ohashi$^{(\boxtimes)}$ and Hiroshi Onuki

The University of Tokyo, Tokyo, Japan
`{ryo-ohashi,hiroshi-onuki}@g.ecc.u-tokyo.ac.jp`

Abstract. In 2023, LeGrow, Ti, and Zobernig proposed a cryptographic hash function (which we refer to as the LTZ hash function in this paper) based on a certain $(2,2)$-isogeny graph between supersingular non-superspecial abelian surfaces over $\mathbb{F}_{p^4}$. The authors claimed that the best-known algorithm for finding a collision in the LTZ hash function is the Pollard-rho style algorithm, whose time complexity is estimated to be $O(p^3 \log(p)^2)$ and whose space complexity is $O(\log(p))$, when measured in the number of multiplications over $\mathbb{F}_p$. In this paper, we first propose a mathematical conjecture on the number of vertices defined over the smaller field $\mathbb{F}_{p^2}$ in the isogeny graphs used in the LTZ hash function. Based on this conjecture, by finding two distinct paths leading to a vertex defined over $\mathbb{F}_{p^2}$, we construct a collision-finding algorithm for the LTZ hash function. Our algorithm reduces the time complexity to $O(p^3 \log(p))$, at the cost of increasing the required memory to $O(\log(p)^2)$, again measured in $\mathbb{F}_p$-multiplications. We implemented these algorithms in Rust and confirmed experimentally that our method finds collisions, on average, 82 times faster than the Pollard-rho style algorithm for primes $p < 1000$.

Keywords: Hash function · Isogeny-based cryptography · Supersingular abelian surface

1 Introduction

Isogeny-based cryptography is one of the promising candidates for post-quantum cryptography, which is secure against quantum computers. The security of isogeny-based cryptography is based on the difficulty of finding isogenies between elliptic curves over a finite field. Currently, most of the isogeny-based cryptographic protocols use supersingular elliptic curves because the isogeny graph of supersingular elliptic curves has an attractive structure for cryptographic applications.

The first isogeny-based cryptographic protocol that uses supersingular elliptic curves is the cryptographic hash function proposed by Charles, Lauter, and

M. Bardet and R. Niederhagen (Eds.): PQCrypto 2026, LNCS 16492, pp. 377–408, 2026.
https://doi.org/10.1007/978-3-032-22698-3_12

Goren [6], referred to as the *CGL hash function*. Roughly speaking, the computation of the CGL hash function is based on a pseudorandom walk in the isogeny graph of supersingular elliptic curves. Since an elliptic curve is a one-dimensional abelian variety, it is natural to generalize the CGL hash function to hash functions using higher-dimensional abelian varieties. The first such hash function was proposed by Takashima [25], which uses superspecial abelian surfaces (i.e., two-dimensional abelian varieties isomorphic to the product of two supersingular elliptic curves). Flynn and Ti [11] pointed out a vulnerability in Takashima's hash function, and Castryck, Decru, and Smith [5] proposed a fix for it. The resulting hash function is referred to as the *CDS hash function*. Note that, under the original initial surface setting of the CDS hash function, collisions can be found in polynomial time (cf. [4, Sect. 5.4]), and hence it is necessary to appropriately choose the initial surface. LeGrow, Ti, and Zobernig [20] proposed another hash function using abelian surfaces, but they used supersingular abelian surfaces which are not superspecial. Recently, Kunzweiler et al. [19] proposed an efficient computing method for the CDS hash function via theta functions, along with a hash function based on superspecial abelian varieties of dimension 3.

The collision resistance of the above hash functions relies on the difficulty of finding an endomorphism with a certain property of an abelian variety, including an elliptic curve. The problem of finding such an endomorphism is equivalent to that of finding a cycle in the isogeny graph of abelian varieties. There are several approaches to find a cycle in the isogeny graphs, and the characteristic p of the finite field is determined by the computational complexity of these approaches:

- As a generic approach for finding a cycle in the graph, the Pollard-rho style algorithm is known. In this approach, we start from the initial vertex of the target hash function, and repeatedly apply a hash function to it, performing a pseudorandom walk on the graph. After visiting about $\sqrt{N}$ vertices, where N denotes the number of vertices in the graph, then we can expect to find the same vertex twice by the birthday paradox. This approach requires $O(N^{1/2})$ hash computations, and only a constant number of vertices need to be stored during the walk.

- In the case of the CGL hash function, the size of the isogeny graph of supersingular elliptic curves is approximately $p/12$. For this graph, a more efficient approach to finding a cycle was proposed by Eisenträger, Hallgren, Leonardi, Morrison, and Park [9]. This approach requires $\widetilde{O}(p^{1/2})$ time, and its space complexity is bounded by a polynomial in $\log(p)$, as in the Pollard-rho style algorithm. In practice, however, it finds collisions in the CGL hash function faster.

- For the high-dimensional case, it is known that the number of vertices in the isogeny graph of superspecial abelian varieties of dimension g is $\Theta(p^{g(g+1)/2})$. In the case where $g \geq 2$, we can reduce the problem of finding a cycle in the isogeny graph to that of finding a cycle in lower-dimensional isogeny graphs by using a method by Costello and Smith [8]. The time complexity of their approach is $\widetilde{O}(p^{g-1})$, and moreover the space complexity is bounded by some polynomial in $\log(p)$. In fact, the cycle obtained in this way does not necessarily correspond to "a composition of good isogenies", and therefore it does not immediately yield a collision in the hash function. However, for the CDS hash function, by combining this approach with the method of Ohashi and Onuki [21], a collision can be found in $\widetilde{O}(p)$ time. On the other hand, we cannot apply this approach to the isogeny graph of supersingular non-superspecial abelian surfaces, which is used in the LTZ hash function.

- In the quantum setting, the claw-finding algorithm by Brassard, Høyer, and Tapp [1] and Tani [26] can be applied. This algorithm requires $O(N^{1/3})$ time and space complexity up to a polynomial factor in $\log(p)$, where N denotes the number of vertices in the isogeny graph. However, Jaques and Schanck showed in [18] that the quantum claw-finding algorithm does not outperform the classical Pollard-rho style algorithm due to the required data structure in the isogeny setting. The attacks by Eisenträger et al. and Costtelo-Smith can be combined with Grover's algorithm [13], reducing the time complexity to $\widetilde{O}(p^{1/4})$ and $\widetilde{O}(p^{(g-1)/2})$, respectively.

Table 1. Time and space complexities of the attacks on the hash functions using the isogeny graphs of abelian varieties. All complexities are measured in terms of the number of multiplications over $\mathbb{F}_p$. The characteristic p of the finite field is chosen such that the classical (resp. quantum) security level is λ bits (resp. $\lambda/2$ bits).

Hash function	Complexity of classical attack		Complexity of quantum attack		Base field	Size of p
	time	space	time	space		
CGL	$O(p^{1/2}\log(p))$	$O(\log(p)^2)$	$\widetilde{O}(p^{1/4})$	$\widetilde{O}(1)$	$\mathbb{F}_{p^2}$	$2^{2\lambda}$
CDS	$O(p\log(p))$	$O(\log(p)^2)$	$\widetilde{O}(p^{1/2})$	$\widetilde{O}(1)$	$\mathbb{F}_{p^2}$	2^{λ}
LTZ (Pollard-rho)	$O(p^3\log(p)^2)$	$O(\log(p))$	$\widetilde{O}(p^3)$	$\widetilde{O}(1)$	$\mathbb{F}_{p^4}$	$2^{\lambda/3}$
LTZ (our)	$O(p^3\log(p))$	$O(\log(p)^2)$	$\widetilde{O}(p^{3/2})$	$\widetilde{O}(1)$	$\mathbb{F}_{p^4}$	$2^{\lambda/3}$

Here, Table 1 summarizes the time and space complexities of the attacks on the hash functions based on the isogeny graphs of abelian varieties. Although the security of the hash function by Kunzweiler et al. [19] is not discussed in detail, the authors estimate its security to be $\widetilde{O}(p^2)$ based on the Costello-Smith attack. However, as mentioned earlier, this attack is not actually valid; therefore, we omit it from Table 1. Their analysis shows that the hash function based on superspecial abelian varieties of dimension 3 achieves greater computational efficiency than the CGL and CDS hash functions. Although they do not provide a direct comparison with the LTZ hash function, the parameter scaling suggests a practical advantage of the LTZ hash function from an implementation standpoint. To achieve a security level λ, the LTZ hash function can use a prime $p \approx 2^{\lambda/3}$, whereas their hash function requires $p \approx 2^{\lambda/2}$. Consequently, even at higher security levels, the prime used in the LTZ hash function often remains within the range of single-machine-word integers (e.g., 64-bit), which simplifies implementations. Therefore, it is important to analyze the collision resistance of the LTZ hash function. In particular, the following question arises:

Is there a collision attack on the LTZ hash function beyond the generic Pollard-rho style algorithm?

In this paper, we give a positive answer to the above question.

Contribution. In this paper, we propose an efficient collision attack on the LTZ hash function. Specifically, we focus on the vertices in the isogeny graph underlying the LTZ hash function that are defined over the smaller field $\mathbb{F}_{p^2}$. By using such vertices, we can construct a collision attack based on an idea similar to the one by Eisenträger et al. [9]. To prove the effectiveness of our attack, we show in Sect. 4 several mathematical properties of these $\mathbb{F}_{p^2}$-rational vertices, and also give a conjecture that their number is sufficiently large, which is verified by our experiments for small primes.

The time complexity of our collision attack in the classical setting is $O(p^3 \log(p))$, measured in the number of multiplications over $\mathbb{F}_p$, which is smaller than that of the Pollard-rho style algorithm, while the space complexity increases to $O(\log(p)^2)$. In the quantum setting, our attack can be combined with Grover's algorithm, reducing its time complexity to $\widetilde{O}(p^{3/2})$, which outperforms the claw-finding algorithm. A comparison of the time and space complexities of our collision attack and previous attacks is shown in Table 1. We implemented our attack in Rust and conducted comparative experiments, confirming that for primes $p < 1000$, it can find a collision in the LTZ hash function on average 82 times faster than the Pollard-rho style algorithm. See Sect. 6 for details of this experiment.

Organization. In Sect. 2, we review several mathematical preliminaries, and in Sect. 3, we present the specific construction of the LTZ hash function. Next, we discuss properties and a conjecture on the $\mathbb{F}_{p^2}$-rational vertices in the isogeny graph underlying the LTZ hash function in Sect. 4. Based on this conjecture, Sect. 5 introduces our collision attack on the LTZ hash function, and provides an estimate of its computational complexity. Finally, in Sect. 6, we show experimental results of our attack, which we implemented in Rust.

2   Preliminaries

In this section, we summarize some mathematical background which will be used in later sections. Throughout, all curves and abelian varieties are assumed to be defined over a field k of characteristic $p > 5$ (a curve always refers to a *smooth* projective variety of dimension one). In addition, all isomorphisms between them are taken to be over the algebraic closure $\bar{k}$ of k.

2.1 Principally Polarized Abelian Surfaces and Their Isogenies

A *principally polarized abelian surface* is defined as a pair $(A, \mathcal{L})$, where A is an abelian surface (i.e., a smooth projective variety of dimension 2 which is also an algebraic group) and $\mathcal{L} : A \to \hat{A}$ is a principal polarization (i.e., an isomorphism to the dual abelian surface, induced by an ample line bundle).

As is well known, every principally polarized abelian surface is isomorphic to either of the following two types:

- the product $E_1 \times E_2$ of two elliptic curves E_1, E_2 equipped with the product principal polarization, or
- the Jacobian variety $\mathrm{Jac}(H)$ of a genus-2 curve H equipped with its canonical principal polarization induced by the theta divisor.

In particular, we refer to the former case as a *decomposable* abelian surface. If a principal polarization on an abelian surface is not specified, then it is implicitly assumed that the canonical one is being considered.

Let $\mathcal{A}_2$ (resp. $\mathcal{M}_2$) denote the moduli space of principally polarized abelian surfaces (resp. genus-2 curves), then the Torelli theorem asserts that the map

$$\mathcal{M}_2 \longrightarrow \mathcal{A}_2,$$
$$H \longmapsto \mathrm{Jac}(H)$$

is well-defined and injective. In other words, two genus-2 curves are isomorphic if and only if their Jacobian varieties are isomorphic. Moreover, it is known that the moduli space $\mathcal{M}_2$ of genus-2 curves has dimension 3, and classical invariants such as the *Igusa invariants* provide a system of generators for its function field. In particular, we review the definition of the absolute invariants of genus-2 curves as given in [2, pp. 73–74].

Definition 1. *For a genus-2 curve H, we define*

$$(j_1, j_2, j_3) := \begin{cases} (J_2^5/J_{10}, J_2^3 J_4/J_{10}, J_2^2 J_6/J_{10}) & \text{if } J_2 \neq 0, \\ (0, J_4^5/J_{10}^2, J_4 J_6/J_{10}) & \text{if } J_2 = 0, J_4 \neq 0, \\ (0, 0, J_6^5/J_{10}^3) & \text{if } J_2 = J_4 = 0, \end{cases}$$

where J_2, J_4, J_6, J_{10} are the Igusa invariants of H. Remark that J_{10} is non-zero, and hence this definition is well-defined. Then, the triple (j_1, j_2, j_3) is called the **absolute invariants** *of H.*

An important feature is that, the set of k-rational points on $\mathcal{M}_2$ is in bijection with the set of triples $(j_1, j_2, j_3) \in k^3$. Then, the following facts hold:

- Two genus-2 curves are $\bar{k}$-isomorphic if and only if their absolute invariants are the same.
- For any genus-2 curve defined over k, its absolute invariants lie in k^3.

In addition, when k is a finite field, for any $(j_1, j_2, j_3) \in k^3$ there exists a genus-2 curve defined over k with these absolute invariants (cf. [29, Remark 1]).

Remark 2. For a genus-2 curve over k, the computation of its absolute invariants requires only a constant number of arithmetic operations in k, since J_2, J_4, J_6, J_{10} are given by polynomials over k of bounded degree (cf. [17, Sections 3–4]).

Fix an integer $N > 1$ coprime to p. For an abelian surface A, let $A[N]$ denote the N-torsion subgroup of A, then we obtain an isomorphism $A[N] \cong (\mathbb{Z}/N\mathbb{Z})^4$. Also, there exists a non-degenerate alternating bilinear form $A[N] \times \hat{A}[N] \to \mu_N$, where μ_N is the set of N-th roots of unity in $\bar{k}$. In particular, when A has a principal polarization, it induces a map

$$e_N : A[N] \times A[N] \longrightarrow \mu_N,$$

called the *N-Weil pairing* of A. We now introduce the notions of isotropic subgroups and symplectic bases of $A[N]$ with respect to the N-Weil pairing:

Definition 3. *Let A be a principally polarized abelian surface. A subgroup G of its N-torsion subgroup $A[N]$ is called **isotropic** if $e_N(P, Q) = 1$ for all $P, Q \in G$. Also, a basis $(P_1, P_2; Q_1, Q_2)$ of $A[N]$ is called **symplectic** if*

- $e_N(P_1, P_2) = e_N(Q_1, Q_2) = 1,$
- $e_N(P_1, Q_1) = e_N(P_2, Q_2) = \zeta_N,$ *and*
- $e_N(P_1, Q_2) = e_N(P_2, Q_1) = 1,$

where $\zeta_N \in \mu_N$ is a primitive N-th root of unity.

In the context of isogeny-based cryptography, we are often interested in isogenies of principally polarized abelian surfaces of the following form:

Definition 4. *Let A and A' be principally polarized abelian surfaces. An isogeny (i.e., finite surjective homomorphism) from A to A' is called an $(\boldsymbol{N}, \boldsymbol{N})$-**isogeny** if its kernel is a maximal isotropic subgroup with respect to inclusion. If such an isogeny exists, we say that A and A' are $(\boldsymbol{N}, \boldsymbol{N})$-**isogenous**.*

Two (N, N)-isogenies from A to A' with the same kernel are equivalent up to an automorphism of A', and hence they are identified. For any principally polarized abelian surface A, the number of distinct (N, N)-isogenies with the domain A is known (cf. [3, Lemma 2.1]) to be

$$S(N) := N^3 \prod_{\text{primes } \ell \mid N} \left(1 + \frac{1}{\ell}\right)\left(1 + \frac{1}{\ell^2}\right). \tag{1}$$

Moreover, the (N, N)-isogenies whose domain is the codomain of a given (N, N)-isogeny can be classified into 3 types according to the structure of the kernel of their composition:

Definition 5. *For two (N, N)-isogenies $\phi : A \to A'$ and $\phi' : A' \to A''$ between principally polarized abelian surfaces,*

- *If* $\ker \phi' = \phi(A[N])$, *then we say that* ϕ' *is the **dual extension** of* ϕ.
- *If* $\ker \phi' \cap \phi(A[N]) = \{0\}$, *then we say that* ϕ' *is a **good extension** of* ϕ.
- *Otherwise, we say that* ϕ' *is a **bad extension** of* ϕ.

By [3, Lemma 2.1] again, for any (N, N)-isogeny, there exist exactly N^3 distinct good extensions. For an integer $n > 0$, any (N^n, N^n)-isogeny $\psi : A \to A'$ can be written as a composition of (N, N)-isogenies

$$A = A_0 \xrightarrow{\phi_1} A_1 \xrightarrow{\phi_2} A_2 \longrightarrow \cdots \longrightarrow A_{n-1} \xrightarrow{\phi_n} A_n = A',$$

where ϕ_{i+1} is a good extension of ϕ_i for all $i \in \{1, \ldots, n-1\}$. For the notational convenience, we introduce the following terminology.

Definition 6. *A sequence* $(\phi_1, \ldots, \phi_n)$ *of* (N, N)-*isogenies of principally polarized abelian surfaces is called a **good (N, N)-sequence** if* ϕ_{i+1} *is a good extension of* ϕ_i *for all* $i \in \{1, \ldots, n-1\}$.

2.2 Supersingular Abelian Surfaces

An elliptic curve E is said to be *supersingular* if its p-torsion subgroup is trivial; otherwise E is called *ordinary*. As a two-dimensional analogue of a supersingular elliptic curve, we define a supersingular abelian surface as follows:

Definition 7. *Let A be an abelian surface.*

- *We say that A is **supersingular** if A is isogenous (over $\bar{k}$) to the product of two supersingular elliptic curves, without polarizations.*
- *In particular, we say that A is **superspecial** if A is isomorphic (over $\bar{k}$) to the product of two supersingular elliptic curves, without polarizations.*

It follows immediately that any superspecial abelian surface is supersingular.

By the Deligne-Ogus-Shioda theorem, any two products of supersingular elliptic curves are isomorphic over $\bar{k}$ to each other as unpolarized abelian surfaces, which shows that all superspecial abelian surfaces are isomorphic without polarizations. The number of principal polarizations on a fixed superspecial abelian surface A, up to the action of automorphisms of A, is approximately $p^3/2880$.

The supersingularity and superspeciality of the Jacobian variety of a genus-2 curve H can be completely determined from the Hasse-Witt matrix of H (we refer to [16, Lemma 1.1] for the criterion). For example, by explicitly computing the Hasse-Witt matrix of $H : y^2 = x^5 - 1$, one can show the following fact:

Proposition 8 ([16, **Proposition 1.13**]). *For a genus-2 curve $H : y^2 = x^5 - 1$, we have the following:*

1. *If $p \equiv 1 \pmod 5$, then $\mathrm{Jac}(H)$ is not supersingular.*

2. *If $p \equiv 2, 3$ (mod 5), then $\mathrm{Jac}(H)$ is supersingular and not superspecial.*
3. *If $p \equiv 4$ (mod 5), then $\mathrm{Jac}(H)$ is superspecial.*

We note that $H : y^2 = x^5 - 1$ is classified as Class (6) in [16], and it is the unique genus-2 curve (up to isomorphism) whose automorphism group has order 10.

Remark 9. The product $E_1 \times E_2$ of two elliptic curves E_1, E_2 is supersingular if and only if both E_1 and E_2 are supersingular. In that case, the abelian surface is automatically superspecial; therefore, a decomposable abelian surface cannot be supersingular without being superspecial.

Next, we consider an abelian surface A defined over $k = \mathbb{F}_q$ with $q = p^r$. The q-th power Frobenius endomorphism on A satisfies the equation

$$\Phi(X) := X^4 + a_1 X^3 + a_2 X^2 + q a_1 X + q^2 = 0 \tag{2}$$

for some integers $a_1, a_2 \in \mathbb{Z}$, and $\Phi(X) \in \mathbb{Z}[X]$ is called the *characteristic polynomial* of A over $\mathbb{F}_q$. This polynomial can be factored as

$$\Phi(X) = \prod_{i=1}^{4} (X - \alpha_i),$$

where each α_i is an algebraic integer such that $|\alpha_i| = \sqrt{q}$. Moreover, the following fact is also well-known (see, for example [28, Section 1]).

Proposition 10. *With the above notation, the characteristic polynomial $\Phi_n(X)$ of A over $\mathbb{F}_{q^n}$ with $n \geq 1$ is written as*

$$\Phi_n(X) = \prod_{i=1}^{4} (X - \alpha_i^n).$$

In addition, the number of $\mathbb{F}_{q^n}$-rational points of A equals $\Phi_n(1)$.

As the following theorem shows, the supersingularity of an abelian surface is closely related to its characteristic polynomial:

Theorem 11 ([12, **Theorem 6**])**.** *If the characteristic polynomial of an abelian surface A over $\mathbb{F}_q$ with $q = p^r$ is given in the form (2), then A is supersingular if and only if $p^{\lceil r/2 \rceil} \mid a_1$ and $p^r \mid a_2$.*

In particular, one can determine the characteristic polynomials of the Jacobian variety of $H : y^2 = x^5 - 1$ over $\mathbb{F}_p$ in the supersingular non-superspecial case:

Proposition 12 ([7, **Example 5.1**])**.** *We assume that $p \equiv 2, 3$ (mod 5). Then, the characteristic polynomial of the Jacobian variety of $H : y^2 = x^5 - 1$ over $\mathbb{F}_p$ is given as $\Phi(X) = X^4 + p^2$.*

In the following, we fix a supersingular elliptic curve E defined over $\bar{k}$. Then, by [22, Corollary 7], for any supersingular abelian surface A over $\bar{k}$, there exists a short exact sequence

$$0 \longrightarrow \alpha_p \xrightarrow{\iota_t} E \times E \longrightarrow A \longrightarrow 0,$$

where α_p denotes the kernel of the p-th power Frobenius endomorphism on the additive group $\mathbb{G}_a$. The possible embeddings $\iota_t : \alpha_p \to E \times E$ are parameterized by $t \in \mathbb{P}^1(\bar{k})$, which is called the *embedding parameter* in [20, Section 2.3]. Also, it follows from [22] that the abelian surface $A = (E \times E)/\iota_t(\alpha_p)$ is superspecial if and only if $t \in \mathbb{P}^1(\mathbb{F}_{p^2})$. Our interest lies in the supersingular non-superspecial case, in particular, when $t \in \mathbb{F}_{p^4} \setminus \mathbb{F}_{p^2}$. For such supersingular abelian surfaces, the following results by Ibukiyama are known:

Proposition 13 ([15, Proposition 2.3]). *Every supersingular abelian surface with embedding parameter in $\mathbb{F}_{p^4} \setminus \mathbb{F}_{p^2}$ is isomorphic (over $\bar{k}$) to any other such surface, as unpolarized abelian surfaces.*

Theorem 14 ([15, Theorems 1.1 and 1.2]). *Let A be a supersingular abelian surface with embedding parameter in $\mathbb{F}_{p^4} \setminus \mathbb{F}_{p^2}$. The number of principal polarizations of A up to the action of automorphisms on A equals*

$$h := \begin{cases} \frac{p^2(p^2-1)^2}{2880} & \text{if } p \equiv 1,4 \pmod 5, \\ 1 + \frac{(p-3)(p+3)(p^2-3p+8)(p^2+3p+8)}{2880} & \text{if } p \equiv 2,3 \pmod 5. \end{cases}$$

If $p \equiv 2,3$ (mod 5), then there exists a unique principal polarization $\mathcal{L}$ on A, up to isomorphism, such that $\mathrm{Aut}(A, \mathcal{L}) \cong \mathbb{Z}/10\mathbb{Z}$. For all other principal polarizations $\mathcal{L}$ on A, we have $\mathrm{Aut}(A, \mathcal{L}) = \{\pm 1\}$.

We note that the principally polarized abelian surface with automorphism group $\mathbb{Z}/10\mathbb{Z}$ in the above theorem is isomorphic to the Jacobian variety of the genus-2 curve $H : y^2 = x^5 - 1$ equipped with its canonical principal polarization.

It follows from Proposition 13 that the $\bar{k}$-isomorphism class of supersingular abelian surfaces with embedding parameter in $\mathbb{F}_{p^4} \setminus \mathbb{F}_{p^2}$ is unique, and we denote it by A_0. For any principal polarization $\mathcal{L}$ on A_0, the principally polarized abelian surface $(A_0, \mathcal{L})$ is isomorphic to the Jacobian variety of a genus-2 curve equipped with its canonical principal polarization by Remark 9, and we write $A_{\mathcal{L}}$ for this. Then, we define the set of $\bar{k}$-isomorphism classes of $A_{\mathcal{L}}$ by

$$\mathcal{V}_p := \{A_{\mathcal{L}} \mid \mathcal{L} \text{ is a principal polarization on } A_0\}/ \cong,$$

which depends only on p. It is clear that the cardinality of $\mathcal{V}_p$ equals h, given in Theorem 14. Additionally, it follows from [20, Lemma 3] that every supersingular principally polarized abelian surface $A \in \mathcal{V}_p$ is defined over $\mathbb{F}_{p^4}$. We finally define the isogeny graph of these principally polarized abelian surfaces as follows:

Definition 15. *For a prime $\ell \neq p$, we denote by $\mathcal{G}(\ell, p)$ the graph defined as*

- *The vertex set of $\mathcal{G}(\ell, p)$ is $\mathcal{V}_p$, and*
- *The edges in $\mathcal{G}(\ell, p)$ are (ℓ, ℓ)-isogenies between two vertices, where two isogenies with the same kernel are identified as a single edge.*

Recall from (1) that $\mathcal{G}(\ell, p)$ is an $S(\ell) = (\ell + 1)(\ell^2 + 1)$-regular multigraph. An important fact, proved in [20, Lemma 4], is that $\mathcal{G}(\ell, p)$ is connected.

2.3 Algorithm for Computing $(2, 2)$-Isogenies

In this subsection, we describe the algorithms used for computing $(2, 2)$-isogenies, which will be necessary later. For simplicity, we assume that principally polarized abelian surfaces in this subsection are all indecomposable (i.e., isomorphic to the Jacobian variety of a genus-2 curve).

In what follows, let $M_{\mathbb{F}_p}$ denote the cost of a multiplication in $\mathbb{F}_p$. Note that the cost of an addition in $\mathbb{F}_p$ is bounded by $M_{\mathbb{F}_p}$, and that the cost of an inversion is in $O(\log(p) M_{\mathbb{F}_p})$. First, we need to define an efficient representation of a $(2, 2)$-isogeny between principally polarized abelian surfaces:

Definition 16. *Let A and A' be principally polarized abelian surfaces over $\mathbb{F}_{p^4}$, and $\phi : A \to A'$ be a $(2, 2)$-isogeny between them. An **efficient representation** of ϕ is a data $\mathcal{D}$ of size $O(\log(p))$ together with the following three algorithms:*

- Domain$(\mathcal{D})$ *returns one of the defining equations of the genus-2 curve underlying A in $O(\log(p) M_{\mathbb{F}_p})$ time.*
- Codomain$(\mathcal{D})$ *returns one of the defining equations of the genus-2 curve underlying A' in $O(\log(p) M_{\mathbb{F}_p})$ time.*
- Eval$(\mathcal{D}, P)$ *takes a point $P \in A(\mathbb{F}_{p^{4n}})$ with an integer $n \geq 1$, and returns $\phi(P)$ in $O(n \log(p) M_{\mathbb{F}_p})$ time.*

For an example of efficient representations of $(2, 2)$-isogenies ϕ, see Appendix A. In the following, we suppose that every $(2, 2)$-isogeny is expressed in an efficient representation. For constructing the LTZ hash function and our collision attack for it, we define the following algorithms:

- CodomainInvariant(ϕ): It takes a $(2, 2)$-isogeny $\phi : A \to A'$, and returns the absolute invariants of A'.
- Conjugate(ϕ): It takes a $(2, 2)$-isogeny $\phi : A \to A'$ over $\mathbb{F}_{p^4}$, and returns an efficient representation of its p^2-conjugate $\phi^{(p^2)} : A^{(p^2)} \to A'^{(p^2)}$.
- Dual(ϕ): It takes a $(2, 2)$-isogeny $\phi : A \to A'$, and returns an efficient representation of its dual $\hat{\phi} : A' \to A$.
- GoodExtension(ϕ, i): It takes a $(2, 2)$-isogeny $\phi : A \to A'$ and $i \in \{0, \ldots, 7\}$, and returns an efficient representation of the i-th good extension of ϕ, where the order of the good extensions is determined by a representation of ϕ.
- IsGoodExtension(ϕ, ϕ'): It takes $(2, 2)$-isogenies $\phi : A \to A'$ and $\phi' : A' \to A''$, and returns whether ϕ' is a good extension of ϕ.

These algorithms can be implemented with time complexity $O(\log(p)\mathrm{M}_{\mathbb{F}_p})$, and space complexity $O(\log(p))$. An explicit description of each algorithm is given in Appendix A. To simplify the notation, we will omit writing Dual and $\mathsf{Conjugate}$ in our algorithms; instead, we denote $\mathsf{Dual}(\phi)$ by $\hat{\phi}$, and $\mathsf{Conjugate}(\phi)$ by $\phi^{(p^2)}$.

3   LeGrow-Ti-Zobernig's Hash Function

A *cryptographic hash function* is a deterministic function $\mathcal{H} : \{0,1\}^* \to \{0,1\}^d$ that takes an arbitrary-length input and returns a fixed-length hash value. It is required to satisfy the following properties:

- *pre-image resistance*: Given a hash value $h \in \{0,1\}^d$, it is computationally hard to find an input m such that $\mathcal{H}(m) = h$.
- *second pre-image resistance*: Given an input m and its hash value $h = \mathcal{H}(m)$, it is computationally hard to find an input $m' \neq m$ such that $\mathcal{H}(m') = h$.
- *collision resistance*: It is computationally hard to find two inputs m and m' such that $m \neq m'$ and $\mathcal{H}(m) = \mathcal{H}(m')$.

Note that the collision resistance is the strongest property among the three.

In this section, we review the construction of the cryptographic hash function proposed by LeGrow, Ti, and Zobernig [20], which is referred as to the *LTZ hash function*. After that, we focus on the collision resistance of the LTZ hash function and describe an existing attack method that solve it.

3.1   Construction

Roughly speaking, the LTZ hash function is derived from the CDS hash function by replacing the $(2,2)$-isogeny graph of superspecial principally polarized abelian surfaces with the graph $\mathcal{G}(2,p)$ introduced in Definition 15. More concretely, for a prime $p > 5$, the LTZ hash function

$$\mathcal{H}_{\mathrm{LTZ}} : \{0,1\}^* \longrightarrow (\mathbb{F}_{p^4})^3$$

is described by the following procedure:

Set-up. We fix an initial edge $\phi_0 : A_{-1} \to A_0$ on the graph $\mathcal{G}(2,p)$ appropriately (we explain later how to choose this). Parse an input $m \in \{0,1\}^*$ as an octal sequence $m_n \cdots m_2 m_1$ where each $m_i \in \{0,\ldots,7\}$.

Walking. There are 8 good extensions of ϕ_0, and we label them $\phi_{0,0},\ldots,\phi_{0,7}$ in a deterministic order. We then define the next edge by $\phi_1 = \phi_{0,m_1} : A_0 \to A_1$, and let $\phi_{1,0},\ldots,\phi_{1,7}$ denote its 8 good extensions. Next, setting $\phi_2 = \phi_{1,m_2}$, we repeat this procedure until the last isogeny $\phi_n : A_{n-1} \to A_n$ is obtained.

Output. The last vertex A_n must be isomorphic to the Jacobian variety of some genus-2 curve H_n by Remark 9, and then we output the absolute invariants (j_1, j_2, j_3) of H_n. We note that j_1, j_2, and j_3 all belong to $\mathbb{F}_{p^4}$, since $A_n \in \mathcal{V}_p$ is defined over $\mathbb{F}_{p^4}$.

Algorithm 1: $\mathcal{H}_{\mathrm{LTZ}}$

Input: A bit string of a message $m \in \{0,1\}^*$.
Output: The hash value of m.
1 Let $\phi_0 : A_{-1} \to A_0$ be the $(2,2)$-isogeny defined as in Section 3.2;
2 Parse m as an octal sequence $m_n \cdots m_2 m_1$ with $m_i \in \{0,\ldots,7\}$;
3 $\phi \leftarrow \phi_0$;
4 **for** $i \leftarrow 1$ **to** n **do**
5 $\quad \lfloor \; \psi \leftarrow \mathsf{GoodExtension}(\psi, m_i)$;
6 **return** $\mathsf{CodomainInvariant}(\phi)$;

Here, the reason why we restrict the isogenies to good extensions of the previous isogeny is to avoid trivial collisions (see [5, Section 7.1] for more details). For the reader's convenience, we give an explicit pseudocode in Algorithm 1. If necessary, one can convert the output of $\mathcal{H}_{\mathrm{LTZ}}(m)$ into a fixed-length bit string.

3.2   How to Choose the Initial Edge

Although the original paper [20] does not make explicit how the initial edge ϕ_0 is defined, we must choose it carefully to avoid trivial collisions. In this subsection, we discuss an appropriate choice.

In what follows, we restrict our attention to the case where $p \equiv 2, 3 \pmod 5$. Let A_{start} be the Jacobian variety of the genus-2 curve $y^2 = x^5 - 1$ over $\mathbb{F}_p$, then by Proposition 8, this is supersingular but non-superspecial. Also, since A_{start} is the unique principally polarized abelian surface (up to isomorphism) which has the automorphism group of order 10, the latter assertion of Theorem 14 implies that A_{start} belongs to $\mathcal{V}_p$, as shown in [20, Lemma 5].

Remark 17. It is not appropriate to simply set $A_0 := A_{\mathrm{start}}$. The reason is that, due to the large automorphism group of A_{start}, it has only three adjacent vertices (cf. [10, Section 4.15]), and therefore no matter how the initial edge ϕ_0 is chosen, there are two distinct good extensions of ϕ_0 with the same codomain. This leads to trivial collisions in the LTZ hash function.

Then, our solution is to employ a technique similar to that used in the CDS hash function, which is described as follows: we compute a $(2^{d+1}, 2^{d+1})$-isogeny with domain A_{start} deterministically, which can be decomposed into

$$A_{\mathrm{start}} \longrightarrow A_{-d} \longrightarrow A_{-d+1} \longrightarrow \cdots \longrightarrow A_{-1} \xrightarrow{\phi_0} A_0$$

for a non-negative integer $d \geq 0$, and we define $\phi_0 : A_{-1} \to A_0$ to be the initial edge in the LTZ hash function. For example, by analogy with the setting of the CDS hash function, a possible solution is to set $d := 10$. Alternatively, a simpler choice is to set $d := 0$, namely, to define the initial edge ϕ_0 to be a $(2,2)$-isogeny starting from $A_{-1} := A_{\text{start}}$.

Note that this choice is not secure in the setting of the CDS hash function as suggested in [4, Section 5.4]. This attack on the CDS hash function uses the fact that the construction of ϕ_0 starts from the product of two supersingular elliptic curves. Since this is not the case for the LTZ hash function, the attack does not apply to it (at least in a trivial way). Nevertheless, the choice of ϕ_0 still remains an important issue, and a more conservative approach would be to employ a trusted set-up, which generates the initial surface while concealing the path from A_{start} to A_0, as in other isogeny-based hash functions.

3.3   Underlying Mathematical Problems

In this subsection, we provide a brief review of the security analysis of the LTZ hash function, as presented in [20, Section 5]. We introduce the following two problems as the underlying mathematical problems of the LTZ hash function:

Problem 18. Given an edge $\phi_0 : A_{-1} \to A_0$ in $\mathcal{G}(2,p)$ and a vertex $A \in \mathcal{V}_p$, find a good $(2,2)$-sequence

$$A_{-1} \xrightarrow{\phi_0} A_0 \longrightarrow A_1 \longrightarrow \cdots \longrightarrow A_n \longrightarrow A$$

for some $n \in \mathbb{N}$.

Problem 19. Given an edge $\phi_0 : A_{-1} \to A_0$ in $\mathcal{G}(2,p)$, find $A \in \mathcal{V}_p$ and two distinct good $(2,2)$-sequences

$$A_{-1} \xrightarrow{\phi_0} A_0 \longrightarrow A_1 \longrightarrow \cdots \longrightarrow A_n \longrightarrow A$$

and

$$A_{-1} \xrightarrow{\phi_0} A_0 \longrightarrow B_1 \longrightarrow \cdots \longrightarrow B_{n'} \longrightarrow A$$

for some $n, n' \in \mathbb{N}$.

It is obvious that the pre-image resistance and the second pre-image resistance of the LTZ hash function both reduce to Problem 18, and the collision resistance of the LTZ hash function reduces to Problem 19. Moreover, Problem 19 reduces to Problem 18. Therefore, for the security of the LTZ hash function, we need to analyze the hardness of Problem 19.

In the original paper [20], the authors claimed that the best-known algorithm to solve Problem 19 is the Pollard-rho style algorithm, which can be roughly described as follows. Let $\mathcal{S}_p \subset (\mathbb{F}_{p^4})^3$ be the set of absolute invariants of the vertices on $\mathcal{V}_p$, and let $P : \mathcal{S}_p \to \{0,1\}^n$ be an injective pseudorandom function for some $n \in \mathbb{N}$. Then, the LTZ hash function can be regarded as a self-map $h : \mathcal{S}_p \to \mathcal{S}_p$, concretely defined by $h := \mathcal{H}_{\text{LTZ}} \circ P$. Starting from a base point $x_0 \in \mathcal{S}_p$, one can find $k \in \mathbb{N}$ such that $h^k(x_0) = h^{2k}(x_0)$, as described in [14, Chapter 4.5]. The expected number k of iterations is approximately $\sqrt{\#\mathcal{S}_p}$, which requires $O(p^3)$ evaluations of the LTZ hash function. Since a single evaluation of the hash function involves $O(\log(p))$ computations of $(2,2)$-isogenies, each of which can be carried out using $O(\log(p))$ multiplications over $\mathbb{F}_p$ as explained in Sect. 2.3, the overall time complexity for finding a collision in this way amounts to $O(p^3 \log(p)^2)$ multiplications over $\mathbb{F}_p$. On the other hand, since only two hash values need to be stored, the required space complexity is $O(\log(p))$.

Implicit Security Assumption. Although not stated explicitly in the original paper [20], the above discussion requires the following assumption related to the isogenies computed in the LTZ hash function:

Assumption 20. For sufficiently large n, the codomains of the $(2^n, 2^n)$-isogenies with fixed domain $A \in \mathcal{V}_p$ are almost uniformly distributed over $\mathcal{V}_p$.

This assumption is based on the weaker conjecture stated below, which is inspired by the conjecture in the superspecial case (cf. [5, Conjecture 3]).

Conjecture 21. For every two vertices $A, A' \in \mathcal{V}_p$, there exists a $(2^n, 2^n)$-isogeny from A to A' for some n.

We note that Conjecture 21 is used implicitly in Problem 18. To the best of our knowledge and efforts, there is no proof of this conjecture. We leave the proof of this conjecture along with the analysis of Assumption 20 as future work.

4   Theoretical Foundations

In this section, we describe the mathematical facts and a conjecture underlying our collision attack on the LTZ hash function. We continue to assume that $p > 5$ is a prime satisfying $p \equiv 2, 3 \pmod 5$, as stated in Sect. 3.2.

4.1   On the Number of Vertices Defined over $\mathbb{F}_{p^2}$

The purpose of this subsection is to present a conjecture (Conjecture 28) on the number of vertices in $\mathcal{G}(2, p)$, as given in Definition 15, that are defined over $\mathbb{F}_{p^2}$. For this purpose, we begin by establishing several lemmas:

Lemma 22. *For any supersingular principally polarized abelian surface $A \in \mathcal{V}_p$, the characteristic polynomial of A over $\mathbb{F}_{p^4}$ is given as $(X + p^2)^4$. Therefore, all the edges on the graph $\mathcal{G}(2, p)$ are defined over $\mathbb{F}_{p^4}$.*

Proof. Let A_{start} be the Jacobian variety of the genus-2 curve $y^2 = x^5 - 1$, which lies in the vertex set $\mathcal{V}_p$, from the assumption that $p \equiv 2, 3 \pmod 5$. Recall from Proposition 12 that the characteristic polynomial of A_{start} over $\mathbb{F}_p$ is given by

$$\Phi(X) = X^4 + p^2 = \prod_{i=1}^{4}(X - \alpha_i),$$

where $\alpha_1, \ldots, \alpha_4$ are the fourth roots of $-p^2$. Then, the characteristic polynomial of A_{start} over $\mathbb{F}_{p^4}$ is given by

$$\Phi_4(X) = \prod_{i=1}^{4}(X - \alpha_i^4) = (X + p^2)^4$$

by using Proposition 10. Equivalently, the p^4-th power Frobenius endomorphism on A_{start} is identical to the multiplication-by-$(-p^2)$ map on A_{start}, which implies that all the $(2,2)$-isogenies from A_{start} are defined over $\mathbb{F}_{p^4}$. Therefore, by Tate's isogeny theorem [27, Theorem 1(c)], each vertex adjacent to A_{start} on $\mathcal{G}(2,p)$ has the characteristic polynomial over $\mathbb{F}_{p^4}$ equal to $(X + p^2)^4$, which is the same as that of A_{start}.

Repeating this inductively, we conclude from the connectivity of $\mathcal{G}(2,p)$ that the characteristic polynomial of any vertex $A \in V_p$ over $\mathbb{F}_{p^4}$ is given by $(X+p^2)^4$. Consequently, applying Tate's isogeny theorem again, we find that all the edges on $\mathcal{G}(2,p)$ are defined over $\mathbb{F}_{p^4}$, as desired. $\qquad\square$

Lemma 23. *Let $A \in V_p$ be a supersingular principally polarized abelian surface over $\mathbb{F}_{p^2}$. Then, the rank of $A(\mathbb{F}_{p^2})[2]$ is 2.*

Proof. First, we show that the characteristic polynomial $\Phi(X) = \prod_{i=1}^{4}(X - \alpha_i)$ of A over $\mathbb{F}_q = \mathbb{F}_{p^2}$ is given by $(X^2+p^2)^2$. It follows from Proposition 10 that the characteristic polynomial of A over $\mathbb{F}_{q^2} = \mathbb{F}_{p^4}$ is given by $\Phi_2(X) = \prod_{i=1}^{4}(X-\alpha_i^2)$, which is equal to $(X + p^2)^4$ by Lemma 22. Hence, we have that

$$(X^2 + p^2)^4 = \prod_{i=1}^{4}(X^2 - \alpha_i^2) = \prod_{i=1}^{4}(X - \alpha_i) \cdot \prod_{i=1}^{4}(X + \alpha_i),$$

and this polynomial is divisible by $\prod_{i=1}^{4}(X - \alpha_i) = \Phi(X) \in \mathbb{Z}[X]$. Since the only possible polynomial of degree 4 with integer coefficients that divides $(X^2 + p^2)^4$ is $(X^2 + p^2)^2$, the claim follows as desired.

Then, again by Proposition 10, the order of $A(\mathbb{F}_{p^2})$ equals $\Phi(1) = (p^2 + 1)^2$, which is divisible by 4 and not by 8. Hence, the rank of $A(\mathbb{F}_{p^2})[2]$ is 1 or 2. Next, let P be a point of $A(\mathbb{F}_{p^2})[2]$, and let Q_1, Q_2, Q_3 be points on A of order 2 such that (P, Q_1, Q_2, Q_3) is a basis of $A[2]$. Denoting by π the p^2-th power Frobenius endomorphism on A, we obtain that $Q_i + \pi(Q_i) \in A(\mathbb{F}_{p^2})[2]$ for all $i \in \{1,2,3\}$. If $Q_i + \pi(Q_i) \neq P$ for some i, then either Q_i or $Q_i + \pi(Q_i)$ is a point in $A(\mathbb{F}_{p^2})[2]$ different from P. If $Q_i + \pi(Q_i) = P$ for all i, then $Q_1 + Q_2$ is a point in $A(\mathbb{F}_{p^2})[2]$ different from P. In either case, the rank of $A(\mathbb{F}_{p^2})[2]$ is at least 2. Summarizing the above discussion, the rank of $A(\mathbb{F}_{p^2})[2]$ equals 2, as desired. $\qquad\square$

Lemma 24. *Let $A \in V_p$ be a supersingular principally polarized abelian surface over $\mathbb{F}_{p^2}$. Then, there exists a symplectic basis $(P_1, P_2; Q_1, Q_2)$ of $A[2]$ such that*

- *both P_1 and P_2 are defined over $\mathbb{F}_{p^2}$,*
- *$(Q_1 + \pi(Q_1), Q_2 + \pi(Q_2)) = (P_1, P_2)$ or (P_2, P_1),*

where π denotes the p^2-th power Frobenius endomorphism on A.

Proof. First, consider the map

$$A[2] \longrightarrow A(\mathbb{F}_{p^2})[2] \,;\, Q \longmapsto Q + \pi(Q).$$

This is a group homomorphism whose kernel is $A(\mathbb{F}_{p^2})[2]$, and hence it is surjective by Lemma 23. Thus, for any $P' \in A(\mathbb{F}_{p^2})[2]$, there exists $Q \in A[2]$ such that $Q + \pi(Q) = P'$. Let e_2 denote the 2-Weil pairing on A, then for $P, P' \in A(\mathbb{F}_{p^2})[2]$ with $Q \in A[2]$ and $Q + \pi(Q) = P'$, we have

$$e_2(P, P') = e_2(P, Q + \pi(Q)) = e_2(P, Q)e_2(P, \pi(Q)) = e_2(P, Q)^2 = 1,$$

which shows that e_2 is trivial on $A(\mathbb{F}_{p^2})[2]$. Therefore, one can choose a symplectic basis $(P_1, P_2; Q_1, Q_2)$ of $A[2]$ such that both P_1 and P_2 are in $A(\mathbb{F}_{p^2})$.

Let $R_1 := Q_1 + \pi(Q_1)$ and $R_2 := Q_2 + \pi(Q_2)$, which are points in $A(\mathbb{F}_{p^2})[2]$. Then, we have

$$e_2(Q_1, R_2)e_2(Q_2, R_1) = e_2(Q_1, \pi(Q_2))e_2(Q_2, \pi(Q_1))$$
$$= e_2(Q_1, \pi(Q_2))^2 = 1.$$

This means that $e_2(Q_1, R_2) = e_2(Q_2, R_1)$. If $e_2(Q_1, R_2) = e_2(Q_2, R_1) = 1$, then we have $R_1 = P_1$ and $R_2 = P_2$. Otherwise (i.e., $e_2(Q_1, R_2) = e_2(Q_2, R_1) = -1$), we have $R_1 \in \{P_2, P_1 + P_2\}$ and $R_2 \in \{P_1, P_1 + P_2\}$ with $R_1 \neq R_2$.

- In the case where $R_1 = P_2$ and $R_2 = P_1$, there is nothing more to prove.
- In the case where $R_1 = P_1 + P_2$, it follows that $R_2 = P_1$. By replacing (P_1, Q_2) with $(P_1 + P_2, Q_1 + Q_2)$, one may assume that $R_1 = P_1$ and $R_2 = P_2$.
- In the case where $R_1 = P_2$, it follows that $R_2 = P_1 + P_2$. By replacing (P_2, Q_1) with $(P_1 + P_2, Q_1 + Q_2)$, one may assume that $R_1 = P_1$ and $R_2 = P_2$.

In each case, the resulting symplectic basis $(P_1, P_2; Q_1, Q_2)$ of $A[2]$ satisfies the desired condition. $\qquad\square$

Here, we introduce the following definition:

Definition 25. *For a supersingular principally polarized abelian surface $A \in \mathcal{V}_p$ over $\mathbb{F}_{p^2}$, let $(P_1, P_2; Q_1, Q_2)$ be a symplectic basis of $A[2]$ in Lemma 24. Then, we classify A into the following two types:*

*(i) We say that A is of **Type I** if $Q_1 + \pi(Q_1) = P_1$ and $Q_2 + \pi(Q_2) = P_2$,*
*(ii) We say that A is of **Type II** if $Q_1 + \pi(Q_1) = P_2$ and $Q_2 + \pi(Q_2) = P_1$,*

where π denotes the p^2-th power Frobenius endomorphism on A. In other words, the abelian surface A is Type I if and only if $e_2(P, \pi(P)) = -1$ for some $P \in A[2]$, and is Type II if and only if $e_2(P, \pi(P)) = 1$ for all $P \in A[2]$.

The following lemma ensures that the type of A is invariant under isomorphisms over $\overline{\mathbb{F}}_p$, and therefore, the above definition is well-defined:

Lemma 26. *Let $A, A' \in \mathcal{V}_p$ be a supersingular principally polarized abelian surface over $\mathbb{F}_{p^2}$, where A is isomorphic to A'. Then A is of Type I (resp. Type II) if and only if A' is of Type I (resp. Type II).*

Proof. By Theorem 14, the automorphism group of A' is either trivial (i.e., equal to $\{\pm 1\}$) or isomorphic to $\mathbb{Z}/10\mathbb{Z}$. In the following, we distinguish the two cases separately, depending on the automorphism group of A'.

If $\mathrm{Aut}(A') = \{\pm 1\}$, let $\iota : A \to A'$ be an isomorphism. Since $\iota^{(p^2)} \circ \iota^{-1}$ is an automorphism of A', we have $\iota^{(p^2)} \circ \iota^{-1} = [\pm 1]$, that is, $\iota^{(p^2)} = [\pm 1]\iota$. Hence, for all $P \in A[2]$, we have

$$e_2(P, \pi(P)) = e_2(\iota^{(p^2)}(P), \iota^{(p^2)}(\pi(P))) = e_2([\pm 1]\iota(P), \pi(\iota(P)))$$
$$= e_2(\iota(P), \pi(\iota(P))).$$

Since $\iota(P)$ runs through all $A'[2]$ as P runs through $A[2]$, the types of A and A' are the same.

Otherwise (i.e., $\mathrm{Aut}(A') \cong \mathbb{Z}/10\mathbb{Z}$), as described after Proposition 8, both A and A' are isomorphic to the Jacobian variety of $H : y^2 = x^5 - 1$. Let ι denote such an isomorphism from A to $\mathrm{Jac}(H)$. Since $\iota^{(p^2)} \circ \iota^{-1}$ is an automorphism of $\mathrm{Jac}(H)$, we have $\iota^{(p^2)} \circ \iota^{-1} = [\pm \zeta_5^k]$ for some $k \in \{0, 1, 2, 3, 4\}$. Here, for each k, we write $[\pm \zeta_5^k]$ for the automorphism of $\mathrm{Jac}(H)$ induced from $(x, y) \mapsto (\zeta_5^k x, \pm y)$ on H, where ζ_5 is a primitive fifth root of unity in $\overline{\mathbb{F}}_p$.

- In the case where $k = 0$, then we obtain $\iota^{(p^2)} = [\pm 1]\iota$. Let Q be the order-2 point $(1, 0) - (\zeta_5, 0)$ on $\mathrm{Jac}(H)$ and $P := \iota^{-1}(Q) \in A[2]$. Then, we have

$$e_2(P, \pi(P)) = e_2(\iota^{(p^2)}(P), \iota^{(p^2)}(\pi(P))) = e_2([\pm 1]\iota(P), \pi(\iota(P)))$$
$$= e_2(Q, \pi(Q)) = -1,$$

  since $\pi(Q) = (1, 0) - (\zeta_5^4, 0)$ from the assumption that $p \equiv 2, 3 \pmod 5$.
- In the case where $k \neq 0$, then we obtain $\iota^{(p^2)} = [\pm \zeta_5^k]\iota$. Let Q be the order-2 point $(1, 0) - \infty$ on $\mathrm{Jac}(H)$ and $P := \iota^{-1}(Q) \in A[2]$. Then, we have

$$e_2(P, \pi(P)) = e_2(\iota^{(p^2)}(P), \iota^{(p^2)}(\pi(P))) = e_2([\pm \zeta_5^k]\iota(P), \pi(\iota(P)))$$
$$= e_2([\zeta_5^k]Q, \pi(Q)) = -1,$$

  since $[\zeta_5^k]Q = (\zeta_5^k, 0) - \infty$ and $\pi(Q) = (1, 0) - \infty$.

In any case, there exists $P \in A[2]$ such that $e_2(P, \pi(P)) = -1$, and this tells us that A is of Type I. Similarly, one can show that A' is of Type I, and hence the type of A and A' are the same. $\qquad\square$

Remark 27. In the discussion of this subsection so far, the congruence condition that $p \equiv 2, 3 \pmod 5$ is employed essentially, *only* at the beginning of the proof of Lemma 22. It should be noted that if $p \equiv 1, 4 \pmod 5$, then all $A' \in \mathcal{V}_p$ have trivial automorphism groups, and thus the latter case distinction in the proof of Lemma 26 is not needed.

Moreover, even if $p \equiv 1, 4 \pmod 5$, as long as there exists *at least one* $A \in \mathcal{V}_p$ whose characteristic polynomial over $\mathbb{F}_{p^4}$ is $(X + p^2)^4$, then Lemma 22 still holds by the same proof as the original one. Therefore, in that case, all the subsequent statements after Lemma 22 remain valid; in particular, the type classification in Definition 25 is also well-defined.

We are now ready to state our conjecture:

Conjecture 28. For primes $p > 5$ with $p \equiv 2, 3 \pmod 5$, we define

$$N_{1,p} := \#\{A \in \mathcal{V}_p \mid A \text{ is defined over } \mathbb{F}_{p^2} \text{ and of Type I}\}, \text{ and}$$
$$N_{2,p} := \#\{A \in \mathcal{V}_p \mid A \text{ is defined over } \mathbb{F}_{p^2} \text{ and of Type II}\}.$$

Then, we have the following:

- If $p \equiv 1 \pmod 4$, then

$$N_{1,p} = \left(\frac{p+1}{2}\right)\left(\frac{p-1}{4}\right)^2, \quad N_{2,p} = \frac{2}{3}\left(\frac{p+1}{2}\right)\left(\frac{p-1}{4}\right)^2.$$

- If $p \equiv 3 \pmod 4$, then

$$N_{1,p} = \left(\frac{p-1}{2}\right)\left(\frac{p+1}{4}\right)^2, \quad N_{2,p} = 0.$$

We have verified by a computer experiments that Conjecture 28 holds for any prime p such that $5 < p < 100$ and $p \equiv 2, 3 \pmod 5$, by exhaustively enumerating all vertices satisfying the required conditions.

Remark 29. For a prime $5 < p < 100$, even if $p \equiv 1, 4 \pmod 5$, it is also verified that every $A \in \mathcal{V}_p$ has the characteristic polynomial $(X + p^2)^4$ over $\mathbb{F}_{p^4}$, and that Conjecture 28 is true (note that, the definitions of $N_{1,p}$ and $N_{2,p}$ make sense by the discussion in Remark 27).

4.2   On the Number of Edges with Good p^2-Conjugate

In our collision attack on the LTZ hash function described in Sect. 5, an edge on the graph $\mathcal{G}(2, p)$ with the following property plays a central role:

Definition 30. *For an edge $\phi : A \to A'$ on the graph $\mathcal{G}(2, p)$ where A is defined over $\mathbb{F}_{p^2}$, we say that ϕ has the **good** p^2-conjugate if it is a good extension of the dual $\hat{\phi}^{(p^2)} : A'^{(p^2)} \to A^{(p^2)} = A$ of its p^2-conjugate.*

Proposition 31. *For a supersingular principally polarized abelian surface $A \in \mathcal{V}_p$ over $\mathbb{F}_{p^2}$, we have the following:*

(i) If A is of Type I, then there exist exactly twelve $(2, 2)$-isogenies from A that are not defined over $\mathbb{F}_{p^2}$. Among these, eight have the good p^2-conjugate.

(ii) If A is of Type II, then there exist exactly eight $(2,2)$-isogenies from A that are not defined over $\mathbb{F}_{p^2}$. All of them have the good p^2-conjugate.

Proof. For a $(2,2)$-isogeny ϕ from A with kernel G, we have that

- ϕ is not defined over $\mathbb{F}_{p^2}$ if and only if $G \neq \pi(G)$,
- ϕ has the good p^2-conjugate if and only if $G \cap \pi(G) = \emptyset$,

where π denotes the p^2-th power Frobenius endomorphism on A.

Let $(P_1, P_2; Q_1, Q_2)$ is a symplectic basis of $A[2]$ satisfying the conditions in Lemma 24. All the maximal isotropic subgroups of $A[2]$ together with the action of π on them are summarized in Table 2 for Type I and in Table 3 for Type II. We note that there are a total of 15 subgroups belonging to the first or second column of each table. These results prove the proposition. $\qquad\square$

Table 2. Maximal isotropic subgroups G of $A[2]$, its p^2-th power Frobenius conjugate $\pi(G)$, and the intersection $G \cap \pi(G)$ for a Type I abelian surface $A \in \mathcal{V}_p$.

G	$\pi(G)$	$G \cap \pi(G)$
$\langle P_1, P_2 \rangle$	$= G$	G
$\langle P_1 + P_2, Q_1 + Q_2 \rangle$	$= G$	G
$\langle P_1 + P_2, P_1 + Q_1 + Q_2 \rangle$	$= G$	G
$\langle P_1, Q_2 \rangle$	$\langle P_1, P_2 + Q_2 \rangle$	$\langle P_1 \rangle$
$\langle P_2, Q_1 \rangle$	$\langle P_2, P_1 + Q_1 \rangle$	$\langle P_2 \rangle$
$\langle Q_1, Q_2 \rangle$	$\langle P_1 + Q_1, P_2 + Q_2 \rangle$	$\emptyset$
$\langle Q_1, P_2 + Q_2 \rangle$	$\langle P_1 + Q_1, Q_2 \rangle$	$\emptyset$
$\langle P_1 + Q_2, P_1 + P_2 + Q_1 \rangle$	$\langle P_1 + P_2 + Q_2, P_2 + Q_1 \rangle$	$\emptyset$
$\langle P_1 + Q_2, P_2 + Q_1 \rangle$	$\langle Q_1 + Q_2, P_1 + P_2 + Q_1 \rangle$	$\emptyset$

Finally, we assume the following heuristic based on Conjecture 28, which will be required for the discussion of the termination of our collision attack:

Heuristic 32. Let ϕ be an edge on the graph $\mathcal{G}(2, p)$. Then, there exists at least one good $(2,2)$-sequence $(\phi, \phi_1, \ldots, \phi_n)$ with $n \leq \log_2(p)$ such that the codomain of ϕ_n is defined over $\mathbb{F}_{p^2}$ and $\hat{\phi}_n^{(p^2)}$ is a good extension of ϕ_n.

In the following, we explain why Heuristic 32 is reasonable. By Theorem 14, the cardinality of $\mathcal{V}_p$ is less than $p^6/2880$. Moreover, according to Conjecture 28, the number of elements of $\mathcal{V}_p$ defined over $\mathbb{F}_{p^2}$ is greater than $p^3/32$. Hence, the ratio of the latter to the former is greater than $p^3/32 \cdot 2880/p^6 = 90/p^3$. On the other hand, the number of good $(2,2)$-extensions $(\phi, \phi_1, \ldots, \phi_n)$ with $n := \lfloor \log_2(p) \rfloor$ is given by $8^n > p^3/8$. By assuming the rapid mixing property of good extensions (Heuristic 20), one may expect the codomains of ϕ_n to be

Table 3. Maximal isotropic subgroups G of $A[2]$, its p^2-th power Frobenius conjugate $\pi(G)$, and the intersection $G \cap \pi(G)$ for a Type II abelian surface $A \in \mathcal{V}_p$.

G	$\pi(G)$	$G \cap \pi(G)$
$\langle P_1, P_2 \rangle$	$= G$	G
$\langle P_1 + P_2, Q_1 + Q_2 \rangle$	$= G$	G
$\langle P_1 + P_2, P_1 + Q_1 + Q_2 \rangle$	$= G$	G
$\langle P_1, Q_2 \rangle$	$= G$	G
$\langle P_2, Q_1 \rangle$	$= G$	G
$\langle P_1, P_2 + Q_2 \rangle$	$= G$	G
$\langle P_2, P_1 + Q_1 \rangle$	$= G$	G
$\langle Q_1, Q_2 \rangle$	$\langle P_2 + Q_1, P_1 + Q_2 \rangle$	$\emptyset$
$\langle Q_1, P_2 + Q_2 \rangle$	$\langle P_2 + Q_1, P_1 + P_2 + Q_2 \rangle$	$\emptyset$
$\langle P_1 + Q_1, Q_2 \rangle$	$\langle P_1 + P_2 + Q_1, P_1 + Q_2 \rangle$	$\emptyset$
$\langle P_1 + Q_1, P_2 + Q_2 \rangle$	$\langle Q_1 + Q_2, P_1 + P_2 + Q_1 \rangle$	$\emptyset$

almost uniformly distributed over $\mathcal{V}_p$. This implies that the set of the codomains of ϕ_n contains approximately $90/8 = 11.25$ elements of $\mathcal{V}_p$ defined over $\mathbb{F}_{p^2}$. In addition, for every ϕ_n with such a codomain, Proposition 31 says that, the probability that $\hat{\phi}_n^{(p^2)}$ has the good p^2-conjugate is at least $2/3$. Therefore, we conclude that Heuristic 32 is reasonable.

5   Our Collision Attack on the LTZ Hash Function

In this section, we describe our algorithm for finding a collision on the LTZ hash function. We first outline the attack in Sect. 5.1, and then provide its concrete pseudocode (Algorithm 2) in Sect. 5.2. The computational complexity of this algorithm is estimated in Theorem 34.

5.1   Overview

Our collision attack is based on the idea in [9], and can be sketched as follows. Let $\phi_0 : A_{-1} \to A_0$ be the initial edge of the LTZ hash function as defined in Sect. 3.2. First, we find distinct good $(2,2)$-sequences $(\phi_0, \phi_1, \ldots, \phi_n)$ and $(\phi_0, \phi'_1, \ldots, \phi'_m)$ where the codomains of ϕ_n and ϕ'_m are defined over $\mathbb{F}_{p^2}$. Let α (resp. β) be the isogeny obtained by composing $\phi_1, \ldots, \phi_n$ (resp. $\phi'_1, \ldots, \phi'_m$) and A (resp. B) be its codomain. We then obtain two isogenies $\beta^{(p^2)} \circ \hat{\alpha}^{(p^2)} \circ \alpha$ and β from A_0 to B since $A^{(p^2)} = A$ and $B^{(p^2)} = B$. The following diagram illustrates the situation:

If $\beta^{(p^2)} \circ \hat{\alpha}^{(p^2)} \circ \alpha$ induces a good $(2,2)$-sequence (that is, it is a $(2^{2m+n}, 2^{2m+n})$-isogeny), then the sequences induced from $\beta^{(p^2)} \circ \hat{\alpha}^{(p^2)} \circ \alpha$ and β give a collision on the LTZ hash function. The remaining problem is to find such sequences, and we explain how to do this in the next subsection.

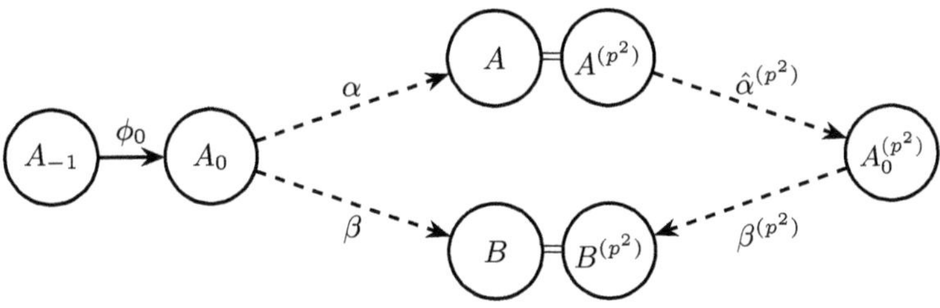

5.2   Description

In this subsection, we explicitly describe our collision attack on the LTZ hash function. For this purpose, we define a tree structure of good extensions:

Definition 33. *For an edge ϕ on the graph $\mathcal{G}(2,p)$, we define the **tree of good extensions** of ϕ as follows:*

- *The root is ϕ.*
- *Each node is a good extension of its parent.*

In addition, if the codomain of a node is isomorphic to $A \in \mathcal{V}_p$ defined over $\mathbb{F}_{p^2}$, then we take the node as an isogeny to A.

In this tree structure, since each node has exactly eight children, the number of nodes at depth n is equal to 8^n.

Additionally, we define the following subroutine to search in the tree of good extensions.

- DFSGoodExt($\phi, N, \mathtt{bool}$): It takes an edge ϕ on $\mathcal{G}(2,p)$, and returns a good $(2,2)$-sequence $(\phi, \phi_2, \ldots, \phi_n)$ of length $\leq N$ such that the codomain of the last isogeny ϕ_n is defined over $\mathbb{F}_{p^2}$, by performing a depth-first search in the tree of good extensions of ϕ. If $\mathtt{bool}$ is given by $\mathtt{true}$, we continue the search until $\hat{\phi}_n^{(p^2)}$ is a good extension of ϕ_n.

Then, our collision attack is described in Algorithm 2.

We finally prove our main theorem:

Theorem 34. *Assuming Heuristic 32, Algorithm 2 always succeeds. Moreover, its time complexity is $O(p^3 \log(p) \mathrm{M}_{\mathbb{F}_p})$ and its space complexity is $O(\log(p)^2)$.*

Proof. First, we show the correctness of Algorithm 2.

- Since the codomain of ϕ_n (resp. ϕ'_m) is defined over $\mathbb{F}_{p^2}$, it is isomorphic to the codomain of $\phi_n^{(p^2)}$ (resp. $\phi'^{(p^2)}_m$). Hence, the output sequences correspond to two isogenies from A_0 to an isomorphic vertex.
- Since ϕ'_1 is a good extension of $\hat{\phi}_1$, we have that $\phi'^{(p^2)}_1$ (resp. $\phi_1^{(p^2)}$) is a good extension of $\hat{\phi}_1^{(p^2)}$ (resp. $\hat{\phi}'^{(p^2)}_1$). Therefore, both of the output sequences are good $(2,2)$-sequences by construction.

Algorithm 2: Finding a collision in the LTZ hash function

Input: The initial edge $\phi_0 : A_{-1} \to A_0$ of the LTZ hash function.

Output: Two distinct good $(2,2)$-sequences that yield a collision on the LTZ hash function.

1   $\phi_1 \leftarrow \mathsf{GoodExtension}(\phi_0, 0)$;

2   $i \leftarrow 1$;

3   $\phi_1' \leftarrow \mathsf{GoodExtension}(\phi_0, i)$;

4   **while** *not* $\mathsf{GoodExtension}(\hat{\phi}_1, \phi_1')$ **do**

5      $i \leftarrow i + 1$;

6      $\phi_1' \leftarrow \mathsf{GoodExtension}(\phi_0, i)$;

7   $N \leftarrow \lfloor \log_2(p) \rfloor$;

8   $(\phi_1, \ldots, \phi_n) \leftarrow \mathsf{DFSGoodExt}(\phi_1, N, \mathtt{false})$;

9   **if** $\mathsf{GoodExtension}(\phi_n, \hat{\phi}_n^{(p^2)})$ **then**

10      $(\phi_1', \ldots, \phi_m') \leftarrow \mathsf{DFSGoodExt}(\phi_1', N, \mathtt{false})$;

11   **return** $(\phi_1, \ldots, \phi_n, \hat{\phi}_n^{(p^2)}, \ldots, \hat{\phi}_1^{(p^2)}, {\phi_1'}^{(p^2)}, \ldots, {\phi_m'}^{(p^2)})$ *and* $(\phi_1', \ldots, \phi_m')$;

12   **else**

13      $(\phi_1', \ldots, \phi_m') \leftarrow \mathsf{DFSGoodExt}(\phi_1', N, \mathtt{true})$;

14   **return** $(\phi_1, \ldots, \phi_n)$ *and* $(\phi_1', \ldots, \phi_m', \hat{\phi}_m'^{(p^2)}, \ldots, \hat{\phi}_1'^{(p^2)}, \phi_1^{(p^2)}, \ldots, \phi_n^{(p^2)})$;

  –   Since the output sequences have different lengths, they are distinct.

Consequently, the output sequences induce a collision on the LTZ hash function, as desired.

Next, we show the termination of Algorithm 2. By Heuristic 32, the calls to DFSGoodExt in the algorithm succeed, and thus the only part whose termination is non-trivial is the **while** loop in lines 4–6. This **while** loop ends after at most six iterations. Indeed, the number of $(2,2)$-isogenies with domain A is 15, among which there are 8 good extensions of ϕ_0 and also 8 good extensions of $\hat{\phi}_1$. Hence, by the pigeonhole principle, there exists at least one ϕ_1' that is a good extension of both ϕ_0 and $\hat{\phi}_1$. Therefore, the algorithm always succeeds.

Finally, let us estimate the computational complexity of Algorithm 2. The algorithm performs a constant number of calls to GoodExtension, IsGoodExtension, and DFSGoodExt. As stated in Sect. 2.3, the former two run in $O(\log(p)\mathrm{M}_{\mathbb{F}_p})$ time and $O(\log(p))$ space. In the calls to DFSGoodExt, we have

  –   The number of detected nodes is at most $\sum_{i=1}^{N} 8^i = (8^{N+1} - 1)/7 = O(p^3)$.

  –   The number of stored nodes is at most N.

For each node, we call CodomainInvariant and GoodExtension once (in particular, if the third argument of DFSGoodExt is $\mathtt{true}$, then IsGoodExtension is also called once). Since these algorithms run in $O(\log(p)\mathrm{M}_{\mathbb{F}_p})$ time and $O(\log(p))$ space, as explained in Sect. 2.3, we obtain

  –   The time complexity of DFSGoodExt call is in $O(p^3 \log(p)\mathrm{M}_{\mathbb{F}_p})$.

– The space complexity of DFSGoodExt call is in $O(N\log(p)) = O(\log(p)^2)$.

This constitutes the dominant part of the algorithm. $\Box$

With quantum computers in mind, our attack can be combined with Grover's algorithm [13], analogously to the attack by Eisenträger et al. on the CGL hash function, thereby reducing the time complexity to the square root of the classical one. As a consequence, the quantum collision resistance of the LTZ hash function is currently estimated to be $\widetilde{O}(p^{3/2})$.

6   Experimental Results

We implemented our collision attack on the LTZ hash function, using Rust programming language. Our code in available in the Github repository

$$\text{https://github.com/hiroshi-onuki/LTZ\_hash\_collision.}$$

In this section, we present several results obtained through computational experiments. Our experiments were conducted on a machine running Ubuntu 22.04.5 LTS with an Intel Core i9-14900 CPU (24 cores and 48 threads), 128 GB of RAM, and Rust 1.88.0 with the `-release` flag enabled. We note that, although our collision attack can be easily parallelized, all experiments in this section were performed on a single core.

6.1   Performance of Our Collision Attack

We ran our implementation for all primes p with $p \equiv 2,3 \pmod 5$ and $35 \le 3\log_2(p) \le 37$ that are parameters expected to yield security levels between 35 and 37 bits and measured the running time. The results are summarized in Table 4.

Table 4. Experimental results of Algorithm 2 for primes p with $p \equiv 2,3 \pmod 5$ and $35 \le \log_2(p) \le 37$, showing the numbers of searched nodes in the depth-first searches in line 8 (resp. line 10 or 13) divided by p^3, the number of cases satisfying the condition in line 9, and the running time.

		#(searched nodes)$/p^3$		The first	Time
		first	second	is good?	(seconds)
$p \equiv 1$	Average	1.1350%	1.4764%	48/61	62,109
(mod 4)	Worst	5.6579%	7.0193%	-	256,715
$p \equiv 3$	Average	1.6520%	1.7365%	40/57	83,787
(mod 4)	Worst	9.6246%	9.5718%	-	346,364

In Table 4, the second and third columns show the numbers of searched nodes in the depth-first searches in line 8 and line 10 or 13, respectively, divided by p^3. By Heuristic 32, these values are expected to be below 100%. The actual values are much smaller than 100%, supporting the validity of our heuristic. The fourth column shows the number of the cases where the sequence $(\phi_1, \ldots, \phi_n)$ found in line 8 satisfies that $\hat{\phi}_n^{(p^2)}$ is a good extension of ϕ_n. The fifth column reports the time required for our collision attack. The detailed results for each prime p are shown in Tables 5, 6, 7, and 8. Also, we confirmed that our collision attack runs in a practical memory size of about 25MB for the range of primes p considered in this experiment.

6.2   Comparison with the Pollard-Rho Style Algorithm

We also implemented the Pollard-rho style algorithm in Rust and conducted experiments comparing its running time with that of our algorithm for all primes p with $p \equiv 2, 3 \pmod 5$ and $100 < p < 1000$. The ratio of the running time of the Pollard-rho algorithm to that of our algorithm is shown in Fig. 1.

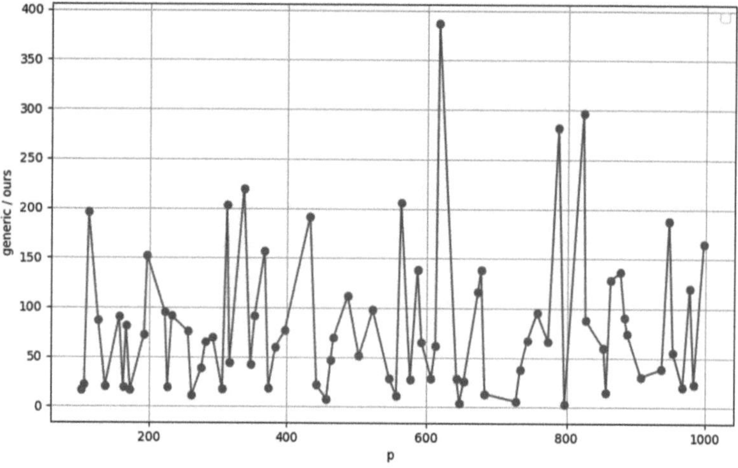

Fig. 1. Comparison of the execution times of the Pollard-rho algorithm and our attack.

In Fig. 1, the ratio ranges from a maximum of 386.865 to a minimum of 3.098, with an average of 81.943. In other words, in the range of primes $p < 1000$, our attack is on average approximately 82 times more efficient than the Pollard-rho style algorithm. Based on the asymptotic complexity analysis, this ratio is expected to increase as p grows larger.

Acknowledgements. The authors thank Marc Houben for his valuable comments on the complexity of the Pollard-rho style algorithm in an earlier version of this paper. This research was supported by JSPS Grant-in-Aid for Young Scientists 25K17225. This research was also conducted under a contract of "Research and development on new generation cryptography for secure wireless communication services" among "Research and Development for Expansion of Radio Wave Resources (JPJ000254)", which was supported by the Ministry of Internal Affairs and Communications, Japan.

A   An Efficient Representation of a $(2,2)$-Isogeny

In this appendix, we give an example of efficient representations of $(2,2)$-isogenies between two indecomposable principally polarized abelian surfaces in Sect. 2.3, together with five algorithms such as GoodExtension.

First, any indecomposable principally polarized abelian surface over a field $k = \mathbb{F}_{p^4}$ of characteristic $p > 5$ is isomorphic to the Jacobian variety of a genus-2 curve

$$H : y^2 = f(x),$$

where $f(x) \in k[x]$ is a square-free polynomial of degree 5 or 6. Then, we consider the set of quadratic factors of $f(x)$ that are pairwise coprime as follows:

Definition 35. *A **quadratic splitting** of a square-free polynomial $f(x) \in k[x]$ of degree 5 or 6 is an unordered triple $\{f_1(x), f_2(x), f_3(x)\} \subset \bar{k}[x]$ of polynomials of degree at most 2 such that*

$$f_1(x)f_2(x)f_3(x) = f(x),$$

considered modulo the equivalence

$$\{f_1(x), f_2(x), f_3(x)\} \sim \{\alpha f_1(x), \beta f_2(x), \gamma f_3(x)\}$$

for all $\alpha, \beta, \gamma \in \bar{k}$ such that $\alpha\beta\gamma = 1$. We remark that if $\deg f(x) = 6$, then each of $f_i(x)$ has degree 2, whereas if $\deg f(x) = 5$, then one of them has degree 1.

There are 15 distinct quadratic splittings of $f(x)$, and they are in bijection with the $(2,2)$-isogenies from $\mathrm{Jac}(H)$, as shown in [24, Proposition 8.2.3]. For a $(2,2)$-isogeny $\phi : \mathrm{Jac}(H) \to \mathrm{Jac}(H')$, we let $\mathcal{D} = \{f_1(x), f_2(x), f_3(x)\}$ be the quadratic splitting of $f(x)$ corresponding to ϕ. The algorithms Domain, Codomain, Eval in Definition 16 can be implemented as follows:

- A defining equation of H is clearly recovered as $y^2 = f_1(x)f_2(x)f_3(x)$.
- A defining equation of H' can be computed as $y^2 = g_1(x)g_2(x)g_3(x)$, where we define the polynomials

$$g_1(x) := \frac{df_2(x)}{dx}f_3(x) - f_2(x)\frac{df_3(x)}{dx},$$
$$g_2(x) := \frac{df_3(x)}{dx}f_1(x) - f_3(x)\frac{df_1(x)}{dx}, \tag{3}$$
$$g_3(x) := \frac{df_1(x)}{dx}f_2(x) - f_1(x)\frac{df_2(x)}{dx}$$

thanks to [24, Theorem 8.4.11].
- For each point $P \in \mathrm{Jac}(H)$, the image $\phi(P) \in \mathrm{Jac}(H')$ can be computed, for example, using the method of [23, Section 4.2].

In addition, one can show that these algorithms achieve the complexities stated in Definition 16. This shows that the data $\mathcal{D} = \{f_1(x), f_2(x), f_3(x)\}$ provides an efficient representation of ϕ.

Next, we fix a deterministic order $\prec$ on $\bar{k}[x]$, and represent ϕ by its efficient representation $\mathcal{D} = \{f_1(x), f_2(x), f_3(x)\}$ arranged so that $f_1(x) \prec f_2(x) \prec f_3(x)$. Let $g_1(x), g_2(x), g_3(x)$ be the polynomials defined as in (3) and write

$$g_1(x) = \ell_1(x) \cdot \ell_2(x) \ \text{ with } \ \ell_1(x) \prec \ell_2(x),$$
$$g_2(x) = \ell_3(x) \cdot \ell_4(x) \ \text{ with } \ \ell_3(x) \prec \ell_4(x),$$
$$g_3(x) = \ell_5(x) \cdot \ell_6(x) \ \text{ with } \ \ell_5(x) \prec \ell_6(x),$$

where $\ell_1(x), \ldots, \ell_6(x)$ are polynomials of degree at most 1. Then, it follows from [5, Proposition 1] that $\{g_1(x), g_2(x), g_3(x)\}$ is the quadratic splitting corresponding to the dual extension of ϕ. Also, the following assertion holds:

Proposition 36 ([5, Sect. 6.1]). *With the above notation, let $\phi_0, \ldots, \phi_7$ be the* $(2,2)$*-isogenies corresponding to the quadratic splitting*

$$\{\ell_1(x)\ell_3(x), \ell_2(x)\ell_5(x), \ell_4(x)\ell_6(x)\},$$
$$\{\ell_1(x)\ell_3(x), \ell_2(x)\ell_6(x), \ell_4(x)\ell_5(x)\},$$
$$\{\ell_1(x)\ell_4(x), \ell_2(x)\ell_5(x), \ell_3(x)\ell_6(x)\},$$
$$\{\ell_1(x)\ell_4(x), \ell_2(x)\ell_6(x), \ell_3(x)\ell_5(x)\},$$
$$\{\ell_1(x)\ell_5(x), \ell_2(x)\ell_3(x), \ell_4(x)\ell_6(x)\},$$
$$\{\ell_1(x)\ell_5(x), \ell_2(x)\ell_4(x), \ell_3(x)\ell_6(x)\},$$
$$\{\ell_1(x)\ell_6(x), \ell_2(x)\ell_3(x), \ell_4(x)\ell_5(x)\},$$
$$\{\ell_1(x)\ell_6(x), \ell_2(x)\ell_4(x), \ell_3(x)\ell_5(x)\}$$

of $g_1(x)g_2(x)g_3(x)$, respectively. Then, they are good extensions of ϕ.

In what follows, let $\phi : \mathrm{Jac}(H) \to \mathrm{Jac}(H')$ be an edge on $\mathcal{G}(2,p)$ with $p \equiv 2,3$ (mod 5), where $H : y^2 = f(x)$ and $H' : y^2 = g(x)$. By Lemma 22, all the edges on $\mathcal{G}(2,p)$ are defined over $\mathbb{F}_{p^4}$, which shows that all the maximal isotropic subgroups of $\mathrm{Jac}(H)[2]$ and $\mathrm{Jac}(H')[2]$ are defined over $\mathbb{F}_{p^4}$. Then, it follows from [24, Table 8.1] that $f(x)$ and $g(x)$ are factored into polynomials of degree 1 over $\mathbb{F}_{p^4}$. Hence, for the efficient representation $\mathcal{D} = \{f_1(x), f_2(x), f_3(x)\}$ of ϕ, we have that each of $f_i(x), g_i(x), \ell_i(x)$ is a polynomial over $\mathbb{F}_{p^4}$. The five algorithms in Sect. 2.3 can be implemented as follows:

- CodomainInvariant(ϕ): Output the absolute invariants of H'. Since H' is defined over $\mathbb{F}_{p^4}$, this can be computed by a constant number of arithmetic operations in $\mathbb{F}_{p^4}$, as explained in Remark 2.
- Conjugate(ϕ): Output $\{f_1(x)^{(p^2)}, f_2(x)^{(p^2)}, f_3(x)^{(p^2)}\}$. Each polynomial $f_i(x)^{(p^2)}$ can be obtained by raising the coefficients of $f_i(x)$ to the p^2-th power, which takes $O(1)$ additions in $\mathbb{F}_{p^2}$. Indeed, if we construct $\mathbb{F}_{p^4} \cong \mathbb{F}_{p^2}[t]/(t^2 - d)$ with some $d \in \mathbb{F}_{p^2}$, then for any $u + vt \in \mathbb{F}_{p^4}$ with $u,v \in \mathbb{F}_{p^2}$, its p^2-th power can be computed as $u^{p^2} + v^{p^2} t^{(p^2)} = u + vt^{(p^2)} = u - vt$.
- Dual(ϕ): Output $\{g_1(x), g_2(x), g_3(x)\}$.
- GoodExtension(ϕ, i): Output ϕ_i defined in Proposition 36. It is necessary to factor each $g_i(x)$ into a product of two linear polynomials over $\mathbb{F}_{p^4}$, which requires computing a square root in $\mathbb{F}_{p^4}$.
- IsGoodExtension(ϕ, ϕ'): Output whether $\phi' = \phi_i$ for some $i \in \{0, \dots, 7\}$.

From the above discussion, it follows that these algorithms run in $O(\log(p)\mathrm{M}_{\mathbb{F}_p})$ time and require $O(\log(p))$ space.

B   Detailed Results

In this appendix, we present the experimental results of our collision attack on the LTZ hash function, described in Sect. 6, for each prime p with $p \equiv 2,3$ (mod 5) and $35 \leq \log_2(p) \leq 37$. Tables 5 and 6 show the results for primes p with $p \equiv 1$ (mod 4), while Tables 7 and 8 show the results for primes p with $p \equiv 3$ (mod 4).

Table 5. Experimental results on the LTZ hash function for $p \equiv 1 \pmod 4$.

p	#(searched nodes)$/p^3$ first	second	The first is good?	Time (seconds)
3253	0.7295%	1.4687%	true	19,204
3257	2.6722%	2.7649%	false	55,338
3313	0.1344%	0.1417%	true	2,949
3373	2.9084%	2.2437%	true	57,360
3413	0.5283%	0.2829%	true	10,435
3433	1.2666%	1.9143%	true	49,374
3457	0.1248%	1.5181%	true	21,358
3517	1.4455%	1.8700%	false	42,531
3533	0.1840%	0.4340%	true	8,026
3557	1.4082%	0.2761%	false	25,222
3593	0.7774%	1.5078%	true	34,630
3613	0.7742%	1.5379%	true	36,599
3617	1.6467%	0.2175%	true	31,423
3637	0.9359%	1.1234%	true	27,196
3673	1.9685%	1.0904%	false	52,013
3677	0.8828%	2.2811%	true	41,712
3697	0.3188%	4.3422%	false	82,941
3733	0.3775%	0.0996%	true	8,141
3793	3.6662%	1.6804%	true	109,999
3797	0.1401%	1.0508%	false	19,109
3833	0.5760%	0.1109%	true	11,440
3853	1.8850%	0.7926%	true	52,193
3877	0.8926%	7.0193%	false	162,217
3917	0.5822%	2.3799%	true	56,441
4013	2.2232%	0.6236%	true	49,747
4057	3.8460%	0.8768%	true	116,987
4073	0.3571%	1.1640%	true	34,901
4093	0.1093%	2.5058%	false	61,097
4133	0.4562%	5.4373%	true	119,781
4153	2.9480%	1.4037%	true	96,005
4157	0.3876%	2.4648%	true	59,477
4177	0.4718%	0.7907%	true	28,346
4217	0.1406%	1.9497%	false	48,797
4253	1.7533%	1.7847%	true	73,184
4273	0.0731%	0.5121%	false	14,036
4297	1.4714%	0.5602%	true	49,141
4337	0.1667%	0.2149%	false	9,243
4357	1.2628%	1.9573%	true	80,142
4373	1.0640%	1.8706%	false	85,576
4397	0.1719%	1.7028%	true	43,792
4457	1.5079%	0.2817%	true	50,771
4493	0.2623%	3.4839%	true	101,164

Table 6. Experimental results on the LTZ hash function for $p \equiv 1 \pmod 4$.

p	#(searched nodes)$/p^3$		The first	Time
	first	second	is good?	(seconds)
4513	0.5242%	1.3952%	true	56,060
4517	0.2961%	0.0735%	true	9,387
4597	0.1615%	1.5010%	true	56,241
4637	5.6579%	0.4922%	true	218,604
4657	1.0994%	0.9443%	true	67,466
4673	3.7523%	0.5686%	false	134,866
4733	0.9277%	0.9783%	true	55,318
4793	0.5844%	0.9697%	true	56,469
4813	1.5671%	2.1137%	true	113,390
4817	0.5109%	5.5784%	true	256,715
4877	1.9020%	0.3706%	true	78,673
4933	0.7224%	0.6621%	true	51,151
4937	1.0915%	0.6708%	true	64,869
4957	0.2418%	2.2691%	true	86,987
4973	0.3158%	0.2851%	true	25,922
4993	0.8801%	0.6917%	true	75,010
5077	2.5897%	0.0422%	true	94,844
5113	0.0687%	1.3861%	true	64,093
5153	0.8448%	1.3341%	true	82,537

Table 7. Experimental results on the LTZ hash function for $p \equiv 3 \pmod 4$.

p	#(searched nodes)$/p^3$		The first	Time
	first	second	is good?	(seconds)
3307	0.8338%	1.1585%	true	21,528
3323	0.9915%	1.2879%	true	25,075
3343	0.7798%	0.4329%	true	14,282
3347	2.7564%	1.7676%	true	55,573
3407	0.4291%	2.0071%	true	34,567
3463	1.3460%	2.4295%	true	48,152
3467	1.1295%	1.1913%	false	28,234
3527	0.2397%	6.2534%	true	93,686
3547	0.7262%	3.5894%	true	55,953
3583	0.2578%	1.7910%	true	35,696
3607	0.6432%	2.0064%	true	39,979
3623	0.8533%	2.4450%	true	51,683
3643	0.0086%	1.3403%	true	22,294
3727	4.1225%	5.0300%	false	154,571

Table 8. Experimental results on the LTZ hash function for $p \equiv 3 \pmod 4$.

p	#(searched nodes)$/p^3$ first	#(searched nodes)$/p^3$ second	The first is good?	Time (seconds)
3767	1.0446%	0.8496%	true	36,550
3803	4.6619%	1.3121%	false	111,046
3823	0.9727%	1.7493%	true	47,020
3847	0.0510%	0.1876%	true	4,308
3863	2.5466%	1.5177%	true	72,808
3907	4.2112%	1.7867%	true	101,110
3923	1.7853%	1.1123%	true	60,548
3943	0.2812%	1.7321%	false	45,623
3947	4.8508%	0.8773%	false	124,157
3967	2.4865%	1.6090%	true	92,877
4003	2.7134%	1.3143%	true	75,936
4007	0.0630%	0.5205%	true	13,859
4027	1.5039%	0.0238%	true	33,873
4127	4.4480%	0.3602%	false	104,673
4243	0.5870%	1.6822%	false	50,468
4283	0.0217%	0.3162%	false	7,839
4327	1.6184%	4.5724%	true	156,197
4363	0.2152%	0.5513%	true	17,931
4423	2.0901%	1.9280%	true	107,997
4447	0.3790%	0.4015%	true	20,676
4463	3.0404%	0.7268%	false	104,570
4483	2.0335%	1.1217%	false	82,928
4507	1.1766%	0.0272%	false	33,235
4523	1.7553%	3.2035%	false	130,494
4547	0.7057%	6.1657%	false	189,359
4567	0.2397%	2.7024%	true	89,306
4583	0.7439%	9.5718%	true	313,677
4603	1.5322%	0.5375%	false	58,156
4643	0.1309%	0.3284%	true	13,471
4663	0.5830%	5.1941%	true	230,453
4703	1.0901%	1.4241%	false	83,571
4723	5.3840%	1.5733%	true	219,436
4783	3.4810%	0.6324%	true	145,468
4787	0.7933%	0.4165%	true	39,146
4903	3.2515%	0.8067%	true	153,387
4943	0.7374%	0.8937%	false	63,786
4967	0.6785%	0.7733%	true	59,894
4987	0.4022%	1.5804%	true	74,001
5003	1.6073%	1.2935%	true	109,181
5023	0.7718%	1.0298%	true	73,707
5087	1.7642%	0.6013%	true	114,135
5107	0.9886%	1.0880%	true	81,388
5147	9.6246%	0.1535%	false	346,364

References

1. Brassard, G., Høyer, P., Tapp, A.: Quantum cryptanalysis of hash and claw-free functions. In: Lucchesi, C.L., Moura, A.V. (eds.) LATIN 1998. LNCS, vol. 1380, pp. 163–169. Springer, Berlin, Heidelberg (1998). https://doi.org/10.1007/bfb0054319
2. Cardona, G., Quer, J.: Field of moduli and field of definition for curves of genus 2. In: Computational Aspects of Algebraic Curves, Lecture Notes Ser. Comput., vol. 13, pp. 71–83. World Sci. Publ., Hackensack (2005). https://doi.org/10.1142/9789812701640_0006
3. Castryck, W., Decru, T.: Multiradical isogenies. In: Arithmetic, Geometry, Cryptography, and Coding Theory 2021, Contemp. Math., vol. 779, pp. 57–89. Amer. Math. Soc., [Providence], RI (2022). https://doi.org/10.1090/conm/779/15671
4. Castryck, W., Decru, T., Kutas, P., Laval, A., Petit, C., Ti, Y.B.: KLPT^2: algebraic pathfinding in dimension two and applications. In: Kalai, Y.T., Kamara, S.F. (eds.) Advances in Cryptology – CRYPTO 2025. LNCS, vol. 16000, pp. 167–200. Springer, Cham (2025). https://doi.org/10.1007/978-3-032-01855-7_6
5. Castryck, W., Decru, T., Smith, B.: Hash functions from superspecial genus-2 curves using Richelot isogenies. J. Math. Cryptol. $\mathbf{14}$(1), 268–292 (2020). https://doi.org/10.1515/jmc-2019-0021
6. Charles, D.X., Lauter, K.E., Goren, E.Z.: Cryptographic hash functions from expander graphs. J. Cryptol. $\mathbf{22}$(1), 93–113 (2009). https://doi.org/10.1007/s00145-007-9002-x
7. Choie, Y.J., Jeong, E.K., Lee, E.J.: Supersingular hyperelliptic curves of genus 2 over finite fields. Appl. Math. Comput. $\mathbf{163}$(2), 565–576 (2005). https://doi.org/10.1016/j.amc.2004.03.030
8. Costello, C., Smith, B.: The supersingular isogeny problem in genus 2 and beyond. In: Ding, J., Tillich, J.P. (eds.) Post-Quantum Cryptography - 11th International Conference, PQCrypto 2020, pp. 151–168. Springer, Cham (2020). https://doi.org/10.1007/978-3-030-44223-1_9
9. Eisenträger, K., Hallgren, S., Leonardi, C., Morrison, T., Park, J.: Computing endomorphism rings of supersingular elliptic curves and connections to path-finding in isogeny graphs. In: ANTS XIV—Proceedings of the Fourteenth Algorithmic Number Theory Symposium. Open Book Ser., vol. 4, pp. 215–232. Math. Sci. Publ., Berkeley (2020). https://doi.org/10.2140/obs.2020.4.215
10. Florit, E., Smith, B.: An atlas of the Richelot isogeny graph. In: Theory and Applications of Supersingular Curves and Supersingular Abelian Varieties, RIMS Kôkyûroku Bessatsu, vol. B90, pp. 195–219. Res. Inst. Math. Sci. (RIMS), Kyoto (2022)
11. Flynn, E.V., Ti, Y.B.: Genus two isogeny cryptography. In: Ding, J., Steinwandt, R. (eds.) Post-Quantum Cryptography - 10th International Conference, PQCrypto 2019. pp. 286–306. Springer, Cham (2019). https://doi.org/10.1007/978-3-030-25510-7_16
12. Galbraith, S.D.: Supersingular curves in cryptography. In: Boyd, C. (ed.) ASIACRYPT 2001. LNCS, vol. 2248, pp. 495–513. Springer, Berlin, Heidelberg (2001). https://doi.org/10.1007/3-540-45682-1_29
13. Grover, L.K.: A fast quantum mechanical algorithm for database search. In: 28th ACM STOC, pp. 212–219. ACM Press (1996). https://doi.org/10.1145/237814.237866
14. Hoffstein, J., Pipher, J., Silverman, J.H.: An introduction to mathematical cryptography. Undergraduate Texts Math., New York, NY: Springer, 2nd ed. edn. (2014). https://doi.org/10.1007/978-1-4939-1711-2

15. Ibukiyama, T.: Principal polarizations of supersingular abelian surfaces. J. Mathematical Soc. Japan **72**(4), 1161–1180 (2020). https://doi.org/10.2969/jmsj/82528252

16. Ibukiyama, T., Katsura, T., Oort, F.: Supersingular curves of genus two and class numbers. Compos. Math. **57**(2), 127–152 (1986)

17. Igusa, J.: Arithmetic variety of moduli for genus two. Ann. Math. **72**(3), 612–649 (1960). https://doi.org/10.2307/1970233

18. Jaques, S., Schanck, J.M.: Quantum cryptanalysis in the RAM model: claw-finding attacks on SIKE. In: Boldyreva, A., Micciancio, D. (eds.) CRYPTO 2019, Part I. LNCS, vol. 11692, pp. 32–61. Springer, Cham (2019). https://doi.org/10.1007/978-3-030-26948-7_2

19. Kunzweiler, S., et al.: Radical 2-isogenies and cryptographic hash functions in dimensions 1, 2 and 3. In: Jager, T., Pan, J. (eds.) PKC 2025, Part III. LNCS, vol. 15676, pp. 265–299. Springer, Cham (2025). https://doi.org/10.1007/978-3-031-91826-1_9

20. LeGrow, J.T., Ti, Y.B., Zobernig, L.: Supersingular non-superspecial abelian surfaces in cryptography. Math. Cryptol. **3**(2), 11–23 (2023)

21. Ohashi, R., Onuki, H.: An efficient collision attack on castryck-decru-smith's hash function. In: Niederhagen, R., Saarinen, M.J.O. (eds.) Post-Quantum Cryptography - 16th International Workshop, PQCrypto 2025, Part II. pp. 89–118. Springer, Cham (2025). https://doi.org/10.1007/978-3-031-86602-9_4

22. Oort, F.: Which abelian surfaces are products of elliptic curves? Math. Ann. **214**, 35–47 (1975). https://doi.org/10.1007/BF01428253

23. Oudompheng, R.: Projective geometry of hessian elliptic curves and genus 2 triple covers of Cubics. Cryptology ePrint Archive, Report 2022/1107 (2022). https://eprint.iacr.org/2022/1107

24. Smith, B.: Explicit endomorphism and correspondence. University of Sydney, Thesis (2005)

25. Takashima, K.: Efficient algorithms for isogeny sequences and their cryptographic applications. In: Mathematical Modelling for Next-Generation Cryptography: CREST Crypto-Math Project, Math. Ind. (Tokyo), vol. 29, pp. 97–114. Springer, Singapore (2018). https://doi.org/10.1007/978-981-10-5065-7_6

26. Oudompheng, R., Pope, G.: A note on reimplementing the Castryck-Decru attack and lessons learned for SageMath (2022). https://eprint.iacr.org/2022/1283

27. Tate, J.: Endomorphisms of abelian varieties over finite fields. Invent. Math. **2**, 134–144 (1966). https://doi.org/10.1007/BF01404549

28. Xing, C.: On supersingular abelian varieties of dimension two over finite fields. Finite Fields Appl. **2**(4), 407–421 (1996). https://doi.org/10.1006/ffta.1996.0024

29. Zobernig, L.: Genus 2 curves in small characteristic. arXiv:2111.07270 [math.AG] (2021). https://arxiv.org/abs/2111.07270

Fault Attacks on MPCitH Signature Schemes

Harrison Banda, Jan Brinkmann$^{(\boxtimes)}$, and Juliane Krämer

Universität Regensburg, Regensburg, Germany
`{harrison.banda,jan.brinkmann,juliane.kramer}@ur.de`

Abstract. In this work, we present two fault attacks against MPCitH-based signature schemes: we present a key-recovery attack and a signature-forgery attack, both of which only need a single successful fault injection to succeed. Focusing on Mirath and RYDE, we provide a detailed analysis of their behavior under the fault attacks presented. In addition, we evaluate the applicability of the same attacks to the other MPCitH-based candidates from round 2 of the NIST signature standardization process (FAEST, MQOM, PERK, and SDitH). Our analysis shows that all six schemes are vulnerable to at least one of the attacks. We validate the practicality of our attacks using the ChipWhisperer setup and discuss countermeasures to prevent the attacks.

Keywords: MPCitH · FAEST · Mirath · MQOM · PERK · RYDE · SDitH · fault attacks

1 Introduction

NIST's search for additional digital signature schemes within the post-quantum cryptography standardization process has brought a new family of post-quantum signature schemes into the focus of the research community: MPC-in-the-Head signatures, i.e., signature schemes which make use of multi-party computation (MPC). In the current second round of the process, six of these schemes are being analyzed: FAEST [7], Mirath [2], MQOM [9], PERK [1], RYDE [4], and SDitH [3]. Since both the MPC-in-the-Head (MPCitH) construction for digital signature schemes in general and the six schemes in particular are rather young, only a few results regarding their physical security exist yet.

A key distinction from other post-quantum signature schemes is that MPCitH-based signatures do not rely on structured algebraic trapdoors for their security. Instead, they rely on cryptographic primitives and zero-knowledge techniques, which simplifies implementation and offers potential robustness against algebraic attacks. MPCitH-based signatures benefit from compact public keys and relatively efficient verification procedures. However, signature sizes tend to be large, and signing can be expensive due to the need to simulate many MPC instances.

© The Author(s), under exclusive license to Springer Nature Switzerland AG 2026
M. Bardet and R. Niederhagen (Eds.): PQCrypto 2026, LNCS 16492, pp. 409–442, 2026.
https://doi.org/10.1007/978-3-032-22698-3_13

Concretely, a digital signature scheme is considered MPC-in-the-Head when it is constructed from a zero-knowledge proof realized through the MPC-in-the-Head paradigm [24]. In this paradigm, the prover simulates a multi-party computation protocol internally ("in the head"), commits to the virtual parties' views, and selectively opens a subset of them for verification. To obtain a digital signature, a suitable one-way function, such as AES or the syndrome decoding function, is combined with the MPCitH construction, and the interactive proof is made non-interactive through the Fiat–Shamir transform [20].

In this sense, FAEST, although categorized by NIST as a symmetric-based signature scheme, is also an MPCitH scheme since it uses AES as its one-way function within the same proof structure. We therefore include FAEST in our analysis alongside the other MPCitH-based candidates, as it follows the same underlying paradigm and shares similar design principles, optimization strategies, and potential fault-attack surfaces.

Since MPCitH-based schemes inherently exhibit a nonzero soundness error, they are susceptible to the Kales–Zaverucha attack [28]. To reduce the probability of successful forgery, the underlying protocol must be repeated in multiple parallel rounds, which directly contributes to the large signature sizes observed in these schemes. To improve efficiency, cryptographic hash functions and GGM tree-based structures [22] are employed for share expansion and commitment generation, optimizing both proof size and verification cost.

To mitigate efficiency drawbacks, most recent schemes adopt advanced frameworks such as Threshold-Computation-in-the-Head (TCitH) [17,18] or VOLE-in-the-Head (VOLEitH) [8], where VOLE stands for vector oblivious linear evaluation. All six MPCitH candidates in the current second round of NIST's additional call for signature schemes make use of TCitH and/or include variants based on VOLEitH. PERK was the last of these to adopt VOLEitH, making the switch in its version 2.1 update, thereby joining FAEST and SDitH, which had already been based on VOLEitH. Despite differences in the underlying techniques, these schemes share structural features such as hashing and tree-based commitment strategies, which, while beneficial to performance, may expose them to physical security threats. Particularly fault attacks seem to be promising from an attacker's perspective, since MPCitH-based schemes rely on deterministic functions which lead to predictable patterns, and hence enable precisely timed faults that can lead to secret-key recovery or fault-enabled signature forgery. In the latter case, an adversary prepares an invalid signature and injects a fault into a deterministic verification operation so that the modified execution accepts the forgery. Throughout the paper, we use the term forgery to denote such fault-enabled signature forgery attacks, unless stated otherwise.

1.1   Related Work

Although MPCitH signature schemes are rather young, they have already attracted some research efforts in the field of physical security: Aranha et al. [5] initiated the research on physical security of MPCitH signature schemes by analyzing side-channel protections. They focused on the Picnic signature scheme, which was an alternate candidate in the third round of the initial post-quantum standardization process by NIST.

They proposed improved masking techniques for the underlying zero-knowledge proof system.

Gordad et al. [21] presented a single-trace side-channel attack targeting the MPCitH paradigm, specifically the TCitH framework. Their work reveals a side-channel leakage in the SDitH algorithm. By exploiting leakage from Galois field multiplication operations, the authors predict intermediate values and take advantage of the structure of the protocol to reconstruct the secret key. The attack is validated both in simulation and on real hardware, achieving full key recovery across all security levels. Most recently, Feneuil et al. [19] studied side-channel resistance of post-quantum signature schemes based on the TCitH framework. They analyzed side-channel leakage paths and introduced three novel tweaks to improve the masking-friendliness of both the Merkle and GGM tree variants of TCitH. They further discuss the applicability of their techniques to VOLEitH-based schemes.

In the field of fault attacks, Mondal et al. [30] analyzed fault injection attacks against zero-knowledge-based signature schemes, focusing specifically on the manipulation of the seed reveal function used in tree-based share expansion. Their work demonstrates that faults targeting seed expansion can lead to the recovery of all intermediate node values, including hidden leaf nodes, enabling full secret key extraction. This analysis is applied to the code-based schemes LESS and CROSS.

Given that MPCitH-based schemes are inherently built on zero-knowledge proofs, this attack model is relevant for such schemes as well. Jendral et al. [27] introduced an instruction-skipping attack on the SHAKE-256 hash function. The attack specifically targets the absorption phase of the hash function and enables secret-key recovery from a single fault injection. This technique has since been adapted to other schemes. For example, it has been extended in follow-up work to MAYO [26], where faults are used to compromise the vinegar seed generation process, again leading to key recovery. The successful transfer of the attack vector to MAYO demonstrates a weakness in hash-based constructions, which are commonly used in many post-quantum signature schemes. Recently, Jendral and Dubrova [25] presented the most comprehensive fault and side-channel analysis to date on a VOLEitH based signature scheme. Using FAEST as a case study, they introduce several attack vectors, including an attack on AES in counter mode to manipulate the generation of child nodes within the tree structure. The authors also generalize their methodology to schemes using similar constructions, such as those based on MPCitH, arguing that the structural similarities make these schemes vulnerable despite implementation differences. However, we show that the said attacks do not work against other MPCitH schemes, since only FAEST uses the AES counter mode for seed creation. In addition to these vectors, Jendral and Dubrova also describe a fourth attack, referred to as the VOLE conversion abort attack, which targets the transformation of the initial seeds within the GGM tree during the VOLE commitment phase and exploits the conversion process to induce aborts and extract information. The authors argue that this attack, although originally studied in the VOLEitH setting, may also be applicable to related constructions, with the SDitH specification being referred to as an example.

Most recently, Sarde and Debande [31] presented the first fault attacks on MQOM. They introduce four differential fault attacks targeting the MQ evaluation phase. Two attacks recover the entire secret key through linear algebra and using one or two random faults, while two others target the MQ system coefficients directly. Their work shows that these attacks remain effective even against masked implementations, highlighting new vulnerabilities in MPCitH-based constructions.

1.2 Contribution

We set out to better understand the physical security of MPC-in-the-Head signature schemes and present a detailed evaluation of fault attacks on RYDE [4] and Mirath [2]. We further assess the applicability of these attacks to the remaining MPCitH-based candidates, all of which are part of the ongoing round 2 of NIST's standardization process for digital signature schemes: FAEST [7], MQOM [9], PERK [1], and SDitH [3].

We present two fault attacks, a key-recovery attack and a signature-forgery attack, both exploiting the structural properties shared among MPCitH-based schemes:

1. The first attack, the key-recovery attack, targets the seed generation process in the GGM tree through fault injection. By forcing intermediate sibling nodes to be identical, the structure of the tree collapses, making it possible to recover all leaf values, and ultimately enabling full secret-key recovery with a single successful fault injection. We identified several attack vectors to achieve this effect. Two of them exploit the fact that the tree nodes are initialized to zero and then skip either the tree expansion or the seed expansion function responsible for computing the node values. The third attack vector ensures that two child nodes obtain the same value by skipping the XOR instruction that is intended to differentiate the sibling nodes.
2. The second attack, the signature-forgery attack, targets the challenge of a linear combination in the Fiat–Shamir transform by manipulating the challenge, often the matrix Γ. By applying a fault during challenge generation within the verification process, the attacker can fix Γ, enabling the acceptance of forged signatures via a Kales–Zaverucha-like attack.

Based on the updated version 2.1 specifications released in September 2025, we analyze all six schemes to determine whether they are vulnerable to the attacks presented in this work. In theory, all six schemes admit both key-recovery and signature-forgery attacks. For Mirath and RYDE, we also practically executed all attacks presented in this work. We chose their reference implementations as target implementations, since embedded implementations are not yet available. Although we do not analyze optimized implementations, our results identify critical issues that must be addressed in hardened versions of these schemes. We describe the experimental setting used to execute these attacks in practice and discuss appropriate countermeasures. Our results are summarized in Table 1. We further assess the transferability of attack techniques from related work to MPC-in-the-Head signature schemes and show that most previously proposed attack vectors are not applicable (see Sect. 3.4).

Table 1. Overview of fault injection attacks on MPCitH signature schemes presented in this work. The key-recovery attack is categorized into three attack vectors: tree generation (**tree**), seed generation (**seed**), and XOR instruction (**XOR**). A checkmark symbol, $\checkmark$, indicates a theoretically feasible attack that we also practically implemented, ($\checkmark$) denotes a theoretically feasible attack with an identified target in the reference implementation, $\circ$ represents a theoretically feasible attack without known target, and $\times$ marks infeasible attacks.

Signature Scheme	Key-Recovery Attack			Forgery Attack
	tree	seed	XOR	
Mirath	$\checkmark$	$\checkmark$	$\checkmark$	$\checkmark$
RYDE	$\checkmark$	$\checkmark$	$\checkmark$	$\checkmark$
SDitH	$\circ$	$\circ$	($\checkmark$)	$\circ$
MQOM	$\circ$	$\circ$	$\times$	($\checkmark$)
PERK	($\checkmark$)	($\checkmark$)	($\checkmark$)^a	($\checkmark$)
FAEST	($\checkmark$)	($\checkmark$)	$\times$	$\circ$

^{a} The XOR attack vector in PERK is only feasible if AES is used for node creation.

1.3   Organization

In Sect. 2, we describe the background necessary to understand the analyzed schemes and the attacks against them. We present the key-recovery attack and the signature-forgery attack, together with countermeasures to prevent them, in Sects. 3 and 4, respectively. Here, we show in detail how they can be applied to Mirath and RYDE. In Sect. 5, we analyze the applicability of the two fault attacks to the other MPCitH signature schemes, namely FAEST, MQOM, PERK, and SDitH. In Sect. 6, we describe the ChipWhisperer setup we used for the execution of the attacks and demonstrate the feasibility of the attacks by successfully executing them on Mirath and RYDE. We conclude in Sect. 7.

2   Background

This section introduces the cryptographic foundations necessary to understand the MPCitH signature schemes analyzed in this work. We focus primarily on

RYDE and Mirath, schemes built upon hard problems in the rank metric and instantiated using the TCitH-PIOP framework.

Section 2.1 provides an overview of the GGM tree structure and the BAVC technique, which are employed to optimize the share-opening process in the analyzed signature schemes. Section 2.2 outlines the MPCitH framework, encompassing both the VOLEitH and TCitH-PIOP formalisms that underpin the analyzed schemes and form the basis of our attacks. Finally, Sect. 2.3 describes the structure of the considered MPCitH schemes, with particular focus on RYDE and Mirath.

2.1   GGM Trees and BAVC

All six MPCitH signature schemes considered in our analysis use GGM trees to distribute secret shares among multiple virtual parties [29]. GGM trees are binary trees, where each node has at most two child nodes, and the structure is generated top-down starting from a root seed. In the context of MPC-in-the-Head protocols, GGM trees are used to commit to additive secret sharings using an all-but-one vector commitment (AVC) scheme, where for a secret split into N shares, $N - 1$ are opened. GGM trees allow for efficient representation of shares, since an opening path can be provided instead of revealing all $N - 1$ shares individually. This path consists of all nodes required to recompute the $N - 1$ leaves, and whenever both children of a parent node are known, they can be replaced by the parent node itself, reducing the number of required nodes in the opening. This path is included in the signature.

To reduce the probability of a successful forgery, the protocols repeat the commitment procedure τ times, corresponding to τ independent parallel iterations of the protocol. The schemes FAEST, Mirath, PERK, RYDE, and SDitH implement the so-called one-tree optimization [6], which enables a batched all-but-one vector commitment (BAVC) approach.

Instead of constructing τ independent GGM trees, a single large tree is generated to commit to all iterations simultaneously. The leaves are organized such that, for each iteration index $e \in \{1, 2, \ldots, \tau\}$, the first τ leaf nodes correspond to the first share of iteration e. For example, the leaf with index τ represents the second share of the first iteration ($e = 1$).

This design improves efficiency because, with high probability, some of the authentication paths associated with unopened shares overlap near the leaves. In this context, we distinguish between hidden nodes, which are not revealed during verification, and revealed nodes, which belong to an opening path that enables the verifier to authenticate a specific leaf from the root commitment.

MQOM further employs the correlated tree optimization [23], which reduces the computational cost of tree generation. In this approach, only one side of each sibling pair is generated using a pseudorandom generator (PRG), and the corresponding sibling is derived using an XOR operation with the parent node, effectively halving the number of PRG calls required.

2.2　MPC-in-the-Head Framework Overview

The MPC-in-the-Head paradigm, introduced by Ishai et al. [24], provides a framework for constructing zero-knowledge proofs from secure multi-party computation protocols. In this approach, the prover simulates an N-party MPC protocol "in their head" where the secret witness is secret-shared among the parties, commits to the views of all virtual parties, receives challenges from the verifier to open a subset of these views, and finally reveals the requested views along with consistency proofs. The key insight is that if the MPC protocol correctly computes the desired function and can tolerate a certain number of corrupt parties, then revealing a random subset of views allows the verifier to check correctness while learning nothing about the secret witness.

The security of MPCitH-based schemes is based on the completeness of the underlying MPC protocol, the privacy against coalitions of up to t corrupt parties, and the binding and hiding properties of the commitment scheme.

A signature scheme is considered MPCitH if it follows the core paradigm of simulating a multi-party computation protocol in the prover's head, committing to the virtual parties' views, and selectively opening subsets for verification. In our analysis, we examine FAEST, Mirath, MQOM, PERK, RYDE, and SDitH, as all of them implement this MPCitH approach. Although NIST classifies FAEST separately as a symmetric-based signature, we include it in our MPCitH analysis because it fundamentally adheres to the same MPC-in-the-Head paradigm.

Recent MPCitH frameworks have evolved to optimize for specific applications, particularly digital signatures, leading to two prominent approaches that will be discussed in the following subsections.

TCitH and the PIOP Framework. Most MPCitH schemes use the TCitH paradigm [17, 18], which is formalized as a Polynomial Interactive Oracle Proof (PIOP) [16]. In this model, the prover commits to a set of polynomials whose coefficients encode the secret witness. The verifier then issues a random linear combination challenge, followed by a request to evaluate the committed polynomials at a randomly chosen point.

Specifically, suppose the goal is to prove knowledge of a witness w satisfying polynomial constraints $\{f_j(w) = 0\}$. In the PIOP approach, the prover samples random polynomials $P_i(X) = w_i X + (w_{\mathsf{base}})_i$, for $i = 1, \ldots, n$, along with an additional polynomial $P_0(X)$ of degree $(d-1)$, where d is the degree of constraints. These polynomials are committed to. The verifier then sends a challenge consisting of random coefficients $\gamma_1, \ldots, \gamma_l$ from an extension field. The prover responds with polynomial

$$Q(X) = P_0(X) + \sum_{j=1}^{l} \gamma_j f_j^{[h]}(X, P_1(X), \ldots, P_n(X)),$$

where each $f_j^{[h]}$ is the homogenized version of f_j. Finally, the verifier selects a random evaluation point z from a public set S and requests evaluations $P_i(z)$ and

$Q(z)$, along with consistency proofs. Soundness is guaranteed because, with high probability, a cheating prover cannot make $Q(z)$ satisfy the expected constraints if the witness is invalid.

VOLE-in-the-Head Framework. The VOLE-in-the-Head paradigm [8] is another powerful framework for constructing efficient zero-knowledge proofs. Instead of committing to polynomials, VOLEitH relies on information-theoretically secure commitments built from Vector Oblivious Linear Evaluation (VOLE) correlations.

In this model, the prover's witness is encoded in a set of linear polynomials over a binary extension field. The core building block is a VOLE correlation: for a length $\hat{\ell}$, the prover holds $(\mathbf{u}, \mathbf{v}) \in \mathbb{F}_2^{\hat{\ell}} \times \mathbb{F}_{2^m}^{\hat{\ell}}$, and the verifier holds $(\mathbf{g}, \Delta) \in \mathbb{F}_{2^m}^{\hat{\ell}} \times \mathbb{F}_{2^m}$, satisfying the linear relation

$$g_i = u_i \cdot \Delta + v_i \qquad \text{for } i \in [0, 1, \ldots, \hat{\ell} - 1].$$

This structure forms a linearly homomorphic commitment to the prover's bits $\mathbf{u}$.

The protocol flow in VOLEitH begins with the prover generating multiple VOLE correlations, one for each protocol repetition. Let τ denote the number of parallel instances executed in a single proof. For each $e \in [\tau]$, the prover samples a VOLE pair $(\mathbf{u}_e, \mathbf{v}_e)$ and commits to it using an all-but-one vector commitment scheme, typically instantiated via a GGM tree. The prover then embeds the secret witness into these VOLE correlations and make use of their linear homomorphic properties to compute proofs of witness correctness.

Next, the verifier issues a challenge Δ, prompting the prover to combine the τ small-field VOLE instances into a single large-field instance. In this step, the verifier also provides random coefficients defining a linear combination of the constraints to be verified. Finally, during the opening and verification phase, the prover opens the relevant commitments and sends a masked version of the combined linear relation. The verifier reconstructs the VOLE correlations from the opened commitments and checks that the relation holds, thereby confirming that the prover's computations are consistent with a valid witness.

Soundness is achieved through the binding property of the VOLE correlations and the randomness of the verifier's challenges. The prover's ability to successfully open the commitments and pass the linear verification check implies, with high probability, that they possess a valid witness. This framework has been successfully instantiated in several post-quantum signature schemes, including PERK (since v2.1), FAEST, and SDitH, and also in the variants of RYDE and Mirath.

2.3 MPCitH Signature Schemes

This subsection provides an overview of the MPCitH-based signature schemes submitted to round 2 of NIST's additional call for signatures. We describe RYDE in detail, Mirath follows naturally because of its structural similarity. For the remaining candidates; FAEST, MQOM, PERK and SDitH, we refer the reader to their respective specifications [1,3,7,9] for further details.

Overview of RYDE and Mirath. RYDE and Mirath share a common structure: both are constructed using the TCitH framework and derive their security from rank-metric problems. RYDE is based on the rank syndrome decoding (RSD) problem [4, Definition 3], whereas Mirath builds on the MinRank problem [13], in particular, its syndrome decoding variant [2, Definition 2]. Both schemes use dual support decomposition [10] to prove knowledge of a low-rank witness.

Dual Support Modeling. Let $\mathbb{F}_{q^m}$ be a finite field extension of $\mathbb{F}_q$, and let $\mathbf{H} \in \mathbb{F}_{q^m}^{(n-k)\times n}$ be a parity-check matrix of an $[n, k]$ linear code over $\mathbb{F}_{q^m}$. A secret vector $\mathbf{x} \in \mathbb{F}_{q^m}^n$ of rank r is decomposed using dual support modeling as $\mathbf{x} = \mathbf{s}\,\mathbf{C}$, where $\mathbf{s} = (1 \parallel \mathbf{s}') \in \mathbb{F}_{q^m}^r$ with $\mathbf{s}' \in \mathbb{F}_{q^m}^{r-1}$ and $\mathbf{C} = [\mathbf{I}_r \parallel \mathbf{C}'] \in \mathbb{F}_q^{r\times n}$ with $\mathbf{C}' \in \mathbb{F}_q^{r\times(n-r)}$. The rank syndrome decoding constraint $\mathbf{x}\mathbf{H}^\top = \mathbf{y}$, with syndrome $\mathbf{y} \in \mathbb{F}_{q^m}^{n-k}$, becomes the quadratic constraint $\mathbf{s}\,\mathbf{C}\,\mathbf{H}^\top = \mathbf{y}$. The witness is $(\mathbf{s}', \mathbf{C}')$, and the protocol proves knowledge of this witness satisfying the constraint.

In Mirath, the error matrix $\mathbf{E} \in \mathbb{F}_q^{m\times n}$ is decomposed as $\mathbf{E} = \mathbf{S}\,\mathbf{C}$, with $\mathbf{S} \in \mathbb{F}_q^{m\times r}$, $\mathbf{C} \in \mathbb{F}_q^{r\times n}$, and $\mathrm{rank}(\mathbf{E}) = r$. Here again, $\mathbf{C}$ is fixed as $[\mathbf{I}_r \parallel \mathbf{C}']$, and the goal is to find $\mathbf{S}$ and $\mathbf{C}'$. The associated constraint becomes $\mathbf{H}\,\mathrm{vec}(\mathbf{S}\,\mathbf{C}) = \mathbf{y}$, where $\mathrm{vec}(\cdot)$ returns a flattened version of the input matrix.

Mirath's interactive proof is similar to that of RYDE. For this reason, we focus on RYDE, and the description extends naturally to Mirath.

RYDE's Interactive Proof. RYDE instantiates the TCitH framework for the RSD problem. For clarity, we summarize the key protocol parameters used. The symbol ρ denotes the number of linear combinations in the first challenge, while τ represents the number of parallel repetitions of the protocol. The parameter N specifies the size of the evaluation set $S \subset \mathbb{F}_{q^\mu}$. The threshold $T_{\mathbf{open}}$ defines the maximum size of openings in the BAVC procedure, and finally, w is the grinding security parameter that determines the expected number of hash queries required to find a valid challenge.

The interactive protocol proceeds as follows:

1. Commitment Phase: For each repetition $e \in \{1, \ldots, \tau\}$
   - Sample degree-1 polynomials:

   $$P_{\mathbf{s}'}(X) = \mathbf{s}' \cdot X + \mathbf{s}'_{\mathrm{base}}, \quad P_{\mathbf{C}'}(X) = \mathbf{C}' \cdot X + \mathbf{C}'_{\mathrm{base}}, \quad P_{\mathbf{v}}(X) = \mathbf{v} \cdot X + \mathbf{v}_{\mathrm{base}}$$

   - Commit using batched all-but-one vector commitment (BAVC) with GGM tree:
     - Generate N seeds $\{\mathsf{seed}_i\}_{i=1}^N$ via GGM tree

- Expand each seed to $(\mathbf{s}'_{\mathsf{rnd},i}, \mathbf{C}'_{\mathsf{rnd},i}, \mathbf{v}_{\mathsf{rnd},i})$ using PRG
- Compute accumulated values:

$$\mathbf{s}'_{\mathsf{acc}} = \sum_{i=1}^{N} \mathbf{s}'_{\mathsf{rnd},i}, \quad \mathbf{C}'_{\mathsf{acc}} = \sum_{i=1}^{N} \mathbf{C}'_{\mathsf{rnd},i}, \quad \mathbf{v}_{\mathsf{acc}} = \sum_{i=1}^{N} \mathbf{v}_{\mathsf{rnd},i}$$

$$\mathbf{s}'_{\mathsf{base}} = -\sum_{i=1}^{N} \phi(i) \cdot \mathbf{s}'_{\mathsf{rnd},i}, \quad \mathbf{C}'_{\mathsf{base}} = -\sum_{i=1}^{N} \phi(i) \cdot \mathbf{C}'_{\mathsf{rnd},i}$$

and

$$\mathbf{v}_{\mathsf{base}} = -\sum_{i=1}^{N} \phi(i) \cdot \mathbf{v}_{\mathsf{rnd},i}$$

- Reveal auxiliary values:

$$\mathbf{s}'_{\mathsf{aux}} = \mathbf{s}' - \mathbf{s}'_{\mathsf{acc}}, \quad \mathbf{C}'_{\mathsf{aux}} = \mathbf{C}' - \mathbf{C}'_{\mathsf{acc}}$$

2. First Challenge: The verifier sends random matrix $\boldsymbol{\Gamma} \in \mathbb{F}_{q^m}^{(n-k)\times\rho}$.
3. Response Polynomial: The prover computes
   $P_\alpha(X) = P_{\mathbf{v}}(X) + \boldsymbol{\Gamma} \cdot \left(\mathbf{H}P_{\mathbf{x}}(X) - \mathbf{y}X^2\right)$, where
   $P_{\mathbf{x}}(X) = (X \parallel P_{\mathbf{s}'}(X)) \cdot [\mathbf{I}_r X \parallel P_{\mathbf{C}'}(X)]$.
   If we let $P_{\mathbf{x}}(X) = \mathbf{x}X^2 + \mathbf{x}_{\mathsf{mid}}X + \mathbf{x}_{\mathsf{base}}$, and $\mathbf{x} = [\mathbf{s} \parallel \mathbf{s}\mathbf{C}']$,
   $\mathbf{x}_{\mathsf{mid}} = [\mathbf{s}_{\mathsf{base}} \parallel \mathbf{s}_{\mathsf{base}}\mathbf{C}' + \mathbf{s}\mathbf{C}'_{\mathsf{base}}]$ and $\mathbf{x}_{\mathsf{base}} = [\mathbf{0} \parallel \mathbf{s}_{\mathsf{base}}\mathbf{C}'_{\mathsf{base}}]$,
   where $\mathbf{s} = (1 \parallel \mathbf{s}')$ and $\mathbf{s}_{\mathsf{base}} = (1 \parallel \mathbf{s}'_{\mathsf{base}})$. Then $P_\alpha(X) = \alpha_{\mathsf{mid}}X + \alpha_{\mathsf{base}}$,
   where $\alpha_{\mathsf{mid}} = \boldsymbol{\Gamma} \cdot \mathbf{x}_{\mathsf{mid}}\mathbf{H}^\top + \mathbf{v}$ and $\alpha_{\mathsf{base}} = \boldsymbol{\Gamma} \cdot \mathbf{x}_{\mathsf{base}}\mathbf{H}^\top + \mathbf{v}_{\mathsf{base}}$.
4. Second Challenge: The verifier sends random evaluation point $z \in S \subset \mathbb{F}_{q^m}$.
5. Open Evaluations: The prover reveals $\mathbf{s}'_{\mathsf{eval}} = P_{\mathbf{s}'}(z), \quad \mathbf{C}'_{\mathsf{eval}} = P_{\mathbf{C}'}(z)$ and
   $\mathbf{v}_{\mathsf{eval}} = P_{\mathbf{v}}(z)$ with BAVC opening proof π for all seeds except seed_{i^*} where
   $z = \phi(i^*)$.
6. Verification: The verifier computes $\mathbf{x}_{\mathsf{eval}} = (z \parallel \mathbf{s}'_{\mathsf{eval}}) \cdot [z\mathbf{I}_r \parallel \mathbf{C}'_{\mathsf{eval}}]$ and
   $\alpha_{\mathsf{eval}} = \mathbf{v}_{\mathsf{eval}} + \boldsymbol{\Gamma} \cdot \left(\mathbf{H}\mathbf{x}_{\mathsf{eval}}^\top - \mathbf{y}z^2\right)$, and checks $\alpha_{\mathsf{eval}} = \alpha_{\mathsf{mid}}z + \alpha_{\mathsf{base}}$ while
   validating the BAVC opening proof.

Non-Interactive Signature via Fiat-Shamir The non-interactive signature is
obtained by replacing verifier challenges with hash outputs
$h_1 = \mathsf{Hash}_1(\mathsf{salt}, \{\mathsf{com}_{e,i}\}, \{\mathbf{s}'_{\mathsf{aux}}, \mathbf{C}'_{\mathsf{aux}}\})$ derives $\boldsymbol{\Gamma}$ and
$h_2 = \mathsf{Hash}_2(\mathsf{Hash}_0(\mathsf{msg}), \mathsf{pk}, \mathsf{salt}, h_1, \{\alpha_{\mathsf{mid}}, \alpha_{\mathsf{base}}\})$ derives $\{i^*(e)\}$.

Grinding: Iterate with counter ctr until $v_{\mathsf{grinding}} = 0$ and BAVC opening has
$\leq T_{\mathsf{open}}$ revealed nodes.

Signature:

$$\sigma = (\mathsf{salt} \parallel \mathsf{ctr} \parallel h_2 \parallel \pi_{\mathsf{BAVC}} \parallel \{\mathbf{s}'_{\mathsf{aux}}, \mathbf{C}'_{\mathsf{aux}}, \alpha_{\mathsf{mid}}\}_{e=1}^{\tau}).$$

Verification: Recompute evaluations from BAVC opening, then verify h_2
matches recomputed hash.

The security of RYDE relies on the hardness of the RSD problem, the soundness of the TCitH proof system, and the security of the Fiat-Shamir transformation.

The parameters (ρ, τ, N, w) are carefully chosen to ensure that the generic forgery attack against five-pass Fiat-Shamir signatures by Kales and Zaverucha [28] remains computationally infeasible. As analyzed in the RYDE specification [4, Section 8.1], the attack complexity is given by

$$\text{cost}_{\texttt{forge}} = \min_{0 \leq \tau' \leq \tau} \left\{ \frac{1}{\sum_{i=\tau'}^{\tau} \binom{\tau}{i} p^i (1-p)^{\tau-i}} + \left(\frac{N}{2} \right)^{\tau-\tau'} \right\}$$

where $p = \frac{1}{q^{m\rho}}$. For all RYDE parameter sets, this cost exceeds 2^λ for the target security level λ, ensuring the attack is infeasible.

3 Key-Recovery Attack on GGM Tree Seed Generation

Recent research has exposed the susceptibility of zero-knowledge signature schemes to fault attacks by targeting their internal seed expansion processes [25,30], particularly when these schemes rely on tree-based structures such as the GGM tree. Our work builds on these insights and shows that the MPCitH-based signature schemes like Mirath and RYDE are vulnerable under this fault model. These schemes in general, rely on a tree structure with $\tau \cdot N$ leaves, which, while optimizing signature size, also increases the attack surface. Each round reveals all but one leaf seed, along with the opening paths required for verification. We show how faults in the seed generation process can reveal the hidden leaf, thereby enabling a secret key recovery. In this section, we identify three attack vectors—namely the expand-tree, expand-seed, and XOR attack vector—that exploit the seed-tree generation to recover the secret key in the Mirath and RYDE signature schemes.

3.1 Attacker Model

We assume an attacker with physical access to the signing device during legitimate signing operations. The adversary is able to induce faults at specific stages of the tree-based seed generation process, particularly during the computation of child seeds from a parent node in the GGM tree. The attacker also has access to the resulting (faulty) signature and the corresponding public information, including revealed opening paths. The goal of an attacker is to use this information to recover the hidden leaf and ultimately the secret key.

3.2 Attack Strategy

For each signature, a GGM tree is generated that realizes an AVC in which all but one secret share (in the form of a leaf node) are revealed. Our key-reveal attack exploits the fact that, with a successful fault injection, it is possible to recover all shares, including the hidden one, in order to recover the complete secret. In our attack strategy, the fault is injected during the tree generation phase and the hidden leaves are selected afterwards during the signing procedure, with the selected leaves containing the information we aim to recover. We identify three potential attack vectors to achieve this.

With the expand-tree attack vector, we target the execution of the complete GGM tree generation. This approach requires that all tree nodes are initialized with known values. If the tree expansion operation is skipped, the nodes do not receive updated values and remain at their initialized state, meaning all nodes of an instance become known.

With the expand-seed attack vector we aim to disrupt the execution of node creation, in which two child nodes are derived from a parent node. Here again, initialization of the nodes with known values is required. Moreover, at least one descendant node must later be selected as a hidden node. Only in this case can a fault attack yield the information necessary for a key-reveal attack.

With the XOR attack vector, we focus on the node computation so that both child nodes derived from a parent node become identical. In many schemes, nodes are generated using AES from the parent node. For Mirath and RYDE the following computation is applied:

$$\mathrm{AES}_k\big(\mathrm{salt} \oplus (\mathrm{bin}_{\lambda-40}(a) \,\|\, \mathrm{bin}_{32}(\mathrm{idx}) \,\|\, \mathrm{bin}_8(0))\big)$$

$$\mathrm{AES}_k\big(\mathrm{salt} \oplus (\mathrm{bin}_{\lambda-40}(a) \,\|\, \mathrm{bin}_{32}(\mathrm{idx}) \,\|\, \mathrm{bin}_8(1))\big)$$

where k is derived from the parent node and the salt is freshly generated for each signature and included in the signature itself. To ensure that both child nodes have the same value, we can skip the XOR instruction that leads to the two nodes being different. For a successful key-reveal, it is necessary that at least one descendant node is later chosen as a hidden node, and that one of the two generated nodes is known. In this case, the sibling node can be inferred to take the same value, allowing the recovery of hidden information.

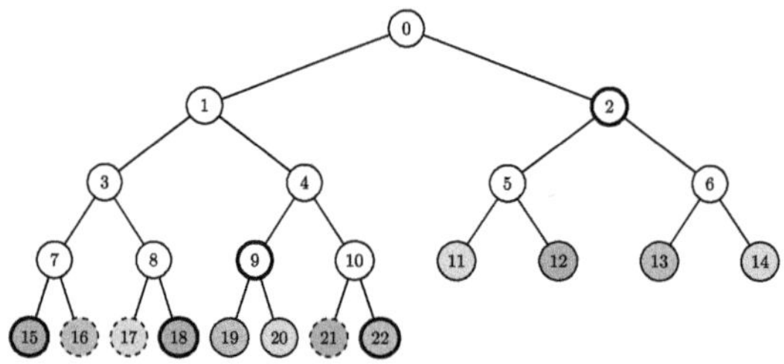

Fig. 1. Example of a faulted batched GGM tree with 12 leaves. Nodes of the same color belong to the same instance. Dashed borders are hidden nodes, while thick borders represent revealed nodes.

As an example, consider a GGM tree with 12 leaves, where $\tau = 3$ and $N = 4$. This means the AVC is executed three times with four secret shares each. In

Fig. 1, a hidden node is selected for each instance. Nodes belonging to the same instance are color-coded, e.g., nodes 12, 15, 18, and 21 belong to instance $e = 2$. A successful attack for the XOR attack vector could occur during the generation of nodes 9 and 10, since node 9 lies on the opening path and, together with node 21, can be used to recover the secret for an instance.

Recovering the Secret After Successful Fault. As noted earlier, our detailed analysis focuses on the RYDE and Mirath schemes, which both rely on the TCitH. These schemes share a similar proof structure for demonstrating knowledge of the witness, meaning that once an attacker successfully recovers the hidden seed from the GGM tree in a particular round, the subsequent process for reconstructing the secret is largely identical in both cases.

We illustrate the recovery procedure concretely using RYDE as a representative example; the same reasoning applies directly to Mirath due to their shared structural design.

Once the attacker recovers a hidden seed, they apply the known signature function `ExpandShare` to each seed and obtain the shares $(\mathbf{s}'_{\mathrm{rnd},i}, \mathbf{C}'_{\mathrm{rnd},i})$. Since $\mathbf{s}'_{\mathrm{aux}}$ and $\mathbf{C}'_{\mathrm{aux}}$ are included in the signature, the adversary can directly solve the following equations to recover the secret $\mathbf{s}'$ and $\mathbf{C}'$:

$$\mathbf{s}' = \mathbf{s}'_{\mathrm{aux}} + \sum_i \mathbf{s}'_{\mathrm{rnd},i} \quad \text{and} \quad \mathbf{C}' = \mathbf{C}'_{\mathrm{aux}} + \sum_i \mathbf{C}'_{\mathrm{rnd},i}.$$

3.3   Practical Attack

In this subsection, we will discuss three attack vectors we have identified to attack the round 2 implementations of the MPCitH-based submissions with the attack strategy explained above. In the following, we evaluate the feasibility of the attacks for each signature scheme and describe how they can be applied to the reference implementation if necessary.

In the reference implementations of the round 2 submissions of Mirath and RYDE, both use the same `ggm_tree_expand` function. Therefore, the attacks described here apply to both schemes. Without loss of generality, we focus on the concrete functions of Mirath. The function `ggm_tree_expand` is located in the file `mirath_ggm_tree.c`. In RYDE, the equivalent function `ryde_3f_ggm_-tree_expand` is defined in `ggm_tree.c`.

*Skip the **mirath_ggm_tree_expand** Function Call:* Before the program calls the function `ggm_tree_expand`, it initializes all seeds of the GGM tree with the value 0. We can therefore skip the function entirely, causing all values to remain at 0.

*Skip a **mirath_expand_seed** Function Call:* In this attack, a call to the function `mirath_expand_seed` is skipped. As a result, the lower-level nodes that would normally be created by this function remain at their initialized value of zero. There are several possible function calls that can be attacked for this scenario. It is sufficient to skip a single `mirath_expand_seed` call assuming it is responsible for creating a subtree that contains at least one hidden leaf node.

Mirath and RYDE utilize a batched GGM tree structure, as outlined in Sect. 2.1, where the path used for the opening varies in each signature due to the random selection of hidden nodes. This randomness prevents most of the single nodes from being statically identified as a guaranteed target for a successful key recovery. To better understand which nodes are most vulnerable to fault injection, we developed a simulation tool that estimates the success probability of recovering the secret key when skipping a specific node. The tool generates batched GGM trees with randomly selected hidden nodes and computes the success probability at each level. Using parameters from `Mirath-1a-fast` with $N = 256$, $\tau = 17$, and $T_{open} = 118$, we performed 10,000 simulations. As expected, the first two levels of the tree always lead to successful key recovery due to their structural inclusion in every opening path. Beyond that, the probability declines: at level 2 it drops to 97.43 %, and at level 3 to 81.88 %, with decreasing probabilities at subsequent levels.

Skip the XOR Operation in `aes_128_expand_seed`*:* In this attack, the exploitation does not rely on initialized zero values. Instead, we force two sibling nodes to become identical by skipping a specific XOR instruction during their generation. Both Mirath and RYDE generate tree nodes using AES, where the encryption key is derived from the parent node. For the message input, the implementation XORs a previously generated salt with a fixed mask. The only difference between the two sibling nodes lies in the first byte of the mask: the left node uses `0x00`, while the right node uses `0x01` (see Listing 1.1). In the reference implementation, both AES calls operate on the same base message `msg`, which is modified in a single instruction. If an attacker successfully skips the XOR operation at line 14, the resulting left and right child nodes become identical. We further believe that the same effect could be achieved through a targeted bit-flip. However, we did not investigate this alternative fault model further in this work.

In Mirath and RYDE, not every skipped XOR operation in the `aes_128-_expand_seed` function results in a successful key recovery. For such an attack to succeed, the targeted seed creation must produce one node that is part of the opening path and another node that is not. This condition ensures that, by knowing the value of the node included in the opening, it is possible to compute the subnodes of the hidden sibling node, which finally leads to a key recovery.

```
1  ..
2  memcpy(msg, salt, sizeof(uint8_t) * 16);
3  msg[0] ^= 0x00;
4  for (size_t k = 0; k < 4; k++) {
5      msg[k + 1] ^= ((uint8_t *)&idx)[k];
6  }
7  msg[5] ^= domain_separator;
8  aes_128_encrypt(&key, msg, dst[0]);
9  msg[0] ^= 0x01;
```

```
10   aes_128_encrypt(&key, msg, dst[1]);
11   ...
```

Listing 1.1. Generation of two seeds in the `aes_128_expand_seed` function.

To extend our analysis from the previous attack vector, we used the same simulation tool to evaluate the practical effectiveness of fault attacks under the parameter set of `Mirath-1a-fast`, specifically with $N = 256$, $\tau = 17$, and $T_{open} = 118$. The tool generates batched GGM trees with randomly selected hidden nodes and evaluates the probability of successful key recovery depending on the targeted node. In contrast to the scenario described for the last attack vector, we define a successful attack here as one in which at least one of the affected nodes is revealed and at least one of them is responsible for generating a hidden node. This tool allows us to estimate the most promising fault injection targets in realistic settings and to quantify their recovery potential based on tree level.

The highest recovery probability was observed at level 3, corresponding to nodes 7 through 14, with a success rate of 47.94 %, followed by level 4 with a probability of 43.18 %. This implies that, for instance, an attack on node 7, which is responsible for generating nodes 15 and 16, will result in a successful key recovery in roughly two signature generations.

3.4 Failed Attack Vectors

While evaluating fault attack resilience of MPCitH-based schemes, we considered several attack vectors that have proven effective in other post-quantum signature schemes. However, we found that these strategies could not be successfully applied to the current round 2 versions of the schemes we analyzed in this submission. This subsection briefly explains why these attack ideas are not transferable.

SHAKE Glitch on Seed Expansion. Earlier versions of the candidate schemes used SHAKE to expand seeds in their GGM tree construction. This opened them to fault injection attacks targeting the SHAKE function. A glitch on SHAKE, such as the one demonstrated in [27] by Jendral et al., could have allowed manipulation of internal outputs, facilitating full seed recovery. However, in the round 2 specifications, SHAKE has been replaced by AES for seed expansion. This change renders the attack infeasible, as the previous fault model, targeting SHAKE, no longer applies.

Instruction Glitch During Seed Reveal. Another proposed strategy stems from the idea of injecting faults during the seed reveal phase using a reference function in a tree structure. Mondal et al. [30] explored how faulting specific instructions can lead to leakage or unintended revelation of multiple seeds. However, these schemes do not implement a reference tree mechanism for seed revealing. Their batched GGM structure does not rely on references function, which makes this form of instruction glitching irrelevant for their implementations.

Counter Skipping in AES. The work of Jendral et al. [25] introduced a *counter increment skipping attack* against schemes that use AES in counter mode, with the aim of producing duplicate AES output. In our context, AES counter mode is used exclusively in FAEST to derive node values in the GGM tree. In the other Round 2 submissions, by contrast, AES in counter mode is employed only within the secret share expansion routine. During this seed expansion, the required secret share value is generated from a seed of the required length, so duplicating AES output via a counter-skip does not generally yield new share material in those schemes. Consequently, the attack described by Jendral et al. is only practically relevant for FAEST and not for the other examined schemes. Moreover, we expect that a counter-skip during seed expansion would reveal little or no additional information about the secret shares in the non-FAEST implementations.

3.5   Countermeasures

As a countermeasure against successful fault attacks on the seed expansion in the GGM tree, we propose several mitigation strategies. The first two attack vectors, which target the functions `mirath_ggm_tree_expand` and `mirath_expand_seed`, are only effective because the tree data structure is initialized with zeros. To prevent the recovery of the secret key through such faults, the tree should not be initilized with zeros and should contain random values. In addition, checks should be performed to ensure that no tree nodes remain equal to zero after initialization.

Furthermore, a general countermeasure against all attacks presented in this section is to include a check that verifies whether sibling nodes in the GGM tree are equal. If such an equality is detected, the signing procedure should abort and output an error instead of producing a signature. This check also mitigates instruction-skip attacks targeting XOR operations. We evaluated the performance impact of this countermeasure and observed that, averaged over 100,000 signatures, the GGM tree computation requires an additional 13,353 clock cycles. For comparison, the Mirath authors report a total signing cost of approximately 5.9 million clock cycles for the `Mirath-1a-fast` parameter set [2]. Consequently, the introduced countermeasure results in an overhead of roughly 0.2 %.

Another effective countermeasure is to validate a signature before it is accepted or used. All fault attacks described in this work result in invalid signatures, and a verification step can therefore detect and reject faulty outputs. For the `Mirath-1a-fast` parameter set, such a verification requires approximately 3.3 million clock cycles, which corresponds to an overhead of about 56 % compared to the signing cost.

It is also worth noting that the use of a batched tree, as employed for performance optimization during the opening phase, can naturally reduce the probability of a successful fault injection due to the increased structural complexity of the computation. For this reason, we recommend adopting a one-tree optimization approach in practical implementations.

Finally, we emphasize that the fault attacks presented in this work explicitly manipulate the control flow of the program. Consequently, control-flow integrity mechanisms can also serve as an effective line of defense. Moreover, it is conceivable that design-level countermeasures specific to MPCitH-based signature schemes could be developed to address these attacks. We leave the exploration of such design-based mitigations as future work.

4   Forgery Attack via Challenge Manipulation

This section introduces a fault-based forgery strategy that targets the challenge of linear combination generated during the Fiat–Shamir transform in MPCitH-based schemes. The attack specifically focuses on the verification algorithm.

Fault injection attacks targeting the verification phase of digital signature schemes have been explored across various cryptographic families. For lattice-based schemes, for instance, it was demonstrated that instruction skip faults, particularly those bypassing correctness or size validation checks, can lead to the acceptance of invalid signatures [11,14]. Very recently, Schneider et al. showed that even hardened elliptic-curve-based verification routines remain vulnerable to single instruction-skip faults, allowing trivial forgeries in secure boot implementations [32]. These findings confirm that verification algorithms represent a critical attack surface for physical adversaries.

Although skipping verification checks through fault injection represents a straightforward attack vector, it is typically well protected in practical implementations [14]. In contrast, our approach provides an alternative by targeting the internal computation of the Fiat–Shamir challenge while maintaining the normal verification flow. This strategy preserves the appearance of legitimate operation while fundamentally subverting the verification of the underlying hard mathematical problem.

Building on practical fault attacks against SHAKE-256 [27], we demonstrate how controlled challenge manipulation enables a forged signature to pass full verification. Although theoretical vulnerabilities in Fiat–Shamir are known [28], our work provides a practical realization of such attacks through fault injection, effectively bypassing parameter-based mitigations.

4.1   Attacker Model

The attacker's goal is to achieve acceptance of forged signatures by the verification algorithm. We consider an attacker with physical access to the verification device who can induce faults during the computation of the Fiat-Shamir challenge Γ. Specifically, the attacker targets the SHAKE function to fix the challenge to a predetermined value.

This model uses practical fault injection capabilities to compromise the cryptographic verification process. We demonstrate how this targeted fault enables effective signature forgery across multiple MPCitH-based schemes while preserving the external appearance of normal verification execution.

4.2 Attack Strategy

The adversary targets the first Fiat–Shamir challenge $\boldsymbol{\Gamma}$ and injects a fault that forces it to equal a fixed, known output. This manipulation breaks the soundness of the protocol by collapsing the verification condition, thereby enabling forgery of signatures.

To demonstrate the feasibility of the $\boldsymbol{\Gamma}$-manipulation attack, we first describe in detail how to apply it to RYDE and Mirath, two MPCitH-based schemes with similar transcript structures and verification conditions. We concretely demonstrate how to fix $\boldsymbol{\Gamma}$ in verification, resulting in a successful signature forgery for arbitrary messages.

Forgery in RYDE and Mirath. Both RYDE and Mirath derive their first challenge $\boldsymbol{\Gamma}$ from a hash function via the Fiat Shamir transform. This challenge is central to verifying the correctness of the witness, as follows: In RYDE, the verifier checks $P_\alpha(z) = \mathbf{v}_{\mathsf{eval}} + \boldsymbol{\Gamma}\big(\mathbf{H} \cdot \mathbf{x}_{\mathsf{eval}} - \mathbf{y}z^2\big)$, and in Mirath, verifier checks $P_\alpha(z) = \mathbf{v}_{\mathsf{eval}} + \boldsymbol{\Gamma}\big(\mathbf{H}\cdot\mathrm{vec}(\mathbf{E}_{\mathsf{eval}}) - \mathbf{y}z^2\big)$. In both cases, the vectors $\mathbf{x}_{\mathsf{eval}}$ and $\mathbf{E}_{\mathsf{eval}}$ are derived from opened polynomial commitments, z is a random eveluation point, and $\boldsymbol{\Gamma}$ serves as a matrix challenge applied to the RSD problem to be verified.

The goal is to produce a forged signature σ^* for any chosen message $\mathtt{msg}^*$ that will be accepted by the faulted verification process. The attack relies on fixing $\boldsymbol{\Gamma}$ to an attacker-chosen value $\boldsymbol{\Gamma}^*$. This allows the attacker to compute a fake witness that causes all verification equations to hold, even though the underlying structure has not been satisfied.

The attack is executed in two phases, as explained in the following.

1. Forgery Preparation:

1. Choose the fixed output $\boldsymbol{\Gamma}^* \in \mathbb{F}_{q^m}^{(n-k)\times\rho}$, that will be forced during verification.
2. Compute a fake witness:
   Zero $\boldsymbol{\Gamma}^*$: If $\boldsymbol{\Gamma}^*$ were the all-zero matrix, then $P_\alpha(X) = P_{\mathbf{v}}(X)$ in both protocols. The verification becomes $P_\alpha(z) = \mathbf{v}_{\mathsf{eval}}$, which holds automatically because $P_{\mathbf{v}}(z) = \mathbf{v}_{\mathsf{eval}}$. In this case, no condition on $\mathbf{x}_{\mathsf{eval}}$ or $\mathbf{E}_{\mathsf{eval}}$ is ever tested; the witness $\mathbf{x}$ or $\mathbf{E}$ could be arbitrary, and the check passes. Hence, a forger who manages to manipulate the Fiat–Shamir challenge $\boldsymbol{\Gamma}$ to be zero could produce a signature that is accepted during verification with a fault, without solving the underlying rank problem.
   General $\boldsymbol{\Gamma}^*$: Generally, any $\boldsymbol{\Gamma}$ that makes the product $\boldsymbol{\Gamma}\cdot(\mathbf{H}(P_{\mathbf{x}}(z))-\mathbf{y}z^2)$ the degree one polynomial will trivialize the proof. The attacker chooses $\boldsymbol{\Gamma}^*$ and then solves for a witness $(\mathbf{s}', \mathbf{C}')$ such that $\boldsymbol{\Gamma}^* \cdot \big((1 \parallel \mathbf{s}') \cdot [\mathbf{I}_z \parallel \mathbf{C}'] \cdot \mathbf{H}^\top - \mathbf{y}\big) = \mathbf{0}$. This system should be easy to solve as the elements of a fixed $\boldsymbol{\Gamma}$ can be used to cancel the remaining terms of the RSD problem for the fake witness.Alternatively, the attacker may fix some entries in $\mathbf{C}'$ and solve the resulting system, which must be in the kernel of $\boldsymbol{\Gamma}^*$.

3. Simulate signature generation: To simulate a valid-looking signature, the attacker takes the following steps:

   (a) For each iteration $e \in \{1, \ldots, \tau\}$, generate the shares and use the forged witnesses to compute $s_{\mathrm{aux}}^{\prime(e)}$ and $\mathbf{C}_{\mathrm{aux}}^{\prime(e)}$, then commit.

   (b) For each iteration $e \in \{1, \ldots, \tau\}$, generate polynomials
   $$P_{s'}(X) = s' \cdot X + s'_{\mathrm{base}}, \quad P'_{\mathbf{C}}(X) = \mathbf{C}' \cdot X + \mathbf{C}'_{\mathrm{base}} \quad \text{and} \quad P_v(X) = \mathbf{v} \cdot X + \mathbf{v}_{\mathrm{base}}$$

   (c) For each iteration $e \in \{1, \ldots, \tau\}$, compute $P_x^{(e)}(X)$ by computing
   $$x_{\mathrm{mid}}^{(e)} = \left[s_{\mathrm{base}}^{(e)} \| s_{\mathrm{base}}^{(e)} \cdot \mathbf{C}_{\mathrm{aux}}^{\prime(e)} + s^{(e)} \cdot \mathbf{C}_{\mathrm{base}}^{\prime(e)} \right]$$

   and
   $$x_{\mathrm{base}}^{(e)} = \left[\mathbf{0}_{m \times r} \| s_{\mathrm{base}}^{(e)} \cdot \mathbf{C}_{\mathrm{base}}^{\prime(e)} \right],$$

   where $s_{\mathrm{base}}^{(e)} = (1 \| s_{\mathrm{base}}^{\prime(e)})$.
   Compute the polynomial $P_\alpha^{(e)} = \alpha_{\mathrm{mid}}^{(e)} \cdot X + \alpha_{\mathrm{base}}^{(e)}$ by computing
   $$\alpha_{\mathrm{mid}}^{(e)} = x_{\mathrm{mid}}^{(e)} \cdot (\mathbf{I}_{m \cdot (n-k)} \| \mathbf{H}')^\top \cdot \mathbf{\Gamma}^* + \mathbf{v}^{(e)}$$

   and
   $$\alpha_{\mathrm{base}}^{(e)} = x_{\mathrm{base}}^{(e)} \cdot (\mathbf{I}_{m \cdot (n-k)} \| \mathbf{H}')^\top \cdot \mathbf{\Gamma}^* + \mathbf{v}_{\mathrm{base}}^{(e)}$$

   (d) Proceed with the simulation by computing
   $$h_2 = \mathtt{Hash}_2 \left(\mathtt{Hash}_0(\mathtt{msg}), \mathtt{pk}, \mathtt{salt}, h_1, \left(\alpha_{\mathrm{mid}}^{(e)}, \alpha_{\mathrm{base}}^{(e)} \right)_{e \in [1, \ldots, \tau]} \right)$$

   and compute the open random evaluation to generate the signature
   $$\sigma^* = \left(\mathtt{salt} \,|\, \mathtt{ctr} \,|\, h_2 \,|\, \pi_{\mathtt{BAVC}} \,|\, \left(s_{\mathrm{aux}}^{\prime(e)}, \mathbf{C}_{\mathrm{aux}}^{\prime(e)}, \alpha_{\mathrm{mid}}^{(e)} \right)_{e \in [1, \ldots, \tau]} \right).$$

This signature is not valid under honest verification, but will become valid once $\mathbf{\Gamma}^*$ is forced during verification with a fault.

2. Fault Injection During Verification: During verification, the verifier computes $\mathbf{\Gamma} \leftarrow \mathtt{ExpandChallenge1}(h_1)$. The attacker injects a fault to force $\mathbf{\Gamma} = \mathbf{\Gamma}^*$, the same value used to generate the fake witness.

Verification with $\mathbf{\Gamma}^*$ should hold from construction by checking the steps below:

1. Computation check:
   $$x_{\mathrm{eval}}^{(e)} = \left[s_{\mathrm{eval}}^{(e)} \cdot \phi(i^{*(e)}) \,\middle\|\, s_{\mathrm{eval}}^{(e)} \cdot \mathbf{C}_{\mathrm{eval}}^{\prime(e)} \right] \quad \text{and}$$
   $$\alpha_{\mathrm{eval}}^{(e)} = \mathbf{v}_{\mathrm{eval}} + \left(x_{\mathrm{eval}}^{(e)} \cdot (\mathbf{I}_{m \cdot (n-k)} \| \mathbf{H}')^\top - \mathbf{y} \cdot \phi(i^{*(e)})^2 \right) \cdot \mathbf{\Gamma}^*.$$

2. Verifying $h_2' = h_2$ and $v_{\mathrm{grinding}} = 0$. Thus, the forged signature is accepted.

4.3 Practical Attack

In this section, we discuss concrete attack vectors from the reference implementations of the various round 2 MPCitH submissions to explain for the attack described above how it can be realized in practice.

Mirath. In Mirath, the challenge matrix Γ is generated by hashing the value `h_sh` with SHAKE. Since version 2.1 of the implementation, two other functions are called for this purpose: first `seedexpander_shake_init` (see Listing 1.2) is executed to initialize hash state, and then, to extract the output bytes into the variable `Gamma`, `seedexpander_shake_get_bytes` is used. The initialization routine `seedexpander_shake_init` first initializes SHAKE with `Keccak_HashInitialize_SHAKE128`, then injects the value of `h_sh` via `Keccak_-HashUpdate`. If a salt is provided it would also be absorbed, but in the computation of Γ no salt is passed. The absorption phase is completed by a call to `Keccak_HashFinal`.

```
void seedexpander_shake_init(shake_prng_t *
    seedexpander_shake, const uint8_t* seed, size_t
    seed_size, const uint8_t* salt, size_t salt_size) {
    Keccak_HashInitialize_SHAKE128(seedexpander_shake);
    Keccak_HashUpdate(seedexpander_shake, seed, seed_size
        << 3);
    if(salt != NULL) Keccak_HashUpdate(seedexpander_shake,
        salt, salt_size << 3);
    Keccak_HashFinal(seedexpander_shake, NULL);
}
```

Listing 1.2. Initialization of SHAKE in Mirath v2.1.

To produce a predictable challenge, an attacker can skip the call to `Keccak-_HashUpdate` so that no input is absorbed into the SHAKE state. In that case SHAKE outputs the digest of an empty input, which is a fixed and known value.

RYDE. In RYDE, the matrix Γ is generated using the `ryde_1f_tcith_-expand_challenge_1` function, which takes both the hash value `h1` and a salt as input. Since the matrix Γ is initialized with zero entries, skipping this function call results in a challenge consisting entirely of zeros. This makes the function a viable target for fault injection attacks. The function `ryde_1f_tcith_expand_-challenge_1` is defined in the reference implementation file `tcith.c`, starting at line 159.

Another attack vector in RYDE is the `seedexpander_shake_get_bytes` in the `ryde_1f_tcith_expand_challenge_1` function. Within the SHAKE function, the variable `random` is used as the target variable. The reason for this is that `random` has the correct file format for the SHAKE results. To write the variable `random` to the matrix Γ, the function `rbc_53_mat_from_string` is called. If this function call is skipped, the values of Γ remain at the initialized state in this case as well.

In [27], a successful attack on SHAKE was presented in which the absorption phase was skipped using an instruction skip. In the SHAKE implementation of RYDE, this is not possible with a single instruction skip, as the `Keccak_HashUpdate` function is initialized with a salt value in addition to the hash value `h1`. By skipping `Keccak_HashUpdate` for the input data, the same function call remains for the salt value.

Furthermore, the function `seedexpander_shake_init` cannot be skipped, because otherwise the pointer `seedexpander` is not initialized and the program would end up in a segmentation fault.

4.4   Countermeasures

In this subsection, we discuss potential countermeasures for forgery attacks targeting challenge generation. We focus on mitigation strategies specifically for those schemes in which we have identified a viable attack vector. As already discussed in Sect. 3.5, the attacks presented here can be effectively prevented by deploying appropriate control-flow protection mechanisms, which ensure the correct execution of security-critical functions and make instruction-skipping faults detectable.

Mirath. In Mirath, the attack becomes feasible only if the SHAKE function is executed without any input. Since SHAKE produces deterministic output, the resulting challenge matrix Γ will always be the same and can be precomputed. As a countermeasure, we recommend verifying during signature verification whether the generated Γ matrix matches this precomputed value. If such a match is detected, the verification process should be aborted.

We note, however, that this countermeasure itself may be vulnerable to a fault injection. If an attacker manages to bypass the check through another fault, the mitigation could be made ineffective. Such second-order fault attacks habe been practically demonstrated against other cryptographic schemes [12]. Therefore, implementing this countermeasure in a fault-resistant way, such as using redundant or hardened checks, is essential for maintaining security.

RYDE. The first attack on RYDE is effective because the challenge matrix Γ is initially filled with zeros. To prevent this, the matrix should not be initialized with zero values. The second attack exploits the fact that the entire computation is performed on a serialized string representation, and the result is only converted into a matrix at the end. As a countermeasure, a comparison should be performed before and after the computation. If the resulting matrix still contains only the initial values, the verification should be aborted.

5   Applicability to Other Schemes

In this section we evaluate the applicability of the attacks presented in Sect. 3 and Sect. 4 to the remaining MPCitH signature schemes. We first deal with the key-reveal attack and then with the signature-forgery attack. For each scheme, where applicable, we present both an attack strategy and a practical attack.

5.1   Key-Recovery Attack on GGM Tree Seed Generation

Attack Strategy for SDitH and FAEST. The attack strategy for these signature schemes is very similar to the approaches used for Mirath and RYDE, which were discussed in Sect. 3.2. For SDitH and FAEST, the secret shares of an instance are summed and combined with the secret to produce an auxiliary value that is included in the signature. Consequently, if an attacker recovers all secret shares for a particular instance, they can calculate the sum of the secret shares and thereby recover the secret itself by combining the sum of the secret shares with the publicly known auxiliary value.

Practicality for SDitH. In SDitH, we found no practical attack vectors targeting tree expansion or seed expansion for key recovery, although such attacks remain feasible in theory; the XOR vector, however, is effective. The SDitH signature scheme constructs a GGM tree similar to the schemes Mirath and RYDE. Starting from a randomly chosen root node, the left and right child nodes are derived by executing an AES encryption on a defined message.

SDitH makes use of structured data types to manage variables, including those used for representing GGM trees. The tree-related structures are initialized through functions such as `ggm_multi_sibling_tree_init` (defined in `ggm.c`, line 457), which primarily set parameters and configuration values. However, the actual node values of the tree are neither initialized nor generated at this stage. Instead, node values are created on demand. As a result, there is no default initialization of the nodes, and attacks targeting the tree expansion (e.g., via `ggm_multi_sibling_tree_get_leaf_seed_commit`, defined in `ggm.c`, line 607) cannot be used to recover the secret key. The seed generation process cannot be skipped either, as all nodes are derived dynamically as required.

Depending on the parameter set and SDitH version, seed generation invokes AES-based functions, such as `aes128_ctrle_oneshot_encrypt_2blocks_ref` (defined in `aes128_ctrle_special_ref.c`, line 25). In this function, the seeds for a pair of sibling nodes are computed, with the counter value `ctr.v8` incremented between the two encryption operations. If the instruction responsible for incrementing this counter is skipped, both sibling nodes receive the same seed value, making a key-recovery attack feasible.

Practicality for FAEST. In FAEST, both the tree-expansion and seed-expansion vectors are exploitable for key recovery, while the XOR attack vector is not applicable. A GGM tree is used to generate the secret shares. The node values for the tree are produced in the function `generate_seeds`, and individual sibling seeds are derived via calls to `expand_seeds`. Unlike most MPC-in-the-Head signature schemes, FAEST does not distinguish sibling nodes by XORing a single bit into the message before AES; instead, AES is used in counter mode to derive the two siblings. Consequently, the XOR-based attack vector is not applicable to FAEST. The nodes are initialized with the following call:

```
nodes = calloc(2 * params->faest_param.L - 1, lambda_bytes);
```

Because `calloc` zero-initializes the allocated memory, the initial values of the nodes are all zero. This enables both the expand-tree attack and the expand-seed attack as potential vectors for key recovery.

Attack Strategy for MQOM. For MQOM, it must be considered that the auxiliary value included in the signature cannot be directly used to reconstruct the secret from the secret shares. The reason for this is that the first λ bits of the auxiliary value are truncated. Nevertheless, the secret can still be derived from the auxiliary value. We consider the following equation for the untruncated auxiliary value $\Delta_x[e]$:

$$\Delta_x[e] = x - \sum_{i=0}^{N-1} \bar{x}_i \, .$$

The first λ bits of x are defined as δ. The parameter λ is used during the generation of the seed nodes: when creating sibling nodes, the right child node is computed as the value of the left child node plus δ. When all secret shares $\bar{x}_i$ are summed, the first λ bits of the result correspond to δ. Consequently, when the sum of the secret shares is subtracted from the secret x, the first λ bits of the result become zero. Therefore, even though the first λ bits are truncated in the auxiliary value, the secret can still be reconstructed from $\Delta_x[e]$ by defining the first λ bits as zero.

Practicality for MQOM. For MQOM, we were unable to identify any attack vector that yields a reliable key recovery in practice. In the scheme, the first seed for the root node is set using the random value `rseed`. All subsequent nodes are derived through a `SeedDerive` function. MQOM employs the *correlated tree optimization*, in which only one value of a sibling pair is generated using a PRG, while the second is computed via an XOR operation.

For the commitment phase, the function `BLC_Commit`, which is part of the reference implementation and defined in the file `blc.c` starting at line 39, is called. This function internally generates τ trees using the `GGMTree_Expand` function. Skipping the `GGMTree_Expand` function is not a reliable fault attack strategy. The corresponding node values (`lseed`) are not initialized and may contain leftover memory values. An attacker who has knowledge of these memory contents might be able to carry out a successful attack. However, in the general case, the resulting node values are random and cannot be linked to any meaningful state, making the attack infeasible. A similar situation occurs if the `SeedDerive_x2` function is skipped. Because the nodes are not initialized, they hold arbitrary and unpredictable memory content, making it impossible for an attacker to reliably control the outcome of a fault and exploit it. Unlike schemes such as Mirath, RYDE, and SDitH, MQOM does not derive sibling nodes using the same message XORed with 1. Instead, different messages are used for each sibling. Therefore, skipping the XOR instruction is not a viable attack vector in MQOM.

Attack Strategy for PERK. The PERK specification [1] details a signing process where the secret witness is embedded into VOLE correlations derived from a GGM tree. If an adversary compromises all seeds in this tree, they can recover the signer's long-term secret key by inverting this embedding process.

1. Reconstruct VOLE secrets: Using all seeds $\{\mathsf{seed}_{e,i}\}$ and the public salt, the adversary executes ConvertToVOLE (Alg. 4.4) and VOLECommit (Alg. 4.5) to recover the prover's VOLE secret $\mathbf{u}$.
2. Extract compressed witness: From the signature component $\mathbf{t}$ and the reconstructed $\mathbf{u}$, the adversary computes:

$$\mathbf{w} = \mathbf{t} \oplus \mathbf{u}_{[0:\ell-1]}$$

   This reverses the witness masking step in P.VOLE-ElementaryVector (Alg. 4.17, line 2) and PERK.Sign (Alg. 4.34, line 12).
3. Decode the permutation: The compressed witness $\mathbf{w}$ is a concatenation of blocks $\mathbf{w}'_i$. Each block is decoded by inverting the PosToWitness encoding (Alg. 4.12), which implements a bijective mapping from a position pos_i to a bit string. The inverse mapping parses the elementary vectors in $\mathbf{w}'_i$ to recover the non-zero position pos_i for each row i of the secret permutation matrix $\mathbf{P}$.
4. Reconstruct the secret key: The set of positions $(\mathsf{pos}_0, \ldots, \mathsf{pos}_{n-1})$ defines the permutation matrix $\mathbf{P}$, which constitutes the functional secret key.

Practicality for PERK. In PERK, every attack vector analyzed can be used to perform key recovery. The node values of the GGM tree are stored in the variable `big_tree`, which is initialized to zero. The tree values are computed by the function `expand_ggm_tree`, and the child nodes are generated inside `ggm_expand_seed`. Therefore, both the expand tree attack vector and the expand seed attack vector are applicable to PERK and can lead to key recovery when exploited.

Since version 2.1 PERK also offers an AES-based mode in which node values are derived using AES. As in Mirath and RYDE, the only difference between the two sibling messages is an XOR operation. Therefore, in the AES mode the XOR attack is also feasible.

5.2   Forgery Attack via Challenge Manipulation

Attack Strategy for MQOM and SDitH. The above attack applies in a similar manner to MQOM and SDitH. In the MQOM specification [9, Section 2.1.2], the security of the 5-round variant relies critically on the linear combination challenge matrix Γ used to compute $P_\alpha = P_u + \Gamma \cdot \hat{F}(P_x)$. If an adversary could fix Γ to zero or another predetermined value, they could completely bypass the multivariate quadratic hardness assumption. Specifically, setting $\Gamma = 0$ would reduce the equation to $P_\alpha = P_u$, effectively eliminating the term that encodes the MQ problem instance. This would allow forgery without knowledge of a valid secret x, as the verification check would degenerate to verifying only the random masking polynomial P_u.

For SDitH, a similar critical dependency exists on the batching challenge $\gamma_1, \ldots, \gamma_m$ used in the linear combinations of instances

$$P_\alpha(X) = P_0(X) \cdot X + \sum_{j=1}^{m} \gamma_j \cdot f_j(P_1(X), \ldots, P_m(X))$$

If an adversary could fix all $\gamma_j = 0$, then $P_\alpha(X) = P_0(X) \cdot X$, completely removing the witness-dependent constraints f_j. This would allow forgery without knowledge of a valid witness, as verification would only check the random masking polynomial P_0. The Fiat-Shamir derivation of γ_j from the commitment h_{lines} is therefore essential to prevent this attack. Additionally, the consistency check matrix M expanded from h_{aux} via `ExpandConsistencyChallenge` ensures that the τ committed polynomials encode the same witness. If M could be fixed, the consistency check would be bypassed, allowing inconsistent witness encodings to pass verification. Both the TCitH and VOLEitH frameworks used in SDitH variants rely on the unpredictability of these challenges for soundness, making them susceptible to similar attacks if challenge derivation is compromised.

Practicality for SDitH. In SDitH, we did not identify any practical attack vector enabling a signature forgery, although such an attack appears theoretically possible. As part of the verification process, the consistency check matrix is generated via the function `both_vole_consistency_check_matrix`, where the variable `cchk_matrix_rng` is defined. This function can be found in the round 2 reference implementation, specifically in `vole_expansion.c`, starting from line 193. This variable represents the challenge used in the check. As in other parts of SDitH, the SHAKE function is used to generate the challenge. To make the SHAKE output independent of the actual input, an attacker might attempt to skip the call to `xof_finalize_and_output`. However, since `cchk_matrix_rng` is not initialized before use, the resulting output cannot be predicted or controlled. As a result, skipping the finalization does not provide any meaningful advantage for an attacker.

Practicality for MQOM. In MQOM, we successfully identified an attack vector that enables a signature forgery. Two different approaches are used to construct the challenge matrix $\mathbf{\Gamma}$, depending on whether a batched tree variant is employed. In the case without a batched tree, the attack cannot be carried out because we do not receive any additional information from the challenge polynomial.

In contrast, when using the batched tree variant, the challenge matrix $\mathbf{\Gamma}$ is generated via SHAKE over the commitment value. This process takes place within the `ComputePAlpha` function (defined in `piop.c`, starting at line 69), where the SHAKE function is executed in three steps: `xof_init`, `xof_update`, and `xof_squeeze`. During one of the `xof_update` calls, the commitment `com` is passed as input to the hash function. If this specific update call is skipped due to an instruction skip, the resulting hash value becomes constant and independent of the commitment. This behavior enables a forgery attack in the batched tree variant, as the generated challenge matrix is no longer related to the actual commitment.

Attack Strategy for PERK. The PERK signature scheme implements a zero-knowledge proof of knowledge for the Permuted Kernel Problem (PKP) within the VOLE-in-the-Head (VOLEitH) framework. The PKP instance is defined by a public matrix $\mathbf{H} \in \mathbb{F}_q^{m \times n}$ and vector $\mathbf{x} \in \mathbb{F}_q^n$, where the prover demonstrates knowledge of a permutation matrix $\mathbf{P} \in \mathbb{F}_q^{n \times n}$ satisfying

$$\mathbf{HPx} = \mathbf{0}.$$

The scheme exhibits a critical vulnerability to forgery attacks when the Fiat-Shamir challenge responsible for constraint combination can be fixed. This challenge, denoted ch_2 in the specification and derived from the hash function H_2^2 instantiated with SHAKE, generates the random coefficients $\alpha \in \mathbb{F}_{2^\rho}^{cn+n+m}$ that linearly combine all proof constraints, elementary vector structure, column summation, and PKP satisfiability into a single master polynomial $f(X)$. The soundness of this construction relies on the unpredictability of α to ensure that any invalid witness produces a non-zero leading coefficient in $f(X)$ with overwhelming probability over the choice of α.

However, if an adversary can predetermine ch_2 through fault injection, they can strategically compute a malicious linear combination that systematically cancels the leading coefficient of $f(X)$ for an arbitrary invalid witness. This manipulation bypasses the core soundness check in V.Check-PKP by ensuring the masked polynomial appears valid despite being generated from a fraudulent permutation matrix $\mathbf{P}^*$ that does not satisfy $\mathbf{HP}^*\mathbf{x} = \mathbf{0}$. Consequently, an attacker can forge signatures for arbitrary message-public key pairs without solving the underlying PKP instance, completely violating the scheme's existential unforgeability guarantees.

Practicality for PERK. In PERK, we identified an attack vector that allows the execution of a successful signature forgery. As outlined in the attack strategy, a signature forgery against PERK can be performed if the second challenge ch_2 assumes a constant value. In the PERK v2.1 implementation this challenge is initialized to zero. The value of the variable `ch_2` is derived by the function `sig_perk_gen_second_challenge`, which computes the hash value used for the challenge. If an instruction skip causes this function to be bypassed, `ch_2` remains zero. Therefore, a successful fault injection that skips `sig_perk_gen_second_challenge` enables a practical signature forgery against PERK.

Attack Strategy for FAEST. Within the FAEST signature scheme's VOLE-in-the-Head framework, the zero-knowledge proof phase relies on a critical challenge for its soundness. This occurs in the QuickSilver protocol, where after a prover has committed to their witness, they must prove that a set of C constraint polynomials $\{p_i(X)\}$ all evaluate to zero. To efficiently verify this, the protocol employs a random linear combination. A challenge vector $\mathbf{r}$ is generated, which is used to compress all constraints into a single, combined polynomial: $P_{\text{combined}}(X) = \sum_{i=0}^{C-1} \mathbf{r}_i \cdot p_i(X)$. The prover must then demonstrate that $P_{\text{combined}}(X)$ is the zero polynomial. The security of this step rests entirely on the unpredictability of $\mathbf{r}$; if even one original constraint is invalid, a randomly chosen $\mathbf{r}$ will cause the combined check to fail with probability nearly 1.

This leads to a devastating forgery attack. If an adversary can subvert the challenge generation; for instance, by forcing a fault in the H_2^2 hash function whose output defines $\mathbf{r}$, they can deliberately set the coefficients of $\mathbf{r}$ to zero. This action systematically breaks the proof's soundness. With $\mathbf{r} = 0$, the combined constraint polynomial becomes zero by construction, regardless of whether the original constraints were satisfied. Consequently, an attacker can forge a signature for any message and public key without any knowledge of the valid secret key, as they can bypass the core proof of knowledge verification entirely.

Practicality for FAEST. In FAEST, we did not identify any practical attack vector enabling a signature forgery, although such an attack appears theoretically possible. For a successful signature forgery, it is necessary that all variables satisfy $r_i = 0$. In the implementation these values appear as the variables `a0_tilde`, `a1_tilde`, and `a2_tilde`. These variables are not initialized to zero in the reference code, and therefore there is no immediate or obvious fault-injection vector that would force them all to zero and thus enable the planned signature-forgery attack.

6   Implementation

In this section, we first introduce the experimental setup used for our fault injection attacks. We then demonstrate the feasibility of the attacks presented in this work by successfully executing them on the Mirath and RYDE signature schemes. By applying the described attack techniques to real hardware, we validate their practical relevance and evaluate their success rates.

6.1   Experimental Setup

For the attacks, we use a setup consisting of a ChipWhisperer Lite, a UFO board, and as an target baord STM32L5HWC [15]. To the best of our knowledge, there is no specific implementation for embedded systems for Mirath or RYDE. Therefore, we implement only the required subfunctions for the experiments, because the entire scheme exceeds the memory requirements during runtime. We choose STM32L5HWC as the target, as it has sufficient memory for these subfunctions and also has a hardware AES module. Communication with a PC takes place via the SimpleSerial protocol. This allows inputs for the implemented functions to be sent, as well as outputs to be received and viewed. On the PC side, a Jupyter Notebook instance is used to control the measurement process and analyze the results.

For the attacks presented in this work, we use clock glitches with the goal of inducing instruction skips. Glitches are injected based on triggers placed in the target program. A trigger is a signal sent from the target device to the Chip-Whisperer, which allows the attacker program to react with specific actions, such as injecting a fault at a precise point in time. To obtain a setup that is as realistic as possible, the triggers are placed around the implemented function rather than directly at the instruction where the fault is intended to occur. In a realistic attack scenario, the adversary does not have precise knowledge of the program state or instruction timing at any given moment. Consequently, the trigger encloses the entire target function instead of a specific subfunction or instruction. This increases the difficulty of the attack, as the adversary must identify the exact point within the function at which the fault should be injected. Such a point can be determined either through program analysis or by evaluating side-channel measurements. Likewise, in a real attack without triggers, the attacker can learn the start time of the target function. For all experiments, we use the clock glitch parameters listed in Listing 1.3.

```
1  scope.glitch.clk_src = "clkgen"
2  scope.glitch.output = "clock_xor"
3  scope.glitch.trigger_src = "ext_single"
4  scope.io.hs2 = "glitch"
```

Listing 1.3. General parameters for the clock glitch attack.

In addition to these settings, Chipwhisperer also has the `offset`, `width` and `ext_offset` parameters to adjust the glitch. We use fixed values for `width` and `offset`, which have proven to be reliable for an instruction skip. To identify a suitable parameter set of `offset` and `width`, we implemented a sample program on the target device and performed a brute-force search over the parameters on this program. The parameter `ext_offset` is used to place the glitch relative to the trigger set. The setting of `ext_offset` is therefore dependent on the respective attack.

6.2 Key Recovery Attack on GGM Tree Seed Generation

For this attack, we implement the subfunction `mirath_ggm_tree_expand` from the round 2 submission of Mirath. The function is the same in both Mirath and RYDE. The seed tree creation uses a salt as input, which is selected each time it is executed. So in order for this salt to be generated, we create a random 32 byte value in the Jupyter Notebook instance, which is passed as input for each execution.

The target of the attack is a GGM tree instantiated with the parameters from the `Mirath1a-fast` version. For a binary tree, $2N - 1$ nodes are required, where $N = 4352$ corresponds to the number of leaf nodes. Since the root node is already given and each seed expansion generates two child nodes from a parent node, the function `mirath_expand_seed` is called 4351 times to complete the tree. Within this function, two child nodes are derived from a parent seed using AES. To accelerate the computation, we use the hardware AES module available on the STM32L5HWC target board instead of the software-based AES implementation used in the reference code.

Instruction Skip on `mirath_ggm_tree_expand` Function Call.
For the key-recovery attacks, we use the function `mirath_ggm_tree_expand` as the core of our implementation. Consequently, this function is the first one called in our partial implementation. To model a realistic attack scenario, the trigger is placed around the entire partial implementation, which causes the call to `mirath_ggm_tree_expand` to occur very close to the trigger point. In our experiments we observed that when `mirath_ggm_tree_expand` is the very first function executed after the trigger, the attack does not always succeed. However, by inserting a `memcpy` operation—as present in the reference implementation—between the trigger and the GGM tree function, we achieved a 100 % success rate with the glitch parameters given in Listing 1.4, corresponding to an expected number of one trial. The insertion of this additional instruction increases the attack window for the fault injection. If no instruction is executed between the trigger and the function branch, parts of the subsequent instructions may already be loaded into the processor pipeline, which can reduce the reliability of the fault and lead to unsuccessful attacks.

```
scope.glitch.offset = -46.6
scope.glitch.width = -5.5
scope.glitch.ext_offset = 13
```

Listing 1.4. Parameters for an instruction skip on the `mirath_ggm_tree_expand` function call.

Instruction Skip on `mirath_expand_seed` Function Call.
To demonstrate the practical feasibility of this attack, we target the `mirath_expand_seed` function from Listing 1.5 and show how to skip its execution. When this function is skipped, the two child nodes that it is supposed to generate remain at their default initialized value of zero.

In the reference implementation, the generation of the GGM tree leaves is performed within a loop structure. As an example, we consider the case where the seed creation for $i = 1$ is skipped. As a result, the corresponding child nodes, labeled as nodes 3 and 4, are not computed correctly and retain the zero value. This creates a fault in the tree structure that can be exploited in the context of key recovery.

```
for (size_t i = 0; i < (MIRATH_PARAM_TREE_LEAVES - 1); i
    ++) {
    mirath_expand_seed(ggm_tree + mirath_ggm_tree_child_0(
        i), salt, i, ggm_tree[i]);
}
```

Listing 1.5. GGM tree creation in Mirath.

We execute the attack from a Jupyter Notebook instance. Here, we also create the random 32-byte salt value and transfer it to the target program via SimpleSerial. We use the `GlitchController` class to record the results. It distinguishes between the events **success**, **reset**, and **normal**. After executing the `mirath_ggm_tree_expand` function, the target program checks whether nodes 3 and 4 of the created tree are the same. If this is the case, the program responds with an "w", otherwise with an "l". The output of the program is then evaluated as **success** or **normal**. If the program no longer responds due to the clock glitch and the target has to be restarted, the **reset** event is tracked.

With an `ext_offset` of 162240, the attack can be executed with a success probability of 100 %, meaning that the fault injection reliably causes the two child nodes to be identical. The reason for this is that the functions used are time-constant, even on random data. To find the correct `ext_offset`, we inserted a loop of NOP instructions at the point to be skipped. During a power consumption measurement, we were able to roughly estimate how many clock cycles had passed. Within the range of the estimate, we could then brute-force the `ext_offset` parameter until we had a successful attack.

As already described in Sect. 3.3, targeting nodes on the first two levels guarantees a successful key recovery with a probability of 100 %, since these levels always include nodes that can lead to the generation of hidden nodes. We validated this result experimentally by performing fault injections against nodes on the first two levels. The 100 % success rate therefore reflects our practical attacks on those levels.

XOR Instruction Skip. In this attack, we demonstrate the feasibility of skipping the XOR instruction during seed expansion. As discussed in Sect. 3.3, the highest probability of achieving a key recovery is obtained by targeting a node at level 3 of the GGM tree. Therefore, we attack the seed creation at iteration $i = 7$. The goal is to ensure that nodes 15 and 16 in the GGM tree receive identical values.

This is achieved by skipping the XOR instruction that distinguishes the messages used to generate the two sibling nodes encrypted by AES. Unlike the function call skip, this fault requires a different offset that targets the XOR instruction. The offset could also be roughly estimated with a power consumption measurement and then brute-forced until a successful attack was detected. With an `ext_offset` of 1296660, we were able to achieve a success rate of 100 % that the generated nodes are the same.

6.3   Forgery Attack via Challenge Manipulation

For this attack, we use a instruction skip to ensure that the challenge used in the target scheme has constant values. To demonstrate the feasibility of the attack, we present two different attacks on the schemes Mirath and RYDE. No attack vectors were found for SDitH and PERK.

Mirath. To demonstrate the practical feasibility of the forgery attack, we implemented the functions required to compute the challenge matrix Γ, namely `seedexpander_shake_init` and `seedexpander_shake_get_bytes`. As previously described in Sect. 4.3, skipping the branch to the function `Keccak_-HashUpdate` inside `seedexpander_shake_init` causes SHAKE to produce the hash value of an empty input. To verify whether the fault injection was successful, we check whether the output of the affected function matches this known empty-input SHAKE output. In our experiments we identified reliable glitch parameters that always skip the `Keccak_HashUpdate` function: setting `ext_offset` to 577 consistently skip the branch to `Keccak_HashUpdate`. As with earlier experiments, this offset was determined using a combination of power-trace analysis and brute-force offset tuning.

RYDE. We have implemented the two functions `hash_sha3_finalize` and `ryde_1f_tcith_expand_challenge_1` from the reference implementation on the board. Two changes had to be made for the code to work. First, explicit x86 assembly code was used for the `rbc_53_elt_get_degree` function, which we converted to ARM assembly. Second, the initialization of the gamma matrix with the `rbc_53_mat_init` function resulted in an allocation error. We have therefore adapted the function so that the pointers generated by this function only point to aligned memory addresses.

As described in Sect. 4.3, we have two possible attack vectors for RYDE. The first attack vector is the function `ryde_1f_tcith_expand_challenge_1`, the second attack vector is the function `rbc_53_mat_from_string`. For an instruction skip in `ryde_1f_tcith_expand_challenge_1`, we set the `ext_offset` to 34398 and achieved a successful attack with a probability of 50 %. For an instruction skip in the `rbc_53_mat_from_string` function, setting `ext_offset` to 70699 resulted in a success probability of 86 %. Consequently, the expected number of trials required for a successful attack lies between one and two for this attack scenario. Again, we were able to find the parameters with a power consumption measurement together with a brute force method. We believe that more successful attacks can be realized with better parameters. We leave this for future work.

7   Conclusion

In this work, we investigated the security of MPC-in-the-Head signature schemes under fault attacks. We introduced two practical fault attacks, a key-recovery attack and a signature-forgery attack, and analyzed their applicability to all six MPCitH-based candidates evaluated in round 2 of NIST's digital signature standardization process: FAEST, Mirath, MQOM, PERK, RYDE, and SDitH.

Our analysis demonstrates that all six schemes are vulnerable to at least one of the proposed attacks. The key-recovery attack, which targets the GGM tree seed generation process, was successfully performed on Mirath and RYDE using a ChipWhisperer setup, confirming its practical feasibility. The forgery attack, which manipulates the Fiat–Shamir challenge computation, was also shown to be effective.

To mitigate these threats, we proposed several practical countermeasures, including initializing GGM trees with random nonzero values, verifying the consistency of sibling nodes, and introducing hardened checks during challenge generation. These techniques can significantly reduce the risk of fault-based key recovery and signature forgery.

Our findings underscore the importance of incorporating physical attack resistance into the design and implementation of MPCitH-based signature schemes, particularly as they progress towards standardization.

Acknowledgments. This work has been funded by the Deutsche Forschungsgemeinschaft (DFG) - KR 5152/2-1 and SFB 1119 - 236615297, and by the German Federal Ministry of Research, Technology and Space (BMFTR) under the project QUORYPTAN (16KIS2034).

References

1. Aaraj, N., et al.: PERK. Tech. rep., National Institute of Standards and Technology (2024). https://csrc.nist.gov/Projects/pqc-dig-sig/round-2-additional-signatures
2. Adj, G., et al.: Mirath (merger of MIRA/MiRitH). Tech. rep., National Institute of Standards and Technology (2024). https://csrc.nist.gov/Projects/pqc-dig-sig/round-2-additional-signatures
3. Aguilar Melchor, C., et al.: SDitH — Syndrome Decoding in the Head. Tech. rep., National Institute of Standards and Technology (2024). https://csrc.nist.gov/Projects/pqc-dig-sig/round-2-additional-signatures

4. Aragon, N., et al.: RYDE. Tech. rep., National Institute of Standards and Technology (2024). https://csrc.nist.gov/Projects/pqc-dig-sig/round-2-additional-signatures

5. Aranha, D.F., et al.: Side-channel protections for picnic signatures. In: IACR Transactions on Cryptographic Hardware and Embedded Systems, pp. 239–282 (2021)

6. Baum, C., et al.: One tree to rule them all: optimizing GGM trees and OWFs for post-quantum signatures. In: Chung, K.M., Sasaki, Y. (eds.) ASIACRYPT 2024, Part I. LNCS, vol. 15484, pp. 463–493. Springer, Singapore (2024). https://doi.org/10.1007/978-981-96-0875-1_15

7. Baum, C., et al.: FAEST. Tech. rep., National Institute of Standards and Technology (2024). https://csrc.nist.gov/Projects/pqc-dig-sig/round-2-additional-signatures

8. Baum, C., et al.: Publicly verifiable zero-knowledge and post-quantum signatures from VOLE-in-the-head. In: Handschuh, H., Lysyanskaya, A. (eds.) CRYPTO 2023, Part V. LNCS, vol. 14085, pp. 581–615. Springer, Cham (2023).https://doi.org/10.1007/978-3-031-38554-4_19

9. Benadjila, R., Bouillaguet, C., Feneuil, T., Rivain, M.: MQOM — MQ on my Mind. Tech. rep., National Institute of Standards and Technology (2024). https://csrc.nist.gov/Projects/pqc-dig-sig/round-2-additional-signatures

10. Bidoux, L., Feneuil, T., Gaborit, P., Neveu, R., Rivain, M.: Dual support decomposition in the head: shorter signatures from rank SD and MinRank. In: International Conference on the Theory and Application of Cryptology and Information Security, pp. 38–69. Springer (2024)

11. Bindel, N., Buchmann, J., Krämer, J.: Lattice-based signature schemes and their sensitivity to fault attacks. In: 2016 Workshop on Fault Diagnosis and Tolerance In Cryptography (FDTC), pp. 63–77. IEEE (2016)

12. Blömer, J., da Silva, R.G., Günther, P., Krämer, J., Seifert, J.: A practical second-order fault attack against a real-world pairing implementation. In: FDTC, pp. 123–136. IEEE Computer Society (2014)

13. Buss, J.F., Frandsen, G.S., Shallit, J.O.: The computational complexity of some problems of linear algebra. J. Comput. Syst. Sci. **58**(3), 572–596 (1999)

14. Calle Viera, A., Berzati, A., Heydemann, K.: Fault attacks sensitivity of public parameters in the dilithium verification. In: Bhasin, S., Roche, T. (eds.) Smart Card Research and Advanced Applications, pp. 62–83. Springer Nature Switzerland, Cham (2024)

15. ChipWhisperer: open source side-channel analysis tools (2020). https://www.newae.com/chipwhisperer

16. Feneuil, T.: The Polynomial-IOP Vision of the Latest MPCitH Frameworks for Signature Schemes. Post-Quantum Algebraic Cryptography - Workshop 2, Institut Henri Poincaré, Paris, France (2024), presentation

17. Feneuil, T., Rivain, M.: Threshold linear secret sharing to the rescue of MPC-in-the-head. In: Guo, J., Steinfeld, R. (eds.) ASIACRYPT 2023, Part I. LNCS, vol. 14438, pp. 441–473. Springer, Singapore (2023). https://doi.org/10.1007/978-981-99-8721-4_14

18. Feneuil, T., Rivain, M.: Threshold computation in the head: Improved framework for post-quantum signatures and zero-knowledge arguments. J. Cryptol. **38**(3), 1–82 (2025)

19. Feneuil, T., Rivain, M., Warmé-Janville, A.: Masking-friendly post-quantum signatures in the threshold-computation-in-the-head framework. Cryptology ePrint Archive, Paper 2025/520 (2025). https://eprint.iacr.org/2025/520

20. Fiat, A., Shamir, A.: How to prove yourself: practical solutions to identification and signature problems. In: Odlyzko, A.M. (ed.) Advances in Cryptology – CRYPTO' 86, pp. 186–194. Springer, Berlin Heidelberg, Berlin, Heidelberg (1987)
21. Godard, J., Aragon, N., Gaborit, P., Loiseau, A., Maillard, J.: Single trace side-channel attack on the MPC-in-the-Head framework. In: International Conference on Post-Quantum Cryptography, pp. 267–293. Springer (2025)
22. Goldreich, O., Goldwasser, S., Micali, S.: How to construct random functions. J. ACM **33**(4), 792–807 (1986). https://doi.org/10.1145/6490.6503
23. Guo, X., et al.: Half-tree: Halving the cost of tree expansion in COT and DPF. In: Hazay, C., Stam, M. (eds.) EUROCRYPT 2023, Part I. LNCS, vol. 14004, pp. 330–362. Springer, Cham (2023). https://doi.org/10.1007/978-3-031-30545-0_12
24. Ishai, Y., Kushilevitz, E., Ostrovsky, R., Sahai, A.: Zero-knowledge from secure multiparty computation. In: Proceedings of the Thirty-Ninth Annual ACM Symposium on Theory of Computing, pp. 21–30 (2007)
25. Jendral, S., Dubrova, E.: Side-channel and fault injection attacks on voleith signature schemes: a case study of masked FAEST. IACR Cryptol. ePrint Arch. **378** (2025). https://eprint.iacr.org/2025/378
26. Jendral, S., Dubrova, E.: MAYO key recovery by fixing vinegar seeds. Cryptology ePrint Archive, Paper 2024/1550 (2024). https://doi.org/10.62056/ab0ljbkrz, https://eprint.iacr.org/2024/1550
27. Jendral, S., Mattsson, J.P., Dubrova, E.: A single-trace fault injection attack on hedged module lattice digital signature algorithm (ML-DSA). In: 2024 Workshop on Fault Detection and Tolerance in Cryptography (FDTC), pp. 34–43 (2024). https://doi.org/10.1109/FDTC64268.2024.00013
28. Kales, D., Zaverucha, G.: An attack on some signature schemes constructed from five-pass identification schemes. In: International Conference on Cryptology and Network Security, pp. 3–22. Springer (2020)
29. Katz, J., Kolesnikov, V., Wang, X.: Improved non-interactive zero knowledge with applications to post-quantum signatures. In: Lie, D., Mannan, M., Backes, M., Wang, X. (eds.) ACM CCS 2018, pp. 525–537. ACM Press (2018). https://doi.org/10.1145/3243734.3243805
30. Mondal, P., Adhikary, S., Kundu, S., Karmakar, A.: ZKFault: fault attack analysis on zero-knowledge based post-quantum digital signature schemes. In: Chung, K.M., Sasaki, Y. (eds.) ASIACRYPT 2024, Part VIII. LNCS, vol. 15491, pp. 132–167. Springer, Singapore (2024). https://doi.org/10.1007/978-981-96-0944-4_5
31. Sarde, V., Debande, N.: Differential fault attacks on MQOM, breaking the heart of multivariate evaluation. Cryptology ePrint Archive, Paper 2025/1895 (2025). https://eprint.iacr.org/2025/1895
32. Schneider, K., Auer, L., Wagner, A.: Fault attacks on ECC signature verification. IACR Trans. Cryptographic Hardw. Embedded Syst. **2025**(4), 1010–1052 (2025)

Author Index